# IRWIN F. GELLMAN

# THE
# CONTENDER

RICHARD NIXON

THE CONGRESS YEARS

1946–1952

THE FREE PRESS

*f*P

THE FREE PRESS
A Division of Simon & Schuster Inc.
1230 Avenue of the Americas
New York, NY 10020

All photographs not otherwise credited
are from the Richard Nixon Library &
Birthplace, Yorba Linda, California.

Designed by Carla Bolte

Manufactured in the United States of America

10  9  8  7  6  5  4  3  2  1

Library of Congress Cataloging-in-Publication Data

Gellman, Irwin F.
    The Contender : Richard Nixon : the Congress years,  1946–1952/
Irwin F. Gellman.
        p.   cm.
    Includes bibliographical references and index.
    1. Nixon, Richard M. (Richard Milhous), 1913–1994.   2. Legislators—
United States Biography.   3. United States.   Congress.   House.
Biography.   4. United States—Politics and government—1945–1953.
5. Presidents—United States Biography.   I. Title.
E856.G45        1999                99-22248          CIP
973.924'092—dc21
    [B]

ISBN 0-684-85064-8

# Acknowledgments

Before I begin to thank those who have contributed to this particular work, I would first like to pay tribute to a friend and scholar. Frank Freidel acted as a mentor to me, found the publisher for my first as well as my second book, and wrote jacket blurbs for my books until he passed away. I miss him. He was the class of his scholarly and gentlemanly class.

David Pletcher supervised my graduate studies, when he and my other major professors stressed two major themes: first, the research had to be exhaustive, and second, the writing had to be the best that I could do. In regard to the former, this book rests extensively on two archives. The first is the Richard Nixon Library & Birthplace. John Taylor, executive director, could not have provided a more conducive environment for my work. Beverly Lindy, assistant to the archivist, could not have provided a more enjoyable setting in which to do my work. However, Susan Naulty, the archivist who cherishes the manuscripts under her control, occupies a special place of distinction. She has gone beyond any call of duty to provide me with every available document up to the last possible moment for my examination.

Second, the National Archives and Records Administration, Pacific Southwest Region, houses the Richard M. Nixon Pre-Presidential Papers. Diane Nixon, the regional director, has made certain that anything that can be made available has been, and Paul Wormser, the principal archivist in charge of this collection, has been exceptional. I cannot thank them and the other members of the staff enough for their kindnesses; they represent professionalism at its best. Milton Gustafson, senior specialist, at the National Archives in College Park, has been a valued resource since I first started writing.

Several other critical collections added breadth to this study. The Jerry Voorhis papers are located at the Claremont Colleges, the Honnold/Mudd Library, under the supervision of Jean Beckner, librarian, special collections; she and her staff could not have been more accommodating to my research needs. The Carl Albert Center at the University of Oklahoma holds the Helen Gahagan Douglas manuscripts, where archivist Carolyn Hanneman and assistant curator Todd Kosmerick made my stay profitable. Paul and Carolyn Glad added to my pleasant stay in Norman not only by providing their warm hospitality, but also by allowing me time to discuss some ideas with Paul.

Various presidential libraries were obvious stops. The Dwight D. Eisenhower Library holds a wide variety of manuscripts, and archivist James Leyerzaft ably provided direction while Kathleen Struss, audiovisual archivist, showed me film and photographs. The Herbert Hoover Presidential Library had a wide range of material dealing with Hoover and his relationship to Nixon that archivist Dale Mayer culled out for me. The Lyndon Baines Johnson Library holds the Drew Pearson collection, and Claudia Anderson, senior archivist, supplied me with his files. At the Franklin Delano Roosevelt Library, archivist Raymond Teichman and Robert Parks assisted me with Laurence Duggan's correspondence with Sumner Welles. Randy Sowell and Dennis Belger, archivists at the Harry S. Truman Library, provided me with material relating to the president's connections to Nixon, and Pauline Testerman, audiovisual archivist, showed me film of the president's conversation with Pearson.

Others who went above the call of duty were: at the University of Notre Dame, archivist William Kevin Cawley helped with the Father Cronin papers; Bonnie Olson, library associate at the Karl E. Mundt Historical & Educational Foundation, Dakota State University, provided data on Mundt's relationship to Nixon; Angela Stockwell, research associate at Northwood University, cheerfully aided with the Margaret Chase Smith papers; at the Hoover Institution Archives, Carol Leadenham, assistant archivist for reference, found letters in the Alfred Kohlberg collection and located a critical memorandum on the 1952 Republican national convention in a miscellaneous collection; Michael Austin, manuscripts assistant, special collections, Harvard Law School Library, reviewed Federal Bureau of Investigation memoranda in the Alger Hiss collection; at Marquette University, Philip Runkel, assistant archivist in special collections, provided material from the Charles Kersten papers; Simon Elliot, university research library, special collections at the University of California, Los Angeles, assisted with the Ed Cray papers; Fred Bauman, at the manuscript division of the Library of Congress, located Nixon's interviews in the Alsop papers; David Roepke, archivist at the John M. Ashbrook Center for Public Affairs, Ashland University, assisted with information from the Victor Lasky collection; Melissa Paul, archivist at the university archives, California State Polytechnic University, Pomona, provided John Balch's essay; Carla Summers, chief manuscript librarian, Department of Special Collections, University of Florida, sent me George Smathers's recollection of his relationship with Nixon; and Gary Kurutz, principal librarian, Special Collection Branch, California State Library, verified the existence of Jesse B. Blue, Jr. At the Federal Bureau of Investigation, Julie Icowsky tracked down Edward Hummer for me, and Linda Kloss sent me another critical document dealing with the FBI's relationship to the House Committee on Un-American Activities.

In the specialized field of oral history, Harry Jeffrey spent several hours with me describing the work of California State University Fullerton in recording the memoirs of individuals connected with Nixon's early career. Jackie Dooley, director of special collections at the University of California at Irvine, provided copies of the oral history projects dealing with Helen Gahagan Douglas and Earl Warren.

I owe a special debt to various public libraries in Southern California. I used the one in Whittier for back issues of the *Whittier News*; in Alhambra, Carol Stone, the library's director, assisted me with early editions of the *Alhambra Post-Advocate*; in Yorba Linda, James Granitto helped me with the early editions of the *Yorba Linda Star*; and from Pomona, Susan Hutchinson sent me articles from the *Pomona Progress-Bulletin*. Even more than the above libraries, the Newport Beach Public Library has assisted me with my research needs with the greatest skill and ingenuity. Sometimes the reference librarians found esoteric material that I did not think that they could ever find. Susan Warren with Susie Hubbs most ably directs the operation; June Pilsitz located information on the Internet and everywhere else; she is a jewel. Sara, Steven, Andrea, Marianne, Claudia, and other staff members could not have been kinder about my seemingly endless requests.

Herbert Klein read a draft chapter on his role in the 1948 primary election and made comments, as did Stephen Zetterberg. They cogently articulated their views, and I listened to their remarks seriously. Ralph de Toledano allowed me the use of his letters to and from Whittaker Chambers; once they were published, I decided to cite to the published record. James Gleason read the chapters dealing with Nixon's senatorial years for accuracy. Marilyn Nielsen introduced me to the works of M. F. K. Fisher; Richard Corngold shared an article dealing with George Marshall's address at Harvard University; Donald Thompson, assistant treasurer in the 1946 election, helped me understand that initial campaign in greater detail; and Hubert Perry talked to me about his father's relationship with Nixon. Lawrence Klein, M.D., interpreted Nixon's medical records for me.

Many scholars have helped me with this project. At the University of California Irvine, Mark Petracca, Jack Peltason, and William Shoenfeld offered their opinions of some of my early drafts. At Whittier College, Joseph Dmohowski, serials, science, and special collections librarian, read my introductory chapter on Nixon's early life. James Patterson reviewed my work on the Taft-Hartley Act. Barton Bernstein and Athan Theoharis looked at my chapters on the Alger Hiss–Whittaker Chambers case. Richard Challener shared the results of his research on John Foster Dulles, Dwight Eisenhower, Alger Hiss, and Richard Nixon.

Chapman University, through the setting that Drs. James and Lynne Doti have established, has provided an ideal place in which to do my work. Leland Estes, chairman of the social sciences division, and Robert Slayton, chairman of the history department, fine scholars in their own fields, have provided continual encouragement. Stephen and Michelle Christensen add to this kind atmosphere with their own brand of aid and comfort. Raymond Sfeir interpreted the value of the Consumer Price Index for me. Gina Wilkenson, who handles interlibrary loan requests, has been marvelous.

The Free Press has demanded nothing less than excellence from me and themselves. Bruce Nichols, senior editor, has given me the best that he has to offer; that essence is mirrored in his superb assistant Dan Freedberg. Ann Adelman has copyedited this manuscript with an eye toward anything that would detract from its smooth flow. David Frost, coordinator of everything that gets the manuscript ready for printing, has been a delight. Elizabeth McNamara could not have been more helpful in providing legal counsel. Yet, above all, Bruce has provided the leadership. Sometimes bluntly but with only the best of intentions, he has insisted that I be better than I thought that I could be. For that raised standard, I am grateful.

ACKNOWLEDGMENTS

While I was researching this work, a negligent driver totaled my automobile. Alan Beyer, my orthopedic surgeon, took care of some of my problems, but my greatest concern was the damage caused to my hands. Dr. Nicholas Rose has worked with me since the winter of 1997. I still have pain, sometimes severe, but he has tried to prescribe medication and treatment that do not interfere with my work. Being doped up does not lend itself to scholarly pursuits. His willingness to cooperate with my compulsive need to write and the treatment at Pro Sport physical therapy, especially Joelle Shoemaker, Joe Donohue, and the rest of the staff, have made the pain almost bearable.

Finally, but not lastly—in fact, initially—my wife Gloria Gae originated the idea of focusing my energies on this project. While, at first, I resisted, I now realize how right she was. For this and the rest of all that she does for me, I am truly blessed and eternally thankful. She is a treasure.

FOR MY WIFE

GLORIA GAE

# Contents

# Preface

Writing this book was not my idea, though I now wish it were. After having completed three volumes dealing with the administration of Franklin Roosevelt, I had planned to commence a fourth one on America's reaction to the Holocaust, a subject that has deeply disturbed me for years. I had already started collecting data on it, yet my wife, Gloria Gae, had continually nudged me to visit the nearby Richard Nixon Library & Birthplace since its opening in the early 1990s. Quite frankly, I saw no need. I was not planning to write anything on the thirty-seventh president of the United States. I was content in my comfortable niche.

Gloria refused to surrender; so I naturally did. One afternoon in early 1995, we traveled, with me grumbling all the way to Yorba Linda, about a half-hour drive from our house. We had a pleasant lunch on the lovely grounds of the library, and after my wife softened me up with food, she suggested that we visit the library's archives. That is one item on an historian's agenda that will just about always spark a positive response. We went downstairs, where Susan Naulty, guardian of every single piece of paper, photograph, recording, and any additional document floating in the ether, cordially greeted us. Before I could even mutter a word, Gloria asked for a tour of the archives, and Susan promptly and professionally agreed. Once she outlined the library's holdings, I was hooked. The amount of documentation there that other scholars had not seen was staggering.

From that day until the present, I have regularly driven to the library to use the materials housed there. After almost four years of study, I am convinced that this collection, when combined with key Nixon material

1

in the National Archives, will be the finest collection for an American politician from the end of World War II to almost the close of the twentieth century. It graphically illustrates the domestic shift from New Deal politics to the right of center; it describes the gradual movement toward bipartisanship in foreign affairs; and it offers the best view on one of the most painful periods of American history, one that almost irreparably fractured the political process.

I have been fortunate in being able to examine every catalogued item in the library's collection covering Nixon's congressional career. I have supplemented them with trips to dozens of other repositories, cited in the source notes at the end of this book. Most important has been the National Archives in Laguna Niguel, where many Nixon congressional and senatorial files that had remained marked "Confidential" were cleared for my examination and have added an enormous richness to this period.

Nixon left the most impressive chronicle of any Republican congressman during the early years of the Cold War, but much of this record has been unexplored until now. I came to this project without any special expectations. In fact, until this volume, I have concentrated on the foreign policies of Franklin Roosevelt. Although I lean toward the Republican viewpoint in my voting habits, my historical research is not affected by my personal persuasion.

What I discovered after four extensive years of research and writing was a Nixon who almost always contradicted previous biographies. Nearly every stage of his early congressional career has been distorted. This does not infer that he was a saint. One incident during a 1952 congressional primary campaign was particularly troublesome, revealing that Nixon had a major lapse of judgment. But neither was he an outrageous Red-baiter, nor a crooked fund-raiser, nor a smarmy politician who smeared his opponents. His victories over Jerry Voorhis and Helen Gahagan Douglas were hard fought and deeply emotional, primarily due to the divisive issues raised during that era. His relationships to Earl Warren and William Knowland have been widely distorted; this especially applies to the circumstances of the trio's actions leading up to and including the 1952 Republican National Convention.

This work hopefully will correct the existing factual record and not be viewed as a partisan attack or psychological interpretation. Readers can draw their own conclusions about why and what Nixon did or did not do, but first they must understand exactly how he acted. I have supplied the perspiration; my wife has regularly given me inspiration; and friends have freely offered encouragement. No one close or related to Nixon has offered or contributed any advice or financial assistance.

I alone am responsible for any errors in fact or interpretation.

*Chapter* I

# THE PREREQUISITES FOR A CONGRESSIONAL CANDIDATE

To Nixonphobes, Richard Milhous Nixon was sinister: a practitioner of skulduggery and the quintessential "Red-baiter." To Nixonphiles, he was a patriot: righteous and virtuous. Throughout his career, inaccuracies and point-of-view attacks or defenses have muddied the historical waters, and the clarity has become murkier since his death. Writers still tend to assume a pro- or anti-Nixon stance, repeating the myths erected by their predecessors rather than analytically examining what really transpired.

Even his youthful upbringing has been appropriated and warped for predetermined posturing. As in any individual's life, some reasons for various decisions cannot be resolved, but the unsubstantiated stories that have survived in Nixon's journey are incredible. To take one early, perhaps even mundane example, several legends have arisen about Nixon's Federal Bureau of Investigation (FBI) job application while he was completing his last year of law school. On April 23, 1937, Nixon applied for employment as a special agent. He was rejected, never even receiving the courtesy of a form letter. For years, he wondered why.

Director J. Edgar Hoover, as much a Nixonphile as anyone, supplied a seemingly rational answer to this baffling question on June 11, 1954. Introducing the vice president before the fifty-third graduation exercises of the FBI national academy, the director claimed that Nixon "was extended an appointment as a Special Agent of the FBI, but having already embarked upon the practice of law, the FBI's loss ultimately became the country's gain." Hoover, in this instance, suggested that Nixon, rather than the bureau, had lost interest. When Nixon addressed the eighty-third graduation exercises for the same event on May 28, 1969, however, he stated that after becoming vice president, he asked Hoover to check to find out the reason for his rejection. On this occasion, the director changed his story, telling Nixon that he had been approved, but Congress had not appropriated sufficient funds for his appointment, and therefore his position had been eliminated.[1]

Nixon haters, for their part, have connected this incident with Nixon's sinister side. Professor Bruce Mazlish, for example, stated that Nixon's failure to be accepted as a special agent demonstrated that "Nixon clearly had not made it on his first try. Psychologically, he must have perceived himself as a failure, like his father." Dr. David Abrahamsen claimed that even though the FBI turned Nixon down, he remained fixated with the bureau because of its emphasis on "law and order." This anxiety, the psychoanalyst surmised, "may have been a reaction to his own antisocial tendencies, which he projected onto other people and which he felt had to be watched."[2]

The existing record, in this instance, presents what occurred and proves both sides wrong. Just over six decades after Nixon applied to the FBI, it released his file. Included in his application was his readiness to serve immediately, to proceed to Washington, D.C., with ten days' notice at his own expense, and to go anywhere in the United States for temporary or permanent duty. As for his current health, he noted two or three "common, slight colds" in the previous three years, but omitted a tonsillectomy in 1935. He did suffer from relaxed inguinal rings in both left and right groins, but these ruptures in his lower abdomen could be repaired easily and would not affect strenuous activities.

He filled out a brief biographical sketch that gave enough vital information so that the agency could easily check his background. Born on January 9, 1913, in Yorba Linda, California, at twenty-four years old he was five foot eleven, weighed 160 pounds, and his blood pressure was 126 over 78. His parents were Francis Anthony "Frank" Nixon, originally from Ohio, and Hannah Milhous, who came from Indiana. Their son Richard was an unmarried U.S. citizen, without any children or debts. From his outline, he started elementary school in Yorba Linda at the age of six, moved on to the East Whittier School in 1923, entered Fullerton High School three years later, transferred to Whittier High School in September 1928, and graduated in two years. He attended

Whittier College from 1930 to 1934, went to Duke University Law School that fall, and expected to receive his LL.B. in June 1937.[3]

Dean of the law school H. Claude Horack reminded J. Edgar Hoover, in a letter sent on May 3, 1937, that he had asked the dean to refer "any exceptional young man" for the position of special agent. Horack recommended Richard Nixon "without reservation" because he was "one of the finest young men, both in character and ability, that I have ever had the opportunity of having in my classes. He is a very superior student, alert, aggressive, a fine speaker and one who can do an exceptionally good piece of research work when called on to do so." He represented the student body of the law school after being elected president of the Duke Bar Association, where he had shown "fine executive ability and extremely good judgment."[4]

Special Agent J. H. Hanson interviewed Nixon during the middle of July in Los Angeles for forty minutes. He found out that his subject lived in Whittier with his parents and two brothers who were in school. Richard had never been arrested or involved in any trouble. He had worked in his father's grocery store part time, interviewed students considering Whittier College during the summer of 1931, and helped with the family business from 1932 through 1935. After entering law school, he was employed as an assistant in the law library and later did research for the dean. He mentioned his election to the major legal honorary society, the Order of the Coif, and his failed attempt to receive a varsity football letter during his college years.

Hanson described his candidate's personal appearance to be good, neat, and ordinary. He was poised, spoke adequately with no foreign accent, was self-confident without being nervous, and demonstrated tact. He answered questions quickly, was resourceful, and was likely to develop executive abilities. For relaxation, he played handball, bridge, and poker; he also swam, went to the movies, danced, and read. Occasionally, in social situations, he drank liquor. He already planned to return to California and take the bar examination commencing on September 7. If his FBI application was rejected, he would practice law. His deficiencies, according to the special agent, were that the prospect had not studied federal procedure, had no investigative experience, and no firearms training.

After this and another interview, Hanson recommended Nixon, who was "above average in intelligence and mental alertness." He possessed "sufficient force and aggressiveness" and had "good common ordinary sense." He expressed his thoughts clearly and had a manly presence. Hanson thought that Nixon "could successfully contact persons of all walks of life and that he would inspire confidence."[5]

Once this recommendation was approved, Nixon next had a medical examination scheduled in Los Angeles, toward the end of July, which he passed, and was cleared to perform "arduous" physical exercise. Special agents from California and North Carolina did background checks in Yorba Linda, Whittier, and Durham. On the last day of the month, Nixon agreed to the FBI terms of employment to be appointed Special Agent in Grade Caf (Clerical, administrative, and fiscal categories within civil service) 9, at $3,200 annually, and on August 3 he had been cleared for appointment. Yet, in the middle of the month, without any explanatory note in the file, his employment was canceled.[6]

The FBI never sent Nixon a letter saying that he had been turned down or gave a reason for his rejection. By winter he eliminated the FBI as a career choice; instead, he decided to join a local Whittier law firm. Within this context, he reported taking the bureau's examination, and that since that test, special agents had "been investigating my character. . . . However unless my present prospects fall through, I shall not accept the job even if it is offered to me."[7]

Hoover's assertions from the 1950s are clearly wrong. Nixon could not have chosen the law over the FBI, for he did not receive notification that he had passed the bar until early November. Second, the director's later assertion that an appropriations reduction was the cause is not supported in the file; Congress had already funded the agency for that year.

In the spring of 1969, Special Agent J. B. Adams looked again into the question and again realized that no satisfactory answer could be discerned. He suggested that Hoover's 1954 remarks be reiterated because they were "consistent with the information which we have in our files." Consistency appeared more essential than veracity for a potentially delicate inquiry.[8]

This case dispels myths about Nixon's initial connection with the FBI without offering any definitive replacement for them. Possibly, the agent who requested that Nixon be deferred until he completed the bar examination was the cause, or with that delay, someone else filled his appointment. Sometimes life does not fit in neat compartments. American history might have been very different if Nixon had joined the FBI at twenty-four years old. Fate intervened to take him down another avenue.

Fortunately for all of us, Nixon's FBI application can definitively answer many of the questions about his early life. As his application to the bureau hints and many other sources confirm, Richard Nixon in 1937 was a driven, popular, and highly successful young adult. He came from solid stock. His father's lineage traced back to Scotland and Ireland. Several relatives fought in the American Revolution and Richard's great-grandfather died during the Civil War at the battle of Gettysburg. Part of the family moved from Pennsylvania to Ohio, where Frank was born on December 3, 1878, one of five children, to a farming family of practicing Methodists, living on the edge of poverty. His mother, Sarah Ann, died of tuberculosis when he was eight, and his formal education ended before the completion of elementary school. He became a laborer, painted houses, made bricks, worked as a potter, and farmed. He also worked as a streetcar motorman in Columbus. During the harsh winter of 1906, his feet suffered from frostbite, and as a result of that hardship, he successfully lobbied to have vestibules enclosed and heated for motormen. Nonetheless, he decided to leave the extreme weather conditions of the Middle West for California. He was not well educated, but he had reliability, diligence, and talent.[9]

Nixon's maternal heritage was also pre-Revolutionary. The Milhouses originally came from Germany and migrated to England and Ireland. James Milhous, an Irish-born Quaker, came to the United States in 1729 and settled in Pennsylvania. Descendants moved to Ohio and then to Indiana where Hannah Milhous was born on March 7, 1885, into an energetic Quaker farming family in Butlerville, one of seven girls and two boys. Since both her parents belonged to the church, she was classified as a birthright Quaker. In 1897, her prominent and prosperous father, Franklin Milhous, an orchardist, moved the family's entire belongings in a freight car to Whittier, California, founded a decade earlier, named after the famous Quaker poet John Greenleaf Whittier. While Franklin attended to the business of establishing a tree nursery and planting an orange grove, his daughter Hannah continued her education, graduated from the Whittier Academy, and attended Whittier College through her sophomore year. By all descriptions, she was deeply religious, well educated, enjoyed music, and was ready to start her own family.[10]

Frank Nixon reached Southern California in 1907, and a year later, he met Hannah at a Valentine's Day party. Instantly attracted to one another, they were married four months later over her family's objections that Frank was not a Quaker and Hannah had not finished college. Their first child, Harold, was born in 1909, and Richard, the second son, came in 1913; Francis Donald, Arthur, and Edward followed. With the exception of Francis Donald, all were given the names of early English kings. Richard was the first child to be born into a modest house that Frank had built in Yorba Linda. The first floor had a kitchen, living room, and bedroom for his parents. To get to the second story, Richard and his brothers had to climb narrow steps upstairs to sleep in a single room of about one hundred square feet, where a man taller than five foot ten had to crouch. He and three other brothers shared two tiny twin beds.[11]

The family settled in Yorba Linda principally because land cost less there than in Whittier. Frank planted lemon trees supplied by Hannah's father on the 12½-acre tract. After Richard gained fame, he sometimes was heralded as the first Caucasian born into that tiny farming community of approximately two hundred inhabitants. With the exception of the housing concentration around the large Sunkist packing facility, his closest neighbor was at least a quarter mile away. The climate was semi-arid. The topography featured rolling hills with few trees. During the powerful Santa Ana winds, sagebrush rushed through the canyons. Plenty of coyotes inhabited the region, filling it with loud howls, but these creatures caused no threat to small children, for there was also an abundance of ground squirrels and jackrabbits.[12]

The social center of the family was the Quaker Church. Frank quickly converted to that religion without having to abandon much of his original faith, for the Friends church attended by the Milhous clan did not follow the meetinghouses of their East Coast forefathers, a faith exemplified by silent prayers and the absence of ministers. Though the Quakers in Southern California shunned water baptism and communion, and some prayed quietly and used "thy," "thee," and "thou" to cast off class differences, while dressing plainly and practicing pacifism, most Quakers filled their church with a minister, sermons, and music. Services were held four times on Sundays and once on Wednesday evenings. The Nixons were not only fully committed to their local church, but revivalism and evangelism appealed so much to Hannah and Frank that the family often journeyed to Los Angeles to hear the major preachers of the era.[13]

Jessamyn West, Richard Nixon's second cousin and author of the novel *The Friendly Persuasion* and other books, remembered at sixteen attending Frank Nixon's Sunday School class. According to her, he was "an ardent and energetic teacher." His room was always filled and had to be expanded to accommodate others who wished to listen. His absolute conviction appealed to her, but not to her birthright relatives, "who were quiet, subdued, inclined to see both sides of every question. Frank saw one side: his; and he was not bashful about letting you know what was wrong with your side." He often was truculent, but congeniality tempered his harsher tone. Preaching to his class, "His cheeks flamed, and his voice trembled. He was the first person to make me understand that there was a great lack of practicing Christianity in civic affairs."[14]

Several years after Frank passed away, Richard remembered hearing about his father's difficulties leaving school at a young age and having to go to work. He had a "tough" childhood, but his son emphasized that his father "was a fighter" and "loved to argue with anyone about anything." Nixon credited his father with instilling a "competitive feeling" in him.[15]

In his memoirs, Richard added to these earlier impressions by providing a much deeper analysis of his father's behavior. He said that Frank grew up almost "penniless" after his mother's death, worked at various trades, and continually "tried to better himself through work." Even when his family desperately needed economic assistance, Frank refused to accept what he considered to be charity. Indeed, his lifelong commitment rested on the "dignity of labor." If that translated into lack of funds, so be it.

Frank was quick "to anger and to mirth." As a child, Richard recalled his father's temper most vividly. When Frank was upset, Richard avoided him. His father also was "a strict and stern disciplinarian." He loved to argue and debate, and his son credited the father with passing those traits on to him. Frank also believed in the "little man" and opposed the "robber barons" who controlled a large portion of America's wealth at the turn of the twentieth century. Despite the connection between big business and the Republican Party, he remained a staunch defender of the GOP.[16]

While Richard, in a 1958 interview, recalled his father being strict, he pictured his mother as "the complete opposite." She was "the gentlest, most considerate woman" of them all. "She would never turn a tramp away from the door." She and Frank argued about this: he wanted someone to work before receiving assistance, but she "ran the house like a charitable operation."[17]

In Richard's memoirs, his mother was a "Quaker saint," a "remarkable" individual whose "most striking quality was a deep sense of privacy." She was deeply religious. At night, before retiring, she "went into a closet to say her prayers." She provided him with a sound educational base. Before Richard went to grammar school, she had already taught him to read. She played the piano in the living room that gave him an early appreciation for music. While the clothes he wore were hand-me-downs, they were clean and pressed. Hannah was the inner strength of the family, completely devoted to her husband as he was to her. The parents, as expected of Quakers, did not drink, smoke, or curse, and that extended to the children.[18]

Richard's first vivid memory was when, at three, he fell off a horse-drawn buggy and sustained a gash on the left side of his head that resulted in an ugly scar. To hide it, he combed his hair straight back for the remainder of his life. He started elementary school in Yorba Linda at six and skipped the second grade. He quickly became an avid reader, and after completing his chores and homework, would read a book or magazine.

The family moved to Whittier in 1922. His father purchased some land on the main road connecting the eight-mile stretch between Whittier and La Habra to open the first gas station on that route. An almost instant success, the family added the Nixon Market, where Hannah baked pies and cakes. The enterprise consumed the entire family. Everyone worked keeping accounts, ordering goods, stocking shelves, spraying for flies, and cleaning up at the end of each day. As Richard remembered: "It was not an easy life, but it was a good one, centered around a loving family and a small, tight-knit, Quaker community. For those who were willing to work hard, California in the 1920s seemed a place and time of almost unlimited opportunity."[19]

When the family moved to Whittier, Nixon entered the fifth grade and participated in his first debate: "Resolved, that it is better to own your own home than to rent." He took the renting argument, and his father spent a great deal of time with his son analyzing that position. Frank badly wanted him to win. He did. For six months in 1925, Richard went to live in Lindsay, a Quaker settlement in central California, to test his musical abilities with Aunt Jane Beeson, one of Hannah's sisters, who had studied piano at the Metropolitan School of Music in Indianapolis. During that short period, he took daily piano and violin lessons. That June, he returned to Whittier, a twelve-year-old, reunited with his family, with piano skills that he would never forget.[20]

Shortly after coming home, tragedy struck when his seven-year-old brother Arthur died after a short illness. Hannah searched internally for strength, while Frank embraced evangelism, closing the gas station on Sunday, believing that keeping his business open on the Sabbath had somehow contributed to his son's death. The oldest son, Harold, had contracted tuberculosis several years before Arthur's death, and for years the family would cater to his medical needs as he gradually grew frailer and frailer. During Richard's last year at high school and early years in college, Hannah had taken Harold to Prescott, Arizona, where the dry climate and high elevation was supposed to help cure consumption. To reduce expenses, she would accept three other patients and administer to them. During Christmas and spring vacations, Frank would drive the long fourteen-hour trip to see his wife and son. Richard would spend parts of two summers there to stay with them and work at odd jobs. When Harold did not improve, they would return to familiar surroundings in the hope that that would somehow assist in his recovery. Nevertheless, after a long battle with this dreaded disease, Harold would succumb in the early spring of 1933. The deaths of these two siblings greatly disturbed Richard, who had been extremely close to his brothers.[21]

Back in the seventh grade, he continued on his debating career. The topic was: "Resolved—That insects are more beneficial than harmful." Taking the affirmative, he won again. Upon graduation from the eighth grade, his mother presented him with a Bible. Every night thereafter he went to bed after reading a few verses. Every day his forensic skills improved and added to his self-esteem.[22]

After completing school in East Whittier, he entered high school in Fullerton during the fall of 1926, and in the yearbook for his sophomore year, he was lauded for his "excellent work" as the representative of the West Coast High Schools in the National Oratorical Contest where he spoke on the U.S. Constitution. During his two years there, he averaged between 94 and 99 out of a possible 100 points. One of the courses in which he received straight As throughout high school was Latin. His mother had learned it and set a high standard for her son. He also was expected to behave. He never got into any trouble.[23]

In his junior year, Richard transferred to Whittier High School, where Richard suffered his first political defeat for presidency of the student body. The faculty mitigated that disappointment by selecting him for the powerful post of student body manager, the individual who handled football ticket sales and advertisements in the yearbook, the *Cardinal and White*. During his senior year, he starred as Aeneas across from his girlfriend, the police chief's daughter, Ola Florence Welch, who played Dido in an adaption of Virgil's *Aeneid*. When he embraced her, they had to wait until the catcalls and hooting stopped to proceed.

No one laughed at his scholastic record, which featured one of the highest grade points at the school. He was president of the Scholarship Society, wrote feature stories for the newspaper, and held memberships in the Latin and Dramatic Clubs. He spoke before the Kiwanis Club for constitutional orators, where he won the ten-dollar first prize; in his senior year, extemporaneous speaking was introduced for the first time. He again won ten dollars from the Kiwanis and twenty from the *Los Angeles Times*. During the district contest, held in Monrovia, he placed second. Only one thing could have stopped him from graduating: he contracted undulant fever and took four weeks to recover. He graduated on June 19, 1930, finishing third in his class and receiving the Harvard Club of California's outstanding student award.[24]

Although Nixon thought that he might be qualified for a tuition scholarship to study at Yale University, leaving Southern California to attend college was never an option. He graduated from high school at the height of the depression, when his older brother's futile fight against tuberculosis had depleted the family's finances. He had to remain at home, and that meant attending Whittier College, which not only provided a good education but also was still closely associated with the Quakers.

At seventeen, he entered college and decided to major in history, where Paul Smith taught him about American politics. A future president of the college, Smith later extolled his student's virtues. Richard Nixon was one of the finest students that the history professor had ever had. He quickly cut through to the essence of the question and had "a fantastic capacity to communicate with people eye to eye, shoulder to shoulder." Albert Upton instructed him in dramatics; and J. Herschel Coffin espoused a conservative brand of Protestantism. He also read and learned to enjoy the novels of Leo Tolstoy. During his first year, Nixon maintained a B average, a B+ as a sophomore, and nearly straight As for his last two years. Three years after graduation, S. A. Watson, dean of the college, called him "an outstanding student" and characterized him as being "a natural leader, an excellent mixer among students or adults, and an outstanding debater." Acting president Herbert Harris claimed that of all the college boys he had seen over the past twenty years, none outranked Nixon.[25]

He energetically participated in extracurricular affairs. He was elected president of the freshman class and also initiated the idea of a social fraternity called the Orthogonian Society, the "Square Shooters," presiding over its inaugural year. And he joined the varsity debate team. During his sophomore year, that group went on a 3,500-mile tour through the Pacific Northwest. In their travels, they stopped in San Francisco, where Nixon had his first drink of hard liquor at a speakeasy. He sang in the glee club, acted as stage manager for a production of *The Mikado* in his junior year, and appeared in dramatic productions. During his final year, he won the presidency of the student body based on a pledge that he would lobby for student dances on campus. The 1934 yearbook *Acropolis* stated that he was "Always progressive, and with a liberal attitude, he led us through the year with flying colors." That year, he received the Southern California Intercollegiate Conference extemporaneous debating award.[26]

He lost his front teeth playing basketball, which required a porcelain dental bridge. He tried out for the football team as a tackle, but was too light and uncoordinated. Still, he attended most practices and warmed the bench for years. Even with his athletic limitations, Nixon had a remarkable effect on the team because of his positive attitude. Coach Wallace "Chief" Newman, one-quarter Indian, ingrained that idea in the young man. The Chief's theory was that if you worked hard, you could beat anyone. Character counted. If you were knocked down, you got up and tried again. When the coach was later asked his opinion of Nixon, he replied that he was "one of the best all-around students Whittier College ever had." Newman also understood that Nixon was not "the husky type" and worried that since his brother Harold had died of consumption, Richard might possibly be prone to overexert himself.[27]

During the summers and after school, Nixon continued to work in the family grocery store, where he purchased and displayed fresh fruit and vegetables. In his last two years at Whittier, he traveled to high schools for the college to interview prospects, earning $250, which happened to coincide with his annual tuition.[28]

Sometime in his senior year at college, Nixon read a bulletin from the recently accredited Duke University Law School, announcing that it was offering tuition scholarships. He applied, was accepted, and left to begin his legal studies in September 1934. Arriving in Durham, North

Carolina, he confronted another culture. This was the South, and the town looked like something out of the Middle Ages. Even more important, rather than being at the top of his class, over half of his Duke colleagues wore Phi Beta Kappa keys out of the approximately one hundred students in the law school.[29]

Duke adopted the Harvard case method of teaching, which meant that students studied hundreds of cases for facts and precedents contained in each one. Professors then called on the students to recite in class and comment on the pertinent information from each case and on which legal theories were applicable. Memorization was essential to succeed in examinations. Nixon had a phenomenal memory, did well on his tests, and served on law review. Registrar Helen Kendall asserted that he was "considered one of the outstanding men in the Law School."[30]

Professor Douglas Maggs instructed Nixon during his entire stay and claimed that he was "one of the best students" at Duke. In addition, as president of the Duke Bar Association, Nixon handled disciplinary problems judiciously. Professor David Cavers edited the quarterly law review journal, *Law and Contemporary Problems*, and also taught Nixon. As for his scholarly achievements, Cavers pronounced that Nixon's articles "were some of the best that had ever appeared therein, and that he had a fine legal mind, and was a trustworthy and conscientious student."[31]

Nixon maintained his tuition scholarship during his entire stay, but that did not pay for his room and board, plus incidental expenses. His relatives provided some money, but he also worked part time. For the first two years, he assisted at the reference desk in the law library. William Roalfe, the librarian, considered Nixon "well above average not only in his work, but in his character and personality, and that he was well liked by students and faculty." In his last year, he did research work for Dean Horack, netting sixteen dollars a month. Ms. Bess Horton, in the student aid department, reported that Nixon did not borrow any money from the university and "all smaller bills that he incurred upon the campus had been promptly paid." When the FBI checked his credit record at the local Merchants Association, the special agent found out that Nixon "had no credit or criminal record" in Durham.[32]

He lived cheaply. During his first two years, he stayed in a rented room for five dollars a month. In his senior year, he moved into a "one-room clapboard shack without heat or inside plumbing" along with three other students, sharing two large brass beds. A metal stove sat in the middle of the room. At night, during cold weather, they stuffed paper in their primitive heater, and the first one to rise would light it so that they could put their clothes on by the heat from the fire. They called it "Whippoorwill Manor," appropriately in Duke Forest, close enough to walk to campus. His landlord, Mrs. Z. G. Henderson, did not charge Nixon because he was selected "as deserving" of free board; she characterized him as "very likable and trustworthy and . . . a rather quiet serious minded boy."[33]

Nixon saved money by usually having a Milky Way candy bar for breakfast. He left his razor blade on campus and shaved each morning in the men's room at the law library. Each afternoon, he played handball in the gym, and afterwards, showered there. His long relationship with Ola Florence Welch in Whittier was fading, but Lyman Brownfield, one of his roommates, recalled that Nixon "wasn't allergic to girls. . . . He liked them—as all of us did. But we just didn't have the money, and the dates were few and far between."[34]

The semester before graduation, Nixon started to plan for his future career. During the Christmas vacation of 1936, he traveled with two of his classmates to New York City to interview for legal positions. Only one firm showed any interest, writing him a month after his trip. By that time he had lost his enthusiasm for beginning a career in a large, expensive city. The following spring, he turned in another direction, applying to the FBI, which had initially responded positively. While he waited for the bureau to decide on his application, he marched in Duke's eighty-fifth commencement exercises as more than seven hundred students received degrees, the largest in the school's history. His family, including his eighty-eight-year-old grandmother, attended; his relatives' pride must have swelled as the announcer declared that Richard had graduated third out of the twenty-six in his class and had been tapped to the legal honor society, the Order of the Coif.[35]

Nixon returned to Whittier to prepare for the California bar examination, scheduled for September 7–10, for seven hours each day, by enrolling in the Nix-Burby course. During one of his interviews with FBI agent Hanson, Nixon affirmed that he hoped to take the test and would be finished by September 11. The agent recommended that Nixon's application be delayed until the 15th, "as I feel that the applicant is very desirous of taking this Bar examination and I believe that he would be a more satisfied employe[e] if he had that opportunity."[36]

While the recent Duke graduate crammed for the bar examination, the FBI interviewed individuals over thirty, but not relatives, gathering information. Essick Perry, a friend of the family who had known Richard his entire life, called the boy "A-1" and labeled the family "outstanding." Captain O. C. Smith of the Whittier Police Department regarded Nixon as "one of the outstanding young men of the community, his character being beyond reproach." Harry Schuyler, who managed the Leffingwell Ranch in town, lived near the family, praised the young man's character, and declared his parents were "industrious people who have enjoyed an excellent reputation." Those not on the list but interviewed randomly expressed similar feelings. W. Q. Dietrich, who operated a nearby service station, called Richard "an industrious young fellow." Mrs. M. Herigoyen, a neighbor, did not know the family well, but claimed Richard had "always been a fine young fellow and he never caused any trouble at any time." Special Agent G. J. Ross concluded the obvious from these references: Richard Nixon was exceptional, a "young man of outstanding attainments and ambition."[37]

Nixon never heard from the FBI. Fortunately for him, the state bar notified him that he had passed the examination and was admitted to the bar on November 9. By the start of 1938, Whittier's oldest firm, Wingert & Bewley, decided to hire him to handle federal income tax issues, estate planning, and divorce cases, an aspect of the law that he found particularly distasteful. His new profession consumed almost every waking moment, even opening a branch office in La Habra, a nearby town of four thousand. Within a year of entering practice, his diligence paid off when the firm was expanded to Wingert, Bewley, & Nixon.[38]

He was shy under certain circumstances, recalling one example shortly after starting his legal practice. His client in a divorce proceeding was a beautiful woman, who began explaining her intimate marital problems to him. This kind of "personal confession" embarrassed him, and he "turned fifteen colors of the rainbow."[39]

To build his business, Nixon had to overcome his discomfort to attract clients. He accomplished this by tying his community volunteerism to his practice. He joined the Kiwanis Club of La Habra, the 20–30 Club, composed of business and professional men in that age group, eventually serving as its president. Whittier College's trustees selected him as the youngest member ever chosen to its board; he became president of the college's alumni association as well as that of Duke's graduates in California. As for politics, he registered as a Republican in 1938 and spoke for its senatorial candidate, Philip Bancroft, in the Whittier area during that contest; two years later, he supported GOP presidential hopeful Wendell Willkie against Franklin Roosevelt's bid for an unprecedented third term.[40]

One other activity that he continued from high school and college days was dramatics. During his first year back home, he joined the Whittier Community Players, where he had a small part in *First Lady* and played the part of the attorney Flint in *The Night of January 16th*. The tryouts for the next production, *The Dark Tower,* changed his life, for he met Patricia Ryan there. As he remembered the event: "For me it was a case of love at first sight."[41]

They would spend more than half a century together. She not only appealed to him because she was very attractive, but they had a great deal in common. They were born within a year of one another, Pat being just nine months older than he. Both came from rural farming settlements, with financially unsuccessful parents who provided them with food and shelter, but had little excess cash. Both excelled in school (both skipped the second grade) and experienced deep personal losses during their educational training: two of his brothers died, as did both of her parents. Each was intensely private, and yet actively participated in extracurricular activities like acting and debate.

Born in the booming mining town of Ely, Nevada, on March 16, 1912, Thelma Catherine Ryan was the name that her Germanic mother christened her, but to William, her father of Irish descent, she was always his "St. Patrick's Babe," and her birthday was observed on March 17 in honor of his country's patron saint. To her father, she was "Pat." The year after her birth, the family moved to Artesia, California, eighteen miles southwest of Los Angeles, where Will operated a marginal 10½-acre truck farm. Her half brother and sister, along with her two brothers, helped with the chores, but during her first year in high school, when Pat was thirteen, her mother died of cancer. Despite that trauma she did well in her schoolwork, participating in dramatic productions, debate, and other extracurricular activities, and graduated with her two brothers in June 1929. Celebration turned to despair the following May 5, when a priest performed the last rites on her father.[42]

Too poor to attend college full time, she enrolled in a junior college in the fall of 1931. She accepted part-time jobs to support herself and entertained herself by taking major roles in local plays. By the fall of 1932, she left school and drove across the country to New York City to work and meet her eastern relatives on her father's side of the family. She worked in a hospital, traveled up and down the Atlantic seaboard, but soon realized that she needed to complete her education to achieve financial security. She returned to Los Angeles, enrolled in the University of Southern California, worked part time to support herself as a salesgirl and extra in the movies, and graduated in June 1937, cum laude.[43]

At twenty-five years old, Pat was five feet five, thin, with auburn-blond hair and brown eyes. She had several job opportunities, but accepted employment as one of 117 faculty members at Whittier High School with 1,821 students. She taught commercial subjects and was the adviser to the Pep Committee along with coaching the cheerleaders. As part of her faculty requirements, she was expected to participate in community affairs. Having enjoyed acting since high school, she joined the Whittier Community Players, where she met Dick at the auditions for *The Dark Tower*. When the review was published on February 18, both were received well.

Dick quickly decided to pursue her alone. She reacted ambivalently and continued to date other men; she had no intention of getting involved in a serious relationship. She hardly ever spent a weekend in Whittier, preferring to meet her dates in Los Angeles. Sometimes Dick escorted her to meet her boyfriends and drove her back home. By the summer of 1939, however, Pat was falling in love. On June 21, the following year, in a simple ceremony at the Mission Inn's presidential suite in Riverside, California, she became Mrs. Richard Nixon.[44]

After honeymooning in Mexico in mid-July 1940, the couple, along with Pat's Irish setter, moved to La Habra Heights, two miles from his law office and the high school, into a rear apartment above a garage, with a living room, bedroom, kitchen, and bath. Typical newlyweds, both worked and played together; they entertained frugally and basically enjoyed their new status as husband and wife. To celebrate their first wedding anniversary, they booked the least expensive accommodations for a two-week cruise on the *Ulua* through the Panama Canal. Their journey was memorable for two reasons: Dick got motion and seasickness, suffering in a cabin next to the engines while the smell of fumes seeped into their cabin. Second, they learned that Hitler had invaded Russia; both hoped that Stalin would win because the couple despised the Nazis. Though he would later build a career opposing the Soviet Union, at the time of this cruise, Richard held no strong anti-Communist feelings.[45]

Upon their return to Southern California, Richard learned that one of his major law professors, David Cavers, had recommended to David Ginsberg, general counsel of the Office of Price Administration (OPA), that he hire Nixon. Although the couple was enjoying married life in the West, both wanted to broaden their experiences. Richard traveled to San Francisco for an interview and was hired. One Sunday, shortly before the Nixons left for Washington, D.C., the news flash came over the radio that the Japanese had attacked Pearl Harbor. When, by January 1942, the couple moved into an apartment in Alexandria, Virginia, and America was at war, Nixon pondered changing his position from civilian to military service.[46]

While he was considering this major decision, he began work as a junior attorney in the tire-rationing section of OPA, while Pat took a job in the price division. In their eight-month stay in the capital, Nixon coordinated various price and rationing controls and won promotions for his diligence. In his short tenure, Nixon experienced both the strengths and weaknesses of the federal bureaucracy. He recognized the need to supervise the supply and demand for scarce products during a time of national emergency, but also saw the inefficiency that was part of a large organization that often fell prey to its own inertia.[47]

Under less than challenging conditions and the belief that he must join in the actual fighting against the Axis, despite his Quaker upbringing and his mother's fervent pacifism, Richard decided to resign from the OPA in August 1942, enlist in the U.S. Navy, and travel to Quonset Point, Rhode Island, for officer training school. Within two months of his arrival, he was commissioned a lieutenant. He immediately requested active sea duty; instead, he was appointed aide to the executive officer charged with building an air station at the Naval Reserve Aviation Base in Ottumwa, Iowa. Pat followed her husband to the construction site and worked as a local bank teller. While Richard helped supervise construction of the air strip for basic flight training, the couple lived in an apartment in town, and their biggest complaints centered on the severe midwestern winter and the food shortages.[48]

Dissatisfied with being landlocked, Richard saw a notice that the Bureau of Aeronautics had requested volunteers for sea duty among officers twenty-nine or younger. Although worried about his safety, Pat supported his decision to fight. In the spring of 1943, he received orders to report to San Francisco. Before debarking, he went back to Whittier to see his relatives. His mother Hannah, he understood, would be upset by his decision to join the fighting, but his convictions called for him to join the armed forces and fight. Pacifism would not impede Axis aggression. As he boarded the train with Pat, those gathered realized he might never return. Turning for one last look, he noticed that his mother maintained her composure, while his "father began to sob." Lieutenant Nixon shipped out in early June for the Solomon Islands; while he was steaming to the South Pacific, Pat decided to remain in Northern California and work in the city as a price analyst for the OPA.[49]

Nixon arrived in Nouméa, New Caledonia, late that month, assigned to the South Pacific Air Transport Command (SCAT), composed of two squadrons of Marine Air Transports and two of Army Air Transports, which used naval officers in charge of ground operations. His principal duties were to bring supplies to combat areas and evacuate casualties. From his first post on the island of Vella Lavella, he wrote Pat on August 24 about the various frustrations. He complained of the monotony, of working every night from 5:30 P.M. to the following morning without even time for a beer. One benefit was that his days were free, which enabled him to study a great deal. Instead of remaining in relative security, he hoped for a better job, "to spend some time in a less civilized place where I would feel that I was doing more." He was working on such a plan and told her: "Keep your fingers crossed and wish hard!"

For Dick, his dwindling expectations of war excitement and his loneliness caused him great pain. "The only thing that matters," he continued, was "that I love you more and more every day." In a postscript, he emphasized: "When I feel blue—I think of our times together—and it has a miraculous effect. You are a real tonic for me! Do write often because your letters are my only happiness now." He dutifully wrote Pat every day as long as he remained in his combat area.[50]

To get closer to combat, in January 1944 he found a way to be assigned to Bougainville, the largest of the Solomon Islands, where Japanese bombers occasionally struck. Everyone received a nickname; his was "Nick" Nixon. For those flight crews who landed at his SCAT station, he inaugurated "Nick's Hamburger Stand," which served free hamburgers and beer to weary flight crews.

Shortly after his arrival, the enemy attacked. He and five others rushed to an air-raid shelter. When the bombardment stopped, he emerged to find thirty-five shell holes nearby and his tent destroyed. Toward the end of January, he wrote Pat, describing the raid and how he and his men got up, put on their raincoats, and jumped into their foxhole only a few feet from that tent. The previous day had seen another, rather different brush with the enemy. After the flight crew that he saw off that morning returned in the afternoon, the alert sounded, and he and the airmen rushed to a trench, where they remained for about a hour until the all-clear sounded. So that his wife would not worry, he minimized the devastation caused by these air assaults: "It really isn't as bad as it sounds and the danger is very small. The only casualties are among those who refuse to get up and go to the foxhole and there are very few people like that!"[51]

Trying once more to get closer to the fighting, he joined New Zealand troops in the middle of February, who went ashore on Green Island, an atoll in the northern Solomons about three hundred miles from his current post. Four construction battalions landed to face light resistance from the skeleton force of 150 Japanese troops who remained there. By the end of March, the Seebees finished construction on a runway. A few days before completion, just about the time dusk turned to dark, an army B-29 bomber that had received major damage in an attack over Rabaul made a crash landing with some equipment still remaining on the field. As the plane's belly seemingly touched down safely, the observers cheered. Elation soon turned to horror as the plane slammed into a bulldozer and erupted into flames. Nixon helped carry away from the wreckage a dead crew member whose wedding band was still on his partially charred hand. After fourteen months in the South Pacific, Nixon's tour of duty was completed. He was awarded a navy unit commendation ribbon for his service with a unit that had displayed "outstanding heroism."[52]

Nixon returned to the United States in August 1944. Immediately after landing in San Diego, he called Pat in San Francisco, and she flew down to meet him. He waited for her at a terminal gate, and once she spotted him, "her eyes lighted up, and she ran to the barrier and threw her arms around me." According to her recollection, she greeted him with "an all-encompassing embrace."[53]

From the third week of August until the end of the year, Nixon was posted to the Alameda Air Station—near where Pat was living—as a first lieutenant attached to Fleet Air Wing Eight. At the start of the new year, he was transferred to the Bureau of Aeronautics in the capital for a month, then went to Philadelphia for another two months, then New York City for four months. In September, he was assigned to Baltimore, where he handled contract termination negotiations with the defense contractor Glenn L. Martin.[54]

During his absence in the South Pacific, the couple had corresponded about what they should do after the end of his tour. They decided to start a family and possibly remain on the East Coast. They had compiled a nice nest egg: he had won some money playing poker, and she lived frugally, which added to their savings. They would need it: Pat got pregnant that summer and was expecting her baby early in 1946. His naval assignment in Maryland, terminating defense contracts, was almost over; he knew that he had better find a new job because he soon would become a father.[55]

He had several alternatives. One option that he had discarded was a professional military career. He would be discharged by the new year. All indications pointed to his resuming private practice. Before the war, he was a bright, well-spoken young attorney who had worked energetically at a prominent Whittier law firm. He had gained additional experience in the federal bureaucracy drafting OPA regulations. During his time as a naval officer, he learned new skills directing a SCAT detachment and terminating multimillion-dollar government contracts. All of this training gave him additional breadth and depth, but he was uncertain where these strengths would lead him.

Yet Nixon had demonstrated a powerful drive toward successfully fulfilling his goals. He had grown up in modest surroundings and had excelled in school, graduating near the top of his class in high school, college, and law school. As his benchwarmer football attitude demonstrated, he was no quitter. Failure was no excuse; often it was the prelude to success.

He had proven himself in school, love, and combat through study, perseverance, and resoluteness. These traits would remain with him for the rest of his life. The question of how to channel these strengths toward the end of 1945 had not been settled.

# Chapter 2

# NIXON'S FIRST PRIMARY

By the fall of 1945, while Nixon was deciding his future, the Republicans in California's 12th congressional district had grown angry and frustrated because they had never won that House seat. Activists embarked on an almost religious crusade to defeat Horace Jeremiah "Jerry" Voorhis, the five-term incumbent. Many in the GOP believed that he had repeatedly been triumphant not because of his attributes but because Republicans had failed to unite behind their nominee. Roy McLaughlin, their sixty-five-year-old conservative standard-bearer in 1944, agreed. If the GOP had pulled together, he would have claimed victory. Using this argument for the momentum to unite, a small group of leading Republicans met at Eaton's restaurant in Arcadia in the spring of 1945, where they formed the Candidate and Fact Finding Committee, ultimately consisting of approximately 109 of the district's party faithful.[1]

One of its most prominent members was the chairman of the Republican Central Committee for the 12th district, Roy O. Day, who issued an open appeal that summer to solicit candidates to run against the incumbent. Twenty-six local newspapers thought this novel approach so unusual that they printed his general requirements on their front pages as a feature story. In it, Day called for aspiring Republicans—preferably young veterans with some education—to present themselves before the committee and seek its endorsement. But those who initially applied failed to impress the committee.[2]

Herman L. Perry, Bank of America branch manager in Whittier and another well-respected committee participant, thought that he had the solution: Richard Nixon. Toward the end of the summer, Perry began asking mutual friends where to find him. Perry got a mailing address, and on September 29, sent an airmail letter to Nixon at his apartment in Middle River, Maryland, asking if he would consider running for Congress in 1946. If so, Nixon should reply promptly. Less than two years after that unexpected letter, Nixon acknowledged that Perry's initiative had changed his life, for until that moment, he "had not the slightest idea that I might be running for Congress."[3]

Nixon was so excited by the proposal that instead of replying by mail, he telephoned Perry to offer himself as a candidate. Temporarily dampening his enthusiasm, Perry explained that Nixon had to go through a selection process to get the committee's endorsement; even then, the nomination was not automatically his. He would have to mount a primary campaign. For the present, Nixon must trust Perry's political acumen and let him maneuver. Grateful for the opportunity, the enthusiastic aspirant instantly placed his future in the banker's hands.

Perry, an old family friend, looked distinguished, was heavyset, graying and losing hair, wore glasses, and dressed conservatively. Born in 1884 at Westfield, Indiana, the son of birthright Quakers, he graduated from high school in 1901 and briefly attended Earlham College, founded by Quakers. He next went to business college in Nebraska, where he took courses enabling him to teach bookkeeping and commercial law. In 1905, he managed a grocery store; the following year, he moved to Whittier to do similar work. Two years later, he switched to banking and remained in it for the next four decades.[4]

Perry had actively engaged in local Republican politics since 1920, believing: "If you want sound men in office you must help select them." In 1932, he was elected to the county's GOP central committee, but soon resigned his post. Disillusioned with the New Deal, he still preached that "every individual should assume his or her share of community or public responsibility." He practiced this credo by serving as a member and later president of both the Whittier College board of trustees and the Whittier Chamber of Commerce.[5]

Although not officially a member of the Republican county organization, Perry was well respected. His opportunity to introduce Nixon's name to the Candidate and Fact Finding Committee came at its first dinner meeting at the Woman's Club in Monrovia on Friday, October 5, 1945. The banker could not attend, but two days before the gathering, he wrote his colleagues that Nixon was "the best available candidate."

He was a relatively young and a "very aggressive individual." Like Perry, Nixon came "from good Quaker stock," had gone to high school and college in Whittier, where he had become a champion orator and debater in school, had been a partner in a prominent local law firm, and was currently a naval officer stationed on the East Coast.[6]

While Perry was busy listing Nixon's virtues, Dick informed his sponsor that he would not be a financial liability to the party because he would "be able to stand the financial expense that the campaign would entail." If he stood a reasonable chance to win the Candidate and Fact Finding Committee's approval, he needed to know so that he could train a successor, since he was finishing up his assignment dealing with contract negotiations for the navy and expected to be discharged in January 1946.

Nixon did not mask his delight at the possibility of running. He had been away from the West Coast for almost four years and was pleasantly surprised "to learn that I was even being considered for the chance to run against Jerry Voorhis." To Nixon, his possible opponent was weak on a number of political issues, but the voters had previously cast their ballots for him solely because he was the best candidate in a mediocre field. The fact that he was not a veteran also hurt his chances. Given the opportunity, Nixon felt "very strongly that Jerry Voorhis can be beaten and I'd welcome the opportunity to take a crack at him. An aggressive, vigorous campaign of a platform of *practical* liberalism should be the antidote the people have been looking for to take the place of Voorhis' particular brand of New Deal idealism. . . . I'm sure I can hold my own with Voorhis on the speaking platform and without meaning to toot my horn I believe I have the fight, spirit and background which can beat him."[7]

Nixon had accurately gauged the minimalist caliber of Voorhis's Republican past adversaries. In his first congressional election, Voorhis benefited from the Roosevelt 1936 landslide. Two years later, his challenger had been so shy that Voorhis had to introduce him at joint appearances. The next contender, who lost by a wider margin, was a commander of a small military school for boys. In 1942, Robert Shuler, a bombastic El Monte minister and radio evangelist, even embarrassed GOP regulars, and McLaughlin was the last victim.[8]

Voorhis had originally entered politics on the platform to End Poverty in California (EPIC) in the bleakest days of the depression. He was espoused by the novelist Upton Sinclair, who ran on the gubernatorial ballot, and who wanted to end direct relief by encouraging farming and basic industries to sustain themselves. That kind of cry appealed to Voorhis, who ran as a Democrat, but he lost badly to the popular incumbent, Herbert Evans.[9]

Born in 1901 into a prosperous family, Jerry readily accepted its deeply held Christian beliefs. He graduated from Hotchkiss, an elite boarding school in Connecticut closely associated with Yale University, and started at Yale in 1919, leaving four years later with a Phi Beta Kappa key. He never considered himself part of the "in crowd," and in many ways, he relished being a maverick. After graduation, Jerry rebelled against the family fortune and decided to live with the poor. He took jobs as a freight handler and a laborer in an automobile assembly factory. In the winter of 1923–1924, he went to Germany as a Christian volunteer to do charitable work, but came home after an illness shortened his stay.

During World War I, the horror of the conflict had convinced him to become a pacifist and a socialist. As part of his conversion, he became vehemently opposed to monopolies, for he felt that they inhibited the rights of laborers. To accommodate his mission to assist the needy, Jerry and his wife, Louise, founded several schools for homeless boys; and in 1927, at the request of his father, who had purchased some land in San Dimas, the couple moved to California, where they established the Voorhis School for Boys. As for politics, Jerry registered with the Socialist Party. Initially, Roosevelt was unappealing; but by 1936, Voorhis fully embraced the president and the New Deal.[10]

Perry joined the Republican battle against Voorhis after Donald Lycan, president of Signal Oil, approached Perry in early 1944 with an intriguing proposal: Lycan would contribute $2,000 to the GOP campaign that year if Perry would direct it. Lycan, due to his prominence in the petroleum business, did not want to publicize his large contribution because it might soil his candidate's chances. Perry agreed to lend his name to the campaign with the stipulation that if he thought that McLaughlin had no chance, Perry would terminate his involvement and return whatever portion of Lycan's funds remained. Perry, in fact, grew so disenchanted that several weeks before the general election he refused to spend Lycan's last $500. Although Perry did not have any intention of launching the Candidate and Fact Finding Committee after McLaughlin's defeat, that money provided the initial capital for the committee's efforts, and in that sense, Don Lycan unknowingly became Nixon's first contributor.[11]

Perry had far greater expectations for Nixon in 1946. McLaughlin, Perry had learned, lost partly because he faced many primary challengers. The current committee's screening process hopefully would significantly narrow the field and thereby reduce the bickering among the Republican contenders. "Old Blood and Guts," General George Patton, Jr., who had a home in the district, was mentioned in the newspapers as a possibility, but he quickly declined. Sam Gist, Jr., a fifty-six-year-old Pomona furniture dealer who had fought in both world wars and was a civic leader, had also advanced his name, but he attracted a lukewarm following. Others like Tom Ball, who had run unsuccessfully in the last primary, were bluntly discouraged. Just by attrition, the field was significantly narrowing.[12]

Unbeknownst to Perry, some Republicans were considering as their first choice Dr. Walter Dexter, a former Whittier College president and current state superintendent of public instruction. Perry had been a confidant of Dexter's and a supporter in his earlier campaigns. Now he was irritated that Dexter had not consulted him. Perry informed Dexter that Nixon's name had already been submitted, and Perry felt that Nixon would make "a very attractive candidate." The last thing that Perry wanted was a hotly contested primary struggle between Nixon and Dexter.[13]

Under this possible adversarial scenario, Perry pressed Dexter to remove himself from consideration, while Roy Day, more than anyone else, was pulling in the opposite direction. He had supported McLaughlin's effort and hated losing. Day gave no quarter and later recalled: "I've never gone on a basis of just playing to play. I like to win and I play hard to win. You have to carry the fight all the way; never get on the defensive. Nice guys and sissies don't win many elections." He knew Dexter and thought that he could win; Nixon was an unknown.[14]

Day committed himself to victory. This, thin, dark-eyed, middle-aged man was born in 1900. The son of a Pomona orange grower, he grew up on a ranch, attended local schools until his junior year in high school, dropped out, and then joined the navy. After finishing his military service, he worked two years as a secretary to the head of the United Fruit Company in Costa Rica, then returned to Arizona, where he became a secretary at Ray Con Copper Company, and pitched semi-pro baseball. One year later, he returned to Pomona to sell classified advertising at the *Progress*, which ultimately became the *Progress-Bulletin*. That was his profession; his avocation was Republican politics.[15]

Dexter had taught Nixon at Whittier College and was impressed with his former student; Nixon, too, had fond memories of his former teacher. Dexter went so far as to recommend Richard Nixon to Day. If Dexter decided against running, Day grudgingly agreed to consider Nixon, but the chairman still pressured Dexter to enter the race. The committee leaders, Day assured Dexter, represented an "excellent cross section of political thinking and wishes in our area." They would endorse "ONE candidate" and unite behind that person. This would discourage others from entering the primary, and for the first time, the Republicans in the 12th congressional district would not be saddled with a minority candidate, a hastily drawn organization, and bruised egos. The party would then be rebuilt "on a new, modern, streamlined basis," and develop a positive alternative to the Democrats, "not just register a protest vote against Jerry Voorhis." According to Day, only a progressive campaign strategy could defeat the Democrats.[16]

Day placed Dexter's name before a pivotal planning session in early October and purposefully postponed the next meeting of the Candidate and Fact Finding Committee until early in November to allow Dexter time to make his decision. But in mid-October, Dexter became seriously ill, and decided against running. He died suddenly of a heart attack on the 21st. Even before that tragedy, Day had accepted Dexter's withdrawal and tentatively decided to support Nixon if he flew to California and present himself for a November 2 interview. If that was impossible, Day and other Republican leaders wanted to arrange a private luncheon with Nixon to evaluate his chances.[17]

While Day and others started to lean toward Nixon's selection, the mere existence of the Candidate and Fact Finding Committee proved somewhat controversial. The *Arcadia Tribune & News*, an independent Republican newspaper, editorialized that Republican leaders were choosing a congressional candidate using Tammany Hall methods, of which the paper disapproved. This ad hoc committee had no authority to choose a candidate from a smoke-filled room. Everyone who wished to enter the contest should have a chance during the primary election: "What the men who are attempting to impose this idea on the 12th District Republicans are saying, in effect, is that you, the voters, are not smart enough to pick a good and worthy candidate to carry the Republican banner in the coming election, so we, the dozen or so of us, who know all the angles, will have to do it for you."[18]

Despite such nagging criticisms, the committee moved forward, and

Nixon, who now realized the importance of his trip, arranged a flight to Los Angeles for himself and Pat. He even encouraged Perry to arrange a meeting with district leaders to express his political views because he "could effectively sum up the reasons why Voorhis can and *must* be beaten in this election."[19]

Filled with doubt, "Nick" Nixon, on October 22, wrote James B. "Jim" Stewart, a comrade who had served with him in the South Pacific. He told Jim that he regularly worked in New York City on termination contracts and had been trying to locate his pal since summer when the navy relocated him to the East Coast. The navy had promoted him to lieutenant commander, and if he stayed in the service until mid-April, the navy promised to make him a full commander. But he and Pat had had enough. They had decided that he would leave the service by the new year and might even move north because both of them thought that there was "no town like New York."

The one alternative that intrigued Nick Nixon was a run for Congress. He was flying out to Los Angeles for a critical meeting where he would present his qualifications and worried that he was going to have a "pretty tough" time. "I guess I need you to promote the deal! I don't know whether it will pan out."[20]

While Nixon fretted, Perry was successfully lobbying McLaughlin, who was convinced that Nixon "would be a strong fighting candidate. If he can make as good a showing upon a personal appearance we should be able to elect him." The former candidate was concerned that voters found Voorhis attractive because he was "a nice appearing young man who poses as a prophet or martyr." Voorhis worked hard, and therefore any direct attack on him or his record would fail to dissuade his admirers. McLaughlin wanted Republicans to present a positive alternative in sharp contrast to Voorhis's unproductive record.[21]

The GOP was already publicizing its upcoming meeting by sending out press releases stating that several potential contenders, including Nixon, planned to seek the Candidate and Fact Finding Committee's endorsement to challenge Voorhis. Day reminded Nixon's backers: "we must remember that we only have one chance to see, know, and if it seems the thing to do—sell Lt [*sic*] Comdr. Nixon to the district."[22]

Nixon arrived in time for a special noon luncheon on November 2 at the University Club in Los Angeles. Gerald Kepple, former state assemblyman from Whittier and currently vice president and general counsel for Consolidated Telephone Company, and Tom Bewley,

Nixon's former law partner, served as escorts. Most in attendance were businessmen who knew how to sell merchandise and exercised considerable influence in Republican local political circles. The GOP national committeeman from California, who happened to reside in South Pasadena and practice law in Los Angeles, McIntyre Faries, went; his friend and ally, Harrison McCall, who owned the Los Angeles Testing Laboratories and was president of the Republican Assembly for the 12th district, was there; Herbert Spencer, president of the South Pasadena Republican Club, came; a representative of the *Los Angeles Times* was there; Lance Smith, chairman of the Republican Assembly in the 49th state district, attended; and Frank Jorgensen, a recent appointee to the Los Angeles County Republican Central Committee and a successful insurance executive, was included, as was John "Jack" Garland, a wealthy real estate developer, who was married to Helen Chandler and automatically became the brother-in-law to Norman and Philip Chandler, owners of the *Los Angeles Times*. Once the participants finished lunch, Nixon rose and explained to the group why he should be considered for the endorsement. He closed: "I'm in your hands. If you want me to run, I will."[23]

Those in attendance were impressed. Several like Garland, McCall, Spencer, and Jorgensen would become lifelong Nixon advocates, contributing time, allegiance, and money to their standard-bearer. Even at this initial stage of his political blush, influential people from various backgrounds saw something in Nixon that engendered confidence: a feeling that he would not only seriously contest the congressional seat but also had a far brighter future.

Following up on his noontime success, Nixon appeared the next evening at the final dinner of the Candidate and Fact Finding Committee at the William Penn Hotel in Whittier. Six potential candidates spoke, and Nixon, dressed in his naval uniform, happened to draw the lot as the last speaker. The program was long, and Nixon therefore decided to make his first political speech short. He pledged to work for free enterprise instead of government control, personified by the New Deal. If he won the committee's endorsement, he would "be prepared to put on an aggressive and vigorous campaign on a platform of practical liberalism," and with the committee's backing, Nixon felt "very strongly" that he could defeat Voorhis. By the time Nixon had finished his presentation of about ten minutes, Day later reflected that he had "salable merchandise."[24]

Nixon thanked Day for the opportunity to present his credentials and flattered him by linking him to "a younger element in the Republican Party represented by men like yourself who are making a real effort to find a winning candidate for 1946. A candidate should welcome the opportunity to run against Jerry Voorhis with such support." The next day, Nixon met informally with a Republican women's group from San Marino, where one guest blurted out that Pat did not "even know what color nail polish to wear." Day never forgot that snide remark; he grew to admire Pat so much that he eventually named one of his daughters after her.[25]

Tom Bewley was overjoyed with the results of Nixon's visit and the surge of enthusiasm within Republican ranks: "I am quite thrilled about your record and appearance. It has at least gotten the party together." Bewley cautiously warned Dick that the Democrats had spies within the Republican Party and would quickly learn about his trip. At present, that eventuality seemed inconsequential because his friends were already lining up committee members' votes for Nixon. Kepple would nominate him, and Thomas Erwin, popular state assemblyman from the area, would make the second. Bewley felt Nixon would win in a landslide and so noted that Day excitedly claimed to have already raised $5,000 with expectations of doubling that figure.[26]

Bewley continued to send Nixon glowing reports. The committee started talking about a landslide and getting a glossy photograph of him in naval uniform, but Nixon's former law partner cautioned that he should not "count your chickens too soon." By the middle of November, Bewley supplied a further update: "The boys have been taking a poll all week and they actually count more than a majority in your favor." The drive to anoint Nixon was accelerating.

Nixon added fuel by writing Bewley: "I'm getting pretty pepped up for this race and hope the boys give me the chance to run. If they do—you can tell them Jerry will know he's been in a real fight because I won't spare the horses."[27]

Nixon's ability to inspire confidence came from the manner in which he treated potential supporters. He welcomed comments and solicited advice. While on the plane back to the East Coast, he read the articles on the atomic bomb that Herbert Spencer had given him a day earlier. Nixon was impressed with Spencer's call for immediate action, while President Harry Truman failed to grasp the urgency for movement. If Nixon received the endorsement, he expected to consult with Spencer, who recognized "the necessity of adopting a constructive liberal program rather than of resorting solely to the usual negative critical attack upon current new deal policies."[28]

Now Roy Day was orchestrating Nixon's chorus. First, according to the chairman, Judge Harry Hunt would drop out of the race and announce for Nixon. Although a Pomona faction expected to nominate Sam Gist, after the first ballot he would move to make the vote for Nixon unanimous. The Whittier contingent, led by Perry and his assistant at the bank, Harold Lutz, was firming up pledges for Nixon. As far as Day was concerned, he was already confirmed. Just after New Year's Day, 1946, Day anticipated kicking off the campaign and intended to push straight through to the election: "Frankly Dick, we feel we have SOMETHING AND SOMEBODY to sell to this district now and are going to do our very best to close the deal." Day was anticipating victory that fall and told the faithful that if only 7,041 voters had switched to Republican in the last election, the party would have won.[29]

Nixon expected to return to California by the new year if he was nominated. He had been studying Voorhis's record during the evenings and on weekends and also had read the congressman's poorly and turgidly argued book, *Out of Debt, Out of Danger*, which proposed direct use of federal credit and an end to interest on the national debt. "I believe there's some ammunition right *there* which can be used to advantage." The Democrats were vulnerable on issues like foreign affairs and labor matters; the latter needed to be handled delicately. Nixon did not expect to focus on Voorhis's failures. He intended to highlight the positive Republican approach.[30]

As for Perry's role, Nixon could not have been more solicitous: "If I get this chance I will always feel that you were responsible and I certainly appreciate all you've done." Perry reciprocated and commented that Nixon had "been easy to sell the leaders." Still, Nixon never forgot his first advocate. Forty-one years later, he wrote Perry's son Hubert that without his father's "help my political career would never have begun!"[31]

The evening meeting on November 28 at the Alhambra YMCA completed the final action of the Candidate and Fact Finding Committee. Day had distributed a page-long list of twenty-three points in October so that everyone understood the voting procedure. Each member could only vote once by secret ballot, and the winner needed to receive at least two-thirds of those present.[32]

Erwin and Kepple, as anticipated, placed Nixon's name for consideration; several other nominations followed. The first ballot split along the expected lines: 63 for Nixon, 12 for Gist, and 2 for Frank Benedict. Then, as previously arranged, Gist's backers called for unanimity, and this gave Nixon the endorsement. Kepple beamed because Nixon had not only won the nomination, but he also had done so without creating bitter enemies. For first time, Republicans in the 12th district were united.[33]

Day phoned Nixon at 2:00 A.M. to give him the news. Later that day Nixon in a letter thanked the members. If elected, he would be responsive to his constituents, and he recognized "the urgent necessity of adopting a practical realistic foreign policy which will have as its primary purpose the avoidance of all future wars." At home, the United States faced reconversion: "The inventive genius and industrial know-how which have made America great must not be stifled by unnecessary bureaucratic restrictions. Economic dictatorship by irresponsible government agencies must never be allowed to become an accepted principle of our American system of government." As for the bitter feuding between management and labor, he proposed "to promote industrial peace as opposed to class hatred and economic warfare."[34]

Perry cautioned his protégé shortly after his pronouncement about making statements before adopting a platform. Nixon was now a marked man, and even unions would start to lobby him: "Watch your step from here on out. Now is the time to walk down the middle of the road and be careful where you go and who you counsel with."[35]

Nixon followed the advice. Until the Republican platform was accepted, he would not make any commitments: "I feel we must be particularly careful to have a progressive platform which will appeal to the rank & file as well as the regular party workers." He looked for ways to broaden his base and turned to Republican college professors on his steering committee who were not professional politicians: "I realize some are pretty liberal but I have some good friends up there and feel that their support & advice would be valuable."

He also was scrutinizing Voorhis's record: "I'm *sure* of what he is because I've talked to too many fellow travelers back here who are wild about him to fall for his 'conservative' line as indicated by his articles & his speeches. We must get the goods from his record." Voorhis had even convinced some Republicans that he was not a New Dealer, but Nixon knew better, as he informed Kepple: "I can assure you that judging from the high esteem in which he is held by some of my old 'Pinko' acquaintances in Washington his voting record has definitely been completely

New Deal." Nixon wanted to speak as much as possible before receptive audiences and already was drafting speeches to be given before service clubs, women's groups, and churches on nonpolitical topics like his military service. In this way, "We can make Mr. Voorhis sweat a bit this time."[36]

Nixon's use of anti-Communist terms like "fellow travelers" and "Pinkos" did not make him an anti-Russian crusader. He had not, as yet, assumed that mantle. He did, however, use emotionally laden phrases that appealed to those in the district like Kepple and others who highlighted the Soviet threat and objected to Roosevelt's postwar internationalism. The combination of the Democratic Party's drive for an American-Soviet alliance and the acceptance of the international Communist movement during the war drove many in the GOP to oppose Truman, work for his removal from office, and replace him with the traditional values of the Republican Party.

Nixon's linkage of Voorhis to the New Deal was essential to the upcoming campaign. The congressman had supported just about every piece of domestic legislation from enlarging federal bureaucracy to enacting labor standards and shorter hours. He had even supported the extremely unpopular Supreme Court packing scheme that had seriously split the Democratic Party in 1937. Voorhis, however, served on the House Committee for Un-American Activities (HUAC) and led in the passage of the Voorhis Act in 1940 that required any political organization controlled by a foreign power or engaged in military activities aimed at subverting the American government to register with the Justice Department. He had strong anti-Communist credentials, but his New Deal activities overshadowed everything else.[37]

Voorhis's votes demonstrated both his strengths and weaknesses in the first postwar congressional elections. In domestic matters, he had totally embraced the New Deal's social legislation and wished to go even further. Under these conditions, he relied on organized labor and other Democratic regulars as his major base for campaign contributions. In foreign affairs, he followed Roosevelt's internationalist approach and called for the United States to accept its international responsibilities rather than returning to prewar noninterventionism. His objectives still appealed to many, especially his party's loyalists, who still pledged their allegiance, vividly remembering Roosevelt had brought the United States out of the depths of depression. However, a large number of postwar Americans no longer blindly followed that legacy. Instead, they gradually moved away from left-of-center politics in favor of a more centrist approach. To that large mass, Voorhis's message had become outdated. The congressman never recognized that shifting political sentiment or the need for him to make his appeal broader to include this new rising constituency.

Combating Voorhis's record was not enough to assure victory. Nixon also needed to articulate his own positions. He tried to draft a statement of principles at his apartment, but they appeared dull. He had not, as yet, formulated the major issues that would eventually reflect the concerns of this newly emerging political base. While his lack of direction troubled him, he was confident that he would perform well in public. "I think we can build a fire under the district which won't die until Jerry Voorhis' goose is cooked!" Nixon would concentrate on "building up a positive, progressive group of speeches which tell what *we* want to do not what the Democrats have failed to do." To win, he had to capture the Republican faithful, the "liberal fringe Republicans," and a few Democrats.[38]

Although just recovering from the flu, Day intended to help as much as possible. He hired Murray Chotiner, a lawyer and public relations specialist for California Republicans, to prepare a news release on Nixon's endorsement and continue to issue regular information on what Nixon was doing. In total, Day paid Chotiner $500 through the 1946 primary campaign to produce ten news releases. He never worked in the general election, but over the next decade, Chotiner vastly exaggerated his initial involvement, angering several early loyalists. Ten years after this first race, Nixon commented that Chotiner made people "sore" by his untruthful statements and enraged the two actual campaign managers during the 1946 campaign. Nixon mythologists have seized on Chotiner's claims to illustrate how the Nixon-Chotiner nexus evolved from the very beginning of Nixon's entrance into politics, but the factual record from this first campaign confirms Nixon's version. Chotiner's involvement beyond the initial press releases was tangential.[39]

While Day and others were preparing for Nixon's return to California, Perry was sending letters of introduction and making appointments for him to see Joseph Martin, Republican minority leader in the House from Massachusetts, and John Phillips, a Quaker Republican congressman from nearby Banning, California. Both veteran politicians had analyzed Voorhis's vulnerabilities.[40]

In the middle of December, Nixon met with Martin as well as Representative Charles Halleck of Indiana, who chaired the Republican congressional campaign and from whom he had also received valuable information on organization and procedure. Voorhis, Nixon discovered, had consistently voted "with the most radical element of the New Deal group. He is definitely lined up with Congressman Vito Marcantonio of New York, [Frank] Hook of Michigan and Helen [Gahagan] Douglas of Hollywood whose political views are not open to doubt."[41]

Nixon also learned that Voorhis had not passed any of his sponsored bills or amendments, although he had introduced more each session than any other member. Everyone agreed that he was "honest, conscientious and able," but he simply did not focus on critical issues. Nixon acknowledged Voorhis's popularity and realized that any personal attack would backfire. He would sell himself and Republican policies, trying to avoid any mention of Voorhis by name. Initially, he would speak in generalities and gradually point to the incumbent's failures, but not too early to permit effective replies. Nixon would not go on the offensive until the summer.

As usual, Nixon carefully sought sound advice. Phillips emphasized a positive Republican program and especially encouraged the establishment of powerful groups of women volunteers. Congressman Carl Hinshaw from Pasadena advised him to concentrate on enthusiastic followers and select a campaign manager who could devote sufficient time to appeal to new voters and woo citrus growers from Voorhis's camp. At first, Nixon needed to focus on nonpolitical speeches and keep precinct workers inactive until just before the primary in early June 1946. He needed to maintain party unity. If he did not succeed there, he surely would lose.[42]

Spencer argued that Nixon had to support "sound economics" and convince labor that he sympathized with their concerns and was willing to listen to their viewpoints. To the older man, the United States needed men like Nixon in the federal government, and Spencer wanted to "send enough young people to Congress to stop this practice of mortgaging the future of your generation in order to keep a group of elderly politicians in power."[43]

While Nixon was preparing for his new adventure, Voorhis was attending to his usual congressional duties in 1945 and preparing for the upcoming campaign. To project a wholesome image to his constituents, he made short motion picture features that portrayed him as a family man—thin, cleanshaven, with dark hair and eyes—who drank milk, went to baseball games with his children, got regular haircuts, and was a habitual pipe smoker. In Congress, he worked hard on matters dealing with the agricultural needs of his district as well as postwar reconstruction. He was especially concerned about the availability of veterans benefits for returning soldiers; a far greater anxiety derived from his fear of the destructive capacity of the atom bomb and how to find a solution to prevent a nuclear holocaust.[44]

Back in the 12th district, his influential father Charles was monitoring his son's political base and kept his son apprised, sometimes daily, on what was happening in the district. Charles served as his son's liaison to the local business community and became heavily involved in Jerry's political career. Born in 1880, Charles Voorhis came from a deeply religious midwestern family with staunch abolitionist Republican beliefs. He started his working career as manager of a hardware store in Ottawa, Kansas, moved to Oklahoma in 1908 as a salesman for Kingmen Plow Corporation, and then to its headquarters in Kansas City three years later. Just before the outbreak of World War I, he moved to Pontiac, Michigan, to work for General Motors. When he retired in 1925, he did so as general sales manager for Nash Motor Corporation and had amassed a sufficient fortune to settle in Southern California and live off his portfolio for his remaining years.[45]

During World War II, Charles became particularly irritated with the emergence of radical elements within the labor movement's growing power inside the Democratic Party. He objected to the arbitrary actions of the Congress of Industrial Organizations (CIO) because it "was drunk with power." Extremists dominated these unions, and Congress had to apply the corrective. Charles knew that the CIO was "saturated with the more radical elements in our society, including the real Communists."[46]

Despite these misgivings, the father was extraordinarily proud of his son's "splendid" political accomplishments. Charles labeled Truman a "conservative liberal," who was performing well, while his son was leaning toward the president, having shifted from a full-fledged New Dealer to his maturation as a moderate Democrat. That summer, the *Progress-Bulletin* in Pomona editorialized that Voorhis was "one of the hardest working men in Washington and one of the best known of the Congressmen." The paper would not be surprised if he decided to run for the Senate in 1946. Such acclaim did not seem to invigorate Jerry, who appeared somewhat ambivalent toward his job. If he lost his bid for reelection, he "would look forward with the keenest pleasure to being in private life once again where the responsibilities of this office would no longer be upon my shoulders."[47]

His father saw no reason for this kind of pessimism; he was certain that his son would be reelected. No Republican had emerged to give him a serious challenge in the summer. By early winter, Charles reported "the more meetings they [the Republicans] hold the more hopelessly they are divided." Opponents were frantically searching for a serious contender and had not produced anyone.[48]

On December 1, Charles informed his son that the Candidate and Fact Finding Committee, in contradistinction to the spirit of the primary laws, had endorsed a Quaker named Richard Nixon. Charles optimistically predicted that his son would retain a large Quaker bloc because of his record. Nixon was "not very well known" and was being discharged from the navy a lieutenant commander: "It is just another campaign that we have to go through but I am quite sanguine as to the outcome. In any event, we have nothing to worry about now." Jerry's reply was as cavalier as his father's: "I am not worried about the matter and we will just go ahead like we have before."[49]

Jerry and his father had badly miscalculated Nixon's success, the extent of his support, and his unifying effect on the Republican Party. Instead, they listened to another political ally, Jack Long, a chicken rancher from Baldwin Park, who wrote the congressman: "At the present time there isn't any too great harmony among the Republicans of the 12th District." Veteran and labor issues were before Voorhis in Congress, and that meant that he could not even return home over the Christmas recess.[50]

Jerry, therefore, decided that he should remain in Washington, D.C., through the primary and rely on his record as a diligent congressman who mirrored the social programs of the New Deal era. That strategy had worked admirably in the past. A limited campaign would spring from amateur politicians like his father and other friends who mailed out introduction-to-candidate letters and who paid for a minimal amount of political advertising in the local newspapers. The front-page headline, NIXON ACCEPTS BID TO OPPOSE JERRY VOORHIS, in the *Progress-Bulletin* on December 21 sparked no serious response.[51]

Nixon lacked name recognition, financial contributors, and a loyal following. He had won the endorsement of a select GOP group called the Candidate and Fact Finding Committee. His middle-class promoters, Perry, Day, Bewley, and others, had convinced a tiny fraction of the constituency to support a young, unknown naval officer. In reality, the committee had few options since it had not found anyone who had created the enthusiasm that Nixon had engendered. In addition, the committee had avoided a divisive primary struggle where each candidate bloodied the other. Rather than concentrate on a weakened survivor, the GOP could focus its attention on defeating the symbol of the abhorrent Roosevelt legacy.

Nixon boldly accepted the call to run against the well-entrenched New Deal incumbent. The challenger countered with his own belief in the Republican principle of private initiative and less government control. Voorhis lacked critical ingredients for political survival; he had grown complacent by running against lackluster opponents. He did not know, nor did he ever bother to learn about Nixon. Rather than follow the first rule of a congressman, which was reelection above all else, he stayed in the capital, expecting just another bothersome contest.

By the time the Nixons returned to California at the beginning of 1946, they faced a pressing complication: Pat was in her third trimester getting ready to deliver her first child. Rather than search for housing at a time of critical shortages, they temporarily moved in with Dick's parents in Whittier. With their accommodations arranged, they turned to the congressional campaign and allocated their wartime savings of approximately $4,000 to support themselves during the race. Skeptical GOP professionals did not give Nixon any chance of winning the general election, but these oddsmakers had vastly underestimated both Nixon's abilities as a campaigner and the commitment of those who supported him and abhorred Jerry Voorhis and his New Deal philosophy. [52]

Even before coming home, Nixon had started to build his political base. Sam Gist, who lost the committee's endorsement, received a letter from Nixon in early December 1945 thanking his former opponent for making the endorsement unanimous. Nixon also took this opportunity to praise Gist for his knowledge of the issues: "I should like to consider you as one of my close advisors throughout the campaign." While Nixon was a political novice, his willingness to reach out for counsel proved immeasurably valuable in winning loyal backers. [53]

By the time Nixon returned to the district, he was ready to campaign over an enormous area. The 12th congressional district included four hundred square miles in Los Angeles County, composed of the San Gabriel and Pomona Valleys. This area of rolling foothills near the coastal range of mountains was generally rural; the largest city was Alhambra, with a population of over 43,000, and smaller communities including Whittier, El Monte, and Claremont dotted the landscape with their streets lined with acacia, eucalyptus, and pepper trees. The inhabitants were primarily white middle class with some Hispanics and African Americans, mainly engaged in the citrus industry and vineyards; some of the population ranched; and others processed meat and chicken.[54]

Mindful that veterans had exaggerated the value of their military service in recent elections, Nixon intentionally minimized his officer rank in favor of appearing as just another civilian who had fought for his country. To accomplish this, he needed clothes because all he had left over from the war were his navy uniforms and "one well-worn suit." On his first stop to John P. Evans, the "style headquarters" in Pomona, the candidate bought a blue suit to wear for his appearances until he could afford to buy another one as an alternative. He chose flashy ties, but Roy Day suggested more subdued ones, "so that people would concentrate on his words not his neckwear." New shoes proved the hardest item to find: Nixon took a size 11-D, and a pair that large needed several months to locate.[55]

While the candidate was assembling his wardrobe, Nixon's executive committee was established. Roy Crocker, a banker from South Pasadena, served as chairman; Gist became vice chairman; Arthur Kruse, another banker, was appointed treasurer; and other appointees came from across the district, including two prominent women: Mrs. Rex Harbert and Mrs. Harvey Stewart. This committee met every Saturday afternoon over lunch to plan strategy. Most encouraged modest contributions between ten to twenty dollars from a large pool of voters rather than relying on a few large donors. The candidate needed to meet with small neighborhood groups, and as he grew more knowledgeable and comfortable with the issues, then the committee would arrange for larger audiences. Republican female groups called the Minute Women, as Nixon had already learned, were essential to the campaign's success. Female volunteers engendered great enthusiasm, working long hours without pay. He called on local newspaper editors and publishers to introduce himself and present his positions; and the committee arranged to hire a public relations specialist to arrange favorable coverage. Finally, Nixon's strategists looked for a campaign manager—not necessarily identified as a "political Republican expert," but someone who was committed to winning.[56]

Nixon, still a novice, followed many of his advisers' strategic suggestions, concentrating on what he did best: speechmaking. Starting in mid-January 1946, he began addressing service clubs like the Kiwanis and Rotary to recount his wartime experiences in the South Pacific. He cast himself as a democratic figure, not an officer, and praised his fellow enlisted men, who cooperated in the war effort and fought for freedom, despite the hot, humid weather and the ration of two gallons per man per day of distilled water for washing, drinking, and cooking. To bathe, the men swam in a lagoon infested with fungus.[57]

His maiden political speech to the GOP faithful came on the afternoon of February 5 before the Alhambra–San Gabriel Women's Republican Study Club, where he pledged to present a positive campaign and eschew negativity. Republicans, Nixon charged, were pushing forward on economy in government, sound money rather than "crackpot schemes," lower inflation, opposition to burgeoning federal bureaucracy, higher wages, and decent working conditions for laborers. His principal theme centered on government control versus free enterprise: "we believe that our future as a nation depends on what we do ourselves, not in what the govt. will do for us." Lillian Amberson, the club's corresponding secretary, wrote him three days after his speech. Her group was "just recovering from the shock that at long last we have such a remarkable candidate for whom we can work." She was buoyant and looking forward to campaigning for his "ideals and convictions."[58]

Her reaction was typical. Nixon usually talked before a receptive audience who wanted to hear the GOP standard-bearer. He spoke about current issues and related them directly to his listeners; he spoke from notes rather than a drafted text, and when he recognized that a theme met with a positive response, he made that part of his regular remarks.

He followed this trial run with his first major address a week later. At the Nixon for Congress Lincoln Day Dinner at the Pomona Ebell Clubhouse, 425 local partisans packed the hall at two dollars a plate. Nixon was introduced as the party's best chance for success. Republicans, he asserted, had been labeled the party of the privileged and big business, but the GOP reached out to all people, not to classes. The party had to promote cooperation between business, labor, and the consumer if it expected to unite all segments of society. In foreign policy, it had to be based on international cooperation and an informed American constituency. A hundred years earlier, Nixon proclaimed, Abraham Lincoln had stood for preserving the Union as did modern Republicanism. With veterans coming home, the nation had to be prepared to incorporate them into a society where a free economy, as opposed to a government-controlled one, existed. Some regulations were essential, but enforcement had to come from well-trained administrators and not crackpots and fuzzy-minded theorists. Like Lincoln, Nixon favored free enterprise. This election was another great postwar test of liberty versus serfdom. Republicans would triumph.[59]

A noticeably pregnant Pat, who had temporarily quit smoking, accompanied Dick. At smaller meetings, she offered brief greetings, but did not speak. That was Dick's function. At the close of his remarks, he answered questions and then left for his next appearance. She sometimes remained to socialize and thank the female volunteers for their efforts. Besides this role, she managed the office and performed secretarial duties.[60]

This routine was interrupted on February 19 when Pat began contractions during breakfast. By 9:00 A.M., she arrived at Murphy Memorial Hospital in Whittier. Since she was almost thirty-four years old, the doctor expected a long labor and told Dick that he would have plenty of time to attend a critical meeting at the Los Angeles Athletic Club.

The physician's prediction was wrong. While Dick was at lunch, Pat delivered a seven-pound baby girl with two double chins and deep blue eyes. The birth was a breach one, feet first, with a broken shoulder. While mother and child recovered, five days passed before the baby became Patricia, shortened to Tricia. News of the birth and photos of the young family were carried throughout the district and provided some of the most effective publicity that Nixon received. The *Monrovia News Post* on March 11 carried the delighted father's remarks as he cradled his infant: "she's the only boss I recognize." Her new father was proud: "Patricia is a lucky girl. She will grow up in the finest state in the union, in the greatest country on earth. She will grow up, go to schools and when the time comes she will register and vote Republican."[61]

Tricia's arrival precipitated another change. The newly created family moved into a rental house, modestly called a small bungalow. The neighbors next door raised minks that squealed loudly and smelled terribly. After three weeks of rest, Pat returned to run the office, and Tricia's birth, if anything, accelerated her parents' pace. From the start of February until the end of March, Nixon appeared before over thirty-five service and civic organizations, generating a tremendous amount of enthusiasm.[62]

While Nixon pursued a hectic speaking schedule, his executive committee in the middle of March named Roy Day campaign manager. Soon after this announcement, the candidate went to the Registrar of Voters on the morning of March 18 for photographs of his filing congressional papers in both the Democratic and Republican primaries, a political tactic called crossfiling. Under California electoral law, any qualified candidate was allowed to file on any party's primary ballot so long as $100 was paid per party filing. Day personally advanced the $200 for his fees and recalled that he "had a hell of a time" getting reimbursed.[63]

While Nixon was seeking to gain name recognition, Jerry Voorhis stayed in Washington, watching the crescendoing spread of strikes, the emerging "iron curtain," the frustration with price and wage controls, and the gradual movement away from New Deal initiatives. Facing opposition in his district from many Republican-controlled newspapers, the congressman used a regular radio broadcast and large mailing list to inform his constituents of his views.[64]

His name was constantly in the local news, but nothing helped present his viewpoints more than his weekly column, published in a variety of local newspapers throughout the district, and called "People's Business." Starting in January and running through March 1946, the congressman discussed foreign policy issues like the significance of Roosevelt's death, controlling weapons of mass destruction, the establishment of the United Nations, and victory over the Axis. Still, he faced the future with optimism and faith: "we dedicate our most earnest efforts, under the guidance of God, to the rebuilding of the world which has been desolated by the most terrible war in history."[65]

As for domestic problems, Congressman Voorhis called for new management-labor legislation to try to settle strikes; he wanted Congress to authorize 2.7 million homes for veterans before the end of 1947 to meet the tremendous demand. To relieve world hunger, he introduced a House resolution to reduce brewers from using 4 million bushels of cereals per month for liquor, and instead, use those agricultural products for relief supplies. Europe's starving appreciated the gesture, but liquor manufacturers in California opposed it.[66]

Charles Voorhis wrote his son on February 8 that the opposition would run Nixon ragged by November 1 "and he will have run out of something new to say long before that time." Charles predicted a "very interesting" contest and "perhaps the cleanest one that you have had to face so far as your opponent personally is concerned. We are all talking about the tough campaign we are going to have and I am stressing that point with all those to whom I talk." But Jerry should not worry because he was going to win. "If it were not for the fact that I feel you are needed badly in Washington I could almost hope that you would not have to go back again."[67]

Charles confirmed that Nixon had been quite active, but voters would quickly tire of constantly hearing "the same thing over and over and over again." By the end of March, Charles thought that Nixon could not maintain his pace for the remainder of the campaign. The father was pleased that his son would remain at his desk until August and then return to the district. That was "sufficient." Jerry agreed with his father that the Republicans had started too quickly, but they were working better than in the past, and with the difficulties inside the Truman administration, voters might link these negative activities directly to Voorhis.[68]

Jack Long presented the congressman with a much more pessimistic picture about how the Republicans were going to try to confuse the people about his voting record and how the GOP regulars were slowly accepting Nixon as their candidate. By the end of March, Long predicted that the Republicans would stage a "pretty dirty" campaign, and Nixon would flood the local media with press releases. At present, local editors had not embraced Nixon: "I guess that they are waiting to see the color of his campaign money." Jerry appreciated Long's insights and local news clippings, but the congressman was not discouraged because he felt that the Republicans had begun an exhaustive campaign schedule too early.[69]

No one questioned Nixon's energetic style. By the end of March, he had appeared before scores of civic organizations with almost as many topics as speeches. He coupled these public appearances with an equal amount of home gatherings. Nixon had completed the first phase of his campaign and was preparing to launch a concerted drive for a primary victory beginning April 1. In order to build enthusiasm and a feeling of participation, he intended to send members of the Candidate and Fact Finding Committee progress reports approximately every ten days, and he wanted "suggestions or advice" that any of these individuals might have, "because I feel strongly that only with the cooperation of all the Republican leaders of the District will we be able to win the primaries in June and the final election in November."[70]

Nixon wrote Voorhis on April 1 to thank him for sending a copy of *Infant Care,* a government publication about raising a child, to his family. Congressmen had regular allocations of 150 copies per month for free distribution to encourage greater information about proper pediatrics, and Voorhis's staff had sent one to the Nixons. Dick also reminded the incumbent that they had met twelve years earlier at a home in North Whittier Heights.[71]

Not to be outdone, Voorhis replied that he hoped the booklet would be useful and that he, too, remembered their earlier meeting. The congressman quickly moved to the present, claiming that he heard rumors that Nixon planned to run for Congress. If he intended to contest Voorhis's seat, the incumbent knew that "the campaign will be a clean, open above board one." After the congressional session adjourned, Voorhis hoped that he and Nixon could share a platform in the form of debates or joint appearances. The congressman added one additional note: his job at the present time was "truly a mankiller."[72]

Rarely during the primary campaign did Nixon directly attack Voorhis. The challenger did allude to the unsound positions taken by the congressman in his book, *Out of Debt, Out of Danger* , but generally he concentrated on their philosophical differences: "I have no personal quarrel with my opponent"; however, they had "two divergent fundamental political beliefs."[73]

Nixon took that message throughout the district through a variety of means while stressing his humble upbringing. His father had owned a grocery store in East Whittier for twenty-three years, and he himself worked his way through school by clerking at the store, operating the service station, and grading fruit in a packinghouse. He joined the American Legion and the Veterans of Foreign Wars, and his campaign committee established veteran groups in all three state districts that composed his congressional district. He spoke to them on their concerns in speeches like "The Veteran in Peace Time" in which he emphasized patriotism and the need for military "preparedness." Americans were practical and did not intend to lay down their arms until they had guarantees for peace. Young veterans knew little about what Congressman Voorhis had done for them. Nixon sounded like their advocate. Older veterans, however, remained staunchly Democrat.[74]

In early May, Nixon spoke before a friendly audience of about one hundred in San Marino, where he called for an end to inflation by reducing government expenditures. Besides constricting government size,

Americans needed to end price controls by allowing private enterprise to expand. As for foreign affairs, the United States had to reject isolationism and cooperate with the development of the United Nations. That meant toppling the "old boys" network in the State Department and replacing it with fresh leadership. He attacked Voorhis for not finding solutions to the red tape that interfered with veteran services. Radical labor groups had endorsed the incumbent and attacked Nixon as labor's enemy, but in reality, he called for labor-business cooperation. To Nixon, America had to return to the freedoms that made it great. Republicans would fulfill the promise of that dream. A Democratic observer reported that Nixon had almost completely memorized his forty-minute address and was "an accomplished public speaker, attorney and debater."[75]

Along with providing information on Voorhis's voting record, Murray Chotiner encouraged Nixon to send his positions on crucial issues to Chotiner's public relations firm so that he could issue an immediate press release. This savvy political operative excluded laudatory endorsements; he wanted substance. Whenever anything important occurred in the district, Chotiner urged Nixon to notify his office immediately.[76]

Chotiner knew, and Nixon quickly came to understand, that positive press coverage was critical. This was especially true of the *Los Angeles Times,* which supported just about every antilabor action and vigorously opposed the New Deal. To lead these crusades, the publishers selected a twenty-eight-year-old Tennessean, Kyle Palmer, as his political editor in 1919, who gradually assumed a major influence in California politics and became the state's "Mr. Republican." Short and stocky, with gray hair, he had an ingratiating manner and a ruthless nature. Palmer enjoyed playing the political insider. He picked Nixon as his protégé and treated him like a son.[77]

Nixon reciprocated by recognizing Palmer's value and thanking him for his favorable coverage. Nixon knew that he was in a "tough race" but that he was receiving "solid Republican support." Palmer responded with articles like the one on May 21 in which he praised Nixon for calling for the elimination of the Office of Price Administration; it damaged rabbit growers because the agency raised the price on feed by 50 percent, but it did not let growers increase the prices for rabbits. "Nixon," Palmer held, was "about the best candidate the Republicans have dug up in years against incumbent, Jerry Voorhis, but unless they get out and hustle for him, push doorbells, talk him up and get the voters out they might as well put up a bale of hay—for Hon. Voorhis is a very good campaigner, a likeable chap—but a New Dealer, straight up and inside out."[78]

Nixon received other assistance. Many Republicans were becoming more enthusiastic and optimistic about winning in November. Physicians backed him because of his opposition to socialized medicine. Whittier realtors supported him because of his position on free enterprise. Several Democrats wrote him and pledged their votes. Robert King, an auditor and income tax reporter, for example, knew and liked the congressman, but this time he was switching candidates: "If you are for the continuation of the New Deal and its bureaucratic control and regimentation of the American people, then you would naturally vote for Jerry." If you opposed them and voted for Voorhis because he was "sincere," then listen to Nixon, who was "sincere" and "fundamentally RIGHT and SOUND."[79]

As Nixon became more comfortable as a campaigner, he moved from friendly, relatively small audiences to larger ones in more hostile Democratic territory to spread his message. Toward the close of the primary campaign, he and Pat decided to go to Voorhis's hometown of San Dimas and the hostile, heavily dominated Democratic territory of El Monte. He wanted to meet all of the newspaper executives and political writers that he had missed because he felt that his publicity was not gaining enough media coverage. From the middle of May until the day of the primary in early June, he expected to cover every town in the district.[80]

While Nixon concentrated on public appearances, home gatherings, and media attention, his campaign chairman, Roy Day, was directing the Republican effort to get his party's voters to the polls. He also needed local advertising, sponsors for these ads, district fund-raising, group endorsements from doctors, veterans, women's organizations, and other associations. They needed to contact friends and have them meet the candidate. From early May until the primary, Day planned five major political rallies of from 200 to 1,000 spectators, strategically placed in the district.[81]

By the middle of the month, Day became even more aggressive. He sent 100,000 Nixon flyers by first-class mail to every home in the district; 50,000 postcards endorsing the Republican slate were going out; thousands of letters from realtors, insurance men, auto dealers, and others were being mailed, appealing to them "to elect NIXON and get NEW BLOOD into Congress—AND GET SOMETHING DONE." Everyone, from veterans committees to Democrats for Nixon, was working vigorously for their candidate, and during the last two weeks, Republicans needed to focus on the election. Day urged Nixon to attend a luncheon at the William Penn Hotel in Whittier toward the end of the campaign: "Better come and see what goes on and a 5 minute pep talk. Do or die stuff!"[82]

As Nixon's campaign efforts were growing in intensity, Jerry Voorhis seemed preoccupied with tangential issues and did not concentrate on the campaign. He planned to return to the district during the congressional recess that spring, but his advisers, especially his father, argued against it. A week in mid-April would be too long before the primary and too short for effective campaigning. He would not be able to see everyone, and some would be disappointed. He should stay healthy, well rested, ready to campaign in August. These arguments helped the congressman decide to remain in Washington, D.C. Although wishing to return home, he could not conscientiously leave the capital with problems like veteran housing shortages and European food relief. Other national concerns like the continuation of price controls also troubled him. As soon as scarcities ended, so would government regulations.[83]

Jack Long summarized conditions in the district at the beginning of April. The campaign committee was raising money for Voorhis's election, and while they were working, he should rest: "Jerry, we might as well look facts in the face. You haven't a chance to win the Republican nomination at the primaries any more than Nixon has to win the Democratic party, so why kill yourself working in the primaries." The district voters were split over Truman's domestic policies, but favored his foreign positions. Since the Republican Party exhibited disunity, Voorhis's chances to win in November had improved; indeed, Long had already declared him the winner.[84]

Charles Voorhis offered his evaluation. The campaign had been conducted quietly and with dignity. "There have been no brass bands and there will be none until we meet you at the train with the Bulldog Band!" Volunteers were sending out literature stressing Jerry's record as an incumbent. His son would win, but the campaign would be hard, and he needed to be well rested. Jerry replied that he was working hard and was feeling fine, but worried about his father: "I only hope you are not over-doing and I would beg you to take it easy and not worry about this darn campaign."[85]

Jerry Voorhis read these assessments as well as those of others who sent him regular correspondence. He was primed as early as the beginning of April that the campaign was "going to be mean and continuous," and hoped his supporters would be energetic because this would be "the toughest race we have ever had and a good deal of hard work will have to be done." By the middle of the month, he had recalled that many city incumbents nationwide were defeated in late 1945 and wondered if this trend foretold his probable future. He confronted another hurdle early in May when he decided to disassociate himself from the Democratic gubernatorial candidate; the Republican Earl Warren was "much the better man."[86]

Voorhis had gained the allegiance of most veterans groups for his wholehearted support. During the primary, Democrats claimed that their man worked hard for the 11 million vets. His record included a bill passed over Truman's veto to renew their term insurance. He voted for every benefit package, assisted their medical treatment, and advocated speedy construction of veteran housing. Veterans associations appreciated that kind of legislative record.[87]

While Voorhis actively sought the veteran vote, he prided himself in every election that he was the champion of the working man. Indeed, as long as he ran as a Democrat, labor unions formed the core of his constituency, and he made no secret of that affinity: "my fundamental desire is to serve the best interest of the common people of this country and particularly those who labor to produce its wealth." Within that sphere of influence, Voorhis depended most heavily on the American Federation of Labor (AFL). Writing to W. J. Bassett, executive secretary of the United AFL, Voorhis reiterated: "I say this in order to try to have you understand how much I prize this endorsement and how much it means to me."[88]

This commitment was uncontestable until the establishment of the Congress of Industrial Organizations (CIO) in the summer of 1943. Sidney Hillman, a socialist and president of the Amalgamated Clothing Workers, established this body and its fund-raising arm, the Political Action Committee (PAC), to provide money to reelect Roosevelt and others whom Hillman desired to assist. During the following summer, Hillman added the National Citizens' Political Action Committee

(NC-PAC) to organize the nonlabor equivalent to the CIO-PAC. Under its guidelines for contributions, half of the money from the unions went to the state and national organizations for distribution and the other half remained with the locals to use as they wished. Since both of these groups were formed to aid Democratic candidates, Republicans vigorously denounced them. These PACs had another weakness exploited by the opposition. Although Hillman vehemently opposed the Communist Party, its members dominated some of the local PACs.[89]

Charles Voorhis was particularly concerned about the CIO-PAC from its inception, and worried that it would dominate the Democratic National Convention in 1944 and damage his son's campaign. Jerry expected to support Roosevelt, but the CIO's radical drift deeply troubled him, and its leadership recognized his ambivalence. He knew that the CIO already exerted tremendous influence on Helen Gahagan Douglas, a Democrat from the nearby 14th congressional district, and he believed that the Communists within the local organizations were trying to cause a breach between them.[90]

Over the next year, Charles Voorhis's anxiety over the CIO-PACs intensified due to the Democratic Party's momentum toward the far left. During the second half of 1945, he objected to the arbitrary actions of the CIO because it "was drunk with power." Extremists now dominated these unions, and Congress had to apply the corrective. The CIO had become "saturated with the more radical elements in our society, including the real Communists." Ironically, while the role of pro-Soviet forces in the CIO was "the most contentious" in its existence, even some of the Communists' severest critics, according to the labor historian Robert Zieger, "have conceded that Communist-influenced unions were among the most egalitarian, the most honest and well-administered, the most radically progressive, and the most class conscious."[91]

Both father and son recognized the potentially damaging complications of the CIO-PAC during the 1946 primary. According to Charles in a letter to his son on April 1, the Hollywood CIO had already endorsed Jerry because he was the only candidate that it could support. Jerry replied five days later feeling that he was "better off without the CIO endorsement and I would have also been better off without the endorsement of the Hollywood PAC group." The congressman did not want any contributions from those organizations, but he did "not want to be discourteous to the people connected with them who are really quite all right. There is too much of a sprinkling of communists among them, however, for us to have any real contacts." He wrote to Long the same day that CIO support would be detrimental to his campaign, due to the feeling that the Communists substantially controlled the California CIO. Jerry faced a profound dilemma: he wanted to appeal to the labor vote and simultaneously reject CIO support.[92]

Jerry Voorhis's connections with the CIO-PAC grew more complicated toward the end of May when Griselda Kuhlman of the Los Angeles Joint Board of the Amalgamated Clothing Workers of America (ACWA-CIO) proudly informed the congressman that "we have endorsed you for reelection to Congress." The union only had about a hundred members in his district, but even though all of his votes did not favor labor, the ACWA appreciated his "liberal contribution" in other areas and would "be very happy to do whatever we can to help." Voorhis appreciated that he had been endorsed "for re-election by the Amalgamated Clothing Workers."[93]

The director of Region 6 of the United Automobile, Aircraft, Agricultural Implement Workers of America (UAW-CIO), C. V. O'Halloran, pledged "to render you my fullest support in your candidacy for reelection." Voorhis had an "outstanding record" in behalf of labor, even when he felt that it had been wrong on issues. The congressman had demonstrated that he acted independently and none of the special interest groups would manipulate him. Voorhis appreciated these comments. Sometimes he had difficulty deciding what was right, but he tried to make the best decision possible.[94]

Loren Grey, PAC director for Region 6, UAW-CIO, had offered to support Voorhis's race several weeks before O'Halloran had written. The congressman replied that he supported the CIO, but he was "deeply concerned over the degree to which the Communists have succeeded in getting hold of some of the organizations, and I definitely do not want their support nor would they be justified in giving it to me from their own point of view." Voorhis opposed Communists in the labor movement, and if Grey accepted that position, the congressman "would be glad and proud to have his support." Grey quickly agreed to Voorhis's conditions and lamented: "At present about all we are able to do for your campaign is to include your name on all of our slates, but I think we will be in a position to give you more substantial help in November." Somehow Voorhis did not consider the endorsements of the Hollywood and UAW-CIO PACs or the ACWA-CIO as fitting into his criteria for PACs. The official California CIO newspaper, *Labor Herald*, at the end of May, placed "NO

ENDORSEMENT" next to his name. To Voorhis, that was taken at face value. His acceptance of local CIO-PACs was excluded, and he maintained his interpretation for the remainder of the campaign.[95]

While Voorhis somehow rationalized a marked distinction between local and state PACs, he acknowledged their decisions. On at least one occasion, he was not even asked for his approval. Toward the end of March, the Los Angeles chapter of the NC-PAC circulated a bulletin that included the selection of Voorhis as one of its recommendations. That group apparently never communicated with the congressman. It just published its own independent slate, and a copy promptly reached Nixon's headquarters.[96]

During the primary, the Nixon campaign vaguely connected Voorhis and the CIO-PAC. Andrew Dunlap, vice chairman of the Nixon campaign finance committee, complained in early April : "The New Dealers have a war chest in the P.A.C. I don't know what it takes to arouse the American people—to make them fighting mad!" At the end of the month, Roy Day said that the PAC had publicly endorsed Voorhis and the congressman was answerable to pressure groups, not the people. Voorhis quickly shot back: "I never sought nor did I receive any such endorsement."[97]

Voorhis, instead, busily tackled his congressional duties, such as working on the coal strike, OPA legislation, the draft, confusion over foreign policy, and a myriad of other issues. He received letters in every mail about Nixon's "excellent campaign." Nixon, Voorhis reasoned, did not have the burden of being an incumbent, nor did he have the responsibility for taking measures that upset people. Voorhis was pessimistic and prepared to lose the election: "I think Mr. Nixon on the whole has a pretty easy task ahead of him. The main point in his favor will be that he was not a Congressman and does not have responsibility for all the things that make the people mad. I just hope that nobody is going to be too disappointed if things go badly in this election, for I am personally quite prepared for such an outcome. This is not to say that I won't do my level best and campaign a little harder than ever as soon as I get home." He expected to "take a pretty dignified position until that time comes and not give any evidences about getting too excited or panicky."[98]

Voorhis had reason for concern. During the last week of May, local newspapers decided on their political endorsements. The *South Pasadena Review* praised both men; but even though the editor personally admired

Voorhis, he had received the CIO-PAC endorsement and was a New Dealer. Nixon, on the other hand, was a young veteran who was "progressive but realistic, has won outstanding recognition for his plain, every-day horse sense, is an accomplished speaker and independent thinker," whom both Republicans and Democrats could back. He would go to Congress as an independent without debts to any group. The *Claremont Courier* followed a similar approach. Voorhis was sincere and honest, but these virtues were insufficient "to see us out of our present muddle and back to a system of free enterprise, individual initiative and responsibility." Nixon would provide new leadership because he was a "practical man and independent thinker." These kinds of endorsements were coupled with advertisements for Nixon a week before the primary election that stated in bold print: THERE'S NOTHING WRONG WITH THE COUNTRY THAT A GOOD ELECTION WON'T CURE![99]

In addition to these paid ads, Nixon received media coverage when he publicly opposed Truman's call for a bill to draft strikers into the armed forces. This, to Nixon, threatened American liberties. The president had already permitted strikers too much latitude in the past, and now was going too far in the opposite direction. If Truman's emergency legislation became law, Nixon contended, it would grant too much power to the chief executive and allow him to destroy both business and labor. Nixon proposed a system of labor-management conciliation, with highly trained mediators: "The need for a constructive approach to the problem of industrial peace is imperative. Labor should not be denied the right to strike but mediation machinery must be set up which will go into action before strikes are called, rather than afterward." By taking these measures, the nation's welfare and the consumer would be adequately protected.[100]

Voorhis countered with his own political advertising. Instead of one ad, his supporters ran several, urging voters to "Keep Jerry on the Job." He had served exceptionally well on the House Agriculture Committee, fought for veterans benefits, kept monopolies from controlling the economy, and was developing a plan for the control of atomic energy. Another ad demonstrated his maturity: Jerry had served five terms representing all his constituents, and the United States was moving into a critical period. The country needed his sagacity and guidance. The *Los Angeles Daily News* reflected these views with its endorsement. According to its editorial, Voorhis was working for a peaceful postwar world and was "an able, articulate spokesman for the common man, a champion of the underdog."[101]

The Voorhis faction miscalculated horribly about their opponent and how his campaign would be waged. Nixon, of course, espoused traditional Republican principles because he believed them, but he said much more in his evolution of his own particular brand of Republicanism. At the end of World War II, the United States stood as the mightiest power on earth, but that had changed abruptly. The Democratic administration did not provide the postwar leadership to keep America moving forward. Instead, the nation stood still. Veterans returned disgruntled; housewives protested high prices; and unions struck for higher wages. To counteract these negatives, the United States demanded new leadership, and Nixon wanted to replace the negatives with positives: "I believe in America and it's our opportunity and duty to do our part in giving the country back to the people." To create the proper environment, the United States had to turn from the New Deal back toward free enterprise. Americans had to reduce the bloated federal bureaucracy and expenditures, halt the momentum toward socialism and nationalization, end price and wage controls of the OPA, assist farmers in crop production, encourage private industry to build more housing, care for veterans' health problems without instituting socialized medicine, and support the G.I. bill of rights in higher education that would decrease class and racial hatred. These measures would drive inflation down and restore domestic confidence.[102]

Nixon was especially concerned with labor-management relations, holding that he was not against labor but for industrial peace. He wished to end union strife, but the administration's policy had been a dismal failure. Republicans had to find a way to balance the interests of labor, management, and the consumer. He opposed compulsory arbitration, but felt that government had an obligation to establish guidelines, and then business and labor played within those rules. Both sides had to cooperate to protect the national interest.[103]

In foreign affairs, Nixon saw an enlightened public as the cornerstone of his policy. Isolationism had been discredited, and the United States had to cooperate with the newly founded United Nations to construct world order. The Russians had bamboozled America at the end of the war and commenced on a path of worldwide conquest. Until the United States won adequate assurances, it needed to hold on to the atomic bomb. Preparedness was key to the struggle between democracy and totalitarianism. Those responsible for the failures in diplomacy had to be removed, and that meant the State Department needed a house-cleaning. The nation had to use its best minds, not an elitist diplomatic corps.[104]

Nixon lectured his listeners on Russian history from 1240 forward and the rule of the czarist dictatorships. He reminded his audiences not to forget Alan Meshikoff, who played center on the Whittier College football team. "Mech" only weighed 160 pounds, but still made all-conference in his junior year. He was "a fighting man if I have ever seen one." He also was Russian, and today 160 million Russians worked for a Communist government that threatened U.S. democracy.[105]

Nixon had another fascination: new frontiers of technology. Television was coming to the public, and air transportation was expanding domestically and internationally as the speed and comfort of airplanes accelerated. Frozen foods were replacing canning and gaining wider acceptance. Laborsaving devices were reaching more consumers. Plastics and electronics enlarged their markets. Nixon regularly turned to the theme of optimistic self-reliance: "We must recognize that our future as a nation will depend on what we do ourselves—not on what our govt. will do for us."[106]

Finally, Nixon spoke out for social legislation "as a matter of humanitarian justice—as a matter of decency." He believed that the Fair Employment Practices Commission (FEPC) helped the Negro in getting a job, but he felt even more strongly that education reduced racial hatred. "We must recognize," he preached, "that in America there is no place for class hatred; we must resist any tendency to build it up because our struggle is in our ability to work together as a team. This is for school, for church, for individuals." Americans all had to pull in the same direction.[107]

Voorhis relied on a decade of failed lessons. Due to lackluster Republican opposition in the past, he had never built a political machine to gauge his opponents. Rather than return home to campaign before the primary, he decided to remain in the capital, representing his constituents in the enormous problems facing the nation. He and his closest advisers believed that Jerry would win votes as a pillar of the congressional work ethic. They ignored the fact that voters and the media wanted to see their congressman, talk to him, and shake his hand. Nixon was visible; he made local news, addressed local concerns, and shook hands. Voorhis did nothing significant to counteract his Republican opponent's challenge. Even more mystifying, that seemed to be the Democratic plan.

While such inscrutable decisions helped bring about political disaster, Congressman Voorhis consciously dictated his position toward labor. Voorhis was the champion of the worker and welcomed AFL endorsements. However, he and his father worried so much about Communist influence in the CIO that they cringed over the prospect of its open support. Even more troublesome was the possibility of CIO-PAC backing. The congressman eventually accepted several PAC endorsements, but only if those local PACs renounced any Communist influence. Voorhis negotiated and received such assurances from the PAC director of the UAW; the congressman knew about the Hollywood PAC's blessings, but was unaware of the Los Angeles NC-PAC chapter's action.

No one in the Voorhis camp, particularly the congressman himself, ever publicly acknowledged his acceptance of certain PAC endorsements or explained his distinction between Communist and non-Communist CIO-PACs. Rather than announce this position, Voorhis doggedly claimed that he never had any CIO-PAC backing. He in fact meant any national or statewide support. Nixon and his supporters sporadically, though just as vociferously, proclaimed throughout the primary that the incumbent had PAC allegiance. Writers have incorrectly concluded that Nixon either exaggerated or lied about the Voorhis-PAC connection. In actuality, Congressman Voorhis was the offending party. Those who point to the Nixon-Voorhis election as the opening salvo of Nixon's march toward chicanery will have to look elsewhere.

With the primary campaigning completed, the candidates awaited the results of the June 4 balloting. Of the 163,613 registered voters, 80,215 were Democrats and 74,604 were Republicans. When the voting was tabulated, only 69,633 people cast ballots:

|  | Reputblican | Democrat | Total |
| --- | --- | --- | --- |
| Jerry Voorhis (D) | 12,125 | 25,048 | 37,173 |
| Richard Nixon (R) | 24,397 | 5,077 | 29,474 |
| William Kinnett (R) | 1,532 | 1,200 | 2,732 |

The Prohibition nominee, John Hoeppel, had been defeated by Voorhis in 1936 for Congress, received several hundred votes, but used his place on the ballot to attack and embarrass the congressman.[108]

When the votes were tallied, Voorhis had received the Democratic nomination and Nixon had won the Republican endorsement. After all the votes were counted, the incumbent had received 7,699 votes more than his challenger.

The primary had demonstrated the power of Voorhis's name recognition and little else. The congressman had remained in the capital maintaining his position enacting the legislative legacy of Franklin Roosevelt and he ran on that platform. Voorhis depended on his followers to campaign for him in the district and several advertisements to remind his constituents of his record. That minimalist campaign was sufficient for another primary endorsement.

Nixon's success did not visibly weaken the strength of Voorhis's incumbency. However, just below the surface, Nixon accomplished several objectives that should have caused the Democrats serious concern. First, the challenger united the GOP behind him and enunciated traditional Republican principles. Second, he was an attractive candidate, who spoke well and provided the enthusiasm that the party faithful needed to run a strenuous general election. Finally, Nixon, who had driven with the will to win, would now concentrate even more to upset the favorite.

For the first time, Nixon was a serious contender.

Instead of dissecting the actual, albeit mundane, events of one of hundreds of congressional primaries, writers have chosen to replace the reality with far-fetched, unsubstantiated rumors and record them as fact. The allegation, for example, that Nixon responded to a local newspaper advertisement to launch his political career is astounding. How Nixon found newspapers from California in Maryland is never even mentioned. Even more fantastic was Voorhis's claim that in October 1945, a large New York "financial house" sent a representative to California, who opposed Voorhis's position on monopolies and monetary system reform and considered him "one of the most dangerous men in Washington," who needed to be ousted from Congress. No name has ever been linked to that wild charge.[109]

Charles Hogan, a staunch Democrat and hardened Nixonphobe, proclaimed that oil companies had recruited Nixon in law school to run against Voorhis. Unaware that Nixon went to Duke in the mid-1930s, Hogan contended with certitude that Nixon "had been bought at Duke by the oil interests." Hogan's smears, alleging that oil barons secretly financed Nixon, have gained credence over the years. In fact, the substantial sum contributed to the 1946 campaign by an oilman came from the balance of Don Lycan's original fund in the 1944 campaign reserve; he never met Nixon until much later. Any charge that Nixon owed anything to these interests in 1945 or earlier was as preposterous as Voorhis's use of the secret "financial house" allegation before the election.[110]

Such unfounded rumors gained credence and persisted. The syndicated columnist Peter Edson, six years after the 1946 campaign, asked Nixon if the circulating stories about his initiation into politics with the backing of one hundred California businessmen were valid, and did each of these alleged contributors give $200 per year to supplement his salary? The reporter personally liked Nixon, but if these allegations proved accurate, Edson would have serious reservations about Nixon's character.[111]

The unreasonable substituted for facts, and the record was not researched. A constant barrage of misinformation dealing with the 1946 primary would haunt Nixon for the rest of his life. Fifteen years after the Candidate and Fact Finding Committee endorsed him, Nixon was still denying the newspaper advertisement fantasy, sadly noting: "the myth is better than the reality."[112]

# Chapter 3

# NIXON VERSUS VOORHIS

Within a week of the primary results, Roy Day informed Republican loyalists that while Nixon had been virtually unknown in January, through a concerted campaign effort, Voorhis's margin of 60 percent in 1944 dropped to 53.5 percent in 1946. The three hundred volunteers who had worked tirelessly would have to extend themselves even more until November. If they did, Nixon could be victorious. As for Day, he resigned as campaign manager and went back to his job in order to support his family and get "acquainted again with my two kiddies."[1]

Day was not quitting due to despair; he was highly optimistic. Wherever Nixon had appeared, he had made a favorable impression. Currently, he was heading for British Columbia for a brief vacation, but upon his return, Republicans would map their strategy for the general election. Some plans had not been revealed, but Day guaranteed: "You will see a fighting two fisted candidate by the name of Nixon tearing into the weaknesses of the incumbent New Dealer with telling effect," who would talk to as many voters as possible and paint Voorhis in his true liberal Democratic colors.[2]

Nixon was even more positive in his mid-July message to precinct workers. Voorhis had made his worst primary showing, and the GOP volunteers were mainly responsible for this result. Nixon could be triumphant in November, but everyone had to try harder because the incumbent had the endorsement of the NC-PAC, a "well organized pressure group." Republicans had to win "voters away from the discredited policies of the New Deal Administration which Mr. Voorhis has consistently supported."[3]

While Republicans energized their volunteers' spirits, party professionals examined the voting patterns by each area and recognized the formidable task before them. Nixon had lost the three state assembly districts (49th, 50th, and 53rd) that made up the congressional district. In each, the conclusions were similar. To win, Nixon had to bring out registered Republicans, convert Democrats, and appeal to independents.[4]

Even though the challenger faced a daunting task, he received encouragement from a friendly press. E. H. Briggs, who wrote for the *San Marino Tribune*, told Nixon to keep the momentum up and avoid blunders. If he accomplished those objectives, there was "a good chance to win." The *South Pasadena Review* advised its readers that Voorhis was vulnerable if they studied his record and backed the Republican contender.[5]

Voorhis viewed the results from a quite different perspective. Encouraged by them, he was "not worrying about this election at all and that he [Charles] shouldn't either." His percentage was slightly less favorable than in the two previous elections, but under the difficult circumstances that existed during the primary, Voorhis thought that his district supporters had achieved a remarkable accomplishment. Gone was the earlier lethargy; he and his staff in Washington, D.C., were mapping campaign strategy by unifying the multifaceted Democratic factions. He intended to win, and until the general election campaign began, a devoted son wanted his father to rest. Charles, however, had other priorities. He was pleased with the primary results due to the large amount of Republican votes that his son received. They had ten thousand more voters go to the polls than the Democrats. If they voted in large numbers and registered more party members for the general election, Jerry would win. Nothing, to father and son, had really changed from earlier campaigns. But both men had grossly misjudged the mood of the electorate.[6]

While Jerry and Charles Voorhis were anticipating the usual, Nixon moved his campaign headquarters from downtown Pomona at 134 West Third Street to a single room at 205 East Philadelphia Street, in one of the oldest buildings in Whittier. From early March, Pat Nixon, with the assistance of three other part-time female volunteers, managed the office. The furnishings were spartan: Ralph Peck contributed a battered desk; Hannah Nixon donated an old leather sofa, hauled over by her son

Donald in his truck; another friend lent a typewriter, and someone else sent over a throw rug.[7]

To replace Day, the Nixon committee turned to Harrison McCall, a well-respected party official. Born in Minneapolis, Minnesota, on July 9, 1888, he attended public schools there and finished his education at the state's university. He married Lotta Shedd in 1916 and moved to South Pasadena five years later to raise his four children. He owned Los Angeles Testing Laboratories, a firm that tested various materials like concrete in construction projects. After business came politics. McCall took an active role in the Republican Party during the 1920s, and in 1936, he directed Fred Houser's unsuccessful effort against Voorhis. McCall was intelligent, worked hard, and liked Nixon. He did not dominate overall strategy like Day. McCall, instead, allowed Nixon to take control. He issued instructions, and McCall promptly implemented them.[8]

The committee divided the 12th congressional district into the three state assembly districts, with prominent Republicans in charge of each area: Ernest Geddes, Thomas Erwin, and Lothrup Smith. To demonstrate the importance of GOP women, two influential regulars, Mrs. Eunice Lowell and Mrs. Genevieve "Gen" Blaisdell, headed those groups. Even with this efficient organization, the perennial question was how to raise the thousands of dollars needed for a successful campaign. Earl Adams, a Harvard Law School graduate from San Marino, and Frank Jorgensen, an early convert from the same town, offered McCall $500 per month until the election. The problem was that neither knew where to raise the money. Jorgensen, Arthur Kruse, the campaign treasurer, and Perry quickly evolved into the finance committee, and Perry once again turned to Lycan and other wealthy Republicans for large donations. They sent some money, but most contributions averaged between fifteen and twenty dollars. When the local GOP finance committee was approached for funds, bitterness erupted, for it did not respond positively to Nixon, a newcomer without a track record. This kind of rejection did not deter Perry. Republicans must donate: "The elimination of this 'New Deal' Congressman," Perry argued, "will bring us nearer to a balanced budget than any investment of a political nature, ever offered."[9]

While Murray Chotiner had ceased writing Nixon press releases because of his major commitment to managing William Knowland's bid to retain his recent appointment as a U.S. senator, Chotiner's assistant, Ruth

Arnold, covered Nixon's activities as part of her work for the GOP in Southern California. She searched out Republican analyses of Voorhis's congressional voting record and researched critical information that the challenger felt was imperative in his future assault on the incumbent. Along with this assistance, Nixon hired a major Los Angeles advertising agency, Lockwood & Shakelford, to buy eighteen billboards for him that struck the Republican national theme: "Time for a Change." Nixon was convinced that this type of advertising boosted name recognition.[10]

Pleased with the results, Nixon believed that the committee had established its broad campaign outline by the middle of August. He immediately eliminated expensive radio broadcasts. Depending on the budget, he planned to use outdoor advertising and bumper stickers. If he had the money, he hoped to buy small newspaper ads. If not, the media campaign would start four weeks before the election. Every district voter would receive a piece of Nixon literature, and special mailings would go to farmers, veterans, doctors, realtors, and others. He also needed money for precinct workers in Democratic strongholds like El Monte and Monterey Park where few Republicans lived.[11]

Returning to his greatest strength, Nixon resumed his hectic speaking schedule. He directly attacked the vulnerabilities of the Truman administration and connected them to Voorhis. At speeches toward the end of July before the Republican Club in Puente and two weeks into August, he accused the Democratic president of corruption, bickering over price controls, confusion in the State Department, and creating crippling strikes. The country also had to rid itself of "commies" and their "fellow travelers." Nixon posed a fundamental choice for his audiences: "The basic issue facing the nation today is whether America is to be a nation in which the govt tells us what we can do and how we can do it in every phase of our lives or whether we want the opportunity to work out our own problems with a necessary minimum of govt controls & direction."[12]

Nixon began associating his opponent with the administration's emphasis on big government and concentrating on Voorhis's links to the CIO-PAC. The challenger pointed out in late July: "I have no personal quarrel with my opponent. I have no criticism of him as a man & if I did I wouldn't use it because I don't believe in that kind of politics." Nixon, however, did attack the NC-PAC as "the left wing sister" of the CIO. He had "no war chest"; people gave to him in small amounts. In mid-August, he proclaimed that his vote was not for sale while Voorhis had accepted PAC money, inferring that Voohis belonged to the special interest groups. Democrats had "unlimited funds," and the people that supplied them were "fanatical in their cause."[13]

Raymond Haight, national committeeman from California, attacked even more forcefully, reflecting the GOP national theme of linking the Democratic administration to flawed domestic security and weakness in dealing with the Russians. He told a district newspaper that Voorhis faced defeat because he, Helen Gahagan Douglas, and other New Dealers in Congress followed "the Communist line." Democrats should not be given the responsibility of negotiating with the Russians; the Truman administration, Haight dejectedly concluded, already had demonstrated its inability to forestall Soviet expansionism.[14]

One of Nixon's supporters, Kenneth Spencer, spoke for many in the GOP who saw a vast conspiracy unfolding. He believed that Franklin Roosevelt had betrayed the United States in his secret dealings with Josef Stalin. Voorhis, to Spencer, "was one of the gang and on his shoulders must rest part of the responsibility for that betrayal." Nixon should expose these shocking revelations because Americans must realize "how they have been hoodwinked and sold down the river." Some thought that Roosevelt had gambled and lost in his negotiations with the Soviet Union, but Spencer went further, convinced that the Roosevelt peace plan "was to take this country into something so near communism that the Russians could not tell the difference." Every American life had been placed in jeopardy; the country, as a result, had become disillusioned, and these transgressions were fair game for the campaign.[15]

Spencer spoke for many Republicans who felt that Roosevelt had betrayed the country. While Nixon sympathized with their feelings, he had not agreed that the president had surrendered the nation to the Russians. He did, however, concede that the Communists were trying to subvert the American way of life, and he would guard against Soviet infiltration.

On Labor Day, Nixon spoke to a friendly crowd in Whittier, announcing a recurring proposition: "It is a satisfaction and a privilege to accept the challenge of the P.A.C." He intended to attack it and other extreme left-wing elements that sought "to eliminate representation of all the people from the American form of government."[16]

Along with these public appearances, Nixon managed the daily routine and gave McCall a detailed list of specific tasks to accomplish. The candidate wanted Nixon for Congress town groups assembled by the middle of the month. Several stories were coming out in the newspapers, and he wanted to capitalize on them. Since Voorhis was wooing veterans, Republicans also needed to entice them. Democrats for Nixon, farmers, and other special interests like realtors and insurance agents should be targeted. Women had to take a larger role, and a Whittier College contingent as well as Whittier Citizens for Nixon had to be formed. To the challenger, everyone who was a potential voter should be identified. Even though the campaign presently lacked funds, as soon as donations increased, the committee would be ready for a mailing from prominent people in the district supporting his cause. As for the opposition, Nixon wanted information: "If possible we should get better reports on Voorhis' activities than we are at the present time. If necessary one person should be assigned the duty of tailing him and reporting on everything he says."[17]

As he formulated these organizational plans, Nixon continuously addressed audiences. On September 11, he spoke before his veterans committee in Whittier about battle-wounded soldiers. To him, these men were entitled to full government protection. He expected to help them with housing, jobs, and education, but he refused to accept pork barrel legislation to assist them. On the 13th, he appeared in front of the Alhambra Jaycees at a luncheon about the value of democracy over totalitarianism. In the United States there were choices, and he hoped that labor and business could solve their own problems without government intervention.[18]

While Nixon had consolidated his forces throughout the summer, the only positive action that Voorhis proposed was holding joint appearances or debates with Nixon after the congressional adjournment. He even composed a letter to his expected opponent for comment within his group of advisers. What the congressman proposed was a series of appearances on the same platform as formal debates or question and answer periods. In this way, voters would familiarize themselves with both candidates and the issues. After Jack Long met with five or six people about this idea, they rejected it. Although Nixon was supposedly a champion debater, they told Voorhis, "with your age and experience, the general public might not take kindly to your challenging a boy like Nixon." In spite of that possible negative, Long was trying to arrange debates with the opposition as long as an impartial moderator served in each contest.[19]

Charles Voorhis led the plans for his son's campaign by working on registration, precinct organization, and voter turnout for November. Jerry would have to reacquaint himself with his constituents' concerns since he had been gone from the district for almost an entire year. The committee was planning a homecoming for him at El Monte High School, and then after a couple of days rest, he would attend a wide variety of meetings until the November election.[20]

To meet this schedule, Jerry anticipated sending his family ahead of him by car. He would leave the capital on August 2 and meet them in Iowa. His two secretaries, Harold Herin and Duane deSchaine, were included in the caravan. From there, they would take a leisurely drive, "since this is probably all the time we will have to get more or less away from work." The party would arrive in California on August 11. This schedule was never met because Jerry suffered from a severe case of hemorrhoids and had to stop in Ogden, Utah, for surgery. As a result of the painful operation, he was physically exhausted and in poor health throughout most of the campaign.[21]

Despite this setback, Voorhis returned to the district with a great deal of favorable national exposure. *Pageant*, in its August edition, stated that his colleagues selected him their hardest-working member. Livid at free publicity for the congressman from a Quaker journal, Perry complained to Errol Elliott, editor of the *American Friend*, toward the end of the month about his praise for Voorhis's efforts on behalf of European relief. At the beginning of September, *McCall's* magazine labeled Voorhis "one of the most conscientious men alive. A clear thinker; he suffers antagonism from both the right and left wings."[22]

Voorhis often won accolades from his colleagues. In his memoirs, Senator Paul Douglas considered Jerry a "political saint." Douglas had met Voorhis in 1936 when the Democrat toured California on the lecture circuit. His friend worked a sixteen- to eighteen-hour day and mastered every subject that he chose. His colleagues referred to him as "Kid Atlas." In the area of banking, Voorhis forced the Federal Reserve Banks to return their net earnings to the Treasury from interest on government bonds purchased by the banks, and this practice saved Americans a billion dollars a year. That was one reason why the House voted him its "most conscientious" member.[23]

These kinds of descriptions increased Voorhis's national prestige, but his long absence from the district did not allow him to benefit from them at home. When the congressman spoke at his homecoming at the El Monte High School on August 23 for almost three hours, the *South*

*Pasadena Review* characterized his presentation as sincere but unrealistic. He had passed one bill of the 125 that he had introduced. He spoke on his pet theories on money and banking. He was a socialist at heart and opposed business. His foreign policy views were clear and correct. He supported the CIO-PAC, but avoided discussing it and his relationship to such liberal fellow Democrats as Helen Gahagan Douglas and Chester "Chet" Holifield. The contest pitting Nixon against Voorhis, the paper predicted, would be an interesting one.[24]

Even with the *Review*'s pessimistic comments, Voorhis had the enormous advantage of incumbency. He had built a strong following within the citrus industry, ranchers, labor unions, and veterans. This coalition had provided the margin for victory over the last decade, and he did not anticipate any defection. He often spoke on the radio, reaching a large number of constituents, and published his column, "People's Business," in the local press. But at the end of July, he had announced a temporary interruption of the column because he did not want to give the impression that he might be using the column as "a means of political campaigning."[25]

This self-imposed limitation weakened Voorhis's political outreach. During his decade in office, he had done little to create an organization. Instead, he depended on his father to supervise the campaigns without any precinct structure. His main structural efforts came from compiling lists of supporters to run newspaper advertisements and to develop a network of volunteers during campaigns. Jack Long assisted in coordinating the efforts with labor, farmers, and local Democratic politicians, but he resented anyone who did not fit in this mold, and therefore trusted only a select few. This time, at least, Voorhis brought his two capital secretaries home to coordinate his campaign efforts.[26]

Voorhis's most glaring political liability centered on his bonds with the CIO-PAC. McLaughlin's unsuccessful attempt to exploit this issue in 1944 possibly gave Voorhis comfort that the connection presented no political hazards. He knew that Communists dominated some CIO unions, but underestimated voter unrest with labor as the Cold War heightened that summer. For those or some other reason, he did not consider this issue a serious challenge to his reelection, nor did anyone associated with his campaign vehemently disagree. Why the opposition attacked the issue so forcefully simply was never addressed. Yet the GOP never let voters forget that Voorhis, the PAC, and unions were intertwined.

Although several prominent Republicans attached Voorhis to the

CIO-PAC, the real acrimony flared up earlier when, on May 27, an editorial in the *South Pasadena Review* accused the congressman of having the CIO-PAC endorsement. The editor later grudgingly admitted that he could not prove that Voorhis ever had it, but the paper's charge had already inflicted the damage. To present Voorhis with a platform to respond to this and other allegations, the Independent Voters of South Pasadena (IVSP), a group composed of New Dealers and liberal Republicans who were disenchanted with the Truman administration, encouraged joint appearances with the candidates for major office in the district.[27]

IVSP chairman Paul Bullock, a Voorhis partisan, led the momentum toward debates. After a speaking engagement was arranged in South Pasadena, he encouraged Voorhis to concentrate on American-Soviet relations and recent labor legislation that the congressman had introduced for special mediation and arbitration courts for disputes. Many South Pasadeneans, Bullock cautioned, thought Voorhis was "a wild-eyed radical " or "a 'stooge' of the CIO-PAC." He needed to demonstrate to the audience his cogent, independent thinking.[28]

To proclaim his public position, Voorhis took out a political advertisement in many of the district's newspapers on September 11, declaring that he proudly accepted the endorsements of the AFL and Railroad Brotherhoods for his reelection, but since he opposed Communists in the labor movement, the CIO-PAC had refused to endorse him: "American labor, American progress, American forward looking political movements cannot be mixed with any labor man who opposes these influences. I can not accept the support of anyone who does not oppose them as I do." In response to that declaration, McCall declared that he had evidence that Voorhis had the PAC endorsement and would "offer the proof at the proper time."[29]

Two days after this cryptic prophecy, the candidates met on Friday, September 13, at South Pasadena Junior High School. The constituents in the area were white, middle-class, mainly conservative Republicans. The day had been hot and smoggy, with the temperature soaring to a high for the year of ninety-four degrees. By nighttime, the smog had dissipated and the heat turned into a balmy, pleasant evening. A capacity boisterous crowd of a thousand, sometimes overflowing into the aisles, crammed into the auditorium to listen to the presentations, with Professor Carleton Rodee of the University of Southern California serving as moderator. Both parties had planted cheering sections in the crowd and designated individuals to pose difficult or embarrassing questions when the question and answer period arrived.[30]

Before the congressional candidates made their joint appearance, spokesmen for the U.S. senatorial aspirants addressed the audience for about fifteen minutes each. Chotiner represented his client, William Knowland, the Republican, and Democratic congressman Holifield of Southern California was the surrogate for Will Rogers, Jr., son of the famous humorist. In addition to representing the senatorial candidate, Holifield deeply respected Voorhis, who had originally encouraged Holifield to run for public office. Holifield and Chotiner held a spirited debate over the Truman administration; Chotiner attacked the Democrats for their left-wing leanings, while Holifield defended the status quo and the New Deal heritage.[31]

When they concluded, Voorhis, who made no special preparations, gave a similar fifteen-minute presentation on the issues confronting Americans in the postwar world, and just as he was concluding, Nixon, who had arrived late, with his wife watching, walked onto the stage to a thunderous round of applause. The two men shook hands, and then the contender attacked price controls, the lower standard of living, and other weaknesses of Truman's policies. He opposed the crescendoing amount of strikes and worried that 125 congressmen were directly tied to the CIO-PAC. He questioned Voorhis's "funny-money" scheme, which would diminish the dollar's value, and received his warmest response when he said: "the time is at hand in this country where no labor leader or no management leader should have the power to deny the American people any of the necessities of life."[32]

Voorhis asked Nixon for proof that the congressman had the PAC endorsement. Obviously ready for that challenge, Nixon reached into his pocket and produced *Action for Today*, a two-page bulletin from the NC-PAC in Los Angeles that had, in fact, included Voorhis in its Political Committee Recommendations on March 27. Nixon walked over with the document in hand; even though some of his supporters knew about this endorsement, still no one had informed the congressman. Surprised, bewildered, Voorhis floundered, blurting out the NC-PAC was not the CIO-PAC. While he fumbled for words, Nixon read the lists of directors of both organizations, pointing out that many names served on both boards.[33]

After the gathering had ended, Voorhis asked Holifield for his impressions of the debate. Recalling the encounter thirty-two years later,

Holifield said: "Jerry, he murdered you. He used every dirty trick in the book." The audience cheered everything Nixon said and booed Voorhis. Holifield counseled his friend against appearing in any more joint appearances. Friday, the 13th, had not been a good day for the incumbent.[34]

Nixon and his supporters were elated. Kenneth Spencer watched the debate and declared his choice the winner. Voorhis did not "look so good" and Nixon "did a fine job of it. . . . I thought you were splendid and that he is very scared and nervous." The Democrats tried to call Republicans reactionary, but the party stood "for practical liberalism, the Democrats for a lot of unworkable socialistic ideas which have no hope of functioning unless we are willing to change our whole theory of government."[35]

McCall was so impressed with Nixon's performance that he hired a large calendar manufacturer to produce thousands of plastic thimbles printed with the slogan: "Nixon for Congress—Put a Needle in the PAC." This novelty quickly became a popular giveaway item at Nixon's meetings.[36]

Voorhis continued on his speaking schedule while developing a strategy to minimize the damage done at his South Pasadena appearance. Deploring Secretary of Commerce Henry Wallace's attack on Secretary of State James Byrnes's foreign policies, Voorhis held that he backed the administration's diplomatic initiatives, while the secretary of commerce, who had close connections with the PACs, refused to follow the administration's foreign policy objectives. Since Voorhis could not condone Wallace's recommendations, he sent telegrams to NC-PAC in New York City and the PAC in Los Angeles on September 18, objecting to Wallace's attacks on the administration and the PACs' apparent support for the secretary of commerce. Since Voorhis approved of Truman and Byrnes's actions, "I hereby request that whatever qualified endorsement the Citizens PAC may have given me be withdrawn."[37]

This convoluted rationale for denying the NC-PAC endorsement provided the Republican challenger with even more ammunition. Nixon had illustrated that the congressman, indeed, had the PAC endorsement and refused to apologize for making a false statement. Voorhis never repudiated the organization or denounced its doctrines. He merely asked for the endorsement to be withdrawn and still voted the PAC line just like Helen Gahagan Douglas and others. By answering the charge of the NC-PAC's "qualified endorsement" with a poorly constructed reply, Voorhis allowed Nixon to leave the impression with voters that the congressman had lied, always knowing that he had PAC support. The Republicans had unknowingly caught him in an impossible situation, for during the primary, Voorhis knew about the Hollywood PAC endorsement; it could hurt him politically, and yet he did nothing to have it rescinded. He also personally negotiated the endorsements of the local PACs of the Amalgamated Clothing Workers of America and the United Automobile, Aircraft, Agricultural Implement Workers of America.[38]

Despite this dilemma, the incumbent hoped that testimonials from prominent Democrats would boost his reelection chances. The Speaker of the House of Representatives, Sam Rayburn, for example, wrote that a Democratic majority in the House was crucial to sustain the president's proposals. Voorhis had been of great assistance and had to be reelected: "Your great energy, your sound judgment, your untiring industry, and your unfailing loyalty to the people and principles have made you one of the most valuable men in the House." Voorhis appreciated this strong endorsement because "Frankly, things are pretty tough this time and some of the quarrels and disagreements among high officials in Washington are not helping any."[39]

The banner headline on September 20 in the *Alhambra Post-Advocate* caused added consternation: WALLACE FIRED FROM CABINET. That day, the candidates' second joint appearance was held before the recently organized Whittier Ex-Servicemen's Association in that city's Patriotic Hall, was restricted to two hundred war veterans, and was limited to issues that affected them. Gone were the booing and heckling from the previous encounter. Voorhis spoke first, advocating support for veterans and their dependents. He wished to restrict commercial building so that contractors would have enough material to increase housing. Nixon followed and called the housing shortage a national disgrace; all controls should be lifted so that private enterprise would have the opportunity to produce whatever was needed. The two argued over government ownership of basic industries and utilities, with the incumbent advocating that certain monopolistic utilities should be government-owned, as well as the Federal Reserve Banks. The challenger countered, opposing further "industrial socialization and federal controls in the United States." During the rebuttal period, Nixon censured the congressman for failing to support the House Committee on Un-American Activities, to which Voorhis replied that he disapproved of making it a permanent congressional committee.[40]

During the last half hour, the candidates answered questions from the audience, with each contestant receiving the same number of questions and then one minute to comment on queries directed at the other. The debate heated up when Nixon accused his opponent of having the CIO-PAC endorsement and read a letter proving his point. Voorhis replied that he had requested the PAC to withdraw its support and added: "A man can not be held responsible for the action of any group, whether it is against him or for him." That was the logical reply, but it came too late and without widespread media circulation.[41]

While the Whittier gathering gave each veteran in the audience a chance to listen to and evaluate both contenders, the Whittier Narrows Dam project offered a distinct advantage to the incumbent. El Monte, already a heavily populated Democratic stronghold, vehemently fought construction of the dam because it would wipe out a section of the town. Reverend Dan Cleveland, a Southern Baptist, who ministered at the Church in the Barn close to the proposed construction site, led the battle against it, and Congressman Voorhis accepted their arguments and served as their champion in Congress. Nixon, too, pledged his opposition, but at least one anonymous writer held that since Whittier was pushing for the dam's development, the challenger was being duplicitous.[42]

McCall, who closely scrutinized the debates, ignored that charge. He believed that the Republican challenger had a real possibility of winning in November. He had attended both contests, and "it certainly was an inspiration to see how Nixon could handle himself after ten months of campaigning while the incumbent has been campaigning for over ten years. It really was better than a boxing match to observe the blow by blow slugging of each candidate. The contest has started the voters talking throughout the district and that is just what Nixon needed."[43]

To provide additional insurance, Nixon hired William "Bill" Arnold, whose father, Fred, had been a Los Angeles newspaperman for over six decades and a friend of President Woodrow Wilson, to handle some publicity writing in the last two months of the campaign. Bill had earlier assisted with the publicity for Earl Warren's first gubernatorial campaign. During the war, Arnold served in the U.S. Air Force, was discharged, and now found himself in the middle of a hotly contested congressional race.[44]

Arnold later analyzed Nixon's strengths. The challenger had a remarkable gift for seizing opportunities and turning them to his advantage. During that first campaign, Arnold asked Nixon how an inexperienced novice had gained such political savvy. He shrugged: "I guess it was through a lot of history reading about guys like Teddy Roosevelt and Woodrow Wilson in their campaigns." To Arnold, Nixon had much more to commend him, demonstrating a degree of sophistication and shrewdness beyond his years.[45]

To build upon Nixon's momentum, McCall called on Voorhis to schedule at least eight more debates, due to the overwhelming public response from the first two. Voorhis accepted more appearances on the conditions that the candidates could find agreeable dates and opening statements would be extended from fifteen to twenty or twenty-five minutes. Nixon promptly consented; all Voorhis had to do was have one of his managers phone Pat Nixon to arrange dates. The committees, during the first week of October, found three mutually acceptable dates later in that month. The Nixon forces could not have been happier.[46]

With four weeks to go before the elections, McCall told the campaign committee that Nixon would discuss the final phase of the election with the members on October 10. When approximately 150 volunteers met at the Garfield School in Alhambra, the challenger asked them to work harder. Although the PAC had a "huge slush fund" to spend on its man Voorhis, Nixon welcomed the opposition of "this radical group," but its large sums of money and paid workers created a difficult situation. He did not have those resources, and his campaign workers would have to redouble their efforts for "those who stand for the American way of life."[47]

While Nixon was pressing his followers to press forward, he also had been wooing William Kinnett, the Republican attorney who had lost in the primaries. As early as May 20, Nixon appealed to Kinnett to "join forces to insure the election of a sound progressive Republican in place of Mr. Voorhis." In mid-October, Kinnett publicly endorsed Nixon and asked his followers to cast their ballots for the Republican standard-bearer. Money was still a struggle. Sometimes donors surfaced at precisely the right moment. Nixon, for example, acknowledged Herbert Spencer for making his contribution "when we were bogged down for lack of funds and you came to the rescue."[48]

Nixon sought to turn his acquaintance with Harold Stassen into a political advantage. They had met in the South Pacific during 1944. Dick described Stassen to Pat as "only thirty-five—a big, good-looking Swede—and I was very impressed by his quiet poise." Elected Minnesota's governor in 1938, at thirty-two, Stassen became the youngest American ever to reach a state house and served several terms before entering the navy, achieving great popularity by promoting reduced taxes, civil service reform, and governmental efficiency. During the 1940 presidential contest, he keynoted the GOP's national convention, then acted as Wendell Willkie's floor manager, and later emerged as a leader of the internationalist wing in the Republican Party.[49]

Shortly before the end of 1945, Joseph Parker, a naval lieutenant who worked with Nixon in terminating contracts, wrote Stassen that before entering the military, Parker had attended the Minnesota state convention that renominated the governor in 1940. Parker added that Nixon, who had worked with him in the navy, happened not only to be "an outstanding lawyer," who "performed an excellent job with a number of our larger contractors," but also had been chosen to run for Congress against Voorhis. Both Parker and Nixon, before they left the service, hoped to meet Stassen in New York City, especially since Nixon was "deeply interested in the Republican party and its liberal future" and wanted to talk to the governor about his views.[50]

Unable to meet at that time, toward the end of the 1946 primary, Nixon wrote Stassen: "I have been very interested in following your campaign to liberalize the Republican Party because I feel strongly that the party must adopt a constructive progressive program in order to merit the support of the voters." He was planning to attend the Pasadena Junior Chamber of Commerce dinner on May 28, where Stassen was the banquet speaker and hoped to speak with him there. Once Nixon won the primary, Stassen offered to assist him in the finals since Stassen saw that the 12th congressional district was a key one in the United States. McCall was so excited about this possibility that in late September, he pledged the plane fare to fly Stassen out to Whittier for "a bang-up meeting" to speak at Nixon's last rally with at least 2,500 people in attendance and a possible radio hookup for California, if not the entire West Coast. Stassen accepted, with the proviso that the California State Republican Central Committee had to approve. It did not, forcing the Nixon committee to abandon the idea.[51]

While Stassen seemed eager to support Nixon, Governor Earl Warren was not. Though a registered Republican, he also attracted essential independent and Democratic voters by asserting his nonpartisanship. His refusal to endorse the entire party ticket displeased many partisans, and although the GOP apparatus supported him, he did not reciprocate. Stalwarts quietly griped among themselves, but publicly they maintained silence. Warren had cross-filed in 1946 and won both major primaries.

His popularity was unquestionable, and his name recognition garnished votes for other GOP candidates with the draw of his coattails, even while many conservatives grumbled.

A native Californian, of Scandinavian ancestry, Warren was born in 1891 and raised in Bakersfield. He attended the University of California, Berkeley, and during his junior year, entered Boalt Hall to combine his bachelor's and law degrees. After World War I, he worked for local attorneys, and in 1924, he joined the Alameda district attorney's office, got married, and became actively engaged in Republican politics. The following year, with the publisher of the *Oakland Tribune*, Joseph Knowland's, backing, Warren was appointed district attorney. In 1926, he ran for that office stressing his independent nature and won in a landslide. During the next two elections, he continued to win large pluralities, and in 1938, he announced as a candidate for California attorney general. He proved just as appealing on the state level as he did on the county, and four years later, he declared for and won the governorship. Even in Sacramento, Warren continued to espouse nonpartisanship and used the wartime crisis to reenforce this theme.[52]

Warren sometimes honored political debts. In 1945, he appointed William Knowland U.S. senator to fill out an unexpired Senate term created by the death of Hiram Johnson that August. The governor owed a great debt to Joe Knowland of the *Oakland Tribune* and also was fond of his son. When Bill stood for election in 1946, the governor enthusiastically endorsed him.[53]

Mac Faries, Republican committeeman from California, interacted with Warren, Knowland, and Nixon during the 1946 campaign. Faries had campaigned for Warren in 1942 and recalled that he "was as always, a loner. He took the position that it was not the thing to do to endorse openly with some exceptions, other party candidates or propositions." Faries recognized that the governor and Bill Knowland were close friends, and the latter had demonstrated in 1946 that he was not a lackey to his influential father. As for the novice Nixon, Faries participated in the first Fact Finding Committee meeting to assess this young naval officer's chances of facing off against Voorhis and backed the group's conclusion that Nixon was the person to challenge the incumbent's collectivist ideas.[54]

While Nixon was unaware of the complicated Knowland-Warren relationship, the governor, true to form, endorsed only one congres-

sional candidate, Bertrand Gearhart from Fresno. Bill Arnold had backed
Warren's initial gubernatorial campaign in the early 1940s and asked him
to announce for Nixon because Voorhis had used a letter from Warren
praising the congressman's proposal for a disability insurance program in
California. Arnold asked Warren to disavow the laudatory letter, or at
least write something nice about Nixon. Warren responded that Voorhis
deserved the compliment, and Nixon would not get any endorsement.[55]

The Warren-Nixon relationship started on the premise that the governor would act independently, without consideration for party loyalty.
Nixon recognized Warren's power and prestige, while also understanding that many GOP conservatives objected to the governor's refusal to
support the party's slate. Nixon might not appreciate Warren's political
decisions, but never underestimated his clout. Even if the challenger disapproved of the governor's actions, he did not voice displeasure. Nixon
could not openly attack Warren's disagreeable actions, for he could not
afford the governor's antipathy.

Voorhis had his own difficulties when the Los Angeles County
Democratic Central Committee proposed extending an invitation to
Wallace to appear in the area. To Voorhis, this was folly; Democrats had
to support Truman and Byrnes's policy of being firm with the Russians.
Voorhis used the radio to announce his support for Byrnes's foreign
policy and call for an end to party bickering and the acceptance of bipartisanship. The differences between Truman and Wallace were clear.
Although Voorhis agreed with Wallace that the Russians had legitimate
concerns, the congressman felt that the United States had to stop "giving ground." Since Stalin had rejected the American proposal on international control of atomic weapons, the secretary of state reacted
appropriately in being firm with the Soviets.[56]

When Nixon and Voorhis appeared at a third meeting, diplomacy
was never an issue. The League of Women Voters and the Claremont Kiwanis Club sponsored this debate in Bridges Hall at Pomona College on
October 11 before a capacity audience of 1,850. On the flip of a coin,
Voorhis went first. Each had an allotted half hour for opening remarks
and ten minutes for rebuttal. A two-man screening committee selected
one question from each political party, passed in from the audience. One
principal issue was the continuation of the OPA, with Voorhis taking the
position of continued enforcement, and Nixon calling for an end to
burdensome regulations. The combatants also discussed monetary pol-

icy: Nixon opposing socialization of any basic, free industry, and the congressman demanding the nationalization of the federal reserve system. Voorhis further suggested secret ballots for union officer elections, as well as strike votes.[57]

With the conclusion of this appearance, Nixon began sending out letters on October 14 written by Chief Newman, Whittier College's popular football coach, who was more than making up for denying Nixon's varsity letter: "The forces opposing Dick are well-entrenched after ten uninspired, unchallenged and ineffective years in office." They were well organized and financed; they needed to be driven out of office: "We have the opportunity to elect to our national Congress a man whose Whittier College background, whose ideals of honesty, fair play and democracy we share." They had to put Nixon in Congress. While that message went out to college friends, consumers of the *Monrovia News-Post*, four days later, read: "ARE YOU SATISFIED WITH PRESENT CONDITIONS?" Vote for Nixon.[58]

During the same interim, Voorhis had to respond to his vicious enemy John Hoeppel's challenge to meet with him in an open forum. This bigot wanted the congressman "to defend . . . his consistent voting of the PAC-CIO Communist and fellow traveler program." The incumbent refused. Nixon's name was never mentioned, but here was another allusion to Voorhis's connections to the Soviet Union.[59]

The combination of the Hoeppel challenge, the Nixon advertisements, the joint appearance in Claremont, and Truman's firing of Wallace still did not produce a strong response from the Voorhis camp. Voorhis's complacency was apparent when he and Nixon met for their fourth appearance at Monrovia High School on October 23, in front of approximately twelve hundred people. The challenger unleashed two new charges. First, he accused Voorhis of being an ineffective legislator; and second, he contended that in the last four years, Voorhis had offered 132 bills but only had one passed into law. That sole piece of legislation moved rabbit ranching from the Department of the Interior to the Agriculture Department. Nixon further claimed that forty-one of Voorhis's forty-six votes in Congress followed the CIO-PAC line. When asked to give his sources for these allegations, Nixon cited the *Labor Herald* and three supplements of the *New Republic*. The congressman replied that he had passed an act to employ the physically handicapped, but Nixon responded that this was not a law, rather, a joint resolution. Upset and astonished, Voorhis stood up to protest, but Nixon supporters loudly booed at the interruption.[60]

Voorhis stayed awake until 4:00 A.M. trying to determine the accuracy of Nixon's charges. The congressman counted twenty-seven and not forty-six votes; furthermore, many were not pro-CIO-PAC. Voorhis responded with his own advertisement: "Truth About Jerry Voorhis and His Voting Record in Congress." His answers were poorly framed and presented unclearly. At one point the ad stated that forty-three "bad" votes had favored the PAC, but they were for such issues as the extension of the Reciprocal Trade Agreements, economic assistance to Great Britain, limitation of the United Nations Relief and Recovery Administration, abolition of the poll tax, and the school lunch bill, which were not necessarily pro-Communist. The three "good" votes were for other things. At another point, the ad said that there were only twenty-seven votes, and Nixon had counted some more than once. The ad only muddied the waters. To many voters, Voorhis remained an ineffective legislator who voted with the CIO-PAC.[61]

While Voorhis fumbled, Nixon and his advocates pushed forward from the 24th until election day. McCall informed Republicans that Nixon for the first time had moved ahead in the polls. The Democratic reaction to this voter swing was to bring James Roosevelt and other prominent Democrats into the district to campaign for Voorhis. The PAC opened an office in Monterey Park to solicit votes for the incumbent, and the GOP fought to counteract that activity. Chief Newman signed another letter: "America needs *new* leadership *now*! A vote for Nixon is a vote for change!"[62]

Newspaper advertisements repeated news stories that Moscow Radio had urged the election of the CIO slate to Congress, and that voters should move against the Republicans who opposed the PAC. Another ad labeled Voorhis a New Dealer who had NC-PAC backing and had voted for the CIO-PAC forty-three out of forty-six times. He also had been a registered Socialist, and "his voting record in Congress is more Socialistic and Communistic than Democratic." In addition, he voted against the Tidelands bill that would have protected Californian property and also against farming interests in labor legislation. If this bombardment was insufficient, one ad emphasized the disingenuous nature of his voting record: DECEPTION OF THE VOTER HAS NO PLACE IN AMERICAN POLITICS.[63]

Money was still a problem. One morning Charles Cooper saw Pat

Nixon almost in tears because the campaign was running out of funds, and she could not send out the mailers unless more donations arrived. Her husband also kept a watchful eye on the prompt payment. When ads did not reach newspapers on time, he reacted strongly: "As a result several of the weeklies won't be able to print our ad answering Voorhis. If we get into this situation again will you please let me know and I will advance the money from my own funds."[64]

Four years after the fact, Pat Nixon recalled their financial plight facing the closing days of the campaign. Many people did not think that her husband had "a very good chance" of beating Voorhis, and therefore, Dick's challenge to the incumbent did not bring out many contributors. As a consequence, she noted, "all our savings went into that campaign."[65]

The last joint appearance was on Monday evening, at 8:00 P.M., on October 28, at the San Gabriel Civic Auditorium in front of the largest audience to listen to the two combatants, with Dr. Charles Lindsley acting as moderator. Over two thousand well-behaved people watched from inside while another several hundred outside heard the contest over a loudspeaker. The incumbent spoke first for twenty-five minutes, defending the Truman administration in its efforts to reduce inflation, expand Social Security, develop a federal housing program, and increase veterans benefits, and calling for government control of public utilities. Nixon, in contrast, spoke about the failures of the Democrats, demanding an end to government controls and pledging to oppose socialization and nationalization programs. He wanted private enterprise to work because it would always do a better job than government inefficiency. A question and answer period followed where each had three minutes to answer questions from the audience and one minute for rebuttal; then Nixon had seven and a half minutes for a closing statement, followed by Voorhis with the same amount of time.[66]

Voorhis attacked Nixon for building his campaign around the ads about the supposed forty-six votes. Voorhis charged that the challenger had counted some votes twice, three, or four times. In reality, there were only nineteen bills involved. These "46 mysterious votes" were invented to avoid real discussion. Everyone knew where Voorhis stood, but Nixon evaded the issues. Where did he stand?[67]

Nixon responded with his own assault. He had brought a copy of the *Congressional Record* to the meeting and repeated his charge that

Voorhis had not enacted any bills into law during the last four years. Voorhis had passed one resolution transferring control of rabbits to the Agriculture Department, but that was not a bill. Nixon concluded: "Therefore I assume you have to be a rabbit to have representation from the Twelfth District in Washington." According to Roy Day, who attended the gathering, the audience burst out with laughter. Voorhis became nervous, upset, and jittery. Day concluded: Voorhis "just came apart at the seams."[68]

Mac Faries also watched the debate and later expressed his ambivalence. He objected to Nixon's use of the Red issue because the challenger was clearly ahead and did not need to attack the incumbent so vigorously. But Nixon had discovered that charges of not dealing strongly enough with the Soviet government were effective. Faries conceded that this issue "was a good issue, a gut issue, and . . . Nixon was honest about it; but I thought he was a bit of the boy debater and a little cold."[69]

Nixon received the loudest and longest applause when he announced his rationale for electing a Republican majority in 1947: "If we send back to Congress the same men who have failed this country ever since V-J Day, in matters of industrial relations, price controls, lack of production and others of the present administration's most notable failures, we will only get another helping of the same. But the American people have had enough and they are going to send a new Congress, a Republican Congress, to Washington next year."[70]

A few congratulated Voorhis on his performance, while many applauded the challenger. Hubert Perry, Herman's son, and his wife watched from a front-row seat while Voorhis was on the defensive all night "as a result of your arguments and rebuttal." His wife thought that Dick's "delivery was terrific." Momentum built. Pat Nixon commented in the final days of the campaign: "Huh, Boy! These people must really believe we're going to win the way donations are coming in!"[71]

The initial returns on election day showed Voorhis in the lead, but by 9:00 P.M., they shifted toward Nixon. By late in the evening, Voorhis knew that he had lost. Nixon, on the other hand, was uncertain of victory until 4:00 A.M., recalling it with great fondness: "There have been many great days since then but none will ever equal that campaign or the thrill of that particular day." He and Pat were happier then than "we were ever to be again in my political career." At thirty-three, he was a newly elected congressman.[72]

Nationwide, 54.3 percent voted Republican and 45.7 percent Democrat. Republicans gained 12 seats in the Senate for a majority and won 246 House seats, an increase of 55, the largest Republican assemblage since 1928. The Democrats retained 188. The 12th congressional district reflected this national trend. The districtwide turnout had exceeded 65 percent in some areas. Nixon had lost eight of fourteen cities in the primary, but won nineteen of twenty-two in the general election. Voorhis retained his Democratic majorities in Baldwin Park, Monterey Park, and El Monte, but lost his home town of San Dimas, 516 to 434, while Nixon took Whittier, two to one:[73]

| Candidate | Vote | Percentage |
|-----------|------|------------|
| Nixon | 65,586 | 56.1 |
| Voorhis | 49,994 | 42.7 |
| Hoeppel | 1,476 | 1.2 |
| Others | 13 | |

On the evening of the 6th, while Nixon thanked his supporters and looked at his victory as a mandate for change, he first paid tribute to his family: "I think today my greatest satisfaction over the results of this election is not for myself but for my wife and my parents. Their happiness over this success is the best reward of all."[74]

The expected congratulations poured in from officials like Earl Warren and his lieutenant governor, Fred Houser. Original sponsors of the Fact Finding Committee applauded his victory. Others like Vernon Hodge, a Republican and principal of an evening school in Los Angeles, praised Nixon: "You fought a grand, clean fight against an adversary who knew no rules and you gave him a sound beating."[75]

Several Democrats praised Nixon. Charlie Cooper, a staunch party member, voted for Voorhis, "but I'm somehow pleased that you won." Nixon had conducted his campaign in "fine spirit and brilliant conduct," and congressional politics had reached a "new and high level" in the district. Aubert Bruce's wife had taught Nixon in high school, where she formed a good impression of him. Even though Bruce and Voorhis were personal friends, the congressman "was in the wrong crowd and I just came to the point where I couldnt [sic] go along any further with him." Bruce even enclosed a small check to help defray Nixon's campaign expenses.[76]

One critic felt that Nixon used lawyer's tactics to win, but won no respect for himself in the process. The writer only hoped that Nixon would be as good a representative as Voorhis had been. Hoeppel expressed some of his hatred toward Voorhis. Never expecting to win, he wanted "to expose what I considered to be the alien-minded, un-American, PAC, Red, Congressional record of the Democratic incumbent."[77]

The local Quaker ministers split over the outcome. Harold Walker of the East Whittier Friends Church, where the Nixons went, offered his congratulations, but O. Herschel Folger of the First Friends Church in Whittier voted for Nixon with "great hesitancy." He was concerned about the "petty politics" and the need to raise the conduct of the participants. Nixon agreed, admitting on several occasions the need "to curb overzealous supporters." Voorhis had similar problems. Some Nixon followers had told him that Democrats had spread rumors that he had spent his wartime service at a desk in Washington, D.C., but now those shenanigans were "under the bridge."[78]

Nixon received his first national exposure on November 18. *Newsweek* identified him as "a husky ex-footballer" who bested Voorhis in five debates. According to the reporter, the defeated congressman described Nixon as having "a silver tongue." *Time* labeled him a Quaker attorney who fought a grassroots campaign that many Republicans considered "hopeless." He passed out his thimbles, hammered away on the issues, and *avoided* personal attacks on his opponent.[79]

While Nixon and his friends celebrated, Voorhis released a statement on November 7 acknowledging that his challenger had won decisively. Voorhis thanked those who had backed him and his righteous causes over the past decade: "I have given the best years of my life to serving this district in Congress. By the will of the people that work is ended. I have no regrets about the record I have written."[80]

Hundreds of sympathetic letters flowed into Voorhis's office providing reasoning for his defeat. Some thought that the Democrats were too complacent, believing he could not lose. Another blamed the failures of the Truman administration, Wallace's disloyalty, and domestic discontent. Several close friends thought that voters had had enough of the Democratic Party and cast their ballots for change. Finally, a very angry supporter blamed the defeat on "a campaign of falsehood and mudslinging" that riled him up. "In a fair fight the best man is entitled to win, but the abuse to which you were subjected goes a little below anything I have experienced or observed in these parts."[81]

Voorhis did not send Nixon a congratulatory letter until early December: "I sincerely wish you well as you undertake the tremendous responsibilities which will soon be yours." Voorhis offered his assistance, and before he left his office, Nixon came in to see him one afternoon. They shook hands and smiled at each other, talked for more than a hour, and parted company, Voorhis thought, as friends. He believed that Nixon would be a conservative Republican congressman, and "I believe he will be a conscientious one."[82]

With this business completed, Voorhis initiated a touching exchange of letters between himself and his father. Charles was proud of his son's accomplishments and bitter over his defeat. Jerry's opposition "had conducted the most vicious and powerful campaign against you that money could buy. Experts from the outside, highly trained in the art of lying and misrepresentation repeating these misstatements over and over again." Vast amounts of money flowed into the district for Nixon and the Republican-controlled press attacked Jerry. Despite these overwhelming obstacles, he still could have been victorious, but "the great surge for a change which swept the country . . . was just too much." On the very last day of 1946, on the way home from his office in the evening, Jerry sent his final letter as a congressman to his father. If he had accomplished anything over the last decade, he owed his success to his number one supporter, his father: "It has been primarily due to your help, your confidence, your advice,—above all to a feeling I have always had that your hand was on my shoulder. Thanks" and "God bless you."[83]

The congressional career of Jerry Voorhis had ended. He published the first account of the defeat in his memoirs, *Confessions of a Congressman* (1948). The real contest, according to the author, centered on the "ins" versus the "outs" and the tremendous sums of money that the Nixon campaign generated. Voorhis admitted that the election was the "bitterest campaign I have ever experienced." Nixon read the book upon its release; his only comment was: "What I am wondering is where all the money went that we were supposed to have had!"[84]

That ended any significant publications about the 1946 election until Ernest Brashear, the labor editor of the *Los Angeles Daily News* who had lost a California state assembly seat in 1950, wrote an article entitled "Who Is Richard Nixon?" in the *New Republic* during the fall of 1952. With the publication of this story, the legend was launched. Designed to denigrate Nixon as the vice-presidential candidate, Brashear wrote that big business had given large sums of money to Nixon in his campaign against Voorhis, and spoke of the vicious rumors Republicans had spread that Voorhis was a Communist Party member. For the first time a new wrinkle surfaced; without any proof, Brashear charged that anonymous telephone callers told their listeners: "I just want you to know that Jerry Voorhis is a Communist."[85]

The allegation gained credence when a biography of Voorhis was released twenty-six years later. The author, Paul Bullock, conceded that Voorhis could have conducted a better campaign, but claimed Nixon had hurled false accusations at the incumbent. Bullock repeated Brashear's story that Nixon supporters used telephone banks to call and whisper that Voorhis was a Communist. Bullock's evidence extended to the hearsay that a Democratic loyalist asserted that a relative who had worked as one of the operators admitted to making calls. During the 1946 contest, Bullock had only said that Congressman Voorhis was "the victim of a national trend the power of which none of us could forsee [sic]. This is not a good year for sincere liberals."[86]

Voorhis embellished these stories in the winter of 1958, repeating patently false allegations. He claimed that Nixon had already been chosen to run against him even before the Fact Finding Committee's so-called want ad. Banks, insurance companies, and oil interests solidly lined up against the incumbent; the charge of the anonymous phones calls labeling him a Communist, of course, was featured. He added, without evidence, new accusations that newspapers had labeled him a fellow traveler. Republicans had spent money on a large advertising agency and billboards, while he could not afford them. These were merely symptoms. The real malaise was that when Nixon got angry, he would "do anything. . . . Any critic of Nixon is labeled an enemy of the country."[87]

This unsubstantiated phone calling eventually evolved as the pivotal issue in Nixon's skulduggery. It became more embellished and perverted with the passage of time. Twenty-five years after the event, Senator Paul Douglas, who had no firsthand knowledge of the 1946 campaign, vividly presented Nixon's villainy. Voorhis, according to the senator, was an anti-Communist who shielded the innocent from unfair charges of being subversive. The Nixon forces had labeled him the Red candidate, and during a week before the general election, telephones began ringing throughout the district. Housewives picked up their receivers and heard: "Good morning, Mrs.——, did you know Jerry Voorhis was a Communist?" "No, I didn't." They would supposedly ask who was calling and receive the reply: "Just a friend who thought you ought to know." The caller would hang up. By the time the Voorhis campaign learned of this attempt at character assassination, it could not respond. Nixon had triumphed and begun his ill-gotten political ascendancy.[88]

While Voorhis and his advocates constructed their tales, Pat Nixon, in her memoirs forty years after the fact, complained that Democrats burglarized her husband's campaign headquarters in 1946: "I wonder why it [the Watergate break-in] is played up so much. No one cared when it [the Democratic burglary] happened to us in '46!"[89]

Just as no convincing evidence of telephone calling has emerged, and no mention of it can be found until Brashear published his allegation, Pat Nixon's memory of a break-in is also dubious. Yet the former misty memory became an enduring myth, while the latter was properly dismissed.

Another incredible myth concerning the campaign dealt with the volunteers that supported Nixon's cause. One of the scores of mistakes in Roger Morris's biography from Nixon's birth through his election to the vice presidency was that the 1946 contest had been fictionalized to appear as if "gifted amateurs" had managed it and that the Committee of 100 was composed of "typical small businessmen and civic leaders chafing at the New Deal." In reality, according to Morris, this was a half truth: "the University Club, Elk Hills, the corporate levies, the vastly larger forces arrayed against Voorhis" really controlled the campaign. Murray Chotiner played a "genuine and decisive role obscured along with the events and trends he determined."[90]

Such sinister exaggerations are false; yet, Morris merely further distorted earlier fantasies like the one printed in "The Merry-Go-Round" column of Drew Pearson on September 24, 1952. In it, the muckraker informed his audience that Nixon had commenced his political career "when a wealthy group of businessmen" in the Pasadena area called the "San Marino Group" determined that he should defeat Voorhis. It was the "country club set" even during the depression when homes sold for a minimum of $15,000. Roy Day, "a local newspaper publisher," worked through the San Marino Group, "the real nucleus of the Nixon movement."[91]

After reading this, Roy Day fumed in a letter to conservative columnist Fulton Lewis, Jr.: "I simply can't stand this habitual liar Pearson attempting to even tear down the background of Nixon in the manner used in his column." Of the original committee, Day who chaired it emphasized, only eight came from San Marino. The group "represented the finest and not the richest citizens of the old 12th District, carefully selected to give a complete cross section of agriculture, business and professional groups. Political leaders of the district had only a 1 to 3 percentage of members to make it an actual grass roots movement."[92]

Publicly, Day issued a denial in the local newspapers that same day. He had worked for the *Progress-Bulletin* in Pomona for the last twenty-eight years as a salesman, never as a publisher as Pearson characterized him. The reporter had lied by asserting that "Nixon was in any way influenced by any so-called millionaires group from San Marino." The committee was taken from the twenty-three local communities, and San Marino was only one part. The group was based on voter registration; in fact, the members felt that voters from the 12th congressional district preferred a candidate from outside of San Marino to reflect the farming and small town atmosphere. Day was so upset at Pearson's misrepresentations that he called for legal action against the reporter.[93]

Morris's and other Nixonphobes' allegations about the professional nature of the 1946 campaign ignore the fundamentals of the political environment and both of the candidates' actions. Critics choose to exclude Day's description, or ignore him, fail to make an exhaustive study of the campaign. If they had, the general shift away from the Democrats and Voorhis's absence from his district in particular created serious problems for incumbents as the congressman already knew.

Starting with a feature story in the local press that produced no candidate and ending with the election of Nixon by a grassroots representation from across the district, they were far from sophisticated. Even Chotiner's minimal role has mushroomed into a grand design that never took place, except later when Chotiner, much to the chagrin of Day and McCall, puffed his importance. Both the primary and general election campaigns were launched in the midst of a swing against the Democratic administration with Voorhis through his own mismanagement, assisting the Republican opposition in its efforts to unseat him. Those who battled along with Nixon in 1946 were not necessarily "gifted," but they were committed. Those nefarious interests that Morris invents did not manipulate the contest. The ideological shift away from the New Deal and those who applauded it did.

The truth of the 1946 contest was much more mundane than later writers have advanced. Voorhis was a popular, fine, decent Christian gentleman; that was beyond dispute. As a professional politician, he failed dismally. He never established a viable Democratic organization; instead, he depended on his father and friends to evaluate voters' likely habits. Rather than return to campaign in the primary when he recognized Nixon's attractiveness, he remained in the capital, allowing Nixon to court newspaper publishers and reporters as well as constituents who wanted to have firsthand contact with their congressional representative. Even when Voorhis returned to the district, he made one blunder after another and clumsily hid the fact that he had several local CIO-PAC endorsements.

The tide of '46 washed strongly in Nixon's direction. The incumbent symbolized the past, a continuation of the New Deal; the challenger represented the new, a shift away from the expansion of government intrusion into the private lives of Americans. These political ideologies were fundamentally at odds with each other and they evoked deep emotional feelings. To trivialize the campaign on the issues of the CIO-PAC and Communist allegations is to minimize the larger view. Two political forces struggled at the end of World War II to court American voters. Nationwide, one beat the other soundly.

Nixon reflected an emerging synthesis between the Roosevelt legacy and the advent of the postwar world. He spoke for the continuation of most New Deal programs while demanding a halt to their worst excesses. An overwhelming majority shared his anticommunism. As the ads implored, November 1946 ushered in a time for change.

Chapter 4

# LEARNING THE
# CONGRESSIONAL ROUTINE

For the several weeks in November 1946 following Nixon's triumph, he and his supporters celebrated. On the 13th, for example, the Whittier Chamber of Commerce sponsored a dinner for $1.75 per person, at which the candidate promised to do his best and exemplify the town's spirit. Eight days later, the Pomona Valley Club held its own supper honoring their man for $1.50 a plate.[1]

From the moment of triumph, Nixon recognized that his constituency opposed the legacy of many New Deal social programs that verged on socialism. He also agreed that American values had to replace any subversive alternatives at home such as the use of books in California public schools advocating the overthrow of government. He knew that the labor strikes of the previous several years had to stop, and that meant limiting unions' gains since the advent of Franklin Roosevelt's presidency. Nixon's election philosophically signaled the victory for moderation in economic matters. He accepted that much of the legislation over the last decade was part of the nation's social fabric, but his triumph illustrated that new proposals would be met with skepticism.[2]

Nixon regularly read David Lawrence, publisher and influential columnist for *U.S. News & World Report*, who warned Republicans in the middle of November against mimicking the Democrats. President Truman and Senator Arthur Vandenberg, Republican from Michigan, had structured a bipartisan foreign policy, and thereby set a positive trend. Lawrence asked the two political parties to extend this cooperation to domestic issues, particularly in regard to new labor legislation. The Republican success in 1946, he suggested, was not a mandate for a counter-revolution, but a signal to move away from the New Deal's assumption that government interference was the solution to people's problems. Nixon agreed. For him, *U.S. News* was a realistic, unbiased magazine.[3]

As the Nixons made preparations to leave for Washington, Dick still kept his law office on the fifth floor in the Bank of America Building, the branch Perry managed. As part of Pat's going-away presents, friends took a week to hand-knit several dresses for her because that fashion was the current "rage."[4]

She and Dick left Whittier on November 26 in a Ford, planning to arrive in the capital by December 2 and stay at the Statler Hotel while they searched for a permanent residence. They had asked Paull Marshall, an attorney who had been a colleague of Dick's in the OPA during 1942, to find them a furnished home or an apartment. Marshall had no luck and even asked the Republican National Committee for a referral, but moderately priced housing was a precious and scarce commodity in postwar Washington.[5]

When Pat and Dick reached the capital, they stayed with friends and then moved into the Mayflower Hotel on December 10. Nixon would receive $1,041.66 per month in salary. The only place he could find was a two-bedroom apartment for $400 per month. The Mayflower had no long-term lodgings for babies, and his parents, along with Tricia, their ten-month-old granddaughter, would arrive just after the new year for his swearing-in ceremony. The situation grew worrisome, but the Nixons optimistically felt that they would find a home.[6]

One reason for their confidence was that the Nixon for Congress Committee had not only paid off the campaign expenses to date, but Art Kruse, campaign treasurer and president of the First Federal Savings and Loan Association of Alhambra, had enough in the bank to send them $300 for expenses until Congress convened. Nixon used the money to pay his own personal telephone bill from the campaign, the cost of the thank-you letters, the press dinner, and secretarial assistance. McCall shortly informed his candidate that all bills had been paid, and many of Nixon's closest supporters met toward the end of December to talk about the establishment of a fund for the 1948 campaign.[7]

Far more immediate concerns than planning for the next election preoccupied Nixon. The first priority was his committee assignment. His preference was the labor committee, but when Congressman Bertrand Gearhart, Republican from California, asked him to rank his choices, he responded differently. First, he selected judiciary, due to his legal training; second, he requested the education and labor panel, where he could make a "real contribution" in labor legislation and draw on his services on the board of trustees for Whittier College; third, he listed expenditures in the executive department, where he would use his experience in the OPA and his negotiations of government contracts for the navy; and finally, he asked for a position on the agricultural body since his district had considerable farming interests.[8]

The Nixons quickly grew accustomed to a "very busy" schedule, in which they had "scarcely a moment" to themselves. The congressman spent considerable time on the composition of his staff. He had worked in the capital at the OPA before the war and recognized the importance of a harmonious and efficient office. He had already hired two individuals from California: Bill Arnold as his executive assistant and Dorothy Cox as a secretary. On December 14, he moved into Room 528 at the top of the House Office Building, a location regularly assigned to freshmen congressmen called "the attic." He was relieved that his building was "marvelously air-conditioned, so we at least are able to work here in comparative comfort." Nixon still needed a good stenographer and happily filled the position by the new year. He had completed his staff, and its members seemed to work harmoniously.[9]

The Nixons, particularly Pat, felt somewhat isolated. Donald Thompson, the assistant campaign treasurer, recalled that initially she felt like a "fish out of water" since she was not part of the Washington "inner circle" and was unfamiliar with the protocol for congressional wives. To make her feel more comfortable, Thompson called Catherine Rippard, the wife of a savings and loan executive, who introduced Pat to the Congressional Club, the "in" ladies' group.[10]

By the summer, the weather reminded Dick of days in the South Pacific. He and Pat tolerated it, but Tricia seemed "to have a rather tough time adjusting herself to the heat." Still, the Nixons were gradually settling into a routine. Dick had fortunately found "a very satisfactory colored woman to take care of the baby. She is just as clean as she can be and does a splendid job in every respect."[11]

The awesome responsibility of becoming a congressman was starting to replace the exultation of victory. Dick was no longer the center of attention; he was one of over a hundred newly elected politicians congregating on Capitol Hill. He was entering the national arena with his highest previous elected office as the president of Whittier College's student body. He had not been part of a powerful political machine, nor did he have a congressional mentor to point the way and protect him from potentially costly blunders.

Frank and Hannah Nixon arrived with Tricia on Thursday, January 2, 1947, the same day that House Republicans caucused to determine likely committee assignments. On Friday, Congress convened with its opening ceremonies, and Nixon's parents, wife, and child watched him take the oath of office. Three days later, President Truman delivered his State of the Union message to the joint session of Congress. The Republican majority sat on one side, the Democrats on the other. Richard Nixon, John F. Kennedy, and Lyndon B. Johnson, three future presidents, listened from the floor. Truman offered a conciliatory tone and focused most of his attention on labor by calling for a ban on jurisdictional disputes, an end to secondary boycotts, binding arbitration in disputes over interpretation of existing agreements, and the appointment of a commission to study labor-management relations.[12]

Nixon began to realize the benefits deriving from a positive image and received press coverage for his stand on the housing shortage when Representative Adolph Sabath, Democrat from Illinois, called on the government to find apartments for congressmen. Nixon rejected this idea. The people, he reasoned, had repudiated big government's meddling in the recent elections. Congress needed to solve the national housing plight, and Sabath's demand smacked of special privilege. Nixon had not found his own housing and refused to accept any preference while veterans and the general public suffered.[13]

In March, the Nixons finally found an unfurnished two-bedroom apartment for $80 per month in a new housing development of low-cost duplexes at 3538 Gunston Road, Park Fairfax, Virginia, twenty minutes from the Capitol. By the time they moved in, Pat and Tricia had already caught the flu, but Dick had assistance because "Nana" and "Grandpa" Nixon moved from California and bought a dairy farm near Menges Mills, in York County, Pennsylvania, about a three-hour drive from Washington, so that they could be near their son and his family. Hannah loved farming, and Frank named the cows for movie stars like Loretta Young, Gary Cooper, and Dorothy Lamour. They also regularly drove to Washington to help with Tricia.[14]

Newspaper coverage for the new congressman was overwhelmingly positive. In a Philadelphia story, Nixon was described as a "tall, husky former football player," who was an attorney and a naval officer in the war. He had defeated an "able" opponent "in one of the toughest campaigns waged in the country." He had already decided to support a bipartisan foreign policy that called for American participation in international affairs. In another article coming from the capital, Elizabeth Oldfield said of Nixon: "Serious and energetic, he is indicative of the change in political trends, the increasing emphasis on youth, and a genuine desire to serve the country. If he bears out his promise he will go far."[15]

Such expressions of support were welcome, but Nixon's primary objective was to play a major role on the House Committee on Education and Labor. He felt that it would "probably have some of the most important legislation in the new Congress." He had anticipated that the Speaker of the House, Joseph Martin, Republican from Massachusetts, would announce the panels in the middle of January and believed that he stood a "fair" chance of getting this coveted seat.[16]

Every House member served on one permanent committee, and just as Nixon predicted, the speaker appointed him to the Committee on Education and Labor. Since many congressmen had lost elections, seniority was determined by a drawing. Nixon drew the lowest rank, making him the most junior Republican on that panel. In a press release in the middle of the month, Nixon declared: "The 80th Congress will undoubtedly adopt a new national labor policy and, as a member of the House Labor Committee, I will work in behalf of legislation which will be equally fair to both labor and management and will also give due consideration to the best interests of the people as a whole."[17]

That statement was inaccurate. Nixon had run on a platform opposing widespread union strikes and CIO-PAC's political influence in the Democratic Party. He clearly wanted to tilt the balance away from labor. Congressmen already had submitted approximately forty labor bills attacking labor's power, and several other bills dealt with federal employment practices and aid to education. Nixon was intensely interested in the latter since he had been a member of the board of trustees at Whittier College. He wanted to know what the college thought of federal aid to education and felt that his former football coach, Chief Newman, probably opposed the idea. Nixon himself appeared skeptical about the concept and was surprised "as to the lengths some of these [eastern] professors go in putting out their propaganda in classrooms." The country needed time to take the appropriate actions: "Too many folks just got into the habit of thinking and talking New Deal and they are having a hard time getting over it!" Despite his interest, his committee did not address federal aid to education during that session.[18]

Nixon started to learn how the House functioned and quickly discovering that speeches on the floor had minimal effect on legislative decisions. That might change during the debates, but he believed that the battles were won or lost in the committees. Besides committee responsibilities, he had to vote on the myriad of bills that came before the House and supported action for increasing allowances for on-the-job training, disabled entitlement to automobiles, long-range disability compensation, and cash terminal bonds. He conceded that his schedule was "certainly keeping me hopping here."[19]

Another dominant congressional issue was the federal budget, and the struggle between Democratic and Republican principles would continue throughout the 80th Congress. The Republican plan of reducing Truman's proposal by $6 billion was based on the assumptions that military expenditures could be cut without endangering the national defense. Many congressional GOP members remained committed to noninterventionism; they were unconvinced that large numbers of U.S. military forces needed to be stationed abroad. Thus, without this large-scale troop involvement and countless examples of waste in the federal bureaucracy, taxes could easily be cut. Tax reduction appealed to Nixon: "The nation is in the hole, deep, and we will never climb out of it until we economize in governmental administration. Furthermore, I believe the great majority of the people would rather spend their hard-earned money themselves than send it to Washington in taxes for the bureaucrats to spend for them."[20]

Housing was another subject of intense debate. Nixon had read a great deal on the problem, especially on "moderate-cost rental housing." Veterans needed living units, and the United States had to streamline regulations to encourage the building of more apartments. Democratic senators Allen Ellender from Louisiana and Robert Wagner from New York joined with Republican Robert Taft from Ohio to co-sponsor a bill that provided for rental units, slum clearance, and easy Federal Housing Agency loans. It passed the upper body, but met substantial House opposition, particularly over the sections dealing with public housing. Many congressmen expected the legislation to encourage private contractors to build rather than put the government in the housing business. Nixon approved of some provisions, but disagreed with the federal housing features. Congress, he predicted, might pass some bill, but as the debate grew more polarized, he saw no likelihood of any housing legislation in the present session. The socialistic sections of the bill had created an impasse that would not be easily surmounted.[21]

Since the government could not agree on a program of housing expansion, Nixon had to reconsider the need for rent control. He opposed both it and socialized housing in principle, but realized that rent controls would become "a very hot issue. . . . I do not believe that controls will be completely abandoned but a percentage increase of some amount will probably be granted." As usual in economic matters, he agreed to compromise, as long as his fundamental beliefs were not violated. When Congress acted in the early spring, it called for an end to controls by December 31, 1947. If a housing shortage had not existed, rent control would have been eliminated. But builders needed time to catch up with demand. Until then, the extension of rent control was the only possible solution.[22]

Nixon recognized the importance of keeping his key supporters informed about national politics and sent them a regular mimeographed letter. In his initial one, mailed in early spring, he emphasized that Congress had reorganized under GOP leadership, and it exercised its prerogatives instead of rubber-stamping executive proposals. He also highlighted his role in shaping new labor legislation and other congressional responsibilities.[23]

Nixon warned his constituents about media coverage of the Republican agenda. Some columnists, he asserted, indulged in deliberate falsification of the facts in order to discredit the Republicans. To the congressman, the public failed to understand that the press still mirrored Franklin Roosevelt's objectives, if not at the managerial level, in the editorial rooms where the American Newspaper Guild ruled. Nixon not only resented what he considered to be slanted press coverage, but he also became disillusioned by the flood of form letters from "so-called church organizations" like the Young Men's Christian Association that sent out "New Deal propaganda." Even though the news media generally painted a flattering portrait of the new congressman, he gradually accepted the GOP position that the press expressed a left-wing viewpoint. This, with a very few exceptions, ultimately became his lifelong belief.[24]

Nixon was learning the congressional routine and also just how expensive being a congressman was. On the last day of January, he confided to McCall that the checks Kruse sent from his campaign committee were vital. The Nixons' living costs from December 20 until January 20 went above $1,500, and that was "a pretty good indication of what you are up against when you first start out. Believe me the Committee sending the money on was certainly appreciated." In his first two months in Washington, he had received his committee assignments, established his office, formed a cordial relationship with Senator Knowland, received considerable media attention, and started to deal with legislative procedures. He traveled a great deal by plane to attend hearings, so as not to be away from the House floor for more than two days. He was serious about developing a record based on attendance and had only missed two votes.[25]

Even though a wide variety of issues crossed his desk, Nixon knew that his main focus during the first session of the 80th Congress revolved around labor legislation. Almost twelve years earlier, Franklin Roosevelt had linked his administration with organized labor by signing the National Labor Relations Act, also known as the Wagner Act, in July 1935. This momentous piece of New Deal legislation, called the Magna Carta of labor, placed the authority of the government behind labor to organize union shops, bargain collectively, and strike. To guarantee these union rights, the act created the National Labor Relations Board (NLRB) as an effective enforcement arm.[26]

Nixon had witnessed the devastating strikes which had broken out across America after returning from his tour of duty in the Pacific. Like Nixon, the overwhelming majority of voters in 1946 called for changes in labor legislation. Historians have often repeated an unflattering and ever-enlarging apocryphal story that Nixon told reporters just after his swearing-in ceremony that "I was elected to smash the labor bosses" and to curb the excesses of those leaders. The remark made Nixon appear an inflexible panderer, who aped his earlier campaign rhetoric against the CIO-PAC. In fact, Nixon's position was far calmer, more flexible, and more impartial than many congressmen at the opening of the 80th Congress, who openly reflected their hostility toward labor.[27]

Truman urged prudence against punitive legislation; but given the divisive environment, the president's conciliatory attitude was ignored. On January 16, Nixon attended a meeting at the Press Club where Senator Taft advised moderation on labor legislation. While the novice congressman was surprised that this influential senator had taken such "a middle of the road program," he optimistically predicted that a bill would pass in the next two weeks and "that some of the current evils will be remedied."[28]

At the beginning of February, Nixon did not understand the complexities of maneuvering in the House or its role in changing labor legislation. Republican Fred Hartley from New Jersey, a committed anti-unionist, chaired the Committee on Education and Labor composed of fifteen Republicans and ten Democrats. Nixon sat at one end of the committee table and looked across at John Kennedy of Massachusetts on the Democratic side. Ten of the Republicans and four of the Democrats had no experience on labor issues, but the committee convened its hearings on February 5 and did not finish until March 13. In those six weeks, the members heard over 130 witnesses.[29]

During the initial stages of the hearings, Nixon did not comprehend the vast gulf that existed between those who cherished the Wagner Act and those who sought to dismantle it. He listened to Vito Marcantonio, the sole representative of the American Labor Party in Congress, vehemently lead the fight against any new labor legislation that would dismember workers' rights. Nixon also recognized that pressure groups were already trying to influence his decisions, and that sometimes they would support him and other times howl their disapproval. He noted that some columnists were attacking the GOP for proposing changes in the Wagner Act. Drew Pearson, according to Nixon "the least reliable correspondent and radio commentator in Washington," already was distorting Hartley's views. The columnist opposed anyone who favored changing the existing law, and Republican freshmen, including Nixon, sometimes commended one another when the muckraking reporter attacked them.[30]

When Nixon presented a well-delivered speech at a Lincoln Day celebration at the Lackawanna County Republican Club in Scranton, Pennsylvania, on February 12, he did not emphasize labor legislation; instead, he concentrated on reducing government spending, lowering taxes, and protecting human rights. He also mentioned an amendment limiting the president's time in office to two terms, and talked of resisting extremist proposals from the left and right, and defending human rights worldwide.[31]

While Nixon was in that highly unionized city, he spoke to laborers and came away convinced that the views of the rank and file did not necessarily coincide with those of their leaders. As he later told his committee colleagues, union members had convinced him that they approved of the labor-management movement, but they opposed certain autocratic powers of the union bosses. Members wanted their own bill of rights, which included secret elections of officers and an independent agency supervising strike votes. Nixon saw merit to these ideas and urged union members to write him about their feelings.[32]

If Nixon hoped for reactions, they poured in. The Scranton-Lackawanna Industrial Union Council CIO wrote that Nixon was only in town for twelve hours, and the council could not locate any union members that he had used for his "so-called" survey. They concluded that he committed fraud. The union's secretary, Elizabeth McMenamin, appended her own letter to Nixon, saying that if he had "a sense of humor you would have enjoyed that meeting." She had lived there her entire life and had joined her union two years earlier. Sometimes her union leaders acted irrationally, as she inferred they had in this case in denouncing Nixon. Other letter writers offered mixed reactions. Some workers agreed that their unions were autocratically run; others defended the labor movement at any cost.[33]

The committee hearings proved contentious. When Edward Wilms, chairman of the Independent Unions of the State of New Jersey, testified on February 21, Nixon wanted to know if Wilms would support annual financial reports to members on the expenditures of union monies. The congressman asked other questions. Could members sue if their unions compromised the rights of the workers or if the union leadership indulged in acts that damaged their privileges? Since he believed that unions, wherever possible, should have smaller units that more accurately reflected their members' interests, Nixon inquired if a provision limiting industrywide bargaining might encourage the growth of more independent unions.[34]

Nixon listened and questioned many labor leaders who testified against changes in the Wagner Act. He came away with a negative or ambivalent impression of union leadership. The only exception was the president of the Western Conference of Teamsters, Dave Beck. He and Nixon had recently spoken, and Beck was "far more reasonable in his attitude than some of the C.I.O. boys." He had "no Communist leanings and is a believer in the free enterprise system." (At that time, Nixon did not know that Beck would turn into a thug.) Even with that acknowledgment, Nixon accepted the Republican argument that labor unions had grown too arbitrary and needed tighter regulation.[35]

By the end of the month, Nixon expressed futility and frustration over what he considered labor's inflexibility: "Union labor could do itself a great deal of good by advocating its own program of remedial legislation, rather than opposing every reasonable proposition which has been submitted to the Congress." He saw the need for the passage of a "strong labor bill" and concurrently believed that the federal government oftentimes interfered too much in the settlement of labor disputes. Nixon, hardly advocating a "smash the bosses" program, hoped for a time when collective bargaining would settle strikes without intervention from Washington.[36]

During the early stages of the labor hearings, Nixon met Charles Kersten, from Milwaukee, Wisconsin, another freshman. They quickly bonded, sharing legal backgrounds, seeking tax reduction, vehemently fighting against Communist infiltration into labor unions, and promoting American aid to Europe as a means of preventing Russian expansionism. Nixon called him "one of the ablest members" of the House, and they would remain friends until Kersten died on October 31, 1972.[37]

Kersten, who gravitated to others who shared similar opinions, probably introduced Nixon to Father John Cronin. Five years older than Nixon, the priest was raised in New York by devout Catholic parents. John attended parochial schools and then studied at Holy Cross College from 1923 to 1925. Two years later, he transferred to the Catholic University of America, where he received his Ph.D. in 1935. In the midst of his educational training, he was ordained as a priest on May 19, 1932, as a member in the Society of Saint Sulpice, a community of secular priests that specialized in the education of Roman Catholic priests. The following year, he became a professor of economics at St. Mary's Seminary in Baltimore, where he remained for thirteen years, writing on economic issues; during the summers, starting in 1941, Cronin directed the Institute of Catholic Social Studies and the Catholic University Summer School.[38]

Besides his academic pursuits, Cronin became deeply involved in Baltimore's labor movement and regularly spoke out nationally to priests and laborist laity in favor of the capitalistic system. As the Axis grew more aggressive, he openly opposed its cause, and after World War II erupted, Cronin's antagonism intensified. He called on Catholics to rid the United States of Communists and fought against their influence at the Bethlehem Fairfield shipyard located at Baltimore's harbor. During 1940–41, an FBI special agent approached Cronin to meet and exchange information. He agreed, and by the end of the hostilities, with cooperation from the FBI, Cronin became a nationally known figure on Communist espionage.[39]

Cronin was rewarded for his specialty in early 1946 by an appointment as assistant director of the social action department for the National Catholic Welfare Conference, the administrative organization of the U.S. Catholic bishops, in Washington, D.C., a position that he held for just over two decades. Kersten had learned of Cronin's research, had talked with the priest, and had introduced Nixon to Cronin as a valuable source of information on Communist penetration of labor unions sometime during the Taft-Hartley hearings. Eleven years after this early meeting, the priest remembered that he and Nixon had initially discussed economic and social problems and that their interaction was personal, not political. It gradually matured into a concerted anti-Communist alliance.[40]

Cronin and Kersten influenced Nixon's position on Communist penetration in union activities. When the labor hearings opened, Robert Buse, president of Local 248, UAW-CIO, at the Allis-Chambers Manufacturing Company in Milwaukee, had to face difficult questioning on whether or not the striking unions were Communist-dominated. Buse categorically denied any "substantial Communist influence" in his union; but when Nixon pressed him about preventing Communists from becoming union officers, Buse refused to support any provision where Communists were disallowed to serve. He opposed labor violence, but would not surrender any of labor's gains. He fought the publication of the union's financial reports on the grounds that management would know the strength of the union and gain an unfair advantage. Nixon saw merit to some of these concerns and favored the establishment of an impartial government agency to conduct secret strike votes.[41]

Nixon looked at the antics of John L. Lewis as a prime example of both labor's arrogance and its strengths. Lewis had taken the United Mine Workers (UMW) out on strike after the government took over the coal mines. Lewis's initial defiance resulted in a Supreme Court decision to fine him $700,000 for contempt, but Nixon resented the fact that that payment came from workers' dues. When the UMW boss appeared before the labor committee, Lewis objected to any change in labor legislation, including government action if the public welfare was threatened. "The cause of the working man," according to Nixon, had "been done a great disservice by union leaders who are arrogant and uncooperative in testifying before Congressional committees." He wanted to "provide greater democracy within unions and thereby lessen the possibility of strikes in the future." Lewis was simultaneously unreasonable and a powerful advocate for his union.[42]

Nixon predicted that Congress would soon pass labor legislation, but understood that the political process was more complex and time-consuming than he had first realized. Committees had to organize, hold hearings, and make legislative recommendations for the proper bills. Both sides demanded to be heard, and as a result, the committee held daily (including Saturday) sessions over ten weeks and had taken almost three million words of testimony. The members hoped to present a bill that would be comprehensive enough to avoid any need for later amendments; this required holding executive sessions and complicated negotiations. The major provisions of the bill were becoming visible: it would outlaw jurisdictional strikes (strikes called by rival unions over which one had the right to work on a job, laws that were designed to preserve traditional nonunion shops) and secondary boycotts (where strikers pressured an uninvolved party in the dispute in the hope that the party would halt its business dealings with the same employer); it would attempt to stop picket-line violence and curb mass picketing; it would contain a worker's bill of rights; and it would curtail industrywide bargaining and the closed shop (the practice of hiring only union workers).[43]

Even before the House saw the committee's proposals, the Lewis testimony and a possible work stoppage in the coal mines focused sharper attention on the pending legislation. Nixon objected to the union boss characterizing the mines as "Krug's slaughterhouse," in a reference to Secretary of the Interior Julius Krug. Nixon believed that the United States had to toughen mine safety codes to protect workers, but Congress also had to enact a new law that would secure the rights of the public when nationwide strikes spread "where they endanger the public health and safety so that we may avoid the necessity of resorting to public ownership and operation of some of our vital industries."[44]

The bill that finally emerged, the Hartley bill, was hotly debated, but overwhelmingly popular among members who advanced union restrictions. Nixon agreed with the majority and gave the closing arguments in the House that the bill was in the best interests of all Americans. This was the time to halt union strife and end the era of costly postwar strikes.[45]

The House passed the labor bill without substantial amendments on

April 17 by a vote of 308 to 107, almost a three-to-one margin. Even the Democrats favored it 93 to 84. Nixon especially approved of the sections that gave rank-and-file workers rights that they never had, but he disapproved of murky provisions on industrywide bargaining and some of the language in the use of injunctions where force and violence was involved. These unclear sections would unquestionably face legal challenges. But even with these criticisms, Congress had addressed the paramount issues. Nixon privately confided to a friend: "It will be . . . up to the Senate and the President to fish or cut bait on the labor issue."[46]

Three days before House passage of the bill, Congressman Frank Buchanan, Democrat from Pennsylvania and former mayor of Mc-Keesport, a town located just outside Pittsburgh, invited twenty-nine-year-old John Kennedy and thirty-four-year-old Richard Nixon to appear at eight o'clock on the evening of April 21 at the Penn-McKee Hotel to discuss the pending labor legislation in front of a prominent civic group called the Junto. Each would present his side and then the audience could ask questions. The evening was cold, and rain kept the crowd down to just over one hundred. Nixon spoke first, declaring that the bill benefited the workingman and did not usurp any fundamental labor rights. The Wagner Act had gone too far against business, and public opinion favored a legislative corrective that would limit disruptive strikes. He chided labor for being uncooperative at the House hearings. Kennedy replied that unions would not be able to prevent themselves from becoming sweatshops if Congress passed the pending legislation; industrywide collective bargaining also would end. Some provisions were praiseworthy, but the bill would strangle the American labor movement.[47]

Usually, the Junto attracted Republican businessmen and professionals with a smattering of other interested parties, but this legislation brought out at least one-third pro-union supporters, who attacked Nixon at the end of the formal presentations. The assault ended by 10:30 P.M., and by midnight, the two congressmen had boarded the Capital Limited for the return trip home. Neither man had made a lasting impression. In fact, the next day's local newspaper printed unflattering photographers of both: Kennedy looked like a grinning high school student with a wide smirk, while Nixon, with an unkempt collar and loud tie, appeared in need of a shave.[48]

Two days after Nixon returned to his office, he wrote about his brief encounter in McKeesport: "Young Kennedy, who is a Democrat and one of my fellow members of the Labor Committee, went with me and we discussed the Labor bill on opposite sides in a spirited but rather clean 'debate.' The reception to my end was good, considering the locale and audience." The first Kennedy-Nixon debate was hardly an auspicious event.[49]

Many years later, Nixon expanded on the episode. As the train headed back to the capital, Kennedy and Nixon drew straws for the lower berth. Nixon won. They talked late into the night—more about international matters than domestic affairs. They represented the same generation, were navy veterans, and went to the House in the same year. Both guarded their privacy, and as a consequence, their seeming shyness occasionally bordered on aloofness. Nixon recalled: "Kennedy and I were too different in background, outlook, and temperament to become close friends, but we were thrown together throughout our early careers, and we never had less than an amicable relationship." Nixon continued: "In those early years we saw ourselves as political opponents but not political rivals."[50]

As soon as the Senate passed its own version of the bill, a conference committee worked to find a compromise that both houses could accept. As for Nixon's stand, he received far more supportive than hostile mail. To one correspondent, he wrote: "I grew up in a grocery store myself in East Whittier, and I know well how hard my own father and mother worked to build up the business they have. They always had a very cordial relationship with the people who worked in the store just as you describe your own situation. It is certainly a tragedy that union organizers can come in and disrupt conditions as they do."[51]

Nixon did not realize that the House bill had shifted the balance too much from labor to business for the Senate's taste, but Senator Taft did. He took a less drastic approach, always looking to limit government interference in the American economy and simultaneously recognizing the votes that he had to have for passage. He favored the right of labor to bargain collectively with management and affirmed the right to strike; at the same time, he hoped to protect the rights of both management and labor. Taft chaired lengthy hearings from January 23 to March 8 and demonstrated fairness throughout his proceedings. He controlled the Senate floor debate with a firm hand, exhibiting equanimity throughout. When the vote was taken on May 13, the Senate overwhelmingly passed the Taft version, 68 to 24.[52]

With both versions completed, Taft and Hartley worked together on

a proposal acceptable to both houses. These two accomplished politicians also understood that they had to draft legislation that might have to
override a presidential veto, for even with large Republican majorities, a
two-thirds vote might be tough. Congress listened and took the middle
ground. In the end, labor retained the right to organize, join unions,
strike, and bargain collectively; none of which was ever in dispute. Jurisdictional disputes between unions, however, now had to be settled without strikes, and secondary boycotts were curbed. Both management and
labor were bound by their contracts. The closed shop was banned, but
the union shop had thirty days to sign up workers after the start of their
employment. Union members had the right of a secret ballot when voting on union issues, and unions had to furnish financial reports and account for welfare funds. Congress prohibited Communist-dominated
unions. If a strike affected the national interest, the U.S. Attorney General had the right to seek an injunction against the strike for ninety days
to allow for government conciliation. This legislation offered something
for both labor and business. It had imperfections, but many thought that
it was a proper corrective.[53]

As the conference committee negotiated, Nixon used the lull to fly
home and speak before the National Convention of Sales Executives in
Los Angeles on Wednesday, May 28. One of his earliest backers, Boyd
Gibbons, Jr., who owned a Ford dealership in the city, had asked him to
come and agreed to pay for all expenses. Originally, Nixon decided
against the trip, but House Majority Leader Halleck encouraged him to
report to his constituents on his congressional activities. Nixon took a
late plane so that he had a chance to sleep and arrived Wednesday morning for his first trip back to the district since his election. His speech
stressed the problems business faced in regard to the Communists in the
CIO. The next morning, he went to breakfast at the Hugheston Mead-
ows sponsored by the Whittier Chamber of Commerce, where 350
neighbors greeted him. He addressed Pomona residents at a luncheon,
and talked at the San Gabriel Town Club gathering over dinner.[54]

A day after Nixon spoke before the sales executives, Gibbons wrote
Pat glowing with pride and admiration: "Your husband is a hero—he is
a great man—he is a great statesman—and he gave the best darned talk in
his career." The car dealer predicted that some day her husband would be
president. With that eventuality in mind, Gibbons had a photograph
taken with Dick: "AND I WANT TO BE ABLE TO SHOW ALL OF MY FRIENDS
THAT I KNEW THE GUY WHEN—!!"[55]

Nixon also used his trip home to release the results of the Nixon Poll. His office had mailed out 100,000 questionnaires to registered voters in early April on several topics and over 13,000 replied. Just over half of those surveyed favored federal aid to education. Almost three-quarters disapproved of Truman's price controls and wanted to outlaw the Communist Party. Most interestingly for Republicans, over 90 percent approved of increasing military preparedness. An overwhelming majority (85%) wanted suspected Communists or foreign agents removed from government jobs. Yet indications also were that the movement toward internationalism was growing. Almost 75 percent favored the proposed labor legislation.[56]

The completed labor bill went to the White House on June 9 for Truman's consideration. Nixon believed that the final effort was "a better one than was introduced in either the House or the Senate." Some weaknesses remained, "but it will accomplish some good despite the criticism which has been heaped upon it." While Congress awaited the president's action, labor and its allies mounted a tremendous campaign demanding his veto.[57]

Truman withheld comment until June 20, when he informed Congress that he had vetoed the Taft-Hartley bill. Nixon was livid. The president, he argued in a press release, had eloquently called for bipartisanship in his State of the Union Address, and Congress had responded favorably. How had Truman responded? He not only vetoed the tax reduction bill, but he also parroted the CIO objections to Taft-Hartley. The president had demonstrated that he was "more interested in catering to labor bosses who might deliver him a few votes in 1948."[58]

The House heard the veto message read at 12:05 P.M., and a little over a hour later, overrode the veto with a vote of 331 to 83; one of the 106 Democrats who defied the president was Lyndon Johnson. All but eight votes for the legislation came from the South or Southwest. Only seventy-one Democrats backed the president, including Kennedy and Helen Gahagan Douglas. When a filibuster prevented swift Senate action, Nixon immediately condemned the senators who resorted to delaying or thwarting the legislative process. Any filibuster was "wholly bad." On Monday, June 23, the upper House voted 68 to 25 to make the Taft-Hartley Act a federal statute. Nixon hoped that American labor would accept the majority's will and avoid "any general revolt against administration and enforcement of the law."[59]

Taft's biographer, historian James Patterson, saw several problems with the act: anticommunism oaths failed to work, the ban on the closed shop was unenforceable, the separation on NLRB functions was confusing, the secret ballot provision was repealed, and employer complaints against their unions had limited success. Even with the Taft-Hartley's weaknesses, it has withstood all attempts at repeal. As Patterson pointed out, it was "the only major change in New Deal legislation to pass Congress, and one of the few important bills ever to be devised and passed wholly without the assistance of any executive department."[60]

While the new congressman concentrated his energies on labor legislation, he never forgot that the voters in the 12th congressional district had sent him to Washington. Those who had cast ballots for him could just as easily vote against him if he did not listen to their concerns, and the most pressing one in 1947 was the construction of the Whittier Narrows Dam. Nixon opposed construction because proponents did not demonstrate any urgency as a flood control measure or for water conservation. Without any pressing need, and with Nixon's vocal opposition, the appropriation for the project was dropped.[61]

While the Whittier dam issue created strong, emotional responses within several specific towns, Nixon calmed their fears and went on to fulfill his everyday responsibilities. He filled vacancies at the U.S. Naval Academy and at West Point. When he received complaints about poor postal service in his district, he called for a house cleaning and the appointment of an efficient replacement. He also called for a comprehensive investigation of the local government with the possibility of home rule.[62]

Reporters asked Nixon on many occasions to summarize the accomplishments of his first congressional session. He replied that the Republican Congress had done well and Truman had opposed it for no good reason. He blamed the president for vetoing the federal budget for only the second time in American history and stressed that if the House had two more votes, it would have overridden him. Nixon also faulted the president for vetoing Taft-Hartley. By the end of the term, he noted that strikes were down, production and employment had risen, and housing starts jumped markedly. The first session had been a "corrective or remedial." The next one would present the opportunity of beginning "a long-range positive program."[63]

# Chapter 5

# NIXON AND HUAC

The single most controversial element of Nixon's congressional career came from a chance appointment on the House Committee on Un-American Activities (HUAC), which he had not sought to join. Throughout his campaign against Jerry Voorhis, Nixon had made much of his opponent's New Deal, socialistic tinge, which bordered on communistic, like the NC-PAC; but in fact, Nixon had only the vaguest idea of any Soviet threat before entering Congress. Only once he began his systematic legislative investigations of communism in America did he arrive at the conclusion that the Russians were actively trying to overthrow the American system of government.

When Nixon announced his two committee assignments on January 13, 1947, he emphasized labor and educational matters. As for his position at HUAC, its main job, according to the young congressman, was to "ferret out un-American activities of government employees to the end that extremists of both the left and the right, whether they be Communist or Fascists, shall be removed from the federal payroll." The committee, however, should not infringe on the basic rights of free speech and press.[1]

More than a decade after Nixon accepted his HUAC appointment, Speaker Joe Martin claimed that he had chosen Nixon because of his legal experience and his desire for that position. Nixon recalled that the speaker had asked him to serve on that body; he had not lobbied for it. Nixon knew that HUAC had a checkered and volatile past. The committee originated with Samuel Dickstein, Democratic congressman from New York City, who spearheaded the movement to create a special committee to investigate Nazi subversion before World War II. Dickstein was passed over for chairman, and Congressman Martin Dies, Democrat from Texas, was selected. Dies had a different agenda than Dickstein and chose to concentrate on both Nazis and Communists. Demagogic and flamboyant, he sometimes used vigilante tactics that brought enduring and righteous hatred on the part of civil libertarians. Due to ill health, Dies retired in 1944, and a year later, the House changed its temporary status to a permanent committee. The committee had received more press coverage since 1938 than any other and had constantly made headlines. HUAC members often had special contacts within the press corps and gave certain reporters confidential information. Some members refused to adhere to their own rules of procedure, and continual leaks of sensitive, unverified material sometimes proved embarrassing.[2]

When the Republicans took control of Congress in 1947, J. Parnell Thomas of New Jersey, who had been assigned to the Dies Committee since its inception, became HUAC chairman. Thomas launched his political career in 1925 by winning election to the Allendale borough council, captured the mayor's race the following year, and took a position on the Bergen County Republican Committee in the depths of the depression. From 1935 to 1937, he served in the New Jersey state assembly, and with the death of Congressman Randolph Perkins, the GOP tapped him to run for the Perkins's seat. Victorious, he went to the House in 1938 from the recently created 7th district, and served on the House Armed Services Committee and the Dies Committee. He passionately spoke out for military preparedness, fought fervently for military control of atomic power, crusaded against foreign "isms," and attacked what he considered was the New Deal for its protosocialism.[3]

With the GOP gaining a congressional majority in 1947, Thomas became the first Republican congressman from the northwestern section of New Jersey to head one of the nineteen permanent House committees in the last two decades. As the senior Republican on the committee, he was almost automatically entitled to that chairmanship. His office was located on the second floor of the House Office Building, where he hung a picture of an American flag behind his desk with the caption underneath: "These colors do not run." Jerry Voorhis, who served on the committee in the early 1940s, called him "a *mean* guy." Robert Carr, professor of law and political science at Dartmouth College, who wrote an early treatise on HUAC, characterized Thomas as

"small, narrow-minded, petty, emotional, vindictive, and blindly partisan." Sometimes he acted fairly, but generally his conduct at the hearings
proved an embarrassment.[4]

Others liked him. Peter Edson, the Washington reporter, described a
man of medium height and stocky: "His somewhat violent coloring—
dark brown eyes, snow-white hair, perpetually pink face and pate—
make him look always angry. About subversiveness, he is." The *Bergen
Evening Record* held that Thomas had gained nationwide "attention,
much praise, and some ridicule." He had attacked Communists for more
than a decade and had been "accused of conducting witch hunts, but
files necessarily closed to the public would reveal how valuable his contributions have been. The gradual elimination of subversive influences
from Government service offers testimony enough to the gravity of the
situation."[5]

Another member of the committee was even more controversial and
certainly more bizarre than Thomas: John Rankin, Democrat from Mississippi. Born in the rural South in 1882, he graduated from the University of Mississippi law department in 1910 and was admitted to the bar
the same year. He was elected to the House of Representatives from his
state's 1st congressional district in 1921 and reelected to it for fifteen succeeding terms until 1953. By the time the 80th Congress convened,
Rankin was easily recognizable. Small, wiry, white-haired, he debated
the issues closest to him and took special delight in baiting those individuals and groups whom he despised, including Jews, African Americans,
Communists, and unionists.[6]

Shortly after the House convened, Rankin spoke on the floor of the
House to link Jews with Communists and then coupled both groups
with "niggers." When Representative Adam Clayton Powell, Jr., Democrat from New York, who was a light-skinned African American,
objected to that racial slur, Rankin answered: "It is not a disgrace to be
a real Negro . . . if I were a Negro I would want to be as black as the
ace of spades. I could then go out with Negroes and have a real good
time."[7]

Nixon along with Thomas made up two of the five-member Republican majority, with four Democrats, including Rankin, in the minority. During 1947, the committee conducted seven sets of hearings in
twenty-seven days and published four reports. The committee's central
focus was Communist subversion. The first hearing opened on February
6 when Gerhart Eisler, a powerful Communist Party functionary in the

United States, testified. All HUAC members attended; Robert Stripling, HUAC's chief interrogator, was present to direct the questioning, but Eisler refused to be sworn in. Since he considered himself "a political prisoner in the United States," he demanded time to make a three-minute statement. Thomas refused, and an unpleasant scene filled with recrimination erupted. At the completion of this spectacle, the committee moved that Eisler should be cited for contempt of Congress. The motion was carried swiftly and unanimously. A federal jury heard five weeks of testimony that summer and reached a guilty verdict in two hours and fifteen minutes. The judge sentenced Eisler to a year in prison along with a $1,000 fine, but before the sentence was carried out, he fled to Eastern Europe, avoiding punishment.[8]

Nixon, angered and shocked by Eisler's performance, went on the radio the day of the hearing to report on his impressions of what he had witnessed. Louis Budenz, former managing editor of the *Daily Worker* and a fervent anti-Communist, had named Eisler the top Soviet agent in the United States during the war and also claimed that Eisler was a fugitive in the Canadian A-bomb spy case. Eisler's sister, Ruth Fischer, had testified that her brother had come to the United States from Russia to direct subversive activities, and called him "an arch terrorist." The committee further recommended to the Justice Department that Eisler be tried for perjury, failure to register as a foreign agent, conspiracy to overthrow the government, and falsification of a passport.[9]

On February 18, in the midst of this episode, Nixon gave his maiden speech on the House floor. As the subject for his opening address, Nixon chose the Eisler testimony, and the congressman reviewed the credentials of this Russian spy who had actively masterminded espionage activities in the United States. During his appearance before HUAC, "His manner and attitude was one of utter contempt." Eisler came and left the United States surrounded by a cloak of secrecy, but his career was "replete with criminal acts against the United States, forged documents, perjury, failure to register as an alien agent." While Nixon defended the freedoms of speech and press, Eisler needed to be expelled from the United States because those rights "did not carry with them the right to advocate the destruction of the very Government which protects the freedom of an individual to express his views."

Radical congressman Vito Marcantonio from New York, the sole representative of the American Labor Party in Congress, responded. Under the current hysterical anti-Communist climate in America, the congressman hoped that fundamental principles would prevail. In this spirit of constitutional fairness, he conceded that Eisler was a Communist, but insisted that he never preached the overthrow of the American government. Eisler had offered to take the oath after making an opening statement, but Thomas had demanded that the witness be sworn in first. Under these circumstances, Marcantonio reasoned that the courts, not Congress, should render a decision on Eisler's actions. This floor exchange between Nixon and Marcantonio marked the beginning of many HUAC motions for contempt citations against Communists who refused to testify. The overwhelming majority regularly sustained the committee's actions, while a handful of dissenters, for numerous reasons, voiced objections.[10]

Along with the task of exposing Communist subversion, Nixon became acquainted with those American authorities who fought the Red menace. On Monday, March 24, for example, the former ambassador to Russia and France, William Bullitt, testified that if the Soviets had the atom bomb, they would have already dropped it on the United States. In fact, the Soviets detonated their first A-bomb in September 1949 with considerable assistance from spies in America. Two days after Bullitt testified, Nixon, for the first time, heard FBI director J. Edgar Hoover warn that a Communist-dominated labor union would oppose the United States if the Russians caused strife abroad. The director branded the U.S. Communist Party a "fifth column if there ever was one" and declared that its purpose was the "overthrow of our Government." The best defense against communism, according to the director, was "vigorous, intelligent, old-fashioned Americanism." California state senator Jack Tenney, chairman of the state committee investigating Un-American Activities, talked about Communist infiltration in the California maritime unions. By listening and questioning these and other witnesses, Nixon started connecting his labor committee with his HUAC assignment.[11]

While the congressman made these links, the loyalty of federal employees became a compelling issue in front of HUAC. To take this issue away from the Republicans, the president, believing that he had to act, appointed the President's Temporary Commission on Employee Loyalty, which submitted its recommendations for preventing government employment of allegedly disloyal people in February 1947. On March 21, Truman promulgated Executive Order 9835 for a federal loyalty program that called for an investigation of every government worker, to be conducted by the FBI. In addition, the U.S. Attorney General was instructed to widen the published list of subversive organizations. The president announced that these procedures would not violate anyone's civil rights. He was mistaken, but with the ever-expanding fear of subversion, the public ignored a loud minority demanding toleration and accepted investigations that often infringed on individual rights.[12]

Parnell Thomas claimed that Truman had filched the loyalty program from HUAC, for Thomas had announced early in 1947 that he would introduce a plan to establish a federal loyalty commission, and on February 27, he had done just that. The executive order preempted his commission, but he quickly became dissatisfied with the lack of zealousness of the federal bureaucracy in carrying out its loyalty mission. By late spring, he demanded that the president immediately act against the "Red fifth-column" in the United States. The Communist menace, he insisted, was real, as Thomas and FBI director Hoover had warned. Now the Attorney General had to take vigorous action at home. "The immunity," Thomas held, "which this foreign-directed conspiracy has been enjoying for the past 15 years must cease."[13]

Nixon approved of Truman's loyalty program to get rid of subversive workers and simultaneously protect loyal ones. Anybody accused had the right to appear before its departmental loyalty board with counsel to present evidence to refute charges against them. If that process failed, the employee had a final appeal before a Civil Service Commission loyalty board as a further safeguard against any injustice. To Nixon, "It is . . . simply a case of chasing the other team's halfbacks out of our own backfield while we are calling our signals in the huddle."[14]

At the beginning of April, Nixon, demanded that the Justice Department publish an updated list of subversive organizations, which had not been revised since 1942. These groups supposedly had increased dramatically, but federal employees did not know which organizations to join after Truman's recent loyalty directive. Some might not know which ones were subversive, especially since front organizations tried to hide their Communist connections to lure unsuspecting liberals. A new list was a necessity. "It's not fair," Nixon argued, "for the government to have a secret list of front organizations which will be the basis of dismissals."[15]

Nixon's measured response toward his HUAC duties was winning acceptance. One Republican stalwart from Alhambra, Dick Cantwell, applauded Nixon's prudence: "Most like your attitude in the affairs of the Un-American Affairs Committee, no one likes a witch hunt, but do want a light shed upon the many questionable organizations now operating." Nixon reinforced such opinions. His private as well as public comments were similar. He privately admitted that the committee was "a pretty hot spot" and that he was doing his "very best to see that we follow as judicious a course as possible in our investigations. In the end I think that such an attitude will pay off in results." Publicly, he insisted that HUAC was focusing the legislative spotlight on subversives, not "liberals." The objective was to hunt espionage agents; as he stated when he accepted the position, he "would not be a party to any witch hunts or persecutions," and that had not occurred. The committee was doing its job of examining Fascists and "ferreting out Communist infiltration into governmental departments, labor unions and the public educational facilities."[16]

Nixon made a clear distinction between the best tradition in the American way of life and those who abused the system. For example, he congratulated Justice Isadore Bookstein of the New York Supreme Court for allowing Paul Robeson the right to sing at Albany High School. Robeson was "a noted colored baritone, a great and inspiring artist in his field. He is also, quite outspokenly, a rollicking Fellow Traveler, if not a card-carrying member of the Communist Party." The judge acted properly by letting Robeson sing but not allowing him to extol Communist virtues.[17]

Nixon also worried about leftists at Whittier College, a topic that was extremely delicate because "the minute you begin to infringe upon academic freedom you alienate the liberals as well as the Communists." Both Nixon and Herman Perry had served on the board of trustees. The congressman cautioned his close adviser that in this affair they had to follow a "middle ground where you can insure freedom without going so far as to openly invite subversive teaching due to lack of care in selecting personnel."[18]

Congressman Karl Mundt, Republican from South Dakota, further helped to shape Nixon's views. As a member of HUAC since 1943, Mundt had run for Congress in 1938, won handily, and was returned to the House with ever-increasing majorities. As World War II approached, he spoke out forcefully for noninterventionism, and even after the war, he continued his skepticism toward international involvement. While Mundt opposed direct European assistance, he pushed for countermeasures to Soviet propaganda, opposed any curtailment in the State Department's Voice of America activities, and introduced a measure to legalize its broadcasts. The bill with amendments passed in June and became law in early 1948, with a ten-million-dollar appropriation for an exchange of students and teachers, books and periodicals, as well as distributing information about the United States through the press, radio, film, and information centers.[19]

Nixon enthusiastically supported the bill. Although hotly contested, especially the provisions dealing with information and exchange proposals, the bill authorized the broadcasting of American information programs to foreign countries and provided student and teacher exchanges. To Nixon, these were essential because the world was in an ideological battle pitting communism against democracy. Propaganda was a powerful tool that the Russians had perfected. The United States had to respond in kind. The Mundt plan promoted mutual understanding between the United States and foreign nations and could correct misunderstandings and misinformation about America that existed in other parts of the world.[20]

While the Mundt exchange proposal became law, another idea for placing restraints on the Communist Party of the United States of America that Mundt had been contemplating since 1945 had taken form in the 80th Congress. The congressman spoke on the radio about restraining, not outlawing, that party. If it was an American political party, then any restriction would be a violation of constitutional rights, but the Kremlin guided the U.S. Communist Party. "I advocate these restraints on Communism," Mundt held, "as I advocated restraints on the Bunds whose activities were guided by Hitler." If democracy worked, the United States would not need to police communism, but both ideologies were not playing according to the same rules: "Communists in this country are guilty of sabotage, propaganda against the interests of the United States in time of war, physical abuse during elections (and murder) plus hundreds of crimes such as draft dodging, passport faking, perjury and lesser crimes."[21]

Nixon embraced this concept as his own, much to Mundt's chagrin, and began referring to it as the Mundt-Nixon or the Subversive Activities Control bill, which would shortly come up before the House for consideration. Nixon felt that the bill represented "a fair and sane approach to the very difficult problem of controlling subversive Communist activities in the United States." The bill's major objectives were to make any attempt to establish a dictatorship under a foreign power in the

United States a crime; to require the Communist Party and its associated groups to register with the U.S. Attorney General; to remove party members from government employment, and to deny passports to party officials like the general secretary of the party, Earl Browder. American Communists vigorously opposed the bill and tried to make it a battle over fundamental rights like freedom of press and expression. Nixon called on liberals and progressives to support the concept over loud Communist objections. He was confident that Congress would eventually pass the measure.[22]

When HUAC investigated UAW-CIO, Local 248, which had been on strike for ten months against the Allis-Chalmers Manufacturing Company in Milwaukee, Nixon heard witnesses assert that the local was Communist-dominated and the strike Communist-inspired. He learned how a small band of Communists came to dominate a 8,700-member union by clever parliamentary tactics, violence, intimidation, and dishonest ballot counting. The leadership had held down wages during the war to keep rank-and-file members dependent on them for assistance and guidance, and subversives had used their positions to distribute Communist literature and organize for their cause. Other witnesses testified about Communist penetration at the strike of the Food, Tobacco and Agricultural Workers against Reynolds Tobacco Company in Winston-Salem, North Carolina, and the United Electrical, Radio and Machine Workers of America (UE) strike in Bridgeport, Connecticut. By the end of the hearings, Nixon became convinced that small numbers of Communists were capable of controlling large unions. He publicly called on the 99 percent of UE members to remove the 1 percent of Communist members who dominated the union and planned "to wreck free trade unionism."[23]

Nixon went on the radio to discuss the connection between HUAC and the Communist threat. He called his and the committee's conduct "judicious and statesmanlike," aware that HUAC's function was investigatory, not prosecutorial. HUAC had uncovered Soviet espionage agents and pressed for their criminal indictments. He had studied Communist penetration in the unions and named several CIO organizations that had been compromised. Nixon opposed outlawing the Communist Party because that action would possibly sanctify and martyr an unworthy beneficiary. Outlawing the party might drive it deeper underground and make it harder to locate. Communists had to be forced into the sunlight, for the way to destroy a subversive philosophy was to sell democracy and the American way of life. According to the congressman, "It is not enough to denounce Communism, Fascism and all other isms which are opposed to the American form of government—the fundamental task which we have to perform in combating such alien philosophies is to make our own way of life so fine that no other system can take root on our shores."[24]

While Nixon actively participated in many HUAC hearings, he did not play a prominent role in its most publicized hearings in 1947 dealing with Communist activity in Hollywood. He had alluded to removing Communists from the movie industry during hearings in late March. A month later, he announced that a special assignment on the labor committee prevented him from joining a special subcommittee, composed of Chairman Thomas, John McDowell, Republican from Pennsylvania, and John Wood, Democrat from Georgia, that would arrive in Los Angeles on May 8 to investigate Gerhart Eisler's brother, Hans, a Hollywood film music composer. The group would stay for a week, but would not hold any public hearings. They were developing the foundation that would "lead to a thorough probe of Hollywood Reds" for a future hearing in Washington.[25]

During those hearings, Adolphe Menjou testified in the middle of May. In his fifties, he had been an actor for twenty-seven years. A linguist, world traveler, and self-proclaimed authority on the movie business, Menjou informed the subcommittee that at least six directors and several actors were Reds; furthermore, Hollywood had become a center of Communist activity due to the propaganda benefits of the film industry. After the Communists had sufficiently softened up the United States, Menjou predicted that the Soviets had plans "to destroy America within the next 15 years."[26]

The Hollywood hearings publicly convened on Capitol Hill on October 20 and continued until the end of the month, directed by a HUAC subcommittee composed of three Republicans: Thomas, McDowell, and Richard Vail of Illinois. The caucus room was at capacity with 391 spectators. During the first week, those who held that Communists had infiltrated the movie industry presented their case. Menjou, dapper as usual, wearing a suit and a homburg, was sworn in, and as he chain-smoked long Pall Malls with the smoke swirling about him, declared that he was "a Red-baiter. . . . I make no bones about it. I'd like to see them all in Russia. I think a taste of Russia would cure them." Nixon attended the first day and questioned Jack Warner about the large amount of

movies that attacked the Third Reich and the paucity of films that opposed communism. By the end of a gentle interrogation, Nixon gladly
proclaimed that Warner Bros. was "contemplating for the first time now
making a motion picture in which they point out to the American
people the dangers of totalitarian communism as well as fascism."[27]

Ronald Reagan, president of the Screen Actors Guild (SAG), also
testified. He agreed that a small SAG clique followed the Communist
Party line, but the group was ineffective. He had no direct knowledge
whether any of these individuals was a Communist, nor any information
about front organizations. When Chief Counsel Robert Stripling asked
Reagan for his opinion on how to stop Communist infiltration of SAG,
the actor's reply was "to make democracy work." *Newsweek* later commented: "Despite his 38 years, the pink-cheeked and sandy-haired
Ronald Reagan looked so boyish that when he arose to speak the room
was filled with oh's and ah's."[28]

Nixon was present, but never questioned Reagan. Still, he had reason to chuckle quietly. The congressman had already had a "long conversation" with Reagan that spring during a recent trip to California.
Nixon had regretted that the subcommittee had not previously contacted Reagan because he would make a good HUAC witness. Nixon
wished that the SAG president would be called at public hearings in
Washington since he was "classified as a liberal and as such would not be
accused of simply being a red baiting reactionary." Obviously, the subcommittee had reconsidered and followed Nixon's advice.[29]

Starting on October 27, the HUAC subcommittee turned its attention to hostile witnesses, who became known as the Hollywood Ten.
The first was John Lawson, a screenwriter whose appearance was violent
and disorderly. When he finished, he was cited for contempt. The next
day brought three more contempt citations for refusal to testify; the following day, there were four more; and the on last day, two more contemptuous witnesses brought the total citations to ten.[30]

During a special session of Congress in November, Nixon led the
effort to have the House sustain the HUAC contempt citations. He asserted that the subcommittee had the power to investigate and protect
Americans from the Communist menace. The chairman asked two
questions: "Are you a member of the Screen Writers' Guild?" and "Are
you, or have you ever been a member of the Communist Party?" By asking these questions, Nixon argued, the committee was pursuing its legitimate legislative function. It had not infringed upon the witnesses'

individual rights, and each had an attorney. The committee was not in the executive position of being able to punish anyone, rightly or wrongly, for their affiliations. Congress overwhelming affirmed Nixon's argument. What had become known as the Hollywood Ten waived jury trials; all were found guilty and went to jail. After their release, all were blacklisted. Most never again regained the stature that they had held the movie business.[31]

Many criticized HUAC's handling of the Hollywood Ten. Eric Johnston, president of the Motion Picture Association of America, accused the committee of making a blanket indictment against his industry. HUAC declared that the movies were filled with pro-Communist propaganda, but did not produce a single film as proof. He concluded: "The communists hate our films because they show a way of life they hate—a life where free men work and play in the ways of freedom—a life where men are masters of their own destinies, and no pawns in the chess game of autocracy—where no one man is at the mercy of another and where the virtues of justice and charity are still enthroned."[32]

Nixon acutely understood the potential dangers of these hearings and warned HUAC that investigators had to build "a good strong case" before inviting any witnesses to Washington. He urged extreme caution to avoid "the criticism which is bound to be heaped upon us in the event we happen to smear a few innocent people along with those who are really guilty." He was partly accurate in his prophesy. Walter Goodman, who carefully studied HUAC's role, concluded that the premise "that movies were being subverted by a Red underground in league with New Deal bureaucrats, was asinine; its [HUAC] methods were gross and its intentions despicable." Every Communist involved in the movie business could not and did not threaten American security. Robert Carr, in his detailed examination, added that HUAC "had failed to demonstrate that Hollywood was a hotbed of Communist activity." The committee members allowed the questioning of unfriendly witnesses to degenerate into whether they were party members and nothing more.[33]

Nixon was exempted from hostile attacks, emerging as a moderate who preached caution and fairness. Early into his membership, he recognized the outrageous conduct of Thomas and Rankin, and avoided inclusion or association with this unsavory duo.

Whatever HUAC's methods, Nixon and a large portion of the American public came to believe that domestic subversion represented a serious menace. Nixon watched horrified at the testimony of men who had dedicated themselves to overthrowing the U.S. government and replacing it with a Marxist model. It was an abomination that the young congressman refused to accept. Nixon supported curbs on the U.S. Communist Party, increased spending for the Voice of America, and active prosecution to remove disloyal federal employees. His positions were not considered radical; much of what he advocated followed rather than led his peers. Like many others, Nixon had moved from vague opposition to the Soviet Union in 1946 to a much clearer evaluation by the end of the following year. He had watched and examined witnesses, had read documents, and talked to experts. By the time that 1947 drew to a close, he was convinced that the Communists were a serious threat to American security at home and abroad.

# Chapter 6

# THE HERTER COMMITTEE

A fter working on the passage of the Taft-Hartley Act and looking directly into the threat that Soviet communism posed to democracy, Nixon unexpectedly received his first foreign policy assignment. He had been interested in American diplomacy since his college days; during his political campaign early in 1946, he had called for enlightened public support for American foreign policies. Isolationism, he proclaimed, had died with the completion of World War II. Nixon was an internationalist. He naively called for an end to secret arrangements and urged Americans to turn the United Nations into an effective organization. He believed in peace through collective security.[1]

Nixon recognized that democracy competed with totalitarianism, and the United States had to watch the Soviet Union, even though the war had wreaked havoc on its very existence. He did not want America to share information on the atomic bomb or provide economic aid that could hasten Russian development of weapons of mass destruction until the Communists renounced their credo of world conquest. He argued that the United States and the USSR had to find a way to coexist in order to guarantee peace.[2]

During the campaign, he had labeled the State Department "Confusion Castle" because it did not provide clear, consistent policies. Now he urged that the diplomatic corps get a thorough housecleaning with a new cadre of well-trained public servants replacing the elitists who were currently employed. He also wanted America to champion the cause of human rights, and this could only be accomplished under a higher standard of public service.[3]

Nixon had agreed with Voorhis in backing the Truman-Byrnes policy of dealing more firmly with the Russians. He opposed Henry Wallace's approval of Soviet domination in Eastern Europe. When Nixon did voice his disapproval, he attacked the Truman administration's muddled leadership and the president's Anglophilism. Nixon's political advertisements had demanded a "realistic foreign policy" favoring guarantees of U.S. freedoms to smaller nations and no appeasement of any aggressors.[4]

Nixon gradually opposed foreign aid, but he voted for then chairman of the Famine Emergency Commision Herbert Hoover's food relief plan as "the only way we can keep the Communists from having things all their own way in Europe." He became more convinced that hungry Europeans would turn toward communism as their most viable option. The United States, Nixon reasoned, had to feed the starving, but also had to develop an economic recovery program for European countries to provide work for their own advancement. He concluded: "The United States cannot undertake to feed the entire world indefinitely and consequently our relief program must be combined with a realistic policy, encouraging all-out protection of goods in Europe and Asia."[5]

Nixon initially linked foreign policy goals with military concerns, but he saw the armed services' preparedness campaign as "a smoke screen to keep Congress from making any substantial cuts in the agencies." He already opposed the president's plan for Universal Military Training, and instead, favored a standby Selective Service act. To crystallize his thoughts further, he and Congressman Charles Kersten had an informal meeting with Secretary of Defense James Forrestal on March 10, at which Nixon reasoned that universal military preparedness was "the best guarantee for peace." To him, the deterrent to war was might, and the United States had to impress any aggressor with a powerful air force and modern weaponry to discourage an attack.[6]

The congressman refused "to go off half-cocked on any subject," and this applied to Truman's Universal Military Training plan of recruiting men for six months to a year for a large pool from which it could then draw. A far better idea would be a program where local communities would be responsible for some military training and also prepare for civilian disasters. Nixon felt that the best way to provide security was to concentrate on aviation, atomic energy, new weaponry, and military specialists, including a division dealing with intelligence.[7]

Nixon held anticommunistic ideas from the beginning. He wrote a constituent on March 11 about his deep concern that the British had announced plans to withdraw from Greece. The United States had "an obligation to ourselves and to all freedom-loving people to give aid and support wherever it will have the effect of curtailing the spread of Communism." He was disappointed that the American people might have to provide financial assistance to the Greeks while the United States was attempting to reduce government expenditures in order to lower taxes and the national debt. But under the current conditions, those objectives moved into second place. "Maintenance of our security," according to Nixon, required "peacetime as well as wartime sacrifices."[8]

The following day, March 12, President Truman addressed a joint session of Congress mirroring many of Nixon's feelings by asking for aid to Greece and Turkey to fight Communist subversion and aggression. He warned that American security and international commitments were involved, for the Greeks needed economic and military aid if the regime had any chance of fending off Communist terrorists. Turkey also needed assistance because it played a critical role in the maintenance of order in the Middle East. The president sternly lectured his audience: "I believe that it must be the policy of the United States to support free peoples who are resisting attempted subjugation by armed minorities or by outside pressures." In that defining sentence as well as throughout the address, Truman had seized the initiative, deliberately used ideological language, embarked on a crusade, and placed the prestige of his office on what has become commonly known as the Truman Doctrine.[9]

Nixon quickly responded to Truman's message with a call for bipartisan cooperation on this subject. The congressman wanted the president to make a clear statement on U.S. opposition to communism at home and abroad. How much money was going to Greece and Turkey, and what about the Chinese, who also faced subversion? Truman had not mentioned these issues, and some had accused the Greek regime of repression. A factual report had to determine whether or not the Greeks deserved American assistance.[10]

Herbert Spencer applauded Nixon's "courageous statement" on Truman's proposals. At last, the 12th district had a representative who thought incisively and who had the courage to speak out. Toward the end of March, Nixon offered another idea that he and eight House colleagues had drafted to stop Communist aggression and strengthen the United Nations. These congressmen introduced House Concurrent Resolution No. 170 to eliminate the veto power used by the Russians to prevent the preservation of peace. The newly formed world body had degenerated into something less respected than the League of Nations. "We either must make the UN work," Nixon argued, "through revision of its charter, or stop relying upon it as an effective means for peace and scrap it."[11]

By the end of the month, Nixon felt that the Truman Doctrine was one of the most serious issues the Congress would consider. He disagreed with those House members who endorsed the idea wholeheartedly without demanding that the administration answer some fundamental questions about its future international and domestic plans. He worried about Communist infiltration in labor unions and other subversive activities that would weaken U.S. defenses in the event of any trouble with the Soviet Union. The Truman administration had to attack any domestic menace before the United States spent money abroad.[12]

Even with these misgivings, the bill easily passed both houses of Congress by early May 1947, and Truman gladly signed it into law. Nixon voted for it since he wanted to prevent another Munich and any more appeasement to the aggressor. Those who opposed the bill, he thought, were either isolationists or pro-Russian. The government had to encourage democracy besides deploring the Communist threat. "We must show to the world that democracy is a dynamic, growing thing; that free peoples must never be content with the status quo of their freedoms." The United States had a duty to lead by example: "in the final analysis, war and democracy are abhorrent to each other and, in contrast, war and totalitarianism are synonymous."[13]

Nixon apparently took no notice of Secretary of State George C. Marshall's commencement speech at Harvard University on June 5. Only twelve hundred words, spoken in less than twelve minutes, many ignored it. Few sensed that it would be the most significant graduation address ever given at that institution of higher learning. Marshall proposed, without fanfare, that the United States was willing to assist Europe if it cooperated in its own economic recovery. The secretary called on the European nations to take the initiative and ended his remarks by telling his audience that the real significance of this plan was difficult to grasp: "And yet the whole world of the future hangs on a proper judgment."

When he finished, the audience of seven thousand gave him tremendous applause, but he received scant notice in the American press. British foreign secretary Ernest Bevin heard parts of Marshall's speech on the radio that evening and phoned the French foreign minister, Georges Bidault, the next day. Their governments quickly accepted the secretary's overture, and with that modest beginning, the Marshall Plan started to evolve.[14]

As the Europeans initiated the momentum toward economic recovery by using American assistance, Nixon argued that international economic intercourse would help keep the peace. "The American people," he asserted, "must be made to realize that a properly developed program of foreign trade is in their own self-interest as well as that of the rest of the world. Unfortunately, there are still too many people, both in Congress and out, who think that the way to solve our international difficulties is to isolate ourselves from the rest of the world and to become completely self-sufficient." The United States, instead, had to import more from other countries. America could not just loan money; it had to increase imports, for "our own wealth will be increased rather than depleted in the end." Embracing international intercourse was the means of preventing another world war.

The young congressman had an unexpected opportunity to discuss foreign policy when Congressman Edward Devitt of Minnesota arranged a meeting with Truman at the White House on July 2, at 10:30–10:45 A.M., for himself and three other Republican congressmen—Nixon, Kersten, and J. Caleb Boggs of Delaware. Nixon recalled his first time in the Oval Office: it was a "big pleasant room," with "no gadgets" except for a pony express confidential pouch. The president had photographs of his family on the table and behind his desk a model plane. Truman greeted them by shaking their hands; then they sat around the desk and discussed Russian intentions, European relief, German rehabilitation, Manchuria, the Balkans, and the Dutch East Indies. Nixon expected to support bipartisanship, but he wanted to know Truman's long-range goals, especially in regard to European economic assistance. To Nixon, relief for its own sake was insufficient. He told the group that "we must assure ourselves of an eventual end to such spending by building toward a peaceable and productive Europe which will be able to stand on its own two feet and take care of itself." Preparing to leave, he turned to Truman and said that one of his Monterey Park constituents, Robert Reece, had fought with Truman during World War I. The president smiled, glad to hear from "one of his old buddies."[15]

Nixon maintained his interest in bipartisan cooperation on foreign policy and publicly called for consultation between the executive and legislative branches before international commitments were finalized. He and nine other congressmen presented House Resolution No. 68, which called for a conference on the United Nations to revise and strengthen it as an effective instrument against war. The United States would be able to determine "whether the Soviet Union is bent on conquest or whether she would be willing to go along with other nations in creating a United Nations which would guarantee her own security." Nixon wanted Russia to "put up or shut up" about world peace. If the Communists refused to cooperate, the other peace-loving nations should proceed without them.[16]

The congressman also called on the administration to develop better foreign food relief programs. The government had large surpluses of some commodities and had not disposed of them. Oranges were excluded from the aid plan, and citrus growers in Southern California were angry that the current excesses of the orange harvest were ignored.[17]

By the end of July, Congress had adjourned. During that interim, Representative Christian Herter, Republican from Massachusetts, was assembling a House committee to travel overseas to explore the possibilities of a foreign aid program. An outspoken internationalist, he had visited Europe to examine food shortages. On March 20, 1947, he had presented a House resolution to investigate European economic conditions with a budget not to exceed $125,000. Approved on July 22, it created a Select Committee on Foreign Aid to be composed of nineteen members to study European requirements and American aid. Charles Eaton of New Jersey, chairman of the House Committee on Foreign Affairs, decided against leaving the country and let Vice Chairman Herter take the lead.[18]

Speaker Martin took a personal interest in naming the members of the committee, quickly selecting eleven Republicans: Eaton, Herter, Nixon, John Kunkel from Pennsylvania, Thomas Jenkins from Ohio, Charles Wolverton from New Jersey, August Anderson from Minnesota, Francis Case from South Dakota, John Vorys from Ohio, Charles Versell from Illinois, and W. Kingsland Macy from New York. The eight Democrats chosen were: Francis Walter from Pennsylvania, William

Colmer from Mississippi, James Richards from South Carolina, Harold Cooley from North Carolina, George Mahan from Texas, Overton Brooks from California, Eugene Keogh from New York, and A. S. Monroney from Oklahoma. Martin picked these men from the twelve House committees concerned with foreign aid. They came from fifteen states, and the majority was, as Philip Pope described it, "conservative, skeptical, if not hostile, to the idea of major American assistance" in European recovery. Half came from urban areas and the rest from rural communities. This mixture became known as the Herter Committee.[19]

On Wednesday morning, July 30, Nixon was pleasantly surprised to read an Associated Press dispatch in the *Washington Post* saying that he had been appointed to the Herter Committee. Although Speaker Martin never explained his reasons for choosing Nixon, there were probably several major ones. He was the only westerner and the youngest member of the group, had regularly followed the GOP leadership in his voting, had vocally backed a bipartisan foreign policy and the Truman Doctrine, decided against cutting foreign relief funds, and supported the State Department information program.[20]

The following day, Philip Watts, executive officer for the Herter Committee, sent out a bulletin on the details of the trip to Nixon. Watts had already made a reservation for him at the Biltmore Hotel in New York City for the evening of August 26; the committee would hold a special conference at 4:00 P.M., and the members and staff afterwards would be given the latest updates on their mission. The *Queen Mary* would sail the next day. Would Nixon be there?[21]

Nixon could not have been happier. He had never dared to ask Martin or anyone else about this assignment because he did not think that he had a chance of going. Nixon wrote the speaker that he was "without doubt the most surprised and pleased person in Washington. I want you to know how much I appreciate the appointment and I sincerely hope that my work on the committee will not be a disappointment to you."[22]

Bill Arnold mirrored his boss's sentiments: "This has been regarded around here as *the* best interim committee to land due to the fact that its recommendations will go a long way toward determining our foreign aid policy at the next session." Nixon left the capital from August 6 through August 20 "for a much needed rest." During this period, Herbert Spencer wrote him on behalf of a group of his closest supporters. They worried about the European and State Department propaganda that Nixon would hear, especially since the Marshall Plan concept was to give money to European states that were already socialistic or communistic. The GOP had to focus on its election goals. The congressional leadership was "wise enough to refuse to be drawn into support of a dangerously unworkable and profoundly inflationary foreign policy." Spencer typified many Republicans who opposed the ideas of the Marshall Plan and worried that Nixon did not. Others added to Spencer's admonition: "Don't let those 'city slickers' take you in camp."[23]

Jack Garland, member of the Los Angeles County Republican Committee and a wealthy real estate developer, who had just returned from the Europe, wrote Nixon, calling for economic assistance to prevent starvation in the war-torn region. The congressman replied almost as soon as he returned from vacation. He promised that he would make a practical and independent analysis of the American foreign aid program and hoped that the committee would make sound recommendations that would lead to future workable programs. He stressed to Garland that the Truman administration controlled foreign policy because Congress did not have "access to the facts. The Foreign Aid Committee . . . has a great responsibility to reverse this trend and to put our relief program on a sound business basis." As for Spencer's advice, Nixon read the letter several times and was taking it with him on his journey. He promised not to accept any State Department propaganda and to make his own judgments and recommendations to Congress based on what the committee decided.[24]

To his constituents, in a bulletin entitled "Under the Capitol Dome," his regular newsletter, Nixon forecast that the second session of the 80th Congress beginning in January 1948 would face raising the minimum wage, tax reduction, Universal Military Training, Social Security benefits, aid to education, and foreign assistance. He pledged that his greatest emphasis would be on the cost of living and the housing shortage.[25]

While Bill Arnold began planning for the upcoming congressional race and preparing for Nixon's visit to the district after his European journey, the congressman focused on getting ready for his mission. Phil Watts, whom the congressman would latesr describe as "a fine fellow," had already informed the committee members that this mission would be strenuous: "No wives, no dinner coats." While Dick traveled in Europe and the Arnolds drove to California, Pat would be in charge of running the office.[26]

On arrival at the Biltmore, Nixon received his passport and ticket.

Rose Mary Woods, the staff secretary, handled these kinds of arrangements and was introduced to the youthful congressman. At 4:00 P.M. the committee assembled for the first time and heard from Charles "Chip" Bohlen, counselor for the State Department, who briefed the congressmen on their mission. He had reached the pinnacle of his influence under Marshall; indeed, Bohlen had drafted most of the secretary's Harvard commencement address for long-term economic assistance to Europe.[27]

After that indoctrination, Nixon boarded the vessel. Christened late in 1934 by the queen of England, this mammoth Cunard White Star vessel, which exceeded the size of any of its competitors, was 1,004 feet in length along the waterline (a world's record at its launching), 118 feet high, and 135 high from keel to the top of its superstructure. Its gross tonnage was 80,773, and it displaced 77,500 tons, far greater than that of any other ships. The luxury liner comfortably slept 2,075 passengers. It had twelve decks, and a main restaurant, the largest room ever built in a ship of 18,720 square feet, that seated 815 persons.[28]

When the congressman described the *Queen Mary* to his wife, he began by saying that it was "just out of this world in every way." He had toured the vessel and declared that it was "just too big to describe." Each of the three classes of passengers had different facilities: their own lounges, movies, dining room, swimming pool, and so on. Even the least expensive tourist class had a nursery, "with toys, children's murals on the walls & nurses in attendance!"[29]

Nixon was assigned a cabin in the first-class section, along with Thomas Jenkins, who chaired the Italy-Trieste-Greece subcommittee, of which Nixon was also a member. Aboard ship for five days, Professor William Elliott of Harvard supervised daily seminars conducted by experts in a special lounge. Nixon grew to respect Herter as the leader of the mission, and they formed a cordial relationship. Herter also invited one of his friends, Allen Dulles, to come, and Nixon met him on the crossing, where they initiated the start of a long friendship.[30]

The evening before the delegation arrived at Southampton, Nixon wrote about how wonderful the weather had been and his impressions of the voyage. The *Queen Mary* was "a fine ship & luckily for me (a poor sailor) it has been a smooth ride all the way." "Our committee," he asserted, "had meetings every morning & afternoon all the way across. The group is a serious one & I believe has some very able members."[31]

The committee disembarked on September 2 and took a train to London. The chaotic appearance of one of the world's great cities shocked Nixon, who was unprepared for the devastation he saw. To add to this terrible situation, Europe was undergoing the second worst drought in a century. Even before the group reached their hotel, they went to the U.S. Embassy and listened to Ambassador Lewis Douglas, a conservative American businessman, who gave them a three-hour overview of European conditions. Not only had the English suffered in World War II, he lectured, but this devastation had had a cumulative effect, beginning with World War I. An entire generation of men had been lost. Currently, the economy was weak, and the Labor Party government dampened recovery by interfering in the free enterprise system. Douglas explained that before the war, even though Great Britain imported more than it exported, its foreign investment covered up the deficit. During the war, Britain liquidated most of its overseas empire, and the Nazis had decimated its merchant fleet. As a result, the current government was confronted with alternatives of reducing imports, and therefore, a lower standard of living, or increasing exports to compensate for the lost colonies and shipping revenue. The election slogan of "Vote Labour—Get What You Want" masked the fact that either option would be extremely unpopular.[32]

The next day, the delegation went to 10 Downing Street for tea with Prime Minister Clement Attlee. From that official welcoming reception, they met for an hour with Foreign Minister Bevin, who in the midst of a monetary crisis the previous day had advocated dividing the gold in Fort Knox to solve the world's financial troubles. Two committee members were bankers, and Bevin faced "a rather rough time during the question period." Despite this gaff, Nixon saw Bevin as the strongest man in the Labor cabinet, who spoke for the more right wing part of his party and had the most realistic viewpoint by opposing any further nationalization of industry.[33]

Stafford Cripps, the top economic minister, had been pushing for austerity measures. Cripps's reasoning impressed Nixon, who concluded that if the government required longer hours in the coal and textile industries or gave workers incentives to pull the country out of its difficulties, then the nation had a chance to survive. If this did not occur, Labor would be defeated in the next spring elections and another party would put an austerity program in place.[34]

While Nixon approved of Bevins and Cripps, John Strachey, minister of food, who represented the far left, preached the unimaginable. Strachey favored the immediate nationalization of the steel industry and wanted to absorb other industries. To him, "If the people of Europe are faced on the one hand with stark reaction and on the other hand with Communism, they definitely will turn toward the Communists." Nixon demurred.[35]

Nixon left England on September 4 for the short flight to Berlin. That and other German cities looked "just like great gaunt skeletons." After his arrival in the early evening, his army driver commented: "There was still the smell of smoke and death in the air." Three million people lived in the rubble, with boys trying to sell their fathers' war medals as souvenirs. Nixon described them as "living there like a bunch of starved rats in ruins."[36]

That evening after checking into the Harnack House Hotel, he went to the Lakeside Club, where the committee members had a buffet supper and met with General Lucius Clay, the American in charge of the U.S. occupational zone, who reviewed the bleak economic conditions. Before the war, Germany had the most productive economy on the continent; currently, it was functioning at 25 percent of its prewar capacity. Other European nations depended on trade with Germany, and if it did not improve economically, the entire Continent would continue to suffer. To Clay, the United States had successfully demilitarized and denazified the country. The most critical job now was combatting acute hunger. Without these relief supplies, thousands would starve. Clay knew that four-power (United States, Britain, France, and the Soviet Union) cooperation had collapsed. Forgetting the humanitarian considerations, the general argued for German recovery so that that nation could serve as a buffer against Soviet aggression.[37]

After that briefing, Nixon and the other committee members headed for the Wannasee station to depart on the night train for Essen in the British occupation zone, a city in the middle of the Ruhr Valley and the center of the Krupp works. When Nixon awoke, he looked out of his window: "As far as the eye could reach all we could see was complete utter desolation and destruction." This region, before the fighting, had been one of the productive areas in the Third Reich. People currently lived in cellars with as many as four to six individuals inhabiting a nine-by twelve-foot room for all their necessities. Many had advanced cases of tuberculosis due to "malnutrition and poor living conditions." A large barn, with little heat and light, served as a hospital for two hundred children with TB, which had caused Nixon to think about his late brother Harold.[38]

Nixon quickly came to the stark realization that there were "no heroes in a defeated country." He found a miner and his wife, along with a young man of twenty-two, who had lost a leg in the war, living under wretched circumstances. The young man had no pension because only those who lost both legs or arms were eligible in war-torn Germany for assistance. A mother and three daughters lived under similar dismal conditions. Her husband was killed in a bombing raid; one son died at Stalingrad; and the other was a Russian prisoner of war, who the woman said "might as well be dead."[39]

Near Essen, the British gave the miners incentive rations to provide additional energy: these consisted of a thin soup with cucumbers spread on top. When Nixon noticed that many men did not eat the food, he walked up to a red-headed boy of fourteen to find out why. The boy replied that he would take it home, and his family would water it down further so they could all share. Indeed, Nixon discovered that almost half of the miners followed this practice. Soup kitchens also provided further nourishment for youngsters, but they too divided their meals with their families.

Representative Eugene Cox, Democrat of Georgia, who happened to be with the mission when it toured this region, had given some chocolate to children around the train and offered his last piece to little girl carrying a baby. The child took none for herself but carefully placed it in the baby's mouth: "When she did that, I just couldn't help myself. I went back to the train, got everything that I had and gave it to the kids. Including my sweaters, soap and some shirts."[40]

Nixon understood that Americans overwhelmingly thought that the Germans deserved these privations or even worse. People in the States, however, had not experienced this kind of agony. Nixon thought that a remark from Congressman Francis Case, chairman of the German subcommittee, who had walked these wastelands, was appropriate: "When civilized people capture cannibals they do not eat them."[41]

The committee left Essen for Frankfurt by automobile and stayed there overnight. From that city, the nineteen members split into five subcommittees, and Nixon was attached to the Italy-Trieste-Greece group that became known as "Jenkins' Raiders," after the head of the group, Thomas Jenkins, with whom Nixon had shared a cabin on the *Queen Mary*. From Frankfurt, his party of four flew to Rome on September 6.[42]

Italy, too, was economically devastated. The coalition government appeared honest, but Prime Minister Alcide De Gasperi lacked leadership qualities. The worsening political and financial conditions created an anarchical situation caused by rising political violence, poor living environments, and the exclusion of the Communists and the Socialists from a new cabinet formed at the beginning of June. As the radical left tried to enlarge its base of followers, the extreme right responded with its own terror. In the midst of this chaos, the government seemed powerless to curb the growing anarchy or to bring the guilty to justice.[43]

Nixon spent several weeks in Rome and left with the conviction that the Italian Communist Party was directly linked to Moscow. During that visit, he talked with Joseph Alsop, a popular American columnist, who thought that the situation was "pretty critical & that unless we intend help we are going to have the Communists sweep Europe this winter."[44]

The embassy had scheduled meetings with major Communist figures, including Umberto Terricini, president of the Chamber of Deputies, who compared with the American Speaker of the House. One major qualification for his standing in the party was that he had spent eighteen years in prison, for anyone who was a Red during the regime of Benito Mussolini either went to jail or left the country. When the subcommittee interviewed him, his luxurious office was decorated with red curtains and walls. Called "the Brain" of the Italian Communist Party, he was small in stature, wore a red flag in his lapel, and acted debonair.[45]

Palmiro Togliatti, the vice premier, looked like a successful American businessman, usually dressing in a neat blue serge suit. The leader of the Italian Communist Party, he spent the war years in Russia, and of all the Communists Nixon met, he found Togliatti the ablest man outside Moscow. He had convinced many Italians that they could be patriots as well as Communists. During recent municipal elections in Rome, Red posters outnumbered all others five to one, and none of them had the hammer and sickle of the Soviet Union. Instead, the party used pictures of Giuseppe Garibaldi, the nineteenth-century hero who united Italy. Togliatti also convinced Italian Catholics who made up 95 percent of the population that they could be both good Catholics and Communists.[46]

The Reds, under his leadership, made concerted appeals to youth.

When Nixon visited one family, he asked a young adult why so many of his age had joined the Communist Party, and the boy took Nixon to the window of his modest tenement apartment and pointed to the Communist Youth Club building where the Red flag of Moscow was flying. Young people could go there for a snack, participate in free athletic events and picnics. He did not submit to any indoctrination programs, but if he wished, he could read Communist literature. Other political parties did not have the funds to finance these programs.[47]

Besides observing these activities in Rome, Nixon and the other three subcommittee members flew to Milan in the north on September 12. Included in the itinerary was a trip to a Alfa Romeo plant in Piedmont that made customized cars and trucks. They toured the plant and spoke with workers, labor leaders, and Vittorio Valletta, general manager of the company, who told the committee that the Communists were losing power and the De Gasperi regime was gaining support. His government would succeed if the United States provided desperately needed assistance. Others were not nearly as optimistic.[48]

The committee spent the next day in Turin, where they visited the famous Martini Rossi winery. The members returned to Milan by evening to attend an opening at La Scala of *Manon*. At the end of the first act, the stage crew shone a spotlight on the box, while the orchestra played "The Star-Spangled Banner." The hectic pace continued the next day with a drive to Venice to talk to farmers, shopkeepers, and workers. Before supper, Nixon went for a swim and commented that "the surf was wonderful." Even though his travels sounded like a congressional junket, Nixon maintained that his journey had "been a hard trip & we are really learning things."[49]

On September 15, the group left for Trieste for a three-day stay that coincided with a crisis when Yugoslav military forces attempted to take over the city. The second largest Mediterranean seaport, nestled at the northern end of the Adriatic Sea, drew most of its trade from northern Italy and central Europe. During World War I, the Italians lost a half a million men there wresting it from Austria. Nixon understood its strategic importance and described the seaport as a current-day Danzig, the Polish city that Hitler insisted be absorbed into the Third Reich. After the war, Marshal Josip Broz Tito, supported by Stalin, asked to incorporate the city into Yugoslavia, a request the Italians bitterly opposed. The compromise which settled the dispute was that the Free Territory of Trieste would become an autonomous political entity on September 15,

1947. Until then, fifteen thousand American, British, and Yugoslav troops would garrison the region under a UN mandate.[50]

Nixon arrived in Trieste shortly before the free-city status was to go into effect. Shops were closed. As he started to unpack his clothes at the hotel, he heard Communists singing the *Internationale* at the "top of their voices" in the street below him. He went to the window and saw a parade of five hundred. Most were young, vigorous, and "full of fight." Many carried the Red flag, and since Communist Party headquarters was next to the hotel, Nixon watched as the marchers "raised their hands in the clinched fist salute of Moscow" as they passed the building.[51]

Nixon found an interpreter and went into the street, where they heard an explosion. A Communist had thrown a grenade from a second-story window into a group of protesters who had formed to oppose the Red parade. One of them had his head blown off. The police were chasing a Communist suspect the size of a football fullback. That day, five people died and seventy-five were wounded by bombs and gunfire. Later, Nixon visited a shop where the female owner echoed the general fear of another European war: "Above everything else they fear another war and they are willing to take almost any steps to avoid one."[52]

Making the situation even more perilous, at 4:00 A.M., a Yugoslav colonel with two thousand troops marched to outpost no. 5, manned by Lieutenant Oaks of Nashville, Tennessee, and twelve U.S. soldiers. The Yugoslavs threatened to kill the Americans, but Oaks stood firm and the hostile forces withdrew. Nixon did not know that the Anglo-American military contingent had warned the Yugoslavs that if they sent soldiers into the city, they would be resisted with force.[53]

Nixon was proud of Oaks's courage and approved of his actions. Trieste had voted against a Red government, and now the Communists were using force to achieve their ends. Communists had taken over Gorizia in northern Italy near Trieste. The Reds had changed the schoolbooks and began indoctrinating children with Communist ideology. Nixon knew that this had to end: "By letting the people of Trieste know that even though they are a small state we will not tolerate imposition of a Communist government upon them by force, we give hope to freedom loving people throughout the world, and with that kind of backing they will have the courage to resist the totalitarian pressure both from within and without their country."[54]

Trieste, in fact, did not become a free territory that September; it would remain divided for seven more years. American diplomatic representatives tried to persuade their distinguished visitors that the United States had to continue political support, maintain a military presence, and provide economic assistance. Before the four politicians left, William Sullivan, the British political adviser in the city, notified London that the subcommittee members were "professing their determination to back financial support for the Free Territory, events of the last few days having aroused in them a crusading fervour to resist communist encroachment on Trieste."[55]

Nixon responded to these warnings by issuing a press release for himself and the three other congressmen who had accompanied him. Even though the Yugoslavs had demanded that the American soldiers holding part of Trieste surrender its control, Nixon urged the American people and Congress to support their armed forces and let the Communist-dominated countries know that the United States would not accept any further expansionist acts. Nixon was convinced that America's political, economic, and moral future was "dependent upon our taking an unequivocal firm position against Soviet aggression in this area."[56]

At the completion of the Trieste inspection, Nixon returned to Rome by train and spent the next few days in the capital. On September 19, he and the other subcommittee members met Giuseppe Di Vittorio, Communist head of all Italian unions. The young congressman had watched most American union labor leaders' appearances before his House Education and Labor Committee. Di Vittorio equaled the best of them, and Nixon described him as "about the smartest guy among the Italians we have met." Having fought in the Spanish Civil War and served seven years in jail, Di Vittorio already had legendary credentials. Physically a big man, he sometimes worked fifteen hours a day and was an astute political observer. He favored American aid as long as it did not threaten his country's independence and told Nixon that he wanted a government where labor had the right to strike. The congressman responded: like the United States, for the USSR barred strikes. After the translation, Di Vittorio replied coldly: "The gentleman and I are not speaking the same language. . . . The reason it is necessary to have the right to strike in a country such as the United States is because workers must obtain their rights from the capitalist reactionaries and employers."

Nixon asked him to criticize American foreign policy, and Di Vittorio attacked it severely. The congressman inquired about the weaknesses in Russia's international stands, and Di Vittorio gave Nixon a similar frozen glare: "Again the gentleman and I are not speaking the same lan-

guage. . . . The reason the foreign policy of the United States is necessarily imperialistic is that it is dominated by capitalists, reactionaries or
employers, and therefore, it is impossible for the foreign policy of Russia
to be imperialistic. Therefore it is not subject to criticism."[57]

Next, the committee members flew to Greece. Upon arrival in
Athens, U.S. Embassy officials gave the party a harsh assessment. Greece
was about the size of New York State, with some 7.5 million people living on the poorest farmland in Europe, of which only 20 percent was
under cultivation. The Nazis had burned over one thousand villages; 90
percent of the transportation facilities had been destroyed, and 70 percent of the merchant marine fleet had been sunk. Some of the populace
was left destitute, and guerrillas from the north near the Yugoslav border
posed a serious problem. In this environment, U.S. officials in Athens
urged the congressmen to aid Greece, defend the country's independence, and stop the spread of communism.[58]

Colonel Lehrer told the subcommittee that he had arrived in Greece
two days after Truman signed the aid bill on May 22, as head of the advanced military advisers. He worked on equipping and training the
Greek armed forces of 120,000, of which 78,000 were combat troops.
The guerrillas had about 15,000 soldiers, who attacked at night mainly
in the northern region. The Greek military, to repel these assaults, was
dispersed in small detachments throughout the country, led by unreliable
commanders in the highest ranks. Inductees were paid six cents per day
to risk their lives. Government civil servants were inefficient and corrupt
and failed to support the military's efforts to destroy the insurgents.[59]

Nixon was determined to see a combat zone. Indeed, even before
leaving the *Queen Mary*, he declared: "We are going to try to get back
into the guerrilla country when we get to Greece." He and Congressman
James Richards flew to the northern port of Salonika on September 23,
"on the edge of the guerrilla territory." The pilot landed with full power
on a 2,500-foot runway, and when the plane stopped, it had at least a
foot and a half to spare. The following day, his party took off at 9:00 A.M.
in an old C-47 without a door and flew west from the seaport over Lake
Vegoritis and its surrounding mountains, before coming to a broad valley in which lay Florina, where the mother of Alexander the Great was
born.[60]

The town had a population of 5,000, swollen by 6,000 refugees.
Frontier posts had been manned because the winter of 1946, because
Florina was only minutes from the Yugoslav border. Nixon interviewed

a captured guerrilla who had been recruited in June and surrendered the day before. He also spoke to three other young Communists. The prefect who was escorting the American delegation stopped an attractive girl of about twenty, who told the Americans that the guerrillas were hunting her brother, and when she refused to tell them where he was, they sliced off her left breast. Nixon asked several Greeks which was worse, the Nazis or the Russians. A typical reply was: "The German is a man, the Communist a beast."[61]

By the time Nixon left Athens, he believed that he had factual proof that the Russians were leading and financing the guerrilla movement. Tito had been supplied with American-made Winchester ammunition and British rifles during the war; these were currently being used to fight the Greek military. Nixon asked the captured rebel guerrilla what his leaders told him he was fighting for, and the guerrilla answered: democracy. Nixon called upon him to name the democratic nations, and he replied: Yugoslavia, Albania, Poland, and Russia. His leaders had said that Great Britain was finished and the United States would not last long. Nixon concluded that "simple peasants" were "being indoctrinated thoroughly in the current Communist line that true democracies are the Communist countries and that nations such as the United States and Great Britain eventually will crumble from within and will be easy prey for the Communist aggressors." The United States could not allow Greece to fall under Communist domination, Nixon believed, for other European countries would then become ripe for conquest.[62]

The group returned to Rome for the last time on September 25 and four days later flew to Paris. During this three-day stay in the French capital, Nixon gained the impression that if the United States halted American aid to France that winter, it would result in a totalitarian regime, probably a communistic one. If the country got through the winter and harvested a good crop the following year, France would be on its way to economic recovery by the end of 1948.[63]

After Germany, France had suffered the heaviest physical destruction in Western Europe, but a larger blow was that to French pride. Nixon talked with several French observers who told him that their people were "suffering virtually from a national nervous breakdown." Indeed, the diplomatic historian Irwin Wall has clearly demonstrated that even though the French argued with the United States over many issues, such as the economic reconstruction of Germany, France needed immediate American assistance to avoid catastrophe. As France confronted ever-greater privation and internal social unrest, its government realized that it had to accept the American conditions for aid.[64]

France also had political problems due to its convoluted multiparty system, which did not place responsibility on any single faction. The French Communist Party was the second strongest in the nation, controlling the labor unions. One half-serious allegation was that Stalin could take over the telephone system any time he so desired. The amount of power the Communists had to disrupt the political process concerned Nixon. He also worried about former president Charles de Gaulle, who personified many of weaknesses in this political system with his unpredictable and impulsive behavior. One French politician told the delegation that "De Gaulle in political matters thinks he has a direct telephone line with God and that in making decisions all he has to do is get on the wire and get the word straight from heaven."[65]

On October 4, the *Queen Mary* sailed from Southampton on its transatlantic crossing. Two days later, on board ship, Jenkins summarized his subcommittee's findings for the entire body. While no Communists held any Italian cabinet position, Jenkins realized that they were a force in the Italian Assembly. If the economy grew, the Communist menace would diminish significantly. The chairman also witnessed the chaos in Trieste and concluded that if Red harassment continued, that seaport could not prosper. As for Greece, the nation faced food shortages and banditry, especially in the north, but as long as the United States continued its economic assistance, conditions in Greece would improve. Jenkins declared that Turkey was improving economically, but the United States had to supply military assistance to quiet constant Turkish fears of potential Russian aggression.[66]

During his travels, Dick had written regularly to his wife, opening each letter with "Dearest," always closing with an endearment, and anticipating a future crossing along with her. He bought presents for his wife, Tricia, and friends, including eight expensive Italian linen placemats and four or five pairs of long black Italian gloves, which sold for five dollars in Italy, but at Saks Fifth Avenue went for between twenty and twenty-five a pair. He purchased some silk ties and scarfs for those outside the immediate family. When Nixon learned that the delegation would have an audience with the Pope, he commented that the Holy Father blessed "everything you carry on your person so I'm going to buy a few crucifixes & have them with me." Margaret, Helene, and Jo, some of his Catholic friends "might like them."[67]

Upon returning to Washington, Nixon faced two imperatives: preparing, first, for the HUAC hearings on the motion picture industry, which convened on October 20; and second, getting ready to fly to the West Coast with his family to promote American economic assistance to Europe. He attended the initial sessions of HUAC on Communist infiltration in the movie business while he made arrangements for his return to California.

Press releases began going out in the middle of October announcing his expected arrival on October 24. Nixon knew that the majority of his constituents opposed foreign aid, and he had to reverse that sentiment. He had booked more than fifty speeches to discuss his European journey, emphasizing the desperate food shortage there and the national self-interest of resisting Communist aggression in the Old World before it reached American shores.[68]

Herbert Klein boosted Nixon's crusade, which the congressman appreciated. This local reporter had graduated from the University of Southern California as a journalism major and served as the sports editor of the *Daily Trojan*. He went to work for the *Alhambra Post-Advocate* as a reporter, and since 1940 as a feature editor with a leave for military service, and met Nixon the green politician during the 1946 congressional campaign. They grew to become personal friends during that race and "used to have a cup of coffee at a small restaurant in Alhambra occasionally and discuss whether we should stay in politics and newspapers."[69]

Once Nixon returned to the district, Klein gave the congressman complete and sympathetic coverage. On October 29, for instance, the reporter covered Nixon's address before 250 members of the Alhambra service clubs at the YMCA "If U.S. aid is stopped in Europe, there is no question but that hundreds of people will starve and the Communists will take over." Nixon would urge Congress to provide strict supervision, but even if that occurred, a European catastrophe might erupt. If the worst did happen, Nixon still declared isolationism dead; the United States had to take an international leadership role. That was the central thrust of the congressman's message, and Klein repeated it fully.[70]

When Nixon was back in California for a second trip in November, he and Klein met for several interviews, producing a series of stories on November 11 through 19 in which they discussed the crises of each country where Nixon had stayed and even included two others (Poland and Finland) that he had not visited. If the British did not receive

American aid, Klein reported on November 11, they might turn to the Soviets. In another short article on the same day, Frank Kuest from Washington bolstered this conclusion by reporting that Congressmen Nixon and Donald Jackson from California favored the Marshall Plan to bolster Western European economies before they fell under the Communist orbit.[71]

The next Klein article depicted Nixon's trip to Germany. The Nazis had been decimated and the Third Reich obliterated. The Allies had destroyed the German will to fight, and in the process created hunger and malnutrition. Without American aid, great starvation would permeate the country. The U.S. mission was to increase German productivity, but never allow its citizenry to resurrect its war machine. Nixon was convinced that the Germans had to recover economically in order to contribute to Europe's revival. The following article focused on Italy, where Nixon had spent most of his time and where he "fell in love with that country." He warned his constituents that Italian Communists were no different from any others; they pledged their allegiance to Moscow.[72]

In the midst of these reports, Nixon addressed a near-capacity audience at Alhambra High School Auditorium on the evening of November 13, where he announced that the Herter Committee would recommend a twofold program when Congress convened for its special session on Monday, November 17. First, it would advocate aid for France, Italy, and Austria to survive the winter; and second, it would call for long-term assistance to enable European economic recovery. In order to accomplish these objectives, the committee wanted an entirely new government corporation managed by the nation's top business executives to direct foreign aid.[73]

While the committee's request for interim aid paralleled Nixon's views on French needs, his comments on his stay in Trieste dealt with brute power. The people there believed that the United States would not allow the Yugoslavs to impose their will on the citizens of that seaport. The United States must never again appease a totalitarian aggressor, "because if we do, a third world war will sweep over the globe with destruction more terrible than ever before." In his memoirs, Nixon would later observe: "One basic rule with Russians—never bluff unless you are prepared to carry through, because they will test you every time." He experienced that elemental test of strength in Trieste.[74]

Although Nixon never went to Poland or Finland, he gave his constituents his impressions of both countries from a subcommittee report on November 17. The former was behind the Iron Curtain, and the Communists were crushing any opposition and eliminating personal freedoms; the state had confiscated private property without any compensation; and the bourgeois class had vanished. Any political group that opposed the regime had been dispersed. The only major Polish institution that still survived was the Catholic Church.

Finland, as Nixon described it, was "just in front of the Iron Curtain," and had a long tradition of opposition to the Russians. The Finns were a freedom-loving people, who rejected the police state and were fiercely independent. Even though Communist sympathizers controlled the government, Nixon predicted that the voters would probably drive out the current regime in the next elections. The country had a long tradition of democracy, and the Soviet Union would never dampen that spirit.[75]

As for domestic policy, Truman gave a speech on November 17 calling for price controls. Nixon opposed these, though as president he would later succumb to the same temptation. The United States had to expand production. If Congress adopted Truman's programs, Nixon warned, "we would sabotage foreign aid completely by restricting production of the very items needed to save the economy of Europe." Within a week after Truman's speech, Nixon had already come to believe that the president would not receive the extraordinary powers he had requested.[76]

The last article in the Klein series appeared on November 19, highlighting Greece. Even though the rebels claimed to represent the peasants and workers of Greece for a more democratic regime, the congressman asserted that he had proof the guerrilla forces were being led and financed from Moscow. He conceded that the present Greek government was inefficient and in some cases reactionary, but the people preferred it to a forceful Communist putsch. Nixon called on the United Nations to guard the Greek border. If that were accomplished, Albanian and Yugoslav troops could not cross into Greece; the guerrillas, therefore, would lose in a matter of weeks. Even if that did not occur, the United States had to rebuild the Greek economy and military. That country could not fall under Communist domination, for other European countries would then be the subjects of similar conquest.[77]

Nixon spoke from conviction, but he spent only five days in Greece and heard the U.S. Embassy and local government side of the argument. An historian of American-Greek relationships during this period,

Lawrence Wittner, with the benefit of hindsight and a detailed record of events, clearly illustrated how Tito—not Stalin—supported the leftists in Greece. The United States, however, did not differentiate between the two dictators; rebellion meant Soviet expansion. In addition, Wittner pointed out that the fighting evolved from internal political strife during the war and matched a corrupt, inefficient regime against Communist and Socialist opponents. This grew into full-blown civil war, and the United States had decided to support a repressive regime that gradually became more brutal. Wittner concluded: "The result was that American policy makers, blinded by Cold War dogma, rejected important opportunities for compromise that might have ended the terrible bloodshed that engulfed Greek life."[78]

Nixon did not have the advantage of history, nor had he studied the Greek situation dispassionately. He had spent his time in Congress developing ways to stop Communist penetration in labor unions and removing subversive elements from infiltrating the American government. Now he had seen war-torn European nations and talked to desperate and poorly educated guerrillas. He combined the sum of these experiences into a crusade to halt the spread of Soviet totalitarianism into Western Europe. The United States had to participate.

Nixon's public relations push ended once Truman called a special session of Congress to debate the Marshall Plan. From November 17 until adjournment just before Christmas, Nixon worked in support of Truman's interim foreign aid bill. He fully subscribed to what Secretary Marshall said at the beginning of the debate: "Whether we like it or not, we find ourselves, our nation, in a world position of vast responsibility. We can act for our own good by acting for the world's good."[79]

Congress formed the debate as a choice between immediate relief or Communist ascendancy in Western Europe. The legislation passed by substantial majorities on December 15. Two days later, Truman signed into law an allocation of $522 million for Western Europe and another $60 million for China, which Congress insisted upon funding to fight communism in Asia.[80]

Truman also asked the special session to address inflation, with increasing pressure for controls against rising prices. Nixon felt that the Republicans had tried to submit a plan to help fight inflation and cope with high prices through the Wolcott bill, which extended controls over exports and rail transportation while also increasing Federal Reserve

Board gold reserves. Truman blocked the bill without presenting any alternative. Congress eventually sent Truman an anti-inflationary package that he reluctantly signed.[81]

Nixon's first year in office was over, and it had been an exhilarating one. He had earned only $11,458, but money did not measure the job. He enjoyed it; indeed, it almost consumed him.[82]

He was already well known on three different fronts: first, as an anti-labor advocate, with his vigorous identification with the Taft-Hartley Act; second, as a member of HUAC, making him a vocal exponent of eliminating any Communist subversion in the federal government as well as the unions; third, as an internationalist member on the Herter Committee. What made Nixon unique was his ability to articulate two apparently dissimilar themes: internationalism and anticommunism. Many anti-Communists were concerned with domestic arenas and inclined not to allocate money abroad. Many internationalists worried more over recovery from wartime destruction than over precisely which political factions came to power in Europe. Yet these two emotionally charged topics awaited a national spokesman and would command a large following.

# Chapter 7

# SHARPENING FOREIGN AND DOMESTIC PRIORITIES

By the start of 1948, the GOP was already considering its political options for the upcoming national elections. It held majorities in both houses and was instrumental in the genesis of the Marshall Plan. Republicans, along with conservative Democrats, vehemently disagreed with the administration's attachment to continuing and even expanding the New Deal's domestic programs. That friction did not seem to trouble the party, for Truman's popularity had plummeted, and the GOP optimistically looked forward to the presidential elections that November.

As for Nixon, he generally agreed with his party's positions. He was working vigorously in support of the Marshall Plan's passage, while concurrently opposing the Democratic domestic agenda. He hoped that this year would be quieter than his initiation to Capitol Hill. Despite the rush of the activities that he had experienced in his first year, he now became a seasoned veteran who had sharpened both his anti-Communist and internationalist beliefs.

When Congress opened on January 7, Truman was expected to present the State of the Union, "and Pat is going to sit in the gallery for the first time and hear him make his speech. Up until this time we have always give[n] the lone ticket which we receive to important visitors, but I felt that she should at least have the chance to see him once!" In his speech, Truman preached a passionate New Deal faith, despite its fading popularity.[1]

Even before Congress convened, Nixon devoted a considerable amount of attention to passage of the Marshall Plan. Truman had signed an interim aid bill in the winter of 1947 after Congress had passed it with large majorities. The congressman foresaw stronger opposition to long-term assistance in the current 1948 session, but expected it would become law after "very sharp debate." Emergency assistance had been based on guesses, but the new legislation needed concise estimates. The United States had to stimulate European economies and to get clearer information on conditions to avoid any thought that the American government could or should meet all deficits caused by a Western European drought and/or shortages of petroleum, fertilizers, and coal. To supervise this massive effort, Congress pressed for the establishment of a special corporate agency with tight congressional oversight that could allocate aid without weakening the national economy. Nixon, like his colleagues, vehemently opposed another executive department that the White House advocated.[2]

While Congress began to hold hearings on extending foreign aid, Nixon reported to his constituents that the "Voice of America" bill had passed in late January and received particularly strong support from Herter mission members who saw "the need for disseminating true information concerning American aid to those who are receiving aid." In addition to basic needs like food and fuel, the United States had to "support a dynamic program of information which will tell the people of Europe where the aid is coming from and our true purpose in giving it to them." To counteract Communist propaganda, the Voice of America demanded adequate funding: "In this bloodless war of words and ideologies," Nixon asserted, "we are now in a position to bring up our heaviest battalions."[3]

The day before the Communists staged a coup d'état in Czechoslovakia, Nixon addressed a radio audience on February 26, speaking from the capital, to discuss aid to Greece. The United States had already appropriated about $300 million with requests for more. Donald Jackson, his House GOP colleague from the nearby 16th congressional district in Los Angeles, told Nixon that Greece had critical strategic importance to America, for that tiny nation guarded the approaches to the Middle East and its vast oil reserves. The present Greek government favored the United States and opposed Russian penetration, which still posed a serious threat. Jackson's call for an international police force to end the region's turmoil was stymied when the Soviets vetoed it at the United Nations, allowing Communist guerrillas in the north to wreak havoc.[4]

In his newsletter, Nixon turned to the problems in East Asia. Truman's diplomacy was flawed and dangerous to American interests: "China, in the present situation, is earmarked for earlier conquest by the Communist international conspiracy than is any European country not already included among the Soviet satellites." Although Chiang Kai-shek's regime was corrupt and inefficient, "the Chinese Communists would only impose a far worse government upon the people than the one we are supporting." Nixon concluded that "our best hope of deterring Soviet Russia from pushing this struggle in Europe to a show-down war is to make sure that she does not in the meanwhile bring about the subjection of China to her rear." For these reasons, he voted in favor of the Chinese Aid Act of 1948, in which the government granted $400 million in aid, $125 million of which could be spent on military equipment.[5]

Nixon regularly spoke to his Californian audience over the radio about Communist aggression. Early in March, he addressed the subject of Eastern Europe. With Congressman Charles Kersten as a guest, they described the Soviet takeover of Czechoslovakia by infiltration. Kersten thought that the Russians had fooled Franklin Roosevelt at the Tehran and Yalta Conferences, which shaped a postwar Europe hostile to the United States; after those defeats, the United States should never again compromise with the Soviets.[6]

Both men, accompanied by an Associated Press reporter, had just visited seven Eastern European bloc embassies. The congressmen had asked each of these Soviet satellites' spokesmen about the international situation, and all had responded the same way: they condemned American policy and refrained from attacking the Russians. At the conclusion, Kersten pressed for a strong military alliance in Western Europe and called for labor-management cooperation. Nixon asked for larger allocations to the Voice of America to counter Soviet propaganda, and for more skillful training for American diplomats so that they might better answer Communist attacks.[7]

With the expansion of the Soviet Union into Eastern Europe, a crisis was emerging. Nixon and Kersten introduced a House resolution in the middle of the month to stop Red aggression by having the United States form alliances with the Western European countries. They asked Congress to "give solemn warning to the conspiracy in the Politburo that any further step of aggression, internal or external, will be actively resisted by every means at our disposal." Through strength, they felt this kind of initiative could stop World War III.[8]

Nixon and nine other colleagues chose another vehicle, chiefly as a symbolic response to Soviet vetoes in the United Nations Security Council, to work for world peace by placing their names on House Concurrent Resolution No. 170, which called for a revision of the United Nation's Charter. Under the terms of the resolution, the United States would support any effective UN action for mutual defense such as a world police force. Permanent members of the Security Council would lose their veto right in matters of aggression, first-strike weapons, and admission to the United Nations. Until these measures went into effect, however, Nixon intended to support the American initiative for an atomic development authority. He wanted an international quota on heavy armaments like warships, heavy guns, and warplanes; but in the meantime, the United States ought to continue its preparedness program.[9]

Although Nixon did not serve on any committee debating the legislation to transform the Marshall Plan into law, he considered it the most crucial matter before Congress at the start of its 1948 session. Instead of government clerks, he supported a special corporate agency where the best-trained businessmen should manage the program; loans should be granted when necessary, and gifts of food and fertilizer where needed; American labor should have representation on the board; and other auxiliary measures such as military and diplomatic assistance should dovetail with this bill.[10]

By April, Congress was finalizing the concepts of the Marshall Plan into the European Recovery Program (ERP), and the bill passed on the 3rd. Nixon reiterated the importance of mentioning free labor along with private enterprise. While serving on the Herter mission, he saw how American unions worked for democratic institutions in Europe and opposed the Communist system. Labor, therefore, had to be included in the plan: "Such evidence of American unity will have a tremendous psychological effect upon those whom we propose to aid." Truman signed the bill into law by the end of the month.[11]

Nixon advised several people to seek positions on the ERP staff, including Herman Perry, who was retiring and looking for a new job. Perry replied as an old-fashioned isolationist. The Truman administration would "just be pouring the money down a rathole to help the undeserving in Europe and tax the people in the United States to death."[12]

Despite such misgivings, global tensions accelerated passage of the ERP. During an inter-American conference in Bogotá, Colombia, violence erupted with the assassination of one of that nation's most visible opposition leaders, Jorge Gaitán. Congressman Jackson, serving as a delegate at the gathering, felt that the rioting was deliberately staged to disrupt the meeting: this was a conspiratorial event that was carefully planned, not spontaneous. Nixon agreed. The Communists had outsmarted the Americans in the western hemisphere, where U.S. prestige was "of the utmost importance to us." In the future, the United States should be prepared for such an eventuality: "Being forewarned, let us be forearmed; let us strengthen or re-build, if necessary, our intelligence forces and ferret out these plots before they are hatched."[13]

As for Western Europe, Italy appeared to have the least stable government. Just before elections on April 18, Nixon feared a Communist victory, jeopardizing ERP's success. But once the ballots were tallied, the Italian Communists lost badly, resulting in the first major Soviet defeat in Europe since the end of the war. The De Gasperi coalition had moved energetically against its foes, and the election results, Nixon declared, gave "final and convincing proof to the oft-repeated contention of democratic forces that the only way Communism can come to power is by conspiratorial seizure, or through the exercise of force and violence."[14]

Toward the end of the month, a mission of forty-eight ministers and laymen from a dozen denominations flew to the capital for three days to work for permanent world peace by constructing an international government. Many politicians greeted them, and Nixon treated several delegates to lunch in the House dining room. They agreed with his idea to strengthen the United Nations, but wished to expand his resolution into some form of global governance. While Nixon opposed this concept, dropping an A-bomb on Russia was not a viable option.[15]

One of his alternatives was the Economic Recovery Program. Americans had three main reasons for the program: humanitarian, economic, and strategic. Though the first, according to the congressman, had been overemphasized, it was vital. The United States, next, needed healthy European economies, for that improved domestic conditions by enlarging international trade. Most important, if America did not come to the assistance of Europeans, then communism would absorb the Continent and damage the long-term interests of the United States. Nixon admitted that the plan had risks and might fail, but uncertainty was acceptable in the face of catastrophe. The United States could not return to its old diplomacy of nonentanglement. Peace and democracy in Europe accentuated U.S. objectives.[16]

Nixon accepted the administration's argument to renew the Reciprocal Trade Agreements Act as another means to strengthen the democracies. Although the fight of protectionism versus free trade continued to be fierce, the congressman believed that the United States "was going to have to accept goods from other countries if we were ever going to have our debts paid off." This, of course, did not apply to his constituents. To protect his own, he objected to tariff reductions for the citrus industry. A freeze early in the year had severely damaged the crop, and for the victims of one of the coldest winters in California, the federal government had loans only if private financing was unavailable.[17]

The congressman opposed many of Truman's military proposals, especially Universal Military Training, predicting that it had a 50 percent chance of passage, and those odds gradually diminished. Several prominent advisers like Herbert Spencer and Herman Perry voiced concern because the bill diverted money from more essential military needs and interrupted the educational process from high school to college. Nixon, as a result of these kinds of comments, gave Universal Military Training a low priority. Airpower was near the top of his list.[18]

As congressman, Nixon regularly dealt with routine military matters. He, for example, selected appointees to the Naval Academy and West Point, but felt that both institutions needed a housecleaning. Early in the year, he nominated twelve appointees to the West Point, but only three would be chosen. Before Christmas 1947, he requested clemency for military prisoners' sentences for minor crimes if they were found guilty before that religious holiday. He supported a law for courts-martial for enlisted men, as well as rights and penalties for both officers and enlisted men. Far more substantial, he introduced a bill to assist the veterans' home-building program by having the Veterans Administration become a secondary market agency for private lending institutions' loans under the G.I. Bill. The federal government had to guarantee veterans loans and needed to act immediately so that veterans could have a fair opportunity to purchase homes.[19]

On the domestic front, Nixon was especially upset over White House corruption. On January 8, he condemned the Truman administration for not stopping illegal grain speculation and blamed the Justice Department for not vigorously pursuing a scandal of ballot box stuffing in Kansas City, Missouri, the home state of the president. To Nixon, such practices were unforgivable: "Corruption within the government in time of war or other emergency constitutes a national shame. But toleration of such acts and protection of those who perpetrate them is disgraceful in far greater proportions. Political expediency as a defense for failure to act is the crowning indignity."[20]

The administration and the Republicans opposed inflation, but each party had its own remedies. While Nixon voted to decrease collectable taxes of Americans by $7.1 billion, he preferred a more modest $4.5 billion reduction. The higher figure, he reasoned, would risk an unbalanced budget that would possibly endanger the national security against any potential foreign attack. He also favored tax breaks for lower-income-bracket earners in this period of high living costs, wanted a $100 increase in the exemption and the removal of six million lower-bracket taxpayers from the tax rolls, included a special $600 exemption to the aged and blind, and proposed a reduction for all brackets as an incentive for production. When Congress sent the president its bill, Truman vetoed it because it cut revenue and contributed to inflation; but the Republican majority, supported by a significant number of Democrats, overrode his veto.[21]

The administration spent excessively, Nixon argued, and private interest groups would not agree to economy measures. He had a particularly difficult time with the bloated federal civil service and hoped "to weed out all unessential personnel, particularly in the upper income brackets, and pay the remaining essential workers an adequate living wage." He was also concerned with what he considered far too many military officers who fraudulently claimed disability. Nixon was not the only frustrated congressman in this regard. To Styles Bridges, Republican senator from New Hampshire who chaired the Committee on Appropriations, "The job of trying to put the Federal government on a more economical basis is the most difficult I have undertaken."[22]

Each group lobbied to keep its advantage, making any economic concessions almost impossible. Congress even increased federal employees' retirement benefits as well as those of retired army and navy personnel. To meet current needs, Nixon advocated increased payments under the Social Security Act to millions of recipients. He claimed that only one out of ten Americans over sixty-five had an independent income sufficient "to provide the bare necessities of life." He introduced two amendments in early April to increase the amount of money a retiree could earn while receiving Social Security benefits. Currently, if a recipient earned over $15 monthly, he or she was denied benefits; Nixon's proposal increased this to $40. The average retired couple over sixty-five presently received $38, and the congressman called for a raise to $65.[23]

Although like most Republicans Nixon recoiled over the administration's social programs, he still voted for housing and education bills that failed to pass the House that session. He initially opposed the Wagner, Ellender, and Taft legislation that contained "socialized housing provisions," but stated he would support legislation that placed "emphasis upon private construction and ownership by private enterprise rather than by government." He carried over that position to his opposition to publicly owned and operated utilities. As for federal aid to education, Nixon agreed with the concept that those states lacking "sufficient taxable property to maintain minimum educational standards" should be allocated funds.[24]

The issues presented at the national level were often less complicated than one that took up quite a bit of his time in 1948: the Whittier Narrows Dam entanglement. Starting in the late 1920s, the Los Angeles County Flood Control District began studying the Whittier Narrows to propose a dam in El Monte; by 1931, its chief engineer, E. C. Eaton, had concluded that a dam was essential to provide additional water to Long Beach. In addition, Whittier came out strongly for the project. The Los Angeles Board of Supervisors, in the midst of the depression, asked for an appropriation, but no funding was forthcoming until the U.S. Army Corps of Engineers approved of the dam as part of the flood control effort. Congressman Voorhis opposed the concept in the summer of 1941, and throughout the war, nothing happened. After the war, the army engineers modified their design to take less El Monte land, but the Reverend Dan Cleveland of the Church of the Barn led the El Monte opposition, with Voorhis's active assistance. They believed that those who lived in the affected region would be deprived of their homes, and land developers would buy the lands below the dam, reaping large profits. This stalemate continued throughout 1946, even though an overwhelming majority approved of the idea.[25]

Water supply was never at stake, though the politics of water was always tricky. Seven affected states—Arizona, California, Colorado, Nevada, New Mexico, Utah, and Wyoming—had agreed in 1922 to the Colorado River Compact, a plan which apportioned river water among them. But Arizona had attempted since then to void this agreement. When Nixon learned in early April 1948 that land speculators were possibly buying acreage in the targeted region, he immediately asked the Bureau of Reclamation to release the names of those who held more than 160 acres there, alleging that "big operators have gained title to large areas of land that would be brought into cultivation should this project be constructed. . . . They have bought this land cheap and are in a position to make a killing. . . . If this is true the situation should be exposed." Nixon asserted that any expanded irrigation activity in Arizona would take precious water from Southern California, which had just gone through a severe drought during which some areas had to ration drinking water. The congressman wanted the Supreme Court to decide the case, while Arizona pleaded for a congressional resolution. The California congressional delegation vehemently opposed any legislation dealing with this topic, and Nixon pledged to investigate the rumors of land speculation.[26]

When Nixon beat Voorhis, rumors connected the new congressman with the pro-dam contingent, but he surprised everyone by announcing opposition to the project primarily because he saw it as premature and a waste of money. One reason was that he discovered a large number of Whittier residents did not like the idea. Another was that the nearby Santa Fe Dam had not been finished during the war, and he felt that the first dam should be constructed before the new project was undertaken.[27]

By early February 1947, Nixon went before the House Appropriations Subcommittee to oppose any funding because the new project required condemning 3,077 acres of land as well as 1,100 homes, displacing 4,000 people. By the middle of the month he believed that the army engineers wanted to continue with the Whittier Narrows Dam to keep a large staff on their payroll. Land speculators also were looking for benefits arising from the project. Nixon was bewildered how the administration could press for any new allocation: "Frankly, the time has come when we have to recognize that we can't have our cake and eat it too, and these people who want to cut the budget and cut taxes are simply going to have to realize that economy begins at home." Nixon himself refused. At the beginning of June, he testified against the dam, while others fought for it. Nixon called for the completion of the Santa Fe Dam first, which might make the Whittier one unnecessary. By the end of the month, the House respected the local congressman's wishes and excluded any funding for the project.[28]

This victory was short-lived. Nixon was glad that the Santa Fe Dam was approved because it would definitely improve flood control in the valley, but Senator Knowland notified him at the end of July that he would include a Whittier Narrows Dam appropriation in the next congressional session. For the remainder of the year, Nixon looked for ways to prevent construction, such as finishing the Sante Fe work and checking to see if the Whittier proposal really met flood control needs. He knew that the new dam would be difficult to prevent and shifted his emphasis to finding some compromise.[29]

In the middle of December, when Senator Knowland announced that he would propose a Whittier Narrows Dam settlement the following spring, Nixon realized that the proposal would be approved. The House Appropriations Subcommittee held hearings on the Whittier Narrows Dam at the end of January 1948. Reverend Cleveland as well as other local supporters lobbied energetically against the dam. Nixon knew that he might delay it in the House, but Knowland would push for it in the Senate. In an effort to find a solution, Nixon met with both factions throughout February and into the middle of March, when the parties found the answer by moving the site a mile and a quarter downstream from the original one. El Monte was satisfied, and the new dam, located in Pico, garnered no organized resistance. When Nixon appeared before the Senate subcommittee, Knowland complimented everyone for reaching a settlement.[30]

Nixon was pleased because the settlement was "pretty fair to all parties." He learned how to maneuver privately in order to gain his goal: "this type of behind-the-scenes work is far more effective than going out and making a speech on the floor of the House before a hall with a dozen listeners." His law partner, Tom Bewley, and another local attorney, Marshall Bowen, negotiated the final agreement, in which both sides made concessions. The Reverend Cleveland, too, was satisfied. The press praised Nixon's contribution, and he was "certainly glad to have that one behind me." By summer, Congress appropriated an initial $250,000 for the dam, and the army engineers had begun working with the local citizens to determine the best location; they also kept in contact with Nixon's office for the remainder of the year in various issues involving flood control and conservation.[31]

During this tense bargaining, Nixon had proven himself a man of moderate views, principled dealings, and hard work. While he did not win national recognition for his negotiations over the Whittier Narrows Dam, a successful conclusion was essential for his prestige at home. He demonstrated similar attributes in dealing with domestic issues at the national level. His growing reputation for prudence and fairness possibly led to his surprise appointment to the Herter Committee, and he made the most of the occasion, which pushed him into the vanguard of the Marshall Plan's enactment. Nixon's greater claim to fame arose out of his legislative duties and also emerged accidentally, but when presented with an opportunity to appear in the spotlight, he welcomed it.

His overwhelming focus in the first congressional session of 1948 centered on his HUAC assignment. By chance, the committee's chairman, J. Parnell Thomas, had been stricken ill on a cruise to Panama late in January. Soon he had to be removed from the SS *Ancon* on a stretcher with a gastrointestinal hemorrhage and flown to Margarita Hospital in critical condition. After being medically stabilized, he was flown back to the capital and admitted to Walter Reed Hospital for immediate emergency treatment.[32]

Thomas's absence moved Karl Mundt of South Dakota from vice chairman to acting chairman, giving Mundt additional prestige during his primary campaign for the Senate. Nixon, too, became a more visible, dynamic member of the committee's majority, with the appointment as chairman of the HUAC subcommittee on proposing legislation to curb or control the U.S. Communist Party. Even before his selection, he was already considering the question of whether the party was an American political party or an agent of the Soviet Union. By the new year, he felt that Congress had a responsibility to investigate the possibility that the party was "engaged in a treasonable conspiracy to overthrow the government of the United States," and dismissed the notion that party membership involved only "religious, social or political opinion."[33]

His subcommittee included two Republicans, Richard Vail of Illinois and J. Hurdin Peterson of Florida, and one Democrat, F. Edward Hébert of Louisiana. They would commence hearings on February 5 for about two weeks in the Old House Office Building in Room 225 with Attorney General Thomas Clark as the first witness. Although public opinion, Nixon believed, wanted the Communist Party outlawed, he realized that this presented difficult constitutional issues. The committee had already heard J. Edgar Hoover's opposition to this idea, and Nixon— for all of HUAC's rigidity—professed an open mind.[34]

Nixon wrote many prominent individuals about sharing their ideas before his committee. Adolf Berle, an original Brain Truster in the New Deal and well-known New York attorney, appeared, objecting to outlawing the party as "unnecessary and ineffective." Its members would not register as part of their civil rights. Morris Ernst, another New York lawyer, who disapproved of HUAC procedures during the Hollywood hearings, thought that the committee had "taken quite a beating in the public press and elsewhere" and "much of it is justified." He too concurred with Berle, but reasoned that such legislation would drive the party underground. John Foster Dulles, a prominent New York attorney and the most influential Republican on American foreign policy, saw difficulties with any bill because the Communist Party was "such a nebulous thing." Some members served under "iron discipline" and were foreign agents, while others viewed the party as an agent of reform and held that this group acted as an outlet for grievances. Finally, Eugene Lyons, presently residing in New York City, who served as a former United Press correspondent in the Soviet Union, was convinced that the party was an agent of Russia. Moscow ran the American branch, and he called for its abrogation.[35]

Congressmen had already offered four different types of bills that would curb or outlaw the Communist Party or register it as a foreign agent, as in the case of the Mundt bill. Nixon pledged "to conduct full and fair hearings." The committee gave "the Communists and other subversive groups their most effective ammunition when we adopt[ed] the same arbitrary methods in dealing with opposition political groups for which we criticise [sic] them in the countries which they now dominate."[36]

With this promise, Nixon spoke before the House on February 3, announcing that HUAC had declared that the Communist Party was an agent of the Soviet Union. Since the party was conspiring to overthrow the American government, he agreed it was a danger to the country. He was considering legislating against the party and was looking for different opinions about possible legislation.[37]

The subcommittee convened on Thursday morning, February 5. Nixon set the tone by asking the subcommittee to determine three things: whether the Communist Party or American Communists constituted a real threat to national security; whether the present laws were adequate to deal with the situation; and finally, whether the adoption of any new law would impair fundamental constitutional rights. Mundt was the first sworn witness. His bill not only called for the party to register as a foreign agent but also for all of its literature to be clearly labeled.[38]

Over the next five days, the subcommittee heard from a wide range of witnesses who agreed with many of Mundt's goals, but cautioned that his proposal raised serious constitutional questions. Some were concerned about individual rights and Communists; others were worried about Soviet expansion and foreign infiltration. The American Legion and the Veterans of Foreign Wars pressed to outlaw the party. When Arthur Garfield Hays, attorney for the American Civil Liberties Union (ACLU), testified, Nixon commented that his board of directors had taken action against Communists on its board, but the ACLU objected to Congress taking a similar measure on the national level. Laughter erupted in the hall, while Nixon and Hays parried about the need for legislation. Hays did not see any real threat, but the congressman vigorously dissented. Throughout the proceedings, Nixon argued that "we must be equally vigilant against the dangers of Fascism and Communism alike," but currently, Congress had "to train the heavy artillery on Communism, because that is the evil of the moment."[39]

On his way to his office on Wednesday morning, February 11, he left his apartment for his car, parked by the curb of his apartment. After walking down three or four ice-covered steps with Tricia in his arms, he slipped and landed on his back and elbows, saving his daughter from injury. Pat phoned Bill Arnold, who lived around the corner, to take Dick, who was in great pain, to Bethesda Naval Hospital for treatment. Upon arrival, three or four sailors had to hold him still under the X ray, with good cause: Nixon had suffered a triple fracture to the left elbow, which would remain in a cast for two to three weeks, and a simple fracture to the right one. His naval doctor manipulated everything into place without surgery or permanent damage.[40]

Nixon returned to his office seven days later with instructions not to overexert himself. Only the left elbow was in a cast, so he could sign letters with his right hand. By the beginning of March, he felt much improved and was catching up on his mail. On the 4th, he went out to Bethesda and had the cast taken off his left arm.[41]

Nixon missed the hearings on February 11 at which Representative Rankin disrupted Berle's testimony by complaining that the Justice Department harassed white Mississippians for allegedly treating African Americans unkindly. During the last two days on February 19 and 20, Nixon did not allow a recurrence of this reprehensible conduct. This time, Nixon concentrated on card-carrying Communists and how to strip the secrecy that surrounded them. On the final day, Benjamin Davis, an African American member of the New York City Council and also of the national committee of the Communist Party, spoke against any bill restricting or outlawing his party. It was the last word of the hearings.[42]

But these hearings might have had a far greater significance to Nixon's relationship with the FBI. Robert Stripling, HUAC's chief investigator, phoned Louis B. Nichols and asked him to check the FBI files for any background on Davis, like his criminal record, aliases, or false use of passports that Stripling could use "as an ace in the hole" for the committee to "throw at him," if necessary.[43]

Nichols, who was the bureau's third most powerful official and was head of Hoover's Crime Records division that served as its vast public relations liaison to the media and the Congress, made no commitment, but told Stripling that he Nichols would see "if anything could be done." Internally, Nichols wrote Clyde A. Tolson, Hoover's closest confidante, that "we should go through the motions at least and the Security Division should prepare as soon as possible a blind memorandum of public source material which can be furnished to Stripling." While the FBI memo did not specifically refer to Nixon, he did serve as the subcommittee's chairman; he and Nichols later became close friends. This committee's efforts might have been the first time that Nixon had directly or indirectly asked the FBI for its assistance in furthering his own HUAC inquiry.[44]

The two most distinguished books on HUAC reflect well on Nixon. Robert Carr reviewed the hearings in 1952 and concluded that they were conducted well, with the exception of Rankin's shameful performance. Generally, "the printed record of these hearings contains many intelligent and penetrating comments on legislation to curb the Communist Party." Sixteen years later, Walter Goodman asserted that Nixon had handled the questioning in a professional manner, which was "several cuts above what the Committee's recent performances had given reason to expect."[45]

Unfortunately for HUAC, this standard did not apply to Chairman Thomas's investigation of Edward Condon. They first clashed at the end of World War II over military versus civilian control of atomic energy and the A-bomb program. Henry Wallace had strongly recommended Condon for the Manhattan Project at Los Alamos, New Mexico, and he worked there during the war. After the German surrender, he applied to visit Russia, but the army blocked that request because of some linkage of Condon to Communists and fellow travelers. During the spring of

1946, Thomas, as the fifth ranking Republican on the House Military Affairs Committee, considered legislation dealing with atomic energy to be the most crucial ever to come before Congress, and urged the placement of atomic energy in a panel of a joint military-civilian board with the armed forces holding a majority; his second choice was an all-military body. If a civilian commission held power, it would be "packed with leftists." Condon, from his position in the federal bureaucracy, argued for civilian control, and Thomas never forgot this opposition.[46]

The HUAC chairman found an opportunity to resurrect his antipathy toward Condon in the spring of 1947, when the Commerce Department implemented a loyalty check and requested an FBI report on Condon since he had been appointed director of the National Bureau of Standards, which supervised all atomic scientists and technicians employed by that division. Thomas, in early July, declared that Condon would be subpoenaed before HUAC to learn about his connections to the American-Soviet Science Society (ASSS). Condon replied that he would be glad to cooperate and would appear without subpoena. He had already opened his ASSS file to HUAC staff members, and the Rockefeller Foundation that sponsored the society would furnish additional material if requested. HUAC contended that the U.S. Attorney General had placed the ASSS a subversive organization list, but the committee garbled Condon's ASSS membership to facilitate exchanges with the Russians with another group on the Attorney General's subversive list.[47]

After an initial improvement, Thomas relapsed and was admitted to Bethesda Naval Hospital for observation and further treatment early in 1948. While confined there, he received espionage reports, and dressed in bathrobe and pajamas, with Vail and Wood in attendance, chaired many secret sessions of a HUAC subcommittee centering on Condon. On March 1, 1948, it published six and a half pages of findings on national security, asserting that Condon was "one of the weakest links in our atomic security." The subcommittee released its report without ever calling him to testify, and rumors circulated that Thomas had deliberately smeared Condon for his refusal to support the military's control of atomic energy. Despite these allegations, Thomas would never bring Condon before HUAC to testify.[48]

The furor over the Condon affair heightened when the *Washington Post* published sections of the letter from J. Edgar Hoover to Secretary of Commerce Averell Harriman. On March 5, Nixon wrote the secretary demanding the release of the letter to HUAC because serious charges had been alleged. Harriman refused and criticized the committee for being "un-American." President Truman added to this emotionally charged situation by issuing an executive order on March 13 to heads of federal agencies and departments not to turn over any files to anyone. Some questioned Nixon why this report was made public without any hearings. Morris Ernst, who testified before Nixon's subcommittee, wrote the congressman: "Even Adam and Eve got a hearing before they were thrown out of the Garden." Nixon replied that Ernst was right.[49]

Nixon, in the middle of March, pressed for HUAC hearings on this matter that would feature the Harriman-Hoover exchange of May 15, 1947. The congressman told a friend that he did not want to criticize Thomas, who was confined to bed, but "I have consistently opposed the issuance of reports concerning individuals or groups unless those reports are based on hearings at which the parties concerned are given an opportunity to present testimony in their own behalf." Many educators had vehemently reacted to the chairman's excesses, and Nixon had made a motion to conduct full hearings within the next two weeks. He was neutral, and if Condon were innocent, "I shall publicly so state my conviction and do everything that I can to see that the injustice to Dr. Condon is remedied from the standpoint of making the public aware of my position." He pledged that anyone coming before HUAC would "receive fair and just treatment."[50]

Nixon admitted that he had a difficult time changing HUAC procedures. He had four colleagues who had agreed to changes, but needed one more "to swing the deal." He hoped to make these alterations before Condon came before the committee because "the eyes of the country will be on the committee at that time." Unfortunately for all concerned, the April 21 hearings were canceled without any reason being given.[51]

Instead, Hannah Nixon, who was visiting for several days toward the end of April, watched her son from the House gallery for the first time debate a House resolution, which directed the secretary of commerce to submit the FBI loyalty report on Condon to the House. He argued that whether Condon was or was not loyal was not germane. What was crucial was that the FBI had written a report suggesting he was a security risk that was the basis for the HUAC subcommittee findings. Nixon argued for the release of the entire letter. The House voted 399–29 in favor, but nothing forced Truman to release it, so the president cavalierly ignored the resolution.[52]

Far more critical to Nixon than the Condon affair was the Subversive Activities Control bill of 1948, also known as the Mundt-Nixon bill, the result of his subcommittee hearings. During a radio broadcast to his California constituents in late March, the congressman declared that this bill had just been introduced in the House by his HUAC subcommittee. Experts on communism and constitutional rights had been heard, and most agreed that legislation was needed because the Communist Party had grown into a massive fifth-column movement whose members had to be prosecuted before it was ready to attack. America, Nixon declared, had never confronted such a nefarious challenge; the Communist Party was a bridgehead for the Soviet Union. The proposal had four major specifics: symbolically, it noted that anyone who wanted to establish a totalitarian government in the United States under a foreign power was guilty of a crime; more to the point, the party and its related organizations had to register with the U.S. Attorney General; federal employees could not belong to it and could not knowingly hire its members; and the U.S. government would deny passports to its members. This was his method of removing the cloak of secrecy surrounding Communist-front organizations. Judicial review, he told his constituents, would protect individual rights.[53]

Throughout the first part of 1948, Nixon dealt with a myriad of foreign and domestic issues, but the one that seemed to compress most of these topics into a central theme was the Mundt-Nixon legislation. Certainly, many volatile questions had nothing to do with it, and other actions like Thomas's fixation with Condon blurred the dominant themes. But from the larger view, Nixon concentrated on his anti-Communist orientation, which now included opposition to the expansion of worldwide communism and its spread to American shores. In effect, he reflected the opinions of a significant portion of American society that was anxious about the growing Red menace.

Few doubted that the Russians directed the U.S. Communist Party. Although its membership was small, the party received a disproportionate amount of attention due to the anti-Communist feeling prevalent in the United States. Open registration of card-carrying Communists to many seemed fair and appropriate since a foreign regime, the Soviet Union, was directing their operations. A minority objected to singling out any political party because that violated the Bill of Rights. This fundamental constitutional distinction rose above the argument of protecting the nation from domestic subversion. HUAC's advocacy of

Mundt-Nixon brought two competing forces to the forefront. The committee advanced the practical; opponents summoned up images of the founding fathers' principles. Each side had powerful arguments in support of its cause.

Nixon preached the crusade against communism, and to many that instantly made him an opponent of civil liberties. That position was incorrect. He was not arguing to abolish the Bill of Rights, but was advocating a method to protect national security. But this was a war in which those who emotionally followed one side or the other gave no quarter. Nixon became a permanent casualty in this struggle.

By symbolizing all that was beneficial under the Mundt-Nixon bill, he came to personify all that was evil. Many historians who have examined the legislation from that simplified perspective, have missed the limited nature of the legislation and concentrated on HUAC excesses. As a natural corollary, Nixon emerged as an irrational member when nothing could be further from the truth. In many ways, he was the voice of moderation during a period of massive shouting against the Red peril.

Chairman Thomas returned to HUAC from his most recent illness in the first week of April to preside over the meeting to recommend the introduction of the Mundt-Nixon bill to the House for its consideration. HUAC dismissed outlawing the party and the philosophical study of communism, but the committee did encourage states to enact similar bills and educate its citizens about the evils of communism. In summation and with unanimity: "We are seeking rather to strike a body blow at the American cadre of the Soviet-directed Communist conspiracy."[54]

Nixon worried that HUAC's own inherent weaknesses would inhibit the passage of Mundt-Nixon: "it isn't what the committee does but the way that it does it that gets it in 'Dutch.'" He still pushed forward in his presentation and repeated that his bill was not to outlaw the party or communist theory. The party could "operate as a legitimate American political party above ground and without foreign connections." But if it tried to establish a totalitarian regime here, that would be a crime. Added hope for moderation came from an announcement in early May that Thomas had gone back to Walter Reed Hospital still suffering from his stomach ailment and would remain there for some period of time. Nixon now predicted passage by a four-to-one ratio.[55]

The Communist Party started its own campaign against Mundt-Nixon by writing Congress that the bill was unconstitutional and would nullify the Bill of Rights. Specific laws already dealt with criminal activities like conspiracy, espionage, and sabotage, and no party member had ever been convicted in federal court of advocating any of the above actions. If the bill became law, the party would not register under it and expose its members to police persecution and blacklisting. The U.S. Communist Party was the party of the American worker and promised to continue its mission.[56]

Thomas's sickness once more changed Nixon's role in passage of the bill. By May 8, the chairman designated Nixon the House floor leader for the upcoming debate. This was quite an honor, even though Nixon knew "the left-wingers will be making me a target during the next couple of weeks."[57]

The price he paid was even more than he bargained, for HUAC released a report on the Communist Party and how it advocated the overthrow of the government using force and violence. Russia, the committee reasserted, controlled the party, which had seventy-five thousand American members and far more fellow travelers. They were relatively small in number, but had gained a disproportionate amount of power. During the congressional debate, Communists were not idle bystanders; they wrote passionate letters and sent large numbers of postcards. Some communications claimed Nixon's techniques were similar to those used by Hitler and Stalin. The *People's World* in mid-May asserted: "The fight against the Mundt-Nixon Bill is the first line of defense of American democracy! It must receive priority as the single most important task facing the labor and progressive movement today." The newspaper issued a call for action by holding emergency meetings of every party club within a day or two, distributing leaflets, sending letters to unions, having open-air gatherings, and fighting the bill in every way possible.[58]

The party received assistance from unexpected quarters. Truman told a news conference on May 15 of his opposition to any measure outlawing the Communist Party because the present laws were adequate to prosecute subversive activities. Mayor William O'Dwyer of New York City, a Catholic and war veteran, opposed communism but objected to Mundt-Nixon because it violated the freedom "to discuss and criticize, freely and openly." The bill was too broad and vague; it established "guilt by mere association, without proof of actual guilt and without the safeguard of a jury trial."[59]

The tone of some letters went beyond vicious. A Texas lawyer in

Fort Worth condemned Nixon for attempting, under the guise of curbing communism, to establish a Hitlerite regime in the United States. He was perverting the Constitution and the Bill of Rights: "Millions, like me, already hate you without even knowing you. Most of us have reasons to be proud of California, and I apologize for the good state [sic] for your presence in Congress."[60]

Nixon realized that Communists were "waging a great propaganda campaign against it [Mundt-Nixon] and are completely distorting the facts as to what it would do." He felt that the bill had "adopted a fair and sane program without going overboard in our attempt to deal with the Communist problem."[61] He never seemed to comprehend the depth and visceral feelings of his adversaries.

Influential leaders reinforced Nixon's beliefs that he had acted properly. From the Democratic side, Attorney General Thomas Clark wrote him on May 11: "I appreciate seeing the bill in its final form and was glad to assist in any way possible during its creation." Republican John Foster Dulles added that the bill was "a praiseworthy attempt to deal honestly and in the American tradition with a very difficult and confused situation." Morris Ernst had misgivings about singling out the Communist Party, but admitted that Nixon's hearings "were as sober and deliberate as any hearings run by Congress in decades." Not unexpectedly, Charles Sullivan, Jr., chairman of the Veterans of Foreign Wars, favored the legislation as "a sensible and fair approach to the perplexing problem that now prevails."[62]

Nixon spoke before the House on May 14 as a prelude to presenting the bill for consideration, announcing that he was "trying to get away from that kind of loose listing of subversive organizations." The bill carefully defined them so that the Attorney General would enact careful procedures to identify Communists. "Member after Member has expressed the fear," Nixon argued, "that this bill strikes at all progressive organizations, that it would protect strikes, smash labor unions, and destroy all liberal groups." This was a false characterization. The legislation identified and controlled those organizations solely under the direction of a foreign Communist government.[63]

Nixon paid attention to John Foster Dulles's advice and wrote him on May 17, informing him that HUAC had accepted an amendment clarifying the administrative procedures to be held before the U.S. Attorney General that was a tremendous improvement over the Justice Department's current ex parte measures. The new ones guaranteed public hearings and the right to cross-examine witnesses. Court review would be based on preponderance of evidence instead of substantial evidence. The bill was scheduled for House debate the next day. Many members wanted a tougher bill, but Nixon had an agreement within HUAC to "resist all such amendments because I feel strongly that this legislation goes as far as we should at this time in meeting the danger." Under present conditions, he thought that Mundt-Nixon would pass with a five-to-one majority.[64]

On the evening of May 19, after a day of debate, Nixon gave the opening statement over a nationwide radio broadcast on the Town Meeting of the Air, sponsored by the ABC network, whose discussion centered on the question "How Should Democracy Deal with Groups Which Aim to Destroy Democracy?" The United States had to act against subversion, and "the liberal who wants to tolerate everything will wake up some day to find that he himself is not being tolerated, but liquidated." He defended Mundt-Nixon's provisions and declared that these would enhance the Attorney General's arsenal in the battle against Communist penetration. He also reasoned that since the United States had appropriated billions to fight Russian expansion abroad, the same rationale should apply at home. Although the three other panelists were lukewarm or hostile to the bill, Nixon had an advantage over Judge Thurman Arnold, who "had too many cocktails before dinner!" Senator Robert Taft and Ralph McGill also participated. Reflecting on his role, Nixon commented that it "was a pretty exciting evening for me going up against an array of big shots." After the broadcast, no one called in with negative comments, while many complimented him. Congressman Alfred Bulwinkle, Democrat from North Carolina, for example, called to say that he had done a "wonderful job." Senator Richard Russell, Democrat from Georgia, commented that the bill was "a mighty good one" and the congressman gave a "wonderful performance."[65]

The following day, Nixon assumed his first-time role handling a floor measure. He denied that the bill interfered with constitutional rights or that it was designed for political advantage in the upcoming presidential election: "No Member of this House," Nixon asserted, "who honestly wants to do something about the Communist menace in the United States, can with good conscience vote against this bill."[66]

Vito Marcantonio managed the opposition, comparing the bill to

"Hitler's edicts." Born in New York City in 1902, Marcantonio served in the House in 1934–36 and returned from 1938 until 1950. His support came from the Italian and Puerto Rican tenement dwellers of East Harlem. A Roman Catholic who wore a crucifix around his neck, one biographer has characterized him as "motivated by Christian morals—a kind of American exponent of Christian Socialism." He was a leading advocate of the deprived and later became state chairman of the American Labor Party (ALP). Disavowing that he was a Communist, Marcantonio neither made many pro-Soviet statements nor uttered an anti-Russian word. He battled against the majority opinion on just about every issue in the 80th Congress. He opposed the hostility to Russia expressed in the Truman Doctrine and the Marshall Plan. In the domestic realm, he voted against Taft-Hartley and fought contempt citations issued by HUAC; he favored civil rights and price controls. As for the Mundt-Nixon bill, it horrified him because he felt that the broad, vague wording violated Bill of Rights' guarantees.[67]

Helen Gahagan Douglas joined with Marcantonio in opposing Mundt-Nixon. One of seven women in Congress, she and Mary Teresa Norton, Democrat from New Jersey, fought against the bill, following the president's wishes. Douglas bitterly declared that the bill would create a hundred Communists for each one jailed. She conceded that the bill would pass the House, but the Senate would kill it.[68]

When the House voted on May 21, Douglas's prediction proved to be an understatement, reflected by a lopsided victory of 319 to 58, without any serious modifications in the one-day-long debate. Eight Republicans joined with forty-eight Democrats in opposing the legislation.[69]

Karl Mundt had flown from Sioux Falls, South Dakota, on the morning of May 19 to help direct floor strategy for his bill. Now that the Lusk-Campbell-Mundt-Nixon bill passed the House by a substantial margin, Mundt was willing to share in "a great victory" and would not protest "the inclusion of Nixon to our sacred circle!"[70]

Not everyone was satisfied. The *New York Times* editorialized that while Communists threatened international peace, the Mundt-Nixon bill did not clearly define its provision and the courts ultimately would have to interpret the meaning of the legislation. The newspaper urged the Senate to clarify the bill and not allow anyone to control American political beliefs: "But the country can properly seek, and the Constitution surely would not deny, proper and adequate safeguards against intervention in American politics by agents of a foreign Power." Others felt irrepressible, fundamental misgivings. D. F. Bulwert, a lifelong Republican from Rochester, New York, wrote Nixon that he was repudiating his party affiliation. "You and the Republican Party," he vented to Nixon, "are nothing but an un-American crew of Fascist bastards bent upon ruining the last free country in the world." His proposal would "Hitlerize America using a few thousand measly Reds as an excuse."[71]

The Senate came to the assistance of those who disapproved of Mundt-Nixon. While the GOP Senate majority leader, Kenneth Wherry from Nebraska, called for a vote before adjournment in four weeks, other Republicans delayed. When hearings were conducted at the end of May, William Foster, national chairman of the Communist Party, charged that the Mundt-Nixon bill had railroaded police state measures through Congress without substantial hearings; he wanted more than just the three days allocated by the Senate. Henry Wallace flew in to testify against the bill and asserted that his third party would never register; this was a kind of Nazi legislation. Claude Pepper, Democrat from Florida, announced that if the bill reached the Senate floor, he would vote against it.[72]

That never happened. The Senate never took any action. The Mundt-Nixon bill died. But Nixon's anticommunism only grew in the process.

*Chapter* 8

# RUNNING FOR REELECTION

N ixon had worked tirelessly throughout his first year in office to build a positive record, not taking reelection for granted. The massive GOP victories in the class of '46 were pleasant, but unexpected. Although his initial race had been exhausting and trying, he needed favorable ratings in order to carve out a safe House seat for himself. Even though his followers energetically supported him, Nixon had no assurances at the start of 1948 that he would win in a cakewalk. His positions on anticommunism and internationalism were popular at home, but he still had to defend them. While he popularized his political positions, he also discouraged Republican challengers from entering the upcoming primary by planning to announce early.[1]

Even cakewalks took time and money. During the first half of 1947, Nixon's campaign committee spent just under $1,900 on expenses, and their coffers were low. Harold Lutz, who served as Herman Perry's assistant at the Bank of America, and others were preparing to start raising money for the upcoming election. Roy McLaughlin, the district's standard-bearer in 1944, praised Nixon's efforts on behalf of the Taft-Hartley Act and assured him that the Fact Finding Committee would energetically back him in the next election so that he could fight against the labor law's repeal. McLaughlin almost immediately solicited district contributors to give $10 or more to the next race, and he also contacted the Republican National Committee for money to promote Nixon's reelection.[2]

Jerry Voorhis had not announced whether he would run against

Nixon, but the latter knew that organized labor would support his former opponent. Nixon hoped to counter the unions with an appeal to
veterans. They had not cast a significant number of their votes for him in
1946, and Nixon expected to do better in 1948. He had advanced a considerable amount of his own money in 1946 and hoped that this one
would cost thousands of dollars less than his first campaign.[3]

To prepare further, William Arnold opened a district congressional
office at the Alhambra Post Office on Monday, September 29, on the
theory that Nixon had a strong base and now should reach out to voters
across the spectrum. Arnold was to try to improve relations with labor
and veteran groups, segments of the population in which the congressman had demonstrated weakness in the 1946 balloting. The presidential
contest with its emphasis on national issues would draw funds from local
contests; therefore, he had to appeal directly to voters on issues that
would specifically appeal to them.[4]

From his capital office, he formed a campaign committee of his
closest advisers. Frank Jorgensen, along with Roy Day and Lutz, were
appointed to a districtwide finance body and began raising money by the
end of October. Arthur Kruse returned as treasurer, and Harrison Mc-
Call, campaign manager for the 1946 general election, served as a liaison
with the national, state, and local Republican organizations. Day had
spoken to many Republicans, who were generally impressed with
Nixon's work. As a result, he hoped to eliminate any competitor who
considered running. In a December letter asking for donations of from
ten to a hundred dollars for the June primary, Day reminded his readers
that Nixon had assisted in structuring enlightened labor reform and had
gone on the Herter mission: "From a political unknown, with your support, he emerged as a winning candidate from our district and again with
your support we will elect him in the primary."[5]

Nixon, as in his first race, would cross-file on both the Democratic
and Republican ballots, and some of his advisers like Perry wanted to
make a "supreme effort" to win both and end all speculation early. Day
agreed, but he warned that an early triumph depended on the opponent
and on available funds. He suggested $5,000 as the fund-raising goal for
his district. He also warned that "radical labor leaders, members of the
Communist party, and Communist front organizations are going all out
to 'get' Nixon. They *have* the money and will *spend* it."[6]

To assist personally in the planning, although complaining about the expense of the trip, Nixon decided to make a rush visit to California by himself, but he cautioned his advisers that he did not want any publicity, would not make any speeches or public appearances, and wanted only his closest advisers to know about the trip. Arriving in Los Angeles on Monday morning, December 29, he remained until January 2, 1948, planning campaign strategy and trying unsuccessfully to convince George Savage, publisher of the *South Pasadena Review,* to become campaign manager. A "bull session" with friendly newspapermen Herbert Klein and Frank Kuest followed later.[7] He stayed in the district for one of the best New Year's Eve parties he had ever attended. On New Year's Day, he accepted the Tournament of Roses committee invitation to sit in the official box for the Rose Bowl Game.[8]

Even with a primary-only strategy, financial needs mounted. Meeting on Thursday evenings at Jorgensen's home in San Marino, the finance committee decided to set $10,000 as a goal for the primaries even without a serious challenger. By the end of January, no Democratic challenger had announced; but someone surely would. Nixon expected Jerry Voorhis to challenge him, never knowing that the former congressman had decided at the end of 1946 against running in 1948. Voorhis had applied for the position of executive secretary of the Cooperative League of the United States and started there on April 1, 1947. His father, Charles, who managed his political campaigns, strongly urged him to stay out of politics.[9]

Although Nixon felt that the best opponent the Democrats could select to challenge him would be a disabled veteran, Voorhis was the most obvious adversary. Right after his defeat, according to Nixon, Voorhis had asserted that he "was going to get revenge next time." On a trip to El Monte that summer, he claimed that more houses were built during wartime than were presently being constructed. Nixon labeled this "a wild statement," for in the last two months the United States "built more houses than in any similar period in twenty years," but Nixon worried that Voorhis was "sending up trial balloons for the next election."[10]

A publicity break brightened Nixon's rising star. The U.S. Junior Chamber of Commerce on January 21, 1948, selected him one of the nation's Ten Outstanding Young Men of 1947. The chapter in Pomona had honored him with its Good Government Award in front of five hundred dinner guests at the end of 1947. That local chapter then nominated him for national recognition, where he was selected as a recipient and given the award at the Read House Ballroom in Chattanooga, Tennessee.[11]

Nixon appointed McCall the campaign manager to coordinate both the Republican and Democratic filings. Nixon also expected McCall to make the formal announcement launching his reelection bid because the congressman liked "the idea of having it appear that the people in the district are carrying the ball and are going to run the campaign."[12]

Nixon also demanded that Charlie Bowen's company, Lockwood & Shackelford, handle advertisements as it had done two years earlier. He was certain that Charlie would be hired, but if there were negotiation difficulties, Nixon told Bowen to let him know, "because I am most anxious that you do the job, and if pressure has to be put on from here I intend to put it on." The finance committee bowed to Nixon's insistence and Bowen's knowledge of the district. Nixon had "a deep sense of obligation to the editors and publishers who have done so much for us in the past." While some enthusiastically had publicized his congressional activities, Nixon realized that additional coverage would be proportional to the amount of money these newspapers received for campaign advertising. Costs continued to climb. The finance group now projected $10,000 for advertising on the assumption that Voorhis would not run and that another $5,000 would be assigned to the campaign manager, his staff, and headquarters. The group had already raised $5,000.[13]

Throughout February the committee looked for signs of the Democratic opposition. Day had heard that someone would shortly be named from Claremont. Toward the end of the month, he predicted that Charlotte Nealy, an attorney from that town, might run with backing from the CIO-PAC, and from John Vieg, a professor of government at Claremont College as well as chairman of the local Americans for Democratic Action (ADA) chapter. Day commented: "She is a capable woman, but should get exactly nowhere with you." Democratic leaders also approached Colonel James De La Vergne of the Veterans Center in Alhambra to run against Nixon without realizing the colonel was a Republican loyalist.[14]

Late in 1947, Nixon had identified Jesse B. Blue, Jr., the son of a realtor and appraiser from Rosemead, who also worked in his father's business, to become a leader in the Democrats for Nixon Committee. "JB" avidly backed Nixon, pledging to help in whatever way possible. Still a registered Democrat, he maintained that status and eventually emerged as the chairman of Democrats for Nixon. Besides Blue, Nixon added Leland Poage of Azusa, a farmer who staunchly supported him, and Reverend Dan Cleveland in El Monte to the membership; each Democratic sponsor needed to be "personally approached so that we can make sure of their loyalty before having them go on our list." Nixon was arranging for some of them to sign his filing papers and intended to issue a press release with their names.[15]

In addition, the campaign committee was working on religious leaders in the Mormon and Catholic Churches to announce for his reelection. The candidate also received welcome news from the recent change in editorship at the *San Gabriel Sun*. Bob Young, the new owner, told him that the paper was going to endorse his reelection.[16]

Throughout the first three weeks of March, the campaign committee continued to speculate on possible Democratic opponents. Henry Wallace had split with Truman at the end of 1947, forming his own third party, and the disaffected Wallace wing might field someone, resulting in a three-person contest. If that occurred, Nixon had no chance of winning the Democratic primary, and therefore the better strategy might be to keep this three-way race up to the general election, dividing the Democratic vote. Perry disagreed. With Voorhis's absence, Perry was "sure that we can take both nominations in June."[17] With six days remaining before the filing deadline, no Democrat had taken out papers by March 22, and that party appeared fractured by the split with the Wallace supporters.[18]

Roy Day could not have been more delighted. Recalling the 1946 campaign, he looked at an autographed picture of Nixon in his office and asserted that campaign had been launched "With what appeared to be a lost cause and ended up with a winner." Day predicted that an unknown might file at the last moment, but that illustrated how desperate the Democrats were. Day hoped that no one would file, and Nixon could "go over and help kick the hell out of Helen Gahagan [Douglas]????"[19]

Day's wish ended on March 23 when Stephen Zetterberg announced that he would file on the Democratic ballot. Zetterberg had been appointed to a Democratic committee to persuade Voorhis to run again, without success. Zetterberg, who had some political experience on the Claremont planning commission, out of sheer desperation allowed his name to be placed on the ballot. Born in Galesburg, Illinois, on August 2, 1916, of Swedish ancestry, he moved to Claremont, attended the local high school, graduated from Pomona College with honors in government, and graduated from Yale Law School in 1942. During World War II, he served in the Coast Guard as a gunnery officer and executive officer on a cutter. After being released from sea duty, he became a legislative assistant to Senator Scott Lucas, Democrat from Illinois, and then returned to California, assisting in Voorhis's failed 1946 reelection bid.[20]

After that defeat, he helped establish the law firm of Carter, Young & Zetterberg. By the time of the 1948 primary, he and his wife Connie had three young sons. Under the best of conditions, he faced severe difficulties, but his legal commitments made matters worse because they prevented him from doing any active campaigning until mid-April; in actuality, he did not even start then, devoting just one month to his political drive. As a matter of principle, the thirty-two-year-old attorney only filed a Democratic petition. A local party leader and head of Americans for Democratic Action, Professor Vieg at Claremont College, promoted his candidacy.[21]

Next, Margaret Porter, an attorney and a registered Democrat from Sierra Madre, had placed her name on the Democratic ballot and on the Independent Progressive Party's (IPP) banner of third-party candidate Henry Wallace. J. B. Blue did not want Nixon to attack labeled "left-wingers." Democrats should throw "mud" at them, and he anticipated assisting those people who were designated to carry out that negative program. Blue was even willing to have his name used "on anything short of libel after I have checked it." After all, he was a registered Democrat who was "100% against anything that looks or smells like Truman or Wallace."[22]

Nixon appreciated Blue's zealousness. He now had a strong nucleus of Democratic supporters in the district, and he believed that they realized that both Zetterberg and Porter on the ballot followed "the left-wing line." Perhaps this was just as good as having no opposition.[23]

On the Republican ballot, in fact, he had no opponents. On the Democratic side, he was listed first and designated "Member of Congress," while Porter and Zetterberg rotated from second to third place from precinct to precinct. Porter ran unopposed as the IPP candidate.[24]

With the opening of the primary campaign on April 1, Nixon headquarters moved into action. Jorgensen, Day, and Lutz prepared a budget with two objectives: winning reelection in the primaries and paying off all bills. The total to be raised was $22,692.31. It would be allocated for newspaper and radio coverage, outdoor advertising, direct mailing, and campaign director McCall's salary and expenses.[25]

Nixon had Herbert Klein of the *Alhambra Post-Advocate* help with campaign publicity on a part-time basis. The newspaper paid Klein's salary during the campaign, and McCall covered expenses like meals. Nixon praised Klein's stories as "outstanding because they are very objective and the facts exactly as they are."[26]

Nixon, throughout April, had his supporters spend 75 percent of their time concentrating their efforts converting Democrats. He encouraged Blue to ignore the Democratic opposition until it acted. The congressman, at present, intended to "hold our fire and show no evidence of need for campaigning." He was designing a mailer with Bowen and a special mailing to Democrats signed by Blue. Nixon also was preparing a poll to be sent out by the end of the month to a hundred thousand district voters that would help identify campaign issues. In the period before television advertising, the committee did little more than pay for billboards, leaflets, and postcard mailings.[27]

The Democrats had started to seek media attention, and Zetterberg was sending out weekly press releases, already getting more publicity in the *Star-News* than Nixon had received in the 1946 primary campaign. The congressman encouraged Democrats for Nixon groups in each community to run ads starting five weeks before the election.[28]

Some Nixon supporters' anti-Communist feelings crept into the campaign equation. Leroy Muffler, one voter, who had came out for John Nance Garner as president in 1932, opposed Upton Sinclair for California governor in 1934, and backed Herbert Hoover for the presidency in 1936, labeled Vieg "at least 'pink' if not exactly 'red.'" Muffler had debated him on several occasions and feared that Zetterberg was "merely fronting for Mr. Vieg."[29]

Ted Clark, a native Californian, who was a real estate broker and a post commander of the American Legion, admired Nixon so much that he requested an autographed photograph for his office wall. Clark crudely compared his anti-Communist antipathy to minorities: "I can tolerate Japs, Mexicans, Negros [sic], Jews, and about every type and color of peoples of this earth, however there is one thing that really gets under the skin and I fear 'em. Rattle Snakes of the so called human variety, better known as Commies."[30]

As the primary drew closer, Nixon remained in Washington to lead the fight for the Mundt-Nixon bill. Several major California papers came out against it in early May, including the *California Eagle,* a major African American newspaper in Los Angeles, calling it "one of the most poisonous pieces of legislation in all American history." The proposal was supposed to outlaw the Communist Party, but in reality the bill would squelch freedom of speech because the U.S. Attorney General could define anything as communistic: "Whether or not you were a member of the Communist Party, if you happened to support some measure such as housing, which the Communist Party also supports, you could be sent to jail for doing so." The state CIO concurred in its *Labor Herald* on the need to bury this "police state bill." The *San Francisco Chronicle,* a powerful, mainstream daily, editorialized that the proposal violated constitutional guarantees. Even the *Daily Trojan* offered no respite: the Nixon plan was "the totalitarian method—the method used by such eminent gentlemen as Tojo, Hitler, Mussolini—and by Joe Stalin. Put our economic house in order, Representative Nixon, and we'll have no need for the Mundt bill."[31]

Following nationally syndicated columnist for *Newsweek* Raymond Moley's declaration that the bill was "an excellent attempt to deal with a grave problem within constitutional limits," many district newspapers took Nixon's side. The *Alhambra Post-Advocate* advocated passage, and the *Monrovia News-Post* felt: "Nothing could be more absurd than the spectacle of men and women, bent on the destruction of the Constitution and the overthrow of the government, hiding behind the Constitution to manipulate its destruction." From Arcadia, the *Tribune* published Nixon's reply to his Communist attackers' false accusations that this was a police state bill. He would not allow the Community Party to intimidate him with its lies and smears: "I welcome the opposition of the Communists and I will resist any effort of Moscow to dictate the policies of my district."[32]

During the last month before the June 1 primary, McCall analyzed the current district that embraced the central-eastern section of Los Angeles County, extending from the Los Angeles city limits on the west to the San Bernardino County line on the east and the Orange County boundary on the southeast. The population was divided into approximately 60 percent urban and 40 percent suburban areas. There were five colleges and a large amount of business and professional commuters to the city; there also were small industrial plants and small-sized agricultural properties. The totals showed that 191,498 people were eligible to cast ballots: 92,472 Democrats, or about 51 percent; 89,321, Republicans, or approximately 49 percent; and 9,705 others. McCall mapped out the three state districts that comprised the congressional area:

|  | 49th district | 50th district | 53rd district |
|---|---|---|---|
| Democrats | 25,000 | 32,413 | 35,059 |
| Republicans | 27,021 | 25,728 | 36,572 |

With only 3,151 more Democrats than Republicans, the latter had almost drawn even with their opposition.[33]

As the Nixon faithful worked tirelessly in California, the congressman could only urge them on from afar. Senator William Knowland offered a testimonial on Nixon's role in the Whittier Narrow's Dam settlement, calling his House colleague "intelligent and energetic"; the senator had "a high regard for the way that you . . . have carried out your responsibilities."[34]

Many district newspapers were endorsing Nixon's reelection by the middle of the month. Regardless of party affiliation, the *Monterey Park Progress,* located in a heavily populated Democratic area, declared that Nixon had the leadership qualities necessary during this time of crisis. The *San Gabriel Sun* praised his excellent record. At the core of GOP allegiance, the *San Marino Tribune* unequivocally called for his reelection because Nixon had "found his way through much of the haze, gaining by his knowledge, his acumen, his tireless work, and above all, his unquestioned integrity, the backing of many of the best men in Congress and appointment on important committees." His media consultants emphasized a simple message: "He Gets Things Done!"[35]

Zetterberg's seemingly lackluster performance boosted Nixon's cause immensely, for he did not appear actively engaged throughout the district, nor was he spending sufficient sums on necessities like stickers and posters. When the Democrat contestant asked Colonel De La Vergne to serve as the chairman of his veterans' committee, Zetterberg received the embarrassing reply that the colonel favored Nixon. Local newspapers occasionally reported on the Democratic candidate's views, such as his proclamation that the best defense against communism was "a strong forward-looking liberal program." He also called for revisions in the Taft-Hartley Act because it contained provisions that created such a tremendous backlog for the National Labor Relations Board that it could never bring its caseload current. With justification, Day concluded that Zetterberg posed such a minimal challenge that Nixon would beat him three to two. The congressman had recently found out that Zetterberg as well as Helen Gahagan Douglas in a nearby district had received the CIO-PAC endorsement. If there were a general election, he would also have to bear that cross.[36]

Zetterberg criticized Nixon's leadership of the Mundt-Nixon bill, calling it one of the most dangerous measures ever to come before Congress because it promised "guilt by association." No one, Zetterberg held, should be persecuted for his beliefs: "If we are to keep America free, we should not allow Americans to be condemned simply because they belong to any organization or club, or simply because they think differently from others of us." The Democratic County Central Committee, the same day, similarly denounced it as tearing away "the rights guaranteed by the Constitution."[37]

Most of Nixon's followers disagreed a hundred percent about this position, but Bowen worried that criticism of the bill was increasing and the congressman's opponents were placing him on the defensive. Nixon could change this direction: "I have no doubt that if you come back here and make one of your sound analytical speeches, you will capitalize on the public interest in this issue." Day, on the other hand, thought that Nixon had "struck a gold mine with the timing of the legislation." He should remain in Washington fighting against communism, while Zetterberg was being endorsed by the CIO and the commies.[38]

Nixon concurred. He told McCall to send out favorable publicity on the legislation and use Zetterberg's opposition against him. Even Congressman John McCormack, Democrat from Massachusetts, and others with similar New Deal backgrounds who always defended Franklin Roosevelt, favored the Mundt-Nixon bill. This was "one time when the CIO went out on a limb without knowing what was in the bill and took the Commie line hook line and sinker." The bill was a good one, and if Zetterberg chose to make it an issue in the November election, "that issue will sink him without question."[39]

Finally, with less than two weeks until the primaries, Nixon made a single, weekend trip home. In order not to miss any congressional sessions, he took off from Washington at 4:30 P.M., Friday, May 21, on an American Airlines DC-6. The need for minor repairs forced the plane to stop in Oklahoma City for more than four hours. Then, after takeoff, the pilot saw the fire alarm flashing for the baggage compartment; he pressed the fire extinguisher button, triggering a system that sprayed the luggage with carbon dioxide. This potential disaster resulted in an emergency landing in Amarillo, Texas. Upon arrival, the pilot discovered that it was a false alarm, but the scare necessitated another five-hour interruption. Twelve hours behind schedule, the plane landed in Los Angeles at 1:30 P.M. on Saturday and the congressman boarded a private plane that flew him to El Monte airfield. Chief of Police O. C. Smith had a motorcycle team waiting to escort him for the eight-and-a-half-minute trip to Whittier.[40]

He was "knocked out" from the prolonged flight. Several hundred enthusiastic supporters greeted him for a luncheon at the William Penn Hotel, where he spoke about American foreign policy, predicting that the United States and Russia would not go to war. That afternoon, Reverend Cleveland held a barbeque honoring him in El Monte. That evening, he held a meeting at the local high school auditorium for seven hundred listeners, where he called on his audience to counteract the false propaganda about the value of the Mundt-Nixon bill in exposing Communists: "Let them come out in the open where we can all see them." The Communist Party was inconsequential in the political arena; its prime objective was to act as a front for fifth-column activities of the Soviet Union. While its American comrades played out a political charade, the hidden agenda of the party was "as a bridge from Moscow and is controlled from Moscow." While Nixon preached to the faithful inside, outside, a group claiming to be from the IPP, who favored Henry Wallace, handed out CIO leaflets opposing the legislation. Over breakfast on Sunday morning, Nixon repeated his call to forty reporters for the passage of Mundt-Nixon as a means to control Communist Party clandestine activities.[41] Upon returning to the capital Monday afternoon, he was "about as tired out as I have ever been in my life." It took him a week to recover fully.[42]

Spending less than $2,000 in the primary, Zetterberg was woefully underfinanced. He went to service clubs, house-to-house, did square-dance calling, and spoke at rallies like the one for Young Democrats at Covina City Hall, promising to back the Marshall Plan and bring about world peace. His political advertisements called for the election of progressives like himself and attacked Nixon's record. The challenger continued to lambast the Mundt-Nixon bill as "guilt by association. . . . If we are to keep America free, we should not allow Americans to be condemned simply because they belong to any organization or church, or club, or simply because they think differently from others of us." Zetterberg reminded his readers that the Democratic Party had given him its endorsement, and by the end of the month, the American Federation of Labor officially endorsed him. Margaret Porter of the IPP somewhat confused the traditional Democratic alliance with labor. The official CIO primary election recommendations backed her in the 12th district and Helen Gahagan Douglas in the 14th. This labor organ proclaimed: "ACT NOW TO STOP MUNDT POLICE STATE BILL."[43]

Zetterberg had another insurmountable barrier placed before him. When Democrats received their sample ballots, Nixon's name came first because of his incumbency, and many voters could easily assume that he was their Democratic congressman. His committee, under instructions, mailed out postcards targeted to Democratic voters under J. B. Blue's name addressed to "Fellow Democrats." Similar advertisements appeared in local newspapers. As Zetterberg walked the district, he learned that many voters were convinced that Nixon was a Democrat and displayed their sample ballots as proof.[44]

Nixon's issue polling was revealing. For example, the respondents only favored federal aid to education by 50 percent. As important to preparedness measures, the draft ranked the lowest at 9.5 percent; Universal Military Training only reached 16 percent; and rebuilding the air force was in first place, at just under 60 percent. Almost 75 percent opposed returning to price controls, and a similar number wanted to outlaw the Communist Party. Just over 75 percent favored the continuation of Taft-Hartley. Over 85 percent did not want individuals associated with fellow travelers or foreign agents to hold federal national security jobs. Finally, over 90 percent felt that under current international conditions, the United States needed to increase its military preparedness. As a result of these tabulations, Nixon discovered that his positions across the board were extremely popular among both Democrats and Republicans.[45]

Besides this poll, Nixon recognized that he needed Democratic support to win and turned to the Democrats for Nixon Committee in print media and over the radio. Reverend Cleveland recorded a radio broadcast played the day before the election. An influential church leader in the San Gabriel Valley, he was especially active in his home town of El Monte: "I am a Democrat and proud that I am. I urge every other Democrat to join me in voting for Richard Nixon. I also urge every Republican to vote for Richard Nixon." Margaret Tate, a well-known Pomona resident, also spoke over the radio and recounted the congressman's list of accomplishments, including the Herter mission, floor leader for the Mundt-Nixon bill, anti-Communist, committed Quaker, and native Californian: "As a Democrat, I feel that every Democrat, and every Republican, should express confidence in Richard Nixon by voting for him tomorrow."[46]

The election fell on June 1. By 2:00 A.M. the next morning, Nixon learned the happy results. Even if Zetterberg's and Porter's votes were combined, Nixon still won by almost 2,000 in the Democratic contest:

| | |
|---|---|
| Nixon | 21,411 |
| Zetterberg | 16,808 |
| Porter | 2,772 |

As of June 5, Zetterberg had not wired his congratulations, and Nixon did not expect him to do this.[47]

His finance committee reported that it had raised $7,071, including a $1,000 contribution from the Republican National Committee, and spent $5,628. Nixon was extremely pleased that many people had contributed to his campaign and that he did not need to depend on "a few very large contributors." Some expenses, such as billboards, were donated, but listed as a donation because it could "be subjected to some pretty serious penalties." Unlike the 1946 campaign in which Nixon had to spend his own personal funds, this time he had not personally spent anything during the campaign. The primary surplus was designated for the general election.[48] Without significant opposition, McCall conducted a minimal effort since the result was a foregone conclusion: Nixon received 141,509 votes, or 86.9 percent of the total.[49]

Nixon's 1948 reelection effort has been glossed over. When mentioned, its significance is minimized or distorted. As a candidate, he based this election on his record. Nixon never smeared Zetterberg, even though Nixon has often been characterized as a compulsive smearer. In fact, he had decided early in the primary not to mention his opponent. The campaign was clean, well run, managed by amateur-turned-professional supporters under Nixon's close guidance.[50]

Zetterberg, who still practices law in Claremont a half century later, remains a Democratic loyalist and argues forcefully that Nixon's primary victory was due to the fact that the congressman campaigned as a Democrat who appealed to new residents as the party's sitting congressman. Zetterberg believes that Nixon, concealing his Republican Party affiliation, used to advantage that his name came first on the ballot due to his incumbency and that his campaign committee promoted the "Dear Fellow Democrat" advertising format, enticing enough unsophisticated Democratic voters, who did not understand the crossfiling procedure, into casting their ballots for him. This was the media strategy in the local newspapers. "This *was* his [Nixon's] campaign, and very difficult to negate in view of the sample ballots," Zetterberg concluded. In what could have been his closing arguments, this attorney summed up his case: "The real issue [in the campaign] was one of marketing Richard Nixon as a 'Fellow Democrat.'"[51]

The fact that the Democratic Party did not finance Zetterberg's challenge decreased the chances even more. Jerry Voorhis's decision late in the contest against entering the race further weakened the Democratic cause. Even after Zetterberg was nominated, Voorhis never materially assisted his successor. Voorhis did come to Zetterberg's office and brought his mailing list and index cards of his supporters. He introduced the challenger to Jack Long, a Voorhis political adviser and district manager, who ably assisted Zetterberg during the campaign.

Zetterberg never understood the incumbent's appeal because "I never perceived him as a particularly likeable person or a particularly warm candidate." Zetterberg underestimated Nixon's attributes. Loyalists not only admired, respected, even worshiped their man; but they also fervently backed the causes that he espoused. Nixon, as Zetterberg recognized, stressed "the Red thing." That was what the nation preferred. The New Deal no longer played in Peoria.[52]

# Chapter 9

# MOVING ONTO THE NATIONAL STAGE

W ith his own reelection guaranteed, Nixon turned to the upcoming battle for the presidency. He understood that the 1948 national elections presented an opportunity for Republicans to regain the White House after a sixteen-year absence. Yet he had no experience at this level. He felt that the GOP would unite as the momentum grew toward the national convention, but he did not have any idea how the California delegates were chosen and naively assumed that their selection in his locality came from the county central committee: "This would avoid a great deal of scrambling among the people who want to go to the convention, and also the people there in the district would probably have a very good idea of who should be given a nod in case there was an argument."[1]

As early as 1947, he was watching potential candidates' maneuvering, especially the efforts of Harold Stassen. Just after Nixon won election in November 1946, Stassen wired his congratulations and delight that the winner would be formulating critical postwar policies. Nixon followed the Minnesotan's presidential possibilities, and early in 1947, declared that Stassen was "one of the best vote getters we have and I only hope that he won't be cut to pieces during the next two years." The congressman met with Stassen on several occasions in the capital through the summer, convinced that he was a viable candidate, "despite the opposition he has from party leaders." At the end of August, Nixon's feeling rose to a higher plane. While Governors Thomas Dewey of New York and Earl Warren of California refused to make statements on the tax bill or Taft-Hartley, Stassen endorsed both of them. As a result of these commitments, Nixon declared that the former Minnesotan governor was "the most electable candidate and probably the ablest man of the bunch. He is definitely not the left-winger that so many party Republicans have labeled him."[2]

That winter Stassen confided to Nixon that he planned to start his 1948 presidential campaign for delegates with a nationwide broadcast in late November, originating from a Milwaukee Auditorium meeting. He intended to place his emphasis on issues where the Truman administration was most vulnerable and hoped that he could depend on Nixon for counsel.[3]

During the summer, Nixon heard from some close advisers about Stassen's Californian visits. That summer, Kyle Palmer, political editor of the *Los Angeles Times,* opened his beautiful Malibu beach house for an informal stag party of twenty to twenty-five Republican leaders, businessmen, and the press to meet Harold Stassen, "one of the party's worthwhile leaders." Harrison McCall went, reporting to Nixon that Stassen handled himself extremely well: "Everyone left the party with a much greater respect for the man." During another trip, Chotiner welcomed Stassen to Los Angeles and invited Herman Perry and his son Hubert to see the Minnesotan during his appearance.[4]

Nixon also watched Earl Warren's efforts. Charlie Bowen, one of the congressman's political confidants, detected a Warren movement for president in the spring. By summer, Nixon felt that the governor would "sweep the state without opposition to speak of, but of course, a lot can develop between now and election time." At the end of November, Nixon joined with other California GOP congressmen and with the state central committee to present Warren to the Republican National Convention for the presidential nomination. Warren appreciated Nixon's "confidence" and expected to keep it: "Our party has a great mission to perform in the next few years, and I shall be happy to work with you in the fulfillment of that mission." Nonetheless their relationship remained formal, with the governor maintaining his independence from the stalwarts and Nixon holding fast to his loyalist image. Nixon heard grumblings from some in the state organization about his "cool detached attitude" concerning the governor's candidacy.[5]

Nixon followed Warren's activities into 1948, applauding the passage of the governor's highway program because it was a difficult fight. He admired Warren "for sticking by his guns." Early in January, the governor traveled to the capital, where his close friend Senator Knowland hosted a luncheon for him. Nixon was one of the guests in the Senate restaurant, where, according to the congressman, the governor was "playing his cards very cleverly in his bid for the nomination." He had made an excellent impression on the newspapermen present, and when asked, he dismissed any interest in the vice presidency. As for Nixon's observations, he did not think any of the front-runners like Dewey and Senator Robert Taft could win, "which means that some dark horse candidate is likely to get it." Nixon believed Warren, Stassen, and General Dwight D. Eisenhower had better chances.[6]

Warren's forces consolidated their power at the state level. When John Barcome, chairman of the Los Angeles County Republican Central Committee, refused to cooperate with the governor, he was forced to resign at the end of February. Warren intended to name his delegation slate at the last moment to confuse Stassen supporters. Charlie Cooper commented that Barcome "had his hide tacked to the wall (partly his own fault) so that now the big boys' state machine is in control." The message was crystal-clear. The California GOP would unite behind the governor or else.[7]

Roy Day was more than just a spectator to these events. From December 1947 forward, he lobbied to be a delegate to the Republican National Convention and openly declared for Warren. Day asked Nixon to write a testimonial, but Nixon reminded him that Warren was "the key man" in delegate selection, and Mac Faries, state committeeman, could exert considerable influence.[8]

Day received the news of his selection as a delegate from the 12th district in the middle of March 1948, and thereafter supplied Nixon with important as well as miscellaneous information about the upcoming convention. Day identified Bernard Brennan, the chairman of the delegation, as "definitely a Warren man." The delegates were traveling east on a special train from San Francisco to Philadelphia. Nixon reported that he too was going, but not as a delegate; Bill Arnold, at his boss's request, received press credentials to cover the happenings. Thus, Arnold would have a better seat at the convention than his employer.[9]

To woo Nixon, one of the governor's representatives, Jessie Williamson, told Nixon how much the governor valued his support and asked him in mid-April to become involved with the state delegation. Faries followed up with Nixon two weeks later, stressing Warren's commitment to a strong Republican program in California. Faries added that

Democrats had a million-vote majority in the state, but even Faries stressed then that the governor was "doing a grand job in holding the State for the Republicans, giving them an opportunity to put forth a Republican Program and convert the Democrats to the Republican Party."[10]

Despite this appeal, the congressman steadfastly remained firm in his devotion to Stassen because he had offered to campaign for Nixon during his 1946 contest. During the Junior Chamber of Commerce award ceremonies in January 1948, the former governor, a previous winner, was the main speaker. At the conclusion of that event, he and Nixon returned to the capital together, where they discussed the Minnesotan's presidential ambitions.[11]

By the end of March, some GOP regulars began to criticize Warren's failure to support Republican candidates and initiated a drive to have General Douglas MacArthur file for the California primary. Chotiner felt that since the general had no chance, this would be a mistake. Nixon concurred, and so did Senator Joe McCarthy, who informed constituents that he would not back MacArthur in the upcoming Wisconsin primary, but instead, came out for Stassen, who was young and vital.[12]

The former Minnesota governor had tapped a source of vitality at the grass roots. From 1948 forward, presidential contenders would have to view primary races as critical; in Stassen's case, he was peaking too soon. He won the Wisconsin primary early in April, and in the middle of the month received another triumph in Nebraska. He had done so well that he pulled ahead of Dewey in the Gallup poll. Several days later, Nixon noted that either Stassen or Senator Arthur Vandenberg from Michigan were his favorites of the candidates. MacArthur was finished, while Vandenberg still had a slight chance. Taft could not win, while Dewey was still a viable contender. Stassen was popular at the grassroots level and was gaining ground. Warren, according to Nixon, should work out some deal with Stassen before the convention. By the end of the month, Nixon slightly changed his position: Taft, Dewey, and Stassen looked strong, while Warren and Vandenberg ran as dark horses.[13]

Nixon likewise examined the Democratic contenders. As he became more knowledgeable about that party, his opinion of Truman sunk to new depths. At the start of April, he commented that "By the time the Presidential election rolls around, we should be well enough organized that we could even beat Eisenhower in that district if the Demos dump Harry and get him to run (let's hope that doesn't happen!)." Near the end of the month, Nixon felt that the Democrats had conceded to nominate Truman, a sure loser in Nixon's opinion.[14]

While Nixon disagreed with the majority of Truman's actions, his reaction never compared with the hostility that the congressman demonstrated toward Henry Wallace, who had declared as an Independent candidate for the White House at the end of 1947. Before even leaving the administration, the secretary of commerce had started attacking Truman's anti-Russian posture, and after announcing for the presidency, he pounded on this theme early in 1948. Colonel James De La Vergne relayed to Nixon on February 5 that Wallace's crusade to bring about American-Soviet cooperation would "probably disintegrate and split wide open, even if in secret," the California Democratic Party. By the end of the month, Wallace went before the House Committee on Foreign Affairs to oppose the Marshall Plan as anti-Russian.[15]

Truman surprised his listeners during a speech on the evening of March 17 in New York City by lashing out against his former commerce secretary. Initially, there was nothing about Wallace and his pro-Soviet views in the draft of his speech, but in the midst of his prepared text, he said: "I do not want and I will not accept the political support of Henry Wallace and his communists." A great burst of applause interrupted him. After a pause, he continued: "If joining them or permitting them to join me is the price of victory, I recommend defeat. These are days of high prices for everything, but any price for Wallace and his communists is too much for me to pay. I do not want to buy."[16]

Presidential politics merged with the Mundt-Nixon bill during May. Early in the month, without a doubt much to Nixon's displeasure, Warren openly opposed outlawing the Communist Party of the United States. Most Communists, the governor reasoned, had not registered. Since this was the rule, he proposed a law that anyone who called for the overthrow of the American government would be tried for a felony. Despite this alternative, Warren pronounced that he might support Mundt-Nixon because it did not outlaw the party and addressed the issue of subversive activities.[17]

Warren's remarks were merely a prelude to the real battle. Stassen and Dewey were moving toward a collision course in Oregon, where they were set to debate the Mundt-Nixon bill. Late in April, Dewey spoke with Mundt for a few minutes, and he, in turn, sent the New York governor a confidential HUAC report. Nixon informed Dewey that the proposal was constitutional: it did not specifically mention Communist

Party; it did not outlaw the party; it only made certain conspiratorial acts illegal where a foreign power sought to establish a totalitarian regime in the United States. If the Communist Party continued to take orders from Moscow, Mundt-Nixon would forbid it. If Communists were merely malcontents, the legislation let them alone.[18]

Nixon pitched Stassen to come out for the legislation because of his visibility as a presidential contender, assuring him that the bill was "a sane and fair approach to the problem of controlling Communism in the United States." The congressman made the same arguments that Mundt had presented to Dewey. When the Minnesotan went on *Meet the Press,* he forcefully backed the bill. Nixon saw this as an endorsement and credited Stassen with a courageous act: "The Communists . . . are waging an all out attack against it and it is certainly gratifying to find at least one public figure who has the guts to support it publicly."[19]

Both Stassen and Dewey recognized the Oregon debate as pivotal. Dewey spent $150,000 there, three times the previous record, and campaigned in Oregon for three weeks. During the closing days of the contest, Stassen linked Dewey with being soft on Communists, and Dewey accepted Stassen's challenge to debate him on May 17 on nationwide radio carried by over nine hundred radio stations to an estimated forty million listeners. The single issue was: "Shall the Communist party be outlawed in The United States?" Dewey opposed the idea and made his position clear before the debate. He objected to "thought control" because he believed that any legislation outlawing ideas violated the Bill of Rights and the Constitution; therefore, he refused to support Mundt-Nixon. Stassen argued for laws that controlled domestic communism, praising Mundt-Nixon, but implying that it would outlaw the Communist Party. At the conclusion, both claimed victory, and when the primary was held four days later, Dewey beat Stassen by less than 10,000 votes: 113,350 to 104,211. Oregon completed the primaries between Dewey and Stassen, and if victory were possible, the Minnesotan had to win there. His loss seriously crippled his drive and reestablished Dewey as the GOP front-runner.[20]

On the day of the debate, Nixon wrote John Foster Dulles, Dewey's principal adviser on foreign policy, to apologize for releasing a statement favoring the passage of Mundt-Nixon. Its publication, Nixon asserted, "did not intend to put you on the spot of urging passage of the bill in its present form and I hope that the press handling of the matter caused you no embarrassment." Dulles's declaration was given more press than the others because of his experience in diplomatic affairs and the Dewey-Stassen debate in Oregon. Despite the garbled stances of both candidates, on the day of the primary Nixon somehow reasoned that the "Mundt-Nixon Bill won the Stassen-Dewey debate since both candidates are for it."[21]

After Stassen lost the primary, Nixon admitted on May 27 that Dewey was increasing in strength. The congressman still maintained that Stassen was a serious contender and even sent a check for the Stassen for President Committee through a friend. He and Stassen had also talked over the last few months, and Nixon believed that the governor "would make an excellent candidate in the event that he gets the nomination." Stassen, Nixon confided to a friend, was flying to California to see Warren about accepting the vice-presidential slot on a Stassen-Warren ticket. Nixon was going to the convention to do "everything that I can to insure the selection of a candidate who will not only run a good race, but who will make a good President." Furthermore, he hoped that Stassen would continue to try to win the nomination at the convention since many delegates remained undecided.[22]

Nixon did not end his mission for the Mundt-Nixon bill in Oregon. Throughout June, he continued to justify its purpose, complaining on the 1st that the Communist Party had waged a terrific battle against the bill. Nixon was gratified that he had spoken before the American Legion in Milwaukee and looked back "upon a visit with a group of real Americans, who I feel are far more representative of the people of the country generally." He hoped that the Senate would act before adjournment, but time was limited, and opponents might threaten a filibuster. If the Senate did not act, he would resubmit the bill at the start of the next session, "because we feel that the country generally wants and needs some anti-Communist legislation on the books." By the middle of the month, he knew that the bill would not pass. He summed up his feelings, recognizing that it "was a very controversial measure but I think that much of the criticism of the bill was based on misunderstanding."[23]

Christopher Emmet, on June 25, defended the proposal in *Commonweal* as a way to attack communism. He pointed out that pro-Communist and Wallace groups demonstrated in Washington against it, and the famous African American baritone, Paul Robeson, led the march. Those factions had "a personal axe to grind since the Mundt-Nixon bill would force them from now on to travel under their true colors." Non-Communist liberals, Emmet urged, should denounce these

agitators, but he realized that they would remain silent. Many civil libertarians endorsed its main provisions, while Emmet pointed out that they
had widespread approval. Mundt had overwhelmingly been nominated
for the Senate by a five-to-one margin. Nixon had become "a rising
young Congressman who has impressed Congress and the press with his
intelligence and sincerity, and with the superiority of his understanding
of Communism over the cruder approach of such veteran members as
Parnell Thomas."[24]

Nixon still had to finish up his legislative work for the current
House session, which was scheduled to adjourn on June 19 for the
twenty-fourth Republican National Convention. To finish in time, the
House held night sessions to complete its heavy agenda. Nixon's focus
did not follow any philosophical design, and at one point he even
extended the New Deal by proposing a "work clause" as part of Social
Security legislation that increased the $15 amount beneficiaries could
earn without loss or reduction of payments to $40 per month. He con-
centrated on the elimination of public housing provisions in a housing
bill; and he introduced a bill to provide a secondary market for GI loans.
On the closing day, he commented to a friend who had lived in the capital: "You know what a rat race it is. I have been fair lucky in getting
some pretty good assignments, thought [sic] tough ones, during my first
term."[25]

By the end of the second session, Nixon had not missed a vote on a
major piece of legislation. He favored curbing executive powers over
reclamation, voted against executive authority for income tax reduction
and for the Republican income tax plan, approved of GI job ceilings
and college allowances, and of extending rent control. He voted for
$200,000 to continue HUAC, as well as for the Marshall Plan, state tide-
lands, the Mundt-Nixon bill, and the draft. In summary, he voted with
the GOP majority on domestic issues, enthusiastically backed the European Recovery Program, and dovetailed it with domestic subversive
control legislation.[26]

With his congressional duties finished, Nixon turned to the Republican National Convention. Back in February, Herman Perry had written Carroll Reese of the national committee and Speaker Martin,
suggesting that Nixon be selected as a keynote speaker. McCall knew
about Perry's initiative and presented the same idea to Mac Faries on the
grounds that the GOP needed to influence young veterans, and Nixon
"could talk their own language and convince them that the Republican

Party is no longer dominated by a group of 'stuffed shirts and old men.'"
Herbert Spencer heard Nixon speak over the radio on April 1 and commented that his message was splendid and sincere. He had "the polished
delivery of highly trained radio orators who practically sing their piece."
These efforts, however, did not produce a positive response.[27]

Before the congressional adjournment, Day, from Pomona, and
John Garland, from San Marino, both of whom represented the 12th
district GOP, joined the fifty-three members of the California delegation in Sacramento pledged to its favorite son, Governor Warren, where
the Republicans unanimously elected Senator Knowland as chairman.
The group had a special fifteen-car train that left from the state capital for
the convention in Philadelphia. The train arrived three hours late on
Sunday afternoon; Warren headed for the Bellevue Stratford, while the
delegation stayed at the Warwick Hotel. That evening, the group caucused, and at its conclusion, Knowland voiced his confidence in his candidate's receiving the nomination.[28]

Before the convention was called to order, Dewey, Taft, and Stassen
appeared as the favorites. Each had to convince a minimum of 548 delegates out of the 1,094 selected to his cause to win the nomination. The
former Minnesota governor denied any vice-presidential aspirations, but
acknowledged that after the first round of balloting, he would be in third
place. Some predicted that Vandenberg with his internationalist emphasis would emerge as the dark horse.[29]

As for Warren, he offered no room to negotiate; he was rigid. He
would accept the nomination his way and went to the convention without any political deals, demanding a liberal program: that was "the Paramount issue of the day." He intended to meet with delegates and win
them over to his cause. He declared: "If the nomination can come along
in an orderly way, thru direct and forthright action, I would be very
happy to have it.

"If it doesn't come along that way, I would be just as happy without it."[30]

Nixon conceded in advance that Dewey looked like the nominee.
Once the convention opened on June 21, Dewey's forces lobbied tirelessly to put their man ahead in the balloting and methodically edged
up in delegate count to capture the nomination on the third ballot.
Throughout the convention, Warren maintained his inflexible position
of "no deal," and Senator Knowland enthusiastically reinforced that position, confidently predicting victory. The governor continually rejected

any suggestion of accepting a vice-presidential nomination. However, once Dewey won the top spot, he turned to his California counterpart with exactly that proposition. Warren, of course, accepted. With two formidable governors from the East and West Coasts leading the ticket, optimism reigned.[31]

While most commentators concentrated on the struggle over the presidential nomination, Nixon, Mundt, and Senator Homer Ferguson from Michigan were fighting for a tough anti-Communist plank in the Republican platform that would commit the party to enact legislation like the Mundt-Nixon bill. It stated: "we pledge a vigorous enforcement of existing laws against Communists and enactment of such new legislation as may be necessary to expose the treasonable activities of Communists and defeat their objective of establishing here a Godless dictatorship controlled from abroad." In fact, the Russian blockade of Berlin began during the convention. In a last-minute maneuver, Nixon talked to Senator Henry Cabot Lodge of Massachusetts, who chaired the platform committee and had the plank included.[32]

After the convention ended, Nixon offered his already habitual assessments: "All of us were very pleased that Governor Warren is on the ticket, because we think he will be a great asset as a vote getter in California and other states where the battle will be close." Warren exhibited a warmth and personality that Dewey had not displayed: "although Dewey is an excellent administrator and fine speaker, he lacks the warmth that is essential to a really effective national campaigner." Despite these weaknesses, Nixon felt that Dewey was "a strong leader," and with Warren's assistance, he would "win the election and make an excellent president." Several congressmen whose races were close recognized Dewey's limitations and were pleased with Warren's selection; he also would be "a big asset to the ticket in the border states and in the marginal city districts." Before the campaign kicked off, Warren thanked Nixon for his assistance at the convention and said he looked forward to the contest and working to elect the ticket. If it won, the governor expected to work closely with the congressman.[33]

To several close friends, Nixon confided some ambivalence over the outcome. Stassen was the most popular candidate, "but the Dewey machine was too well financed and too well organized to be stopped." The New York–Pennsylvania combination was just too powerful. Stassen might have won, but he wanted a draft movement, and without Dewey's backing, that was an impossible scenario. Nixon wished that Stassen would remain an active Republican: "He is, without question, the strongest man the party has among the voters and his type of leadership is what we are going to need in the years to come." Warren's selection was a slap at the New York governor because he intended to name someone else. Still, just about everyone seemed satisfied with a Dewey-Warren ticket because it was "a very strong team."[34]

Nixon returned to the capital for his next major event, but in this case all he could do was wait, since Pat was getting ready to deliver their second child. On the evening of July 4, one of the hottest Independence Day's in years, Dick drove his wife to Columbia Hospital, within a fifteen-minute walk of the White House. She was assigned to a corner room with some cross-ventilation. At 3:00 A.M. on Monday, the 5th, Dick, who was waiting in the lounge, learned that Pat had delivered a nine-pound baby girl. They named the baby Julie.[35]

Five days after admittance, Pat left the hospital for her two-bedroom duplex apartment. Life was a strain, and with the terribly hot weather, Hannah had become ill caring for Tricia; now Pat had to walk up and down the stairs administering to her mother-in-law as well as to both daughters. Eleven days later, Nixon reported that Pat would probably remain at their Virginia apartment with the children while he flew back to California.[36]

The Democratic National Convention opened on July 12, also in Philadelphia. After a titanic platform fight, Truman was nominated late in the evening on the 14th, and in the early hours of the next day he stirred the exhausted delegates to a frenzy by promising them victory. Attacking the 80th Congress as worthless, he recited the GOP platform, written less than two weeks ago, to tackle such issues as aid to education, inflation, housing, and increased Social Security benefits. He intended to resurrect the crusading days of New Deal liberalism, and therefore summoned Congress for a special session to deal with these critical issues on July 26, the day Missourians called "Turnip Day," which launched Truman's famous crusade against the "Do-Nothing" Congress.[37]

Before the president called Congress into special session, Nixon had planned to remain with Pat at their apartment for at least a month and maybe more before returning to the West Coast. Initially, after winning both primaries, he had intended to arrive in California in the middle of August and remain there until the next session of Congress in January 1949; later, he compressed this to part of September to some time in November. The new parents were relieved that Dick would not have to mount a vigorous campaign because they desperately needed a summer vacation.[38]

Nixon recognized that Truman had challenged Congress to a battle that would be waged until the November elections. He also worried about a Republican victory in one respect, communicating with his associates during the middle of June in California about the patronage problem because if the Republicans won, this was "going to be a big headache." Nixon recommended "a small group in the district who could take the heat off of me when the job seekers start to come around." He set guidelines in the first part of July by deciding not to become involved in the central committee disagreements or control of the party apparatus. Nixon would depend on the recommendations of local representatives for appointments rather than initiate them from his office.[39]

Truman convened Congress on Monday, in the last week of July, and Nixon had "no idea whatever how long it is going to last." It could continue until October, and it would be contentious. The day the session opened, Truman promulgated an executive order to promote equal opportunity in the federal civil service and the armed forces; he clearly expected to end military segregation. On July 27, the second day of the session, Truman went before an angry Republican majority and resubmitted proposals for housing, price controls, and other legislative initiatives that had already been rejected. The GOP was in a quandary over how to respond to the president's demand that Republicans live up to their own platform promises.[40]

The Californian congressional delegation expectedly split on party lines. The four Democrats were enthusiastic for Truman's actions. Helen Gahagan Douglas vigorously praised the president for his executive order. Nixon did not respond to the desegregation initiative, but, instead, called the Truman entire message to Congress "simply dishonest." Nixon argued that the president deplored high prices, yet he proposed government housing, higher minimum wages, federal health subsidies, federal aid to education, larger Social Security benefits, and more money for the United Nations. These pieces of legislation had to fuel inflation. Nixon and his party felt that the disagreements between the GOP and the administration were so huge that the American voters would make their decision on which course they chose in November. This was the standard Republican stance, but politically, it proved disastrous.[41]

While Nixon reacted to the Democratic agenda, he also was concerned about Communist expansion abroad and subversion at home.

Early in the year, the Soviets had ousted the Czechoslovakian regime through a coup d'état. A grand jury on July 20 indicted twelve high-ranking officials of the Communist Party, the first indictments under the Alien Registration Act of 1940, better known as the Smith Act, which made it a crime to advocate the overthrow of the government by force or violence. Nixon, in view of the Red assumption of the Czech state, applauded the indictments because he felt that these American Communists had been rightly brought out into public view, and their indictments were long awaited, "since there can be no doubt that these top leaders of the party do work in the interests of replacing our form of government with a Soviet dictatorship through the use of force and violence, if necessary."[42]

Their trial would, Nixon believed, furnish valuable information on how to revise the Mundt-Nixon bill to meet subversive activities not covered under the Smith Act, for the United States needed legislation to ferret out Russian spies and front groups because they constituted a real menace.[43]

In the midst of heightened Communist concerns, HUAC chairman Parnell Thomas, still confined to bed, set his committee's agenda for the fall: resumption of the Hollywood hearings, a week-long Condon hearing, three days of hearings on Communist infiltration of African American organizations, issuance of visas to well-known Communists like Mrs. Earl Browder, and discussion of communism in the maritime unions connected with shipments of uranium and "heavy water" to Russia. Thomas consulted with Karl Mundt, as acting chairman, about these topics, and he recommended immediate hearings on July 26 due to the large number of investigations. He was making his first bid for a Senate seat, and even though the special session had interrupted his campaign plans, he decided to take up the visa issue first because he would receive good publicity. As for Condon, Mundt reacted cautiously; he did not want a repeat of the earlier fiasco.[44]

The priorities changed abruptly when Thomas revealed that he had subpoenaed Elizabeth Bentley to come before a HUAC executive session of "espionage activities in the Government." She had finished her testimony before a New York special federal grand jury that had recessed and also had appeared in secret session before a Senate committee investigating the espionage activities of William Remington. The assistant attorney general in charge of the criminal division, Vincent Quinn, and U.S. District Attorney George Fay, tried to delay her public hearings, but

Thomas prevailed. She would speak openly, and he asserted that Bentley would reveal the scope of Soviet spying in America. She had been a Russian courier, confessed her transgressions during the war to the FBI, and became a double agent through the fall of 1946. Her appearance at the end of July would be a prelude to public hearings that would begin around September 1, when Thomas expected to consider five matters: "The first would be the Condon case."[45]

Some felt that Bentley's testimony was flawed and questioned her veracity. Father Cronin, however, was not among those who doubted her information. He knew that the FBI had been pressing its espionage investigation for eighteen months, had blasted the grand jury for not revealing the extent of Communists in the American government, and had lashed out at Attorney General Clark for his failure to indict former New Dealers who spied for the Soviets.[46]

On July 31, a Saturday morning, HUAC met at 10:45 A.M. in its committee room with Thomas presiding and six other members present, including Nixon, to hear from Elizabeth Bentley, who was always guarded. The chairman remembered that auspicious opening: "The caucus room . . . began to look like opening night for a Broadway hit." The chair, Mundt, and John Rankin opened by calling for the grand jury to prosecute spies. Nixon was silent. Bentley, now known as the "Red Spy Queen," introduced herself by providing her background. Born in New Milford, Connecticut, in 1908, she graduated from Vassar College in 1930 and received her master's degree from Columbia University five years later. She joined the U.S. Communist Party the same year and served as a Soviet courier during the war. She then named a number of people who were Communists; Harry Dexter White, former assistant secretary of the Treasury under the administration of Franklin Roosevelt, was the most prominent and caused the greatest stir.[47]

Nixon prevented any discussion by her of charges against Remington, who was under Senate inquiry. She discussed other contacts, and Nixon interrogated her on Lauchlin Currie, who had worked in the Roosevelt White House as a special assistant, but she was not acquainted with him. Nixon had her state for the record that the Russians knew that they were committing espionage in the United States. He commended Bentley for coming forward to expose Communists, but wanted corroboration of her testimony by the FBI director. The committee adjourned by late afternoon without disclosing its next witness.[48]

Bentley's sensational accusations made press headlines over the weekend. Thomas must have been particularly delighted with the allegation that she might connect his old nemesis Condon with other Communists. Bentley, for example, knew that Nathan Silvermaster worked for Soviet intelligence, and Condon had known him. FBI director Hoover might be summoned to corroborate Bentley's accusations, but although twenty-nine subpoenas went out to individuals to appear in the next ten days, the director was not included.[49]

Calling a special session of Congress had brought forth a double-edged sword. Truman had placed the Republican majority in Congress on the defensive. It needed to act, but instead, argued with the White House over political differences. This intransigence allowed the president to shape his winning outline by attacking the "Do-Nothing" Congress during the upcoming campaign. While he gained a political advantage here, neither he nor anyone else realized that in recalling Congress, he also permitted Thomas to reopen his vendetta against Condon. Initially, hearings were to resume in September; but with Bentley's availability and willingness to testify, along with Thomas's wish that she would implicate Condon, Communist subversion was unexpectedly the first item on HUAC's July agenda.

To much of this political maneuvering, Nixon was a spectator. He had gone to his first GOP national convention, saw how Dewey won his nomination, and optimistically predicted a Republican victory. Since he was already assured reelection in November, he had time to campaign for his party and its candidates. He would make the passage of Mundt-Nixon an issue, as well as the ousting of the Czech democratic regime and the indictment of American Communist Party members for spying. All of these events played to his strong suit of combining internationalism and anticommunism.

When Thomas was deciding on the HUAC agenda, Nixon was not asked for any input. Even when the chairman revised his schedule to have Bentley testify, Nixon was not consulted. Present for her media appearance, he anticipated further hearings on domestic subversion, and without any major labor or education legislation under serious consideration in his House committee, and with the special session delaying commencement of the general elections, Nixon could concentrate on HUAC proceedings. He played no role in selecting the topics under discussion at the end of July and had no reason to predict that his duties would be altered. The first week of August, however, would bring about a radical change.

## Chapter 10

# NIXON: CHAMBERS
# VERSUS HISS

By the beginning of August 1948, President Truman had already brought Congress back into a special session to force the Republican majority to make good on its national platform, recently adopted by its presidential nominating convention, or to embarrass the GOP before the electorate for refusing to act positively. Like most of his Republican colleagues, Nixon cavalierly dismissed the White House strategy of attacking Congress in order to win election. It was so transparent he thought that the public would not be deceived.

Just as Nixon did not accurately predict the national trends leading up to the presidential elections, he had no inkling what was about to face him during the HUAC hearings in the special session. He attended the first HUAC meeting at the end of July to listen to Elizabeth Bentley's spectacular account of Soviet infiltration in the federal bureaucracy, testimony that the Justice Department tried unsuccessfully to obstruct due to its own ongoing investigations. Almost immediately after leveling her sensational charges, several of the most prominent men that she had accused issued public denials. These prompt responses led to demands for corroboration. Some independent source had to substantiate Bentley's charges.[1]

Chairman Parnell Thomas announced on August 2 in a small newspaper column that Whittaker Chambers had been subpoenaed to testify the next morning. Born on April 1, 1901, in Brooklyn, New York, Jay Vivian Chambers came from an unstable, relatively poor family. He graduated from high school in 1919, and already a gifted writer, published his first article at seventeen. He entered Columbia University and worked on the school newspaper, but dropped out of college after his junior year. With this end to his formal education, he traveled to Germany in 1924 for several months, returned to the United States, had his first sexual relationship—an affair with a married woman, and then his first homosexual encounter. While exploring his sexuality, he joined the Communist Party in 1925 and went to work for the *Daily Worker*. The following year, his brother committed suicide and Whittaker met Esther Shemitz, whom he married five years later. During this period, as he published more and assisted in editing *The New Masses,* he embarked on a clandestine career as a spy for the Russians. From that moment until leaving the party, he was actively engaged in Communist activities in Washington.

From late 1937 to early 1938, Chambers began to consider breaking with the party, then defected and hid in Florida. He resurfaced in 1939 to begin a journalistic career at *Time* magazine in New York City, and just before the outbreak of World War II, he met with Assistant Secretary of State Adolph Berle to inform on his former comrades. Two months after this conversation, the assistant secretary recorded in his diary that he was not impressed with Chambers's allegations, but still, Berle told Marvin McIntyre, one of Franklin Roosevelt's private secretaries, about the interview, who promised to discuss it with the president. Berle had discharged his duty and never heard back from McIntyre about this matter.[2]

Chambers resumed his magazine job. As his skills improved, he was given greater responsibilities, and by the end of the war, he was promoted to senior editor in charge of the foreign news section and had molded the columns under his direction to a fervent anti-Communistic slant. On most occasions, Henry Luce, the magazine's publisher, agreed with his editor's viewpoints over strong objections from some foreign correspondents. Only Chambers's health limited the effectiveness of his crusade against communism. In August 1945, he drove himself to the point of collapse, suffering a heart attack. Even after his temporary incapacitation, *Time* followed his approach. The routine of getting a weekly out, however, had become onerous, and so to relieve pressure, Chambers left foreign news and switched to another Luce enterprise, *Life*. By the summer of 1948, at the pinnacle of his career, Chambers was making a comfortable living.[3]

On Sunday, August 1, 1948, Chambers's routine started to change radically. As he sat in his office on the twenty-ninth floor of the Time-Life Building at 9 Rockefeller Plaza in New York City, the phone rang. David Senter of William Hearst's Washington news bureau called to tell Chambers that HUAC had subpoenaed him. He had heard the names of several congressmen on the committee, but he had not closely followed its proceedings. As Chambers entered HUAC's offices on the morning of August 3, he only recognized the HUAC director of research, now a rabid anti-Communist, Benjamin Mandel, who had been the business manager of the *Daily Worker* when Chambers was employed there.[4]

Once Robert "Strip" Stripling, HUAC's chief investigator, assembled the staff and the committee members, they went into executive session to evaluate Chambers's credibility. What they saw was a pudgy, balding man, with a round face shaped something like that of a bulldog, relatively short and poorly dressed, wearing a rumpled suit, who bore a vague resemblance to the popular film actor Charles Laughton. Stripling swore in the witness as David Whittaker Chambers, the name that he had assumed in 1940. From this unimpressive first glimpse, the congressmen had to decide whether or not Chambers could verify Bentley's statements. During his initial fifteen-minute examination, he spoke in a monotone, without emotion, denying that any espionage rings had operated in Washington. This would prove a lie, but Chambers did admit that federal officials, whom he named, had formed a Communist cell in the capital. That disclosure was sufficient to demand that Chambers be heard publicly.[5]

Once in public session, Chambers recited his upbringing and his association with the Communist Party, omitting any references to espionage. He read from a prepared text that named Donald and Alger Hiss as members of an underground group in Washington, emphasizing his friendship with Alger, a high-ranking State Department official during the Roosevelt years. Chambers said that he implored Hiss to leave the party in 1937, but Hiss refused and cried at their parting.[6]

Nixon, who remained silent during the closed session, now questioned Chambers about the individuals with whom he had discussed these charges. The witness replied that Isaac Don Levine, a prominent editor and journalist specializing in anti-Communist causes, had taken him to meet Assistant Secretary Berle in the fall of 1939. Chambers had mentioned the Hiss brothers and others to him, but no action was taken. Nixon asked for more examples. Chambers replied that sometime during 1943 he went to the FBI. Once more, his revelations did not stir action.[7]

These declarations failed to excite the committee members, but the *New York Times* page one headlines named the Hiss brothers, Nathan Witt, Lee Pressman, John Abt, Victor Perlo, and Henry Collins as Communists. The *Washington Daily News* acknowledged that the Justice Department had already heard Bentley's and Chambers's accusations, spent $500,000 over the last three years trying to verify them, and failed to uncover any evidence to back them up.[8]

The HUAC investigations, according to acting chairman Karl Mundt, were "proving very interesting. If the White House refused to cooperate in turning over personnel files, we will crucify the administration. If they do, we are going to be able to dig out more stuff to plague them in the fall campaign." This damaging material, from Mundt's perspective, was a welcome addition to the Democratic turmoil at the time when the Wallacecrats, the Dixiecrats, and others were self-destructing.[9]

Donald Hiss, an attorney associated with the prestigious Washington law firm of Covington, Burling, Rublee, Acheson, & Short, was not nearly as smug. The day of Chambers's appearance, he wrote Mundt denying any connections with the Communist Party and insisting on coming before the committee to make a statement under oath refuting the accusations. Donald said he had never been a member of any front organizations or a Communist Party member. He did not know Chambers, nor recognize his photograph: "Any interested person could easily have discovered these facts by inquiry of any of the distinguished, respected and unquestionably loyal Americans with whom I have been intimately associated."[10]

When HUAC reconvened at 10:30 A.M. in the caucus room of the Old House Office Building on August 4, Mundt presided. Before coming to order, he read telegrams from two of the twenty-five-odd individuals whom Chambers had named as Communists. The second came from Alger Hiss, who declared: "I DO NOT KNOW MR. CHAMBERS AND INSOFAR AS I AM AWARE HAVE NEVER LAID EYES ON HIM." Alger asked to appear the next day when he was scheduled to be in Washington, and the acting chairman granted that request.[11]

Nathan Gregory Silvermaster was sworn that morning. The fact that Bentley had identified him as a secret Soviet agent who was connected to Condon was never established because Thomas was too ill to confront Silvermaster. When questioned, Silvermaster denied Bentley's accusations and then pleaded the Fifth Amendment, marking the beginning of the mass usage of invoking the right against self-incrimination in front of the committee. With the completion of Silvermaster's testimony, Condon ceased to be a target for inquiry.[12]

Nixon, on August 5, acknowledged that the special session had been "somewhat hectic, particularly since our Committee became involved in the rather sensational Bentley case." He had not, as yet, grasped that Chambers was the pivotal personality. At 10:30 A.M., in the same caucus room, with Mundt still in the chair, Alger Hiss was sworn in as the second witness of the day. He started his extraordinary performance by presenting an impressive biography. Born in Baltimore on November 11, 1904, he had graduated from Johns Hopkins University with a Phi Beta Kappa key and received his law degree from Harvard in 1929. After graduation, he served as a clerk to the legendary associate justice of the Supreme Court, Oliver Wendell Holmes. During the presidency of Franklin Roosevelt, Hiss moved to the capital to work for the Agriculture Department and eventually transferred to the State Department, assigned to the trade agreements division, where he served as a close associate to Assistant Secretary of State Francis Sayre. By the end of the war he was promoted, attended the Yalta Conference, and served as the head of the conference secretariat at the San Francisco gathering which designed the United Nations Charter. He now lived in New York City, where he was employed as president of the prestigious Carnegie Endowment for International Peace.

Having pronounced his outstanding credentials throughout the hall, Hiss immediately slammed Chambers. While admitting to knowing Collins, Pressman, Witt, and Abt, Hiss said he had never been connected with the American Communist Party and had never heard of Chambers until 1947, when two FBI agents questioned him: "So far as I know, I have never laid eyes on him, and I should like to have the opportunity to do so."[13]

By the time he finished reading his written statement, Hiss had emerged the victor, and the committee's tone of examination was almost semi-apologetic. Nixon, a month after Hiss's appearance, wrote that he was favorably disposed to believe Hiss over Chambers because Nixon was well acquainted with people in the city who were "very friendly with Donald and Alger Hiss." The congressman began by asking Alger who had suggested that he come to Washington, and he replied that Judge Jerome Frank had asked him to come. When the congressman inquired of Alger for additional individuals who had vouched for him, Alger, mindful that HUAC oftentimes brought up names recklessly, reluctantly added associate justice of the Supreme Court Felix Frankfurter to the list. The congressman also wanted to know if Hiss knew Harold Ware, a suspected Communist, and Hiss replied that he was casually acquainted with him. Nixon could not understand the vast discrepancies between the two witnesses' testimony unless this was an unusual case of mistaken identity.[14]

When shown a photograph of Chambers, Hiss claimed not to recognize him. He wanted to see his accuser in person: "If this is a picture of Mr. Chambers, he is not particularly unusual-looking. He looks like a lot of people. I might even mistake him for the chairman [Mundt] of this committee." The audience erupted with laughter.[15]

At the end of the hearing, Hiss thanked the committee for his fair treatment. Nixon, before recessing, asked Hiss if HUAC should investigate Communists in the government and prevent security risks. Hiss concurred, and Mundt thanked him for testifying forthrightly. The committee adjourned at 12:15 P.M. At the conclusion of the proceedings, Congressman John Rankin of Mississippi rushed up to the witness, shook his hand, and congratulated him, for he was the first to ask to testify in order to deny the charges leveled against him.[16]

Hiss's testimony stunned the committee. Nixon was not predisposed to believe Chambers more than Hiss. Nixon later recalled that Hiss had made "a most favorable impression," and his appearance had "blasted us off our chairs." Nixon estimated that 90 percent of the audience, including the reporters, thought that Hiss was innocent, and that Chambers had lied. Nixon remembered that Mary Spargo, reporter for the *Washington Post,* told him to repudiate Chambers, or Nixon would be "a dead duck." However, the congressman also believed that the allegations of alcoholism, craziness, and homosexuality regularly leveled against those who renounced their Communist beliefs and turned against their former comrades was a "typical commie tactic" to discredit party members who had switched sides.[17]

Mundt stated the obvious: either Hiss or Chambers had lied. The committee would meet later to decide if either had committed perjury, or if this was a strange case of mistaken identity. Gloomy committee members assembled in executive session at 3:00 P.M. that afternoon. Democrat Eddy Hébert from Louisiana wanted to drop the matter and send both men's transcripts to the U.S. Attorney General for possible legal action. Nixon along with Stripling resisted this option. The chief investigator, a year later, remembered that they were "vaguely dissatisfied with some of Hiss's answers, though it was difficult to place our fingers on the exact points." Nixon, a month after Hiss's testimony, conceded that he "was rather insolent toward me from the time that I had insisted on bringing Frankfurter's name in, and I am convinced that from that time my suspicion concerning him continued to grow." To turn suspicions into concrete evidence, the committee formed a special subcommittee, led by Nixon, to go to New York City to confront Chambers in executive session. So that HUAC would not again be subject to such embarrassment, Mundt concealed the group's real mission, telling the press that another witness in the Bentley case was living in New York and the subcommittee was going to interrogate him.[18]

President Truman added to HUAC's inferiority complex that day during a press conference. When asked if the spy scare on Capitol Hill was "a 'red herring' to divert public attention from inflation," the president, to reporters' laughter, answered affirmatively and read a statement that federal employees' records relating to their loyalty would be referred to the White House; none would be sent to any congressional investigations. The federal grand jury and the FBI had already completed their inquiries on these subjects without sufficient evidence for any indictments. The current House and Senate actions, Truman asserted, served "no useful purpose. On the contrary, they are doing irreparable harm to certain people, seriously impairing the morale of Federal employees, and undermining public confidence in the Government. And they are simply a 'red herring' to keep from doing what they ought to do."

A reporter inquired if Americans were entitled to know about the information assembled during these investigations. Truman replied that the congressional committees had not "revealed anything that everybody hasn't known all along, or hasn't been presented to the grand jury. That is where it has to be taken, in the first place, if you are going to do anything about it. They are slandering a lot of people that don't deserve it."[19]

These remarks haunted the subcommittee. Composed of Nixon, Hébert, and McDowell, plus staff, this group left the capital quietly that evening for New York City. Before departing, Nixon told reporters that his committee was going to question a "mystery witness who could crack the spy probe wide open." He characterized the subcommittee's interrogation of Alexander Koral as "highly important," but refused to elaborate any further. The deception succeeded. In actuality, Koral's testimony was short and practically worthless, but it served the purpose of hiding the subcommittee's real intentions of interviewing Chambers again.[20]

On Saturday, August 7, the subcommittee convened at 10:30 A.M. in the Federal Court House, No. 2, Foley Square, to interrogate Chambers, who sat by himself across from Nixon, the principal examiner. Nixon immediately raised the issue of Hiss's unequivocal denial that he ever met Chambers, who replied that he had not seen Hiss since 1938, at which time Hiss called him Carl. Nixon asked for proof that Hiss was a party member, and Chambers replied that he collected party dues from Hiss; Hiss also gave his car to a Washington car lot operator who turned it over to a party organizer.

The witness minutely described Alger's habits and lifestyle: he had difficulty hearing from one ear; his mother and sister still lived in Baltimore; and his wife hated her first husband, Thayer, and had a child from that failed marriage. Nixon also wanted information about Hiss's children and family nicknames. Chambers provided some and described his trips to Hiss's homes, including their living quarters, furnishings, dogs, and maids. He recalled that Alger and his wife, Priscilla, were amateur ornithologists and how excited they became when spotting a prothonotary warbler. The witness talked about a 1929 Ford black roadster that the family owned. Finally, Chambers, at Nixon's prodding, consented to a lie detector test, if it proved necessary. He was telling the truth and had nothing to hide.[21]

Nixon, on a very hot summer afternoon, consumed almost the entire amount of a two-hour-forty-minute session. Hébert asked a few questions toward the end due to his skepticism about Chambers's veracity, but at the conclusion felt that the witness knew Hiss well or had a great deal of information concerning him. Nixon appreciated Hébert's skepticism "because it kept the rest of us from going off half-cocked."[22]

From the end of this first week in August, Nixon assumed charge of the investigation. Chairman J. Parhall Thomas was physically incapacitated. Moreover, he faced a series of sensational allegations, beginning on August 4, in Drew Pearson's column for hiring a stenographer and having her pay him a kickback over a four-year period. Three days later, Pearson published an article about another kickback scheme with one of Thomas's clerks and added that the congressman had received money for helping to keep a soldier out of the fighting in World War II.[23]

Mundt also had other priorities. He expected to return to South

Dakota between August 15 and 17 to launch his senatorial campaign. He, however, conceded that "We are head over heels in the most exciting and time consuming activities in which I have been engaged since coming to Congress—the current hearings and investigation in connection with the Communist espionage activities which have so seriously permeated the Executive Department." The other two Republican congressmen on the committee, McDowell and Vail, were in the midst of hotly contested reelections that they would lose. Since Nixon had already won both primary votes, he had more time and became so obsessed with the Hiss–Chambers conflict that he spent up to eighteen-hour days on it. Almost a quarter century after the fact, Nixon asserted: "I've never worked as hard in my life."[24]

From the time the president repeated his catchy "red herring" phrase, in Nixon's mind, he justified HUAC's further proceedings. The president had declared that the hearings were worthless, and as a result he refused to act or even cooperate with Congress. Since the federal grand jury had finished its inquiry without indictments, and the conflicting statements of Chambers and Hiss were insufficient to reopen their case, Nixon felt he had every right to find out which man was telling the truth.[25]

Shortly after Truman left the White House, Drew Pearson interviewed him on television about the "red herring" remark and the legislative failures of the 80th Congress. The former president doggedly insisted that he never used the phrase. Several decades after the event, Nixon chided Truman for repeating the "red herring" declaration, not understanding why he purposefully baited the committee, and what, if anything, stopped him from investigating the legitimate charges brought out by Bentley and Chambers. "The *cover-up*," much on Nixon's mind in the fall of 1972, "is what hurts you."[26]

Liberal newspapers that Nixon read such as the *New York Times* and *Washington Post* opposed HUAC's investigation. On Sunday, August 8, the *Post* editorialized that perjury had obviously been committed and the matter should go to the courts for adjudication. To date, the committee had acted shamefully: "As things stand, it is the committee which is subject to the most serious indictment of all."[27]

Despite such criticism, Nixon moved ahead on several fronts. Stripling was assigned to check various aspects of Chambers's account, and by Monday, August 9, he verified Hiss's assignment on the Senate Munitions Committee as well as his duties at the Agriculture Department early in the New Deal. Stripling also looked into the Agricultural Department's legal staff when Jerome Frank was general counsel to the Agriculture Adjustment Administration and was responsible for hiring Hiss.[28]

The next morning, Thomas chaired the session in the usual caucus room at 10:00 A.M., and the committee spent the time interrogating several witnesses who failed to make any startling disclosures. Thomas had returned to the capital from New Jersey and was trying to help resolve the dilemma over which man, Hiss or Chambers, was lying.[29]

Mundt, who attended these sessions, believed that they were "certainly producing some startling and sordid facts on the workings of Communist Espionage within our Executive Department. It just doesn't seem possible it could happen here—but it has." He thought the committee had demonstrated that the administration had shown poor judgment in hiring certain disloyal individuals to direct domestic and foreign policies. Mundt could not understand "our President's position in not wanting to expose these people of questionable loyalty."[30]

Nixon called William Rogers, chief counsel for the Senate Special Committee to Investigate the National Defense Program, to read Chambers's secret transcript. Senator Homer Ferguson, who chaired that Senate subcommittee, had introduced Nixon to Rogers at the end of July 1948 so that they could share data. Rogers's pleasant personality and legal résumé impressed Nixon. Although the two were physical opposites, they had much in common. Both were born in 1913 and lost two brothers before reaching adulthood. The two men were scholastic achievers, finishing at the top of their classes in high school, receiving scholarships during their undergraduate and professional training. They were chosen for law review, were tapped for the same legal honorary society, and passed the bar in the same year. When the United States went to war, the navy trained them in the same Quonset class, and they were both stationed in the Pacific theater.[31]

The distinguished-looking chief counsel was tall (six foot one), weighed175 pounds, with blue eyes and blond hair. He was a competent lawyer, but not an exceptional orator. Many years after meeting Nixon, Rogers recalled that he was especially taken with Nixon's emphasis on being fair to Hiss; the congressman expected to solve the riddle presented by the two antithetical witnesses and "apologize if Chambers was lying and Hiss was telling the truth." Based on his experience as a prosecutor, Rogers concentrated on the many details Chambers had marshaled concerning Hiss's private life.[32]

After talking with Rogers, Nixon had dinner with Congressman Charles Kersten, who shared many similar beliefs on the Communist menace. Nixon also let Kersten read Chambers's account. After finishing it, Kersten suggested that his friend should allow John Foster Dulles to examine it, for Kersten had already heard rumors that Hiss was trying to get Dulles and other Carnegie board members to come out publicly in his favor. Before Dulles issued a potentially embarrassing statement, he should at the very minimum have the courtesy to read what Chambers said. Agreeing with that advice, Nixon called Dulles the next morning, August 11, and set up a meeting for later that evening.[33]

Thomas made headlines that day by charging Soviet officials with paying Bentley at least $2,000 in October 1945 as compensation for her job as a courier. The only session that day began at 10:00 A.M. in the same caucus room with the chairman presiding. After fighting in World War II and being a federal employee for fifteen years, Henry Collins testified that he lived in New York City, directing the American Russian Institute, and read a statement denying Chambers's allegations. He refused to answer any questions about Communist connections that would incriminate himself, but steadfastly denounced Chambers and Bentley. Elizabeth Bentley was sworn in next to reiterate her account of Collins's subversive activities.[34]

That afternoon, Bert Andrews, Washington bureau chief for the *New York Herald Tribune,* went to Nixon's office. The congressman had called him the day before and asked: "Can you come up and talk to me about the Hiss case for a couple of hours? . . . I need some advice." The reporter had not been assigned to the hearings, but "out of curiosity," the previous day, went to the HUAC hearing room to listen to Lee Pressman repudiate Bentley's accusations that he was a spy and then he watched her reaffirm that he was involved in espionage. Andrews suggested to Congressman Clarence Brown, Republican from Ohio, who was visiting the proceedings, that each be given a lie detector test. They shook their heads, and as Brown was leaving the room, he told Andrews that the committee would not "go for it. They've already asked Whittaker Chambers if he'll take a lie detector test. He said he would, so they want to wait and ask Alger Hiss if he'll take one. They don't pair."[35]

Andrews was about to become a key player in the Chambers-Hiss investigation. Raised in San Diego, California, he dropped out of Stanford University to become a vagabond newspaperman. Consumed by his profession, he settled in New York, writing for the Hearst paper, and became a political conservative who still voted for Roosevelt in 1932 and 1936. Andrews's writing was mediocre, but he was a skilled reporter who searched out the news and tried to scoop his colleagues. He chain-smoked Chesterfield cigarettes and drank expensive bourbon to excess. A series of articles in 1947 about the State Department's unjustified removal of ten employees who were released without any explanation as security risks had won him a Pulitzer Prize. In spite of his shortcomings, he maintained a reputation as an ethical reporter who kept confidences.

Nixon had briefly been introduced to Andrews and had heard about his impeccable reputation for objectivity. The congressman during their meeting declared that he was one of the most baffled persons in the capital and the "most puzzled member" of HUAC. Chambers and Hiss directly contradicted one another, and Nixon did not know whom to believe. In his notes from the interview, Andrews scribbled the congressman's reflections: "Chambers sounded completely convincing. Hiss sounded the same way. In fact, Hiss made such an impression that a number of the committee members want to drop the case right now and go on to something else. They think they've got a potato that's too hot to handle and they're afraid of the repercussions, what with the election coming up in November." Under these circumstances, Nixon asked Andrews for an unbiased evaluation of Chambers's confidential transcript, with the proviso that he could not publish anything until all the newspapers had received the document. After finishing the transcript, Andrews, too, concluded that Chambers knew Hiss.[36]

Nixon and Kersten later boarded a train with Chambers's transcript for the long ride to New York City. When they arrived at the Roosevelt Hotel, Nixon met John Foster Dulles for the first time, as well as his brother Allen, who had accompanied Nixon on the Herter mission. At the start of a lengthy conversation, Nixon asked both lawyers to read Chambers's observations concerning Hiss's private life and render their professional judgment on whether or not Hiss knew Chambers. After the brothers completed their review, Foster paced the floor with his hands crossed behind him as was his practice when contemplating critical matters, concluding: "It's almost impossible to believe, but Chambers knows Hiss." Allen concurred. While the brothers' findings were not definitive, Nixon had saved Foster, chief diplomatic adviser to the Republican presidential contender, from possibly damaging repercussions if he had sent out any statement on Hiss's behalf. Two years later, Foster thanked Nixon, recalling "very well your sound and sober judgment."[37]

Probably to protect his own prestige, Foster hid two critical facts from the congressman. First, Dulles never admitted that he, as the designated chairman of the board of trustees, had propelled Hiss into the Carnegie presidency. Second, at the time Dulles had received two letters alleging Hiss's Communist affiliations, but he dismissed them. Later, in the summer of 1952, Dulles would draft a memorandum that presented the unmistakable impression that he had played a minimal role in Hiss's selection.[38]

Nixon returned to the capital on August 12 in time to read Truman's second declaration that the hearings constituted a "red herring" to deflect public attention from the Republican Congress's failure to pass his anti-inflationary recommendations. He later added that the hearings were "one of the strongest type [of odors] you can smell." Anti-Communism was emerging as an emotional partisan issue.[39]

The reviews of Chambers's account by Rogers, Kersten, Andrews, and the Dulles brothers prompted Nixon to visit Chambers at his farm in Westminster, Maryland, a rural area two hours from the capital, where he met Esther, Chambers's wife, and discovered that she and Whittaker, like Priscilla Hiss, were Quakers. Chambers invited his guest to sit on the porch. He then described Henry Collins's apartment in detail and provided special information about Harry Dexter White and George Silverman. With these additional pieces of the puzzle, Nixon returned to the capital more convinced than ever that Whittaker had told the truth.[40]

Nixon also worked through Hiss to uncover the truth. Nixon had been studying lie detector tests over the past several months and had confidence in those administered by Dr. Leonardo Keeler of Chicago. In a letter on August 13 to Thomas, Hiss wrote that he had not as yet come to a decision about the test, since he had found out that many scientists as well as the FBI doubted its value and no federal court relied on it. Nixon phoned Keeler the next morning, who responded that some judges used lie detectors, as did the War Department. He admitted that the test did not work for "low-grade feeble minded and certain types of psychopaths. The best results are within the so-called normal to intellectual groups."[41]

HUAC's staff was minutely filling in the details for Hiss's biographical sketch. By August 13, the investigators had gathered information on Alger's mother, Mary, and her two other sons. His movements from Baltimore to Cambridge, Massachusetts, were traced. He had rented a house at 2831 28th Street, N.W., in the District of Columbia from

July 1934 through June 1935, had applied for a Washington driver's permit on June 5, 1934, and had owned a 1929 Ford coupe, motor #A-2188811, and bought a Plymouth in October 1935 and another Plymouth in September 1937.[42]

These behind-the-scenes activities did not interrupt the Friday, August 13, hearings. Lauchlin Currie spoke first and presented his outstanding credentials: a Harvard doctorate and service as an administrative assistant to Roosevelt from 1939 to 1945. He spoke freely, vehemently denying Bentley's accusations. When Nixon asked him if he knew that Silvermaster and Silverman were Communists, Currie said that he did not and only met them occasionally. At the conclusion of his examination, he pronounced that the committee had given him a fair hearing.[43]

Harry Dexter White, who also received a Harvard Ph.D., came next to denounce both Bentley's and Chambers's charges to the applause of the audience. Nixon asked if White ever met Chambers; White had no recollection. Due to a serious heart illness, he took a five-minute break, and upon his return, agreed with Nixon that these public sessions had to be based on the presumption of innocence if they were to be fair. Thomas examined White about his connections with many economists with alleged Communist bonds. White replied that he was disappointed with this coincidence, but he was unaware that any of these individuals had spied for the Russians.[44]

The last witness, Donald Hiss, was sworn in and denied ever meeting Chambers. Nixon questioned Donald about that statement and his relationship with Alger. The congressman had examined his testimony and that of Chambers, concluding "that perjury has been committed in this case." While the committee did not have a duty to reach any findings, a court did. If Chambers had made false declarations, his career would be destroyed. Nixon had spoken to him on August 12, and Chambers was expected to come before HUAC again under oath to repeat his accusations. Donald agreed that if he were lying, he should go to jail, and the same applied to Chambers. That concluded the hearings for the week. The committee would reconvene on Monday, when Alger Hiss would reappear. In evaluating Nixon's role, William White of the *New York Times* commented that the congressman was "at pains to try to keep the committee on a legally sound path and has a considerable reputation for fairness to witnesses."[45]

Nixon prepared for the next round by driving out to Chambers's Westminster farm both days. On Saturday, the congressman visited the rural farmhouse with Stripling, who by that time believed Chambers. Strip, the congressman thought, had "almost a sixth sense" discerning "Red-baiters" from those who really wished to assist the committee.[46]

Sunday was even more crucial. Nixon had asked Bert Andrews to grill Chambers to determine if he were telling the truth during their conversation in his office and had phoned Chambers for permission to come see him with a newspaperman, whom Nixon did not identify. Nixon reasoned that an impartial reporter's objectivity would somehow limit his liability. If Chambers were lying and wrongfully attacking Hiss, "it would be a death blow to effective and necessary investigation of the Communist conspiracy in the United States." To Nixon, Andrews was a fail-safe device, and the reporter was delighted to have an opportunity to scoop his peers.[47]

Nixon and Andrews arrived around 2:00 P.M. The congressman parked his car in the driveway near Chambers's barn, and they walked to the somewhat dilapidated farmhouse, where Chambers ushered them into the living room. Their host was puffing on his pipe, and at first, said he did not want to talk with Andrews because the reporter had initially recommended Hiss for the job at the Carnegie Endowment and had been antagonistic toward HUAC. Andrews agreed that he had been critical of State Department loyalty procedures and fought for those who were fired without proper hearings. Most had been reinstated or allowed to resign without any stigma. Chambers, he added, was about to be "railroaded much the same way, even though you may be telling the truth." At present, Chambers had a better chance of an indictment than Hiss, whose background and prominent friends provided him with credibility. Nixon concurred. Chambers ought to talk to Andrews.

Their host thought a moment and then gave his consent. With that, the reporter asked him about rumors spreading through the capital about him being a drunkard, being institutionalized in a mental hospital, and having a homosexual liaison with Hiss. Chambers flatly denied these accusations. The congressman next produced four glossy eight-by-ten prints of Hiss's residences, which Chambers had never seen. He not only identified them but also described the furnishings inside. The reporter turned to the common interest that Hiss and Chambers had in ornithology, and Chambers produced two books on birds that Hiss allegedly had given him. Andrews monopolized the three-hour interview. After completing his grueling examination, he believed that Chambers knew Hiss quite well.[48]

Andrews and Nixon agreed on three points: first, Chambers and Hiss were acquainted; second, records for the 1929 Ford that Hiss had purchased, supposedly given to the Communist Party, had to be found; and finally, the two men needed to confront each other. Nixon also learned how much Andrews resented Congressman Rankin's slurs against African Americans and Jews, as well as the miscues in the Condon debacle. HUAC had smeared witnesses without cause and disgusted many observers, including Andrews.[49]

Now Hiss had his chance to prove his veracity. Nixon went to an executive session at 2:00 P.M. for his special HUAC subcommittee, composed of himself, Hébert, and McDowell, with Thomas presiding. Nixon, clearly in charge, set the tone of the gathering by telling the witness that HUAC was trying to decided which man was lying. The congressman was looking for third-party corroboration. Hiss admitted hearing Whittaker Chambers's name in May 1947 when two FBI agents visited him in New York City and mentioned Chambers. Hiss recalled that the name stuck in his mind because it was distinctive and unusual. He remarked that Chambers looked familiar to him and that he had noted this during his first HUAC appearance. Hiss also speculated that Chambers might have known him because Hiss had hundreds of people going through his home since living in Washington.

The congressman interrogated Hiss about being a party member, a charge that the witness rejected. Nixon asked about knowing Chambers as Carl, and Hiss denied knowing him under any alias. The witness admitted knowing Collins and Pressman, but Hiss never recalled visiting their apartments. Hiss gave the background of his two children, as well as that of his wife Priscilla, who were all currently at their summer home in northern Vermont.

Disappointed that the committee had given Chambers any credence since he was a confessed Communist, Hiss refused to make any identification through a photograph, preferring to meet Chambers and hear his voice. The witness then asked if Nixon had ever stayed at Chambers's farm, and the congressman denied spending the night, but never volunteered that he had visited Chambers on three separate occasions by himself and with Andrews or Stripling. Congressman Hébert listened intently to this exchange. The Democrat, who had an open mind about deciding which of the witnesses was committing perjury, told Hiss, "whichever one of you is lying is the greatest actor that America has ever produced."[50]

After a short break, the session resumed. Hiss seized the moment to suggest that someone called "George Crosley," a freelance reporter whom Hiss had met during the depression in Washington, might be the man in the photographs that Hiss was shown during his first HUAC hearing on August 5. Hiss described Crosley's teeth as in great need of dental work and his wife as having "strikingly dark" complexion. This, to Nixon, gave him an edge, for only he knew that Esther Chambers had such skin color. The Crosleys had been house guests, and they had rented an apartment from Hiss. Hiss and Crosley had lunch together on several occasions and once drove from the capital to New York City. Hiss had given Crosley his old Model A Ford, but Hiss did not remember how he transferred the title of the car to Crosley.

Nixon continued his laborious inquiry. Hiss did not suffer from poor hearing in his left ear, as Chambers alleged. He provided nicknames for his wife and children that did not correspond with Chambers's account. McDowell briefly interrupted to ask if Hiss had ever seen a prothonotary warbler. Hiss responded enthusiastically that he had near the Potomac River, not realizing that the congressman was confirming Chambers's recollection of Hiss's sighting of that rare bird. By the conclusion, Nixon maintained that "as it stands at the present time it is your word against that of Mr. Chambers." Nixon asked if Hiss would take a lie detector test, but before Hiss decided, he wanted to study the request. Stripling examined Hiss briefly about possible Communist connections, but he replied that he had none. Hiss could not understand why Chambers had given such damaging testimony against him.

At the end of the subcommittee meeting early that evening, Thomas informed Hiss that HUAC unanimously decided to hold a public hearing on August 25, at which time Hiss and Chambers would meet. Nixon expected to take Priscilla's testimony in New York City the following day, and her husband thanked the committee for its courtesies.[51]

Some of Chambers's secret testimony had leaked to the press, and the August 16 session also reached the front page of the New York Times, where C. P. Trussell revealed that Chambers was willing to take a lie detector test, though Hiss declined. They would confront each other on August 25 at a public forum to determine which one had been truthful.[52]

Nixon and Stripling went over Hiss's testimony that evening in Nixon's office. They suspected that Chambers had told the truth, but they still harbored doubts. Stripling left by midnight, while Nixon remained to sift through the evidence in the early morning hours of August 17. He phoned Stripling at 2:00 A.M., instructing him to summon both Chambers and Hiss before the special subcommittee that afternoon in New York City at a suite in the Commodore Hotel. Delay, Nixon recollected fourteen years later, would give the liar additional time to prepare for the public hearings; "a sudden and more or less unexpected confrontation," Stripling recalled, would be more effective.[53]

Stripling had Congressman McDowell, one of the committee members who knew Hiss, wire him to meet at the hotel that evening. At first, Hiss balked, but then grudgingly consented. Nixon sent Chambers a telegram: "ESSENTIAL THAT YOU CALL ME AS SOON AS POSSIBLE TODAY."[54]

Chambers did not receive this message. He had planned to leave his farm that day and go to his New York City office, but his intuition prompted him to switch tickets and head to Washington. Reaching the capital about noon, he went to the HUAC office, where the staff greeted him with relief. Without any explanation he was rushed to Union Station and they boarded a train for New York. As the locomotive sped north, Chambers sat alone, smoking his pipe without any idea what was about to transpire. The committee learned on the ride that Harry Dexter White, who had recently testified, had suddenly died of a heart attack. Although later accused of scheduling the confrontation to divert attention from White's death and the possibility that pressure from his HUAC testimony precipitated the attack, Nixon accurately contended that he had already made his decision to bring Chambers and Hiss together.[55]

Donald Appell, one of the HUAC investigators, quietly took Chambers to the hotel in midtown Manhattan and put him in one of two bedrooms in the suite. Chambers and Nixon sat next to one another, with their backs to the window and a vacant seat for Thomas, who arrived late. The pictures on the wall happened to be Audubon prints, a fitting reminder of earlier testimony. A man sat with his back to Chambers. That person, who had not as yet glanced at him, was Alger Hiss, who sat in a chair several feet from the table facing the congressmen.[56]

Nixon informed Hiss that Chambers had been brought to the city for identification purposes since Hiss had mentioned a third party in his examination, George Crosley. The announcement agitated the witness, who claimed that he was disturbed by his friend Harry Dexter White's sudden death. Hiss was additionally agitated that the *New York Herald Tribune* had published leaks from the subcommittee that he had been asked to take a lie detector and that his wife would soon be interrogated.[57]

After Chambers walked in and sat on the couch, Hiss turned, asked him to open his mouth to see his teeth, and then requested that he speak. When Nixon interrupted Hiss to swear Chambers in, Hiss became angry and Nixon annoyed: "I suggested that he be sworn, and when I say something like that I want no interruptions from you." Hiss indignantly replied that in view of White's tragic death, Nixon had no right "to use that tone of voice in speaking to me, and I hope the record will show what I have just said." Nixon remembered the incident another way: "his manner and tone in doing so was insulting in the extreme."[58]

Hiss would not concede that Chambers and Crosley were the same person and insisted that the portly man read something aloud. Chambers, who had recently resigned as a senior editor at *Time,* grabbed a copy of *Newsweek* and read from it; the selection of that rival magazine amused everyone except for Hiss. The congressman then covered earlier testimony: Hiss had met Crosley in Washington during the New Deal, leased him an apartment for three months, gave him a Ford, and traveled with him to New York. Hiss was still uncertain that Chambers was Crosley, and Chambers refused to admit using both names. Nixon thought that Hiss's insistence on looking into Chambers's mouth to examine his teeth and listening to him speak was incredible. The congressman later characterized Hiss's machinations as "one of the most unconvincing acts that I have ever seen put on by a supposedly intelligent man."

While Hiss struggled through his tortuous process of identification, Chambers immediately recognized Hiss and accused him of being a Communist and paying party dues. Hiss abruptly changed his tactic, declaring: "I am now perfectly prepared to identify this man as George Crosley." Claiming to know Chambers only as Crosley, Hiss grew angrier, rose from his chair, walked over to Chambers shaking his fist, and challenged him to make his accusations without congressional immunity: "May I say for the record at this point, that I would like to invite Mr. Whittaker Chambers to make those same statements out of the presence of this committee without their being privileged for suit for libel. I challenge you to do it, and I hope you will do it damned quickly." Louis Russell, one of the HUAC investigators, was concerned that Hiss might strike Chambers and gently grabbed Hiss's arm to prevent this. His voice rose: "I am not going to touch him. You are touching me." Then Hiss resumed his seat, conceding a certain familiarity with the photographs from the August 5 hearing, but still insisting that he could not identify Crosley from them.[59]

The subcommittee took a brief recess to agree unanimously that Hiss recognized Chambers as Crosley, a man whom he met early in the New Deal. The assembled congressmen reaffirmed that HUAC would meet on August 25 in public session to examine both men. Nixon would remain until the next day to take Priscilla Hiss's testimony because she had to return to Vermont to care for her children. Alger would accompany her. As Thomas was about to adjourn the meeting at 7:15 P.M., he thanked Hiss for appearing. Hiss replied: "*I don't reciprocate.*" He resented the committee's methods and phoned Dulles in the evening, declaring "that the Committee and I were now at war."[60]

After Hiss left, the room remained silent for a moment. Strip glanced at Chambers, and in a Texas drawl, totally deadpan, inquired: "Ha-ya, Mistah Crawz-li?"[61]

Hiss held a press conference that evening at which he claimed to have identified Chambers as Crosley, whom he now regarded as a "dead beat." He had been a renter and "never paid one cent on the apartment . . . and in addition to that he touched me for $30 or $40." Hiss added a note of incredulity about the episode. HUAC had earlier scheduled both men to meet later that month, and there was "something funny" about the committee's forcing them to appear in the hotel that day without notice.[62]

Nixon recounted his version of these events three week later. While Chambers was in total control and seemed to be enjoying the proceedings, the congressman recalled that Hiss "was visibly shaken, and had lost the air of smoothness which had characterized most of his appearances before the Committee and before and after this time." This was a defining moment, for Hiss "acted the part of a liar who had been caught, rather than the part of the outraged innocent man, which he had so successfully portrayed before that time." He seemed to hate Chambers, and once "Hiss finally admitted that he knew Chambers, he did so in a very loud, dramatic voice as if he were acting in a Shakespearian play."[63]

After this hearing, Andrews published an article asserting that Nixon was primarily responsible for the meeting. The congressman knew that one of these men was lying and had set out to determine which one.

Each presented his story, and afterwards Nixon declared: "Mr. Hiss gave the impression to the public that he had never known his man at all under any name." Hiss now admitted knowing Chambers as Crosley. The congressman ultimately would find the truth. Frank Conniff, another columnist, wrote that he had watched Nixon on several occasions, "and his plodding but logical approach is the direct opposite of the flashy forensics that usually capture headlines." He staged the confrontation: "Thanks to preserving plodders like Congressman Nixon, the soiled linen is finally being hung out to dry. It's high time, too."[64]

Nixon plodded on. He fit Priscilla Hiss, accompanied by her husband and Charles Dollard, a colleague from the Carnegie Foundation, between two other witnesses. By that morning, Nixon noticed that Alger "had completely regained his composure and was the smooth elegant gentleman that he had been previous." She, in her ten-minute interrogation, confirmed that she remembered Crosley as a "sponger" from the New Deal period, but only vaguely recalled him and his wife. Afterwards, Nixon conceded that he should have been more aggressive in examining her on Communist connections and should not have allowed Alger to attend the session. Nixon returned to Washington that afternoon and prepared for the upcoming confrontation with Hiss on August 25 by driving the HUAC staff harder than ever before to decide which man was truthful. Alger had far greater immediate troubles. That same day John Foster Dulles asked for his resignation; but Hiss requested and received permission to remain in his position until the HUAC hearings ended.[65]

Chairman Thomas charged Truman with purposefully concealing espionage inside the federal government by obstructing the HUAC investigation. Thomas later voiced his opinion on the radio about recent events, highlighting his primary objective in calling these espionage hearings. He claimed that besides the spy rings associated with Bentley and Chambers, a third one that former New Deal officials operated would be implicated. Silvermaster would prominently figure in these alleged activities, and Condon, whom the federal loyalty board had exonerated, would be at the core.[66]

The *Chicago Daily News,* in an editorial, summarized the developments on Thursday, August 19. Nixon was now credited with "breaking" the case because he had pressed to find out which man was lying. HUAC hoped to explore other issues, but Nixon persisted and made

Hiss admit that he recognized Chambers, had rented him an apartment, and had given him a car. Though Truman still doggedly held that it was all "a red herring," one of his advisers admitted that he might have to "choke on that fish" before the hearings concluded, due to Nixon's steadfastness.[67]

The president did not listen to those who cautioned moderation and at a press conference he blasted HUAC's investigation for infringing on the Bill of Rights. Nixon immediately responded to Truman's attack. The congressman shared the president's "great concern over civil rights . . . and because of this I think that it is essential to conduct an absolutely thorough investigation into communism in the United States and the Government." Nixon called upon the White House to cooperate with his committee and guarantee fairness.

The congressman had also pressed Hiss to consent to a lie detector test. By August 19, Hiss had talked to professionals, and due to the unreliability of the polygraph, he decided against taking one. This decision disappointed Nixon, but since Hiss had refused, HUAC, Nixon proclaimed, would not make Chambers submit to one.[68]

As HUAC grew in prominence, Nixon increasingly cemented its fortune with his own. He wrote constituents that the committee had "been quite busy with the current spy investigations and my time has hardly been my own." He hoped to discuss the recent hearings and the need for legislation after his return to California, although the HUAC hearings would possibly "continue for some time." Roy Day wrote that he was "getting a big kick" out of these hearings: "It especially pleases me because some people thought you were running down blind alleys with your committee work at first, but now they are strangely quiet. I'd love to be there and get in on some of the intrigue—or maybe I'd just love to be there??"[69]

Bert Andrews, by now a vociferous Nixon cheerleader, continued the momentum in a Sunday piece for the *New York Herald Tribune:* HUAC had almost dropped the case after Hiss's appearance, but it continued because Nixon and others felt uncomfortable about Hiss's evasiveness.[70]

During the last full week of August, Nixon worked feverishly. On August 23, a HUAC investigator found the Bureau of Motor Vehicles transfer certificate of Hiss's 1929 Ford roadster in the summer of 1936. It had not gone to either Chambers or Crosley, but to William Rosen, an automobile dealer with possible connections to the Communist Party. The staff, at Nixon's direction, started to search for the individuals involved in this transaction.[71]

Nixon, as the sole HUAC member present, convened his subcommittee that Tuesday in executive session at 10:05 A.M. in its committee room to hear additional testimony. Before the meeting, Hiss was already attacking HUAC in the press for its unfair treatment. In spite of his complaints, Nixon went ahead, calling Louis Budenz, former managing editor of the *Daily Worker* and party member, to confirm that Abt, Pressman, and others were Communists. Budenz said he had heard Hiss's name brought up as a party member in 1940 and 1941, and Nixon clarified that Budenz's opinion "was gathered not simply from one casual mention but from several mentions of Mr. Hiss as being under Communist discipline."[72]

That Wednesday, August 25, anticipated by the *New York Times* as "Confrontation Day," was a hot morning and ended in an equally stifling evening. HUAC convened, with Thomas presiding. Besides the chairman, Mundt, McDowell, Vail, and the sole Democrat, Hébert, as well as the staff led by Stripling, were present. The ground rules were simple: only members could ask questions; neither Hiss nor Chambers could cross-examine each other. The committee looked out onto a standing-room audience, filled with reporters, klieg lights, and technicians operating newsreel and television cameras recording, for the first time, a major congressional hearing.[73]

Thomas called Hiss first, who made an opening statement in which he identified Chambers as George Crosley, whom Hiss had not seen since 1935. Chambers was sworn next, contradicting Hiss, and claiming to know him after 1935. Starting with this dispute over dates, Nixon along with his colleagues and Stripling concentrated on the record generated by Hiss's three previous appearances. Nixon, who emerged as Hiss's inquisitor, set the guidelines. The central issues were the real or imagined character, George Crosley, the disposition of the Ford to Crosley, and the apartment lease between Hiss and Crosley.[74]

Under a barrage of questions, Hiss maintained that he had given the Ford to Crosley, the only time that he ever had done such a thoughtless thing. Nixon, however, could not conceive that Hiss would surrender a car in the midst of the depression to a man who failed to pay his rent. Louis Russell interrupted the witness to present evidence that the Ford was sold to Cherner Motor Company on July 23, 1936, with Hiss's notarized signature attached to the transfer document; Hiss said he forgot ever signing a bill of sale. Committee members discussed an oral lease with Crosley to Hiss's apartment in 1935 and argued over its duration. Neither Hiss nor the committee produced anyone who recognized Chambers as Crosley, and no one found any reference to him as a reporter or any publications under that byline. At 1:05 P.M., the committee took an hour-and-a-half break.[75]

At the beginning of the afternoon session, Nixon resumed his inquiry into the Ford's disposition. Hiss recollected that he had permitted Crosley to drive the car in 1935, but he possibly had not completed the sale until the summer of 1936, for the title remained in his name until that time. Nixon then summarized Hiss's earlier testimony and highlighted inconsistencies. Hiss, of course, disagreed with Nixon's arguments as well as his conclusions.[76]

Mundt questioned Hiss on his failure to recognize Chambers from the photographs shown to him on August 5. Nixon interrupted, recalling how Hiss had requested that Chambers open his mouth to see his teeth at the Commodore Hotel twelve days earlier. Nixon asked: "My question may sound facetious, but I am just wondering: Didn't you ever see Mr. Crosley with his mouth closed?" Although the audience chuckled, Nixon was serious, as was Hiss. The latter replied that Chambers's most striking feature was his bad teeth. Mundt then showed Hiss early and recent photographs of Chambers for identification purposes. Although Mundt felt that Hiss had left a false impression of not recognizing Chambers during his first appearance, Hiss denied misleading anyone. Mundt next turned to Hiss's discussion with John Foster Dulles about the FBI's investigation of him and a possible Communist connection. Hiss recounted his conversation with the agents in 1947, where he heard, for the first time, that Chambers had accused him of being a Communist. Mundt later connected Hiss to the Democrats' failed China policy that allowed the Red Chinese to evict the Chiang Kai-shek from the mainland and commented to his wife at dinner after Hiss's first appearance that he "had been taken in by his [Hiss's] suavity," but now believed that Hiss could be a Communist.[77]

Hébert wanted Hiss to explain why he did not immediately recognize Chambers from the photos on August 5. The witness responded that he did not associate Chambers with Crosley that day and did not think about the connection until August 16. Hébert also asked Hiss later how Chambers discovered Hiss's fascination with the prothonotary warbler, and Hiss contended that he told many people about sighting that rare bird.[78]

Stripling focused on Hiss's association with alleged party members like Abt, Pressman, Collins, and Perlo. Hiss asserted that he did not know Perlo and was never in Collins's apartment. Furthermore, he stated that he never knew these individuals were Communists.[79]

Nixon finished his examination of Hiss by forcing him to make numerous damaging admissions. Hiss knew Chambers under another name. Hiss let Chambers use the Ford and then gave it to him; he loaned Chambers up to $150; and he drove Chambers to New York City. When asked to place the last time he saw Chambers, Hiss replied no later than the fall of 1935, while his adversary placed the time much later. Mundt listened to this devastating exchange. Originally, he thought that Chambers had a case of mistaken identity or had falsified his testimony before the committee, but now he had no reservations that Chambers knew Hiss reasonably well.[80]

Hiss defended himself by arguing that Chambers had a decade to study his movements. He was a confessed Communist who, by his own admission, had lied. Hiss had a distinguished record of government service. Hiss then inserted a series of testimonials into the record from prominent people like three former secretaries of state: Cordell Hull, Henry Stimson, and Edward Stettinius, Jr. Hiss's reputation was impeccable; he asked the committee to look deeper into Chambers's background to see if the rumors of emotional problems or mental institutionalization were accurate. When Nixon inquired where Hiss received this information, the latter declined to give a source; it was merely gossip. Hiss again challenged Chambers to make charges against him that he was a Communist outside of the privilege created by the congressional hearing room so that Hiss could sue for libel and slander.[81]

Chambers testified late that afternoon. He alleged that J. Peters, the underground director of the Communist Party, had introduced him to Hiss. Chambers had never given Hiss any money to sublease an apartment or pay for the Ford. Since they were both Communists, he said, Hiss willingly shared. When Chambers broke with the party, he had tried to convince Hiss to do the same because "Mr. Hiss was certainly the closest friend I ever had in the Communist Party." Chambers recounted his visit to Berle in 1939 to expose Communists in the federal government and his disclosure that Hiss was a party member. Chambers said that he had no reason to tell falsehoods because he was only damaging his career and position in his community. He had never been convicted of any crime and never spent any time in a mental institution. Communists employed these smear tactics against their enemies, he asserted. He warned that Communists were still in the federal government and had to be rooted out.[82]

As the testimony concluded, Chambers struggled to maintain his composure. He did not hate Hiss: "We were close friends, but we are caught in a tragedy of history. Mr. Hiss represents the concealed enemy against which we are all fighting, and I am fighting. I have testified against him with remorse and pity, but in a moment of history in which this Nation now stands, so help me God, I could not do otherwise." He fought for emotional control in the silence that gripped the room.[83]

At the conclusion of Alger Hiss's first appearance before HUAC, the audience had overwhelmingly applauded his spirited defense and congratulated him. Now, after nine and a half hours of grueling testimony, he stood practically alone with his lawyers. He saw HUAC as an adversary trying to impeach him. The committee, he asserted, "increased its efforts to create an impression with the public that I had been inconsistent and contradictory while Chambers had been uniformly consistent and accurate. My testimony continued to be adversely characterized, and selected passages were taken out of context. I did not find that the Committee's attitude toward me became either fairer or more impartial." He never again appeared before HUAC's hostile members.[84]

Soon after all this, Nixon assessed his role in the drama. Although he had not proven conclusively Hiss's guilt, he had "pretty much discredit[ed] Hiss in the eyes of most of the press boys." Many wondered if Nixon had kept Hiss "on too long and was going into too great detail. In the end, however, it paid off." The next day, newspapers began crediting Nixon as the chief HUAC examiner during the Hiss–Chambers confrontation. Roscoe Drummond, in the *Christian Science Monitor,* mirrored what many thought: HUAC still needed to decide which man was telling the truth.[85]

Nixon also revealed on August 29 that Chambers, still a secret operative in 1937, had been hired for a federal position, which he obtained through others Bentley had named. As a result, the congressman concluded that the Chambers and Bentley cells were connected. The U.S. Attorney General responded to the pressure to reopen the investigation of Communist activities by calling another grand jury for mid-September. Nixon asserted: "If it hadn't been for these hearings . . . the grand jury would have been forgotten until after November."[86]

Nixon had returned to the capital by afternoon. The oppressive heat of the past four days broke somewhat with a shower. He had no expectations for Hiss's salvation because "the evidence now points definitely to the fact that Chambers was substantially correct in his remarks concerning Hiss. I feel that the burden of proof is now on Hiss to disprove the Chambers' charges." The Hiss-Chambers record was "pretty interesting," and it read "just like a detective story."[87]

Rather than examine the fundamental issues surrounding the Chambers-Hiss confrontation of August 1948, Nixon's critics have chosen to focus on a particular allegation of lying. Some claim that Nixon knew about Alger Hiss's Communist associations before the special session of Congress that summer. Most authors have maintained that Father Cronin told Nixon about Hiss's Communist connections in the spring of 1947, at least a year and a half before Chambers appeared before HUAC in the summer of 1948. This assertion suggests opportunism: if it is true, why did Nixon wait so long to expose Hiss? The contention rests solely on interviews with the priest starting in 1958 that lasted through the 1980s. In 1990, Cronin not only repudiated his earlier position but also supported Nixon's declaration that he never knew about Hiss until Chambers uttered Hiss's name at the HUAC hearing on August 3, 1948.[88]

Some writers added to their thesis by suggesting that the priest provided Nixon with a 1945 document to bolster their claim. Toward the close of October 1945, Cronin distributed the findings of a year's study with the publication of THE PROBLEM OF AMERICAN COMMUNISM IN 1945: Facts and Recommendations: A Confidential Study for Private Circulation, 146 mimeographed pages of text followed by a long index, which went to the Catholic bishops in the United States, restricted to approximately 200 copies. Divided into five sections, the report covered world communism and the United States, the American Communist Party, communism in the labor movement, communism and the public, and communism and Catholicism.[89]

Hiss's name was mentioned four times. The first time, on page 16, he was lumped into the group of "fellow travelers" or "Communist sympathizers"; Cronin stated: "Alger Hiss of the State Department would fit into this niche." In the second and third instances, on page 37, he was included with two others who had infiltrated the New Deal, and an editor of a nationally known magazine was going to publish more about him if he became UN permanent secretary. Finally, on page 50, he was listed with five other fellow travelers.[90]

Cronin's treatise was not definitive. Chambers, Bentley, Silvermaster, and many others in the summer hearings were not mentioned, while the Librarian of Congress and famous American poet, Archibald MacLeish, was identified as assisting Communist propaganda. Dean Acheson was described as "deceived" into following Soviet policy; Communists had supposedly manipulated Secretary of Interior Harold Ickes and former vice president and Secretary of Commerce Henry Wallace, who were "basically liberal, rather than Communist-minded, but . . . they are subject to undue pressure from the Party." Many of its statements did have merit: Harry Dexter White in the Treasury Department was close to the Communist Party. Cronin, who had little involvement in foreign affairs, featured these individuals as well as many others far more than Hiss. Cronin did not intend that Nixon would ever review this document. No Nixon archives have a copy, nor is it ever referred to in any correspondence.[91]

Cronin and Nixon met occasionally after the passage of the Taft-Hartley Act to discuss economic and social problems. The first reference to the priest in the congressman's calendar came on April 12, 1948, with the cryptic comment, "Father Cronin's man," which appeared in the midst of the Condon affair and the debate over the Mundt-Nixon bill, a measure the priest enthusiastically endorsed. Father Cronin was not recorded in the calendar again until two meetings in July and another in late December 1948; the initial mention of Cronin in correspondence came on September 29, when Nixon wrote a memorandum to Stripling about a phone call from the priest concerning an engineer at Bell Aircraft in Buffalo who furnished a camera to Soviet agents in 1944 to photograph blueprints and then gave the information to the FBI, a lead that might be worth pursuing. Besides these facts, Nixon never told anyone during or after the August hearings that he had heard Hiss's name before the summer of 1948. The record is clear. Alger Hiss did not cross Nixon's radar until his name came up at the HUAC hearings.[92]

For all involved, the fact that the HUAC hearings became partisan produced a tragedy. Each side moved away from flexibility to stake out rigid lines. Neither Truman nor the Republican majority would bend. Voices were raised; partisans initiated angry exchanges that supporters mimicked; and little was accomplished. This failure to find a middle ground climaxed during the confrontation between Hiss and Chambers. By the end of that hearing, Hiss bore the onus of proving his innocence. No longer was he the aggrieved party, but rather, part of the infiltration of Communists in the federal government.

Commentators argued over whether he deserved this personal degradation, but they missed the larger future import. With Congress and the White House shouting at each other over Communist penetration, no one devised a solution to be certain the administration removed any serious security risks. Truman and his GOP antagonists fought without any hope of a solution. Thus, when Joseph McCarthy came to the forefront, Republican leaders had no reason to muzzle his erratic antics. His anti-Communist harangues, as bizarre as they became, grew partially from the frustration of the administration's unwillingness to treat the Chambers–Hiss matter and its larger implications in a bipartisan spirit, as well as the Republican intransigence to work with the president. The ascendancy of McCarthy could have only arisen in such a divisive environment. That was an awful byproduct. The deep emotional scars that resulted were a terrible price to pay.

*Chapter* **II**

# THE PUMPKIN, FATHER CRONIN, THE FBI, AND DUGGAN

Nixon now thought that the Hiss–Chambers confrontation was completed, as he wrote in a long letter summarizing the affair to John Foster Dulles. In this aspect, Nixon could not have been more mistaken. On the evening of August 27, Chambers appeared on a relatively new national radio program, *Meet the Press.* Correspondent James Reston of the *New York Times* served as moderator. One of the first questions came from Edward Folliard, a reporter for the *Washington Post,* who asked if Chambers would now accept Hiss's challenge to make his charges publicly, without congressional immunity from lawsuits. Chambers paused momentarily and then responded: "Alger Hiss was a Communist and may be now." After leaving the studio, a messenger caught him walking down Connecticut Avenue on this hot, humid night, and handed him a message with a telephone number to call immediately. When Chambers reached the *Time* offices, he called the number, and an angry Nixon answered: "it [*Meet the Press*] was a damned outrage." Chambers agreed; the interviewers had acted as inquisitors, but he still did not think that Hiss would sue him.[1]

He was wrong. Hiss's defenders insisted that Hiss sue to prove his innocence. His action against Chambers for making false statements was filed in Maryland Federal District Court, just a month after the *Meet the Press* interview. A U.S. marshal served the defendant the same morning at his farm, and Chambers trumpeted to the press that he welcomed the lawsuit: "I do not minimize the audacity or the ferocity of the forces which work through him. But I do not believe that Mr. Hiss or anybody else can use the means of justice to defeat the ends of justice." With that pronouncement, Hiss asserted that his reputation was further injured, and the request for damages jumped from $50,000 to $75,000.[2]

While Chambers was preparing to defend himself, he went before a federal grand jury in New York for the first time, on October 14. Thomas Donegan, special assistant to the Attorney General, asked him why he had broken with the party and what if anything he knew about espionage. Chambers replied truthfully to the first question and lied on the second one, replying that he had no knowledge of any spying.[3]

During the initial pretrial depositions in early November, Chambers took offense at the manner in which plaintiff's lawyers personally attacked him and his wife. In addition, they asked, through discovery, for any written documents that he had received from Hiss during the 1930s to prove their intimate relationship and gave him slightly less than two weeks to produce them. During that interim, Chambers went to New York City and retrieved an envelope that he had left for safekeeping with his cousin, Nathan Levine, to hide in the late 1930s. On November 15, Chambers handed his legal team four pages of handwritten documents and sixty-five pages of typed State Department material from early January through April 1, 1938. When Hiss's lawyers asked Chambers on November 17 to produce his written communications with their client, Chambers turned over this data, and two days later, Hiss's attorneys informed the criminal division of the Justice Department of the file's contents. The supervisor of that division, Alexander Campbell, rushed to Baltimore, took control of the documents, and imposed an order of secrecy on the entire affair.[4]

Two weeks later, on December 1, two articles in capital newspapers dealing with the Chambers-Hiss case piqued Bert Andrews's curiosity. In Jerry Klutz's column "The Federal Diary," the writer claimed that the Hiss–Chambers case would shortly make news. Since Hiss had filed his libel suit, the attorneys had taken depositions from the principles and other witnesses. "Some very startling information," Klutz alleged, "on who's a liar is reported to have been uncovered." Another article told a different story. A United Press dispatch in the *Washington Daily News* quoted Justice Department sources that the Attorney General was getting ready to drop his investigation due to lack of evidence. One unnamed official stated that without additional concrete data, "it would be unwise to take it before a grand jury."[5]

While Andrews investigated, both parties to the case shied away from any comment. One Justice Department confidant did say to Andrews that there was "too much dynamite in it." The reporter phoned Nixon and advised him to contact Chambers because he had "produced something terrific in Baltimore."[6]

Andrews's suspicions resulted in Nixon and Stripling driving out to see Chambers at his Westminister farm in the late afternoon of December 1. Their host knew exactly why they had come and proceeded to tell them that he had dropped a "bombshell" in the libel case by withholding material. Initially, he had not wanted to damage anyone, but Hiss's attorneys had treated his wife ruthlessly and labeled him a homosexual and mentally unbalanced. Chambers admitted that he had something more, but spoke cryptically, for he too had been cautioned about court sanctions.[7]

At 10:00 P.M., after Nixon and Stripling returned to the capital, Nixon phoned Bert Andrews, who then took a taxi over to the congressman's office. During their two-and-a-half-hour conversation, Nixon lamented about traveling to Chambers's home and returning empty-handed; the reporter convinced his host to serve Chambers with a blanket subpoena to produce all of his documents. If anything arose from that production, Andrews would notify Nixon, who was about to go off on a cruise.[8]

Before leaving his office, Nixon called Louis Nichols, an assistant director of the FBI, at home to inform him that Chambers had withheld documents that, as Nixon said, would "substantiate and vindicate his position," and had turned over "some highly incriminating documentary evidence" from the State Department that Chambers and Hiss had given to the Russians. Amazingly, even though the Justice Department had received some of this material, it had seen nothing illegal, and the FBI had not investigated any further.

Here were allegations beyond Communist penetration in the federal bureaucracy. These were, for the first time, charges of espionage. Nixon was angry. He planned to reopen the Hiss-Chambers hearings on December 18 and would subpoena Chambers's documents. He was calling Nichols so that the "FBI would not be caught off base," or receive any criticism. Nixon specifically asked that the FBI not search for the documents and withhold Nixon's conversation from the Attorney General because he "would try to make it impossible for the Committee to get at the documents." Nichols, of course, advised J. Edgar Hoover about the phone conversation with Nixon and suggested that the director find out from Campbell if he had "any documentary evidence" that the FBI had not received. The director replied that he had queried Campbell on that exact point, and Hoover wanted Nichols to watch for the Justice Department's answer.[9]

The next morning, while rushing to leave on the ten-day cruise with Pat and several other congressional couples, Nixon was faced with distractions. He phoned Stripling at home for a meeting to draft a subpoena for Chambers in order to get the material that Chambers had withheld. Stripling, caught in a traffic jam, arrived after Nixon had already left for an eight o'clock train to New York, but the congressman managed to contact Stripling to reiterate his orders for everything that Chambers possessed. By the afternoon, Nixon had embarked aboard the *Panama*.[10]

Stripling, acting on Nixon's orders, called Chambers, who happened to be coming to Washington, and asked him to stop by the HUAC offices. Before leaving his farm, Chambers hid three small aluminum cans and two other rolls of microfilm that he had refused to mention to Nixon and Stripling the previous evening. Chambers chose the perfect hiding place: a pumpkin patch, just outside his farmhouse. He randomly selected a pumpkin, hollowed it out, and placed his precious material inside, then drove to Baltimore, and went on to Washington, arriving before noon. Upon entering the HUAC office, Stripling handed him an unexpected subpoena.[11]

Stripling then assigned two of his investigators, Donald Appell and William Wheeler, to accompany Chambers to his farm. Arriving in Westminister at approximately 10:45 P.M., Appell and Wheeler watched their subject turn the lights on outside his house so that he could see into the pumpkin patch; he then searched for the hollowed-out one that contained the film and the cylinders. Upon finding the right pumpkin, he removed the contents, took them over to the two men, and said matter-of-factly: "I think this is what you are looking for."[12]

While Appell and Wheeler were hurrying back to the capital late that Thursday evening, Andrews, through his own independent sources, learned that the libel action had uncovered something so secret that the government refused to release the material. The reporter as promised radiogrammed Nixon: "INFORMATION HERE IS THAT HISS–CHAMBERS CASE HAS PRODUCED NEW BOMBSHELL. STOP. INDICATIONS ARE THAT CHAMBERS HAS OFFERED NEW EVIDENCE. STOP. ALL CONCERNED SILENT. STOP. HOWEVER, JUSTICE DEPARTMENT PARTIALLY CONFIRMS BY SAYING 'IT IS TOO HOT FOR COMMENT.' STOP."[13]

Nixon did not receive Andrews's communication until Friday. While he relaxed on board ship with Pat, the two investigators delivered their contents to Stripling. When the three men began to examine the film and saw that it was stamped STATE DEPARTMENT, STRICTLY CONFIDENTIAL, along with Assistant Secretary of State Francis Sayre's name and a date, Stripling knew that this was explosive material, for Hiss had worked under Sayre during that period. Stripling scurried to locate the committee's members to have them rush back to the capital for consultations.

Stripling was politically astute enough to know that the Republicans would demand to control the investigation until the Democrats resumed the House majority in the next congressional session. However, the chief investigator faced a dilemma: with Parnell Thomas under federal indictment and Congressmen McDowell and Vail having lost their reelection attempts, Mundt and Nixon were the only members of the Republican majority who had any ongoing authority; therefore, they had to race back to Capitol Hill and take command. With that realization in mind, Stripling called Arnold to place pressure on Nixon to return to Washington. Stripling wired Nixon that evening: "SECOND BOMBSHELL OBTAINED BY SUBPOENA 1 A.M. FRIDAY. CASE CINCHED. INFORMATION AMAZING. HEAT IS ON FROM PRESS AND OTHER PLACES. IMMEDIATE ACTION APPEARS NECESSARY. CAN YOU POSSIBLY GET BACK?" The ship's purser brought the message to Nixon while he and Pat were having dinner at the captain's table with congressional friends. Nixon realized that Stripling would not have sent this message unless the documents were explosive.[14]

As acting chairman, Mundt dictated a press release from his home in Madison, South Dakota. HUAC, he stated, had subpoenaed material from Chambers the previous evening which turned out to be "microfilmed copies of tremendous importance" that were removed from the State Department and given to Chambers for transmittal to Communist agents. This proved "a vast network of communist espionage within the State Department" that far exceeded anything HUAC had thought possible. HUAC now had proof of a Red underground in the United States. Mundt would return to the capital as soon as possible and had radiogrammed Nixon to do the same. He urged the other members to come back for a public hearing: "The evidence before us is so shocking that I do not feel justified in delaying action a day longer than required."[15]

Chambers recognized the beginning of the press frenzy Friday morning when a photographer appeared at his farm looking to get a picture of the famous pumpkin where he had hidden the documents. Later that day, reporters published that startling new evidence about Hiss had been discovered and how Chambers had disclosed proof against his adversary. These revelations prompted Attorney General Thomas Clark to recommend that the grand jury in New York reopen its investigation. Special assistant to the Attorney General Thomas Donegan, who was supervising the grand jury, went to Washington to confer with his superiors.[16]

Even with the attention that the grand jury accorded Chambers, neither the FBI nor the Justice Department had yet contacted him. That neglect abruptly changed. Chambers understood the magnitude of his actions when the FBI interrogated him at 5:00 P.M. at his attorney's offices in Baltimore. They talked casually, then had dinner, and with the preliminaries over, examined him until midnight. Before they finished, a U.S. marshal served him with a subpoena to testify immediately before the New York grand jury. This action disturbed Chambers, for he knew that the federal proceeding now had precedence over HUAC. Until the Justice Department inquiry ended, the committee could not examine him without federal permission. But to Chambers, that concern was outweighed by the fact that the FBI had finally placed the full weight of its investigatory powers to gather evidence against Hiss. He drove back to his farm pleased.[17]

The major dailies on Saturday, December 4, carried front-page stories on the hollowed-out pumpkin. The *New York Times* headlines stated: "HOUSE UNIT SEIZES FILMED U.S. SECRETS AT CHAMBERS' HOME." The *Washington Post* added: "MICROFILMS FROM CHAMBERS INDICT REDS STOLE SECRETS OF STATE, NAVY DEPARTMENTS."[18]

While newspapers reported minute-by-minute revelations, Stripling posted a twenty-four-hour guard on the office to protect the evidence. When Justice Department officials asked to examine the documents, Karl Mundt, as acting chairman, gave permission, but ordered Stripling under no circumstances to surrender the originals. George Fay, U.S. district attorney for the District of Columbia, and Raymond Whearty, first assistant to the assistant attorney general, arrived at the offices shortly before noon, and began reading.[19]

Andrews that morning wired Nixon aboard ship that the documents were "INCREDIBLY HOT. LINK TO HISS SEEMS CERTAIN. LINK TO OTHERS INEVITABLE. RESULTS SHOULD RESTORE FAITH IN NEED FOR COMMITTEE." The columnist implored the congressman to return: "YOU SHOULD BE HERE TO

GET LIONS SHARE CREDIT YOU DESERVE." The committee would meet on Tuesday and the grand jury would expire on December 14. "MY LIBERAL FRIENDS DON'T LOVE ME NO MORE. NOR YOU. BUT FACTS ARE FACT AND THESE FACTS ARE DYNAMITE. HISS'S WRITING IDENTIFIED ON THREE DOCUMENTS. NOT PROOF HE GAVE THEM TO CHAMBERS BUT HIGHLY SIGNIFICANT. STRIPLING SAYS CAN PROVE WHO GAVE THEM TO CHAMBERS." Andrews signed off: "VACATION WRECKER."[20]

Arnold radioed his boss that, if he wished, Arnold would charter a navy plane to fly him back to the United States. Both Arnold and Stripling felt that Nixon needed to come back and chair the committee. Arnold reiterated: "ANDREWS BELIEVES BE GRAVE MISTAKE FOR YOU PERSONALLY TO LET ANYBODY ELSE GRAB BALL AFTER YOU HAVE CARRIED IT SO LONG." With Mundt, Thomas, and Stripling prodding him, Arnold contacted Secretary of Defense James Forrestal to help arrange for Nixon to leave the *Panama* and immediately return to Washington. Mundt had announced a Tuesday HUAC meeting and insisted that Nixon be present.[21]

Nixon succumbed. He requested plane reservations for himself and Pat on December 7 and anticipated arriving in the capital the next day. If that was too late, the navy should get him at sea, and Arnold needed to make those arrangements. Nixon cabled emphatically: "ESSENTIAL I ATTEND HEARING TUESDAY ARRANGE NAVY PICK UP BY ALL MEANS." The *Panama* anchored in a little cove on the leeward side of Aklin Island, south of Jamaica, to drop off Nixon. Crew members lowered the congressman into a lifeboat for a rendezvous with an amphibian Coast Guard air-sea rescue plane for the 475-mile trip to Miami. In an interview aboard a speeding crash boat that took him ashore from the seaplane, he declared: "For the first time we have documentary evidence—it is no longer just one man's word against anothers."[22]

Sunday, December 5, Chambers met in New York City with the president of *Time*, Roy Larsen, a friend of Hiss as well as Chambers. They talked about the events of the past few days with seven or eight other executives, without ever bringing up severing Chambers's employment with *Time*. When the others left, Chambers, alone with Larsen, offered a reluctantly accepted resignation.[23]

A half hour after Nixon arrived in Washington, he was back in HUAC's offices with Stripling working until the early morning. They privately agreed upon strategy: first, they decided that the committee would not release the "pumpkin papers" to the Justice Department until

HUAC was assured that a vigorous prosecution was guaranteed; second, they planned to hold public hearings and call a series of witnesses, including the former undersecretary of state during the Roosevelt administration, Sumner Welles, to explain the secret classification of the documents in question.[24]

Early the next day Nixon, Stripling, and Andrews examined the microfilm while Chambers testified before the grand jury in New York City. They noticed emulsion numbers on the side of the film. Andrews wondered if these could date the film. Stripling called Keith Lewis, the Eastman Kodak Company representative in the capital, to come over to the HUAC office that afternoon. Lewis did so, examined the film, and said that he would use its emulsion numbers to attempt to date the microfilm. He called his experts, and after twelve minutes, they called back. Lewis relayed their findings to the disbelief of his audience: "Sorry . . . but those films were manufactured ten years later than you think they were." According to Lewis, the film had been produced after 1946; it could not have been used to photograph State Department classified material generated in the mid-1930s. Nixon, Stripling, and Andrews almost collapsed. Lewis's findings meant that Nixon had been the victim of an incredible hoax. The chief investigator's credibility was destroyed and Andrews was subject to possible libel action. Nixon recalled what seemed to be an awful half hour during which "we were all convinced that we had been taken in on a gigantic fraud."[25]

Feeling betrayed, Nixon rang Chambers. Without saying hello, the congressman, in the harshest voice possible, told Chambers that an Eastman Kodak employee asserted the film had been manufactured in the mid-1940s, and not in 1938 as Chambers had sworn. He replied: "It cannot be true . . . but I cannot explain it." The congressman answered that his subcommittee was coming to New York that evening and expected Chambers to be at the Commodore Hotel at 9:00 P.M. "We're going to get to the bottom of this," Nixon declared. Chambers promised to be there. Nixon said: "You'd better be there."[26]

Three hundred reporters were waiting for a press conference outside Nixon's office, expecting him to reveal the contents of the microfilm. The prospect had turned into a nightmare, but Nixon and Stripling, despite the embarrassment of being duped, decided to meet the press. "This," Nixon reminisced, "would be the biggest crow-eating performance in the history of Capitol Hill."[27]

But Nixon was spared. Just before the scheduled press gathering,

Lewis received another call. The Eastman Kodak experts in Rochester had checked their findings and discovered that such film was produced in the 1930s. Stripling gave out a Texas yell and leaped on a couch. They all sighed. Nixon phoned Chambers's attorney and told him about Kodak's error.[28]

Nixon held a brief conference so that the subcommittee could catch their taxis and rush to Union Station for the 4:00 P.M. Congressional Limited bound for New York City. When the group arrived, John Mc-Gohey, U.S. attorney for the Southern District of New York, and Donegan met it at the Penn Station platform. The nature of the material was confirmed, but who would get to use it was not. The committee's revelations, from the Justice Department's position, could compromise the federal grand jury probe by interfering with its inquiry, and the attorneys in charge accompanied the subcommittee, headed by Nixon and Mc-Dowell, to the Commodore Hotel, where they argued about any further HUAC public hearings on the Hiss-Chambers case. Nixon violently disagreed; he distrusted the Justice Department's motivation to pursue the case vigorously. Both sides ultimately compromised: the Justice Department received enlarged copies of the microfilm, and even though Chambers was under the grand jury's subpoena, Donegan allowed the subcommittee to question Chambers. When Nixon and McGohey spoke to the press, the congressman promised to work with the U.S. attorney, who frigidly replied: "We hope they will live up to it."[29]

The subcommittee then interrogated Chambers under oath. He told them how he had complied with the HUAC subpoena for the "pumpkin papers," and how he gathered documents from Alger Hiss at his home, where his wife Priscilla copied them on an old Woodstock typewriter. He added that he had also received developed microfilm from Harry Dexter White. He had taken these pilfered documents to Colonel Boris Bykov of the Soviet secret police; on one occasion, the Russian spy gave three expensive rugs to George Silverman, White, and Hiss as a sign of the Soviet Union's appreciation. Chambers had originally withheld the full truth from the committee, he said, because he did not wish to destroy his Communist friends' lives.[30]

The next morning, Chambers again testified before the grand jury in New York. When reporters crowded around him and asked him for information, he generally replied with "no comment." However, after the grand jury adjourned at 1:30 P.M., Chambers disclosed that he had filched classified documents for a prewar Soviet espionage ring and hidden them for a decade. When McGohey spoke to the press after Chambers's testimony, he announced: "we are closer than we ever have been before to a final conclusion—we feel that we are finally getting some real evidence."[31]

The media frenzy for grand jury activity was duplicated on Capitol Hill. Stripling and Wheeler testified how they received the "pumpkin papers," how they were dated, and how they were printed. The public daily read about spies, and how HUAC and the grand jury were proceeding. Truman once more blasted the committee in the press for its "red herring" headline-hunting investigation: the inquiry only drew the public's attention away from the failures of the Republican 80th Congress. Mundt expressed amazement, and Nixon responded that "the President's statement is a flagrant flouting of the national interests of the people." Besides Truman's refusal to cooperate in the investigation, Americans depended on HUAC to find the truth out about these spies. "The President," Nixon proclaimed, "by continuing to obstruct the committee, is helping to keep the facts about the stealing of American top secrets by Communists from the American people."[32]

In Tuesday's newspapers, Nixon elevated HUAC's rivalry with the Justice Department to another level by announcing that "the grand jury will indict Chambers for perjury." Only a handful associated with the Hiss-Chambers saga ever understood that this statement came as a result of what Nixon later described as his back-channel relationship with Father John Cronin and Edward Francis Hummer, an official of the Washington, D.C., headquarters of the FBI. Hummer's leaks to Cronin began after the release of the "pumpkin papers." In this instance, they forced Attorney General Clark to reverse course and bring the FBI into the inquiry. From that point forward, Cronin regularly supplied Nixon with inside information on the Justice Department's deliberations.[33]

Attorney General Clark never realized that Hummer had breached departmental security. Hummer, a "lifelong Republican" appointed to the FBI during Truman's presidency, was a fervent anti-Communist, who had met Cronin in 1946. They opened a dialogue over the Hiss-Chambers matter because the Attorney General intended to indict Chambers rather than Hiss. As the evidence mounted supporting Chambers, Clark withheld these findings. This duplicity disturbed Hummer so much that, according to the priest, he began supplying the results of the FBI inquiry to Cronin, who then daily passed these on to Nixon.[34]

HUAC's members universally shared the opinion that the Truman administration obstructed the committee's objectives and prevented FBI cooperation. Nixon recognized these bureaucratic restrictions that the Justice Department placed on its own investigatory agency. Now he was involved with espionage and that led him into direct contact with the FBI. During the debate over the Mundt-Nixon bill, Nixon acknowledged that the FBI worked closely with HUAC in generating information for its use. However, the Justice Department refused to let Hoover comment on his investigations to the committee. Even though the director might have seemed to want to cooperate, Chairman Thomas maintained that Attorney General Clark "was repeatedly evasive" and "did everything in his power to block the committee's efforts."[35]

Nixon's personal relations with the FBI worsened when two special agents went to the HUAC office on the afternoon of December 8 to obtain a copy of the microfilm. Nixon stated that two copies had been made: one for the New York grand jury and the other for HUAC. He would not approve making another copy. If the FBI needed one, it should get the one being utilized in New York. The congressman was unaware that the FBI already had a grand jury copy, but the bureau was uncertain if HUAC had anything more and was using this request to determine whether the committee had withheld any material. If HUAC said that it had given everything to the grand jury, the FBI already possessed all of the committee's documentation.

After the meeting, former special agent Louis Russell, who was currently a HUAC investigator and whom J. Edgar Hoover described as "a reliable source close to the committee," confidentially told the two FBI men that Nixon "was out to embarrass the Bureau, if possible, in connection with this matter and that he also intends to do everything he can to get the Director before the Committee to testify."[36]

That evening, two former special agents saw Nixon, who showed them copies of the Chambers-Hiss documents. Nixon, according to these men, "was very anxious" to get typewriter specimens from the typewriter used by Priscilla Hiss to compare with his material. Nixon also was "extremely mad" at the Attorney General and Campbell "for not having more vigorously prosecuted this whole matter," but "had nothing but praise for the Director and the Bureau." He exaggerated the length of time that he had discussed the Hiss–Chambers affair with the FBI, for the former agents reported that "he had worked very close with the Bureau and with Mr. Nichols during the past year on this matter." That could not have been the case.

Nixon hoped to turn over the entire Hiss–Chambers affair to the FBI because only it was "capable of fully investigating the espionage angles of the case." In fact, HUAC was considering approaching Truman with such an offer. However, Nixon cautioned, "if the matter were not properly handled the House Committee intended to blast their disclosures in the public press because they felt that without a doubt those who were responsible for stealing the government's secrets should be held accountable." After digesting this information, Hoover concluded: "This fellow Nixon blows hot & cold."[37]

Assistant Attorney General Campbell and U.S. Attorney Fay were understandably concerned about any breach of protocol. They requested HUAC to refrain from questioning anyone who might testify in New York and keep data on the inquiry from the public; in the spirit of cooperation, HUAC members could testify before the grand jury and supply it with documents. The intent of the Justice Department was clear. Campbell called on HUAC to stop any action "which may preclude the successful prosecution of any criminal case arising out of this subject matter and which may be detrimental to the internal security of this country."[38]

While the Justice Department pressured HUAC from one side, Nixon applied some from his end by briefing Acting Secretary of State Robert Lovett about the investigation and showing him the documents. Nixon wanted Lovett to "bring the true facts of the case" to the president, and the acting secretary promised to do that, for according to the FBI, Truman's "red herring" remarks had caused "considerable embarrassment to the State Department." Lovett was busy trying to improve State Department public relations, assuring the public that his agency had already changed its codes and made them as secure from espionage as was feasible. The staff that handled sensitive documents from the highest officials to the lowest ranks had been fully screened for loyalty. These improved procedures over the last decade, Lovett asserted, provided far greater security than in the period when Chambers was stealing documents.[39]

This activity was only a prelude to the HUAC public session that evening. Mundt called Isaac Don Levine, editor of the anti-Communist

*Plain Talk,* to tell him that the Justice Department was going to indict Chambers, and HUAC was going to hold a special emergency meeting. Mundt swore in Levine, with a large number of reporters present, and had him repeat the story of the initial meeting that he and Chambers had with Adolf Berle. Nixon conducted most of the interrogation and had Levine affirm that if the FBI had acted then, it could have undoubtedly prevented the theft of the "pumpkin papers." Nixon did not trust the White House or the Justice Department to undertake a vigorous investigation. He feared that the Attorney General was preparing to indict Chambers for perjury when he was clearly no longer a threat to American security. If the Justice Department tried Chambers, that action would destroy any ability to indict those in charge of the Russian spy ring "because the star witness against the other individuals will have been an indicted and convicted perjurer." Nixon admitted that Chambers had originally been untruthful, but still the only way to bring the Red menace into the open was through the testimony of confessed agents like Chambers.[40]

The next day, Thursday, December 9, Andrews asked President Truman if the government needed to know who stole the State Department documents, to which he answered affirmatively, and without prodding, proceeded to assert that the HUAC inquiry was still a "red herring" and that the committee needed to be abolished. Mundt quickly chided the president for his obstructionist attitude and added: "If this is a red herring, let's publish them [the State Department documents]." The jurisdictional battle between the executive and congressional branches of government appeared to be becoming more intransigent on both sides.[41]

Despite the complaints, HUAC pressed on. On Friday, December 10, Chambers came before HUAC in a public hearing. Nixon used the occasion to praise him. Of course, the congressman conceded, Chambers spied, but "we should recognize that this evidence which has the effect of bringing before the American people for the first time effectively the real essence of the Communist conspiracy and its real danger, is available only because this man was willing to risk a jail sentence, the loss of his position, and criticism of his family and of himself from now on."[42]

Mundt was less complimentary. He chided Chambers for not telling the committee everything during his first appearance. If Hiss had not sued him in a slander suit, Chambers would not have had to produce the evidence to defend himself, and HUAC would never have seen the documents. In correspondence, Mundt admitted that he did not "have too much sympathy with Chambers," but the fact that "he is turning in the evidence to convict himself . . . it makes one realize that he must have had a tough struggle with his conscience." Espionage agents had been exposed, and that was the critical point.[43]

Mundt was confident. He believed that HUAC had "kicked over quite an ant hill in this latest espionage hearing. I think we are going to have a sordid story to reveal to the public to show how our government officials engaged in espionage activities against this government during the war and afterwards." He was "trying to avoid spectacular head-lines or glaring statements. The President's attitude, which I can not understand at all, has made this pretty difficult. It seems incredible to me that he could miss the significance of this disclosure." The next week would reveal even more: "In spite of the cold water that Truman is trying to throw on the Committee, I feel confident that we will expose some very underhanded dealings in high places in government."[44]

Nixon was scheduled to appear before the grand jury early Monday morning, but a derailment interrupted his train schedule, delaying his testimony until 2:15 P.M. During the next hour, government attorneys and the congressman argued over who should control the "pumpkin papers." Nixon refused to surrender them because the House, through HUAC, had not voted to release them.[45]

The grand jury demanded the material by issuing a subpoena to Nixon, who next found himself threatened with a contempt citation. He countered with the threat of invoking congressional immunity, for HUAC had instructed him to keep the microfilm. The ordeal angered both sides, but they eventually reached a solution whereby the congressman promised to allow the FBI to examine the documents the following day in the capital. Later that evening, Nixon repeated one of his foremost concerns to the press: "The indictment of Chambers for perjury without anyone else would constitute a whitewash because it would be impossible to bring out the truth regarding other people." Many people sided with the White House in its battle against HUAC. Syndicated columnist Marquis Childs felt that the Chambers-Hiss affair was unfolding like a Mack Sennett movie comedy. Congress was trying to usurp the law enforcement and punishment powers of the executive branch, and HUAC was the most glaring example. It had created a circus atmosphere, an example of which was a twenty-four-hour guard kept on the "pumpkin papers."[46]

The pace of the investigations accelerated. The FBI found the old Woodstock typewriter on which Chambers alleged that Priscilla Hiss had typed documents produced at his Baltimore deposition. In New York, the grand jury again questioned Hiss, who insisted that he never furnished documents to Chambers, had not seen him after January 1937, and had no idea how Chambers obtained his typewriter. Former assistant secretary of state Berle testified that if he could repeat the events of early September 1939, he would have acted more energetically. However, he did not recall Chambers mentioning the Hiss brothers as part of an espionage apparatus. By 5:00 P.M., Nixon told Campbell that he had issued a statement that HUAC would not call any more witnesses until the grand jury had finished its inquiry.[47]

That Wednesday, a little before noon, the first significant snowstorm of the year dropped four inches in New York City. While the snow was still falling, the nineteen grand jury members filed into Judge John Clancy's courtroom a little after five-thirty, where attorneys, three rows of reporters, and radio and newsreel representatives waited; no photographers were allowed. Donegan told the judge that Hiss had been unanimously indicted on two counts of perjury: he had lied about not seeing Chambers since January 1937 and about not giving Chambers documents. The *New York Times* headlines the next day read: "HISS INDICTED FOR PERJURY IN COMMUNIST SPY INQUIRY."[48]

Nixon's secretary brought him the news as it came over the wire. This phase of HUAC's investigation, he told the press, was finished, but other leads needed to be followed. The congressman found relief in the indictment, which was a "vindication" for the committee as well as "a tribute to the fine work of the FBI." Nixon concluded: "It is a justification for our many months of work. . . . We started at the beginning against overwhelming odds and we were opposed by the Administration and many commentators and news analysts who honestly disagreed with us."[49]

When reporters asked the president for his reaction to Hiss's indictment, Truman asserted that he had not altered his opinion of HUAC's spy hearings; they were still a "red herring." Later in the evening, while Attorney General Clark was attending a dinner at the Waldorf-Astoria Hotel, the press asked for his opinion. The indictment did not surprise him, nor did he think Truman would change his characterization. Nixon, for his part, stated he felt sorry for the president; the media had jockeyed him into an untenable position, and "He's fairly stubborn and it now appears he's stuck with his story. Rather than the herring being on the hook, I think Mr. Truman is on it."[50]

Even before the Hiss trial began in June 1949, Nixon closely followed the preliminaries, and others reported to the Justice Department and the FBI about the congressman's actions. HUAC investigator Russell continued to update the FBI about Nixon's contacts with Chambers. Nixon phoned Nichols at the end of June to urge the FBI to reinterview Henry Wadleigh, a former State Department employee, who had testified before HUAC in the Hiss matter. Wadleigh had worked with Hiss in the trade agreements division of the State Department, but this tall, gaunt, forty-four-year-old economist, who chain-smoked and nervously rubbed his palm on the witness stand, invoked the Fifth Amendment, and refused to answer any question concerning the possible delivery of secret documents to Russian agents. He unequivocally denied being a Communist or a fellow traveler, but would not say whether he were acquainted with Chambers and only grudgingly admitted that he knew Hiss while they were State Department colleagues. Wadleigh, Nixon alleged, since his HUAC appearance had a "guilt complex" over not divulging everything that he knew about Hiss. Nixon felt that "if Wadleigh could be gotten into the right mood . . . he might come through."[51]

Nixon also sent recommendations to the prosecution team through Victor Lasky, a reporter for the *New York World-Telegram*. The congressman warned that Hiss made an excellent first impression before HUAC and would do the same before the jury until he crossed into "unexpected territory." Hiss was vulnerable on many points, but needed to be cross-examined for at least three days. This would risk boring the jury, but Nixon cautioned, "I would risk losing the jury rather than to let Hiss get off the stand with his exterior veneer unshaken." Lasky wrote the prosecutors that Nixon appreciated the "excellent job" that they were doing at the trial and wanted Donegan to know that Nixon wished him good luck in the case. Nixon believed that Donegan had originally been antagonistic toward HUAC because he had been caught in the middle of the conflict between the Justice Department and the committee. The congressman had sent Lasky an analysis of the HUAC testimony given by Chambers and Hiss, and Lasky thought that the prosecution team should review it.[52]

The trial lasted until July 8, when the jury returned hopelessly deadlocked. Those who voted for acquittal refused to talk to the press. Hiss made no comment, and his $5,000 bail was continued. Lasky, who had grown to admire Nixon, published his reaction, mincing no words. Nixon demanded an immediate investigation of Samuel Kaufman as the presiding judge, charging him with bias toward Hiss: "His prejudice was so obvious and apparent that the jury's 8 to 4 vote for conviction came frankly as a surprise to me." He asked why the judge refused to oust a juror who, in Nixon's opinion, allegedly made favorable statements about Hiss at the opening of the trial. Nixon, as usual, acted on his dissatisfaction. The congressman vented: "When the full facts of the conduct of this trial are laid before the nation I believe the people will be shocked." Nixon intended to determine if Kaufman was fit to serve on the bench.[53]

The capital weather was turning hot by the middle of the month, and at the end of July the city was "having a record heat wave." The heat that Nixon and other critics had placed on Judge Kaufman was also having the desired results: "I think we have already accomplished our major purpose which was to see to it that an able, experienced and impartial judge would be assigned to the case when it comes up for trial the second time."[54]

Hiss was tried again that winter in front of another judge, and on January 21, 1950, Mrs. Ada Condell, foreman of the second Hiss jury, after they had deliberated for almost a day, pronounced Alger Hiss guilty on both counts of perjury. Alger and Priscilla Hiss sat quietly in the courtroom to hear a verdict that carried a maximum sentence of ten years and a $4,000 fine. First, his attorneys would exhaust the appeals process.[55]

Nixon went on the ABC Radio network that evening for an interview with Bert Andrews, in which Nixon announced that "high officials" serving in the Roosevelt and Truman administrations concealed that fact that they knew Hiss was a Communist agent. He declared that Truman would "have further reason to regret his red herring remark."[56]

Many supporters sent their accolades, but none pleased him more than former president Herbert Hoover's wire the next day:

THE CONVICTION OF ALGER HISS WAS DUE TO YOUR PATIENCE AND PERSISTENCE ALONE.

AT LAST THE STREAM OF TREASON THAT EXISTED IN OUR GOVERNMENT HAS BEEN EXPOSED IN A FASHION THAT ALL MAY BELIEVE.[57]

Nixon graciously acknowledged those comments, recalling that he and Hoover had met during the first days of his congressional campaign.

The two Quakers were drawing closer by the start of the new year. Hoover had earlier been in the capital and had confidentially asked Nixon for copies of every HUAC report since its inception, although Nixon thought that Hoover had received everything, including the documents that Chambers insisted Harry Dexter White had given him and copies of four classified documents found in the "pumpkin papers." He also provided a list of names identifying Communist infiltrators in the State Department. In January, Hoover held a private meeting with Nixon at his Waldorf-Astoria Towers apartment in New York City. Thanking Hoover for the audience, the younger man could not have been more solicitous: "You can be sure that your suggestions and advice will prove most valuable to me in the months to come."[58]

Nixon had discussed how to end his role in the Chambers-Hiss controversy, and as a result of a conversation with Chambers, planned to conclude his involvement in the affair with a speech before the House in a few days: "After that I intend to say nothing further about the case because I think it would be most unfortunate to make a political football out of the result and eventually thereby make a martyr out of Hiss."[59]

Nixon perceived his address as the climax to the controversy, but Secretary of State Dean Acheson unwittingly and dramatically altered that ending. Hiss had worked for Acheson in the State Department for six months during 1936. Both came from the eastern establishment; both were New Dealers. During Acheson's confirmation hearings in January 1949, he admitted being friendly with Alger Hiss. Donald Hiss, who had joined Acheson's law firm, had much closer bonds to the nominee.[60]

Four days after Hiss's conviction, on the morning of January 25, Acheson had determined that to remain silent on it would be a cowardly act. During a press conference, he refused to comment on the legal aspects of the case since it was under appeal, but discussed his moral dilemma. Whatever the outcome, "I do not intend to turn my back on Alger Hiss." He then referred to chapter 25, verse 35, of the Gospel from St. Matthew. He should have quoted it and the verse that follows: "For I was an hungered, and ye gave me meat; I was thirsty and ye gave me drink; I was a stranger and ye took me in; Naked and ye clothed me; I was sick and ye visited me; I was in prison and ye came unto me." Reporters could have featured that Acheson had expressed his loyalty to an old friend. Instead, the headlines spotlighted his support of a convicted perjurer, who, if the statute of limitations had not run out, would have been charged with espionage.[61]

Nixon declared: "Disgusting." Congressman James David from Georgia wondered: "How long can Americans be expected to show respect for Acheson when he hugs to his bosom those who have betrayed their country?" Most Democrats were silent. Later that day, Acheson admitted that he could have used better phraseology than "I do not intend to turn my back on Alger Hiss." The secretary went to the White House to offer his resignation. Truman, eternally loyal, refused to accept it. Acheson's sympathetic biographer David McLellan praises him for this gesture of conscience, but says that his defense of Hiss "was singularly ill-conceived given the fevered state to which the Cold War had already pushed the American people."[62]

The day after Acheson spoke out, Nixon rose in the House chamber and addressed his colleagues on "The Hiss Case: A Lesson for the American People." Opening with a demand for a "complete overhaul" for the federal employee loyalty checks, he further accused the administration of deliberately refusing to investigate Hiss and White. He called for a reopening of Chambers's spy charges and accused Truman of knowing about Hiss in November 1945 from the interrogation of Igor Guzenko, the Soviet code clerk who broke open a Russian spy ring in Canada. "The tragedy of the case," Nixon argued, was that "the great majority of them [secret agents] were American citizens, were graduates of the best colleges and universities in this country, and had yet willingly become members of an organization dedicated to the overthrow of this Government." To prevent reoccurrences, the congressman offered five recommendations. First, he called on the administration to support the FBI and J. Edgar Hoover. Second, he asked for the statute of limitations on espionage to be extended from three to ten years. Third, HUAC needed active support in its quest to expose subversion. Fourth, the federal employee loyalty program should be radically rewritten. Finally, and most critically, the United States had to enact educational programs that would teach Americans about democracy and communism so that they would understand both systems.

Americans had to learn from the Hiss lesson. Traitors could now penetrate the highest levels of government and supply material to the Soviets that would damage U.S. national interests. America represented the free world and had a duty to expose the Communist conspiracy, "to roll back the Red tide which to date has swept everything before it, and to prove to peoples everywhere that the hope of the world lies not in turning toward totalitarian dictatorship but in developing a strong, free, and intelligent democracy." By April 11, Nixon's office had sent out 280,000 reprints of the speech and more were being processed.[63]

Many were skeptical about altering federal loyalty procedures. The congressman's idea, they felt, would turn the United States into a police state with J. Edgar Hoover acting as turnkey. I. F. Stone foresaw: "Behind Nixon's proposals there advances the shadow of the police state." James Weschler, editor of the *New York Post,* concurred and wrote Nixon that the Hiss case was an unfortunate commentary on the period. Weschler was worried about future implications since the FBI already had sufficient powers, and the director had ample opportunity to solve the case, but never did. "One of the greatest paradoxes in the present Republican position," he observed, was "that you voice deep concern over encroachments on individual liberty, and yet propose sweeping powers for a police agency."[64]

House Democrats from California Chet Holifield and Helen Gahagan Douglas, liberals in their party, had consistently opposed HUAC and proclaimed that "the Committee has continuously abused its powers." These two announced that they intended to present an amendment to the rules of the 81st Congress that would "direct this Committee to use procedures in its hearings that will protect the civil rights of American citizens."[65]

Nixon publicly rebutted these charges. While admitting that HUAC had made some mistakes in the past, Truman's hostility toward the committee's objectives was equally obnoxious. He and other HUAC members might have made errors in their hearings, but even with mistakes, the committee should continue unimpeded because it acted when the Justice Department did not: "I firmly believe that the whole inquiry would have died if the Department of Justice had been able to smother it and if it had not been for the work of the committee in bringing the facts into the open."[66]

All of this posturing between the White House and HUAC, after Hiss's indictment, seemed to be subsiding. The hell that ensued, however, soon resurfaced when Laurence Duggan, president of the prestigious Institute of International Education (IIE), an organization that funded the largest student exchange program in the United States and received part of its budget from the Carnegie Corporation, jumped, fell, or was pushed out of his sixteenth-floor private office on 45th Street, just off Fifth Avenue, on December 20, 1948, and struck a pile of snow near the entrance to the building. An ambulance rushed him to Roosevelt Hospital with fractures and internal injuries, where he was pronounced dead on arrival. The local police disclosed that he was wearing one overshoe; the other was found in his office near a chair where his coat and hat were draped. A "big, low-set, heavy window" was open in his office, and the snow on the ledge had been partly brushed away. He appeared to be heading home to his wife, three sons, and a daughter. There was no sign of a struggle, nor did he leave a suicide note.[67]

Born on May 28, 1905, in White Plains, New York, Duggan went to the Roger Ascham School in nearby Hartsdale, transferred to and graduated cum laude from Phillips Exeter Academy in New Hampshire, and then matriculated from Harvard with similar honors. Duggan quickly decided to pursue a diplomatic career and entered the foreign service in 1930, specializing in Latin American affairs. Within four years of Roosevelt's ascendancy, Assistant Secretary of State Welles had promoted Duggan three times to the position of chief of the division of the American Republics. From 1937 forward, he became the second most influential person in shaping hemispheric affairs. But Secretary of State Cordell Hull forced him to resign in the summer of 1944 on suspicions that Duggan had been disloyal. After his departure from the State Department, Duggan started a profitable consulting business in Latin America, served briefly on the United Nations Relief and Rehabilitation Administration (UNRRA), and succeeded his father as IIE president toward the end of 1946.[68]

Duggan looked like a clone of Hiss. They were one year apart in age: Hiss was forty-four, Duggan forty-three. Both were establishment Ivy Leaguers and New Dealers. Both had risen to important State Department posts during Roosevelt's presidency. Hiss's Carnegie Endowment and Duggan's IIE drew their budgets from the same source.

Was Duggan's death linked to a Red plot? That evening, a reporter located Mundt and Stripling to pose that question. They phoned Nixon, and just before midnight, the three men discovered that Isaac Don Levine, in secret HUAC testimony on December 8, had recalled that Chambers, in 1939, had given Berle six names as part of a Communist cell in the capital, and Duggan was one of those individuals. During an early morning press conference on December 21, Nixon and Mundt released this information. Just as the two were about to leave, a reporter asked Mundt when he would reveal the identities of the other five. Tastelessly, he shot back: "we'll name them as they jump out of windows."[69]

Mundt later responded more tactfully. "Confronted with a serious decision in the middle of the night," Mundt concluded, "Nixon and I—perhaps mistakenly—decided against concealing from the public and the police anything in the record which might be helpful in determining the circumstances of a mysterious violent death in New York. In doing so, we had no other purpose or motive than that." They faced severe criticism, but "it is difficult to know what would be a wiser decision should we be confronted with such a perplexing problem again."[70]

The FBI added to the rumors of a spy link when the agency divulged that it had routinely questioned Duggan at his home on December 10. The United Press found Levine in Mexico City for his son's graduation, and he recounted his conversation with two FBI agents a day earlier before departing for Mexico. Levine told the agents that Duggan was "an idealist and I believed him to be a high-minded person who may have committed some ideological errors." On his return to the United States, he told reporters that Chambers never said that he had received documents from Duggan. Levine did admit that Chambers had mentioned Duggan in connection with Russian spies, but had no firsthand knowledge and had made no charges against Duggan. Mundt and Nixon had released misleading statements.[71]

Since the grand jury was meeting that morning, reporters asked Donegan to comment on Duggan's death. The lawyer said that Duggan had not been scheduled to appear before the jury, but refused go any further. Donegan graciously would not talk about "a man who is dead and is not here to give his side of the case." Francis Sayre, who was waiting to testify in the corridor, stated that Duggan was one of his closest friends in the State Department and a major figure in the creation of the Good Neighbor policy with Latin America. Chambers, who also was present, claimed that he never received documents from Duggan, never met him, and never had direct knowledge of his Communist connections.[72]

Sumner Welles, a cherished friend of Duggan, told the media that his colleague was a loyal American. Welles said that he had recently received an optimistic letter (dated October 6) from Duggan that proved he would not commit suicide, but Welles misled the media about the contents of that communication. Along with some favorable comments about Hans Rosenhaupt, who was director of graduate student admissions at Columbia University, and a brief pleasant chat with Phil Bonsal, who was Averell Harriman's political adviser, Duggan minimized the upcoming surgery, announcing that he was "going into the hospital in a few days for a little repair on my back." Foul play, Welles wired Mayor William O'Dwyer, might have been a factor in his death, and the city needed to launch an immediate, intensive murder investigation. Berle and Sayre dismissed any stories that Duggan was a Communist. Duggan's wife, Helen, said that the couple was aware that his name had been mentioned at a secret HUAC hearing, but they "just scoffed at the whole thing." He had no connection with Chambers. "This is the biggest lot of hooey I ever heard," she declared, "It just isn't so—not any of it." Helen said that her husband had spinal disk surgery in November, but he had fully recovered. She soon altered her position to allow for the possibility of an accidental death. While her husband was feeling better, he still suffered from paroxysms of pain and semifainting spells. He had no reason to commit suicide, but he might have fallen out the window while trying to open it.[73]

Donald Shank, the secretary of the IIE board, confirmed this hypothesis. He stated that Larry had been "perfectly normal" at Monday's staff meeting, but realized that Duggan had been "a very ill and tired man for some time." To Shank, Duggan "was a thoroughly over-worked man."[74]

That evening, Edward R. Murrow, who had known Duggan for eighteen years, spoke on a CBS Radio broadcast about the murkiness clouding his death. On Levine's hearsay testimony, an honorable man's reputation was being ruined after his death. The broadcaster had been chairman of the IIE board when it selected Duggan. Duggan had taken the job at personal economic sacrifice because of his belief in IIE's mission. Another evening broadcaster condemned the mystery that now engulfed Duggan's passing. His friends argued that he fell and Chambers denied labeling him a spy. "So the character and reputation of Laurence Duggan has been damaged," the speaker concluded, "terribly, after his death, by second-hand evidence which is repudiated by the man who is supposed to have given it."[75]

The New York medical examiner, Thomas Gonzales, who released his findings from an exhaustive autopsy done on Duggan, found "no evidence of criminality." Duggan died from "a fall or a jump." Responding quickly to pressure, Nixon appeared on NBC Television to clear the damage done to Duggan's name: "Whittaker Chambers' statement clears Duggan of any implication in the espionage ring. That is the best evidence."[76]

Attorney General Clark also worked to ameliorate the stain that now marred Duggan's reputation by issuing a statement that deviated from the Justice Department's normal refusal to disclose the contents of its files. "To prevent an injustice being done to the family of a former employee of the government," Clark declared, "the FBI investigation has produced no evidence of Mr. Duggan's connection with the Communist Party or with any other espionage activity. On the contrary, the evidence discloses that Mr. Duggan was a loyal employee of the United States Government."[77]

Clark vaguely sketched an outline of Duggan's interview with the FBI. During their conversation, Duggan informed the agents that two different individuals had approached him in the mid-1930s about joining a Communist spy ring. He refused and had no links with any espionage efforts. Duggan had provided the names of these men, and the agency was following up on those valuable leads. Still, the *Washington Post* pondered: Why had not Duggan told his superiors ten years earlier about these advances?[78]

From the day Duggan died and for the next week, Mundt was regularly attacked for smearing Duggan. Mundt's crack about jumping out of windows exacerbated the situation. Some called for a retraction; others branded his actions irresponsible and condemned him for headline hunting; a few demanded his resignation. Nixon was also criticized for this role in HUAC's handling of Duggan's death. A Quaker from Indiana wrote him that Nixon's violent actions had "put the blood of Lawrence [sic] Duggan on your hands." Others agreed that he acted disgracefully in making a false accusation and should exercise more restraint in the future.[79]

Drew Pearson, on December 27, then published a column on Duggan that astonished all and exonerated his accusers. The article was especially devastating because Pearson and Duggan were friends. The reporter had discovered that Duggan had attended Communist meetings in Alexandria, Virginia, in 1932. With this disclosure, Duggan's earlier actions troubled Pearson, especially his sympathy toward Loyalist Spain in the 1930s and fraternization with admitted Communists. Pearson conceded that Duggan had been a Communist and had committed suicide. The deceased, Pearson later reasoned, had become a Communist during the depression, but by the time he joined the foreign service, he had left the party: "He was a farsighted and idealistic public servant under whom our Good Neighbor policy reached a genuine peak of success."[80]

From the 1930s onward, the FBI had collected bits of data about

Duggan's links with the Russians. Noel Field, a suspected Soviet agent, was a close friend of Duggan's, who lived with him when they were bachelors in the capital, but never appeared to recruit him. Frederick Lyon, who served with Duggan in the diplomatic corps as a specialist in espionage, in 1945, "characterized Larry Duggan as a Communist," but added that his father was "a radical left-winger and to the best of his knowledge, not a Communist." During his December 1948 interview with two FBI agents, Duggan admitted that Frederick Field, a longtime friend, a Harvard classmate and roommate, had approached him in 1936 or 1937 to work for the Russians; Henry Collins, Jr., a social acquaintance since 1934, too, had lunched with him in June 1938 about supplying information to the Soviets. Duggan never explained why had he taken over a decade to divulge these encounters.[81]

Duggan was never accused of anything, and HUAC had not subpoenaed him at any time. Yet the heated arguments over how Laurence Duggan died and whether he was or was not a Communist spy still continue. In the September 1995 edition of the *American Spectator,* columnist and commentator Robert Novak pronounced with certitude that Duggan was a Soviet agent. A scholarly book in the same year entitled *The Secret World of American Communism* by Harvey Klehr, John Haynes, and Fridrikh Firsov named Duggan a "Communist source" in the diplomatic corps. And the recently released Venona intercepts, secret Soviet communiqués broken by U.S. intelligence during World War II, appear to point ominously toward Duggan as a Russian spy.[82]

On Tuesday afternoon, December 28, 1948, Mundt and Nixon, accompanied by Stripling, Wheeler, and Appell, went to Westminister to hold one more executive session with Chambers. Because of the agreement between HUAC and the Justice Department over questioning during Hiss's grand jury proceedings, this meeting was convened in rural Maryland. The former Communist spy wanted HUAC to understand the vast scope of the Red menace. "The most important thing," he highlighted, "for everyone to understand is the duration and the dimension of the conspiracy rather than the characters of the persons involved or what seemed to be the chief protagonists." The only way to end Soviet subversion was to outlaw the party: "the Communist Party, particularly that part of it which is deliberately submerged, which is the greater of three-quarters of the iceberg, cannot exist if this atmosphere and alliance with the sympathizers is cut off." This ended Chambers's testimony before HUAC.[83]

On the last day of the year, the committee issued two reports that reviewed its accomplishments. One presented an overview of its investigations into the motion picture business, labor unions, and atomic energy. The other dealt exclusively with the Hiss-Chambers affair. Both concluded that espionage was a serious threat to national security and that this criminal activity against the United States needed to be exposed. The administration's refusal to cooperate, the invocation of the Fifth Amendment, and the refusal to produce documents further hampered the committee's mission. HUAC recommended passage of the Mundt-Nixon bill, strengthening espionage laws, increasing penalties for contempt of Congress, examination of immigration laws, tightening passport visa requirements, and, of course, continuing the committee. "As a result of this decade of service," the annual report asserted, "the House now has at its disposal the greatest file against un-American subversive forces which exists anywhere in the world today."[84]

Mundt completed his work on these reports late on December 30, resigned his House seat as of midnight, and was sworn into the Senate at noon the following day. Mundt never could understand why HUAC took such an enormous amount of criticism for trying to protect the national interest. The Hiss-Chambers case was "the very first time that any agency in government has exposed the spy activities even though the evidence was in the hands of the Department of Justice. If we had not done it, the story would never have been revealed. And poor Harry Truman just doesn't know what is going on around here on this matter. It is too bad that we are going to be forced to have him leading us (if he does any leading) for the next four years." HUAC suffered a real loss with Mundt's senatorial victory. Congressman Thomas was still confined to Walter Reed Hospital. He would eventually go to federal prison. Stripling, with his tasks completed and exhausted from the attacks on him and HUAC, resigned after eighteen years on Capitol Hill to go back to Texas. Vail and McDowell lost their reelections. Only Nixon remained.[85]

The consequences of the "pumpkin papers" spectacular splash across the nation a half century ago reverberate to this day. Newspapers reconstructed everything from descriptions of the pumpkin patch, to Nixon's frantic journey to the capital, to the deliberations of the New York grand jury, to the indictment of Hiss and Duggan's tragic death. These events made front-page stories that are still remembered.

Alger Hiss was the driving force behind these events. He had challenged Chambers to make his charges in public so that Hiss could serve him with a lawsuit for libel and slander. Hiss's attorneys, through discovery proceedings, began the chain that climaxed with Chambers's turning over classified documents with Hiss's handwritten notes.

Even before the "pumpkin papers" emerged, Nixon confidently believed that Hiss had committed perjury and felt that the evidence led to the inescapable conclusion that he was a Soviet agent. While Nixon's opinion of Hiss declined, the congressman's feelings toward Chambers became stronger. Indeed, they continued to see each other and maintained a friendly relationship until Chambers died in 1961. Nixon and Hiss only exchanged words four times in their lives, but those meetings remained fixed in the public conscience to this day.

The advocates of public servants who were driven to disgrace vociferously defended their fallen, but righteous, heroes. Duggan, for his supporters, experienced the ultimate defamation. He was saddled with being named a Communist spy after dying mysteriously. He suffered the indignity of Mundt's jibe about jumping out of windows. This, to his defenders, smacked of more than just bad taste; it went against the American tradition of fair play. Acheson would not let this happen to Hiss. After his conviction for perjury, the secretary of state promised not to turn his back on his friend: a remark that infuriated critics and that Acheson himself saw as so damaging to the administration that he offered his resignation.

Nixon staunchly fought Communists in the government. In his mind, treacherous federal bureaucrats, who had benefited from the fruits of the United States and had turned their allegiance to the Soviet Union, had to be ousted from the administration. No longer was this an issue of Communists penetrating the civil service. It had become a case of actual espionage, in which those who owed so much to America had sold out to the Russians. The Hiss-Duggan-Acheson elitism, to Nixon, came to personify the threat to American survival and the continuation of democracy. To reinforce these opinions, prominent individuals like former president Herbert Hoover showered Nixon with accolades.

Compounding these practical and philosophical differences was the Byzantine fabric of government. Hummer spied on his colleagues in the Justice Department and gave information to Cronin, who passed it on to Nixon. Nixon went public about the U.S. Attorney General office's plan to indict Chambers to halt any such option. At the other end of the spectrum, Lou Russell, a HUAC investigator, was a mole for the FBI, who warned his former employer that Nixon was going to try to embarrass J. Edgar Hoover and the bureau. To protect his agency, the director followed Nixon's movements and concurrently warned the Attorney General about Nixon's supposed nefarious intentions. Rather than concentrating on the search for truth, this bureaucratic intrigue and infighting with spies spying on spies was a sad commentary on the operations within the federal government.

As disappointing as these machinations were, they pale by comparison to the White House's role. The real damage to governance of this period was the steadfast, rigid refusal of Truman and his advisers to recognize that the United States had to address the question of Communist espionage rather than just dismissing it as partisan politics. Revelations of espionage swept the nation, calling out for action, and yet the president remained a partisan Democrat. The administration rebuffed GOP initiatives to form a united front concerning the Red menace.

This intransigence brought extremists in the Republican Party to the surface. Their solutions, as expected, were unacceptable to the administration, but some Republicans doggedly demanded sweeping actions. One of these eventual sponsors was Joe McCarthy, who spoke for a disillusioned and disenchanted minority. He zealously demanded the removal of all Communists from the federal government by using police state measures. This was no longer petty politics; this became McCarthyism. More than just a symbol of national malaise, it tore at the American character. So much so that it would become a form of national insanity.

Rather than evaluate these crucial underpinnings regarding the Chambers–Hiss drama, close to the end of the millennium two beautifully designed, expensive coffee-table books devote two pages each to the Chambers–Hiss controversy and reflect current political correctness over Nixon's sinister role in this episode. Harold Evans in *The American Century* highlights that Nixon never revealed he knew about FBI files on Hiss. American Broadcasting Company's evening news anchor Peter Jennings goes further in *The Century,* asserting that Nixon was "being fed incriminating documents on Hiss by the FBI." The congressman therefore demanded that Hiss and Chamber confront each other to "prove which one was lying." These misrepresentations demonstrate how mythology has mushroomed into the fiber of the national conscience.[86]

# Chapter 12

# NIXON, COMMUNISM, AND THE TRUMAN TRIUMPH

While Nixon was consumed with the events swirling around the Chambers-Hiss affair from the beginning of August until the end of December 1948, President Truman tried to relegate that embarrassment to a secondary level. He was concentrating on the far larger prize, winning a presidential election. Nixon, during the campaign, attempted to spotlight both his investigation and the president's lack of sensitivity to it, demonstrating that Truman did not deserve to sit in the White House for four more years. Each man had his own agenda with his own priorities. Though they regularly crossed swords, their differences did not interfere with their election victories. However, their rhetoric and evolving partisanship during the 80th Congress created deep schisms that were never healed. Nixon always had to confront those who claimed that he had hounded Hiss to prison in his callous political ascendancy. Truman also faced never-ending criticism, holding office for four frustrating years filled with turmoil, disappointment, and war, not to mention a hardening of the anti-Communist line.

As Nixon was making preparations for his campaign, on August 13, Truman tagged the GOP congressional majority as the "Do-Nothing" Congress. Republicans, according to the president, refused to accept his legislative initiatives to implement the planks in their recently adopted platform. Why should Americans trust the GOP to enact critical laws if it won the national election?

Representative Mundt was anxious about Thomas Dewey, the Republican presidential candidate's actions, but not in regard to the legislative matters. Mundt could not reach Herbert Brownell, Dewey's campaign manager, on August 12, so instead talked to Leonard Hall, a Republican colleague from New York who directed the congressional campaign committee, about the Hiss-Chambers situation, "which, for the time being at least, is in such a fluid state, it may break loose in any direction and, of course, it is highly important that Tom Dewey does not commit himself in any way which might prove tremendously embarrassing and troublesome if the outcome of this tangled web of evidence should take a surprising and nation-rocking turn." Mundt felt that John Foster Dulles would not be drawn into the imbroglio unless Democrats raised questions about his sponsorship of Hiss for the presidency of the Carnegie Endowment, "but in the remote event that Hiss should be proved guilty of the charges which Mr. Chambers persists in repeating about him, we certainly do not want to jeopardize Tom's campaign through such a development."[1]

By the beginning of the second week of August, Nixon planned to return to California immediately after the congressional adjournment sometime in late August or early September. He directed his campaign committee members to pay particular attention to newspaper advertisements, "just to keep the publishers on our side—more or less as a goodwill gesture in effect." After flying home, he would remain there until election day, speaking to a wide variety of audiences. Rather than discussing the Mundt-Nixon bill, he intended to address the subject of "Cold War Treason," which provided him with a vehicle "to go into the very interesting developments of the current espionage investigations as well as the need for legislation."[2]

As for Pat and the two young children, they would remain in their suburban Virginia apartment, "due to the obvious difficulties in attempting to move all the infant paraphernalia across the country." While Nixon considered his family's logistics, Frank Jorgensen sent word that the finance committee had reimbursed Nixon for his primary expenses. Jorgensen, furthermore, did not think that the Henry Wallace candidate would run against Nixon; but even if she did, the committee had already reserved space for newspaper advertisements and was prepared for his tour throughout the district.[3]

Nixon expected to speak for his GOP colleagues who were facing difficult reelection contests. One of his closest friends in Washington, who was waging a difficult battle, was Congressman Kersten, who asked his friend to do everything possible to get vice-presidential candidate Warren to give a campaign speech in Milwaukee. Nixon agreed and promised to contact Warren: the California governor would give "a tremendous boost for the ticket and to your candidacy because he is your kind of candidate." Nixon kept his word. He wrote Warren, urging that he tour the Middle West to aid Republican congressmen, especially Kersten, who was "one of the most outstanding of the new crop of young Republican progressives of the House and has a very tough fight in his own district." Kersten would lose this election, but would remain a Nixon admirer for the next quarter century.[4]

By the last day of August, Nixon had mapped out his own agenda. He would campaign in California until the middle of October, would fulfill his state obligations, and from then to election eve would travel across the country and speak for the national ticket. From his viewpoint, the GOP had to combat Democratic distortions of the Republican congressional record because the opposition was "pulling all the stops" to confuse voters. The Republican National Committee was "doing a greatly improved job and is leaving no stones unturned. I also think that the current investigations of Communist infiltration into the government are having a very strong effect upon the voters." Nixon saw the spy hearings having a "far-reaching effect on the national campaign." Victory was not a certainty, but if Dewey won, Republicans would assume a "great responsibility" to address this vexing issue.[5]

By the end of the summer, Nixon had emerged as a minor celebrity within the Republican Party. He had assumed a leadership role in the investigation that led to the unmasking of Hiss and other government infiltrators, and he began to gain a reputation as a powerful and popular speaker who articulated GOP positions in a clear and cogent fashion.

The congressman had a conversation with John Foster Dulles in New York City and hoped that he, "for his own sake and Dewey's as well, will be able to announce in the near future that Hiss has left the endowment." Dulles had, in fact, met with Hiss on August 18 and asked him to resign, but relented when Hiss requested a continuance until the HUAC hearings had been completed. From that moment, Dulles began distancing himself from Hiss, and at the beginning of September, as chairman of the board, he appointed James Shotwell, an influential scholar who had taught at Columbia University and worked at the Carnegie Endowment since 1924, to substitute for Hiss. Dulles's attendance at the opening of the United Nations annual meeting later that month in Paris, further postponed the Endowment's resolution of what to do next.[6]

On September 7, the day before Nixon returned to California, he wrote Dulles about the upcoming Republican national campaign. Dewey, to the congressman, had to pledge to seek out disloyal government employees and remove them from office without any consideration of the political consequences. After taking the oath of office, he needed to cooperate with congressional investigations that sought to eliminate subversives from executive departments. Civil rights had to be defended, but the new president had "the duty to do everything possible to defend the rights and security of the great majority of the people from the Communists and others who are determined to destroy those rights."

Nixon also wanted Republicans to call upon Truman to act in the spirit of bipartisanship with Congress to rid the federal government of Communists. If he refused, the GOP should charge him with placing petty politics above the national interest "because of his fear of what a full-fledged investigation would reveal." That scenario would offer an excellent response to the president's "red herring" tag line and to the fact that he was "playing the least defensible kind of politics in refusing to allow the executive agencies to cooperate with the investigation."

Nixon, furthermore, thought that Dewey should emphasize strengthening espionage laws. Attorney General Clark had testified before HUAC early in 1948 that these statutes needed to be improved, but he had not taken any action. Under the present circumstances, inactivity was inexcusable. Never once during the second session of the 80th Congress had the administration made any legislative recommendations for controlling domestic subversion. The Truman administration was "completely vulnerable and should be attacked without question during the campaign." Dewey should demand that the government vigorously enforce the existing laws and advocate further study to improve them.

Nixon was even considering a statute that would deny federal employees the right of pleading the Fifth Amendment before congressional committees. Canada, Nixon pointed out, had uncovered its Russian agents because witnesses before its commission could not protect themselves under a self-incrimination privilege in matters concerning national security. While he conceded that Americans might not be willing to take such drastic action, some measures might be acceptable to the public. Several American army reserve officers, for example, appeared before HUAC and invoked their Fifth Amendment rights. Nixon believed: "It would certainly be a safe and popular proposal to revoke commissions of officers who plead this defense in matters affecting national security."

The Democratic president, the congressman concluded, could also be attacked for his failure to prosecute and deport alien Communists. J. Peters's name had been in the newspapers over the past several days. He had been living in America for twenty-two years, and during that time, he had operated a Soviet spy network. But the Justice Department had only just allowed immigration officials to start deportation proceedings against Peters as well as many other Communists. Nixon recognized that deportation was a sensitive political issue with many minority groups, but he thought that this could "be handled tactfully enough" and developed into "a very powerful issue."[7]

That same day, George Gallup, director of the American Institute of Public Opinion, published data that reinforced Nixon's opinions: the public believed that HUAC was unearthing valuable information and dismissed Truman's "red herring" charge. Almost three-quarters of the sample thought the president's view was wrong: 84 percent of Republicans, 71 percent of Democrats, and 65 percent of Independents, though Wallace backers agreed with the White House. Four-fifths of the Americans surveyed had been following the hearings and wanted them continued.[8]

Early on the morning of September 8, Nixon departed from Municipal Airport on American Airlines flight no. 1 for Southern California. His speaking schedule was fully booked. He refused to extend his remarks on Communist infiltration in the government over the radio because he believed that his speeches did not adapt well for broadcasts. He generally spoke for about thirty minutes without a written script, but brought quotes for the media to use. Upon arrival, he described his influential role in the HUAC hearings and called for the passage of the Mundt-Nixon bill. With Dewey's ascension to the White House, he promised, an attorney general would be appointed to enforce the laws against domestic espionage. "The administration policy obstructed the work of the spy hearings by failing to provide even the barest employment records of those charged with espionage," he declared, and then offered a challenge: "If Mr. Truman had nothing to hide, let him open the books and prove his 'Red Herring' charges."[9]

His first evening in Whittier, Nixon gave a major address in which he again attacked Truman's position. Some congressional witnesses, he insisted, pleaded the Fifth Amendment as an admission of guilt: "One by one they took the stand, and one after another they refused to answer our questions—some that had absolutely no reflection on their alleged spy activities." Nixon demanded a strengthening of espionage legislation, but that alone was insufficient to confront the Communist menace. The cure was education, "where we can get at the cause. We must fight this thing in our own homes, our schools and our communities."[10]

Meanwhile, at the centennial gathering of the American Association for the Advancement of Science on the evening of September 13, Truman cautioned that scientific experimentation for national security projects might "be made impossible by the creation of an atmosphere in which no man feels safe against public airing of unfounded rumors, gossip and vilification." Afterwards, he "smiled broadly" and shook hands with Edward Condon, who sat on the platform as the president addressed the audience. This was the same scientist whom J. Parnell Thomas accused in a 1948 HUAC report of possibly giving atomic secrets to the Russians. Thomas eventually served time in prison for padding his office payroll, while his archenemy Condon was never tried for spying, though those allegations lingered for the rest of the scientist's career.[11]

Nine days later, the president, aboard his campaign train, told a group of California Democratic leaders that HUAC was "more un-American than the activities it is investigating" and predicted that the HUAC chairman would lose his reelection bid. In a speech at Oklahoma City toward the end of the month, Truman continued his assault. As long as he resided at 1600 Pennsylvania Avenue, Republican anti-Communist overreaching would never be a problem. The GOP was creating "the false impression that communism is a powerful force in American life. These Republicans know that this is not true."[12]

A month later, on October 27, in a speech at Boston, Truman responded energetically to GOP attacks that his administration had created the environment that allowed for a Communist threat. Insisting that the 80th Congress's economic actions had depressed America's prosperity, Truman affirmed: "The real threat of Communism in this country grows out of the submission of the Republican Party to the dictates of big business, and its determination to destroy the hard-won rights of American labor."[13]

While both Nixon and Truman squared off over real fundamental differences concerning HUAC and the Red menace, a third player intimately involved with HUAC had been mortally wounded that fall. The president's criticism of the committee and its chairman J. Parnell Thomas was not nearly as devastating as Drew Pearson's newspaper series on corruption in Thomas's congressional office. When his secretary, Helen Campbell, resigned, Thomas refused to comment. Next, seventeen lawyers, mostly attached to the Democratic Party and Wallace's third party, living in his district, demanded an investigation of the accusations that Thomas had padded his staff's payrolls, placed his wife's aunt on county relief, kept two soldiers from the fighting fronts during the war, and attempted to defraud an insurance company. These violations of federal statutes triggered an FBI inquiry into how Thomas ran his office. Nixon had not heard much talk about the Pearson-Thomas affair on the West Coast, but thought that "an indictment of Thomas would be a very foolish move upon the part of the Justice Department so soon before the election."[14]

Nixon felt dejected, but Thomas faced far less pleasant prospects. Although reelected, when called before a federal grand jury to testify about alleged irregularities like payroll padding in his congressional office, he followed his attorney's ironic advice by pleading the Fifth Amendment. Even employing his right against self-incrimination did not shield him; the grand jury indicted Thomas and his former secretary on charges of defrauding the government.[15]

Herman Perry, now retired, counseled his protégé not "to make any decisions that may injure your future progress." If Thomas was guilty of the charges brought against him, many Democrats would "attempt to crucify every activity of your old committee." Nixon had to proceed prudently.[16]

While Thomas embarrassed HUAC and Truman spoke out against the committee and its actions, Nixon addressed California audiences in the third week of September, stressing that until the United States elected a Republican president, it would never learn about the expanse of the Communist network in America. During the last week of the month, he flew back to the capital to assist in finalizing HUAC's unanimously approved report on Soviet espionage activities in connection with the development of the atom bomb. The Russians, the committee suggested, had tried to get information on the weapon and placed spies in several top-secret installations. Agents did transmit data overseas, but

HUAC could not evaluate the scope of the espionage and its benefit to the Russians. The damage, indeed, was extensive. Klaus Fuchs and Ted Hall smuggled Los Alamos documents to the Soviets that considerably accelerated their research efforts. When Nixon anticipated dire results at a Washington press conference, he did not have any knowledge of these spies, but he named Clarence Hiskey and his former wife Marcia Sand as American scientists who had passed American secrets to the Reds. He had no doubt of their guilt, and as a consequence, considered the administration derelict in not prosecuting them.[17]

Nixon flew back to California with his wife and two children on September 28, where he labeled the president's recent attacks on HUAC irrational and illogical: "In view of the shocking disclosures by the committee of existence of atomic energy espionage ring and the administration's failure to prosecute, the President's comments would seem to be the most weak and unconvincing he has yet made." On the morning of October 6, he reassured a Long Beach chamber of commerce audience that "a real and successful effort is being made to rout Communists and their friends from positions in the government where they serve the interests of a possible enemy." At the conclusion, he was warmly praised and received enthusiastic applause.[18]

A week later, on October 14, Nixon began his speaking tour for the Dewey-Warren ticket to audiences who anxiously waited to hear about the Chambers-Hiss hearings. As audiences increasingly acknowledged Nixon's oratorical skills, the number of listeners grew. Nixon's popularity was spreading so quickly that the GOP faithful flocked to hear him at sold-out meetings. Congressman George MacKinnon of Minneapolis, Minnesota, who was a Republican colleague on the education and labor committee, booked two speaking engagements for Nixon on the Communist menace and European recovery. The MacKinnons, friends of the Nixon family, had given Julie a cradle and implored him: "For god's sake don't let us down as the invitations are going ou[t] right now."[19]

After that appearance, Nixon reached New York City by Tuesday evening, October 19, to participate in the prestigious *New York Herald Tribune* Forum on security and freedom at which his friend Bert Andrews was chairman. Mrs. Helen Reid, the newspaper's owner and a prominent moderate Republican, especially appealed directly to Nixon to participate because this discussion would increase his national visibility. Nixon argued forcefully for Congress to manage loyalty hearings and keep Communists out of the federal government. HUAC was imperfect, and its procedures needed improvement, but the committee had successfully attacked the clandestine activities of the Communist Party.[20]

From New York, Nixon flew to Kansas City for two meetings, followed by Tulsa, and Utah before the end of the month. After midnight on October 26, as he prepared for a 4:00 A.M. plane departure, he assessed where the campaign was heading: "Dewey is a cinch—but Truman seems to be gaining this past week." Unless the New York governor won in a landslide, the GOP might not win the Senate. Fortunately for the party, "Warren is *very* well thought of every place I go." According to the congressman, Warren seemed "probably more popular than Dewey. I just hope we haven't been too overconfident. The big Truman crowds have everybody worried."[21]

Just before the November balloting, Nixon believed that Dewey would easily win Ohio. The Gallup poll had Truman winning in Missouri, but the Republicans had not given up there due to the president's links to the Pendergast machine. The farm vote, traditionally GOP, was splitting. Truman campaigned more actively than Dewey, but Nixon did not know if this would narrow the governor's lead. Still, the congressman saw Dewey sweeping the election, while Andrews saw a closer contest than most predicted.[22]

The Truman victory on November 2 stunned Nixon, Republicans, and even Democrats. Despite all of the polling to the contrary and pundits' estimates, the president won. As an astonished Charles Voorhis put it: "I confess that I never was more surprised in my life."[23]

Nixon was not only disappointed at Truman's triumph; he also witnessed Democrats in many cases doing far better than the head of ticket. They did so well that the Democrats resumed majority control of Congress. The Saturday evening after the election, Nixon spoke before the Republican Assembly at the Huntington Hotel in Pasadena, where he offered a diagnosis of the party's ills and prescribed a cure. Above all, the GOP needed a program to sell. The party had to reorganize and establish a constructive program to replace the Democratic agenda. The party had to do more than just oppose. If it did not, the Democrats would establish a socialistic state. The GOP also had to bring in young people just like the opposition had done; in addition, Republicans had to appeal to veterans and independents. The president promised an unworkable farm program, but Republicans failed to offer a positive alternative. "If you tell a lie often enough," the congressman concluded, "it will be believed."[24]

Truman, Nixon conceded in the middle of November, was an excellent campaigner. He had misrepresented the accomplishments of the 80th Congress, but the GOP had not adequately corrected his falsehoods. Nixon now predicted that the White House would push price controls, renew the Office of Price Administration, public housing, and federal aid to education, possibly institute compulsory health insurance and repeal of the Taft-Hartley Act. He urged his congressional colleagues to unite for the 81st Congress.[25]

By the end of the month, Nixon worried that the new Democratic Congress might even try to eliminate HUAC. Its work, however, transcended "political lines and they [their activities] must not be allowed to lapse merely because of a change in the political alignment of the Congress." Nixon admitted that HUAC had made errors, but even so, the committee should continue its investigations because it acted when the Justice Department did not: "I firmly believe that the whole inquiry would have died if the Department of Justice had been able to smother it and if it had not been for the work of the committee in bringing the facts into the open."[26]

On the last day of the year, now a national celebrity, for the first time Nixon was featured on the cover of *Fortnight,* "The Newsmagazine of California." The illustration showed an attractive characterization of him in the foreground; in the background was a key, attached to a five-pointed star inscribed with hammer and sickle, touching a pumpkin that had been cut into two with several frames of microfilm appearing through a crack and closed shut by a padlock. The accompanying story featured his role in the Chambers–Hiss affair, his reelection, work on the Whittier Narrows Dam project, and his upcoming congressional assignments. As for his HUAC slot, another article revealed that no congressman had applied for a seat on the committee, and Nixon was leaving his reappointment up to the GOP leadership. If asked, he would leave, but if it wanted him to stay, he would. For all of these congressional activities in 1948, he grossed $13,100.[27]

The column speculated that Richard Nixon would break with the GOP leadership in the 81st Congress and join with young progressives in his party if the old guard stalwarts held to their obstructionist practices and did not adopt positive proposals to counter Democratic ones. The first question facing the second-term congressman was: Would he retain his HUAC and labor seats? Since California citrus growers were facing a horrendous crisis caused by severe weather, falling prices, and discriminatory freight rates, he had expressed interest in an agricultural assignment. He also intended to take an active part in the dispute between California and Arizona over ownership of the Colorado River's water supply. Finally, many wanted to know if he would run for the U.S. Senate in the next election. His stock reply: "Run for the Senate? Why not? Everybody else is."[28]

Of course, the rush of events connected with the "pumpkin papers" temporarily overshadowed the unhappiness at Republican losses in the election. Throughout December, Nixon shone brighter than before. He was the crusader who hurried back from the Caribbean, who coordinated the evidence that revealed not only Communist penetration in the federal bureaucracy but also for the first time proof of espionage. By the time he had finished holding up microfilm for news photographs, testifying before the grand jury, and dealing with Duggan's mystifying death, Nixon had moved onto the national stage. He was a celebrity, which brought him fame and thereby attention. From a political vantage point, he grew into an accomplished speaker who commanded a wide audience. The GOP had a young, rising star.

Nixon, without question, was lucky. He had no advance warning about the August confrontation, his unexpected role as anti-Communist spokesman for the GOP, or the hollowed-out pumpkin. In each case, he turned the unknown into something positive. He worked tirelessly to prove that Hiss knew Chambers; he volunteered to speak for the Dewey-Warren ticket; and he recognized his opportunity in December by racing back to the capital and embracing the unexpected. More often than not, he acted with skill and thoughtfulness. He made his own luck.

*Chapter* **13**

# STEPPING SIDEWAYS
# TO MOVE UP

N ixon's stardom created by his participation as a GOP member of the House majority ended abruptly when the Democrats took control of Congress in January 1949. They had no intention of giving him a forum to enhance his prestige; therefore, from the commencement of his second term, his role changed instantly and dramatically. Instead of being the center of attention, he merely sat on the minority side of the aisle. Aside from his mundane congressional duties, his rise inside the GOP continued, where he became identified with the moderate wing of the Republican Party in domestic affairs and with the internationalist faction in foreign matters. Although he had not anticipated the flow of the philosophical currents of his party, he was moving swiftly in the direction that the majority was heading.

What remained was the daunting awakening that Truman was in the White House for four more years, and on his coattails came a Democratic Congress. Adding to that despondent chord, at the start of the year, both Dick and Pat were recovering from the flu brought on by the tension and hard work of the last month. He hoped that the upcoming session would "let up just a bit."[1]

Due to Democratic control of Congress and the presidency, Nixon worried that "many of us aren't going to be able to recognize the country by the time some of this legislation which Truman wants goes through the mill, but time, however, may tell a different story." The Nixons watched the inauguration on January 20 with gloom: "It was an extremely cold day, both from the standpoint of the weather and from the standpoint of the enthusiasm which Republicans displayed!"[2]

The House, however, convened on January 3 and overwhelmingly voted to continue HUAC. GOP minority leader Joe Martin asked Nixon to continue on the committee, "and I am afraid there is going to be considerable pressure for me to do so from the Republican side." He quickly consented to remain and "take some heat" for continuing in that controversial post. Those who opposed the committee worked vigorously against it, but he dismissed them: "The loud screams which you are hearing now from the left wing is an indication of how bad the situation is because they are simply trying to cover up their own shortcomings."[3]

The Democrats named five new HUAC members; each one was a lawyer and three were former judges; John Wood of Georgia served as chairman. The Republicans included past chairman Thomas, who shortly would go prison, Nixon, and Harold Velde of Illinois. When the House voted to continue appropriations, the result was an overwhelming 352 to 25. Although the committee almost doubled the amount of its sessions in 1949, it would receive far less publicity. The majority would careful avoid any repetition of the 1948 fiasco.[4]

At the start of January, Nixon concentrated on rebuilding the Republican Party and agreed with an editorial in the *Omaha World-Herald* on January 26 heralding the rebirth of the GOP. The paper declared in its editorial, "God Hates a Coward!", that Republicans had not had the courage to speak out against the socialist state and Democratic proposals leading in that direction. Republicans had to reverse their course and stand up for their principles, if the party had any chance of winning elections.[5]

The last week of January in the capital had been unusually warm, but on the very last day of the month, the city had about five inches of snow. He and Pat still had mild cases of the flu, and as a result, he had not "been able to work as many hours as I normally do." He was just finishing answering mail that had accumulated since he was last in the district, for he had been "virtually swamped with work during the first days of the session."[6]

As with all congressmen, local issues remained on his agenda. Bitterly cold temperatures in Southern Californian during the winter of 1948–49 caused sheer misery for citrus growers. For an antibureaucracy Republican like Nixon, this presented a quandary. Some members of the congressional delegation proposed a moratorium on government loans to ameliorate the farmers' plight, but others objected. Some farmers had lost 40 percent of their crops. Loan extensions were easily obtainable, but the administration refused to supply disaster payments even to those who had lost the most.[7]

By the start of February, Nixon conceded that all the federal bureaucracy could do for the farmers was refinance their government loans in those cases where the farmers were unable to meet their obligations. Nixon agreed with Truman's refusal of "disaster" relief, "which would eventually break the government completely because it would cover freezes, hurricanes, earthquakes and the like." Tom Bewley, the congressman's law partner, in the middle of the month described the breadth of the devastation to Nixon in readily understandable terms for anyone who was raised there. Four or five days earlier, Whittier had snow in the afternoon at a time when the smudge pots had been removed from the orchards. Whatever sympathy Bewley elicited was squelched when Mayor James Pettit of Pomona at the start of March proposed a relief program that would cost $500 million. The idea, according to Jack Anderson, chairman of the subcommittee for the California delegation handling the citrus freeze issue, was ridiculous.[8]

Toward the end of February, Nixon participated in *On Trial,* a public service of the New York City Bar and ABC Radio in the evening: a mock trial with two sets of advocates, cross-examinations, and summations. The question for debate was: Should the government loyalty oath program be abolished? William Rogers asserted that it should not, declaring that less than 0.3 percent of all government workers were subject to investigation. Nixon then testified to lend credence to Rogers's propositions, and he also applauded the FBI for protecting civil rights. Current criminal statutes, he held, were inadequate to prevent unfit employees from entering the payroll of the federal government; hence the loyalty oath was essential, and approximately one thousand disloyal workers had left due to loyalty checks. The process removed questionable employees, while boards of inquiry and an appeal process guaranteed the innocent their rights. The opposing side rejected Rogers and Nixon's arguments. The loyalty program was aimed at amorphous and undefinable subversives. To use one glaring example, HUAC had egregiously attacked Condon on J. Parnell Thomas's whim, demonstrating how easily someone could direct the program against liberals. That was indefensible; the loyalty oath program needed to be abolished.[9]

Besides this radio broadcast, Nixon aired his own recorded programs in the district, touching on his congressional duties. He noted to friends that he had been "too serious and formal" in the 1948 segments and would attempt "to lighten it up and bring a little more human interest into it" by March 1949. He had also begun bringing people from home on his show because there was "nothing like local interest and local color to build up a listening audience."[10]

He received unexpected favorable national publicity when the *Saturday Evening Post* published "How to Pick a Congressman" in the middle of the month. Eunice Lowell, an influential woman in local Republican circles and an adamant Nixon booster, had encouraged two freelancers, Lynn Bowers and Dorothy Blair, to write an article based on the interest in the Hiss-Chambers case coupled with the novelty of how Nixon was initially selected to run for Congress in 1946. They interviewed him shortly before the November elections for a half hour and sent him a copy of their article for review. According to Nixon, the authors "had a considerable amount of garbled information and a number of corrections had to be made." For example, they had Nixon debating Voorhis in the primary instead of the general elections. Some statements were still iffy, but remained in the draft. Despite such mistakes, he was pleasantly surprised that the magazine took the story.[11]

The article featured Roy Day; Herman Perry was mentioned for initiating the call to Nixon to appear before the Fact Finding Committee; and Harrison McCall was included for managing the final campaign. Nixon had asked the magazine to delete a statement on communism, but they ran it anyhow: "Anyone who thinks communism in this country is just an idea . . . is crazy as hell." He suggested to Bewley that "If anyone raises a question on it, you might explain that I did not write the article and have no control over what goes in it." He then conceded that the quote reflected his viewpoint, but he did not want a such blunt declaration in print. He found some degree of solace: "At least, it isn't as bad as Truman!"[12]

While Nixon enjoyed this type of image building in the media, he was busily trying to prevent the repeal of the Taft-Hartley Act. Shifting from his pessimistic viewpoint at the beginning of the year that Truman would be successful in changing the law, Nixon cautiously predicted that opponents of repeal might prevail despite the Democratic majority. In fact, repeal floundered. Nixon proposed various amendments to clarify some of the act's provisions. In the end, nothing passed.[13]

Republicans in 1949 learned once again how to leverage their minority status. When the House Committee on Veterans Affairs rammed through a veteran pension bill in March, a Republican committee member, Glen Davis of Wisconsin, expressed chagrin to Donald Jackson of California on the House floor. They retired to the Speaker's Lobby and planned ways to summon effective opposition. Their solution was to assemble a group of younger GOP legislators for a meeting in Jackson's office the following Wednesday at 5:00 P.M. They chose John Byrnes of Wisconsin and Walter Norblad of Oregon; John Allen and Nixon came from California, Charles Porter from Michigan, Norris Cotton from New Hampshire, John Lodge from Connecticut, Kenneth Keating from New York, Thruston Morton from Kentucky, Caleb Boggs from Delaware. Gerald Ford from Michigan also was chosen, as were Charles Nelson from Maine and Harold Lovre from South Dakota.

After the initial meeting, Davis and Jackson and these thirteen men met every Wednesday after adjournment or at five o'clock on a rotating basis in the various congressmen's offices. Membership was kept to the initial number, chosen after open discussion by secret ballot. The group had no organization, officers, or rules, but Jackson took responsibility for sending out notices for the dates, times, and places of the gatherings. He even named the body, without anyone remembering how it was derived. This was the birth of the Chowder and Marching Club.[14]

This seemingly picayune club somehow has been magnified into a major event, and Nixon's role in its founding, purpose, and political methods has been grossly distorted to fit the objectives of psychoanalytical historians as proof of Nixon's emotional instability. Fawn Brodie is the worst example. In her *Richard Nixon: The Shaping of His Character,* she describes the Chowder and Marching Club: "Another shrewd political move [in 1947] was Nixon's organizing the fifteen Republican freshmen congressmen into the Chowder and Marching Club—Gerald Ford [he could not be a member in 1947; he was not elected until 1949] was a charter member—with a reputation for being underdogs and 'square,' not unlike the old Orthogonian Society [a social club that Nixon helped form during his freshman year at college]." Her facts are inaccurate and her premise is flawed: first, Nixon did not initiate the idea; second, the fifteen members were not all freshmen; third, Ford did not win his congressional seat until 1949; and lastly, its members certainly were not "underdogs."[15]

Returning to California over the Easter recess, Nixon faced a hectic schedule. He addressed the annual banquet of the Merchants and Manu-facturers at the Biltmore Hotel Tuesday night, then spoke before the Re-publican Assembly at the Biltmore Bowl honoring him Wednesday afternoon, and hosted a breakfast meeting in Pomona on Thursday. Dur-ing these addresses, he reiterated that the Democrats were responsible for the failures of the 81st Congress; Truman was appeasing the Commu-nists, and Republicans had to offer constructive alternatives in domestic and foreign policy matters.[16]

Many of the political positions Nixon espoused resulted partially from a district polling letter posing nine questions that he had drafted at the start of the year. Replies started coming in at the beginning of March and ultimately exceeded the responses over the past year. He even con-sidered mailing out more because the returns were "coming in by the thousands!" Supporters in Alhambra for asked another twenty-five thou-sand, and Pat added: "I'm down helping with these *stacks* of mail!!!"[17]

Nixon published his interpretation in early April editions of the local newspapers, concluding that most respondents disapproved of Tru-man's Fair Deal. His sample was obviously skewed to reflect his backers' opinions. Of the total 205,000 voters in his district, the congressman sent out 125,000 questionnaires with only 30,000 responding. The high-est disapproval rating of a little over 81 percent came in response to a question about Truman's $4 billion income tax increase. But num-bers were almost as high in favor of the Taft-Hartley Act and HUAC. Just under 69 percent disapproved of a national health insurance pro-gram, as well as a federal public housing program for the construction of government-subsidized low-rent housing projects. Just about half wanted federal rent controls ended the next year, and even fewer ap-proved of increasing Social Security payments to retirees at age sixty.[18]

In the middle of May, Nixon flew to Indiana to be the principal speaker at the eighteenth annual Institute of Foreign Affairs meeting at Earlham College, a Quaker-associated institution of higher learning. President Thomas Jones praised his "intelligence, character, and tact to-gether with your convincing arguments [which] impressed us greatly." Jones was proud of his institute and Nixon's religious affiliation: "Any doubts that liberal Quakers or others may have had concerning your vig-orous prosecution of Un-American activities were removed by your speech."[19]

Other Quakers were far less receptive. Perry toward the end of 1948 expressed his feelings about the American Friends Service Committee:

"I think many of these Quakers are pink and are getting to be really agents or to [sic] friendly with the Commies." This group, according to Nixon, had invited Alger Hiss to speak at its summer session in New England and was actively working for his acquittal. Nixon did not equate Quakers with Communists, but he did believe that the latter duped his co-religionists. Bewley had often had to defend Nixon before Quaker groups; on the other hand, the congressman was being constantly bombarded with inquiries as to "why the Quakers have allowed themselves to be so completely sucked in by the Communists."[20]

In early 1950, H. J. Bourne, a Quaker, telegraphed Nixon: "I INTEND TO FIND OUT ABOUT YOU. YOUR QUAKERISM IS PUTRID." Perry, the son of a Quaker minister, responded for his protégé: "I am sure that Congressman Nixon's Quakerism and Americanism will stand the test. He never would have been chosen for his present position had he not been sincere and honest." Nixon now wondered "where the Quakers stood on this whole matter of Communist infiltration in this country." He and Perry discussed the fact that Dr. Klaus Fuchs, the British scientist who worked at Los Alamos during the war and had recently confessed that he had transmitted atomic secrets to the Soviets, was a registered Quaker.[21]

The congressional recess began at the end of the summer, and the Nixons drove in leisurely fashion back to California, not arriving home until the weekend of September 10 for a quiet visit. Dick planned no speeches, hoped solely to talk with a few intimate friends about future political plans, and wanted to spend some time at the beach.[22]

One other major reason for returning was the fact that they were building their first home, at 14033 Honeysuckle Lane, in South Whittier. For the last three years, they had lived in an apartment in suburban Virginia that rented for $80 monthly, with electricity and water included. They also shared a family car to help save enough for a down payment. Bewley watched the construction in California, and by the end of May, assembled color charts for tiles, walls, and other areas so that Pat could choose the colors for the rooms. Like most new home buyers, the Nixons were anxious because the house cost $13,000. Dick had a problem with the ventilation, while Pat was concerned that the windows did not open properly. Still, they plunged forward. Dick sent $84.03 to the Bank of America for the costs of his loan. He thought about cashing in some war bonds to reduce the amount that he was having to finance, but eventually decided to place $5,000 as a down payment and encumber the property in the amount of $8,000 on a twenty-year mortgage with the Federal Housing Administration. By the middle of September, they took occupancy, and by October, were planning a housewarming for their friends. Pat was pleased. Dick had a piano, and the family liked to sing while he played. Julie was still too young for school, but Loma Linda Grammar School was nearby for Tricia to go to kindergarten.[23]

By the third week of September, Nixon had flown back to the capital for the remaining days of the session to focus on reducing government expenditures. Three concerns were paramount to him: long-range spending programs that would dampen any possibility of national bankruptcy, enactment of the Hoover Commission recommendations for greater bureaucratic efficiency, and reduced government expenditures "across the board."[24]

As a member of the minority party, his committee responsibilities were reduced. He no longer chaired anything. Still he reintroduced a form of the Mundt-Nixon bill early in March, but when HUAC took no immediate action, he did not have the votes to force consideration. Meanwhile, aid to education, introduced under the Barden bill, caused considerable attention. Nixon supported aid to poor states. Republicans, including Nixon, backed the Kearns bill because it limited assistance to nine states that had to initiate their own satisfactory programs for improvement. Many southern Democrats and New Dealers in the North conversely favored federal aid to education across the country. When the Democratic bill was defeated, Nixon received a dozen letters from school superintendents and teachers in the district accusing him of being the ringleader of the opposition.[25]

He was also concerned with an adequate Social Security program for senior citizens: "I shall continue to work to develop a sound pension system in the State but one that is free from control by any self-appointed pension dictator." He was not nearly as vehement about rent control. Initially, he favored ending it in three months, but when that failed, Nixon reluctantly voted to continue it. During the next session, he expected to vote against it.[26]

He concentrated on only one foreign policy issue. While many Republicans favored the United World Federalists, he felt that they went "too far in that direction [world government] from a practical standpoint." The organization was not a Communist front, nor did he saddle it with that label. Some left-wingers belonged to the group, but good people joined, including fifty Republican colleagues who had introduced a House resolution exploring the idea of a world government a few weeks earlier. Nixon supported strengthening the United Nations to deal more firmly with aggressor nations, but he felt that establishing a world federal government in place of the United Nation was an unrealistic alternative.[27]

Without hope of the passage of any significant legislation in foreign or domestic matters, Nixon returned to California. That respite allowed him time to accept more paid speaking engagements. He earned his highest income to date: $14,223.[28]

Columnists commented on Nixon's growing stature. Raymond Moley, an original member of the New Deal's brain trusters, wrote that the youthful congressman was a rising star. He had voted, according to Moley, "as a moderate conservative," who worked diligently to revise the Taft-Harley Act, broke the Hiss case, and supported bipartisanship in foreign affairs. At the start of 1950, *Newsweek* called Nixon the "most outstanding member of the present Congress" in an article on Republican resurgence. A month later, Fulton Lewis, Jr., a conservative commentator, told a San Diego audience that Nixon was "one of the truly great youths to cut a swath across Congress."[29]

Some in the media focused on Pat. As a couple, she and Dick seemed ideal: parents who concentrated on their children and did not participate in the capital "social whirl" or entertain often. Pat admitted: "we just do not like big parties." She worked as a volunteer in his office, her husband emphasized, in contradistinction to some Democrats who paid their wives a salary, as Truman did with Bess when he was a senator. Pat helped Dick out "a lot in my correspondence but never has been nor never [sic] will be on the government payroll." She embraced her husband's career: "It's Dick's work; he loves it. I wouldn't have it any other way."[30]

During the first session of the 81st Congress, Nixon emerged as HUAC's ranking minority member. He tried to apply pressure to get action, but Chairman John Wood moved slowly. When, for example, in the recent New York trial of eleven Communist Party leaders, their attorneys, several of whom belonged to the National Lawyers Guild, behaved outrageously in court, Nixon wanted the staff to conduct a preliminary inquiry as the prelude to an investigation of the guild as a Communist-front organization. Nothing happened. When the Senate reported its version of the Mundt-Nixon bill in early March, Wood did not present a companion bill until late summer.[31]

The Nixon family—Harold, Donald, Frank, Hannah, and Richard (right)—poses for a 1917 portrait. Their Sunday best belies the poverty of Nixon's youth.

A rare picture of Richard Nixon as an Orthogonian at Whittier College from 1930 to 1934.

Nixon in repose at Thumb Butte in the Grand Canyon

Nixon (right) with another soldier, identity unknown, in the South Pacific sometime in 1943 or 1944.

From soldier to statesman.
Herman Perry's casual—and
innocuous—letter of inquiry
of September 29, 1945.

Later, in the hands of
unfriendly post-Watergate
historians, the letter would
take on a sinister aspect.

13044

## Bank of America
NATIONAL TRUST & SAVINGS ASSOCIATION
### Whittier Branch

Whittier, California
September 29, 1945

Lt. R. N. Nixon, USNR
B. A. G. R.
50 Church Street
New York, New York

Dear Dick:

I am writing you this short note to
ask you if you would like to be a candidate for
Congress on the Republican ticket in 1946.

Jerry Voorhis expects to run--regis-
tration is about 50-50. The Republicans are
gaining.

Please airmail me your reply if you
are interested.

Yours very truly,

*Perman*

H. L. Perry

HLP:G
Airmail

P.S. are you a registered voter
only

Two of the men who helped to make Nixon the politician. At left, Herman L. Perry, the branch manager of Whittier's Bank of America and an active participant in local Republican politics. It was Perry who first championed Nixon as the Republicans' hope in the 1946 race against Jerry Voorhis. At right, Murray Chotiner, the ingenious Republican political consultant, who offered advice in 1946 and went on to take a more active role in Nixon's 1950 campaign for the Senate.

A pleased but slightly aged Fact-Finding Committee smiles for the camera at the group's four-teenth anniversary dinner at the Flamingo restaurant in Arcadia, California. Pat and Dick Nixon are standing on the far right, toward the rear.

Incumbent Representative Jerry Voorhis, from a primary campaign brochure. Voorhis never took Nixon seriously—until it was too late. (Special Collections, Honnold/Mudd Library, Claremont Colleges, Claremont, California)

**AMERICA NEEDS NEW LEADERSHIP NOW!**

*Elect*

**RICHARD M.**

# NIXON

**WORLD WAR II VETERAN**

**YOUR CONGRESSMAN**

Two 1946 campaign promotions. Above, a poster depicts Nixon as a fresh-faced political outsider. Below, a brochure shows Nixon relaxing at home with his "No. 1 enthusiasts."

## YOUR VETERAN CANDIDATE

Dick Nixon is a serious, energetic individual with a high purpose in life—to serve his fellow man. He is a trained scholar, a natural leader and a combat war veteran. He has acquired the "human touch" the hard way—by working his way through college and law school; by sleeping in fox-holes, sweating out air raids; by returning from war confronted with the necessity of "starting all over again."

There is in Richard Nixon's background much that is typical of the young western American. There are the parents from the mid-west, the father who has been street car motorman, oil field worker, citrus rancher, grocer. There is the solid heritage of the Quaker faith; the family tradition of Work—and Service.

The effects of this background show in Richard Nixon. He has worked in a fruit packing house, in stores, as a gas station attendant. He has made an outstanding success of his law practice. He played college football ("not too successfully," he says); maintains an intensive interest in sports.

Of course, the No. 1 Nixon-for-Congress enthusiasts are Mrs. Richard Nixon, born Patricia Ryan on St. Patrick's Day, and six-months-old baby daughter Pat. Mrs. Nixon is a public servant in her own right, having worked for the government as an economist while her husband was fighting for his country in the South Pacific. Like so many other young "war couples," the Nixons resumed civilian life on a financial foundation comprised solely of War Bonds purchased from the savings of the working wife and sailor husband.

Mr. and Mrs. Richard Nixon have been very busy this year. Individually or jointly, they have (1) been looking for a place to live; (2) practiced law; (3) been taking care of their little girl; (4) been active in veterans' affairs, particularly those relating to housing for Whittier College veteran-students and their families; (5) been looking for a place to live again; and (6) they have been campaigning to ELECT RICHARD M. NIXON TO CONGRESS.

**For New, Progressive, Representation in Congress**

**VOTE FOR**

**RICHARD M. NIXON**

ON NOVEMBER 5

MR. AND MRS. RICHARD M. NIXON AND PATRICIA

*"I pledge myself to serve you faithfully;*

*To act in the best interests of all of you;*

*To work for the re-dedication of the United States of America as a land of opportunity for your children and mine;*

*To resist with all my power the encroachments of foreign isms upon the American way of life;*

*To preserve our sacred heritage, in the name of my buddies and your loved ones, who died that these might endure;*

*To devote my full energies to service for you while opposing regimentation of you;*

*To remain always humble in the knowledge of your trust in me."*

Richard M. Nixon

**ELECT**

**RICHARD M.**

# NIXON

**WORLD WAR II VETERAN**

**YOUR CONGRESSMAN**

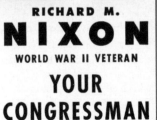

From left: J. Curtis Counts, Virginia Counts, Leah Smith, and Pat and Dick Nixon on vacation in the summer of 1946 a a newly built bridge over Lake Washington, Seattl

The morning after Nixon's 1946 election to Congress, some of the major players in his campaign gather for a photographer. From left: Harry Schuyler (family friend), Thomas Bewley (law partner), Wallace "Chief" Newman (Nixon's football coach at Whittier College), James Gerard, Rex Kennedy (owner and editor of the Whittier *Daily News*), a triumphant but tired Nixon, Rex Chandler (mayor of Whittier), Ralph Thyness, Herman Perry, Ray Cole, Lewis Sawyer (president of Whittier National Bank), and Dr. William Jones (president of Whittier College).

The Herter mission. From left: Congressmen George Mahan of Texas, Richard Nixon, Thomas Jenkins of Ohio, and James Richards of South Carolina are welcomed to Europe in Athens by an unidentified greeter.

Nixon returns to the district to campaign for reelection in 1948 with the help of Pat Hillings (left) and an unidentified partisan.

A photo shoot for the campaign yields this gem: the Nixon family on a duck-feeding outing.

A billboard used in the reelection campaign. Critics would later claim that Nixon's billboards had been bought with illicit funding.

Swearing in. At left, the accuser, Whittaker Chambers, is sworn in before HUAC on August 25, 1948. At right, the accused, Alger Hiss, takes the oath the same day. (Copyright © *Life*)

Squaring off. Later the same day, the lines for the courtroom battle that would keep the nation riveted were drawn. Nixon, despite current popular opinion to the contrary, was fair and, until the evidence became overwhelming, nonpartisan. On the left sits Chambers, sweaty and uncomfortable before a forest of mikes and the attention of a nation. (Copyright © AP/Wide World Photos) On the right, Hiss, the pride of liberals, lean, forceful, and—until the end—convincing. (Copyright © Corbis–Bettmann LLC)

## Helen Gahagan Douglas

- Born, 1900; Boonton, New Jersey.
- Educated at Barnard College.
- International Star of Stage and Opera.
- Married Screen-Star Melvyn Douglas in 1931; they have two children.
- Resident of California since 1931.
- Widely traveled in America, Europe, Asia.

- Gave up opera career in 1937, to fight Nazi-Fascist propaganda in America, and to warn that war was coming.
- Member of President Roosevelt's Advisory Committee on Civilian Defense.
- Member, William Allen White Committee.

- Took a leading part in attempt to solve problems of migratory workers, 1938.
- Member, Advisory Committee, W.P.A. and N.Y.A.
- Democratic National Committeewoman, 1940.
- Vice-Chairman, Democratic State Comm.
- Board of Governors, Californ Housing and Planning Commission.

- Elected to Congress, 1944, 1946, 1948.
- Member, Foreign Affairs Committee.
- Exposed Communist propaganda in famous speech, "My Democratic Credo," in spring of 1946. This speech has been widely quoted and often reprinted.
- Alternate Delegate to United Nations General Assembly at Lake Success.
- Featured speaker at two Democratic National Conventions.
- Received support from 17 state delegations for Vice-Presidency at 1948 convention, which she discouraged, stating that she was for Senator Barkley.

## THE DOUGLAS FAMILY

Helen and Melvyn Douglas with their two children, Mary Helen 11, and Peter, 16. Melvyn now starring in a Broadway play, is a veteran of both World Wars. Too young in the first one and too old in the second, he nevertheless managed to make the grade both times. Enlisting as a private in 1942, he spent almost three years abroad, and emerged a Major. The Douglases were married in 1931.

### HELEN GAHAGAN DOUGLAS HAS NO NEED TO MAKE PROMISES; HER RECORD IN CONGRESS IS HER PLEDGE AND HER BOND

**SHE HAS SUPPORTED:**

- All measures calculated to strengthen the United Nations.
- "Point Four," to export technological skills and help the world rebuild itself.
- International control of the Atom.
- Liberalization of the D.P. Bill.
- The Marshall Plan.
- Rent and Price Controls.
- Housing, both Low-Rent and Middle Income.
- Higher Minimum Wage.
- Women's Equal Pay.
- F.E.P.C. and Anti-Poll Tax Laws.
- The Brannan Plan.
- Central Valley Development.
- Entry of Oriental Wives of American Citizens as Non-Quota Immigrants.
- Veteran legislation.

**SHE HAS PROPOSED:**

- A minimum Federal Pension of $75 per month, as a matter of right, for men over 65, and women over 60.
- Repeal of war-time excise taxes.
- A flat $100-a-year cut in income taxes for every tax-payer and each of his dependents.
- Restoration of excess-profits taxes.
- The Farm Bankruptcy Act of 1949.
- Federal Standards of Housing, Health and Education for Migratory Workers.

**SHE HAS FOUGHT:**

- Monopoly.
- Taft-Hartley.
- Discrimination.

Helen Gahagan Douglas, "California's national figure" and "one of its ablest representatives" in two 1950 senatorial campaign brochures. Above, the Douglas family. In her memoirs, Helen would complain bitterly over anti-Semitic comments directed at her husband, Melvyn. Nixon, she said, was the source. Below, another brochure celebrates Douglas's famous speech on the House floor in which she used ordinary groceries as props to prove that her male colleagues had little concept of the cost of providing for an American family.

---

### AS A MEMBER OF CONGRESS, HELEN GAHAGAN DOUGLAS HAS FURNISHED LEADERSHIP.

- She led the fight against premature lifting of controls and correctly foretold what decontrol would mean.
- She led the three-year battle for low-rent housing.
- She was an acknowledged leader in the months-long fight to gain approval for the Marshall Plan.
- She was in the fore of the long struggle to retain Southern California's steel production.
- She was—AND IS—a leader in the fight against the Taft-Hartley Act.
- She led off in the fight against monopolistic exploitation of Atomic Energy, and co-authored the McMahon-Douglas Bill, which set up the Atomic Energy Commission.
- She arranged the hearing on the Bill for Court Adjudication of the California-Arizona dispute over Colorado River Water.
- She has consistently led the long fight for cheap Central Valley power.

### As A Senator She Will Be Doubly Effective

Vote—DOUGLAS—June 6

### Champion of the Budget

A Cost-of-Living Speech comes to the Floor of the House in Mrs. Douglas' market-basket. Of this speech, the BIRMINGHAM NEWS said:

*"There is not a housewife, we dare say, who didn't cheer Mrs. Douglas when she hauled baskets of groceries into the House to show her male colleagues what they were doing to the American home-maker."*

Helen Gahagan Douglas Campaign Committee
Alexandria Hotel, Los Angeles, MAdison 6-5621

### For Peace And Security . . .

## HELEN GAHAGAN
# DOUGLAS
### FOR U. S.
# SENATE
#### FROM CALIFORNIA

On January 17, 1950, Nixon, now convinced of Hiss's guilt, asked for a new probe. Media coverage of the trial, as the upraised paper attests, was thorough. Nixon, hitherto practically unknown to the public, was thrust triumphantly onto the national stage. (Copyright © Corbis–Bettmann LLC)

## DOUGLAS-MARCANTONIO VOTING RECORD

Many persons have requested a comparison of the voting records of Congresswoman Helen Douglas and the notorious Communist party-liner, Congressman Vito Marcantonio of New York.

Mrs. Douglas and Marcantonio have been members of Congress together since January 1, 1945. During that period, Mrs. Douglas voted the same as Marcantonio **354** times. While it should not be expected that a member of the House of Representatives should always vote in opposition to Marcantonio, it is significant to note, not only the **great number of times** which Mrs. Douglas voted in agreement with him, but also the issues on which almost without exception they always saw eye to eye, to-wit: Un-American Activities and Internal Security.

## Here is the Record!

### VOTES AGAINST COMMITTEE ON UN-AMERICAN ACTIVITIES

Both Douglas and Marcantonio voted **against** establishing the Committee on Un-American Activities. 1/3/45. Bill passed.

Both voted on three separate occasions **against** contempt proceedings against persons and organizations which refused to reveal records or answer whether they were Communists. 4/16/46, 6/26/46, 11/24/47. Bills passed.

Both voted on four separate occasions **against** allowing funds for investigation by the Un-American Activities Committee. 5/17/46, 3/9/48, 2/9/49, 3/23/50. (The last vote was 348 to 12.) All bills passed.

### COMMUNIST-LINE FOREIGN POLICY VOTES

Both voted **against** Greek-Turkish Aid Bill. 5/9/47. (It has been established that without this aid Greece and Turkey would long since have gone behind the Iron Curtain.) Bill passed.

Both voted on two occasions **against** free press amendment to UNRRA appropriation bill, providing that no funds should be furnished any country which refused to allow free access to the news of activities of the United States. 11/1/45, 6/28/46. Bills passed. (This would in effect have denied American relief funds to Communist dominated countries.)

Both voted refusing Foreign Relief to Soviet-dominated countries UNLESS supervised by Americans. 4/30/47. Bill passed 324 to 75.

### VOTE AGAINST NATIONAL DEFENSE

Both voted **against** the Selective Service Act of 1948. 6/18/48. Bill passed.

### VOTES AGAINST LOYALTY AND SECURITY LEGISLATION

Both voted on two separate occasions **against** bills requiring loyalty checks for Federal employees. 7/15/47, 6/29/49. Bills passed.

Both voted **against** the Subversive Activities Control Act of 1948, requiring registration with the Attorney General of Communist party members and communist controlled organizations. Bill passed, 319 to 58. 5/19/48. AND AFTER KOREA both again voted **against** it. Bill passed 8/29/50, 354 to 20.

AFTER KOREA, on July 12, 1950, Marcantonio and Douglas and 12 others voted **against** the Security Bill, to permit the heads of key National Defense departments, such as the Atomic Energy Commission, to discharge government workers found to be poor security risks! Bill passed, 327 to 14.

### VOTE AGAINST CALIFORNIA

Both recorded **against** confirming title to Tidelands in California and the other states affected. 4/30/48. Bill passed 257-29.

### VOTES AGAINST CONGRESSIONAL INVESTIGATION OF COMMUNIST AND OTHER ILLEGAL ACTIVITIES

Both voted **against** investigating the "whitewash" of the AMERASIA case. 4/18/46. Bill passed.

Both voted **against** investigating why the Soviet Union was buying as many as 60,000 United States patents at one time. 3/4/47. Bill passed.

Both voted **against** continuing investigation of numerous instances of illegal actions by OPA and the War Labor Board. 1/18/45. Bill passed.

Both voted on two occasions **against** allowing Congress to have access to government records necessary to the conduct of investigations by Senate and House Committees. 4/22/48, 5/13/48. Bills passed.

ON ALL OF THE ABOVE VOTES which have occurred since Congressman Nixon took office on January 1, 1947, HE has voted *exactly opposite* to the Douglas-Marcantonio Axis!

After studying the voting comparison between Mrs. Douglas and Marcantonio, is it any wonder that the Communist line newspaper, the Daily People's World, in its lead editorial on January 31, 1950, labeled Congressman Nixon as "The Man To Beat" in this Senate race and that the Communist newspaper, the New York Daily Worker, in the issue of July 28, 1947, selected Mrs. Douglas along with Marcantonio as "One of the Heroes of the 80th Congress."

REMEMBER! The United States Senate votes on ratifying international treaties and confirming presidential appointments. Would California send Marcantonio to the United States Senate?

### NIXON FOR U. S. SENATOR CAMPAIGN COMMITTEE

| NORTHERN CALIFORNIA | CENTRAL CALIFORNIA | SOUTHERN CALIFORNIA |
|---|---|---|
| John Walton Dinkelspiel, Chairman | B. M. Hoblick, Chairman | Bernard Brennan, Chairman |
| 1151 Market Street | 820 Van Ness Avenue | 117 W. 9th St., Los Angeles |
| San Francisco—UNderhill 3-1416 | Fresno—Phone 44116 | TRinity 0661 |

◀ 111

The infamous "pink sheet" used against Douglas from mid-September to election day. The document linked Douglas with Congressman Vito Marcantonio of New York, who had built a national name for himself by fighting for labor and other more radical causes. Douglas, who resented the sheet's allegations, would later point to it as the cause of her downfall.

Nixon on the campaign trail. Right, shaking hands with Bill Knowland at a campaign appearance. Above, with prominent actor and Republican activist George Murphy in early 1950 in Los Angeles. Below, in Arroyo Grande, California, on April 20, 1950. Pat Nixon (on the far left, holding a basket) distributes the famous "Nixon for Senate" thimbles.

Nixon, depicted during an uncommon performance, celebrates his victory over Douglas on November 8, 1950, to the delight of a rapt audience.

Below: the Republican Finance Committee dinner of March 29, 1951, in Los Angeles. Seated (from left): Nixon, Goodwin Knight, and William Knowland. Behind them (from left): Congressmen Carl Hinshaw, John Phillips, Norris Poulson, Donald Jackson, and Pat Hillings.

Rose Mary Woods, Nixon's indefatigable secretary, takes dictation sometime in 1951 or 1952.

Nixon and Harrison McCall talking in 1955.

The Republican National Convention in Chicago in July 1952. Above, an excited Dick Nixon hugs Pat at the podium. Left: a triumphant Dwight Eisenhower at the same podium. Below: Nixon meets with Eisenhower and Governor Earl Warren of California in Eisenhower's suite on July 12, 1952. It was a meeting of which much would later be made. (Copyright © AP/Wide World Photos)

Richard Milhous Nixon, toward the close of the Congress years. After having enjoyed one of the most supersonic rises in American history—from unknown to vice president in just six years—he is a man with a lot to be smiling about.

Joseph McCarthy, the junior senator from Wisconsin, who had started using anticommunism as a political issue in 1949, encouraged this kind of legislation. Born in 1908, he was raised in rural Wisconsin and worked his way through Marquette University Law School in 1935. He became a controversial circuit judge. After the Pearl Harbor attack, he enlisted in the U.S. Marines, went to the South Pacific, and soon thereafter shamelessly lied about his military honors. In the Wisconsin senatorial primary election of 1946, he upset the incumbent Robert LaFollette, Jr., and went on to win the general election. Once in the upper chamber, he began lashing out at reputed Communists. The fact that he drank heavily did not help his unsavory reputation.[32]

On January 22, 1950, McCarthy suggested that the Hiss conviction really signaled that "It is time that Acheson clean the Communists out of the State Department or resign and let President Truman appoint someone who will." On February 8, the senator spoke before a Republican group in Wheeling, West Virginia, where he announced that he had a list of Communists who worked at the State Department. Shortly after returning to the capital, he met with Nixon to get material to bolster his contentions. During their conversation, Nixon warned him not to exaggerate, but McCarthy did not listen. Due to the seriousness of his attack, in the third week of February the Senate quickly moved to establish a foreign relations subcommittee, chaired by Millard Tydings, Democrat from Maryland, to investigate the Wisconsin senator's allegations.[33]

By the end of the month, Drew Pearson informed his readers that McCarthy had phoned Nixon and asked about four hundred names in a secret report on alleged subversives. Pearson, who personally detested McCarthy as well as his politics, furthermore inferred that Nixon and McCarthy were closely connected, when in fact they had only casual contacts. The columnist argued that the senator realized his popularity was slipping and had chosen anti-Communist rhetoric to boost his ratings. In addition, Pearson claimed that Senator Taft publicly admitted "egging McCarthy on." The reporter conceded that the State Department should eliminate any Communist employees, but most had already been ousted: "Now it has got to a point where anyone who was sympathetic to Russia during the war is in danger of being called a Communist."[34]

On the last day of March, Nixon reacted publicly to McCarthy's demands for loyalty files from the Truman administration by recommending that the senator be removed from investigating the charges that

Communists had infested the State Department. Instead, Nixon unsuccessfully urged the president to appoint a commission of jurists for an impartial inquiry. With that dismissal, Nixon resumed criticizing the White House for not moving aggressively against Soviet espionage. He conceded at the start of May that McCarthy had exaggerated and should have stated that "there were 150 to 200 in the State Department who have been members of Communist-front organizations." In spite of this error, Nixon wanted McCarthy's accusations fully examined: "If Sen. McCarthy is wrong, he should suffer. But we should not have people in government who are security risks. The present loyalty program is inadequate."[35]

The rise of McCarthy and his allegations accelerated calls from across the country for Nixon to speak. At a Lincoln Day banquet in Laramie on February 6 in the jammed Wyoming Room of the Plains Hotel, Nixon called for a GOP victory that year to prevent any further slide toward socialism. The administration had to rid the government of Russian spies in high-ranking positions, and since Truman had not energetically pursued that goal, Nixon blamed him for espionage agents providing sufficient information so that the Soviet Union could drop an atomic bomb in September 1949, five years ahead of schedule. Stalin was currently developing a hydrogen bomb, and that too, to Nixon, was the White House's fault. Truman was not a Communist himself; he simply refused to pursue people like Hiss energetically. Nixon next attended another dinner in eastern Idaho where he stated: "Like the exposed top of an iceberg, the Alger Hiss case is only a small part of the whole shocking story of Communist espionage in the United States." During a stop in San Francisco before the Council of the American Legion, he maintained that the only preventative against a future war with the Russians was that the United States had "to wage an aggressive offensive against Communism."[36]

James Udall, a friend from Nixon's days in the navy, flew the congressman in a private plane to San Jose on February 11 to speak before twelve hundred guests at the Scottish Rite Auditorium. There he repeated his charge that the administration did not act forcefully to prosecute Hiss, but laxness did not translate into complicity. "Don't think that President Truman," Nixon underlined for his constituency who distrusted the White House, "or any other Administration official is a Communist or an apologist for Communism."[37]

Before departing for Los Angeles on Friday, February 24, to address the Young Republicans of California the following day, he was "right in the middle of an attack of the flu bug, which seems to be roaming all over Washington." Due to his illness, Congressman Gerald Ford helped prepare the material. Nixon addressed 350 Young Republicans from 28 counties, as well as many influential party leaders, at the Hotel El Tejon. He asserted that Truman had provided the means for a Republican victory by his advocacy of socialistic programs like the repeal of Taft-Hartley Act and compulsory health insurance.[38]

By the summer of 1950, Nixon had unequivocally cast himself as a moderate Republican on domestic issues. He opposed "wild government spending," "state socialism and deficient spending programs." He advocated a national pay-as-you-go pension plan because the Social Security Act was inadequate for retired citizens. He opposed the Brannan Plan that guaranteed high farm prices and low consumer costs because it would force higher taxes. He objected to Truman's compulsory health insurance plan, and in its place offered a voluntary one. He objected to lending institutions charging high fees to cover financing costs on veterans' housing, sponsored legislation to give food surpluses to needy families; voted against bookmobiles, argued for a halt of taxes on western farm shipments to eastern markets, and supported the repeal of unpopular wartime excise taxes like the one on kitchen ranges.[39]

Nixon also focused on legislation relating specifically to California. He charged Truman with being indifferent to its needs by jeopardizing resources, especially to the central Arizona water project. The Senate had already approved a billion-dollar irrigation project that hurt California's effort to protect its water rights from the Colorado River. The congressman pledged to fight in the House and expected to testify before the public land committee.[40]

Nixon wanted to "stop the Federal Government's campaign to seize the tidelands of all coastal states, which is but another dangerous attempt to establish an all-powerful Super State in America." During a speech given in Long Beach, California, he warned that the Truman administration's attempt to control the tidelands could adversely affect the nearby Belmont Shores–Naples shoreline. "I have voted and stand for California's ownership," Nixon underscored, "and against further federal encroachment."[41]

Nixon, like most congressmen, urged statehood for Hawaii and Alaska. They were part of the U.S. outer defenses on the West Coast and vital to the nation's security. Nixon referred to General Dwight Eisenhower's warning that Alaska was the weakest point in America's defenses and concluded that the United States was in potential peril if another war in Asia erupted: "With Russia a mere hop and a skip from our Alaskan shores, it is foolhardy to neglect our West Coast defenses any longer."[42]

In a San Francisco address, he warned against isolationism. The State Department, Nixon judged, had been discredited. He asserted that "the most important decisions affecting the lives and security of the American people are to be made in the field of foreign policy." His suggestions were: first, that containment was a negative policy and did not work; second, that the United States had to expand the role of the Voice of America in the propaganda war; third, that the administration had to expose the Communist conspiracy so that Americans would recognize the acute danger; and last, that the federal government had to remain solvent and not spend the people into bankruptcy by expanding foreign aid extravagantly.[43]

As long as the United States had the greatest military might, Nixon believed that the Soviets would not initiate any war. Keenly aware of the need for protection against aggressors, he had grown more vocal in his call for the establishment of universal military preparedness as the best method to preserve peace after the Russians detonated an atomic bomb and China fell to the Communists late in 1949. Since the United Nations obviously had not obtained the capability to guarantee international tranquility, the United States needed a powerful military presence. He especially emphasized "a mighty air force and modern weapons, with all other defense factors, including manpower, assigned a place in the over-all scheme commensurate with their relative importance."[44]

With Mao Tse-tung in control of mainland China, many anti-Communists not only furiously attacked Mao's totalitarian regime but also cried out against the administration for "selling out" Chiang. Nixon and several other congressmen called on the administration to stop importing peanuts and dried eggs from China as well as crabmeat from Russia. The Red Chinese were depriving their own people, and Truman helped these Asian Communists "while stabbing the starving Chinese people in the stomach." These products also took jobs from American workers. "The dollars earned by these imports are unquestionably used by the communists to finance the espionage and subversive activities of communist agents in this country," Nixon asserted. "Why just for peanuts, gentlemen?"[45]

By the end of 1950, Nixon had probably gained as much as possible from the drama of Chambers-Hiss. HUAC members had thrived on controversy, and their adversaries, often with good cause, accused them of going to excess. Although sometimes lumped with the extremists on the committee, Nixon did the best to disassociate himself from them by separating himself from the sometimes outrageous and despicable behavior of members like Thomas and Rankin. Nixon's prudence, in contrast to their antics, gave the impression that his responses were reasonable. He flourished in this atmosphere of charges and countercharges, and at the end of his service, the leading scholars of HUAC saw Nixon in a positive light. In fact, long after HUAC shut its doors, Nixon remained the only member of Congress to reach the presidency based, at least partially, on his anti-Communist stance.

First, he would have to take a smaller step to the Senate.

Even before the votes were counted in 1948 giving Nixon another House term, Roy Day was looking forward to the 1950 U.S. senatorial election in California. He wrote to Nixon: "I have been throwing out feelers on the Senator deal and the reaction seems good." Day felt that the congressman could beat any other Republican in the field "with proper financing and organization." In fact, Nixon had thought about that already. Earlier that summer in the midst of the special session of Congress, Nixon and his supporters gave serious consideration as to whether or not he should challenge incumbent Democratic senator Sheridan Downey in 1950.[46]

In the late spring of 1949, James De La Vergne, who had backed Nixon in his first two successful House contests, wrote an article in the *Alhambra Legionnaire* about the upcoming race. For no apparent reason, he cavalierly dismissed Downey, and in his place suggested Congresswomen Helen Gahagan Douglas from the nearby 14th district to run on the Democratic side. He also pegged Nixon to run against her. She was "a liberal democrat with some conservative ideas whereas Richard M. Nixon is a conservative with some liberal tendencies. Here we have two people who can and will stand up and tell their stories very effectively. Perhaps the debates will not compare with the Lincoln-Douglas debates but they will be plenty good. I'll pay two bucks any time to hear these two representatives talk and so will you." Both would make their decisions about the race soon: "Helen of Troy and Richard the Lion-hearted. What a battle that pair will wage." Douglas read the story, thought that Nixon would be amused, and sent a copy to "Richard" signed "Helen."[47]

Helen Gahagan Douglas addressed him as Richard. Underneath that pleasant formality, they were political opposites. She supported hardly any conservative positions and he openly rejected the New Deal for its latent socialism. As early as first campaign in 1946, he alluded to Douglas as a New Dealer who leaned to the far left. He regularly deplored her votes against HUAC, anti-Communism, and the Mundt-Nixon bill. Their political differences extended to personalities, too; they simply had no use for each other.

Even before mailing that letter to Nixon, Douglas had been contemplating running against Downey, a heavyset sixty-six-year-old lawyer who had come to the Senate supported by the Democratic left in 1938, but had gradually shifted toward big business, corporate farming, and oil interests. One of his major programs was the enactment of the Central Valley Project (CVP), which brought cheap power and water to California's central valley. Delays came from the vigorous struggle between public and private power interests and the limitation of 160 acres per landowner benefiting from the plan. The issues grew more complicated when Secretary of Interior Harold Ickes during the New Deal and for a brief time after Roosevelt's death came to the assistance of the small farmers. Downey argued to exempt the CVP from the acreage limitation, while the small farmers, organized labor, and others fought him.[48]

To Douglas, Downey was increasingly vulnerable for his conservative positions. Though his record on labor issues was mixed, she unequivocally called for the repeal of the Taft-Hartley Act, proclaiming: "Free strong labor unions express the healthy determination of free men to remain free." She had won three elections and defeated her Republican opponent in the last one by a margin of two to one. The *New Leader,* a socialist weekly, in the middle of the summer, proclaimed that she had achieved statewide as well as national acclaim and had emerged as an "outspoken liberal" who had refused the support of Wallace in 1948 and campaigned as an "honest liberal, running on a militant program refusing Communist aid." She was a serious senatorial contender who could win enthusiastic AFL and CIO endorsements.[49]

Helen Gahagan was raised in a privileged environment. Her father encouraged her to go to and finish college, but she rebelled and became a stage actress and opera singer. Early in her career, she appeared opposite Melvyn Douglas as her leading man; they fell in love and were married in the spring of 1931. The following year, she became a Democrat, voted for FDR, and gradually emerged as a party activist. She won the position of California's national Democratic committeewoman in 1940, and within four years, she ran for Congress and won by a slim margin. Entering the House with gusto, she proved a liberal New Dealer who energetically supported the president and First Lady Eleanor Roosevelt. Douglas stood for reelection two more times in the 1940s, and on each occasion, victory came by larger margins than before. By the end of the decade, her voting pattern was clearly identifiable. Her outspoken advocacy for the New and Fair Deals was unassailable. She promoted civil rights and agreed to rent controls; she voted against Taft-Hartley, the Truman Doctrine, HUAC appropriations, and loyalty oaths.[50]

While Douglas contemplated her decision to run, Nixon assessed his chances within the GOP. He had received many inquiries about the senatorial contest, but remained noncommittal. The president of the Young Republicans of California and the state commander of the American Legion had assured him of their backing if he decided to run. Perry had already called upon his protégé to run and met with Day, Lutz, Cooper, and Jorgensen at Jorgensen's San Marino home to establish a finance committee to raise the funds.[51]

Before the meeting, Jorgensen gathered his own intelligence. He met with Bernard Brennan, the influential GOP politician who had served in critical positions for the Republican Party in Los Angeles; he had also been a city attorney, president of the Kiwanis in Glendale, and a director of the Metropolitan Water District. During a three-hour dinner on February 15, Brennan asserted that he was a hundred percent behind Nixon for senator. Jorgensen was excited, because "due to his [Brennan's] wide experience . . . we would be able to bring into your [Nixon's] campaign a great many individuals that we might have difficulty in enlisting otherwise."

In addition to Brennan, Jorgensen added that David Saunders, "a young aggressive and progressive worker" who had directed the Stassen for President campaign in California during 1948, was a Nixon admirer. Kyle Palmer and "Chic" Hansen of the *Los Angeles Times* favored Nixon. As that newspaper went, Jorgensen reasoned, the *San Francisco Chronicle* and the *Oakland Tribune* would follow. He estimated the primary cost at more than $50,000. Since Nixon was relatively unknown in Northern California, he would need to accept some speaking engagements there to gain more exposure. Under these circumstances, Jorgensen pledged to lay "the groundwork for the putting together of an organization and to have secured for you the endorsement as nearly as possible of all these influential people and newspapers."[52]

By the start of March, Nixon was swamped with his regular mail plus a large amount dealing with the campaign. He allowed his name to be discussed as long as no one indicated that he had been consulted, since he did not want "to get myself into a position where everybody is shooting at me because of the fear of my becoming one of their rivals for his nomination." The congressman had good cause for optimism. Brennan, according to Nixon, was "one of the top men in the party and there is no man I would rather have on my side in the event that I had the opportunity to run."[53]

To evoke a Nixon consensus, Saunders, on May 19, officially announced the organization of a nonpartisan group, California Volunteers for Good Government, of which he became president and whose singular purpose was to draft Nixon as the Republican senatorial candidate in the upcoming primary. Following the filing of papers in Sacramento, Saunders pronounced that this nonpartisan, civic-minded group had unanimously acted without the congressman's authorization and chose Richard Nixon for the race. If he agreed, California Volunteers would energetically support his nomination and election, for Nixon had demonstrated intelligence and courage while serving in Congress, and "his fearless stand for American principles of democracy has won the admiration and respect of voters of every party."[54]

Nixon had not been told that the committee was going public, and the story caught him by surprise. The congressman, however, did not think "it would be wise to be too critical of them because I am confident that their action was with the very best intentions, and in the end it may not prove to be harmful at all."[55]

Nixon carefully gauged his chances. He talked with Senator Knowland about the possibility, who responded that if Nixon appeared as the best candidate, he would happily support him. Nixon assured the senator that he would not run without the governor's and Knowland's approval, for his decision depended "to a great extent on what Knowland and Warren finally decide. My own feeling at the moment is that if they give me the 'green light' I should like to do it." He wanted Palmer to understand his position, underlining: "I recognize the risks involved but if solid Republican support is assured I think the opportunity would be so great that I could not afford to turn it down."[56]

Nixon also had those who advised against the run. Tom Erwin, a popular state assemblyman who had backed Nixon in 1946, counseled against any race, due to Downey's strength and the organizational split within the GOP. Gerald Kepple, an original member of the Fact Finding Committee, argued against the challenge because Downey was too entrenched; furthermore, Kepple did not want Nixon to jeopardize his House seat.[57]

Jorgensen and others lobbied for Nixon's return to California immediately after Congress adjourned. If he announced, Jorgensen wanted $25,000 in the bank. Some money would come from within the state, and Bert Mattei, an executive from San Francisco for the Honolulu Oil Company, had pledged to Jorgensen that easterner contributors had offered him "a substantial amount of money." His offer was appreciated, but Mattei's strained relationship with Governor Warren complicated the situation. Since there was "no love between the two of them and we must be most cautious of Warren's relationship," Jorgensen stepped carefully. Reflecting on the confidential nature of his advice, Jorgensen ended his note to Nixon: "I am destroying a copy of this letter; hope you do the same."[58]

Tantalizing stories of secret oil money smeared Nixon throughout his elections. Indeed, Mattei was not Nixon's first petroleum contributor. Don Lycan, president of Signal Oil, who provided the seed money in 1944 for the Republican congressional challenger, indirectly was. Two years later, Perry used the excess from that campaign to launch Nixon's effort. Harry March, one of Lycan's associates, also met with the candidate in 1946, but he apparently offered very little advice and no funds to Nixon. During his reelection campaign, contributions were limited and the contest was decided in the primary. As a result of these two races, neither executive showed significant "big business" involvement, let alone the taint of oozing, clandestine oil dripping into campaign coffers.

As Nixon geared up for his senatorial race, Mattei offered his assistance, which was enthusiastically welcomed. He introduced the candidate to his friends to solicit donations, but any deep involvement by Mattei was squelched because Warren found him objectionable, and Nixon could not afford to offend the governor by appointing Mattei to a fund-raising position in the senatorial contest. Once Nixon made this decision, Mattei did not have any official role in the race, nor did any oil magnate appear to make an overly generous contribution.

The rumor and consequent charge of large amounts of secret cash coming into the Nixon campaign from petroleum interests cannot be verified, but still persist. Proving what really transpired through the thorough documentation left from Nixon's finance committee and other records has been a daunting task; confirming allegations emanating from whispers and gossip without supporting data cannot be taken seriously.

Some of Nixon's support depended upon the strength of his opposition. Tom Erwin disapproved of Nixon's running for the Senate, but Nixon believed he might change his thinking if Douglas entered the race. The congressman intended to await her decision. If she did announce, he "had probably better come to California so that we can make some definite plans." Until Nixon examined every possible vantage point, he would not declare because "it's a pretty tough job any way you look at it."[59]

Throughout the remaining days of the summer, Nixon slowly moved toward proclaiming his candidacy. First, he wanted to be sure that he could handily win the Republican primary. Loyalists across the state continuously updated him on his prospects; Jorgensen noted that Goodwin "Goodie" Knight, California's Republican lieutenant governor, in all likelihood would run against him.[60]

Early in June, Nixon hired J. Patrick Hillings, who had just passed the bar, to work part time in his California office and monitor the movement of potential senatorial contestants. Hillings instantly became a Nixon loyalist who hoped that his boss would enter the contest despite concern over the candidate's relative youth and inexperience. Born in 1924 to a poor Irish, Catholic family from Los Angeles, Hillings went to the local schools. He received excellent grades and played sports, was graduated at the top of his 1941 high school class, and received a scholarship to USC, where he excelled as a straight A student in journalism. After completing his undergraduate degree, he went into the armed forces and fought in the Pacific. On discharge, he returned to his alma mater for law school in 1946, and while on campus, helped establish the first Young Republican club there. Although he and Nixon had never met, Hillings contacted the congressman to speak before a law school audience to a packed room of three hundred. The performance so impressed Hillings that he volunteered at Nixon's district office to answer correspondence.

Nixon eventually hired Hillings for district assignments, which would help pay for some office rent while Hillings was struggling to establish his own legal practice. Nixon liked the twenty-five-year-old veteran, who had "tremendous possibilities and is bound to go places"; he protected Hillings from other older GOP workers, who were jealous of his accomplishments. Hillings responded in kind. More than four decades after their first conversation, Hillings remembered Nixon as "the most brilliant man I have ever met."[61]

Along with these grassroots efforts, Nixon was pleased when Kyle Palmer, of the *Los Angeles Times,* and its publisher, Norman Chandler, promised the newspaper's endorsement. By the end of the summer, he felt that the *Times's* decision was "the most decisive factor on our side at the present time and it is important that we keep that support at all costs." Indeed it was.[62]

Nixon fixed an arbitrary day in July to make an announcement, but then postponed it until the end of August. He flew home for consultations and made an allegedly nonpolitical tour of Northern California to see how receptive audiences were to his candidacy. Some still considered Downey unbeatable, but a Douglas challenge would dramatically brighten GOP prospects. Despite the murky political waters, Nixon was ready to plunge in: "Being somewhat of a gambler, it would seem to me that the gamble on the state-wide race is not as great as the one we took going against Vorhees [*sic*]. Of course, some people will say that there was not so much to lose then as there is now, but I am not inclined to agree."[63]

By the end of July, Nixon had just about decided to enter the contest and asked Perry to gather a group of close supporters to review the entire matter. If Nixon received "substantial support from the party leaders," and Knight did not announce, he would consider that "the die had been cast and we were going to get into the race." He had told House colleagues that "unless the Republicans do make substantial gains in both the House and the Senate in 1950, which necessarily would mean a Republican trend, I seriously doubt if we can ever work our way back in power. Actually, in my mind, I do not see any great gain in remaining a member of the House, even from a relatively good District, if it means that we would be simply a vocal but ineffective minority." If a GOP trend developed, the Senate looked attractive. "If the trend is not on, rewinning the House seat might prove to be a rather empty victory."[64]

Nixon left for California at the end of the month and arrived the weekend of September 10. During his trip, he vacationed and met with his closest friends about the Senate. Both Saunders and the Young Republicans rallied to his cause. Saunders sponsored a private luncheon in the California Room of the Alexandria Hotel in Los Angeles for Nixon to meet members of his California Volunteers committee, who encouraged him to run and promised to raise money for him. The California Young Republicans president, Joe Holt, with Hillings's assistance, at the executive committee that represented twenty-five clubs unanimously passed a resolution urging Nixon to run. Hillings observed: "Things look very good and the movement is growing. The Young Republicans are solidly behind you."[65]

For two weeks, Nixon traveled throughout the state assessing his chances. On the evening of September 25, his departure date to return to Washington, Jorgensen, who had come to trust Brennan, learned from him that Knowland would line up behind Nixon. The next morning, Jorgensen and Brennan met with Murray Chotiner and asked him to serve as campaign manager. Even though they warned him that funds were scarce, Chotiner was "very willing and anxious to assume his part of the campaign." Jorgensen, at this moment, had totally erased his earlier pessimism, telling Nixon: "Nowhere have we met with adverse thinking on your running for the Senator. Everybody seems to agree that you can make the best bid but you will have a hell of a tough job in the finals."[66]

Nixon concurred with these conclusions. His travels to the northern part of the state had reinforced his feeling that he would find enthusiastic backers there. He wished to run, was predisposed to do so, and was ready to be persuaded to go in that direction. As he said, he was a gambler.

By the start of fall, Douglas also increased her pace toward running. At noon on October 5, she appeared as the guest on a radio interview show and surprised her audience by announcing that she was definitely going to enter the race and would make a formal statement in the coming days. Douglas anticipated that she would be accused of socialistic and Communist connections, but said that in reality, she symbolized the spirit of liberalism and was the candidate of the people, while Downey represented big business and the Central Valley Project.[67]

Nixon loyalists reported the welcome news to their leader. Jorgensen effusively exclaimed: "Our luck seems to be holding and I am sure that enthusiasm is mounting each day among those people who we have confidentially advised that your campaign is a certainty." The Douglas announcement stunned Bewley, but he quickly composed himself and energetically prepared for the struggle ahead: "We are all thrilled to death and excited as hell." Nixon's entrance into the contest, as far as Bewley was concerned, was a foregone conclusion, "and I feel that you can lick the socks off her. This is really going to be a campaign and I think one of the most interesting campaigns in the United States." Even oil operators told the Quaker attorney that their men working on the rigs supported Nixon in spite of their union affiliations. Others backed Nixon for the wrong reasons: "Women have no business in Congress. With a great influx of (most) 2nd and worse class people to this state; looks like we are headed for the 'sticks.' Their kids are or will be voting."[68]

From her announcement until the close of the year, Douglas attacked Downey with increasing ferocity and highlighted such issues as reclamation: "Believe me, Downey is done for—and should be. He has turned his back on the people of California and its future. . . . Be it lack of vision or venality, the results are the same." Downey opposed public power and the Central Valley Project in favor of private utility companies. He did not assist the elderly or, for that matter, the rest of his constituency. Douglas, on the other hand, represented and reflected the mandate of the Democratic Party and would "carry the fight into every county, city, town and hamlet in the state." She was pleasantly surprised that California newspapers received her announcement positively.[69]

Douglas realized that if Downey lost the primary, her probable GOP opponent would be Nixon. She already claimed to have some information on his previous "dirty tricks," demonstrating that the legend of Nixon the dirty campaigner was growing, based mainly on the Voorhis CIO-PAC incident. To Douglas, Nixon typified the flawed logic of the Republican Party. If she faced him in the general election, the issues would be "very clear cut. I can't think of a better opponent from the point of view of the Democratic Party platform."[70]

Within two days of Douglas's radio broadcast, Nixon decided to seek the Republican nomination and informed his closest advisers to tell whomever they wished in confidence. But when the *Whittier News* interviewed him over the phone, he publicly replied that no decision would be made until his return to the district. Before going north, he had addressed an audience at the Whittier High School auditorium, believing that he had to "give greater responsibility to the new faces our campaign will attract than has been the case in the past." He would take definite stands that clearly delineated the differences between himself and his Democratic opponents, and would "wage an aggressive, hard-hitting campaign against the Socialist Welfare State policies which have been consistently supported by" Downey and Douglas.[71]

In this contest, Nixon chose Murray Chotiner to manage the contest because he had "a record of managing successful campaigns for Republican candidates in the past and so far, his knowledge and experience have proved to be very valuable in the opening stages of my campaign for the United States Senate." Nixon quickly came to rely on Chotiner for directing the daily routine of the campaign as well suggesting strategy. He had played a minimal public relations role in Nixon's 1946 campaign and even less two years later, but the congressman had confidence in Chotiner's political skills.[72]

Born on October 4, 1909, in Pittsburgh to Jewish parents, Murray lived most of his childhood in Columbus, Ohio, until the family migrated to Southern California in 1920. He went to Los Angeles High School, graduated, and attended University of California at Los Angeles until he enrolled in Southwestern Law School. At nineteen, he received his diploma and waited for two years to take and pass the bar examination. Immediately he opened a law practice, and a year later, he entered politics by campaigning for Hoover's reelection. He had dutifully supported every GOP presidential candidate since then. Chotiner had lost his own primary bid for the state assembly in 1934. Despite this defeat, he remained active in Republican county and statewide organizations and participated in the Los Angeles Jewish Community Relations Committee. His work in planning Knowland's 1946 triumph attested to his managerial skills, and he had directed the Dewey-Warren 1948 effort in Southern California. By 1950, Chotiner was considered a professional campaign manager for the GOP who had already directed a successful senatorial contest.[73]

In 1972, Jerry Voorhis spoke for those who viewed Murray Chotiner almost as a Rasputin-type manipulator. Voorhis alluded to himself as "the first victim of the Nixon-Chotiner formula for political success." In fact, Chotiner did not have any significant role in the Nixon campaign after Voorhis returned to California. His charge that he was the "first victim" of Nixon and Chotiner's "formula for political success" has no basis in fact. Day had hired Chotiner during that primary for limited public relations purposes, and even then Chotiner spent the largest amount of his time orchestrating Knowland's victory. Day and McCall managed Nixon's Republican upset.

The GOP national committeeman from California, Mac Faries, knew Chotiner well and felt that those who labeled him "Nixon's hatchet man" were unfair. Chotiner was "a hard driver, and he drove himself harder than others, but it took him awhile to develop judgment in the driving of others." Hillings, a close friend, insisted that Chotiner "was not ruthless and cruel." He was bright, controversial, and gruff. "People thought he was a dirty tricks man," but Hillings contended that "he was smarter than his critics."[74]

On October 25, Jorgensen, as chairman of the 12th congressional district for the Republican Central Committee of Los Angles County, informed his friends that Nixon would be making "an important announcement" over the Don Lee Mutual network, with statewide coverage, at a dinner held at the Ebell Club in Pomona at 7:00 P.M. on November 3. Guests needed to make reservations immediately: "The time is short and it is my desire that each and every one of the elected Republican Committeemen and leaders of the Republican organizations in the District attend this meeting."[75]

That Thursday evening, the hall was filled to capacity. President George Benson of Claremont College introduced Richard Nixon after reviewing his congressional accomplishments and calling for his election to the Senate. Then Nixon rose, and in a fourteen-minute address, stressed that he had beaten a well-entrenched and popular opponent in 1946. Once in office, he had helped to expose the Communist threat, but now the United States faced an even greater peril: Democratic programs that were destroying American freedoms and pushing the nation toward state socialism. The Fair Deal was "still the same old Socialist baloney any way you slice it." Republicans had to find constructive alternatives to Truman's proposals. Nixon promised to find them, and the audience applauded.

This contest, Nixon stressed, would be difficult. He reiterated that the campaign was "simply the choice between freedom and state socialism." There was only one way to win: "We must put on a fighting, rocking, socking campaign, and carry that campaign directly into every county, city, town, precinct and home in the State of California. I will wage this type of campaign, but only with the help of thousands of volunteer workers can we succeed. We will tell the people the truth . . . . We will raise a banner of freedom which all people regardless of party, call follow. If we do this, we cannot help but win."[76]

Nixon and Douglas had a great deal in common. Both represented constituencies from Southern California in the House: she for six years and he for four. They were energetic, worked tirelessly, represented clearly definable points of view, and were optimistic. Each had loyal followings who truly believed in their congressperson. This almost blind allegiance evolved into something larger than life; both individuals personified all that was holy in their followers' political beliefs.

Their respective entrances into the race were revealing. Douglas concentrated on attacking the incumbent Downey. She loudly condemned some of the senator's personal and professional positions. She was a crusader for Democratic virtue, while the sitting senator, she claimed, had lost the vision of his party and advocated positions that did not necessarily address the needs of his constituency. Douglas openly questioned the worth of the titular head of the Democratic Party in California and made her attack personal and divisive as well as philosophical. She insisted that she symbolized the New Deal, while Downey marched to a conservative beat.

Nixon took an entirely different approach. He first preached to the choir, then moved to enlarge it into a statewide consensus. His method of winning the nomination grew by calculated steps. He had already gained the *Los Angeles Times*'s endorsement, effortlessly nudged Senator Knowland, neutralized any potential animosity from Governor Warren, and built upon independent advocates like the California Volunteers. In order to enhance party harmony, Nixon offended as few as possible. Announcing for the Senate, he stressed traditional Republican values before those who wholeheartedly embraced them.

Nixon had none of the primary hurdles that Douglas had to overcome. He did not have to address Downey's competence. Nixon happily watched the two Democrats insult each other, while he confined his mission to building harmony within his party and shaping his financial and political structure, with Chotiner serving as an adept campaign strategist and organizer.

Nixon, even at this early date, knew that the confrontation between Downey and Douglas would benefit Republicans. All he had to do was preserve GOP allegiance and watch the Democrats self-destruct, at least for now.

*Chapter* **14**

# THE 1950 PRIMARY

The U.S. Senate contest in California during 1950 has become the stuff where legend has replaced fact. "Tricky Dicky" smeared Helen Gahagan Douglas, the "Pink Lady," thus relying on the anti-Communist hysteria to propel the dirty trickster into the upper House. The record, however, paints quite a different scene. Helen Gahagan Douglas was far to the left of many Democrats, let alone Republicans. Besides her close attachment to New and Fair Deal policies that the majority of her party was abandoning, she ran a campaign without the benefit of an effective statewide staff, clearly defined strategy, or an adequate fund-raising scheme. Along with these Herculean disadvantages, a large segment of the Democratic Party had rejected her unswerving advocacy of liberalism. By the time of the general election, she had been thoroughly smeared, not by Nixon but by her own party. Faced with widespread Democratic desertion that she was unable to prevent, Douglas never united the warring factions of the Democratic Party to battle against the Republican enemy. Her painfully inept stewardship—not Nixon—guaranteed her demise.

Murray Chotiner, as manager for Nixon, had a clear vision: "I would like to see the campaign follow the positive psychology that Congressman Nixon is a candidate for United States Senate, and not that he is running against anyone else." He hoped to focus on core Republican issues and demonstrate that excessive government spending contributed to the high cost of living. The election would be difficult enough, and therefore, he did not want to target labor unnecessarily. He rejected any assault on the "welfare state."[1]

Nixon generally followed this counsel. He worried about the "trend of being 'against' everything" and expected "to wage my Senatorial campaign on an affirmative rather than negative approach on the problems of the day." He promised rapt audiences "an aggressive campaign without double-talk or pussyfooting," and was confident that he could win the election.[2]

While Brennan and Chotiner concentrated on Southern California, an influential San Francisco attorney, John Dinkelspiel, served as campaign chairman in the northern headquarters. Aylett Cotton, another prominent lawyer in the Bay area, was also drawn into the campaign, although both advocates were relatively unfamiliar with Nixon's qualifications. By the end of November, Cotton had seen Nixon five times and liked him better with each succeeding meeting. "If we get behind him," the San Fransican argued, "maybe we can elect somebody for a change. I really don't think I have ever been more impressed with anyone than I have been with Nixon." By the new year, Cotton had evolved into a loyalist, for Nixon was "a liberal in the true sense in that he is in favor of progress but against the so-called liberalism that makes people stand in line to get a 'handout' from an official in Washington."[3]

As in most campaigns, smooth operations needed coordination. Nixon and David Saunders talked on the phone about the mission of the California Volunteers. Initially, the group solely backed Nixon, but as the primary grew nearer, some members wanted to endorse other candidates. The congressman would not comment on anyone else that the group might endorse, but he did worry about the group's direction. Saunders assured Nixon that "our first consideration will be that we do nothing that could fairly jeopardize your candidacy. Such action would also injure our effectiveness and mitigate against the principle [sic] objectives of our organization." His volunteers would only work for Nixon in the primary, but he could not prevent some of them from working for other prospects in the future.[4]

Inevitably, nerves were frayed and egos had to be soothed. Pat Hillings and Mildred Younger, an influential Republican in Southern California, had a disagreement over the timing when to endorse Nixon. While these two quickly reconciled, Joe Holt, who directed field operations for Nixon, disagreed with Younger on other matters. Roy Day, in turn, disliked Holt's pomposity and accused Herman Perry of making "vicious accusations" against him. Day saw only one option: "I deeply resent your statements and action toward me and can take no other course than to withdraw to make the position of Nixon a smoother one." Day's venting was brief; after Nixon's primary victory, he rejoined the campaign.[5]

Hurt feelings, no matter how upsetting, took second place to raising money. From September to November, contributors gave anywhere from $10 to $100 each, totaling between $8,000 to $10,000. From November 1949 through January 1950, the committee collected another $3,000 to $6,000. These were not inconsequential sums, for Douglas was busy raising money at that time. Nixon recognized that Dana Smith, the finance chairman, and others were working diligently to get contributions: "Without doubt, the most difficult task in an election campaign is to obtain financial support before the 'band-wagon' psychology begins to take effect and from all accounts you [Morgan Adams, Jr.] and the other members of Dana's group have done an outstanding job." Mac Faries recalled that he never had trouble with Nixon on this topic: "He was a fair-minded man; he was also smart enough never to bring up the matter of his funds personally or directly with me or the group. He was . . . a smarter man than some cared to think, and smarter than a number of his advisors and supporters."[6]

At the start of 1950, candidates for statewide office in California faced a far different political landscape than a decade earlier. While the population of the United States had expanded modestly to 152 million by that year, the rate of growth in California had mushroomed by 53 percent, bringing the population to 10,630,000. Of the total 4,500,000 registered voters, 58.4 percent were Democrats and 37.1 percent Republicans. In sheer numbers, the party of FDR had a tremendous advantage over the GOP. Yet, as the fund-raising effort demonstrated, the GOP faithful were more willing to donate to Nixon than were contributors to Douglas's coffers.[7]

In mid-January, Douglas officially opened her campaign headquarters in Los Angeles and San Francisco to demonstrate to Downey that she was "a serious candidate" and was vigorously contesting his seat. The Fair Deal, she conceived, kept the United States from moving toward conservatism on the right or socialism on the left. Voters had elected FDR and Harry Truman because they defended free enterprise and protected personal rights: "Government" was "the means of coordinating our efforts so that we can work together to obtain goals which would be impossible to us as individuals." She now was soliciting followers to help build "grass roots support" for her vision.[8]

On several occasions, Downey challenged Douglas to a series of debates, but she refused, uncomfortable in that forum. Instead, she dared him to publish his views on pensions and the Central Valley Project. He, in turn, declined to answer her in print. Both thereafter engaged in their own separate campaigns, defining issues as they saw fit and demanding replies that seldom followed. Name-calling grew louder and nastier.[9]

Earl Desmond, Democratic state senator from Sacramento, also announced for Downey's seat. His platform included support for the CVP, state ownership of its tidelands, an anti-Communist domestic policy, and pensions for the aged and needy blind. In many ways similar to Downey, Desmond was another respected voice from central California who was on the centrist side of Douglas's liberalism.[10]

Financing was a constant strain for Douglas. With a fund-raising organization vastly inferior to Nixon's, this weakness would ultimately prove to be a major factor in her undoing. After delivering eight or nine speeches a day, during brief moments to rest she was on the phone trying to find contributors. Knowing that "there will be unlimited money spent against me, and the sources from which I feel I can accept money are very few," she put herself in an impossible position. In the middle of October, she wrote: "Every penny we can scrape together is going to carry on our expenses and we . . . are appealing to the public for funds to see us through." To the former secretary of the interior, Harold Ickes, she pleaded: "You don't know anyone who has any money, do you? We have a campaign on and no money—and I mean *no* money."[11]

Despite the constant shortage of funds, Douglas kicked off the official opening of her campaign on the last day of February 1950 with a statewide radio address. When rumors that Downey might retire surfaced that day, she cynically perceived that his "apparent intention of quitting springs from his fear of growing support for my own candidacy." She mused that Downey's staff had "seized this opportunity [her announcement] to grab headlines. It's strictly a political maneuver." Despite poor health, he might reluctantly run, and that would "give him more headlines and make him look pretty noble."[12]

Douglas underscored her support for the Fair Deal, calling for expanded Social Security benefits for retirees. Truman's national health insurance bill was not "socialized medicine"; it targeted Americans who were unable to afford care. Thousands of people were pouring into the state without any means of livelihood, resulting in mass unemployment throughout California, and she therefore proposed legislation to provide public works jobs for those without employment. Finally, since agriculture was depressed, she called for revisions to support farm income, protect perishables, encourage consumption, initiate a school lunch program, conserve natural resources, and preserve the family-sized farm.[13]

During the first three months of 1950, Nixon concentrated his efforts on gaining GOP support. At the end of January, the California Republican Assembly candidates' committee convened at the swank Del Monte Hotel for $40 per night in Pebble Beach. The two main contenders for the senatorial race were Nixon and Frederick Houser. Initially, a subcommittee recommended the latter by a vote of 6 to 3, but when the entire assembly's vote was taken, Nixon squeaked by with a narrow 13–12 endorsement. The full assembly would meet in San Francisco, and the preliminary decision could be reversed, but that never happened.[14]

Nixon later wrote Philip Davis, a Los Angeles attorney and a close friend of Judge Houser. The congressman knew that the judge might decide to run against him. If Houser did so, many of Nixon's acquaintances would support the judge. Nixon wrote: "You can be sure that there will be no hard feelings as far as I am concerned." Meanwhile, Raymond Darby, a Los Angeles supervisor, was considering running for the Senate, but also was flirting with challenging Governor Warren. Harrison McCall believed that Darby could not be "that gullible for if he does decide to switch again [from the gubernatorial to senatorial campaigns] he will become the laughing stock of the community."[15]

As potential opponents like Houser and Darby tried unsuccessfully to dampen Nixon's momentum, his organization grew stronger. Friends in the 12th district were tapped. Boyd Gibbons, who helped establish the "amateur group" in 1946, asked to resurrect the idea on a statewide basis. Brooks Terry, a friend and neighbor of the Nixons for twenty years, had powerful ties with veteran groups; Jack Drown, a former Stanford University football star who was married to Pat Nixon's best friend Helene, accepted the Long Beach chairmanship; Henry Kearns from Alhambra, a former leader in the U.S. Junior Chamber of Commerce, might direct the campaign in the 12th district; the California Volunteers contacted businessmen and other professionals. Finally, an advertisement that spring urged volunteers to "Join the NIXON COMMITTEE of 10,000 Today!" by sending five dollars.[16]

Chotiner arranged for interviews between potential donors and the congressman. A. G. Wood of Carpinteria was a wealthy supporter, and Nixon had to see him. J. S. Kauffman, a Democrat from West Covina, promised financial assistance and the names of other potential contributors, but was angry when no one contacted him. Harry Schuyler, a local "prima donna" who was an old family friend, was a bit irked that Nixon had not paid more attention to him. Someone had to soothe his hurt feelings.[17]

While these matters were being resolved in Southern California, Dinkelspiel directed the northern effort and hired Harry Hancock, who owned a San Francisco public relations firm, to act as Chotiner did in Los Angeles. Nixon had met Hancock and came away impressed: "I think he certainly is the answer to our northern California problem as far as heading the campaign is concerned." To cover central California, Dinkelspiel hired William Queale to travel through the valley towns and build an effective organization.[18]

Nixon tried to bring his sectional campaign committees into closer contact by asking Brennan to consult with Dinkelspiel and Hancock twice a week in order to form a liaison "to work the northern people into our campaign planning and strategy more effectively than we have in the past." Brennan, Chotiner, and Jorgensen traveled to San Francisco in mid-March to get Northern California input. The complaints that they heard were that Nixon's speeches had been too long and that he was devoting too much attention to his advocacy of the Mundt-Nixon bill, HUAC, and "the red-herring situation." Jorgensen agreed that "too much emphasis on the Red situation will make you look like an Old Maid looking under the bed too frequently!"[19]

Nixon was not deterred, stressing that as the campaign accelerated, various issues including the Hiss affair would be highlighted. In a letter to Brennan, he pointed out that "outside of so-called intellectual circles, the Hiss case has been tremendously effective in getting us the support we need." Bert Mattei had sent $100 for reprints of Nixon's congressional address that followed Hiss's conviction. The congressman was mailing out fifty thousand copies to Democrats in Southern California and another thirty thousand to the northern portion. Over seven thousand newspapers received copies.[20]

After the San Francisco meeting, Brennan wrote Nixon a five-page letter and then destroyed his copy "as this is strictly a heart to heart talk, and your destruction of the letter will then leave it in that category." Brennan held both Dinkelspiel and Hancock in high regard. They, however, wished that Nixon would soft-pedal communism, due to local opinions. Brennan disagreed with this approach: "to the man in the street communism is a vital issue and you will gain more votes than you lose by continuing your present course." Dinkelspiel argued against attacking Downing because Douglas was already doing so, but Brennan again dissented. Douglas's attacks on the senator as a tool of big business made him a moderate candidate, and that perception might deliver him Democratic votes that Nixon could capture. But Brennan concurred with the northerners that Nixon's speeches were too long and that he said, "Now, in conclusion," at least four times. As a candidate, he should limit his talks to thirty minutes. Eventually Brennan thought that Nixon would reach the presidency, but that he needed to act moderately. His move from the House to the Senate was as sudden as a whirlwind; Nixon should not wish to present the illusion that he hoped to capture the White House in 1952.[21]

Throughout, Nixon was an effective fund-raiser. Mattei helped arrange meetings with potential contributors like those at the Bohemian Club in San Francisco. That event, according to Nixon, "was probably the most effective meeting of potential contributors that we have had during the course of the campaign." Still, contributions did not come in quickly enough to satisfy everyone. John Hunt, chairman of the Southern California finance committee, reported in early February that he needed $16,400 for that month's expenses. March expenditures were "exceptionally heavy" due to billboard costs, and the committee had been $7,000 short in February. By the end of March, Hunt was still troubled: the campaign needed another $16,000. However, by April the shortfall was raised.[22]

With Nixon aspiring for higher office, Pat Hillings decided to announce for Nixon's seat in the House. The congressman felt that his protégé would do "a bang-up job" and keep the 12th congressional district working for Nixon's senatorial campaign. Despite these benefits, Nixon wanted Hillings off the congressional payroll since he had become an announced candidate. "If Drew Pearson or some other smear artist learned about it," Nixon worried, "they would probably do a pretty nasty job on both of us." He himself would attempt to find Hillings some money for expenses during his campaign. "This," Nixon predicted, would be "a pretty rough period, as I know from experience, and I should warn you that you will have to be prepared to subsidize yourself for the next year, because it is tough to get money for campaign expenses let alone something for the candidate!" Hillings received the Fact Finding Committee's endorsement. While Nixon agreed with the choice, he was concerned that Hillings's victory might spark a fight in the district and fragment GOP unity because of the personal animosity between the two rival factions.[23]

As Nixon anticipated, political infighting in the district flared. The mayor of Claremont, Stuart Wheeler, refused to accept the Fact Finding Committee's recommendation and embarked upon a bitter primary contest against Hillings. Perry recommended that Brennan and Nixon should meet both men and force whichever man lost to support the other in the general election. Their bickering, according to Perry, was not only hurting the congressional campaign, but it was also "having a most disastrous effect on our chief object, Richard M. Nixon." Their fighting could lose the House contest, the Senate, and the surrounding districts.[24]

Such fear did not stop Nixon from filing nomination papers for the U.S. Senate on March 20 on both the Democratic and Republican ballots. By the end of the month, his schedule for the primary race had been arranged. Commencing a nonstop campaign on April 3, throughout the rest of that month and ending on election day, including Sunday nights, Nixon would cover all fifty-eight counties, especially those where he was unknown. Sometimes he would speak six to eight times a day. He would travel in a bright yellow 1949 Mercury station wagon. On the wood-panel sides, signs in big, bold letters read: NIXON for U.S. SENATOR.[25]

Nixon's first objective, according to Chotiner, was to dispel the impression that Downey was "invincible, and a conservative." Amidst rumors that the senator was under pressure to withdraw, Republican confidants like Congressman Norris Poulson from the nearby 13th district hoped that Douglas would win the primary "because it will then be duck soup for you." Nixon thought that Downey was vacillating about retiring and showed signs of "weakness and indecision." If he decided to drop out of the contest, gossip was that Truman would give him a good political appointment. Nixon had also received unverified information of a poll illustrating Downey losing strength and Nixon with greater appeal than anyone had expected. "This may or may not be true," Nixon declared, "but at least it is an interesting story!" Downey, according to Nixon, did not want to run, "but decided to stay in after the major Democratic leaders told him that they felt Douglas would have a tough time defeating me in the final campaign."[26]

On March 29, just before Nixon embarked on his tour, Senator Downey decided to withdraw from the campaign, citing ill health. Rather than declare for Douglas, he announced that he would endorse Ralph Manchester Boddy, editor and publisher of the *Los Angeles Daily News*, who had quickly filed to run in the race. The Democrats were in disarray.[27]

Douglas ignored Boddy's entrance, launched an exhaustive speaking schedule, and strengthened her hold on organized labor, Democratic loyalists, and minorities. She proclaimed that labor had "now united behind me, and my position is much stronger." John McCormack, Democratic House majority leader from Massachusetts, considered her "one of the ablest Members of the House," who had "made an outstanding record." Even more important, "Not only does Helen Douglas possess unusual ability, and outstanding courage, but above all, she is LOYAL."[28]

Douglas readily embraced the liberal label. With Downey gone, she believed her prospects looked "much better." Yet at no time did she ever seriously consider seeking a rapprochement, neutralizing, or even soliciting Downey's support. She dismissed his surrogate's challenge, but if necessary, she would point to Boddy's "acts of omission as well as commission." She also quickly discovered that "The plot is the same but with a different leading man. The people who backed Downey are now backing Boddy." With inadvertent pressure, one Douglas loyalist noted that Boddy initially treated Douglas "with kid gloves, and we don't want to be the side which can be accused of causing a serious breach in the Democratic Party, the sort of breach that couldn't be healed after the primaries." After Douglas and Downey's deluge of personal insults raining down on one another, this more civil approach was long overdue.[29]

Douglas's themes remained consistent, favoring the New and Fair Deals, never deviating from her principles: "I have not been content merely to ask for legislation implementing those programs, but I have striven with all my might and purpose to achieve them, and I shall continue to do so, if elected to the Senate." She denied any sympathy toward communism or socialism. J. Edgar Hoover, Douglas declared, had her "full support in the discharge of his assigned duties."[30]

Douglas worked against Nixon throughout the primary. At the end of March, she told reporters that she would defeat him in the general election. She privately wrote the editor of the *Sacramento Bee,* Walter Jones, to lobby against any Nixon endorsement. "Officially," she warned, "our margin for error in preserving our liberties is narrow today, but in the hearts of the people I believe there is a wide and sound judgment which will not accept his record." Nixon had helped bring Hiss to trial, but California needed more than a policeman: "In short, this is no time for California to send a 'kid' to Washington to do a man's work."[31]

While Douglas spoke out against her antagonists, she paid scant attention to her own amateurish and inadequately funded organization. Chotiner, in contrast, ran an orderly, professional operation with a determined mission. By the time his candidate started on the road in early April, Chotiner had completed the staffing for the primary. He was arranging for a television film and four radio addresses to attract votes and had chosen a news commentator to introduce Nixon, ask him questions, and conclude by telling the audience where the candidate would appear next. By the end of the month, Chotiner could state: "Things are moving along in grand shape, and I am not being overly optimistic when I say we are going to give you another Republican United States Senator."[32]

Chotiner also planned a direct mailing to Democrats and allocated advertising calling on Democrats to vote for Nixon. Chotiner and others even hoped that Nixon might capture the Democratic primary as he had done in 1948. During a series of breakfast meetings of his closest advisers, they took this possibility seriously: "A continued upsurge of public demand for Nixon's election must be encouraged with every possible weapon. No punches will be pulled in a drive toward a smashing glorious victory of far-reaching national significance."[33]

Kyle Palmer used the *Los Angeles Times* to promote the congressman. On Sunday, April 2, for instance, he wrote an editorial entitled "Cutting Teeth Is No Fun," predicting that the GOP had an excellent candidate and an "auspicious" opportunity to win the Senate. Judge Houser had decided not to challenge Nixon. Downey had withdrawn and Boddy assumed the retiree's mantle against "the left-wing candidacy" of Douglas, who was not only facing Boddy but also the conservative Earl Desmond, who had spent the past sixteen years in the state senate. In later articles, Palmer continued his praise for the congressman, whose speeches were "winning support over the State and—there is no question at all where, why and for what he stands." Palmer characterized Boddy as colorless; he needed to try "in a political sense, of course—to slap her [Douglas] around a bit."[34]

Through most of April, Boddy and Douglas, on the basis of their vastly differing political viewpoints, were trying to attract voters rather than attack each other, but toward the end of the month, Boddy gave Douglas a dose of the venom that she had so far reserved for Downey and Nixon. Boddy's and other newspapers referred to her as "decidedly pink" or "pink shading to deep red." Toward the end of the month, Boddy in his *Daily News* gave her a label that would stick to her for a life-time: "the pink lady." Rather than this infamous tag attaching to Nixon, it came from a fellow Democrat, reflecting the deep divisions within Douglas's own party.[35]

Like Douglas, Nixon adhered to an exhausting schedule. A typical day illustrates: On Thursday, April 6, at 7:15 A.M., he met Jack Polzin, chairman of his campaign for Kings County, where he had an informal buffet breakfast and spoke for about twenty minutes. From 9:00 A.M. to 10:00 A.M. he called at the newspaper, met local merchants, and visited agricultural camps. He then drove twenty-one miles to Hanford, greet-ing local farmers en route. Once in Hanford, he met Juliys Jacobs, who managed the only daily paper, the *Sentinel*. That afternoon, he presented a thirty-minute speech on "1950—The Year of Decision" and then shook hands. After lunch, Nixon drove five miles west to speak on KNGS, the local radio station. He returned to Hanford at 2:55 P.M. for a "Coffee Klatch" at a local café, then left for LeMoore, ten miles away, to call on the local newspaper owner there. By 5:45 P.M., Pat joined him and the couple left for Fresno County. At 7:30 P.M., Rex Pressey, who was handling the meeting there, greeted them at the Chevrolet Garage and drove them to the Sunset School auditorium, where Nixon spoke. They finished at 10:00 P.M. and departed for Los Angeles.[36]

Unlike Douglas, however, Nixon devoted considerable time to the organizational needs of his campaign. After the first week of the tour, Nixon returned to Los Angeles, where he directed Chotiner in the south and Hancock in the north to send out follow-up letters and press packages about the campaign. He felt that county chairmen needed to appoint more locals to the organization. As for street events, they were only successful with careful planning and plenty of advertising; auditorium audiences were disappointing, but breakfasts, luncheons, and inexpensive dinners were excellent ways of drawing crowds.[37]

Nixon stuck to his "message": wherever he appeared, he repeated his themes. Before the annual meeting of the Lumber Merchants Association of Northern California, he demanded new leadership and said that his program constituted "an alternative to the present bungling approach to curing our headaches." Truman was leading the nation on the path toward socialism and was ignorant of the Red threat at home. In foreign affairs, Nixon supported reciprocal trade agreements to benefit American exports. He also backed Herbert Hoover's proposal to reorganize the United Nations without Russian participation: "The change is due and will come," Nixon affirmed. "The United Nations, with Russia in it, constantly exercising the veto power, is powerless to avoid the third world war."[38]

While Douglas campaigned alone, Nixon took his wife with him. Dick said that Pat went "along for the scenic effect but that she also goes as my secretary." She also happened to be "an accomplished stenographer," who had taught business courses. While Dick spoke to crowds, Pat distributed thimbles with the inscription:"Safeguard the American Home." By the end of the campaign she had passed out over sixty-five thousand of them. Impressed by Pat, Marjorie Sharpe of ABC Radio's *Ladies in the News* followed the candidate's wife around for a day. When asked if she was proud of her husband, she replied: "Prouder than anything in the world."[39]

On May 3, Douglas received crushing news from the primary campaign in Florida where a Democratic liberal ally, Senator Claude Pepper, faced his earlier protégé, Congressman George Smathers. The challenger worked energetically and defeated the incumbent overwhelmingly. Douglas observed: "The loss of Pepper is a great tragedy, and we are sick about it. There is all the more reason now that a real job has to be done here in California and in other states." She was convinced that Pepper's defeat stemmed from smears. "What a vicious campaign was carried on against him. No doubt the fur will begin to fly out here too." In fact, Boddy already was attacking her, and she expected the assaults to increase. "It is revolting," she protested, "to think of the depths to which people will go."[40]

The primary campaign, she recognized, clearly was getting "rough." Except for three days when she returned to Washington for a debate on housing legislation, Douglas had no intention of flying back to the capital again until after it was over. The next four weeks until election day would be "heated ones. However, I do not expect to retaliate in any way against the opposition unless their campaign [Boddy's] sinks to a real low." Boddy mailed out countless pamphlets portraying Douglas as a disloyal American and a traitorous Democrat. Despite these blasts, she cautioned supporters not to respond in kind: "The only way we can counteract them is to go out and work a little harder to get the vote out."[41]

On the evening of May 10, Boddy staged a rally in Los Angeles at the Ambassador Hotel for one thousand committed followers at which he lashed out at Douglas, proclaiming that he had "indisputable evidence of a state-wide conspiracy on the part of a small subversive clique of red hots to capture, through stealth and cunning," the California Democratic Party; but they would be rejected in the primary. This "red hot" clique, according to the candidate, posed a real danger, and its objectives were clear: "They seek to create chaos and confusion and thereby to make themselves the main cogs in the Democratic Party and then to use the party to serve their own twisted purposes. . . . What has happened in these central committees betrays the 'red hot' blueprint of subversive dictatorship." This "clique" would lose in the primary election because the party had awakened and shaken off the "paralyzing influence" of a minority. Here was hyperbole far beyond anything Congressman Nixon had employed.[42]

Retiring Senator Downey punctuated Boddy's attack twelve days later by delivering a devastating statewide radio broadcast lambasting Douglas. He was retiring after two terms. He had known the congresswoman during her three terms. Presented in a dispassionate and antiseptic manner, he listed the reasons for opposing her qualifications and House record in "a scathing analysis." Sometimes he agreed with her voting record, but overall "Mrs. Douglas does not have the fundamental ability and qualifications for a United States Senator." She had been an actress and took the spotlight, "But she has shown no inclination, in fact no ability, to dig in and do the hard and tedious work required to prepare legislation and push it through Congress." Downey listed her shortcomings. She had tried to keep Henry Wallace on the Democratic national ticket in 1944. She voted against the Truman Doctrine. She opposed HUAC funding when 348 voted for it and 12 against; she and Vito Marcantanio of New York were two of the most vocal antagonists. In her eagerness to campaign, she had abandoned her congressional responsibilities and had the worst attendance record of any California House member, only twenty-nine of the fifty-four roll calls in the first quarter. "Her record," he concluded, "clearly shows very little hard work, no important influence on legislation, and almost nothing in the way of solid accomplishment. The fact that Mrs. Douglas has continued to bask in the warm glow of publicity and propaganda should not confuse any voter as to what the real facts are."[43]

Douglas struck back on May 26 in an address at Fresno, where she reaffirmed her support for the Fair Deal, claiming that its goals had not been fulfilled because "We still do not have a working liberal majority in Congress." She emphasized her opposition to communism and proposed a citizens' commission on Un-American Activities headed by Eleanor Roosevelt and Herbert Hoover: "Of course traitors should be brought to justice, but we should and must end once and for all these despicable attempts to use the red smear to stampede the American people into reaction." Ruth Lybeck, Douglas's assistant state coordinator, defended Douglas's "policy of consistency and honesty—no matter how many votes it may cost her—we must tell you the truth."[44]

By the start of May, Nixon, according to Perry, was booked "every hour until the evening of" the primary. His main activity remained public speaking. Before a San Francisco group, he declared the death of isolationism. The United States needed to crusade on both sides of the Iron Curtain against the Red threat. Truman had initiated socialistic proposals, tolerated Communist infiltration, and implemented an unwise fiscal policy. Nixon demanded an end to "wild government spending" and called for federal government to return a fair share of the taxes that it collected to Californians. At the Biltmore Bowl in Los Angeles, he argued to retain the major provisions of the Taft-Hartley Act "to get the government out of industrial relations to the greatest extent possible." In Eureka, he called for the development of water, power, and mining resources because the state had to create "new business and industry, new jobs and opportunities, for a greater California." The Nixon parade, personified by the station wagon, rolled on tirelessly. [45]

His strenuous efforts paid off with major endorsements in Northern California. The San Francisco Chronicle liked Nixon's bipartisan foreign policy, support for the Central Valley Project, and opposition to the 160-acre limitation. The paper objected to the Mundt-Nixon bill, but felt that the congressman would act responsibly. "Nixon is a winner," the paper claimed, "and we think that with him in the Senate California would be a winner, too." The *San Francisco News* and the *San Mateo Times* added their approval.[46]

Nixon's committee decided, against the odds, to "make a concerted effort for the Democratic nomination." Polls taken in early April gave an indication that Nixon could win on both ballots, and in the middle of May, Chotiner still thought that the congressman might win both primaries. When Boddy attacked Nixon for trying to capture the Democratic standard, Nixon counterattacked, demanding that Democrats have a chance to vote against the Truman administration. Voting for Nixon represented a vote of no confidence. With a week and a half to go until the balloting, the committee still harbored some hope that Nixon would be victorious. On June 1, Dorothy Cox finished sending out a Democratic mailing. The next day she conceded: "it looks like Helen will get it, although a lot of people predict he [Nixon] might win in the primaries."[47]

In a last-minute political mailing before election day, Democrats for Nixon asked voters to cast their ballot for the congressman "As One Democrat to Another." Three days later, the *Los Angeles Daily News* angrily charged that Nixon had authorized "a viciously false circular" in which "Nixon, Republican, misrepresents himself as a Democrat." In the same issue, the Veterans Democratic Committee, composed of seventeen individuals, published a full-page ad warning every Democrat that Nixon was masquerading as one of them. Vote Democratic in the primaries, they urged: "Look at 'Tricky Dick' Nixon's Republican Record!" Although this uncomplimentary label has been attributed to someone else much later in the campaign, this was the first major use of "Tricky Dick."[48]

On June 2, the Nixons returned to Southern California for the final days before the voting. Boddy's camp realized that he would lose: "So it'll be Dick and the 'lady' in the fall." Nixon and Arnold had traveled to all of the California counties, driven fifteen thousand miles, and Dick had given six hundred speeches. Dorothy Cox confided to a co-worker in the congressman's Washington office: "The campaign has been a rugged one and frankly, Mr. Nixon has been going on nerves for about the last three weeks. Both he and Mrs. Nixon look awfully bad, so I know that your having the work caught up as much as possible will be a great relief to him."[49]

The Nixon campaign ledger ended in the black. Early in March,

Nixon contacted Senator Ralph Owen Brewster, Republican from Maine and head of the senatorial campaign committee, asking for the $5,000 contribution from his fund that traditionally was sent during the general election. Two months later, the check arrived, adding to the coffers, and the Committee of 10,000 had also raised more money than expected.[50]

The Statement of Vote on June 6, 1950, provided the final tally:[51]

|  | Republican | Democrat | Write-in |
|---|---|---|---|
| Manchester Boddy | 156,884 | 379,077 | |
| Helen Gahagan Douglas | 153,788 | 734,842 | 2,326 |
| Richard Nixon | 740,465 | 318,840 | |
| Earl Desmond | 60,613 | 96,752 | |
| Ulysses Meyer | 18,783 | 34,707 | |
| Albert Levitt | 15,929 | -0- | |

Democrats had a 900,000 plurality over Republicans in registration, and with 418,756 votes, more Democrats than Republicans had voted. Nevertheless, Nixon had beaten Douglas by 169,349 votes.

Herman Perry predicted that Nixon would need a united front to win in November. His contender had built a smooth, efficient organization, traveled throughout the state, developed a strong following in the north, raised enough money to pay off his primary debts, and faced a tough opponent. Nixon, like Douglas, was positive about a November victory, expected to campaign energetically, and was ready for the ordeal. Unlike her, he had moved into the political center while maintaining his appeal to the conservative right. His job would be to convince uncommitted Democrats to rally to his cause.[52]

Nixon and Douglas met only twice during the primary, never with the intent to debate. One encounter came during a meeting before the Commonwealth Club in San Francisco, at which Nixon waved a hundred-dollar check from "Eleanor Roosevelt" and read the accompanying note: "I wish it could be ten times more. Best wishes for your success & kindness regards to you & your lovely wife." After listeners gasped, he admitted that he had originally shared their feeling of amazement until he saw that the contributor was Eleanor B. Roosevelt, who lived in Old Orchard, Oyster Bay, New York, and was Mrs. Theodore Roosevelt II. She came from the other side of the Roosevelt family. The audience roared with laughter while Douglas fumed.[53]

The other instance occurred in Beverly Hills. Nixon, according to Bill Arnold, who was accompanying him, arrived on time and addressed the audience first. Douglas was late, and when she marched onto the stage, Nixon played to the onlookers by gesturing to his watch. The audience laughed at the spectacle, while Douglas wondered why. She spoke with Nixon sitting in back of her. To show his disapproval over what she was saying, he started to fidget, crossing and recrossing his knees as a sign of impatience. Again the audience laughed and again Douglas did not understand why. After she finished her remarks, Nixon rose to speak once more. Rather than listen, she left early. Arnold realized that if this had been a debate, and if points had been awarded for speechmaking, his candidate would have won. That judgment came from the Nixon camp. Obviously, Douglas partisans took the opposite position.[54]

Douglas took several serious liabilities into the general election. Her addresses were convoluted and boring. Her state organization was hampered by a campaign chairman with little knowledge of California politics and local committees that varied in their leadership. Inadequate funding was a recurring theme. She heavily relied on labor, and with that dependence came unions' association with CIO-PACs and their links to Communist influence. If that was not debilitating enough, Boddy constantly hammered away at her leftist leanings. Finally, only a few women had served in the Senate, and many voters would not cast their ballots for a female.[55]

So far, Nixon watched the Democratic Party tear apart without impetus from the GOP. He did not smear her; there was no need. The Democrats were self-destructing.

*Chapter* **15**

# DOUGLAS VERSUS NIXON: THE ISSUES

As Nixon prepared for the fall campaign, he and his followers continued to be devastatingly methodical. Nineteen of his closest advisers
held a confidential workshop at the San Ysidro Ranch, 90 miles from Los
Angeles near Santa Barbara, on the weekend of June 10 and 11, where
the committee divided the state into three regions: northern, southern,
and central valley. By the end of the meeting, Brennan not only chaired
the southern region but now coordinated the entire state effort. As soon
as Perry returned from the gathering, he foresaw the Nixon forces "looking forward to a very aggressive campaign for the November election."[1]

The finance committee was fully operational and had established a
fund-raising goal of $197,987.93 for the general election campaign in the
southern region. Throughout the remainder of the race, Dana Smith sent
out weekly budget summaries, which divided expenditures into public
relations, literature, administrative, field and volunteer, staff headquarters,
and Democratic volunteers. To August 12, for example, the committee
collected $11,175.93 and expended $10,875.93; advertising through September 15 totaled $12,399.20; Chotiner's expenses through August 27
were $6,822.23, going for secretaries, field volunteer coordinators, post-
master, station wagon, telephone, Brennan, Murray Chotiner & Associates, furniture, rentals, letters, stickers, supplies, gas, and travel.[2]

One donation stunned Bill Arnold. Congressman Jack Kennedy, on
intimate terms with colleague George Smathers, was also friendly with
Nixon. One day JFK dropped off $1,000 from his father Joseph for the
campaign against Douglas; Nixon and his staff were astounded. Long

after the fact, in a conversation with Speaker of the House of Representatives Thomas "Tip" O'Neill, Joe raised that figure to $150,000. The
elder Kennedy exaggerated outrageously, telling Tip that he had given
that huge sum to Nixon because Douglas was a "Communist."[3]

During the summer, the Nixon committee also produced a *Manual
of Information* that outlined the general themes of the campaign. Nixon,
it asserted, would be an effective senator and an independent thinker and
voter. He would build a stronger America, oppose communism, and
promote California's development. Republicans liked him. Real Democrats could not follow Douglas, and nonpartisan groups, above all
else, wanted the issues addressed. "ABOVE ALL, Dick Nixon is human. He
came from the people, and is still of the people, a regular guy. He is not
infallible, and may make a mistake, but he will always stand on principle,
and act with sincerity and forthrightness."[4]

In truth, the campaign would be fought largely against Douglas and
communism rather than on local issues. Hearing that she had been the
only congressional member to defend the Yalta agreements at their announcement, Nixon wanted a copy of that speech and any specific references to her and Communists. He also asked for material that showed
she was connected with the Civil Rights Congress, was associated with
Communist-front organizations, or had benefited from a CIO-PAC
contribution of $954 in her 1944 race.[5]

The Nixon campaign, furthermore, was intent on comparing
Douglas's voting record to that of Vito Marcantonio. The New York
congressman had been associated with Communists since his arrival in
the House during the mid-1930s and spoke boldly for the poorly educated and economically underprivileged among his Puerto Rican and
Italian constituents. Although never a Communist Party member, he was
often linked to the party. During the 80th Congress, he fought against
HUAC's contempt citations against Communist witnesses as curtailing
civil rights, the Truman Doctrine for being imperialistic, and the Marshall Plan for its anti-Russian implications. He seldom made pro-Soviet
proclamations, but never uttered a word against Stalin's foreign policies
either. Marcantonio opposed the Taft-Hartley Act as antilabor, and in
the 81st Congress, argued for its repeal. He favored the Fair Employment
Practices Commission and opposed the legislation that replaced the
Mundt-Nixon bill. As for foreign affairs, he constantly attacked Truman's European policies in Europe and objected to aid to Chiang Kai-
shek. He ran a distant third for New York City mayor in 1949 on the

American Labor Party (ALP) ticket, never perceiving that his constituency might be moving away from his philosophy. "Despite the struggle over the future of the ALP," biographer Gerald Meyer concluded, "Marcantonio and the Party shared the same basic commitments."[6]

On July 20, a "pink sheet," literally one pink-colored piece of paper that compared Douglas's voting record with that of the radical congressman Marcantonio, was inserted in Nixon's official campaign manual. The top of the page read in bold dark letters: "DOUGLAS-MARCANTONIO VOTING RECORD." Marcantonio was described as "the notorious Communist party-liner"; it was further noted that Douglas had voted with him 354 times since 1945.

"Here is the Record!" followed in smaller dark lettering, highlighting the votes against HUAC, the Selective Service Act of 1948, loyalty checks of federal employees, the Mundt-Nixon bill, congressional investigations of Communists and other illegal activities, and the Greek-Turkish aid bill that was the cornerstone of the Truman Doctrine. Since Nixon entered Congress, he had "voted exactly opposite to the Douglas-Marcantonio Axis!"

Her Democratic primary opponents and the press had already helped associate Douglas and Marcantonio, as noted in the pink sheet. The *Daily Worker* of New York, a Communist organ, on July 28, 1947, chose each one as "One of the Heroes of the 80th Congress," while the Communist *Daily People's World* at the end of January 1950 named Nixon as "The Man to Beat" in the current Senate race. The pink sheet concluded: "REMEMBER! The United States Senate votes on ratifying international treaties and confirming presidential appointments. Would California send Marcantonio to the United States Senate?"[7]

Nixon received many letters applauding his anticommunism. William Elliott, a professor of government at Harvard University and a lecturer on the Herter mission, hoped that the congressman would become the spokesman "for the sane middle-ground defenders of American freedoms against what amounts to intellectual treason." Others were even more blunt.[8]

Nixon also explored the gender issue by having Chotiner correspond with Republican congressman Homer Angell of Oregon, who, in 1938, successfully challenged the Democratic incumbent, Mrs. Nan Honeyman, who happened to be one of Eleanor Roosevelt's bridesmaids. During their race, he refused to attack her, fearing that would sharpen resentment against him among female voters. Angell said as much to Chotiner, who answered, "I still think we are right, but thought you should see this letter. Douglas is a different person from Honeyman."[9]

Douglas, for her part, was struggling to keep her coalition and to broaden her Democratic base. She did not appeal to women in as large numbers as she hoped. Her only staunch financial supporters were the labor unions, the most vocal of which was the CIO. To a large number of the voters, its association with Communists made its high-profile backing a curse, not a blessing.

She worried that the Boddy supporters were joining her cause very slowly, if at all. She spoke with Truman about it, who promised to force the publisher's key backers to support her. Douglas felt that the chief executive would come to California to campaign just for her. She was "sure the President will," but she was wrong. Truman refused, for example, to come to California and speak in the governorship race for James Roosevelt because of his opposition to the president at the 1948 national convention. After losing to Warren by 800,000 votes in the primary, Roosevelt proceeded independently and headed the statewide ticket without effectively coordinating the California Democratic Party. Edmond "Pat" Brown, the nominee for state attorney general, also conducted a separate campaign. As a consequence, the three major statewide Democratic nominees fragmented the California effort.[10]

Douglas knew that Nixon would be a formidable adversary and understood that she would be asked about her anti-Communist views. After returning to the capital, she attempted to question Nixon on his commitment to prevent Soviet expansion by bringing up the congressional package for Korea that lost by one vote in January, was resubmitted for consideration, and was then passed three weeks later. Nixon had voted against it the first time, but she should have realized that she had little chance of attacking him from the right. Her chief strategy was to reaffirm her faith in the Fair Deal: "the way to keep communism out of America is to keep democracy in it." Throughout the campaign, that message was lost in the shrill clamor over her being "soft on Communism." Without an effective method to combat those charges, she would revert to raising the question of Nixon's own commitment to anticommunism—an inadvertent recognition of the issue's pivotal importance and a losing strategy if there ever was one.[11]

Though Nixon had run a positive primary campaign, the fall would be different. He examined Claude Pepper's loss in Florida as a prime example. George Smathers's defeat of the Senate incumbent had featured a notorious brochure, *The Red Record of Senator Claude Pepper,* that appeared by the thousands a week before the balloting and had the expected devastating effect. The pamphlet featured a red-and-white cover with a photograph of Pepper looking startled. Pictures inside showed the senator with such fellow travelers as Marcantonio. The nickname and the bitterness over "Red Pepper" were never forgotten.[12]

Karl Mundt wrote Nixon that Republicans had used this pamphlet to demolish the senator and added that many of the photos included Douglas's picture. "It occurs to me," Mundt advised, "if Helen is your opponent in the fall that something of a similar nature might well be prepared." After Smathers's triumph, Nixon visited the victor, probably his closest friend from the Democratic ranks, at his office for an explanation as to how he had won. Attacking the incumbent, Smathers said, was the only way to win.[13]

After conferring with Smathers and Jack Garland, a close personal adviser, about J. D. Stetson Coleman, a Chicago resident who intended to raise money for the California race, Nixon wrote Coleman that he was facing a similar confrontation as Smathers. Nixon stressed: "We have a real fight on our hands since Mrs. Douglas has the complete support of the radical elements in the state as well as heavy financial support from labor organizations." In the meantime, Nixon's Monterey campaign chairman learned that a great deal of money had been raised from out-of-state contributors to defeat Pepper and urged that Nixon get that list to contact those people.[14]

World events intervened just after the primary to underscore anticommunism's leading role in the race when the North Koreans sent ten combat divisions across the 38th parallel separating the North from the South, in a surprise invasion on Sunday morning, June 25. Truman, who was at home at Independence, Missouri, was immediately notified, and just as rapidly, decided to use the UN Security Council's approval to send U.S. troops to South Korea. By the time the president addressed the nation and called up the reservists, the North Koreans had pushed their enemies back to a small perimeter around the southeast area called Pusan. By the end of the month, America and sixteen other nations, however, had allocated troops for an Asian land war, and a legendary hero from World War II, General Douglas MacArthur, assumed command of UN forces. Korea was initially a popular war; finally, the democracies were fighting to halt Red expansionism.

Of course, this was a boon to Nixon's chances for victory. Yet, at first, opponents tried to attack him over the conflict. Drew Pearson in his Washington column wrote that Douglas almost single-handedly fought for aid to South Korea in January 1950, while Nixon voted against it. The CIO *News* also wrote that Nixon had voted against the appropria- tion of $60 million in military assistance to South Korea five months be- fore the invasion. During a speech to the California Federation of Young Democrats on July 22, Douglas said that she had helped to write the first Korean Aid bill, while Marcantonio and Nixon voted against it. Nixon took violent exception. Marcantonio had voted against the bill because it ran counter to Russian objectives. Nixon had voted against it as a protest; the bill had not included aid to Formosa. Douglas dismissed his reason- ing. She continued to point to this no-vote to illustrate Nixon's failure to support Korean defense and proudly defended the administration's Point Four and Marshall Plan as a means to battle totalitarianism.[15]

Privately, she wrote a supporter that the United States should pursue peaceful solutions to international problems by enhancing the power and prestige of the United Nations. The United States had to retain its mili- tary might in order to defend countries like South Korea from Commu- nist aggression. Still, she hoped for international disarmament: "I do not think it would do much good to outlaw the hydrogen bomb and the uranium bomb if at the same time we do not outlaw or restrict other weapons as well."[16]

Nixon did not publicly respond to her charges throughout July. He had flown back to the capital after Independence Day and concentrated on the upcoming campaign as well as on his congressional duties. He had even refused to make any dates for speaking engagements because the Korean conflict made adjournment uncertain. In the middle of the month, Nixon joined with twenty House GOP colleagues endorsing the Declaration of Republican Principles that called upon his party to offer constructive alternatives to Democratic programs.[17]

Douglas wrote Truman on August 1, commending him for placing American military forces behind the United Nations in Korea. Her hope was that the United States would lead in a collective security action under UN auspices and she recommended that the General Assembly act in regard to the Korean conflict without amending its charter.[18]

In a speech before the national convention of International Oil

Workers of America in Long Beach, California, Douglas praised the president's leadership in Korea. She thought that some "leftists" were trying to get people to support the Communist Party's position on Korea, while those on the far right was equally despicable. "It began with McCarthy and his irresponsible, demagogic and false charges against the State Department and the administration," she said. "McCarthyism is the last resort of desperate politicians, and McCarthyism has come to California." Like McCarthy, she charged, Nixon had been untruthful in his anticommunism, based on his Korean aid vote.[19]

Jack Drown, an intimate friend and ardent Nixon admirer, was present to hear this speech. According to Drown, the president of the union told the friendly but not too enthusiastic audience that labor could not afford to have two Republican senators and quoted from the Bible: "Thou shalt not plow with the ox and ass together." Douglas was given a standing ovation.[20]

Douglas's attempt to link Nixon with both McCarthy and Marcantonio was unconvincing. Her logic failed on its face. Nixon was not an ally of the Wisconsin senator, and in fact, distanced himself from McCarthy throughout the campaign. At any rate, as Donald Crosby, S.J., in his study of McCarthy and the Roman Catholic Church, has declared: "the 1950 elections were clearly no test of McCarthy or McCarthyism." Anticommunism had been incorporated as a staple of partisan politics long before that time. Her association was not taken seriously.[21]

Two Los Angeles newspapers toward the end of July responded to her public attacks on Nixon. The *Examiner*, in an editorial, asserted that only fourteen House members, including Douglas, had voted against the Federal Security Act that gave the heads of federal agencies the right to deny employment to security risks. Kyle Palmer, in the *Sunday Times*, felt that Douglas was an actress who too often changed her appearance. "Her somewhat ridiculous linking of Nixon with her old legislative pal and collaborator, Marcantonio of New York," the political editor sarcastically said, "smacked more of the comedienne than of her more accustomed roles as a star in the tragic dramas, but she was in there, pitching."[22]

The *League Reporter*, the weekly capital publication of the American Federation of Labor, compared Marcantonio's record with those of the two candidates and arrived at very different conclusions. "If Californians make their choice on the basis of the record," the union organ declared, "Democrat Helen Douglas is a 10 to 1 favorite. Her record proved her to be top Senator caliber." Once again, however, the sole evidence linking Nixon to Marcantonio was the single Korean aid vote.[23]

Why a labor paper and Douglas herself decided to attack Nixon on the Korean Economic Aid bill was mystifying. Her Democratic opponents in the primary had embarrassed her by attaching her name to Marcantonio, calling her the Pink Lady, and stressing that she was unfit for the Senate. The GOP would certainly do the same. In addition, Nixon's greatest asset was his anti-Communist stance, culminating with the conviction of Hiss. To criticize him in that arena played directly to his strength.

Douglas's only real hope was to frame the campaign not as a test of anticommunism, but rather as a contest between civil liberties versus suppression. Here, too, she was placed in an untenable position. At the beginning of a patriotic war against the Soviet peril, the hostility against the Russians overwhelmed the wish to protect individual rights. Pressure to adopt a successor to the 1948 Mundt-Nixon bill accelerated, and in late July, Senator Mundt urged citizens to write their congressmen to back his new antisubversion proposal. With American troops dying in Asia, the nation should stop domestic spying. As a consequence of these kinds of arguments, toward the end of August, the House passed legislation authorizing Communist registration and initiating preventive detention of suspected subversives.

Douglas dissented vigorously. She agreed that traitors needed to be exposed and prosecuted and security risks be removed from government service, but she also argued that disloyal individuals could already be tried under numerous statutes, and machinery existed to oust security risks from the federal government. In a statement of August 29, she maintained, "I will not sacrifice the liberty of the American people on the altar of hysteria erected by those without vision, without faith, without courage, who cringe in fear before a handful of crackpots and their traitorous Communist cronies." This bill infringed on American liberty: "I will not be stampeded by hysteria nor will I waver for political expediency."[24]

Nixon stuck with the loyalty issue. In his newsletter the "Washington Record" to his district constituents, he happily informed them that the bill had won by a lopsided vote. Its major provisions closed loopholes in espionage laws, forced Communist Party members and their associates to register with the U.S. Attorney General, disallowed party members to work for the federal government or obtain passports, made party allies label themselves Communists. The bill did not outlaw the party, nor prevent the study of theoretical communism, nor attack "liberal" organizations and unions. Nixon concluded: "this bill seeks only to fight communism in the United States on the same realistic basis that we are already committed to fighting it abroad."[25]

He also sought to reestablish his presence as a leader in the anti-Communist movement by calling for a UN police force to repel worldwide Communist aggression in order to prevent future Koreas. He feared that the USSR intended to stimulate conflicts to sap American military strength. He had already introduced a congressional resolution two years earlier, along with thirteen other House colleagues, calling for a UN international police force to guarantee peace.[26]

While Nixon remained in the capital, his committee was preparing to launch the campaign. The staff checked Helen and Melvyn Douglas's files at HUAC as well as with Jack Tenney's Committee on Un-American Activities in California, which concentrated on Communist activities in the state from 1945 to 1949. The Republican National Committee examined her association with Communist-front organizations, her foreign and domestic policies, and relationship to the CIO-PACs. In an August 24 press release, Brennan announced that Congress would adjourn in early September and his candidate's campaign would "move into high gear." The contest would concentrate on Nixon's record versus Douglas's.[27]

On August 30, Brennan released a statement contrasting Douglas's "soft attitude toward Communism" with her "new role" as a "foe of Communism." She had voted 353 times with Marcantonio. Brennan listed many examples and included the testimonials from the *Daily Worker* naming both "heroes." She was also one of only twenty to vote against the House antisubversion legislation.[28]

The assault on Douglas had just begun. Hancock notified local chairmen that Douglas had misrepresented their candidate's position on the first Korean Aid bill. Nixon had only voted against it on January 19 because Formosa had been excluded, and when the second bill on February 9 included assistance to that island, he had "supported it wholeheartedly." The congresswoman had distorted the facts by alluding solely to the first vote. Since Truman and Acheson had refused to defend Formosa, the congressman used the first vote to register a protest against them. Truman had more recently changed his position and committed American forces to defend that island.[29]

Raymond Moley wrote a column entitled "Nixon vs. Douglas" in the August 28 edition of *Newsweek*, noting California's burgeoning population, the stark differences between the two contestants, and the debate over party responsibility for the Korean War. Moley painted the race in the broad stroke of government interference versus individual freedom. "On this issue," Moley told his readers, "Nixon is a moderate conservative; Douglas, a radical. Inside the polling booths, this would be a vote for or against Truman, with Douglas 100% behind him."[30]

Perry, on the same day, wrote a letter to the *San Diego Tribune* alleging that if Douglas and her supporters had backed military assistance to Korea in 1949, the Communists would not have invaded. The *Bulletin* went further, claiming that Douglas had lied about Nixon's voting record on aid to Korea. Nixon had consistently backed military aid to prevent Red expansion, while Douglas had not: "The opposition's campaign strategy appears to be cut from a pattern of distortion, misrepresentation and falsehood."[31]

Nixon opened his campaign from Washington on August 30, the day after the House passed the Communist Control bill, broadcasting his views over KECA Radio on Wednesday, at 8:45 P.M. He acknowledged that the single most important issue currently facing Americans was the Korean conflict: "If we do not win it, a world war is certain." The current fighting was confined to a relatively small area, but the bloodshed caused inflation at home and the loss of American soldiers. When World War II ended, the United States was the dominant superpower, and now Russia had the atomic bomb and the largest land army. In 1945, democracies had a nine-to-one advantage over Communist nations in population. Without firing a bullet, the Soviets had gained 600 million subjects.

The Truman administration, he asserted, had blundered badly. In February 1950, Secretary Acheson stated that Korea and Formosa were outside the American defense perimeter, which led the North Koreans to believe that they could attack. After the invasion, the president made the proper decision to defend the South, and that meant wartime controls with cuts in nondefense spending and increased taxes. Since the United States was fighting the Red peril abroad, it also had to enact legislation to confront the Communist conspiracy at home.

Nixon proposed a vague program to win the peace: American economic and military strength; a UN police force composed of free world nations; and improved labor-management relations. The United States had to implement a consistent foreign policy that recognized international communism as a threat to the world democracies. "We must recognize," Nixon argued, "that economic aid to countries abroad without adequate military aid is a waste of money." Americans had to fight an ideological battle to win people's minds. He called for Acheson's resignation. The United States needed a new secretary of state and new leadership in Washington.[32]

Before Nixon returned home, some signs of dissension within his campaign committee still existed. Perry informed his student that some actions in the Los Angeles office "were inexcusable." Roy Day, at a statewide gathering late that month, failed to get along with Johnnie Reilly, one of Nixon's friend. Some women in the 12th district also disapproved of how Day treated them and wanted to punish him. Even Perry fought with Day over local issues, but they had "buried the hatchet and have continually worked together ever since." Nixon might need to have Day agree to cooperate or retire him from the campaign. Outside Whittier, Perry observed, "no work was done for your primary campaign in the 12th district. If this personal feud is continued, we must have some new faces in the campaign—or else." The congressman paid careful attention to Perry's advice, admitting that Day was difficult but that a solution would have wait until his arrival in California: "It may be better to let him work in other parts of the county and to leave the Twelfth to Johnnie [Reilly] and get some new faces into the picture."[33]

On Labor Day, Douglas opened her fall campaign by addressing the AFL in Pasadena and the CIO in Sunland, where she emphasized that "every labor organization in California" had endorsed her. Her cry was to pass the Fair Deal programs, for both Nixon and Warren were "tools of the lobbyists," and in general, "Republicans are frightened little men, cringing politicians, who have no real hope in America." In front of these receptive audiences, she labeled the GOP the party of privilege and special interests. Nixon was using the "big lie" against her, although she never defined its meaning. He opposed labor and social legislation such as controlling credit and excess profit taxes. He, of course, voted for Taft-Hartley, just as the National Association of Manufacturers mandated. While she voted for wartime production expansion, the Republicans balked. She also backed the Fair Employment Practices Commission, a larger military force, support for the United Nations, and assistance to developing nations. As for the current Mundt-Nixon bill, she dismissed it as "thought-control."[34]

Douglas addressed a radio audience for the first time for half an hour in her final push on September 6 at 8:00 P.M. She warned listeners that her adversaries would exaggerate what she stood for: "We can be sure the opposition will distort my record of militant support of the Democratic program of President Roosevelt and President Truman. We can be sure the opposition will misrepresent the reactionary record of my opponent—beside whom Bob Taft [Republican senator from Ohio] is a flaming liberal." She had assisted in drafting the Atomic Energy Act, worked on the House Committee on Foreign Affairs, supported the Marshall Plan, reciprocal trade agreements, stockpiling strategic materials, and aid to Korea.

Nixon, she hammered, had "demonstrated time and time again that he has no real comprehension of the challenge of communist imperialism." He had voted against reciprocal trade agreements, and both he and Marcantonio had voted together in 1949 to cut funds from NATO, a bill she helped write. Nixon originally opposed the Korean Economic Aid bill and his claims that his vote was because the bill did not contain funds for Formosa were untrue.

While he disapproved of social legislation, she promoted it. He voted for a repressive labor law, while she wanted to repeal Taft-Hartley. She was one of twenty who cast votes against anti-Communist legislation similar to Mundt-Nixon. She refused to restrict individual rights: "America must be protected against spies and saboteurs and traitors. I stand squarely behind the laws to suppress their activities, but I will not sell American liberties down the river of fear conjured up by the Mundts and the Nixons, the McCarthys and the Cains [Senator Harry P. Cain, right-wing Republican from Washington]."[35]

The parameters of the political debate were emerging. Already, in several crucial respects, the playing field was unequal. Nixon's anticommunism was extremely popular, especially at the height of the Korean War's escalation. As a consequence, he had greater appeal to contributors, and even some powerful Democratic fund-raisers deserted her for him.[36]

Mounting adverse publicity about her own and her husband's association with Communists multiplied Douglas's concerns. She complained about a whispering campaign against the Jewish heritage of her husband, whose real name was Melvyn Hesselberg. He later went on the radio to praise his wife and defend his honor since he had been "informed that certain devious persons are attempting to defeat her by taking advantage of my absence from the state to spread malicious rumors to the effect that I am, or have been, a Communist or fellow-traveler." He was not, he affirmed, and had resigned from the Hollywood Democratic Committee after Culbert Olsen's 1938 gubernatorial election, sensing that the group harbored some Communists or their sympathizers. "I repeat," Douglas pronounced, "that anyone who calls me a Communist or fellow-traveler is either a fool or a deliberate liar." But, according to the Douglases, his denial could not erase smears and harassment, and a media blackout. She admitted that some newspapers supported her, but not many. Frustrated over such rejections, she struck out, calling Nixon "Tricky Dick" and "pee wee."[37]

From the posting of the primary results until the middle of September, Douglas attacked Nixon, while he stayed in his Washington office and did not respond to her charges. His media advocates and his California staff answered them instead. Chotiner saw no reason to react and later chose this moment as the turning point in the contest. "The two campaigns never met on the issues," he pointed out "until the Douglas people made a fatal error and came to use . . . OUR issue. She discussed Communism and tried to show that you were the friend of the Communists and that she was their opponent. Of course she could not sell that bill of goods."[38]

Commentators from every point on the political continuum would later accuse Nixon of having waged a dirty campaign to beat Douglas without analyzing what actually transpired. To pundits, he smeared her and somehow those smarmy tactics translated into her defeat. The fact is, throughout the primary, Nixon had hardly mentioned any opponent. In the fall, she attacked first. Ultimately, any "smears" paled beside the strength of anticommunism's popularity. Voters approved of Nixon's position and his ongoing fight against the Russian menace. By playing to Nixon's strength, Douglas's initial strategy did more than backfire; it doomed any possibility of her November victory.

*Chapter* 16

# FIFTY-ONE DAYS IN THE FALL: NIXON VERSUS DOUGLAS— REALITY AND LEGEND

Before dawn on September 15, 1950, General MacArthur risked his amphibious troops on a bold surprise attack at Inchon harbor with the largest invasion fleet since World War II. U.S. and South Korean Marines landed on a rainy day, in the midst of the smoke from a bombardment. Other allied soldiers broke out of the Pusan perimeter, driving the enemy north. Within two weeks, UN forces recaptured the capital, Seoul, routed the North Koreans, and pushed them across the 38th parallel. For the first and last time during the Cold War, a Communist capital, Pyongyang, fell to UN troops. At least at that brief moment, Americans were jubilant that Soviet expansionism had experienced a humiliating reversal.

A few days after UN soldiers forced the enemy into retreat, Nixon returned home, anxious to begin an exhaustive schedule that would last until election day. Opening his "Kick-Off" rallies on September 18, Nixon, with Pat accompanying him, appeared in one day at four California cities. Using James Udall, his World War II buddy, to chauffeur him to each place in a private plane, he participated in a breakfast meeting in San Diego, then a rally at the Biltmore Bowl in Los Angeles in the afternoon, followed by another at Fresno, and a mass meeting in San Francisco in the evening. This was the first time a statewide nominee for major office had accomplished such a feat.[1]

During his Los Angeles appearance, Nixon spoke before twelve hundred listeners, comparing his record with Douglas's: "It just so happens that my opponent is a member of a small clique which joins the notorious Communist party-liner, Vito Marcantonio of New York, in voting time after time against measures that are for the security of this country." According to the candidate, the congresswoman did not comprehend the scope or the peril of the Communist conspiracy at home or abroad, did not understand the fundamentals of a strong foreign policy, and had not studied military defense. While he spoke, the "pink sheet" was passed out.[2]

Before Nixon addressed an audience at the Scottish Rite Auditorium in San Francisco, John Dinkelspiel, the northern campaign chairman, promised: "Nixon is not going to pull any punches about Mrs. Douglas' record. It's an extreme left-wing record, pure and simple and Nixon will blast it right down the line because he does not believe the California electorate wants that kind of representation." When the candidate spoke that evening, he pledged "no name calling, no smears, no misrepresentations," but he would reveal Douglas's record, which would disqualify her "from representing the people of California in the U.S. Senate." He lumped Douglas and Marcantonio together as the most vocal HUAC critics, and then chided her. If she "had had her way, the Communist conspiracy in the United States would never have been exposed and instead of being a convicted perjurer, Alger Hiss would still be influencing the foreign policy of the United States."[3]

Nixon immediately challenged Douglas to debate, for she was "out of harmony with the Democratic majority," as he would demonstrate. Initially, she agreed to meet him, but suddenly withdrew, claiming that her failure to appear came from pressing business in Washington. James Roosevelt, instead, appeared in her place on the evening of September 20, and at the end of the formal presentations, Nixon received prolonged applause, having to appeal for quiet so that the question and answer period could commence. The debate proceeded, and according to the *Los Angeles Times,* "was kept on a high tone." Nixon informed the audience that Congress had no emergencies pending that forced Douglas to return to the capital; yet overall she had the worst attendance record of any California House member. She had also earlier said that FBI director Hoover was against the loyalty bill, but Nixon produced a telegram from him stating that he intended to enforce the legislation if it was passed. Roosevelt stressed his personal distaste for the bill. Nixon responded that Roosevelt did not understand the real danger.[4]

A few days later, Nixon helped to enact the anti-Communist policies that he espoused. After Truman vetoed the McCarran Omnibus Internal Security bill on September 22, Nixon flew to Washington the next day to vote to override at the last session of Congress. The vote in the House was 286 in favor, including 161 Democrats and 125 Republicans, to 47 against, one of whom was Douglas; the Senate vote was 57–10, with 26 Democrats and 31 Republicans in favor. Nixon used the occasion to criticize Douglas for opposing the registration of Communists while millions of young Americans had to register for the draft to fight the North Koreans abroad. She bitterly confided to a friend: "I feel this red hysteria had become so great that we are threatened with the loss of the state."[5]

Through a constant stream of press releases, Nixon made his positions clear on the Korean War. He wanted to assure peace after the fighting, and therefore, the United States had to build a powerful military and cut domestic expenditures. In addition, America had to guard against the Red Chinese sending forces to capture Formosa. To register further disapproval of Mao's aggressive impulses, the United States should oppose Communist China's admission to the United Nations. Besides these military and diplomatic initiatives, the Russians had to be fought "on the ideological level. Communism, after all, is an idea—an evil and malignant idea—and you cannot destroy an idea with bullets alone."[6]

Dan Green, editor and publisher of the Democratic *Independent Review* in Los Angeles, disagreed and argued that Douglas was being defamed for being an alleged Communist. He charged: "Representatives of her senatorial opponent Tricky Dick Nixon, are the chief mouthpieces for this partisan effort to crucify Mrs. Douglas with a continued repetition of the Greatest Lie Ever Told in a political campaign in the entire West." This was the national campaign on the state level, and the lie, which McCarthy, Nixon, and Republican senator William Jenner of Indiana evoked, was based on Hitler's theory that if you constantly told falsehoods, they would eventually be accepted. In public Douglas's adversaries were cagey, but the fallacious whispers persisted that she was a Communist. In reality, she was a great woman and "the implacable foe of Communism."[7]

James Roosevelt needed more than just glowing testimonials to beat Earl Warren. On September 28, he wrote the president about the critical situation in California. To win, Roosevelt and Douglas were "going to have to produce something unusual." They did not have Nixon's financial resources, and during the final ten days of the campaign, he anticipated that "the opposition will use every dirty trick known from Florida to North Carolina, and of course, will completely blitz us." If Roosevelt did not make a respectable showing against Warren, Douglas would also be damaged. Roosevelt had recently debated Nixon, who, if elected to the Senate, FDR's eldest son predicted, "would really provide a thorn in the side of the Democratic Party. He is a smooth and capable person, who . . . never in any way [would] consider [the] appeasement of the Democratic Party!"

Roosevelt proposed that Truman fly out to California on November 3. Such a trip "would completely knock the opposition over and any screams that might go up would be completely ineffective in the remaining time before the election. It would rally the Democrats—and we have a winning majority of them. If we can even get a reasonable portion of this majority to vote the Democratic ticket, we cannot lose." Roosevelt's desperation did not soften Truman's memory of the fact that FDR's son had tried to dump him from the 1948 Democratic ticket; the president rejected the plea.[8]

Truman further demonstrated his disdain in the middle of October. After meeting with General MacArthur on Wake Island to discuss conditions in Korea, Truman flew to San Francisco, specifically announcing that he had "no political appointments whatever." Despite this declaration, Roosevelt tried to make some political gains by declaring that he was invited to the presidential box at the theater where Truman was scheduled to speak during his stopover. In fact, Roosevelt was not invited to sit with the president. He and Douglas arrived early; she sat in the center aisle, second row, and he was behind her. After completing his address, Truman left for the capital without any endorsement for either Democratic hopeful.[9]

October, the last full month of campaigning, played out almost like a holy crusade. Each side's knights rode into the fray to champion their leaders. Neither side seemed concerned with the rational basis of the issues; each simply tried to gain an advantage. The candidates, staff, volunteers, and voters became consumed with proselytizing for converts.

Robert "Bob" Hicks, district superintendent of El Monte Union High School, for example, praised Nixon: "You certainly have put on a grand campaign, a campaign which has made all of your followers mighty proud of you and happy that they have joined up with you in what we consider next to a holy cause." He did not see how Douglas could beat Nixon and had not talked to any outstanding Democrat who was voting for her: "If that 'gal' and 'Jimmy' can be laid on the shelf we shall all breathe more freely."[10]

Converted Democrats preached even more dogmatically. Former congressman Alfred Elliott from Tulare, who had retired after six terms, declared: "all of Nixon's qualities and abilities add up to the stature of true statesmanship. He always puts his country first, and we Democrats can vote for him with the assurance that we are voting for a real American." Albert Armor, chairman of Kings County Democrats for Nixon, stated: "We are all Democrats. However, we are Americans first, Californians second and Democrats third." Oliver Carlson, Southern California director of Democrats for Nixon, who had managed the FDR labor effort in 1940 and had been Governor Olsen's director of public relations, asserted that Douglas was "*not* a true Democrat and should *not* be sent to represent the people of California in the United States Senate."[11]

William Malone, San Francisco County Democratic chairman and former Northern California campaign chairman for Boddy, who in the primary had viciously attacked Douglas, now applauded her. "I feel," he added, "Nixon is one of the most reactionary Republicans in California. . . . He has raised a phony issue to campaign on, and that's the only issue he's been able to find, a smear." *Labor's* entire front page featured Douglas, calling her its best friend and Nixon its worst enemy. "Take any . . . legislation of vital importance to workers and their unions," the newspaper averred, "and the story is the same—Mrs. Douglas always on the right side, and Nixon on the wrong one." The *Press Democrat* in Santa Rosa charged that Nixon ignored those domestic programs which kept America strong, and Douglas fought the greatest threats of unemployment, slums, and poverty. Nixon dismissed housing, low wages, and hunger; he voted against Korean assistance, but accused Douglas of causing the war. The paper warned that "the Republicans talk about housing and decent wages, but they do nothing about it, because only if nothing is done about it can they win support and get in their licks."[12]

In a statewide radio broadcast on the evening of October 2, Douglas pledged to continue on the domestic path of the Fair Deal and to stand with Truman, Attorney General J. Howard McGrath, and J. Edgar Hoover "in the fight against Communism and Communists in this country." Both she and Nixon agreed that the Russians were the common enemy, but she preferred proven leaders rather than "my young

Republican opponent who is hiding his reactionary record behind a Red smoke screen." She accused him of voting incorrectly on Korea, for if he had voted properly, the war might have been averted. If the United States had followed his advice in Asia, the nation might have even been engaged in a war with mainland China. Once more she was unsuccessfully trying to attack him from the right.[13]

In the meantime, articles began to appear in the press contrasting Pat Nixon the homemaker to Douglas the actress. Mrs. Nixon was "friendly and poised, with a quick warm Irish smile, is not one to seek the limelight, but neither is she self-effacing and uncomfortable before an audience." She happily did her own housework and made her own budget. It was an effective tactic; many housewives cast ballots for the Nixon family, who mirrored the traditional role.[14]

Nixon's committee sought to buttress the areas in which the Republicans were perceived as weak. Fresh attention was devoted to getting voters from poor and minority communities. Dorothy Cox appreciated the work of Adela Rogers St. Johns, a political reporter for the Hearst chain. Though she was "a bit on the 'frumpish' side," she "would be an asset among low-income groups. Too many people associate the idea of a well dressed women [sic] with Republicans and the filthy rich, and for that reason among certain groups, Mrs. St. Johns would be just a plain Jane like the rest of them."[15]

When Nixon commended an African American division in Korea on September 11 for its courageous service, Chotiner circulated that story to African American publications. On October 5, the Los Angeles Sentinel, which had a circulation of 25,000 and the largest advertising volume of any Western African American newspaper, editorialized that although it still liked Douglas, but it could not support her for the Senate. "We are amazed at her weak-kneed stand on the issue of Communism, and its fellow travelers." African Americans were bound to a national vision that Nixon personified.[16]

Nixon's campaign staff remembered to reach out to ethnic groups. Crossing Catholic boundaries, Consuelo Castillo de Bonzo, prominent Democrat and well-known civic leader in the Spanish American and Mexican American communities, made her decision: "Regardless of creed, origin or nationality, I sincerely hope and believe that a vote for Richard Nixon for United States Senator is our best guarantee for keep our country free and strong." Reyes Gutierrez addressed the Hispanic American voters over the radio and urged them to vote for Nixon.[17]

Democratic Jewish Americans were also targeted. Rabbi Merritt and Gustav Goldstein, registered Democrats, were voting for Nixon because he was the best candidate. Mr. Goodman, a general sign contractor, left his party because its candidate was unacceptable.[18]

Douglas's media strategy was problematic. She had an inferior press relations division that feebly sent out a few mimeographed sheets, while the Nixon campaign distributed releases on just about every subject. When announcements of Democratic defections were printed, Douglas's replies were inadequate. George Creel, a former Democratic National Committee officer, for example, speaking for sixty-four prominent members of his party, publicly repudiated the congresswoman. The *San Jose News* editorialized that it was not surprised by what the Creel group had done: "Nixon's record . . . has been 100 per cent loyal to the United States. It is not surprising that Creel and his friends prefer him to the left-wing Mrs. Douglas, particularly since the Korean War has more sharply revealed the aims and plans of the Communists." The Douglas camp did not respond effectively.[19]

While Douglas's written responses were sporadic, her assaults were not. During the second week of October, Douglas forces began taking the offensive. The forty-eighth convention of the California Federation of Labor denounced Nixon as "an outstanding enemy of organized labor" and called upon each local council in the state "to devote every possible resource to defeat Richard Nixon."[20]

Vice President Alben Barkley was the first of many leading Democratic personalities to visit California to endorse Douglas. The vice president arrived in Los Angeles on the 9th, and at a press conference explained Douglas's vote against HUAC: "she voted her conscientious convictions." She then spoke, asserting that the issues in the campaign had been "diverted by a smokescreen fired up by men driven to desperation by the gnawing pains of political hunger." She lumped Nixon with Senators McCarthy and Cain.[21]

Attorney General McGrath arrived on October 16, blasting HUAC and asserting that Douglas voted correctly in opposing it. The FBI, McGrath declared, was sufficient to investigate Reds, and he insisted that the Justice Department, not HUAC, had exposed Hiss. Nixon responded with a blistering attack, amazed that McGrath would criticize HUAC on the Hiss case: "The whole country knows that, if it had not been for the persevering action of the committee and that if it had been left to the Attorney General's Department, Hiss would never have been exposed." When he praised Douglas for voting against HUAC and the McCarran Act, he and she were minority voices, for the large majority of their party, Nixon accurately pointed out, had voted for both measures.[22]

On the same day that McGrath was promoting Douglas, the *Gilroy Evening Dispatch* reported on a speech that McCarthy gave in San Diego. The newspaper asserted that Warren had disassociated himself from the Wisconsin politician and the Democrats should have covered his visit. "In our minds," the reporter thought, "the linking of McCarthy and Nixon will do the Republican candidate little good, and even may cause him some harm, for we believe that the American people, with their sense of fair play, have become disgusted with the harmful, irresponsible type of representation as provided by the senator from Wisconsin."[23]

While Douglas was hoping to gain from Truman's stop, from administration spokesmen's testimonials, and from McCarthy's visit, Nixon was shifting into a higher gear. At a dinner meeting in San Diego, he charged that she and five other already defeated congressmen had sponsored resolutions for the United States to leave mainland China. He cited a statement that she made in 1946: "We all know communism is no real danger to the U.S." On the evening of October 16, he decried her for recently describing him as "a young man with a dark shirt," an obvious allusion to the Nazis.[24]

According to Bill Arnold, who traveled with Nixon throughout much of the campaign, his boss "bent over backwards to prevent criticism of him for using unfair tactics." Still, Douglas's snide remarks provoked Nixon. When he first heard them, he vented to Arnold: "Did she say that? Why I'll castrate her." Arnold joked that that was impossible, but Nixon responded: "I don't care, I'll do it anyway."[25]

The congresswoman's committee continued with a provocative media blitz: "EXPOSE THE 'BIG LIE' For Yourself!" According to Douglas, the GOP had no programs, only smears. The party was composed of Nixons and McCarthys hurling hysterical invectives with "nothing to offer voters except a brush dipped in red paint." Nixon had sponsored the McCarran Act, which held that anyone who supported Communist-dominated foreign nations' positions was guilty of subversion. Yet, by casting an earlier vote to cut military assistance to Europe, China, and Korea, "He supported a policy advocated by Communist Russia." If the McCarran Act had already passed, "Nixon could have been arrested and punished under the terms of his own bill!"[26]

Another negative advertisement read: "The difference between Douglas and Nixon is the difference between a clear, sunny day and a black stormy night. On almost every score, he's wrong and she's *right!*"

The campaign was getting personal, yet Nixon's momentum was accelerating. As expected, the *San Diego Union* announced for him on October 15. More surprisingly, the liberal *San Francisco News* followed suit five days later. The *Los Angeles Times* announced its support and chided Will Rogers, Jr., for following Douglas's position on communism: "If Helen had her way there would have been no Un-American Activities Committee, no Communists exposed in Congress—just send the men and money over to Europe and Asia, while the Reds and traitors gnaw away unmolested in the U.S.A." George Dixon, in his "Washington Scene" column, was astounded that the congresswoman was even in the race: "the fact that Helen Gahagan Douglas had the nerve to run for Senator in the first place, or any public office in the United States of America, has baffled me." The *San Bernardino Evening Telegram* considered Douglas too radical and Nixon deserving of the victory.[27]

The last full week of October saw the crusaders coming to shrill verbal jousts. Douglas, on the evening of October 23, spoke over ABC Radio praising Truman's foreign policy and his wish for peace. While she backed the Marshall Plan, reciprocal trade agreements, and the Point Four international economic assistance program, Nixon, who wore an anti-Communist cloak, had "voted time and time again to defeat, to discredit or to render ineffective our far-sighted efforts for peace in the world and our efforts to build a strong America at home." She cried out that Nixon, Knowland, McCarthy, and their followers did not understand the threat from abroad and how to meet it. "The blindness of my opponent," she stressed, "to the requirements of a strong foreign policy is matched by his blindness on domestic policies." Nixon had voted against slum clearance, low-cost housing, rent control, Social Security, farmers' funds, FEPC enforcement, portions of the Displaced Persons bill, minimum wage increases, water and power resources restrictions, and the lunch program. Publicly, she told voters that he was "throwing up a smokescreen of smears, innuendoes and half-truths to try to confuse and mislead you." She despised any form of totalitarianism and "the cheap thinking that is being injected into this campaign in California and throughout the country."[28]

Privately, she admitted to a supporter: "the one-sided propaganda and name calling this campaign has reached a new low in American politics." "I am confident," she optimistically exclaimed, "that the people of California will not cast their votes on the basis of lies, innuendos and distortions. I have too much faith in democracy to believe that!"[29]

Powerful advocates came to Douglas's aid and supported the picture she had painted of her opponent as part of the privileged minority. Drew Pearson, for one, advanced his liberal friend's cause. Fifteen hundred listeners heard him give "a most helpful plug for your cause." In a radio broadcast at 8:00 P.M. over the ABC network, Pearson reported that Nixon had been appealing to Texas oilmen to contribute to his race. "As a result all kinds of money has been pouring into California for Nixon's campaign." Later that month in his column, Pearson claimed reactionary Democrats, powerful ranchers, utility companies, and oilmen conducted the most sophisticated and "cut-throat campaigns against her I have ever witnessed." The most unfair charge was contained in the pink sheet. By linking both Douglas and Marcantonio to government control of public utilities and the tidelands, the pink sheet inferred that Douglas and Marcantonio had similar Communist sympathies. These were not Communist issues, but ones that had an impact on a vast number of Americans. Nixon, Pearson conceded, did well on the Hiss case, "but this brand of unfair politics is not going to help him with the fair-minded American electorate in the long run."[30]

During that same week, Nixon appeared on the radio to attack Douglas for making five glaring misstatements. He charged her with conducting a campaign that had "degenerated into a calculated program of evasion, misrepresentation, double talk and smear." From that point until election day, "I am going to take the gloves off and lay the situation between myself and my opponent squarely on the line." Douglas had accused Nixon of importing outside speakers and receiving secret advice. She, in fact, was covering up her own carpetbaggers. She refused to debate Nixon. She had him voting with Marcantonio three times, while she voted with him 354 times. Nixon voted aid to Korea, despite what Douglas said, and he had never given comfort to the Communists. He had not misstated her record and challenged her to give an instance where he had: "If it is a smear involved, let it be remembered that the record itself is doing the smearing and Mrs. Douglas made that record. I didn't."[31]

Nixon and Knowland conducted a round table discussion on American foreign policy in which they announced their support for the administration's commitment to stopping the spread of communism in

Europe. However, both condemned the State Department's position in Asia, which resulted in the loss of China. The United States also compromised its international leadership by surrendering Asian territory to the Russians. Knowland was shocked that Douglas had recently defended the Yalta agreements and conceded the Soviets their expansionist gains. Nixon never wanted "our diplomats to lose what our fighting men have won at great sacrifice." Americans for Democratic Action (ADA) had recommended that the United States withdraw its recognition from Chiang as the legitimate ruler of mainland China; the administration, instead, should recognize and vote to seat Red China if it did not engage in the Korean conflict and force a military solution in Formosa, where Chiang led the de facto regime. If this position was accepted, both Nixon and Knowland saw the possibility of another Yalta. Douglas was a member of ADA's foreign policy panel, which supported the admission of China into the United Nations and U.S. recognition of Red China.[32]

Advertising from the Nixon campaign started to appear:[33]

### Votes Affecting American Security and Foreign Policy

|  | Douglas and Marcantonio | Nixon |
| --- | --- | --- |
| Greek–Turkish Aid Bill | Against | For |
| Free Press to UNRRA | Against | For |
| American Supervision of UNRRA | Against | For |
| Selective Service Act of 1948 | Against | For |
| Mundt–Nixon Bill | Against | For |
| Security Bill (after Korea) | Against | For |
| Loyalty Bills | Against | For |
| Contempt Citations | Against | For |
| HUAC Appropriations | Against | For |
| California Ownership of Tidelands | Against | For |

Ralph de Toledano described the California political climate for his *Newsweek* readership by the end of the month. He had met and befriended Nixon during the Hiss trial and wrote *Seeds of Treason: The True Story of the Chambers-Hiss Tragedy* (1950), using detailed interviews with the congressman. De Toledano felt that Warren would easily beat Roosevelt, but the fight between Douglas and Nixon was heated. With 42 percent of voters concentrated in Southern California, both candidates would be fighting fiercely for voters there in the last frantic week of the campaign.[34]

Others made more scientific predictions. In two California polls taken by Mervin Field, Nixon led on October 12 with 39 percent, Douglas had 27 percent, and 34 percent were undecided. He had a wide lead among Republicans, and she led with Democrats, but he was also gaining a strong Democratic following. At the end of the month, Nixon held 49 percent, Douglas 39 percent. Even with a ten-point spread, eight days before the election, Field thought the race was still to close to call. (Later polling methods might have allowed for certainty that Nixon was, in fact, far ahead.) Osman Reichel, director of the bureau of political research in San Francisco, who had made astonishingly accurate prognoses in past elections, forecast that Nixon would win by 500,000 votes.[35]

The shrill cries from the two camps became louder and more extreme. Douglas's last large-scale advertisement was just one illustration of how Nixon used the big lie:

> HITLER invented it
> STALIN perfected it
> NIXON used it.[36]

She too used Marcantonio as a foil to show that Nixon was the congressman that the Kremlin loved:

| | Date | Douglas | Nixon | Marcantonio |
|---|---|---|---|---|
| Aid to Korea Bill | 1-19-50 | Y | N | N |
| Export of Scarce Material | 2-17-49 | N | Y | Y |
| Bill to Cut Military Aid | 8-18-49 | N | Y | Y |
| Reciprocal Trade Agreements | 2-9-49 | N | Y | Y |
| Interim Aid to Europe and China | 12-10-47 | Y | N | N |

Charles Voorhis wrote his son on November 3: "We are nearing the end of about the dirtiest campaign that I have ever witnessed here in California. Both sides have used up about all of the mud that could be manufactured." Charles was still uncomfortable, facing a dilemma over whom to vote for in the senatorial election. He personally liked Douglas, but opposed her political positions. Under no circumstances, however, would he vote for "little Dick."[37]

As the election grew nearer, some of the support that Douglas had clamored for began to materialize. President Truman told a press conference that she was one of the administration's most valued assets on bipartisan foreign policy, and that he had depended on her help for legislation dealing with international matters. The president also relented and spoke out for Roosevelt. Manchester Boddy announced for her; the *Eastside Sun* endorsed the entire Democratic ticket. The *Sun-Reporter*, the largest African American newspaper on the West Coast, came out for Warren and Douglas. Nixon's voting "against the vital issues affecting the masses shows that he lacks the elementary knowledge and appreciation of the dangers which threaten our American way of life. His demagogic support of the McCarran-Mundt-Ferguson-Nixon Bill, despite President Truman's veto of same, shows that this man Nixon would destroy fundamental American liberties in his rabid quest for a seat in the U.S. Senate."[38]

On November 2 at noon, before a partisan crowd of two thousand in Union Square, San Francisco, Douglas dubbed Nixon "tricky Dick" and predicted that if he won, the United States could face another depression. She claimed that he knew "nothing about foreign policy and Communism," or he would not have voted against the Korean Aid bill and cuts in the Marshall Plan. She blasted Nixon for trying to "steal" Democratic voters by harping on her votes and not discussing his own record. Later that night, she declared that Republicans had to steal Democratic votes if they were going to win, and she would "not tear up the Bill of Rights to protect myself in a smear campaign."[39]

Throughout the campaign, hecklers followed both candidates to pose embarrassing questions. One of the most difficult for her to answer was whom she was voting for for governor. If she publicly endorsed Roosevelt, then she might lose the backing of Governor Warren's followers. In San Diego on November 3, after trying to dodge the choice for governor, she responded to GOP heckling by stating: "I hope and pray he [Roosevelt] will be the next governor and he will be if the Democrats voted the Democratic ticket."[40]

This declaration delighted Nixonphiles. Although Warren had announced in late October that he had no plans to endorse anyone, after hearing that Douglas came out for Roosevelt, the governor said: "I might ask her how she expects I will vote when I mark my ballot for U.S. Senator next Tuesday." Brennan followed up Warren's inference by declaring that this meant the governor was voting for Nixon, and he, in turn, would vote for Warren.[41]

Two days before the election, on November 5, Douglas maintained that voters would "not turn their backs on the Democratic program" and blithely equated Nixon with McCarthy. A day before the election, her campaign ran a political cartoon advertisement that had McCarthy and Nixon putting logs on a fire and fanning it, alleging false charges, Red-baiting, fear, smears, and phony claims. Douglas asked voters if they wanted to follow the successes of FDR and Truman or the party of the Great Depression. She was "confident that the people of California will show with their votes their disgust at the campaign tactics of my opponent and send me to the United States Senate."[42]

That evening, Humphrey Bogart introduced Melvyn Douglas to a radio audience. He had not intended to make any campaign address, "But I am angry. I am angry because of the tactics that have been used by her opponent, and those who support him." The Douglases had been falsely attacked for being Communists. He agreed that his wife and Nixon were opposites, but she had a positive program; the GOP had none: "We must not let the McCarthys, and the Nixons, shake that keystone loose," which referred to the smears and innuendos.[43]

While the Douglas campaign ended its effort on the theme of smear and fear versus the continuation of the Fair Deal, the well-organized Nixon committee orchestrated an ever-increasing crescendo, culminating on election day. By November 1, public relations, including radio, television, advertising, outdoor billboards, direct mail, stickers, and postcards, were monitored. Chotiner planned for the last rally the day before the election to "keep our crowd pepped up," comprised of a caravan consisting of a half dozen cars and a station wagon to go to each Los Angeles headquarters with Nixon, who would stay there ten to fifteen minutes. Nixon reiterated: "Truth is not smear. She made the record. She has not denied a single vote. The iron curtain of silence has closed around the opposition camp."[44]

That evening, with the actor Dick Powell as the narrator, Nixon broadcast *Seeds of Treason* over the radio, in which he reviewed the melodrama of the Hiss-Chambers case. After the candidate completed a long discourse on the subject, Powell said that Attorney General McGrath was speaking for Douglas when he erroneously asserted that Nixon had not broken the Hiss case. Nixon had recommended a bipartisan approach to squelch the international Communist conspiracy, but Truman had dismissed it. Powell urged his listeners to vote for his candidate because Nixon had seen the seeds of treason, and he "for one was grateful."[45]

The Nixon camp brought out prominent Californians for the days before the election. Actors like Charles Coburn, Adolphe Menjou, and Randolph Scott lent their names, and former African American UCLA football star Kenny Washington also endorsed Nixon. Actress Irene Dunne declared that Nixon had exposed Hiss, and speaking for the Committee of Ten Thousand, she urged everyone to vote for Nixon. In another spot, she emphasized the wholesomeness of the entire Nixon family and repeated that he had worked hard to expose Communist infiltration in the federal government.[46]

A giant rally was held on the evening of November 2 at the Hollywood American Legion Stadium, with Dick Powell serving as master of ceremonies, the popular entertainer Dennis Morgan singing, and co-chairs Dunne, Harold Lloyd, Washington, and Mrs. Goetz heading the list of dignitaries. Nixon spoke, charging Douglas with distorting his record and attacking her for using the false "big lie" theme.[47]

Throughout the last days of the campaign, Nixon attacked Douglas for being "soft on communism." He reiterated her opposition to HUAC, the Truman Doctrine, the McCarran Act, and many other pieces of legislation, but he now added a new ingredient that Manchester Boddy had injected into the picture with the entrance of Chinese Communist troops into the Korean conflict on November 5. Once Nixon confirmed that Chinese Communist soldiers had been introduced in the fighting, he demanded that the State Department release a statement that the United States would not recognize Mao or sanction China's UN admittance. He continually hammered Douglas for her association with the failed administration policy in Asia. She had joined, according to Nixon, "with a small banker's dozen clique who vote against these security measures."[48]

While he was getting ready to conclude his campaign, newspapers from across the state published their endorsements. The *Los Angeles Examiner*, a Hearst paper, rejected Douglas's Fair Deal attitudes in favor of the congressman: "An overwhelming majority for Mr. Nixon is clearly indicated as an expression of well-earned confidence, as a measure of safety, and also as a deserved rebuke to those who undermine confidence and imperil safety." In San Bernardino, the weekly *Sun-Telegram* thought that he would stop Communist penetration, while she did not believe it was a serious menace, and thus exercised poor judgment. The threat was real. Bill Henry, columnist for the *Los Angeles Times* and radio commentator, reflected many constituents' opinions, believing that Nixon would be "the best Senator this State has had in my lifetime. Not only has he the intelligence, courage and other basic qualities but he has a proper sense of proportion." Unstated but clearly understood was that Douglas did not.[49]

The candidate had his own spots. "This election," he exaggerated to his audience, "was the most important in American history." He wanted to live in peace by making America economically sound and by building a powerful military. He placed security above partisan politics and wanted to make certain that Californians had peace and freedom. He would fight the Communist fifth-column menace as well as corruption.[50]

Throughout the campaign, Dana Smith had handled the fund-raising efficiently and effectively. He urged backers to target Democrats who opposed the "pink lady," Republicans who wanted to give solely to their candidate, and out-of-state contributors. By the third week of September, Bill Arnold had already reported that he was "really getting swamped" with checks coming into the campaign's coffers. At the end of the month, the costs for advertising and billboards alone reached $22,609. For that amount, Northern California had 287 boards, central region had 91, and the southern peaked at 396.[51]

By October 5, the Nixon campaign had received $106,828.84 and disbursed $92,647.92. The committee was communicating with the public through every major media network and had purchased a half hour on ABC Radio for $1,081. Another $1,000 went for six movie star television film spots. Toward the end of October, the Nixon campaign had taken in almost $150,000 and had spent almost all of it. By election day the committee had met its goal of almost $200,000. Even though Douglas did not leave exact figures for her campaign, Nixon certainly raised more money, both a signal and a cause of Nixon's greater momentum.[52]

On Tuesday, election day, the Nixons expected to cast their votes at the Whittier American Legion Hall at 7:00 A.M., but they had difficulty finding a baby-sitter and that delayed them by half an hour. Dick cast his ballot with Pat watching. He appeared happy and gave the okay signal. Douglas voted in Hollywood: after spoiling the first ballot she received, she completed another one.[53]

The Nixons thanked their volunteers and sent out ten thousand cards to workers before election day about how well the campaign was progressing and how he was encouraged by the favorable polls. A large undecided bloc still remained, and volunteers needed to remain vigilant until the completion of the balloting. Throughout the day, Nixon appeared on short television campaign spots. One called for America to remain strong: politically, militarily, and ideologically. Another declared that the United States was fighting in Korea to guarantee peace, security, and freedom; he would make certain of that commitment. He placed "security of America first" against the Communists as a nonpartisan issue.[54]

Nearly seventeen hours after the polls closed, Douglas had lost decisively. She conceded: "I personally shall continue to work for the Democratic Party program, which I firmly believe is in the best interests of the people at home and abroad." She did not send the traditional message of congratulations to her opponent.[55]

Of the 5,244,837 registered California voters, 3,685,961 voted for either Nixon or Douglas. He received 2,183,454 votes and she 1,502,507; his plurality was 680,947, at 59 percent the largest senatorial victory in the United States that year. Chotiner's analysis of the election illustrated how badly she was defeated, even when compared to Warren's lopsided, almost two-to-one victory over Roosevelt.[56]

| | Douglas | Douglas% | Nixon | Nixon% | Nixon Lead |
|---|---|---|---|---|---|
| Northern California | 597,206 | 37 | 776,211 | 57 | 179,005 |
| Central California | 106,710 | 32 | 153,623 | 59 | 43,913 |
| Southern California | 798,591 | 37 | 1,253,620 | 61 | 455,029 |
| Totals | 1,502,507 | 37 | 2,183,454 | 59 | 680,947 |

Douglas held her left-wing base, Democratic loyalists, and those who despised Nixon, but little more than that. She earned every vote that she received. San Mateo County, in Northern California, for example, gave her 49.9 percent in the primary, while Nixon received 36.2 percent. In the general election, she plummeted to 35.2 percent and he jumped to 64.8 percent. For his home territory of Orange County, he received 52,187 votes, or 73.7 percent, against her 18,520. Only 9 precincts out of 320 failed to give the congressman a majority.[57]

The newspapers demonstrated clearly voter sentiment. Fred Arnold, columnist for the *Los Angeles Herald Express* and father of Nixon's chief legislative associate, Bill, declared that Warren's and Nixon's vote tallies in that region were "in tune with the nationwide revolt against left-wing socialistic policies of the national administration." Even in far more liberal Northern California, the *San Francisco Examiner* chided Truman for becoming involved in the senatorial race by offering Douglas his backing. The voters had repudiated her, for "They knew the Congresswoman as belonging to the 'be kind to Communists' element."[58]

Throughout the campaign, the Douglas committee constantly complained that the newspapers did not give her as much coverage as Nixon. Harold Tipton, Douglas's state coordinator, for instance, praised the *Santa Barbara News Press* for "some degree of objectivity which most newspapers had not given her." The Stanford University Institute for Journalistic Studies examined those charges and found that, surprisingly, Douglas had received 52.6 percent of all coverage, while Nixon had 47.4 percent. The institute had sampled twelve California dailies consisting of Democratic, Republican, and Independent viewpoints, from September 1 to November 7, in which the news was reduced to 8,081 statements. The report, also surprisingly, concluded that the campaign had not been "overwhelmingly negative in nature."[59]

Nonetheless, myth gradually merged with reality. Most historians have let the "smear" moniker stick without ever carefully testing it. Though at least some writers note that both sides attacked each other, they somehow attribute Nixon with initiating and setting the smarmy tone. Somehow this unseemly symbol submerged the crucial importance of the issues. In truth, the ideological and issue-oriented differences could not have been clearer, and voters responded overwhelmingly. Douglas never had a chance.

Douglas's reflections on her defeat more or less admitted as much, centering on the changing times. To Walter Reuther of the United Auto Workers, less than a week after the balloting, she wrote: "We made a good fight—we put on a good campaign, and I am ashamed of none of it." The nation had shifted away from the Democrats: "We lost in California because the opposition was able to split the labor vote and the women's vote. . . . Actually there was nothing that we did or did not do that would have made any difference in the result."[60]

Arthur Schlesinger, Jr., wrote her a few days after the election, expressing how depressed he was with what he understood "was an unusually unfair and dirty campaign." A friend, George Outland, was far more philosophical: "It was one of those years when probably nothing would have changed the result—even had limitless funds been available, I am afraid the temper of the times would have been difficult if not impossible to counteract." Charles Voorhis painted an even clearer picture. The election was unusually dirty, but "Helen did not have a chance, largely because of the dissension and bickering within the democratic party, and the fact that labor did not vote solidly for her." The main reason for her defeat, however, was that she "had been entirely too radical and careless."[61]

In the meantime, the Nixon camp celebrated. Even Governor Warren, who had refused to endorse Nixon, sent congratulations through intermediaries, and former president Herbert Hoover wired: "YOUR VICTORY WAS THE GREATEST GOOD THAT CAN COME TO OUR COUNTRY."[62]

Those allied to Nixon in the anti-Communist crusade were ecstatic. De Toledano wrote that his "cup brimmeth over" to Whittaker Chambers, who earlier had written Nixon that the Chambers family was "happy for the nation that could put a man like you in the Senate—we think there aren't many of them."[63]

A month after losing, Douglas asserted: "What the election demonstrates more clearly than anything else is the intensive job which liberals must undertake to win again in 1952. This is a challenge which we shall and will meet." By mid-December, she added that higher taxes, the entrance of Chinese troops into the Korean War, rising prices, and McCarthyism had hurt her chances, but no one was at fault for her defeat. She was "proud of the fight we made. There will be another battle on another day, and I know we will be in it together."[64]

Over time, however, a faulty memory replaced the reality. Throughout the remainder of the 1950s, Douglas refused to discuss Richard Nixon with many people. To some, she expressed her frustration. At the end of October 1952, she portrayed Nixon's campaign against her as "a truly vicious one." He did not discuss issues, but attacked Democratic integrity and loyalty. Only a tiny portion of these assaults on her were printed: "The whispering campaign is what was so vicious. People were paid to deliberately spread lies—and, of course, the biggest one was that my husband and I were Communists." Nixon was "much too wise to have called me a communist in so many words." However, his campaign was based on the assumption that she was a Communist: "The pink sheet gave the impression to the reader who was not too well acquainted with the workings of Congress that there was a Marcantonio program presented in the House of Representatives which I supported 354 times."[65]

During the 1960 presidential election, Douglas went on the campaign trail to attack Nixon and blasted at his campaign tactics in order to turn Eisenhower Democrats from the GOP. She enthusiastically supported JFK and Lyndon B. Johnson, and was "nauseated at the thought of voting for Nixon." She reminded voters that Nixon had used McCarthy techniques against her in 1950.[66]

While Douglas sporadically compared her defeat with that of Voorhis in 1946, others were slowly beginning to bind the two losses into one knot. Dr. Remsen Bird, who spent two decades as president of Occidental College in Pasadena, urged Douglas toward the end of 1955 to ferret out Nixon's evil nature. Nixon replaced Voorhis, Bird alleged, by using "lies, innuendos, exaggerations and smear a-plenty, and he [Voorhis] was lost to the government, and it was a great loss!" This academic knew that Nixon was a horrible person, but did not have the details and was writing the father and son to get them. Bird also wanted a statement from Douglas "of exactly what he [Nixon] did do that was hitting below the belt, and by this method of planting fear, lying and misrepresentation."[67]

During the 1960 presidential campaign, the claim that Nixon had subjected Voorhis and Douglas to smear campaigns was magnified. Nixon denied the allegations, but they were cemented in the American psyche by a rush of national publicity. Morris Rubin, just before the election, in "The Case Against Nixon," for *The Progressive,* charged that anyone who read the record could not "escape the conclusion that he has violated every principle of decency and fair play." Without citing sources, Rubin contended that Nixon connected Voorhis to the Communists and the CIO-PAC, supposedly knowing that these accusations were false. Four years later, Nixon used the "pink sheet" against Douglas to link her to Marcantonio. Nixon used the "big lie." The conclusion: "to achieve power, he has corrupted the truth, smeared his opponents, betrayed his friends, invoked ugly innuendo and the furtive accusation as his major weapons of political warfare, and relied heavily on a capacity for slippery evasion of commitment that enables some of his supporters to hail him as a conservative and others to embrace him as a liberal."[68]

During the 1970s, after Watergate and the endless stream of analysis of Nixon's early years in politics, the smear stories multiplied. Former McGovern campaign manager Frank Mankiewicz, in *Perfectly Clear: Nixon from Whittier to Watergate*, highlighted every nasty thing said about Nixon in his early campaigns. He never won a free election, defined by the author as "one untainted by major fraud." Without identifying any documentation, Mankiewicz recited the CIO-PAC charge against Nixon "in the classic definition of fraud, known by Nixon to be false." He also related the charge that Nixon had phone callers saying, "Did you know Jerry Voorhis was a Communist?" Finally, Mankiewicz argued absurdly that had Nixon not won both primaries in 1948, Stephen Zetterberg would have probably beaten him in the general election.[69]

Beginning in the mid-1970s and finishing in the early 1980s, the Women in Politics Oral History Project conducted a series of interviews with Helen Gahagan Douglas and many of her admirers, vividly demonstrating the weaknesses of oral histories done twenty to thirty years after the fact. While several Nixon supporters were included, the majority of the interviewees sounded like Alice De Sola: "I always disliked Nixon, quite apart from what he did to Helen. What he did to Alger Hiss infuriated me. I still think Hiss was framed." Philip Noel-Baker, a British diplomat, thought that Douglas should have defeated Nixon, but he used dirty tricks and she lost. As a consequence, he became "Tricky Dick" in England: "Nobody trusted Nixon after that. . . . I thought him very second-rate." Judge Byron Lindsley, who chaired the Douglas campaign in San Diego, made the wildest accusation: that 500,000 phone calls were made in his city and Los Angeles charging Douglas with being a Communist. None of his friends received any, and he could not cite a single recipient. Mary Keyserling, who held high-level posts as an economist in the federal government, also pronounced Nixon guilty in attacking Voorhis and Douglas. Nixon, she told her interviewer, was dishonest and had an "evil spirit."[70]

In her own memoir, published two years after her death, Helen Gahagan Douglas reinforced the story that Nixon had waged "a vicious campaign to discredit" Voorhis. Nixon had supposedly attacked his opponent for trying "to thwart the work of HUAC in order to protect communist spies." One of Douglas's campaign workers' daughters, the bizarre tale continued, had spent a day at Nixon headquarters, assigned to a room filled with people using telephones, saying, "Good morning. Do you know that Jerry Voorhis is a Communist?" Nixon's sole goal in the 1950 campaign was to find Democratic voters, and according to

Douglas, the only way to accomplish this was to destroy her integrity. After thirty years of reflection, Douglas concluded that Nixon had no scruples: "There's not much to say about the 1950 campaign except that a man ran for the Senate who wanted to get there, and didn't care how."[71]

Ingrid Winther Scobie, an historian who examined Douglas's career for over two decades, came to a different finding: Douglas lost because of the fragmentation of the Democratic Party, Boddy's assault on her, the popularity of Governor Warren over James Roosevelt, and the power of the GOP within California. No woman could have won the Senate race that year, due to the discrimination against females. Furthermore, Douglas was a radical liberal, and her political extremism cost her votes. Scobie felt that Douglas's "idealism" may have hurt her chances the most. "But her lack of political experience and her inflexible stands on political issues, along with gender questions, eroded the support of the Democratic Party in 1950."[72]

Other writers in the 1990s have not followed Scobie's example of careful documentation. If smears were insufficient reasoning for Douglas's defeat, the titanic sums that Nixon allegedly gushed into the campaign have taken second place. Nixon haters have claimed that he raised astronomical sums to swamp his opponent. Such allegations are without merit, but this theme has been taken to new heights with sinister accusations of ill-gotten monies, raised from clandestine sources.

Two far-fetched examples of these arguments come from Roger Morris and Greg Mitchell, respectively. Without citing to campaign spread sheets or other relevant accounting data, Morris, with a doctorate from Harvard in government, claimed in his biography that a major reason for Nixon's victory was that he had been "richly financed, mostly in secret," guessing the fund-raising at $1–$2 million. Mitchell, who wrote a recent book specifically on the 1950 senatorial election, declared without any supporting figures: "Money poured in to [Nixon] headquarters from near and far." Mitchell continued on this path by challenging a headline that Douglas spent more than Nixon without identifying any hard evidence on what each candidate raised. Mitchell accurately reported that Nixon had not supplied the full extent of his fund-raising activities to the state, but failed to add that campaign finance reporting in 1950 was full of loopholes, and few, if any, reported all of their contributions. Mitchell then jumped to a fantastic estimate of $4,200,000, as "surely closer to the mark than the official figure" of $4,209.[73]

Neither Morris nor Mitchell provided detailed evidence to support their claims. In fact, the campaign, as was the practice in 1950, was relatively short. Nixon spent two months in a station wagon during the primary traveling across the state and blitzed the state for another seven weeks from mid-September until election day. He in all likelihood outspent Douglas, but big business did not bankroll Nixon with enormous sums.

After the Senate race, Nixon dismissed most complaints that he had smeared Douglas. In reply to a letter in the summer of 1952, he denied ever engaging "in a personal campaign of vilification against Mrs. Douglas in the 1950 campaign, or that I ever stated or implied that she was either a Communist or fellow traveler." Nixon concentrated throughout that campaign on the differences between his and Douglas's congressional records: "Neither in my own case nor in that of my opponent did I at any time place any interpretations on the records, but merely recommended that these records should speak for themselves."[74]

However, during the 1952 presidential contest, gossip circulated that the vice-presidential nominee was anti-Semitic, anti–African American, and anti-Catholic. Dinkelspiel dismissed these accusation as "an outright lie. As you probably know, he is a Quaker with the broadest outlook towards all groups and classes." Chotiner asked those who said that Nixon had passed out racial or religious materials in the senatorial contest to produce them for examination. No one met his challenge.[75]

By the end of the year, Nixon felt that he had made progress combating the "hate" stories. "It is absurd for anyone to say that I attacked Mrs. Douglas during the 1950 senatorial campaign on the ground that her husband was Jewish, or that anti-Semitic groups were behind me. The truth of the matter is that at no time did I attack Mrs. Douglas' husband on any ground, and the truth is further that I have always repudiated and will continue to repudiate any attempt by an anti-Semitic group which tries to attach itself to my campaigns."[76]

Rather than racial motives, Chotiner supplied an incisive analysis of the race to a campaign school for the Republican National Committee before forty-eight state chairmen at the Sheraton Hotel in Washington, D.C., during the early fall of 1955. He liked to employ themes, not slogans that the opposition could twist. As for dirty tricks, "I believe it is a smear to attack an individual on things that have no relationship whatsoever to the campaign. If you attack his personal life, if you attack

members of his family, if you made an attack on things that do not go
into the question or whether or not that man would make a good public
official, that is a smear. But it is not a smear, if you please, if you point
out the record of your opponent."

Nixon talked about a strong America and domestic communism,
while Douglas promised federal handouts. Since he could not "out-
promise a New Dealer," Nixon stuck to his theme. Refusing to discuss
her issues, Douglas grew desperate and started debating his issues. With
that decision, she lost, for "she could not sell the people of California
that she would be a better fighter against communism than Dick Nixon.
She made the fatal mistake of attacking our strength instead of sticking
to attacking our weakness."

Republicans in 1950, Chotiner reasoned, had to sell their candidates. They needed to reach every party member and establish separate
organizations for Democrats and independents; besides these major
groups, the committee needed veterans, women, physicians, and other
special interest organizations. Polling helped to determine the candidate's and opponent's strengths and weaknesses. Direct mail was critical
to communicate with the electorate. Newspaper and outdoor advertising was essential. Radio and television had become as integral as the
speaker's bureau.

Chotiner ended his presentation with four things his audience had
to have to run a campaign: "a thick skin," a "sense of humor," a "thick
neck," for those who wished to cut your throat, and a "strong back," for
those who were ready to plunge a knife into it. When Nixon ran for the
Senate, he had chairmen for all fifty-eight of the state's counties, and between forty-five to forty-seven of those men were under the age of
thirty-five. The party needed young blood and Nixon had one of the
best run offices on Capitol Hill, with many youthful individuals on his
staff.[77]

Nixon, in his memoirs, reviewed the literature reiterating the
Douglases' complaints. His explanation was elementary: Californians
simply disapproved of a left-wing woman whom they perceived was
"soft on communism." She "waged a campaign that would not be
equaled for stridency, ineptness, or self-righteousness" until George Mc-
Govern's presidential bid twenty-two years later. Even late in his political
life, Nixon occasionally faced misquotes like the alleged apologetic remark: "I was young then, I'm sorry." There was "no basis in fact for this
statement." Despite continual denials, it still persists.[78]

The age of Roosevelt had ended without Voorhis and Douglas comprehending its consequences. Rather than economic depression, Americans confronted inflation fears at home and the rising Red peril from abroad. Democrats like Voorhis and Douglas did not understand the significance of this shift. Nixon did and exploited that advantage.

Nixonphobia turned into a cult, and its visceral hatred cannot be overemphasized. Its followers cling to unproven or erroneous happenings to demonstrate how Nixon had smeared Voorhis and Douglas. Consumed by hatred, these Nixonphobes turn to the very methods that they swore their antagonist implemented. The record paints quite a different picture. Both Democrats, Voorhis and Douglas, suffered from a lack of organization and strategic suicide. Both spoke from the left of center and never realized that their political survival depended on catering to the needs of their constituents rather than crusading on a path that the vast majority refused to travel.

*Chapter* **17**

# COMMUNISM AND KOREA

Three issues referred to as "C-2, K-1"—Communism, corruption and Korea—dominated congressional debates from the summer of 1950 through 1952. The last reared its head first once the North Koreans invaded the South. As a candidate in early November 1950, Nixon briefly touched upon rumors that Red Chinese "volunteers" had joined in the Korean conflict. At the height of the campaign, however, Nixon was not much concerned with the implications of this military movement; instead, he used mainland China's aggression to prevent American recognitions and admission of Mao Tse-tung's regime to the United Nations. American officials as a whole seemed indifferent to the possible entry of Chinese soldiers, having already anticipated bringing the troops home by Christmas.

Despite such euphoria, the Chinese Communists had been warning the United Nations since its forces started pushing the North Koreans closer and closer to their common border on the Yalu River that volunteers might enter into the conflict. Just after Thanksgiving, in a fierce winter, as temperatures dipped to twenty-five degrees below zero, with bugles blowing, 500,000 Red Chinese, who had infiltrated quietly across the frozen river, attacked UN soldiers, forcing an immediate allied retreat. The optimism of ending the war turned again to fear of losing it.

Nixon now saw the Korean War as Truman's debacle and felt that the paradox of a GOP landslide in a state with a heavy Democratic majority was "due to the fact that the people of California were concerned as never before over the international situation and the manner in which our foreign policies have been administered by the representatives of the party in power. The voters . . . had lost confidence in their leaders to protect the security of the country and decided it was time for a change."[1]

Nixon listened to the powerful GOP voice of John Foster Dulles on Southeast Asian affairs. As American representative to the United Nations, Dulles made a speech on November 27 noting that the United States had forty-four military advisers on Formosa and defended that island with the Seventh Fleet. Americans had not blockaded the island, nor had they any territorial interests there. The U.S. Air Force also had been holding maneuvers near Manchuria, and the Soviet Union had incorrectly accused the Americans of violating its airspace. In fact, he said, the administration had no aggressive intentions. He insisted that the United States would persevere in Korea.[2]

Two days before the end of the year, Dulles spoke more generally about America's five-year response to the Communist challenge, arguing that Western civilization had dominated the world for a thousand years and wondering if the Communists would now emerge as the dominant force. America, he declared, had established a fairer income tax system and had enacted Social Security legislation without resorting to communism. America, Dulles conceded, still had faults, but was moving in a positive direction by slowing Communist advances. The free world had industrial superiority and military deterrence, while the Russians had to defend an enormous area with an unwieldy totalitarian regime. Still, Dulles and most Americans worried that China's entry into the Korean conflict spelled trouble.[3]

The failed policies of the Truman administration in Asia, according to the GOP, especially the fall of mainland China to the Communists and the escalating war in Korea, contributed to the disenchantment of a large bloc of Americans. After Red Chinese troops in massive numbers routed UN soldiers, drove them from the North Korean capital of Pyongyang, across the 38th parallel, and quickly recaptured Seoul and Inchon, Jack Garland, an original member of the Fact Finding Committee, was comforted "to know that you [Nixon] will be on the floor of the Senate next Monday, ready to represent California and the American way of life, which made it possible for you to rise so quickly and so brilliantly to such a high national position." Herman Perry echoed widespread conservative frustrations that for a decade, the Democrats had betrayed the country, and believed that General George Marshall, Secretary of State Dean Acheson, and "every known pink who has been in or is still in the State Department for treason against the United States" were culpable. For them, Nixon was not just an improvement but a savior.[4]

During the third week of November, Senator Downey announced that, due to health considerations, he would retire at the end of the month, allowing Nixon to fill his unexpired term and thereby gain a little seniority for committee assignments. Warren confirmed that Nixon would receive the interim appointment, and the incoming senator flew to Sacramento on November 22 for a lengthy interview with the governor covering water problems, federal tidelands legislation, and construction projects.[5]

Nixon was sworn in on Capitol Hill on December 4 with approximately fourteen Californians watching. He was now a member of the upper chamber of Congress, where old traditions of respect and seniority held great power, even more than in the House. Nixon wrote one constituent that "during the first couple of months of my service in the Senate it would be well to maintain the respectful silence which the senior Senators expect of a new member."[6]

Before he could turn back to the Korean situation, he had to dissolve Bewley, Knoop & Nixon; the remaining partners announced the formation of their new firm. Unless Nixon needed the extra office by the elevator, Bewley was going to release that space. As he told Nixon, "It has been a mighty fine partner relationship and we hope the same feeling will always continue." Even though the senator did not receive any income from the partnership during 1950, he, too, shared the feeling that it had been a pleasant arrangement. Nixon still retained his Whittier law office and thanked Bewley for his hospitality. Nixon would only be in the office for about three months at most, while the majority of his time would be spent traveling throughout the district. When someone needed to be impressed, he could borrow an office and set up his interviews on Saturdays as he had done in the past.[7]

Nixon, due to his extensive campaigning, had netted only $12,728 for 1950. After his victory, Dana Smith, who had directed the financial aspects of the campaign, recognized that Nixon's followers wanted him "to continue to sell effectively to the people of California the economic and political systems which we all believe in." Smith and others knew that this cost money that Nixon did not have, and therefore, many back-

ers had to "set up a pool" to continue on an annual basis "to meet expenditures which seem necessary to accomplish this objective." Smith
hoped to raise $20,000 to $25,000 annually, and "only included in our
group of people who have supported Dick from the start so that it does
not provide any way for people who are 'second guessers' to make any
claim on the Senator's particular interest." The range of contributions
started at a minimum of $100 and peaked at $500, "so that it can never
be charged that anyone is contributing so much as to think he is entitled
to special favors."

Smith and Bernard Brennan would manage the fund through "a
trust account subject for review." No one would receive any salary or
other compensation so that everything possible went toward the primary
objectives: allocation for transportation and hotel expenses for trips to
California over Nixon's official mileage allowance; reimbursement for
long-distance telephone calls and airmail during his stays; payment for
Christmas cards and other materials that kept contributors informed;
and finally, donations for media advertisements publicizing Nixon's
statewide appearances.[8]

While Smith commenced the establishment of this special fund,
Nixon dealt with family concerns. His parents enjoyed their Whittier
home, but his father, according to Nixon's sister-in-law, Clara Jane, typ-
ically had "a couple of good days then a poor one. He apparently has to
be careful not do too much because of his heart condition." His parents'
health would increasingly be a concern to Nixon.[9]

Dick and Pat were also preoccupied with buying a new house. The
two-bedroom apartment in suburban Virginia was simply too small. Pat
commented: "my cloths [sic] are even hanging on doors—we're bursting
at the seams." By the middle of February, they had bought one in Spring
Valley, a pleasant residential area in Washington, D.C., for $41,000 with
a $21,000 down payment. It was still under construction and would not
be ready until the spring, but Nixon hoped to sell their California home
in the meantime because of the substantial down payment. Building was
delayed until June 15 at the earliest, and Pat told friends how much she
was "looking forward to the new home."

By the early part of July, according to Dick, Pat was "keeping very
busy making the necessary arrangements" to complete the move and had
chosen a southern pine desk for him; and by the middle of the month,
they had moved to their residence at 4801 Tilden Avenue, N.W. This
seven-room, two-story, white brick home had three bedrooms: the par-

ents took the master one; Julie, who had just had her third birthday, and Tricia, who was six and on the verge of first grade, shared another; and his parents used the third on their frequent visits. Assistant Attorney General Peyton Ford lived next door, and two houses away was Senator Herman Welker, Republican from Idaho, who kept "some of the boys from taking themselves too seriously. This is a fatal occupational disease in this business as you know!" Dick proclaimed: "We feel that by the time we elect a Republican President in 1952 everything should be squared away so that we can do some entertaining!"[10]

This was far more than just a house to Pat Nixon. She was coming up to her fortieth birthday, and throughout 1951, as she prepared to move, then settle in, then finally grow accustomed to her new environment, she confided to her best friend Helene Drown about the various family changes. She playfully admitted to Helene that her home was not like the Drown mansion with five bedrooms in an exclusive Southern California community of Rolling Hills. When the Drowns phoned the Nixons long distance that fall, Pat wrote: "You'll just have to take it off on your income taxes as charity—a shot in the arm for two poor souls!"[11]

The Nixons obviously were not as financially secure as the Drowns, but the senator and his wife fit snugly into the middle class. In order to buy the Spring Valley home, they sold their Whittier residence and hoped "to break even" on the sale. They used their California furniture, but needed new carpeting. Pat found out that prices had doubled since she had last priced it. As she prepared to move, she anxiously remarked: "I have moved so many times and the actual process has always been gruesome. Dick is always too busy, at least *his* story, so I do all the lugging, worrying and cussing." Despite such concerns before the move, by the end of the year, Pat seemed somewhat satisfied. The house was "in fair shape using or recovering much of what we already had." She had some help from a decorator "who dreamed up the dramatic touches such as silver tea paper on one wall of our bedroom with a mural by a local starving artist." One wall in the living room was mirrored and the others were aqua. The cornices, draperies, and the fireside chairs were peacock blue. They needed more accessories, "but we also need some cash so - - - !"[12]

Julie and Tricia were "extremely well" at the beginning of the year; by then, both had had their tonsils removed. Tricia was going to kindergarten, and the mothers in the community had just started a nursery school, with paid teachers and each mother's assistance every ten days. "I hope Julie will go because I could use a little free time for errand-doing, shopping, etc." A new medium also provided some time for relaxation: "We fell for television too and the children are now watching it. . . . Tricia likes cowboys or horror stories so Julie has little chance."[13]

Pat also employed a cleaning girl twice a week, "My days out! Otherwise I have stayed closer to home than any time since we have been here. With all our expenses I really haven't tried to find anyone so far but dread the time I do as they are hard to find here too." She admitted that this helped "some," and she enlisted Dick to help with the chores: "Our lawn is 2 ft. tall—Dick mowed it once and boasted blisters." If their gardener did not come soon, "Dick said he'd take another try at it. I'll telegraph you when it happens."[14]

Her wardrobe needed updating early in the year, and she expected to have "to get a few dressy duds soon." Her dressmaker in California, Elissa, was doing one fancy dress with a "slim underskirt of knife pleated SATIN with top & tunic of silver patterns of lace which she backed with nylon net to give it body." Toward the end of the year, her need for clothes on the household list was about eightieth. "Other than the one suit," she pointed out, "I haven't bought a pair of nylons but I'm afraid I'll have to do something before the season gets in full swing." Pat wished that Elissa lived closer, and "I would have her create a couple of numbers." Pat had already written her about a new dinner dress, but also wanted other things.[15]

Even with money worries, two growing daughters, and the responsibilities of running a new house, Pat lived an exciting life that revolved around her husband. Early in the year, she reported: "So far we have been swamped with visitors and are not able to see even half of them." Dick left on Friday for five days on his Lincoln Day tour in the middle of February. That evening, she met him in New York City and saw *Call Me Madam*, "which was a riot." At noon on Saturday, Dick spoke at an event and then they went to a cocktail party hosted by Ralph de Toledano, "with a *most* interesting guest list" like the former Communist spy, Hede Massing. That evening, Mrs. Theodore Roosevelt entertained them at dinner with the president of Chase Bank, Winthrop Aldrich, Clare Booth Luce, Peter Grim who designed Rockefeller Center, William L. White the author, and two former ambassadors. "It was as impressive a group as we have ever 'broken bread with.'" By that fall, she was "a widow" because Dick had committed himself to a speaking tour that "he couldn't back out" of. As soon as he finished, Dick would travel to California where he had over five hundred requests to speak, attending only a small fraction of the events that he had invitations for.[16]

His new Senate office in Room 341 would ultimately have fourteen employees. Receptionist Dorothy Cox, a staff member since 1946, welcomed visitors. Gemma O'Brian, Marge Ackerson, Pat Wright, and Marian Budlong also shared that office's secretarial duties, with Betty Lewis and Loie Gaunt working downstairs in the mail room. The administrative assistants included William Arnold, who had served Nixon since his first days in Washington and concentrated on publicity matters. James "Jim" Gleason, a veteran just about to turn thirty, with a wife and two children, was a Catholic with strong anti-Communist convictions. He had achieved an excellent scholastic record, graduating from Georgetown University Law School, and had gone into private practice. Nixon hired him early in February to research various legislative issues.[17]

The third and last administrative appointee to arrive was John J. "Jack" Irwin, born on March 16, 1908, in Mount Clemens, Michigan. A devout Catholic, he went to St. Mary's parochial school in Port Huron, moved to Los Angeles in 1928, and attended Loyola College of Law in the evening while working in a law office during the day. Admitted to the bar in 1932, he was an assistant U.S. attorney in 1933–37, and then served as local counsel for the Federal Deposit Insurance Corporation. He helped organize the Young Democrats in 1932 and served as its chairman, but during the 1950 senatorial campaign, he switched from the Democratic Party to work tirelessly and enthusiastically for Nixon's committee. After the election, the senator asked Irwin to join his staff. He agreed and left a successful ten-year partnership at Sanner, Fleming & Irwin. Before flying east, he had to recover from an appendicitis operation. Shortly after his arrival on Capitol Hill in January, the staff described Irwin as "a perfectly charming gent [who] fits in beautifully."[18]

Another newly hired employee in the outer office guarding Nixon's door was his private secretary Rose Mary Woods, who, like Gleason and Irwin, was Catholic. Born in Sebring, Ohio, a town of about five thousand, her parents had a total of five children, three girls and two boys. She had graduated from McKinley High School with top awards in commercial studies and came to the capital in 1943: "I went there seeking opportunity, but I was scared, starry-eyed, and naive." She served as staff secretary for the Herter mission, where she met Nixon and later saw him and Pat at a party. After winning the senatorial contest, he asked her to become his secretary. Woods inquired around Capitol Hill about him, heard favorable reports, and accepted his offer in early February, two days before Gleason joined the staff.[19]

By the beginning of February 1951, Nixon had acquired a full secretarial complement; his office was receiving between five hundred to seven hundred pieces of daily mail that had to be answered. Late that month, the flu had been passed through the staff, and in the middle of March, Nixon admitted that he "had a little bout with the flu and am just now getting around to catching up on some of my correspondence."[20]

By the end of March, he designed the primary function of his administrative staff to handle constituents' problems so that he could devote his time to the legislative process. One of his principal aides should be in the office at all times. All three were capable: two lawyers, who concentrated on legal issues, and a public relations expert. Someone had to deal with lobbyists "more to get them off our neck than anything." The senator wanted everyone seen: "it wasn't a pleasant task but that we had to take the 'bad with the good' and that occasionally a crackpot had something to offer—to bear in mind the case of Whittaker Chambers whom everyone thought was a crackpot!"[21]

Outside the Washington office, Nixon had problems with the perception of his relationship to Murray Chotiner. After winning his coveted seat, the junior senator frequently consulted his former campaign manager. Without charge, Chotiner helped with Nixon's travel arrangements to California and coordinated his speaking engagements with those of Knowland's. Since Chotiner's office was closed on Sundays, Murray provided his and his assistant Ruth Arnold's addresses and phone numbers for emergencies.[22]

Some people wondered how much Nixon relied on the adviser and where Chotiner fit in the senator's organization. Too many, according to Perry, believed that Murray was the "unofficial representative for Dick in California," even while Perry represented that Brennan was Nixon's chief spokesman. Brennan objected to any hierarchy; whoever wished to contact Nixon, Brennan referred to his office. No one, he declared, spoke for the senator, and that included Chotiner, who did provide some free technical advice. "This way," Bernie thought, "Dick can always be the one who is in contact with his people instead of having to do it through others."[23]

Nixon referred to Chotiner as "one of the most objective and astute political observers in the country." He occasionally attended a Democratic political meeting, "as one John Q. Public, in order to make a firsthand observation of the opposition party," and evaluated Truman's successful selling of his anti-inflation bill, which would halt rising prices, while his opposition's proposals would not. He analyzed criticisms of Nixon's senatorial operations, as well as traveling throughout California and sending the senator a comprehensive report on the conditions there. Brennan accompanied Chotiner on this trip and observed that everyone had confidence in Murray's skill during the primary and general elections. Brennan was "more resolved than ever to fight the battle with anyone that starts a critical program as far as your continued use of Murray is concerned." Dana Smith concurred: Chotiner had done "a whale of a good job."[24]

Nixon, throughout the remainder of his relationship with Chotiner, had to balance his friend's assets and liabilities. He worked hard, offered good advice, and was loyal. Yet Murray was loud, he exaggerated his importance to the senator, and he led individuals to believe that he had greater authority than, in actuality, he had. Despite this puffing, Nixon recognized that Chotiner's benefits far outweighed his weaknesses.

While in the midst of structuring his organization and deciding where everyone fit, Nixon established an informal set of guidelines for cooperation between him and California's senior senator, Bill Knowland. Born in 1908, son of a congressman, publisher of the *Oakland Tribune* and staunch Republican, Bill was an avid Republican even while attending the University of California at Berkeley. After his graduation in 1925, he worked for his father's newspaper, won election to the state senate, and almost immediately formed a close bond with Earl Warren. When Warren decided to run for California attorney general in 1938, Knowland supported that decision, as well Warren's announcement to run for governor four years later. Although Knowland was inducted into the army before his friend won the gubernatorial election, Warren did not forget the support from Bill and his father. When Senator Hiram Johnson died on the day that the atomic bomb was dropped on Hiroshima, the governor paid a personal and professional debt to Bill by appointing him at thirty-seven to fill the deceased's unexpired term.[25]

When both Nixon and Knowland were candidates in 1946, the former appreciated Knowland's willingness to appear with him in the 12th district at campaign functions. During that initial period, Murray Chotiner not only briefly assisted the congressional aspirant but for the first time assumed the role of professional campaign manager for Knowland. When his opponent, Will Rogers, Jr., despite his famous father's name, ran a lackluster race, he was easily defeated.[26]

Nixon and Knowland had always been closely aligned. Not only were they both conservative Republicans in their domestic views, but they also agreed on many foreign policy issues such as support for the Truman Doctrine and the Marshall Plan. Nixon also defended Knowland, who was scorned as the "senator from Formosa" for his advocacy of the Nationalist Chinese position. Nixon felt that too many Californians did not recognize "the great service he [Knowland] has rendered to the country in pointing up the dangers which that situation presents to the very security of the nation." After assuming his Senate seat, Nixon and Knowland rotated returning home so that at least one of them would always remain on Capitol Hill.[27]

Nixon now turned to lobbying for committee assignments. He wished to serve on the Senate Armed Forces Committee, but since Knowland already was a member, Nixon eventually settled for the Committee on Labor and Public Welfare. His other post was the Committee for Expenditures in the Executive Departments, successor to the Truman committee that had acted in a watchdog capacity over the defense industry during World War II. Initially, his request for this was rejected, and he was assigned to the far less desirable District of Columbia Committee. But when Arthur Vandenberg, Republican from Michigan, who was slowly dying of cancer, agreed to take that post and relinquish his seat on expenditures, Nixon had that plum. Joseph McCarthy, the GOP ranking member of that committee, claimed that every senator asked to be on it, with a single exception, but he had named Mundt and Nixon "because of their great background of experience in investigating work." McCarthy had also "bumped" off Margaret Chase Smith from Maine because she openly criticized him on the Senate floor. This was his "first open act of revenge," and according to Smith, it is designed "to retaliate for my Declaration of Conscience," a speech given on the Senate floor in McCarthy's presence, on June 1, 1950, attacking his extreme, unsubstantiated statements about Communism in the federal bureauacy.[28]

Nixon appreciated McCarthy's action. After the Wisconsin senator had written a speech for the Senate floor to be delivered on December 6, 1950, he sent a copy to his new colleague for suggestions. McCarthy wrote about his concern over the Korean conflict. Even though the Truman Doctrine had been successful, the Marshall Plan had not provided for military assistance. As a consequence, the United States fought communism in one-third of the world with military aid; in another region with economic support; and in Asia, the third area, McCarthy repeated his continual charges against "The Hiss-Acheson-Jessup-Lattimore-Vincent Plan to turn all of Asia over to the Communists and to then cooperate with those 'friendly' Communists." Secretary Acheson and his misguided followers, McCarthy alleged, had failed there, and the administration should allow General Douglas MacArthur's forces to attack the Red Chinese wherever appropriate, give the Nationalists military equipment for guerrilla attacks on the mainland, allow Chiang to move against Mao, blockade Chinese ports with the Seventh Fleet, provide Western Europe with military capabilities, and encourage the free nations to withdraw recognition of Communist China. McCarthy concluded that the United States had been betrayed, and that situation had to be remedied.[29]

Nixon did not send any written recommendations, but within a week of McCarthy's address, McCarthy, Drew Pearson, and Nixon were guests of Ginnie Steinman, a local socialite, at the exclusive Sulgrave Club in Washington for dinner. McCarthy's and the columnist's mutual distaste had deepened since McCarthy's Wheeling speech, which attacked Dean Acheson, a Pearson friend, and was full of indiscriminate accusations of federal employees being Communists. Pearson began maligning the senator with increasing frequency in his column, and McCarthy eventually replied to Pearson with his own vicious speech on the Senate floor. When they confronted each other at the end of the party in the men's cloakroom, an altercation ensued. McCarthy said that Pearson threatened that if he (McCarthy) spoke against him, then the reporter would "get" him. McCarthy immediately "slapped him in the face. I slapped him hard."

Pearson denied any injury, offering this blow-by-blow description: McCarthy had kicked him "twice in the groin. . . . As usual he hit below the belt. But his pugilistic powers are about as ineffective as his Senate speeches. I was not hurt." The reporter added that he did not retaliate since so many women were present.[30]

Nixon inadvertently happened into the cloakroom while the two men were fighting and separated them. The fight was brief, but quickly became legendary. Joe Holt, the energetic worker in the California senatorial campaign, wrote his candidate: "Wish you had slugged Drew

Pearson for me!" Perry jokingly informed his pupil that the Lions Club of Whittier was so angry at the publicity given to this bout that it "almost sent you a letter of Censure" because Nixon should not have interfered and "should not have shown your Quaker training in stopping the fight!"

Many conservatives wanted McCarthy and Nixon to work closer together. Whittaker Chambers, a month after the bout, wanted Nixon to say hello to McCarthy: "He, for one, knows that you must go forward. You can't stand still, you won't go back—in war, in politics." In spite of this encouragement, however, Nixon maintained his distance, recognizing McCarthy's recklessness.[31]

Yet Nixon had no intention of attacking McCarthy either, since the latter supported the general anti-Communist crusade. By the end of January 1951, Nixon spoke before several audiences and called for an inquiry into government loyalty and internal security programs. Some critics claimed that McCarthy had been irresponsible with his accusations of Red infiltration in the State Department, while others blamed the administration for creating a crisis in confidence. In either eventuality, the United States had to be strong both at home and abroad to halt the spread of international communism.

Running through many of Nixon's lectures were references to the Communist menace and the urgency of alerting citizens to that danger. The senator reminded listeners at the noon session of the U.S. Chamber of Commerce, on May 1, that since the end of World War II, the Russians had absorbed over eight major governments and millions of people. According to the FBI, he noted, the United States had forty-three thousand active members of the Communist Party. In order to prevent revolts, the nation had to remain strong to stop espionage agents like Hiss. To accomplish this objective, Nixon asked for more HUAC funding for "rooting out and exposing the potential 5th columns at home."[32]

For the most part, Nixon dismissed many of McCarthy's outlandish charges about Communist penetration in the State Department, but the junior senator from California did say, on March 20, that he hoped that the Wisconsin senator's allegations would have a "good thorough nonpartisan investigation." However, Nixon recognized the divisiveness that McCarthy was precipitating. That winter, for example, Charlie Cooper, a Whittier friend who was a Democrat and a Nixon supporter, identified McCarthy as "the most dangerous senator since Huey Long." On October 25, when asked about inviting McCarthy to speak, Nixon hedged, agreeing that McCarthy was "a big drawing card and although he is admittedly a controversial figure at the present time, from all reports he is a very effective speaker." At the end of January 1952, in a poll ranking senators, fifty leading American political scientists placed Paul Douglas, Democrat of Illinois, first, and the Wisconsin senator last, at ninety-fifth; Nixon, who had been in that august body for a year, was seventy-first.[33]

Without question, Nixon comprehended the double-edged sword that McCarthy wielded. McCarthy blustered against the Communist menace in the State Department, but he had few facts, exaggerated them, or even lied to bolster unfounded allegations. Nixon was too circumspect to follow the Wisconsin senator's lead blindly. Instead, he agreed with some of the general accusations that McCarthy outlined and called for investigations. However, Nixon himself never stood close enough to McCarthy to be spattered by his mud. He was savvy enough to maintain a safe distance in public and on the Senate floor.

As the upcoming 82nd Congress began its deliberations, according to the San Francisco Chronicle, it would be Democratic in name only; the Senate had forty-seven Republicans and forty-nine Democrats and the administration's opponents really controlled that body. The GOP had to cooperate with Truman and not abuse its gains: "Clearly the people are seeking new leadership, but they will not accept it unqualifiedly until it can demonstrate its dynamic purpose." The country had drifted from the Fair Deal toward the center, and initiatives like socialized medicine, the Brannan Plan for farmers, and repeal of the Taft-Hartley Act were no longer attainable.[34]

Nixon disapproved of Truman's budget message because it included funds for Fair Deal programs in spite of his State of the Union message, in which the president pledged to cut nonessential spending. One of Nixon's first votes was against extending rent control and allowing local decontrol as authorized by the Los Angeles City Council. He became a member of the Committee on Labor and Public Welfare where he favored an amendment to the Taft-Hartley Act to eliminate the union shop election requirement and opposed unions' coercion of their members about fines and other punitive measures due to the failure to participate in political activities or to give money for a designated candidate's campaign.[35]

He consistently emphasized the need to cut nondefense federal spending to a minimum in order to stop inflation. "Once our productive power is destroyed," he feared, "all will be lost." He stressed "pay-as-you-go basis" for the defense programs. "Whether we like it or not,"

Nixon reasoned, "that means high taxes until the defense appropriations can eventually be reduced."[36]

Although he generally disapproved of price and wage controls, Nixon was one of the first to demand them as necessary under wartime conditions, and supported the Defense Production Act with its price control provisions that allowed an administrator to roll back certain increases. If Truman had properly enforced these articles, he felt, they would have stopped inflation and encouraged expanded production. Nixon reluctantly voted to extend this legislation because the enormous military budget and inflationary forces would "be set in motion which can not be controlled without some action on the price and wage control front." This was not the first time that his lack of an economic background would yield to the temptation to assert nonexistent control over such basic market processes.[37]

In other ways, he preferred free markets. He voted against licensing of all businesses, federal building and operation of new plants, rent controls on business establishments, and price rollbacks. He worried about the effect of the excess profits taxes on small, growing corporations and pledged to give those firms needed relief. On infrequent occasions, he increased the civil service umbrella, preferring to place Post Office employees under federal guidelines rather than continue political patronage.[38]

Nixon opposed programs that he feared bordered on socialism like proposals for subsidized medical schools. He voted against the administration's Brannan Plan, a plan to assist agriculture with farm subsidies, but supported the current agricultural parity program because its abrupt elimination would be too drastic. When an appropriation bill was presented that ended some "excessive subsidy payments and food destruction programs," he would back that objective, but he was wary of any massive overhaul.[39]

Certain rights belonged to the states, such as voting against the federal government for denying assistance to those states that made welfare recipients' names public. He voted in favor of "the quitclaim bill to renounce any interests of the Federal government in the tidelands," but Truman vetoed it, arguing national defense required federal ownership and operation. Finally and most critically, Nixon devoted considerable attention to the Colorado River project, which gave water rights to Arizona that California claimed. Even though the Democratic majority in the Senate passed the bill, Nixon opposed it as "extravagant and infeasible," and he pronounced to a constituent, "you can be sure that our fight against it will be continued."[40]

Nixon felt deeply about suspending the statute of limitations for all offenses involving official duties of congressmen and government employees while working in the federal bureaucracy. That summer he introduced a bill to revise existing laws that dealt with breaches of the public trust that expired three years from the date of the offense's commission. Since these public servants concealed their cupidity, he hoped that this might be a deterrent. Himself a veteran who used his housing benefits, he called on the Veterans Administration "to assist veterans in their efforts to purchase homes." If a veteran had accumulated "enough money for a substantial part of a normal down payment, he by all means should be assisted in easy term financing for the balance of such payment."[41]

Economic pressures to raise salaries at the height of the Korean War plagued Congress. When mail carriers demanded a raise, Nixon refused to commit to an increase until he was convinced that the budget could absorb a hike. After the House Committee on Banking and Currency rejected the administration's defense housing bill and forced Truman to make significant changes in it, the senator confidently stated that "the days when the Administration could send down any kind of a bill on housing, medicine or other welfare programs and get it rubber-stamped are gone."[42]

One option for expanding social programs that he favored was charitable giving. He wished to increase the incentives for these kinds of gifts rather than limit them, "because I think in the end it would pay off real dividends, both monetary and otherwise." Private institutions should be given a larger role in both educational and welfare programs, and the federal government should expend less for those purposes.[43]

Nixon approved of international cooperation. "While I believe that during these times the free nations must maintain adequate systems of collective military security, I have long felt that we have not placed enough emphasis upon other methods which might prove effective in avoiding armed conflict." He called on the United States to maintain its UN membership. Even though that organization had disappointed many, "the United Nations should be strengthened rather than scuttled." As senator, he moved to expand the Voice of America to promote democracy, for it had to win the ideological war over communism. To encourage this, he co-sponsored an amendment to raise the government radio program appropriation from $63 million to $85 million.[44]

Nixon recognized the importance of lowering trade barriers, but thought that the State Department had not given "adequate protection to American industries which are in competition with industries in foreign countries" under the reciprocal trade agreements program. He encouraged international economic intercourse to obtain repayment on the American funds loaned abroad, but he hoped the diplomatic negotiators would seriously consider the adverse consequences to domestic business.[45]

Despite his opposition to Universal Military Training during his House tenure, he now changed that position, favoring some type of program to have combat-ready military forces so that the United States would never again be surprised. The Korean conflict had demonstrated America's inadequacies without sufficient numbers of trained soldiers who could resist enemy aggression. While compulsory military training was unpopular, the current bill provided for "constant maintenance of a trained reserve of military personnel."[46]

Nixon, as a member of the subcommittee on health of the labor and public welfare committee, was invited to be an American delegate to the Fourth World Health Organization (WHO) Assembly in Geneva, Switzerland, which met from May 6 through 26. Though unable to leave Washington until May 11, he took off on his first trans-Atlantic flight on Saturday, attended the conference for four days, and was sufficiently impressed to vote to restore the UN special agencies appropriations, which the House had cut. Nixon still opposed American support for more than one-third of the UN budget, but felt that the WHO reduction was "unwise because it in effect would have required our representatives abroad to abrogate commitments for the budget of the United Nations agencies which had previously been agreed upon."[47]

Along with the political debates on Capitol Hill, Nixon faced growing, divisive factionalism at Whittier College. He had resented some Quakers at his alma mater who had supported Douglas. William Jones, a Congregationalist, president of the college since 1944, led the liberals there, and during the debate over Universal Military Training he spoke out against it. Perry championed the conservatives on campus, differing from his co-religionists by calling for efficiency in government to avoid national bankruptcy and believing that every American should be drafted. Even conscientious objectors should go into the medical corps. If the Korean conflict lasted five or ten years, "under the old scheme we will have no one left but the incompetents and those of poor health."[48]

Tom Bewley knew that college administrators and their supporters were aware that Nixon felt that these individuals had been hostile toward his anti-Communist crusade and had tried to impede his 1950 campaign by withholding alumni lists during the election. Even though Jones and other trustees had made donations to Nixon's committee, Bewley informed them that the congressman was so hurt by their actions that he did not wish to speak on campus. To Nixon, Bewley admitted that the present administration had made some errors, but he thought Nixon should reconsider this decision, demonstrating that he was "much bigger than any petty differences of the administration"; this would place him in a position to exercise "some influence in the coming days."[49]

Nixon relented and served as master of ceremonies at the Whittier College Golden Anniversary Development Fund dinner celebration, which was held at the Ambassador Hotel in Los Angeles on the last day of March, to raise money to construct new buildings and improve existing ones. Nixon had John Foster Dulles speak on "Peace in the Pacific," which the CBS network carried as a major foreign policy statement over 197 of its radio stations. Dulles outlined the terms of the Japanese peace treaty. Rather than a harsh agreement, in which the victor subjugated the vanquished, this one restored Japan to the international community as a sovereign nation, albeit without any significant military force. Dulles stressed that the main goal of the treaty was to have the Japanese "live with others as good neighbors." The war in the Pacific that began at Pearl Harbor was over, but Dulles warned his audience that Korea still posed a threat to Asian as well as American security.[50]

Even though the event raised a great deal of money and won additional prestige for the college, shortly after the banquet, President Jones announced his resignation. Nixon urged the trustees to select Dr. Paul Smith, who was the senator's favorite teacher and a product of the University of Wisconsin where he accepted Wilsonian progressism. The senator even asked Perry to remain on the college board to make his choice known. By the end of May, Smith had become president, pleasing Nixon, who wired and phoned his congratulations. Nixon and Perry pledged their active support.[51]

Born in 1897, Smith had been raised on a farm north of Richmond, Indiana, graduated from Earlham College in 1919, and completed his doctorate in history at the University of Wisconsin eight years later. By that time, he already was serving at Whittier College as chairman of the department of history and political science, and as both a teacher and an administrator he scored high marks. He was the first president drawn from the faculty, and as the eighth president of the college, he faced a budget crunch caused by the war and a serious drop in enrollment. Still, Perry and Nixon were hopeful that Smith's selection would bring older college alumni back to campus and initiate a campus atmosphere more to their liking.[52]

Nixon, to Perry, was critical of Whittier's recent history, believing that "some of our Quaker friends have had a tendency to confuse true tolerance with appeasement. What we have to recognize is that if we want real peace, a policy of appeasement is one that under no circumstances should be adopted." When the chairman of the American Friends Service Committee (AFSC) in Whittier, R. L. Warren, asked about Nixon's stance on Universal Military Training, the senator replied that "an adequate pool of men trained for combat and available for duty on short notice" was essential during those troubled times. He favored a program for all able-bodied youth to receive military training rather than the Selective Service Act, opposed a permanent military training system, and wanted a discontinuance clause when international conditions improved.[53]

Further friction centered on the seventeenth annual Institute of International Relations meeting, which the AFSC sponsored for the purpose of giving "expression to varying points of view—in keeping with the Town Meeting tradition which is so fundamental to our democratic processes." Perry did not accept that mission and asked Congressman Donald Jackson, who had replaced Nixon on HUAC, to have the speakers' list examined for their political leanings. Several names came back as having close Communist connections. When the AFSC denied these allegations, Perry exploded. Even though disagreeing with total pacifism, he had originally supported the committee, but now it was "under the influence and infiltration of Left-wingers." He was worried: "As far as the Quakers are concerned, I think they have been *duped* and *mislead*," and the institute harbored "a bunch of *Socialists* and *Left-wingers*." He and other Quakers were trying to get the conference moved off campus.[54]

Congressmen Hillings and Jackson, at Nixon's instigation, decided to help Perry expose the speakers who belonged to or were associated with Communist-front organizations. Both Republicans spoke on the House floor about the institute and mentioned Maynard Kreuger, a professor of economics at the University of Chicago and vice president of the American Federation of Teachers, who ran the vice president alongside Norman Thomas on the Socialist Party slate and Henry Cadbury, Hollis Professor of New Testament at Harvard University and AFSC's chairman, who had no Red attachments. After these remarks, Jackson learned that the institute would probably move off campus, which delighted him. Nixon wished for "a growing realization of the present danger among members of the Quaker faith. Certainly there is among those members of Congress who were born and reared in the Quaker tradition. Peace is an objective which is sought by all of us, but many of us are unwilling to accept a peace which we are convinced means ultimate slavery." The new president disappointed Perry by encouraging the unhampered exchange of ideas, but he was clearly a Nixon admirer, thinking so highly of his godson that even before reaching the presidency Smith had moved to endow a Richard M. Nixon chair.[55]

Nixon concentrated most of his attention in 1951 on international affairs and what would become known as the "Great Debate." By the time of his election, the new senator was visiting more frequently with Herbert Hoover, who invited Nixon to his New York apartment in the Waldorf-Astoria Hotel. Before that meeting occurred, Hoover, on December 20, 1950, delivered a major address on television, attacking the foundation of the administration's foreign policy. Though Truman labeled the speech isolationist, that was an exaggeration. What Hoover proposed was, first, defending the Americas by securing the Atlantic and Pacific Oceans; furthermore, he did not want to send American troops to Europe and Asia, and thereby invite another Korea. Europeans had to defend themselves and build their strength against Soviet aggression rather than totally depend on the United States.[56]

Almost immediately after Hoover's address, over a hundred wires of approval reached Nixon. Scheduled to leave for New York shortly, the senator hoped to see Hoover and added that "your comments will have an excellent effect in developing a more realistic approach to the critical problems we face today." The former president was "indeed heartened by your support. At least we have the animals stirred up!"[57]

Nixon agreed that many were moved to action and believed that any future American assistance should be conditioned on those nations' willingness to help themselves. Constructive debate over U.S. actions in foreign affairs was essential "to reach definitive and effective decisions that will safeguard the nation, our people and our way of life." Due to the administration's failures abroad, the country was placed in a "desperate position," and he wanted to remove those responsible for those mistakes and replace them with "individuals who will devote themselves to the task of developing a new, consistent and realistic policy, one which will place the security of the United States above all other considerations."[58]

Senator Taft quickly followed Hoover, emphasizing that America's allies had to protect themselves and the democracies had to win the battle of ideologies in which the United States united the non-Communist nations. Attention to preventing the Communist menace at home was a direct corollary to international initiatives. Government at every level had "the right to protect itself by aggressive and affirmative action against the clear and present danger presented by the world communist movement."[59]

Nixon listened carefully to both Hoover's and Taft's addresses, and even though he did not agree entirely with them, he thought that "neither of the speakers can properly be called 'isolationists' for the positions they have taken." America had to expand its military capabilities because the USSR might do so. The United States probably would not reach the Soviet Union's troop level, and he had not been persuaded that the administration should commit massive military forces to Western Europe, but he did realize that Acheson and other foreign policy leaders "should be replaced by men whose judgment will have the confidence of the American people." Since Truman refused to contemplate these changes or take positive actions in Asia, senators from both parties were demanding that the president receive congressional approval before sending more American soldiers to Europe, and any further military and economic assistance would be predicated on those nations' willingness to contribute to their military revival.[60]

He commended a radio broadcast which Congressman John F. Kennedy gave after a five-week European tour commencing at the end of 1950 to examine Western European conditions in the face of Soviet expansion. JFK had traveled to three NATO countries: Great Britain, France, and Italy; he also visited Yugoslavia, Spain, and Italy. His conclusion was that the Continent had not made enough sacrifices to protect itself from attack and needed to do more. "We can and will survive despite Europe," he stressed, "but with her it will be that much easier. But Europe must know . . . that freedom is born and held only by deep sacrifice." Nixon had talked to others who had gone there to get firsthand impressions and "thought Jack Kennedy's report was one of the clearest and most objective which has been made up to this time."[61]

Nixon spoke out regularly across the United States on the "Great Debate." Addressing the Beacon Society of Boston, a group of New England industrial and business leaders on Saturday, January 6, 1951, at the Algonquin Club, Nixon asserted that American policy in Asia had failed and was shaky in Europe. The United States needed new leadership and had to decide whether to stay in or get out of Korea. Since there were political considerations, the administration should consider applying sanctions, even bombing China, and increasing propaganda. As for Europe, American policies had succeeded economically but failed militarily. One audience member praised the speech, referring to Nixon as the "whiteman's hope." His call for consideration of bombing was hotheaded, but mirrored many of his colleagues. After further debate, Nixon backed off of this idea.[62] A day later, he spoke to the Washington, D.C., League of Republican Women at the Mayflower Hotel, announcing that he would praise Acheson when right and criticize him when he was wrong. Nixon believed that the secretary was loyal, but had implemented questionable policies. Nixon rejected isolationism, but now proposed an American military *withdrawal* from Korea, followed by economic sanctions against the Red Chinese. In its place, the United Nations needed to take a leadership role.[63]

Many citizens supported Herbert Hoover's call for a shared responsibility from European and Asian allies. "The time has come," Nixon declared, "when either the United Nations should recognize the obvious fact of Chinese Communist aggression and take effective action to meet it, or the United States should withdraw its troops from Korea." As for the specter of isolationism, Nixon privately wrote that he ignored it, and instead, decided to propose "developing a constructive program of our own, rather than by directly attacking those who advocate the isolationist position."[64]

Nixon used a Lincoln Day event in mid-February to test themes and assess audience reactions. The GOP, he said, had to provide new leadership with better solutions to domestic and international problems. The United States had to apply efficiency to government programs. If this did not occur, Americans might win the war but lose economically. In addition, the administration had allowed Communists to outsell democracy. "Our task," Nixon pronounced, was "to prove to people everywhere on both sides of the iron curtain that the hope of the world today does not lie in turning toward dictatorship of any type but that it lies in the development of a strong, free and intelligent democracy." He again shifted his Korea position, stating that the rearmament of Western Europe and the continuation of the Korean War were equally essential to the future of American security. He also demanded a halt to Russian expansionism and called for an economic blockade of Red China.[65]

Many of Nixon's statements dealing with foreign policy seemed inconsistent. In reality, he was reflecting the confusion within his party and his own mind. He recognized the need for the Great Debate to decide on the direction of American foreign affairs, and this dialogue meant that many different approaches needed to be articulated and discussed. Sometimes he blustered; other times he understated his case. But throughout the process, he was clarifying the basis of his own internationalism.

Spring was an attractive period to be in the capital, and as Nixon pointed out, this was "the one time in the year when Washington is really fit to live in!" On Monday, April 2, both Nixon and Knowland were in the Senate chamber due to the tense international situation and important legislation about to be proposed. A resolution on sending American troops to Europe would be raised. Even though a vote might not come for two more days, if either of them were not in their seat, they "would be subject to heavy criticism." The junior senator was also getting ready to end his period of self-imposed silence; his "period of apprenticeship" was about over, "and you probably will be hearing from me from time to time in the future on current issues." As for the senior senator and many of his GOP colleagues, they were miffed that the president had not consulted them over the Korean War and other foreign policy matters.[66]

Soldiers stationed in Korea kept Nixon informed about battlefield conditions. Arthur Paik, a friend of the family who lived in Whittier, was a sergeant and described the inflation at the PX where it rationed items in short supply so that black marketeers could not make enormous profits. Charles Cooper, a lieutenant commander on the front line, also sent his observations.[67]

Stationed in the South Pacific during World War II, Nixon knew about the legendary leadership capabilities of General MacArthur and approved of his appointment to lead UN forces in Korea, but the senator had no idea of the irreconcilable differences fomenting between the White House and MacArthur. The general called for an expansion to mainland China, which the president and the Joint Chiefs of Staff rejected. As MacArthur grew more insubordinate, the president became convinced that he had to be replaced; finally, MacArthur's behavior became so antagonistic to the administration's objectives that Truman abruptly fired him.

The unexpected announcement on April 10 reverberated in the Senate—as in the rest of the nation—with demands for the president's impeachment. For three days Nixon received between seven thousand to nine thousand wires and hundreds of thousands of letters in protest. The day immediately following the news, Senator Robert Kerr, Democrat from Oklahoma, argued for Truman's limited war over MacArthur's proposed expansion into Red China. Nixon chose this moment, with the backing of many Republican senators, to make his maiden address, asking why the general was fired and whether his recommendations were sounder than the failed Asian policies of the administration that resulted in the birth of Red China. To Nixon, without Chinese encouragement, the North Koreans would never have attacked.[68]

Nixon asserted that the Communists had done a "hatchet job" on MacArthur. "If any group in this Nation is happy today over the action of the President," the senator proclaimed, "the Communists and the stooges for the Communists are happy, because the President has given them exactly what they have been after—General MacArthur's scalp." Nixon and many other Republicans now approved of the general's position for winning the war by attacking the Red Chinese. If the United States allowed it to grow in strength, mainland China would ultimately consume all of East Asia. Nixon foresaw dire consequences: "once Asia falls, war becomes inevitable so far as the United States is concerned, and it will be a war which we will eventually lose, because the odds in manpower and the odds in resources will be irrevocably on the other side."[69]

Nixon argued for stopping all trade with Communist China, bombing enemy bases across the Yalu River, receiving significant assistance from the United Nations, and permitting the Chinese Nationalists on Formosa as well as guerrilla forces on the mainland to assist in the victory. At the end of his remarks, the galleries applauded him, and the presiding officer had to threaten to clear the spectators who were cheering. Pat Nixon, who watched, commented: "Dick spoke very sensibally [sic] about the matter being beyond party politics, etc., and the galleries clapped while [Vice President] Barkley rapped for order in a most irritated fashion."[70]

Nixon followed up his statement with a press release. Truman claimed to have fired MacArthur for disobeying orders, while the general's real crime was proposing a military solution by taking the fight to mainland China. The president had tried to frame the debate as a limited war versus a world war, but that was not the question. The major decision was whether the president was going to continue the status quo or allow the military commanders in the field to win the war. Nixon wanted to find out from Truman how he expected to be victorious without appeasing the Red Chinese. Chotiner made certain that, within an hour of his office receiving Nixon's declaration, the media had it.[71]

The senator continued his verbal assault on the administration at the National Metal Trades Association in Chicago on April 18, calling Truman's reaction to the general's arrival in the United States "a gross insult to General MacArthur and to the American people." Rather than fire him, Nixon said that the president should have removed Acheson, for he personified the failure of the administration's Asian policies. During the last three wars, the United States had had Democratic presidents, an unenviable record for maintaining the peace. Nixon reiterated MacArthur's outline for ending the war with honor, and reminded his listeners that 90 percent of the soldiers in Korea were Americans. By the next day, Nixon returned to the Capitol to hear MacArthur's historic address to a joint session of Congress; if possible, he admired MacArthur even more after that poignant appearance.

The avalanche of mail continued to pour in, supporting Nixon and MacArthur. Pat Nixon "was impressed into a 14 hour non-paying job" when the office received approximately 6,000 telegrams and 30,000 letters. Dick Powell, who had volunteered in the 1950 campaign, wrote: "We've very proud of you out here [in Hollywood], Richard—keep up the good work. I'll be very happy to work with you at any time on anything so just feel free to call on me for any little assistance I am able to give." Raymond Cramer, the new pastor of the East Whittier Friends Church where Dick and his family prayed, approved. "We have been shocked and dismayed at the despicable manner in which our President has desecrated his high office, stooping to personal animosity and revenge in the manner in which he has handled the MacArthur situation." The pastor demanded Acheson's removal: "While we as Friends are committed to a policy of peaceful settlement of our difficulties, we also feel that where there is a disease, the only cure is to reach the source of the infection and deal with it in a way which will open the door to recovery."[72]

On May 1, Nixon spoke to a national radio audience over America's Town Meeting of the Air in Toledo, Ohio, several months after truce talks had begun, asserting that the United States had three options in Korea: leave; win on the battlefield; or political settlement. The senator preferred victory, but the firing of MacArthur squelched that. Despite that impossibility, Nixon repeated the general's steps for a successful conclusion and reminded his radio audience: "the way to end the war in Asia is to win the war in Korea." Senator John Sparkman, Democrat from Alabama, answered for the administration, stressing that the general was ousted for refusing to obey orders. Nixon framed the issue in terms of appeasement, while Sparkman outlined the debate as civilian versus military control of government. The wide gulf between the two men did not provide any room for compromise.[73]

During MacArthur's congressional testimony in early May, Nixon watched and marveled how admirably the general had done in the three days of hearings; he only wished that the proceedings could have been televised. Nixon later recalled that MacArthur's testimony was "the greatest performance before a Congressional committee that I have ever seen. He answered questions without referring to files or experts and took the very best cross examination that the Administration could throw at him without ever once becoming involved in a major contradiction." Afterwards, the senator introduced a resolution deploring MacArthur's removal. It went nowhere, but reflected many Americans' disappointment.[74]

By the second week of May, Nixon again called for the bombing of Chinese bases, if the Reds continued to supply the North Koreans; in addition, he urged that the United States should consider a possible naval blockade as well as air reconnaissance missions over the mainland. At the end of World War II, the United States had "9 to 1 in our [democracies'] favor, but today they [Communists] are 5 to 3 against us."[75]

On the last day of May, seventy-five thousand listeners who tuned in to Fulton Lewis's broadcast responded to a radio poll designed by Nixon. The conservative audience overwhelmingly disapproved of the administration:

Would you vote for Truman today? Nixon asked; 73,632 said no and only 1,510 yes.

Would you have MacArthur report to Congress? 72,840 yes and 2,679 no.[76]

Nixon remained heavily booked with appearances throughout the latter half of May and into the early part of June. At the request of Senator Everett Dirksen, Republican from Illinois, he presented the commencement address and received his first honorary degree from Bradley University in Peoria on the 11th. Three days later, he addressed the fifty-second convention of the National Association of Retail Grocers in Chicago, repeating his themes concerning State Department confusion, the need for victory in Korea, and the failure of America's Asian policies. In another week, he spoke before the Iowa Manufacturers Association, using MacArthur's firing to enumerate the growing number of Truman's misdeeds.[77]

By the middle of summer, the war had stalemated at the 38th parallel. The United Nations and the North Koreans had negotiated a cease-fire and armistice talks began. Nixon hoped that these signaled peace, but most politicians in the capital viewed the talks "with a considerable amount of skepticism." Everyone wished for peace, but did not believe that "the Commies are really going to leave." This was a period when prayers were necessary, and the senator looked toward God for guidance. Still, even with the truce, America should not "drop our guard, either at home or abroad."[78]

Communism and Korea had evolved into two major issues that the Republican Party would use in the 1952 presidential campaign to defeat the Democrats. Throughout his brief tenure in the Senate, Nixon addressed both themes. Although many tried to connect Nixon's fight against Soviet expansionism with the antics of Joe McCarthy, that linkage never stuck. Even though Nixon's enemies continually lumped him with the Wisconsin senator, they had little in common, being worlds apart in temperament and intelligence. McCarthy lived in his own world—a world filled with imaginary images that caught the public's fancy. His success was directly connected to the frustration of a superpower unable to solve complex international tension. Nixon had no easy answers, only complicated ones.

Nixon devoted a considerable amount of time to foreign affairs. The Great Debate, as Nixon perceived it, had grown from midwestern Republican traditions. Hoover and Taft symbolized those who objected to the Truman administration sending American soldiers around the globe without restrictions, forcing the United States to defend Western Europe when it needed to protect itself. The White House responded that such thoughts were malevolent because this was a return to isolationism. It was not; but it *was* less active than Nixon chose to be.

In Korea, the White House had entered into a righteous fight, but without articulating clear goals at the start or later on. When Chinese volunteers smashed through UN lines and crushed any dream of bringing American troops home, disillusionment began to fester. The unexpected firing of General MacArthur allowed disenchantment to spill out onto the American political stage. Nixon believed that with his departure, this "police action" no longer was a patriotic war, but part of the bickering between the two political parties.

Truman, for one, grew even more extreme in his partisanship. The champion of the Fair Deal had no opportunity to enact his domestic imperatives until he ended the Korean fighting. Under these trying conditions, he needed cooperation to push through his programs, but he refused to build a consensus with the Republicans. And with the Democratic majority holding a bare edge, 1951–52 was bound to be an unpopular period. On the other side, the GOP did little to muzzle Joseph McCarthy, who constantly embarrassed the administration.

Nixon stepped into the Senate when his activist anticommunism was not built on consensus; it had emerged in the midst of the acrimonious shouting from Truman down Pennsylvania Avenue and McCarthy up on Capitol Hill. What both men personified made for great press coverage, but did little to reach a compromise. The deep dissension between the two national parties over philosophical communism and Russian appeasement had existed since the advent of the New Deal. The Red menace took on new meaning with communism, as magnified by the domestic espionage of Alger Hiss, and the stalemate in Korea, taken to the zenith in talk about Truman's impeachment with the abrupt firing of Douglas MacArthur.

These deeply divisive differences between Democrats and Republicans were not settled by compromise because each side saw its cause as righteous. Truman crusaded to stop the spread of communism by sending troops to Southeast Asia and pushing back the North Koreans. He would not go further. Many in the GOP argued that this was inadequate. The Democrats had already "lost" mainland China to the Reds and that affliction was spreading around the globe. Herbert Hoover's and Robert Taft's roles in the Great Debate were only symptoms of how to face the greater danger of how and when the free world would confront Stalin. Even the heart of democracy, the United States, had been penetrated by Communist infiltrators.

Nixon reflected these titanic struggles facing America. No longer was he willing to seek an rapprochement with the administration, for it was wrong. His cure was new leadership. No longer would he accept White House rationale over how to deal with international communism. Truman had gone into Korea with no strategy for victory and had fired MacArthur, the military symbol of any hope for triumph. Nixon reacted with anguish, as did most of his GOP colleagues. Yet Nixon expressed his disappointment eloquently through a multitude of speeches to the Republican faithful across America. By the time of the GOP presidential nominating convention, he had helped to present communism and Korea as referendums that Americans would accept or reject at the polls. To Nixon, the Democrats had to defend their failures. On an up or down vote, they would lose. No compromise was possible. To Nixon the political cheerleader, the Republicans had to win to preserve the Union.

# Chapter 18

# CORRUPTION IN THE
# HIGHEST PLACES

When Harry Truman had been a senator, he won a reputation for fighting waste and wrongdoing in the negotiation of defense contracts during World War II. Scandal, however, plagued his presidency. As a product of Missouri machine politics and Tom Pendergast's boss system, Truman was intimately involved in cronyism. As Alonzo Hamby pointed out in his biography of the president, "Truman, displaying an ill-formed sense of public relations, was not just inept in dealing with such charges; he behaved so willfully as to seem almost a conscious co-conspirator with his enemies."[1]

Some appointments, such as that of Omar Bradley to head the Veterans Administration, were above reproach; but others proved embarrassing. Edwin Pauley, a Democratic crony, had his nomination as undersecretary of the navy withdrawn for failure to divulge connections with oil interests. The president's staunch commitment to such individuals, according to historian Andrew Dunar in the only scholarly study of the Truman scandals, "seemed to confirm the notion that Truman had instituted government by crony, practicing Pendergast politics on a national scale."[2]

Terms like "fixer," "expediter," "five percenter," and "influence peddler" connoted those who offered favors at a price to win government contracts, procure federal loans, or have a beneficial review of tax returns. Some had ready access to the Oval Office, and the greatest test of Truman's unswerving loyalty was Harry Vaughan. They had met in 1917, when they both were artillery officers, and became lifelong friends.

Vaughan served as treasurer for Truman's 1940 senatorial campaign, became his executive assistant, was promoted to military aide to the vice president and then to the president. Unfortunately for Vaughan, he was not savvy politically, but was fiercely loyal and a wonderful raconteur. His problems resulted from poor judgment and from choosing associates who used him; but Truman suffered from Vaughan's indiscretions.

During the summer of 1949, Vaughan provided a feeding frenzy for the national press corps. The Senate subcommittee on Expenditures in the Executive Departments investigated his relationships to many individuals, including John Maragon, an "influence peddler," who eventually went to federal prison for perjuring himself before a Senate committee. Mundt and McCarthy, along with the committee's chief counsel William Rogers, led an examination of Vaughan that ultimately cleared him of allegations that he was crooked. However, the committee's antagonism toward Vaughan almost guaranteed that Truman would stand behind his friend and call the investigation a partisan assault.[3]

As the national media zoomed in on those who surrounded the president and had profited from that association, Nixon joined the bandwagon. Joseph Major, for example, who worked for the Government Service Agency (GSA) as a purchasing agent, had served with the president in World War I and was close to Vaughan. Attacked as another "influence peddler," Major defended his purchases from associates by declaring that he was only assisting them. Criminality, as Nixon pointed out, was not charged, but Major's actions demonstrated "a lack of understanding as to what the real issue is—not whether what he did is legal, but whether it is morally right." Federal agencies that dispensed large sums of money and made Democratic insiders wealthy were symbols of administration graft.[4]

Other sensational senatorial inquiries had already shaken the administration. Estes Kefauver's special committee to investigate organized crime in interstate commerce started to probe racketeering early in 1950. After careful preparation, the committee held well-publicized hearings in many major cities examining the role of organized crime in those localities. When he had completed testimony in Florida concerning the mob, politicians, and money, Kefauver used television to expose Mafia operations in Chicago. Kansas City was another stop and an indirect slap at the president's home state, where the committee linked Democratic politicians to local gangsters.

Truman resented these urban-oriented investigations that damaged his party more than the rural-based GOP and doubted Kefauver's political sagacity as well as his party loyalty. But once the senator showcased mobsters on national television during late January 1951, his committee blossomed into an overnight sensation. Millions watched Kefauver question gangster Frank Costello on his connections to Tammany Hall, the Democratic club that influenced New York City patronage; the committee confronted the former mayor and current ambassador to Mexico, William O'Dwyer, on why he had not taken aggressive action against the mob and even impeded promising investigations. O'Dwyer had no satisfactory answers, but Truman retained him as ambassador. Possibly afraid of prosecution, O'Dwyer remained in voluntary exile until 1960. At the conclusion of the hearings that spring, Kefauver emerged as a national celebrity. He also guaranteed Truman's and the big-city Democratic bosses' antipathy to any aspirations that Kefauver had for the presidency.[5]

Senator J. William Fulbright, Democrat from Arkansas who chaired a subcommittee of the Senate Committee on Banking and Currency, felt that the Reconstruction Finance Corporation (RFC) was making loans to profit those inside the administration and started a probe of RFC loans early in 1950. His two main subjects of influence peddling were E. Merl Young, whose family came from Missouri and was close to Truman's, and Donald Dawson, a graduate of the University of Missouri, who had campaigned for Truman in each of his campaigns and had become director of personnel and chief dispenser of patronage at the White House in 1947.

The committee recommended restructuring the RFC, but Truman refused. Fulbright, on February 2, 1951, then released a report, "Study of the Reconstruction Finance Corporation: Favoritism and Influence," which accused the corporation of acting against the public interest by succumbing to political pressure and implying that the administration had refused to stop this unsavory behavior. Truman responded with his accustomed pugnacity by calling the report "asinine," an extraordinarily harsh public characterization, and accusing Fulbright of refusing to see him about this information. The senator called the president a liar and released damaging testimony about the activities of Dawson, Young, and others. Although Truman eventually capitulated by reorganizing the RFC according to senatorial guidelines, Fulbright, as much as any of Truman's political adversaries, had tarnished the presidency, and the White House never forgot it.[6]

During the Fulbright inquiry, the committee caused a national outcry when it learned that Young had given his wife, Lauretta, a White House stenographer, a $9,540 natural royal pastel mink coat as a gift from Joseph Rosenbaum, an attorney for a company that had received an RFC loan, which Young had helped to obtain. Young would eventually serve time in prison for perjury, and mink coats became symbols of high-level government corruption.[7]

Reaching several million readers toward the end of May, an article entitled "The Scandalous Years," by Fletcher Knebel and Jack Wilson in *Look* magazine, listed a wide variety of cronyism and criminal activity within the federal bureaucracy. The authors began: "Political morality in Washington has sunk to the lowest depth in a quarter of a century." Since Truman had assumed the presidency in 1945, four White House staffers had been implicated in "undercover deals"; two presidential friends had been convicted of fraud and a third had been indicted; fourteen high federal officials had been exposed as influence peddlers; nine administration members had accepted valuable gifts, including mink coats; ten federal agencies had been implicated in shady manipulations; and almost nine hundred civil servants had been caught improving their personal wealth through their public posts. Truman had pardoned fifteen convicts in his first year in office and made no White House announcement about their release; he quickly commuted an income tax evader's sentence, and a wealthy Democratic contributor, Joseph Schenck, the movie mogul, was pardoned for the same crime.

The article made scores of sensational charges. When David Bennett, president of Albert Verley & Co., a Chicago perfume business, had asked to travel to Europe during the closing days of the war when air transportation was severely limited, General Vaughan had put him on a priority flight, and Bennett returned with $53,405 worth of perfume. The day he landed, he sent several expensive frozen-food units to Vaughan, Bess Truman, and others, valued at $390 each. John Maragon, a former Kansas City bootblack whom Vaughan liked, flew off on a priority flight to Europe and returned with more perfume. He was later fired, but not before he gave a $300 donation to the Democratic Party. The article also pointed out that as late as December 1945, Truman was still paying dues to the Pendergast Club, another sign of condoning corruption.

In the spring of 1946, Deputy Commissioner Stewart Berkshire of the federal alcohol unit had overruled his own field office and issued a federal liquor license to Lew Farrell, a Des Moines, Iowa, gambler, who had a police record for carrying a concealed weapon. About a year later, Peter Lektrich, a licensing officer in the Commerce Department's division of international trade, approved an export license for 100,000 pounds of scarce steel pipe to oblige an old friend, Robert Mistrough, an "expediter" for elicited licenses. These were legal; fake export permits sold for as much as $10,000. Fired for that indiscretion, Lektrich soon found employment under the clerk of the House.

In May 1947, a Kansas City grand jury had indicted seventy-one people for perpetrating fraud in a city election. Before the trial, thugs blew open the vault at the Jackson County Courthouse and stole impounded ballots. On August 13, pardons for four mobsters associated with Al Capone were linked to the Justice Department and the White House. The next month, Truman denounced more than eight hundred federal employees who were involved with grain speculation totaling $213 million; the president's private physician, Brigadier General Wallace Graham, had invested at least $22,500 in the scheme and did not close out his account until almost the end of the year. During the 1948 presidential campaign, Charles Binaggio, a top Kansas City mobster, had raised money for Truman; in the spring of 1950, Binaggio and Gus Gargotta, his chief henchman, were murdered on a city street. Nixon read the article and said that if Truman ran for reelection, these revelations alone were enough to defeat him.[8]

Alonzo Hamby summarized the results of the machinations of Vaughan, Dawson, and Young, the investigations of Fulbright and Kefauver, the murders of the gangsters in the streets of Kansas City and its crooked politics by the end of 1950. All tarnished the White House seal, and Truman should have protected himself from further injury, but he did not. This allowed his enemies to redouble their efforts in this vulnerable area "for an increasingly credible claim that the president of the United States tolerated corruption, consorted with crooks, and might be at least a bit of a crook himself."[9]

By the start of April 1951, with Nixon now in the Senate, the Committee on Expenditures in the Executive Departments, on which he served, initiated an investigation into the RFC. He welcomed these hearings "to clean out the corrupters," and hoped that the committee would "take a long and hard look at a number of situations in the government where there have been indications of illegal activities."[10]

After several months of investigations, Nixon spoke before the Lake

County Republican Picnic in Illinois on September 16, to announce that his subcommittee probe of influence peddling had reached the chairman of the Democratic National Committee (DNC), William Boyle. During the proceeding week, the committee had questioned several witnesses about Boyle's exerting influence to obtain loan approval by the RFC to the American Lithofold Corporation of St. Louis after a series of earlier requests had been denied. Boyle had publicly stated that he had nothing to do with that loan, but the company's treasurer testified that three days after Boyle had telephoned the RFC chairman, the loan was granted. Since his law firm had represented American Lithofold during some of these negotiations, Nixon wanted Boyle to explain his firm's connection with the company.[11]

Ralph de Toledano of *Newsweek* told Nixon that he believed Truman had "whitewashed Boyle" and was trying to delay any inquiry. De Toledano did not want to give the president that opportunity and hoped to highlight Boyle's role at publicized hearings. "If you remember," the journalist reminded Nixon, "what brought you the most attention during the Hiss case was your charge that the Justice Department was trying to queer the prosecution of Alger [Hiss]." Nixon had to increase the pressure: "What's more, once you get rolling, I'll be able to help. As a matter of fact, I've been pressing for a cover story on you. This will be the perfect peg."[12]

Boyle, in his late forties, was more than just another politician who had been selected as chairman of the DNC early in 1949; he was a Kansas City Democrat and a Pendergast machine veteran whom the president liked. As a former police chief and a prosperous attorney, Boyle moved to the capital in 1941 to act as assistant counsel for the Truman committee, became his personal secretary, and managed his vice-presidential campaign in 1944; some credited him with masterminding the presidential campaign of 1948. After assuming leadership of the party, he proved to be an excellent fund-raiser, but many blamed him for the Democratic losses in 1950.[13]

The subcommittee convened on what was referred as the Boyle-RFC-Lithofold matter on September 27. Senator Clyde Hoey, Democrat from North Carolina, opened the proceeding by allowing Boyle to read a statement into the record, recounting his version of the American Lithofold story. Boyle stated that he had only received $1,250 in fees from the company, even though the *St. Louis Post-Dispatch* in a sensational summer exposé reported that he was paid $8,000. He vigorously defended his actions: "If a person seeks an appointment with an official of any governmental agency or with Members of the Senate or House, I feel it is not only proper for the staff of officials of the Democratic National Committee to make such appointments, but it is their duty to do so."[14]

Nixon asked Boyle how much he received from his legal practice; what was his relationship to the company, and what else he did for it besides the RFC contact. Boyle replied that he had done nothing else. Nixon pressed him on his phone call to the RFC; if Boyle made the contact as chairman of the DNC, "the fact that the introduction is made, constitutes influence." Boyle dissented.[15]

Within a week after Boyle's appearance, Nixon issued a statement requesting information about $1,271 that the DNC chairman had paid to Turney Gratz in 1949, a RFC employee who received $10,330 per year; during 1948, furthermore, Boyle had paid Gratz $2,130 for an undetermined reason. The senator wanted to call him as a witness to determine what services he performed for Boyle that required payment. At first glance, Boyle seemingly had acted improperly by supplementing the income of an RFC official; at least, that was Nixon's reasoning.[16]

On October 4, Guy George Gabrielson, chairman of the Republican National Committee (RNC), testified about a loan that he had negotiated for Carthage Hydrocol Company with the RFC. Nixon only cursorily examined his involvement, but four days later he released a statement calling on both Boyle and Gabrielson to resign from their posts: "The basic issue is whether a high official of the National Committee of either major political party should be in a position where he can profit financially from the influence which he may be able to exert with government agencies." Boyle admitted that he had received $1,250 from American Lithofold and the only work he did for this fee was to make an appointment with RFC officials. The loan was quickly approved after every staff examiner, agency review board, and the board of directors had rejected it.

Gabrielson's facts were different, but the same logic applied. Although unpaid as RNC chairman, the only client that he represented before the RFC was Carthage Hydrocol, of which he was president and general counsel. Before becoming chairman of the company, his RFC loan was granted, and his only request to the RFC after becoming RNC chairman was rejected. Yet Nixon argued that Gabrielson could not simultaneously be RNC chairman and a company president who applied for a RFC grant. The appearance of influence peddling, Nixon argued, damaged the GOP, "because the charges against him [Gabrielson] will constantly be used to camouflage and confuse the issue and to protect those who are really guilty of corruption in high places of Government." Nixon did not accuse either Boyle or Gabrielson of doing anything illegal, but both men, he argued, had to resign, and their replacements should be individuals "who are in a position to profit neither directly nor indirectly from any dealings with the Federal Government."[17]

Boyle understood the message, and despite Truman's strong defense, the DNC chairman resigned on the evening of October 13. De Toledano observed a president who "looked haggard and confused. The attacks are beginning to tell [and] the scandals will grow bigger, not smaller. One topnotch fighter with a little knowledge of judo could finish Harry off. But all we have in the Senate is a bunch of Hessians."[18]

Some Republicans disagreed with Nixon. Boyle acted illegally, while Gabrielson was innocent; therefore, Nixon should not have asked for the latter's resignation. Many more, however, approved of the senator's approach. His nonpartisanship played well. The *Daily Sun* in San Bernardino, California, applauded him. James Guthrie, editor and publisher, commented in the middle of October: "the public resents the goings on in Washington and is displeased with both Boyle and Gabrielson. They have no place in the Washington picture because they have failed to live up to what the people have a right to expect of them."[19]

By the end of the month, most of Nixon's advisers agreed that Gabrielson should have resigned, that by placing his personal interests above the party's, he had demeaned the GOP. The senator had encouraged the RNC chairman to resign after learning that Boyle intended to quit. Nixon hoped that Gabrielson "should, if possible, beat him [Boyle] to the punch," since ordinary voters would not comprehend the subtle differences between each man's transactions. Nixon protected his flank by insisting on knowing about anyone who offered any staff members a gift. As a general rule, he insisted they never accept anything from anyone who had a matter pending in his office.[20]

As the year ended, Nixon was convinced that only a small fraction of graft in the administration had been uncovered. He heard rumors that Vaughan had been "shaking down companies who are getting war contracts" in return for insurance and annuity policies. Congressional investigations such as that into the disposal of surplus property in the

Philippines in 1946–49 were pending. He was correct; the bulk of the Truman scandal controversies were still to come in 1952.[21]

Nixon remained at the capital throughout most of January 1952 preparing for upcoming committee meetings, "with particular emphasis on the necessity to restore integrity and honesty in high places." Fundraisers were critical, but the obligation to expose corruption would be powerful ammunition to shoot at the White House.[22]

When Truman appointed Attorney General J. Howard McGrath in the second week of January to end government corruption, many in Congress were outraged. Scandal had shaken the foundations of the Justice Department, and Nixon said: "The public will have no confidence whatever in an investigation of the justice department by the justice department." He also renewed his demand for the firing of Secretary of Treasury John Snyder, who ran the graft-laden Bureau of Internal Revenue.[23]

Hundreds of local bureau collectors either resigned or were dismissed. Many were eventually indicted and convicted of charges that ranged from bribery to embezzlement. The assistant commissioner, Daniel Bolich, was investigated but never tried; its chief counsel Charles Oliphant resigned for accepting gifts; and by the end of 1951, fifty-seven bureau officials had been removed. That same year, Assistant Attorney General T. Lamar Caudle, who directed the tax division, was dismissed and subsequently convicted of conspiracy.[24]

Nixon now announced that he had designed a program to halt the wave of corruption in the federal government. He did not pretend that the plan would prevent all abuses, because dishonest people would remain in the civil service and laws would be disobeyed; therefore, "Congress must never relax its efforts to expose crooked public servants and uncover illegal practices." But he did offer several reforms: federal employees had to be allowed to testify before congressional committees; the statute of limitations had to be extended for prosecution so that employees could not depend on time to prevent the discovery of their misdeeds; if a national political party committed an offense, it should pay compensation; political parties' employees had to be stopped from influencing any U.S. agency; and finally, the treasury secretary had to divulge tax collectors' cases where anything less than the amount owed was paid.[25]

The Attorney General then announced on February 1 the appointment of Newbold Morris as a special assistant to remove wrongdoers from government. Not only was he the son-in-law of the famous jurist,

Learned Hand, but Morris was a senior partner for the prestigious New York law firm of Lovejoy, Morris, Wasson & Huppuch. He was a liberal Republican who presided over the New York City Council. Assigned an office in the Justice Department, he was expected to "make enough dent so that maybe they'll remember me as a guy who started a new era of decency."[26]

Despite these credentials, Nixon denounced Morris's selection as "a complete phony by the White House" to direct any investigation into government corruption. The senator disclosed that Morris was a subject of a Senate committee inquiry into the sale and use of surplus American tankers. When the senator's critics cried smear, Father Cronin joined the fray by arguing that the Attorney General should not have endorsed Morris's inquiry without a careful background check.[27]

Congressman Charles Potter, Republican from Michigan, was far more hostile, asking Morris to quit because he had been used to front for Communist organizations by selling goods to the Red Chinese, and Senator Mundt called upon Morris to answer charges about his association with those groups. The new appointee immediately denied involvement in any ship deal, though a Senate committee was investigating how the China International Foundation, of which he was president, had purchased ships at such a low price. "I never bought or sold a ship," he proclaimed, "and never received one dollar in the form of salary or otherwise as head of the China International Corporation."[28]

In fact, the Senate subcommittee on Expenditures in the Executive Departments had been receiving information of a possible ship scandal since the spring of 1951. Investigators had learned in 1947 that the China Petroleum Corporation (CPC), an official agency of the Chinese Nationalist government, had been allocated American funds for oil purchases. Since the Chinese lacked tankers for transportation, the China Trading and Industrial Development Corporation had hired Houston Wasson, a partner in Morris's firm, to secure tankers from the U.S. Maritime Commission for charter by the CPC.[29]

Since a non-American owned corporation might not receive favorable consideration by the commission, United Tanker Corporation (UTC) was formed on December 10, 1947, and on the same date, Morris submitted applications to the Maritime Commission from the China Trading and Industrial Development Corporation to buy two tankers, using funds from the Chinese government and its citizens.[30]

The applications were refused. With that avenue closed, UTC ac-

quired stock by paying $2.5 million in a corporation that already had
been allocated for tankers in 1949. In addition, the parent corporation
donated eighty thousand shares of its stock to China International Foundation, Inc., formed in Delaware, with Morris as president, to sponsor
fellowships for Chinese students doing research at U.S. universities. The
foundation received about $284,000, mostly from UTC stock, from
1949 to 1951.[31]

Before these complex transactions were taken to the Senate investigating committee, Admiral E. L. Cochrane, the Maritime Administrator,
informed Nixon in early March 1951 that over two hundred vessels
under the Merchant Ship Sale Act of 1946 were sold to foreign ownership and registry, and after the sales, information that the commission
had on these vessels was fragmentary. The Chinese had purchased two
tankers to transport petroleum products from June 1949 to June 1950
between Communist ports, and the ships' charters allowed them to trade
with whomever they wished; however, no other American flag tankers
had engaged in trade with the Communist bloc. After October 12, 1950,
the Maritime Commission changed its rules, and U.S. commercial vessels had to have specific approval to trade with fourteen identified Iron
Curtain countries. No one had requested permission.[32]

A month later, the Chinese Embassy acknowledged that CPC had
bought two American tankers from the Chinese government to haul
crude oil from the Middle East to Formosa. UTC along with CPC chartered these ships from China Trading. Once the Red Chinese controlled
the mainland, CPC stopped using the tankers. The Nationalist government on Formosa did not know what UTC was presently doing because
it was a private corporation and not under the supervision of Chiang's
regime.[33]

At the end of January 1952, Admiral William Smith, chairman of
the Maritime Commission from 1946 to 1949, said that he had discussed
UTC deal with Morris before his group had chartered the two tankers
under the American flag. Shipping had experienced a significant reduction since World War II due to a dwindling demand for petroleum
goods. The admiral, therefore, saw no problem with the transaction, and
the Bureau of Internal Revenue had been consulted for an advanced tax
ruling for American Overseas Tanker Corporation. Smith, several
months later, admitted meeting briefly with Joseph Casey, who spearheaded the purchase of these tankers, but Smith did not have any knowledge that Casey's investors were going to sell the vessels from American

Overseas Tanker to another corporation at a profit. Under the law, Smith believed, that speculation would be unlawful and he did not know of any tax avoidance scheme.[34]

During Nixon's biweekly radio report on February 27 to California from the capital, the senator talked about Morris's role in the government corruption scandal and his inability to get the administration to cooperate with his probe. Nixon pointed to the growing list of shocking exposures concerning graft in the administration. As for Morris, the committee was investigating his connection to Casey in the tanker deal whereby his investors had leased tankers through an American corporation to a parallel Panama enterprise. By transferring title from U.S. control, the owners saved $1.4 million in taxes; the Bureau of Internal Revenue was examining that transaction. Initially, Chinese nationals supplied the bulk of the capital to buy the tankers, while Morris put up six dollars. The two tankers had chartered oil from Russia to Red China. Nixon wondered how these ships could enter into that kind of contract and how Morris could probe corruption under the cloud concerning the questionable circumstances of his own dealings. To Nixon, Morris served as a prime example of unacceptable, abhorrent behavior for government workers who had "to do what is right and not what is wrong."[35]

On the next day, Morris denied that his firm had ever represented the so-called Casey group. Chinese capital financed the United Tanker Corporation, he said, and the Maritime Commission gave its approval after full disclosure that the tankers were under the control of U.S. citizens. His law partner Wasson was involved with the enterprise for four years, using the tankers to carry oil from the Persian Gulf to Formosa refineries as part of the Chinese Nationalists' postwar economic assistance program. No American, he insisted, ever acted as an agent for Chinese interests.[36]

Early in March, Nixon wrote Admiral Cochrane of the Maritime Commission that the Senate subcommittee had established that two of eight surplus tankers acquired by the Casey group, composed of Washington, D.C., attorneys, had been used to transport petroleum products between Communist satellites and had netted a profit of $264,410. To date, the investors' gain amounted to $1,267,200, The senator made an urgent request to find out if other surplus tankers were used in a similar fashion. Nixon expected to call Morris to testify and explain his role in these transactions.[37]

In the midst of these revelations, Morris appeared on television on March 2. Roy McLaughlin, who had unsuccessfully run against Voorhis in 1944 and supported Nixon thereafter, reported his daughter's reaction to Morris for the senator: "He [Morris] seems to me to be sort of a nut—a good deal like Jerry Voorhis." The senator quickly responded that McLaughlin's child had "made a pretty correct appraisal of him [Morris] in every way!"[38]

On March 11, Newbold Morris testified. A tall, fifty-year-old New York attorney, he immediately launched an aggressive assault by declaring that, according to his wife, he was "just on the assembly line . . . two weeks from now they'll [the senators] have another victim." He then provided a sarcastic bit of faint praise: "Senator Nixon, you have been mild this morning, but over a period of months I have resented the aspersions you have cast upon my integrity, and I am glad to have a chance to tell you to your face."[39]

The next day, Morris reappeared and issued a press release accusing congressional committees of ruining the lives of individuals who had testified before them. He was a target of "insinuation by diseased minds in this chamber [the Senate]." "For the past ten months," Morris complained, "I myself personally have been subject to character assassination and my life subject to innuendo and misrepresentation by certain members of this committee." He encouraged voters to cast their ballots against those offending senators, Nixon, Mundt, and McCarthy; they were especially unfair to him and cruel to Secretary of State Acheson.[40]

Nixon immediately answered in his own press release. The committee, according to the senator, had heard from twenty witnesses about the disposal of government-owned surplus tankers, and Morris was the first who refused to cooperate in getting the facts. His testimony was "one of the most disgraceful performances I have ever seen before a congressional committee." He was flippant, rude, and contemptuous. Nixon called upon Truman to replace Morris with "someone better qualified to handle" corruption in the federal bureaucracy.[41]

Attorney Jack Irwin, one of Nixon's legislative assistants, sat in on Morris's testimony. He noted that when McCarthy asked Morris about associations with subversive organizations, Nixon stopped that line of questioning as not pertinent to the inquiry. The senator, however, did question Morris carefully on his disclosures to the Maritime Commission. Morris proclaimed his innocence, but all of the commissioners refuted that position. If Morris had made full disclosures, they would never have approved the transfer.[42]

The reaction to the Morris-Nixon exchange was extreme. One detractor wired the senator: "MORRIS PINNED YOUR EARS TO YOUR PANTS." Katherine Bryan, a GOP follower from New York City, was delighted that Morris had "finally spoken for those Republicans who deplore the revolting methods used in some of the Investigating Committees of Congress. The never confirmed charges, the misuse of Senatorial immunity have sickened and disgusted all Republicans that I know."[43]

The *Washington Times-Herald* editorialized that Morris came to Washington as a reformer, but all he did was to cause friction. Truman had made mistakes during his long tenure, but Morris created disaster within a month of his arrival. "So far as we recall, never has anyone alienated so many so soon or so fully, as this so-called 'Abraham Lincoln' Republican, who turns out to be only another loudmouthed Manhattan hick who came down here thinking everybody is really as dumb in fact as it would be convenient to him for them to be."[44]

Frank Chelf, Democrat from Kentucky, chaired a House Committee on the Judiciary subcommittee to investigate the Justice Department, with the first hearing on March 26 concerning the appointment of Morris. The Chelf Committee looked solely at the Justice Department and asked how Morris could be hired since Attorney General McGrath had received correspondence in the summer of 1951 in regard to Morris's questionable financial dealings with the tankers and the foundation that supported Chinese university students. McGrath's own criminal division was investigating Morris, but the Attorney General replied to House inquiries that he had no knowledge of Morris's questionable dealings before his selection. Although candidates for such sensitive jobs were usually investigated, Morris had not been.[45]

As for comments on current administration scandals, Nixon could not see how Morris could carry out his "clean-up boss" mission as an impartial observer. To those in the audience who followed the underworld connections to the former mayor of New York, Mr. O'Dwyer was presently ambassador to Mexico because he had "too many powerful friends in the right places." Once again, Nixon contended that the Truman administration was riddled with graft.[46]

Finished with the subcommittee's hearings, Morris battled on a second front against his boss McGrath. Morris sent out a questionnaire from the office of the special assistant to the Attorney General in late March, to all officeholders, including McGrath, who not only refused to fill it out for violations of privacy but also won Truman's consent that the questionnaire should not be distributed.

By the start of April, any Morris-McGrath cooperation was impossible, and on April 2, the Attorney General and the president were seen shouting at one another. While Truman and his staff were meeting on the following morning, he learned that McGrath had fired Morris. No one at the White House gathering defended the Attorney General's action; in fact, the consensus called for McGrath's resignation. Truman phoned and informed McGrath that his resignation would be announced later that day.[47]

The Chelf Committee evaluation of the Newbold Morris matter was scathing. McGrath had hastily hired Morris without any background check. After distributing his questionnaire, he was summarily fired, with no replacement. Even though Newbold Morris was appointed to clean up executive corruption, the Attorney General never cooperated actively or even acted in good faith. As the Chelf Committee reported, "It was an awkward, bungling attempt by the Executive Department, through the Department of Justice to investigate its own branches. It failed ingloriously, leaving the task to committees of the legislative branch and demonstrates the imprudence of permitting those under investigation to choose the investigators and dictate the methods of investigation."[48]

If possible, Nixon was even more outraged. Whereas earlier he had been dogging Morris, now he turned on McGrath. He felt that Morris was chosen "to perform a 'whitewash' job, but was dismissed when it appeared that he intended to pursue a thorough housecleaning of corruption in the government." Yet Morris had still been a bad choice. During his brief stay in the capital, "he showed a basic emotional instability and lack of the mature judgment which is essential for anyone who is to be granted the unprecedented broad powers to conduct a government-wide investigation of corruption." The entire episode was a disgraceful display by a failed administration.[49]

Nixon tried to reward those who exposed corruption and had introduced a bill in the Senate to reinstate William Burkett to his seniority and former status at the Bureau of Internal Revenue before the Morris affair. Burkett had voluntarily resigned on August 18, 1950, as a senior special agent attached to the bureau in the Treasury Department's San

Francisco office so that he could publicize misdeeds and testify before the Kefauver Committee, providing evidence of bureau corruption in Northern California and Nevada. A federal grand jury later indicted tax collector Pat Mooney and his chief deputy, Mike Schino, for selling bogus mining stock as a bribe to settle pending disputes of individuals facing serious tax penalties.[50]

Burkett used his notoriety to enter San Mateo County politics, where he had lived for sixteen years, but was presently residing in Sacramento. At thirty-eight years old, he had a wife and two children, was a licensed accountant and had been a naval intelligence officer during World War II. Even though ten others had already entered the primary race for the House, many groups urged Burkett to run, comparing him to Nixon on youth, legal training, and wartime naval service.[51]

Nixon introduced the Burkett bill without any knowledge about his possible congressional aspirations. When the senator privately found out that Burkett would not receive the local Fact Finding Committee's endorsement, he commented: "Frankly, I was very much put out when I learned that he was using my name in building himself up and I am glad that the people of the Fact Finding Committee were not taken in by this tactic." Burkett did not do badly. He returned to his job as executive vice president of the Inter-Association Unemployment Insurance Company, which was financed for at least two more years. Burkett would probably remain in that job, and Nixon stayed out of that primary fight.[52]

Commissioner John Dunlap agreed with Nixon and others that most malfeasance in the agency came from the political appointees. The current housecleaning had not been completed, but Dunlap assured Congress that the major problems had been solved. Although it approved Truman's overhaul, Nixon opposed the plan that placed bureau collectors under the civil service without any clear method to accomplish that objective. Examinations for top officials were included without any outline as to how or when that would occur, nor did the program expose past graft or help to stop it in the future. Nixon was also disappointed that political cronies had not been eliminated. Future legislation would have to address that issue.[53]

On March 20, Nixon suffered his own embarrassment when the House Committee on Ways and Means subcommittee on administration of the internal revenue laws, chaired by Cecil King, Democrat from California, found out from Senator Ralph Owen Brewster, Republican from Maine, who chaired the GOP committee for senatorial contributions in the 1950 elections, that Nixon and Milton Young of North Dakota had besieged him for money to use in their primaries. Since the senatorial committee could not advance funds for primary campaigns, Brewster "took the perhaps somewhat unusual procedure of intervening myself personally." He borrowed $10,000 from a commercial bank, but did not wish to create any misunderstanding about contributing to those two primary campaigns because "I was afraid my actions might be misunderstood." He therefore had Henry Grunewald, a personal friend and acknowledged capital "influence peddler," act as a funnel for the transaction by writing two checks for $5,000. Each candidate received a check from Grunewald for his own primary and repaid Brewster directly, not through Grunewald. Then both men received the standard $5,000 contribution given to Republican senatorial candidates for the general election. This mini-scandal, like so many others in the realm of campaign finance, died quickly.[54]

The corruption probes were the most sensational domestic issue that Nixon engaged in during his senatorial term. At the acme of the accusations, Truman held a press conference at Key West, Florida, during a vacation in the middle of March 1952 to defend the honor of his administration. Alluding to the crescendoing criticism at the height of the embarrassment over the Newbold Morris matter, the president declared: "My people are honorable—all of them are." In reply to a suggestion from Senator Knowland that Truman should return from his holiday to the White House to clean house, Truman added: "My house is always clean. What are you talking about?" In response, reporters said that they were asking about newspaper and editorial criticism of some White House employees' ethical and moral standards, to which the president stated: "It isn't true. Point blank—categorically, it's just not true."

Throughout most of the interview, Truman appeared in good humor. However, when asked if Mrs. Merl Young, the White House stenographer with the mink coat whose husband was a major target of the RFC probe, had been fired, Truman answered: "No comment."

By any standard, Truman's partisan defense of the charges against his administration dealing with graft and corruption was disingenuous, for he knew that serious breaches of the public trust had taken place. Despite this fact, Andrew Dunar, in his authoritative *The Truman Scandals and the Politics of Morality* (1984), concluded that these scandals never personally tarnished Truman. The president's blind spot was that he would not censure or disassociate himself from friends and acquaintances who took advantage of their public trust. The president, rather than look at the merit of many of the charges that ultimately ended in criminal convictions, chose to perceive these attacks as politically motivated.[55]

Jules Abels, a GOP conservative activist during the Truman presidency, offered a diametrically opposite viewpoint. There were hundreds of corrupt Democrats who answered to the sordid names of "fixers," "five percenters," or "influence peddlers." His book, *The Truman Scandals* (1956), took readers through a virtual compendium of corruption and graft; the most serious violations were an outgrowth of the chicanery in the Bureau of Internal Revenue. Tax Commissioner Joseph Nunan and Assistant Attorney General T. Lamar Caudle, in charge of the tax division, went to jail for tax fraud. They were only two of the multitude who went to prison, were fired, or resigned their positions under suspicion of wrongdoing. As for the RFC investigations, Merl Young, the most prominent offender, went to prison for perjury for lying before a congressional committee.[56]

While graft had reached the White House in the administrations of Warren Harding and Ulysses S. Grant, their transgressions were minimal when compared to the epidemic proportions under Truman. "The unprecedented debauchery in government," Abels asserted, "which flourished during the Truman administration occurred only because of a prevailing moral climate which made it possible or promoted it." The president did not take effective measures to halt the venality, and his administration also sometimes shielded wrongdoers or blocked investigations. "The frauds were revealed not because of the administration," Abels concluded, "but in spite of it."[57]

Examining Truman's actions over his long political career, Alonzo Hamby in his biography wrote that "Truman dealt with the corruption issue as a politician of the past. He was perfectly willing to continue a vast bureaucracy with huge sums of money to hand out and countless points of access from supplicants and grafters, and to assume that some impropriety and petty graft were part of the process of government— messy and distasteful perhaps, but unavoidable." If Republicans screamed, they in reality were "partisan hypocrites" who followed the same practices.[58]

That lame excuse should not absolve Truman for his refusal to address this issue squarely. He and his staff were well aware of the embarrassment that the corruption question was posing. Even a sympathetic biographer like Robert Ferrell retained the deep anxiety that the assistant press secretary to the White House Eben Ayers felt and periodically recorded in his diary: Vaughan was loyal and would not personally injure the president, but he did; when the deep-freezer units' story erupted, Ayers placed the blame solely on Vaughan "for his troubles and the troubles he has brought on the president and others. He seems to have no realization of what harm he has caused the president and other people."[59]

Truman, according to Ayers's observations, refused to believe that his appointees were guilty of any wrongdoing. He told his assistant press secretary that General Graham or Ed Pauley might be speculators, but they did nothing illegal; when Matthew Connelly, a presidential aide, brought Truman some papers that dealt with a Reconstruction Finance Corporation request from Ed Crump, the Democratic political boss in Memphis, Tennessee, Truman instructed the Reconstruction Finance Corporation to turn it down and tell Crump that the president had ordered it. Congressional investigators and muckrakers like Drew Pearson, according to Ayers, tried to connect Vaughan with "five percenters" like Colonel Hunt and John Maragon, but the president reassured Vaughan that "he had gone through things like this and knew what it all was."[60]

Truman doggedly defended his friends, an admirable trait that many authors have alluded to. It has allowed Truman to highlight his hallmark of personal integrity and point to the motto on his desk in the Oval Office: "The buck stops here." While the legend continues to grow, Truman's honesty and willingness to make tough decisions must be tempered with the unsavory fact that a great deal of sleaziness existed within his administration. That too must be part of his lasting legacy.

# Chapter 19

# "ELECTABILITY" AND OTHER ISSUES

The ever-increasing reliance on "C-2, K-1" in Nixon's speeches arose directly from the causes that the GOP attributed to Thomas Dewey's shocking loss in 1948. In the Republican postmortem of that race, the party felt that the New York governor went down to defeat because he did not differentiate between Republican and Democratic principles. Nixon like many other regulars was devastated and felt a sinking sense of despair for the party's survival if it did not capture the 1952 presidential prize. To accomplish this, Nixon believed that Republicans had to concentrate on two fundamental factors: first, the GOP had to select its best possible candidate; and second, the party vigorously had to attack the Truman administration for its failures on communism, Korea, and corruption. Both of these efforts would successfully fuse into the objective of recapturing the White House.

Nixon's first choice to lead in this assault was former Minnesota governor Harold Stassen. Indeed, Nixon spoke briefly with him at the Army-Navy football game and met again in Los Angeles to discuss future plans during late 1948. Nixon was convinced that Stassen would be "one of the most effective leaders of the party during the next four years" and felt that the former governor was "following a policy of watchful waiting at the present time." During the spring of 1949, Stassen, then president of the University of Pennsylvania, discussed legislative matters like federal aid to education with Nixon, while the senator wanted Stassen to meet Joe Holt, "a close personal friend," and a California delegate to the last Republican National Convention. Throughout the remainder of the year, both men communicated regularly, and the former governor's early endorsement of Nixon's senatorial announcement was much appreciated.[1]

This mutual respect and encouragement of Stassen's presidential aspirations continued into 1951 as the Minnesotan echoed many of Nixon's positions. In the domestic realm, Stassen announced his support for federal aid to education for economically disadvantaged school systems in the South; in foreign affairs, he called for Acheson's resignation, charged Truman with being "soft" on communism, and condemned the administration for its alleged complicity in the Communist conquest of mainland China. Stassen's presidential proponents invited Nixon to a two-day, invitation-only, confidential gathering at Amos Peaslee's estate in Clarksboro, New Jersey, on June 23 and 24, that included Warren Burger, Dana Smith, Joe McCarthy, and Governor Val Peterson of Nebraska, to discuss Stassen's presidential bid.[2]

By late summer, however, Nixon had eliminated Stassen as a viable candidate, feeling that he could not obtain the necessary GOP support to win the nomination. When both were mentioned to appear on a program for the Young Republicans in San Diego County, Bill Arnold, at his boss's direction, squelched it. When invited to travel to St. Louis at the end of December to hear Stassen announce officially for the presidency, Nixon begged off. He was correct to separate himself from the former governor. By the time of the convention, Stassen had been totally discredited and the subject of ridicule.[3]

At the end of January 1951, Kyle Palmer, an astute observer of California GOP politics, had written Nixon that Senator Robert Taft, Republican from Ohio, known as "Mr. Republican" for his staunch partisanship, was the leading contender in the presidential sweepstakes of 1952. Despite rock-solid advocacy from conservative Republicans, the columnist felt that Taft "should not be our man," then sarcastically added, "but maybe I'm just a hick and can't see things as they should be."[4]

Within three weeks, Nixon replied, observing that Taft's stalwarts were especially well organized in the Middle West and the South, while Republicans in New York, Pennsylvania, and Maine seemed to prefer Ike. Nixon, too, admired Taft "as probably the ablest man in the Senate," but he and others whom he had talked with worried that the Ohioan "would be difficult to elect." His followers pointed to Taft's overwhelming reelection victory in 1950 to refute that sentiment. Besides, unless others who disapproved united behind another attractive candidate, the senator from Ohio would easily capture the nomination.[5]

So Nixon expected Taft to face Truman, but he also speculated that the Democrats might turn to Senator Paul Douglas of Illinois or Fred Vinson, chief justice of the Supreme Court. Either man would jeopardize Taft's ability to win the election. In that case, Republicans needed to organize immediately if the senator were going to be the nominee.[6]

At the start of 1951, Governor Warren had not declared as a candidate. Despite that fact, Nixon had given major speeches in key states with crowds from ranging six hundred to two thousand, and received a warm reception with the following statement: "There are many of us in California who think that Governor Warren rendered a great service, not only to his state but also to the nation, when he defeated a man by the name of Roosevelt by over one million votes in a state which has a million more Democrats than Republicans." Some thought that if Warren had been the Republican nominee in 1948, the GOP would have won. Some were already asking him to run in 1952.[7]

Hostile gossip interfered with Nixon's goodwill message and complicated his relationship with Warren. Remarks surfaced like the one in Arthur Caylor's *San Francisco News* column, which claimed the senator had refused to attend a dinner where Warren was present because Nixon felt that "Warren, a notorious lone-wolf, gave him no help when he needed twice that much. It's a feud that could queer Warren's presidential chances—not with the people, but with party big-wigs at the convention." Major contributor Roland Woolley heard that Nixon had "unfriendly feelings toward Governor Warren, supposedly based on developments during last fall's campaign." The senator denied the story and asked Brennan to see that Woolley "get the record straight." Brennan had lunch with him and resolved any misunderstanding.[8]

While Stassen, Taft, and Warren were expected to announce as presidential candidates, General Dwight D. Eisenhower was the wild card in the Republican poker game. Many, according to Nixon, believed that the general was a Democrat, but the senator disputed that contention: "Eisenhower has strong support everywhere. If he indicated his willingness to run as a Republican, there would be no question whatever that he would get the nomination."[9]

Truman gave Nixon his opportunity to determine if Ike, indeed, would run as a Republican when the president appointed Nixon to travel to Geneva as an American representative to the World Health Organization Conference. Before leaving in the second week of May, Nixon received word from Alfred Kohlberg—a vocal advocate for the Nationalist Chinese, a supporter of General MacArthur, and a fervent admirer of Joe McCarthy—who relayed a message from Eisenhower, commander of the Supreme Headquarters Allied Powers in Europe (SHAPE), that the general wanted Nixon to make an appointment to see him in Paris to talk about the issue of domestic subversion. Nixon enthusiastically accepted, and on the day of his departure, their meeting had been confirmed.[10]

Nixon was excited. He had first seen Ike on June 19, 1945, when the general received a tumultuous welcome in New York City, spoke at City Hall, and saw the Boston Braves defeat the New York Giants, 9 to 2. The young naval officer was working in the Bureau of Aeronautics at the time, negotiating the termination of war contracts on the twentieth floor at 50 Church Street, while Ike was riding by below in his ticker-tape parade. Nixon watched him standing in the back of his car with both arms raised high over his head, a gesture that would become a political trademark. The next time Nixon saw Ike was following the funeral cortège of General John Pershing in the middle of July 1948, leaving from Capitol Hill and proceeding to Arlington National Cemetery. Generals Eisenhower, Omar Bradley, and George Marshall walked on foot, while others went in automobiles. Later that year, Nixon heard the general brief colleagues at the Library of Congress on European conditions.[11]

In late July 1950, Nixon attended the annual Midsummer Encampment at the Bohemian Grove, an extraordinary gathering of influential and powerful American males presided over by Herbert Hoover. Nixon was profusely grateful for the invitation: "It was one of those rare experiences of a lifetime, and clearly apart from any political consideration, I wouldn't have missed it for anything." He made many contacts, had a chance to meet potential backers, and attended a luncheon at which Ike was present. The general, as Hoover's guest, sat to the right at the head of the table, while Nixon, senatorial candidate, was near the foot. Although he heard Ike speak at the encampment on several occasions, they were not introduced.[12]

Eisenhower and Nixon still had not met to that point, but the general scrupulously had followed the congressman's role during the

Chambers-Hiss melodrama. In the spring of 1948, during his brief tenure as president of Columbia University, Eisenhower was asked and honored to join the board of the Carnegie Foundation. As its president, Alger Hiss periodically corresponded with Ike, as did John Foster Dulles, chairman of the board, to keep the members apprised of the unfolding case. Eisenhower initially approved of Hiss's actions before HUAC and defended his innocence: "it does strike me as curious, rather as incomprehensible, that there can be any recognized or legal procedure whereby the reputation of a man can be almost destroyed merely on the basis of another's startling conclusion." After Hiss filed his libel suit, Eisenhower maintained that as long as the issue was before the courts, the trustees must not prejudice the case by taking any action.[13]

After the conviction of Hiss, H. L. Hunt, a Texas millionaire, wrote Ike that the foundation should have fired Hiss before his trial because Dulles had known that Hiss had been under suspicion of being a Communist for quite some time. Ike respected the Texan's judgment, and wrote him on August 1, 1950, that in two recent speeches, he himself had unequivocally declared: "Any citizens of this country who embrace Communism can be considered nothing less than traitors." Yet, even in the campaign against subversives, "we must be very careful to preserve the essentials of Americanism, including . . . the complete equality of each of us before the law." A month later, the general reiterated his opposition to anyone being tried in the court of public opinion, but conceded that "the more highly placed such an individual is, the greater his crime." Hunt had given Ike *Seeds of Treason,* the best-seller by Ralph de Toledano and Victor Lasky, which was largely based on Nixon's recollections. After Ike finished the book, he expressed deep concern about "the presence of any disloyal man in a government position."[14]

Ike was consistent in his treatment of Hiss. Initially, Hiss remained president of the Carnegie Endowment Foundation on a paid leave, but after the grand jury indicted him, he resigned to help with his defense. Throughout this ordeal, Ike demanded that the accused be treated fairly: mere allegations were insufficient to force him out of his job; the courts should render a judgment first. After Hiss's conviction, Ike turned to the seriousness of the crime and his antipathy toward traitors. *Seeds of Treason* reinforced the general's favorable impression that Nixon had examined Hiss fairly and had helped to expose a dangerous espionage ring in the United States.[15]

With this background, Nixon and Eisenhower each had positive opinions of the other, and each had his own personal reasons to get better acquainted. After Nixon completed his assignment in Geneva, he arrived in the French capital. Before meeting with Ike, he conferred with Ambassador to France David Bruce, and his counselor to the Paris embassy, Cecil Gray, ambassador to the Soviet Union, as well as with Chip Bohlen, and others.[16]

Even though Ike's calendar was divided into fifteen-minute appointment intervals, Nixon and his host spent almost an hour together starting at 10:30 A.M. on May 18. From the senator's vantage point, he described it as a "nice visit" and said he was "very impressed with his [Ike's] understanding of the nature of the problems we face both abroad and at home in respect to the Communist conspiracy." Ike had emphasized that "the ideological phases of the conflict against Communism in Europe were just as important, if not more important in the long run, as the military and economic."[17]

A month after this first exchange, Nixon stressed in a press interview that although he and the general had never discussed politics, Eisenhower might seek the presidency, and if that happened, he would do it as a Republican.[18]

This personal evaluation was more than wishful thinking. Of likely GOP candidates, polling data demonstrated that Republicans would vote for Eisenhower. In June 1950, he stood at 39 percent, with Taft at 15 percent; at the end of September, the general rose to 42 percent and the senator's rating did not change; in the middle of December, Eisenhower slipped to 35 percent and the Ohioan climbed to 24 percent. During 1951, the polls sometimes showed a 30-point spread for Eisenhower over Truman. Such diverse people as Charles Voorhis, Henry Luce, and Drew Pearson recognized Ike's presidential qualities.[19]

As ever, Nixon consulted with Murray Chotiner to identify winning issues for the 1952 race. One major theme of their dialogue resulted from Oklahoma senator Robert Kerr's speech at the Western Democratic Conference in Denver on the evening of May 23, where he labeled Democrats as the party of the Fair Deal while the Republicans personified a warlike mentality. Chotiner noted that he hoped the GOP would not attack the Fair Deal or Korea, but would concentrate on "*corruption and moral decay in the government."* People wanted decency in the federal administration, and voters were dissatisfied with corruption under the Democrats. If Truman refused to respond to these charges, his silence was admission of guilt; if Democrats answered, the myriad of scandals would convict them.

The GOP, Chotiner emphasized, would not unite on MacArthur, the Korean War strategy, social legislation, or foreign policy. "But they will be able to UNITE on the issue of giving the American people DECENT government again." If the party did not single out that one issue, Republicans could lose the election. Everyone needed to rally around that overarching theme. If the GOP did not do so, it would miss a wonderful opportunity "by not concentrating on the BIG ISSUE which the Democrats *cannot answer."*[20]

The logic of this argument impressed Nixon so much that he circulated copies of Chotiner's letter to Republican leaders across the nation. Senator Wallace Bennett of Utah agreed, as did Joe McCarthy. Congressman Claude Blakewell of St. Louis had used corruption as his sole issue in his 1950 campaign, and "I should like, with modesty, to state that my election was a trial run on Chotiner's strategy."[21]

Others disagreed. Senator Wayne Morse of Oregon responded that the party had to unite the liberal and conservative wings. Kenneth Wherry of Nebraska saw "Administration immorality, wasteful spending and exorbitant taxes" as the main points. RNC chairman Guy Gabrielson believed that while moral decay was a major factor, so was "the bumbling and fumbling of the Administration on foreign policy."[22]

On Thursday, June 28, speaking from the capital over a nationwide radio hookup, Nixon tested many issues, including corruption, while keynoting the biennial Young Republicans Convention of one thousand delegates in Boston. Beginning with foreign affairs, he argued that the Democrats had failed in the battle against communism, the war in Korea, and the rise of the Red Chinese. The GOP should keep the nation strong militarily, and as the global leader of anticommunism, the best minds should be tapped, including Democrats and generals like Douglas MacArthur. As for domestic policy, Nixon stressed that Democrats were socializing America's basic institutions, creating inflation, and destroying free enterprise. To reverse these trends, first, the government had to reduce spending to a minimum due to wartime conditions. Second, inflation had to be attacked by using price controls, demanding a balanced budget, and maintaining high productivity. Third, the United States had

to reverse any move toward socialization and restore individual initiatives. In addition, the United States had to move forcefully against the
Soviet "fifth-column" movement. The Democrats had employed traitors like Harry Dexter White and Alger Hiss, while the GOP was patriotic and would quickly expunge subversive influences from the federal
government.

Finally, the senator turned to his most critical point, which was "to
reestablish the high moral standards of Government service which have
been responsible for our great success as a nation in the past, and which
are so sadly lacking today." The Truman administration ran rampant with
corruption and graft. While the White House insisted that its administrators had done nothing illegal, employees received mink coats, freez-
ers, luxury vacations, tips for commodity insider trading, and worse.
Nixon claimed that "never before in our history have we seen corruption defended and condoned by those in high places." Republicans had
to restore "moral integrity" to the national government.[23]

This powerful speech reinforced Nixon's position as a rising star in
the party. Alvin Derre, Republican County Central Committee chairman from San Francisco, called it "outstanding" in presenting GOP intentions. Perry Gwin in Los Angeles wrote the senator that this was the
first talk that he had heard in twenty years that offered positive Republican options. Voters were not looking for Democratic mistakes; people
knew about them. "What the people are now looking for is a savior.
They want to know how and why the Republicans would do better and
Sen. Nixon is the first Republican to make a speech on 'Why Republicans Would Do Better.'"[24]

In addition to events on the national level, Nixon turned his attention
that spring to Bill Knowland's reelection bid. If the party was going to
win the presidency next year, the GOP had to do well in congressional
races. To accomplish this and give Knowland a boost, Nixon delivered the
principal address at the quarterly meeting of the Los Angeles County Republican Central Committee dinner in Los Angeles on March 30, urging
his listeners to cast their ballots overwhelmingly for Knowland as a vote of
confidence: "It's time to clean out the corruptors—get mad and stay mad
until November 1952—and the American people will do just that!"[25]

Nixon agreed that Knowland should make major political appearances at home to get the maximum press coverage, and he immediately
needed to obtain Warren's endorsement: "If the Governor does not care

to endorse Republican candidates in 1952," Perry predicted, "he does not have any honorable reason to expect support from members of the Party." Nixon concurred, emphasizing Warren might possibly support Knowland because of the criticism directed at the governor "for his inaction in the 1950 campaign." More importantly, Warren and Knowland were close friends.[26]

Nixon and Knowland also had good relations. First, they agreed philosophically on many issues. In foreign policy, they favored the Marshall Plan and the Truman Doctrine, but passionately objected to the firing of General MacArthur. The junior senator acknowledged that his colleague had been "one of the most articulate and able critics of the Administration's policy in the Far East and I am sure that they will leave no stone unturned in their efforts to defeat him."[27]

GOP national and state politics merged on August 18, when Brennan wrote Warren, Knowland, Nixon, and Faries that California's Republican leaders had to present a united front at the national convention with a delegation pledged to the governor so that the state would play a major role in determining the presidential candidate. Brennan proposed a meeting of a small group including those above, plus state chairman Tony Delap and some others, like Murray Chotiner, who were professional managers. Nixon quickly agreed.[28]

Early in November, that plan matured into Warren's favorite-son candidacy when Knowland asked the California GOP to endorse the governor's presidential ambitions. On the 8th, both senators, the Republican congressmen, and some state politicians wrote to encourage the governor to run and pledged to support him.

Bewley immediately warned Nixon that anti-Warrenites would withdraw their backing from him if the senator promoted Warren. Perry, one of those with hurt feelings, called the initiative "very premature," and said he was "not just going to believe this kind of bunk." For Perry and many others, Warren was too moderate, not vocal enough in his anticommunism, and had not endorsed the Republicans' statewide ticket in the past.[29]

Nonetheless, Warren announced for the presidency on November 14. Writing to Perry, Nixon recognized that any alignment with Warren could lead to desertion from the conservative wing, and therefore, he tried to distance himself from Warren's cause and apologized for his decision to introduce Warren at a GOP meeting in the San Diego: "You can be sure, however, that I will not use the occasion to nominate him for President!" Soon afterwards, Nixon attended the California State Central Committee, where he complimented the governor; Aylett Cotton, who observed Nixon's masterful performance, congratulated him on doing "an excellent job of walking down the middle of the Warren controversy in your disc jockey speech."[30]

Nixon explained his decision to back a favorite-son candidacy. With neither Ike nor Taft expecting to mount any primary fight in California, Nixon wanted the most forceful delegation that the state could muster. That required the most influential political leaders serving as delegates. Then, if the governor were eliminated as a viable prospect, Nixon expected the delegation to turn to the contender who had the best chance of winning in 1952. It was a classic example of kingmaker strategy.[31]

Herman Perry was livid: "Hardly a day goes by but what I come across one of our enthusiastic supporters with whom I have to argue and reason relative to your present position in the forthcoming Presidential election." Perry wrote later, "I am having one H. of a time trying to convince people to be realistic about your support of Governor Warren. Every body [sic] seems to think you have sold out your friends in California. I tell them no."[32]

Despite such harsh admonishments, Nixon actively promoted Warren's candidacy when visiting New York City in the first part of December. He conferred with Leo Casey, who had seen Warren at the American Bar Association Convention and had pledged to work for him in the East and Midwest. Nixon told Brennan about this discussion, who, in turn, contacted Casey about starting his campaign activities. Brennan recognized Warren had to act promptly, but understood that "Earl's normal reaction is against getting under way until late in the game. I am just as concerned as you are that the delay may be so long as to be damaging."[33]

Already the front-runner, Taft had announced in October. Appearing at the Bohemian Grove earlier that summer, he left a positive impression, but had not won many over to his side. Yet polls of a Truman-Taft race showed a slight edge for the senator.[34]

When Nixon met with General MacArthur in New York City in the middle of December, the general modestly complimented Taft as the best candidate to oppose Truman, saying that the senator stood for everything that the president opposed. At the close of the month, de Toledano reported on the current presidential sweepstakes: "The biggest news here is that Taft is sewing up delegates at a tremendous rate. So unless the West Coast comes to Ike's rescue, it looks as if Taft will win the nomination, almost by default. My emotions are mixed."[35]

Many in the Nixon camp rejected Taft. When Dana Smith, campaign treasurer during Nixon's senatorial contest, asked if he could become involved with the Ike campaign that July, Nixon did not dissuade him. That winter, when Smith approached Jack Drown to come out for Ike, Drown hesitated until Nixon encouraged him to take that step if Drown believed in Eisenhower's cause. Bewley conceded that the general was the best vote-getter, but not a party man. "The average voter, however, is very much pro Eisenhower." As Bewley and Nixon had previously discussed, they needed a change in Washington, and "the only way to get it is to get a sure winner."[36]

Nixon had this opinion graphically reinforced while riding on a train with Congressman Bill Colmer of Mississippi, who foresaw a southern Democratic revolt because of that party's hatred of Truman. The congressman's first choice was Ike, to which Nixon responded: "if Eisenhower were nominated he would carry most of the South against any Democratic candidate."[37]

The dilemma was that "if." Eisenhower, throughout 1951, remained reticent. Cyrus Sulzberger, publisher and reporter for the *New York Times,* regularly chatted with the general. During early spring, the reporter believed that Ike disapproved of the "social or political philosophy" of the Truman administration and disagreed with American diplomacy that had abandoned Chiang Kai-shek due to his refusal to allow Communists in his government. Ike was much closer to Herbert Hoover and Taft, despite their disagreements over NATO.[38]

By the end of the summer, Cliff Roberts, a "very close friend" of Ike's, felt that he would run. In the late fall, Sulzberger sensed that the general wanted the Republican nomination, and during the second week in December, after an hour and a half's conversation with Ike, Sulzberger hoped the general would be "drafted at the Republican convention, runs and is elected."[39]

Although Nixon was not a party to Eisenhower's agonizing over whether he should run for the White House, he was grappling with his own health problems, wishing to "take that good long vacation that Pat and I have been trying to get in for the past five years." By early fall, Nixon admitted that the current session had been "a long arduous" one, and he and his wife needed a rest. "In fact," speaking in the third person, "the Senator has been somewhat under the weather and the doctor has told him not to come in unless it is absolutely necessary. Nothing serious, but just too much prolonged work without a rest. He has never had a day's vacation in the five years he has been in Congress, and none after the campaign, then this session has been a little rugged, so altogether, it's beginning to take its toll."[40]

By the middle of September, everything was canceled on doctor's orders, and Bewley insisted on "your getting clear out of the country for the month of October and hope that you and Pat will do just that." On the afternoon of October 9, they left for Sea Island, Georgia. The setting was beautiful. Although the sun shone for only two days due to a nearby hurricane, they both relaxed for two full weeks. As Pat put it, "It was a real rest for Dick but not long enough."[41]

Nixon had given forty-five speeches in twenty-one states in 1951, mostly during congressional recesses. He was so well received that Selma Warlick, director of the National Concert and Artists Corporation, booked him for paid engagements. After several talks, Warlick received excellent reviews from the groups to which he had spoken: "all of them expressing praise of your speech and presentation."[42]

As a result of these paid addresses, Nixon's income jumped to $19,870 for 1951 from just over $7,000 for the previous year. His official expenses also had climbed. To a public servant of modest means, his patrons' trust fund supplementing his senatorial income had become essential. Christmas cards cost $2,537.25; recording facilities for his messages to California were another $165.30; reimbursement for office expenses came to $125.65. Much of this and other incidentals Dana Smith paid for through the special fund.[43]

At the end of 1951, Nixon's overriding concern was the future of his party. *U.S. News & World Report* graphically illustrated "Why Republicans Worry." Half of the American voters had grown to voting age after Herbert Hoover left the White House, and records indicated that Republicans were now a minority party. If Republicans were going to win, the newsmagazine postulated, they must capture two out of every three independents, who traditionally tended to vote Democratic. Relying on these statistics, the GOP had to decide whether it would pick a new face like Eisenhower, assuming he would enter the race, or an old well-known character like Taft and hope to win on the issues.[44]

The old versus the new was precisely Nixon's dilemma throughout 1951. First, the GOP needed a presidential winner. He had eliminated Stassen, had deep trepidations over Taft, hoped for an Eisenhower declaration; but without that, Nixon had to settle on the favorite-son candidacy of Warren as a means for California to come to the convention as a formidable bloc. Knowland and other Republicans had to win if the GOP was going to triumph. Second, Nixon hammered at Truman on the C-2, K-1 topics. His speeches helped party stalwarts identify the rallying cries for the uncertainties of the upcoming year and associate the issues with Nixon, the spokesman who cogently articulated them.

When Senator Henry Cabot Lodge, Jr., campaign manager for the Eisenhower forces, released a letter on January 6, 1952, to Governor Sherman Adams of New Hampshire stating that Ike had permitted his name to be entered in that state's Republican primary, the political landscape dramatically changed. Though the general refused to return home from Europe to campaign, he said he would accept the nomination if it were offered.[45]

Almost immediately after that announcement, derogatory stories about the Eisenhowers began circulating. Anonymous slanderous rumors started spreading that the general's health was deteriorating; his wife, Mamie, was a drunk; his alleged wartime romance with his driver, Kay Summersby, still flourished; and a divorce was in the offing.[46]

When Nixon discovered that an extremist fringe group called the Partisan Republicans of California had issued "some very defamatory literature" directed against Ike, the senator wrote him on January 17 for two purposes. First, he explained that this group had "opposed me during my race against Helen Gahagan Douglas as well as her on the ground that I was an internationalist and, therefore, friendly to the Communists!" Nixon assured the general that the great majority had dissociated itself from such fringe organizations: "As a Californian, I am ashamed of the fact that we seem to attract so many crackpots to our State." The general quickly thanked Nixon for his letter, declaring that these groups did not typify the "fine people of California." Such attacks were "occupational hazards" for individuals like him and Nixon, but they were vexing. Ike added that he was "grateful for your concern."[47]

Second, the letter gave both men the chance to reestablish contact. Nixon remembered "with great pleasure" their conversation in Paris, and said he hoped to see Ike in the future. "I want you to know," Nixon continued, "that I am among those who believe you are rendering a great service to the country under very difficult circumstances and I want to take this opportunity to wish you well in the days to come."

Eisenhower replied that he appreciated Nixon's NATO backing: "I believe we agree on its importance to the security of the United States and to the world in general." Ike hoped that the senator would find another opportunity to visit Europe: "then I can have a chance to discuss with you our progress over the last year."[48]

By the start of February, Nixon moved closer to backing Eisenhower, wishing that he would return to the United States. The senator declared on the 2nd: "The political pot is really boiling and I only hope that Eisenhower can see his way clear to come back to the states about a month before the convention. I, frankly, believe this will be necessary if he is to get the nomination." To those who wished to take an active part in the Eisenhower drive, Nixon urged them to contact Dana Smith of the Eisenhower Volunteers of Los Angeles.[49]

While Ike remained in Europe, he won a stunning victory over Taft in New Hampshire, followed by a big win in Minnesota. Newspapers began to clamor for the general's return to the United States and for him to state his position on issues forthrightly.[50]

Nixon realized that "Mr. Republican" still controlled many GOP stalwarts who worked at the grassroots level across the nation and within the RNC. Nixon perceived the Ohioan's strength significantly improving in the Middle West, but noted that he had not developed a real base in California. "In any event," the senator wished, "let's hope that we can nominate somebody next July who won't have been killed off by the Republicans themselves!"[51]

Taft had loyalists in the Nixon camp. Former Nixon law partner Tom Bewley was "for Taft—first, last and always. I hope you [Herman Perry] are too—he *can* be elected." George Creel, who led the Democrats for Nixon in 1950, pulled for Taft, but felt the momentum for MacArthur swelling. Perry saw the benefits of a MacArthur-Taft ticket and presented it to his protégé toward the end of March. After visiting with MacArthur, Senator Mundt was also ready to back him for the presidency and make Taft vice president, a wonderful combination that he thought the public would embrace.[52]

Although MacArthur attracted avid anti-Communists like Mundt and Perry, Nixon stayed in the mainstream. He continued to chart the shifting national polls in 1952 that tracked Ike and Taft. In the middle of February, they were tied among GOP voters; in early March, the senator led the general inside the GOP by 1 percentage point, while Ike had a large advantage with independents; in the second week of April, Ike had a 37 percent to 34 percent edge over Taft.[53]

In such a fluid situation, Nixon also concentrated on the composition of Warren's favorite-son slate and believed that he would be asked to become a member. He added: "it is essential that we get the strongest possible group as members of the delegation so that it can do the right job at the proper time."[54]

Although Warren and Nixon had different motives to see that the favorite-son slate was victorious, both men attempted to look for ways to cooperate even though gossip continually surfaced about their disagreements. The *Los Angeles Examiner* in the middle of January ran Harry Lang's column, "Looking Around," reporting gossip that Nixon, acting as an undercover go-between for months, had brokered a deal between Ike and Warren whereby the governor would withdraw at the last possible moment to support the general and accept the vice-presidential spot. Nixon denied the truthfulness of the story: "I only wish that I had that much influence with either of the two gentlemen concerned!" Still, many were suspicious of Nixon's support for a governor with whom the senator had never worked closely. On the 21st, Nixon responded to rumors that the governor had been trying to win a Supreme Court appointment by swinging his delegation to Ike. Nixon denounced any suggestion that Warren was empowered to make any deals for the delegation if he could not win the nomination.[55]

Toward the end of January, the governor appeared to reach out to Nixon when Brennan suggested that Nixon should phone Warren for an appointment. Kyle Palmer added that the governor had unsuccessfully tried to reach Nixon on several occasions to congratulate him for his various accomplishments. By the middle of February, Nixon reciprocated by declaring the governor to be "the strongest dark horse in the race." To the senator, Warren was "electable," and his chances were rising as the possibilities of a deadlock between Taft and Eisenhower increased. Refusing to speculate on which of the two leading contenders would take the second spot, he highlighted his two major considerations: "I will withhold judgment until I see which can best support and sell our program. I am interested both in principles and electability."[56]

Nixon doggedly maintained that the best way for California to influence the Republican National Convention was to make certain that the Warren slate won. Nixon encouraged Harvey Hancock in San Francisco in mid-March to work energetically for the delegation: "We have to win this one or else!" On March 21, he explained that a powerful California bloc would be able to unite with other delegations in their quest to select the best candidate: first supporting Warren; and if he dropped out, later emerging as a large swing vote.[57]

On March 24, the names of the seventy-member Warren for President delegation for California's June 3 primary were released. Nixon's most avid supporters were Jack Drown, a close personal friend; Roy Crocker, a banker and supporter since 1946; Pat Hillings, protégé and congressional successor; and Warren Brock, a wealthy farmer from El Centro. As alternates, Nixon had Frank Jorgensen, an original 1946 backer; John Dinkelspiel, who led the Northern California 1950 campaign; Murray Chotiner; Athalie Clarke, owner of the mammoth Irvine Company property; Harrison McCall, general election manager for the 1946 contest; Ray Arbuthnot, a wealthy rancher; and Bewley. Some, like the actor George "Murph" Murphy, were sympathetic to Nixon, but not directly aligned with him. These choices undoubtedly pleased the senator and his followers, but even if these individualists pledged absolute fealty, Nixon controlled less than 10 percent of the voting delegates and their alternates.[58]

Many GOP conservatives who backed Nixon continued to deplore his support of Warren. George Bobbitt from El Monte considered the governor "as big a spendthrift as Truman ever dared to be." William Gamble from Beverly Hills was extremely disappointed, conceding that the governor had integrity, but everything else was questionable: "This was not the Richard Nixon I had built up in my mind. Warren failed to come to bat for you as he should have . . . has carried water on both shoulders . . . is too much of an opportunist . . . too controversial a personality in our own party within the state . . . and not sufficient in stature to warrant your endorsement."[59]

Once again, Perry was furious. On January 9, Nixon tried to calm him: "I can appreciate all the beefing you must be having to take on the Warren situation. I am inclined to think, however, with Eisenhower in the picture the race will soon narrow down to one between him and Taft with Eisenhower eventually winning. You can be sure that I intend to have a very frank heart-to-heart talk with Bill Knowland within the next couple of days on the delegation situation and that I shall let him know the type of opposition which has developed on the Warren deal."[60]

This soothing failed. On March 10, the retired bank manager as-

serted that Warren had "pushed Dick around . . . asking all kinds of favors and concessions from him." This certainly did not assist in the creation of a united front and the breach might even damage Knowland's
reelection expectations. Eight days later, Brennan informed Perry that
the composition of the Warren delegation would please him since "Dick
has been consulted right along and will have a good many of his gang in
the picture." Perry grumbled; he was still pessimistic, but was impressed
with the inclusion of some Nixon followers in the delegation.[61]

In reality, Nixon had no intention of challenging the hold of a popular governor; neither did Taft. When a group led by Congressman
Thomas Werdel from Bakersfield at the beginning of 1952 decided to
spearhead an anti-Warren slate that favored Taft, he discouraged it, recognizing that the governor was too well entrenched. Despite this rejection, Werdel's organization pushed ahead, and Werdel openly attacked
Warren's policies on the House floor. On the last day of February,
Werdel announced that his Independent/Republican delegation would
be "uninstructed" so that each delegate could vote as he or she wished.
Nixon added the obvious, that "you have to admire them for their
guts."[62]

Although the senator respected many within the Werdel group, he
discovered that Gregory Bern and Major Robert H. Williams of the
Williams Intelligence Survey, an anti-Semitic front for the Partisan Republicans, which employed smear tactics against its adversaries, possibly
had aligned with the Werdel faction. If a properly timed article proved
the connection, Nixon felt that it would have "a devastating effect since
the Partisan Republicans seem to be spearheading the independent slate.
[Yet] I wouldn't do it . . . if you [Brennan] find they have carefully
screened all of that gang out of their delegation." Nothing came of this
suggestion. On March 29, the Werdel group announced its membership
for the primary ballot and its opposition to Warren "as a New Deal Tru-
manite."[63]

While worrying about the delegates to the national convention,
Nixon faced another unpleasant primary decision. Since his congressional election in 1946, he had adopted a strict statewide policy of not
intervening in any primary races. He followed this until Joe Holt faced
off against Jack Tenney in the 22nd congressional district. The latter had
served in the state senate and had warmly promoted Nixon in the 1950
senatorial race. The former was a twenty-eight-year-old marine, who
had recently returned from Korea with a Purple Heart and had been

Nixon's field organizer in 1950. Nixon felt that Holt deserved his support. Immediately after Nixon endorsed him, Tenney wired Nixon: "ET TU BRUTE."

Nixon encouraged Holt to run because he represented "the type of new, young leadership which the Republican Party and our country needs to restore the confidence and faith of the people in the government." He extolled Holt's virtues and praised his loyalty: "I became greatly impressed with Mr. Holt's qualities of leadership and integrity when he served faithfully and effectively as field director of my senatorial campaign in 1950. He was with us from the start, when the outlook was decidedly bleak, and contributed in large measure to the ultimate success of that campaign."[64]

Chotiner, Holt's campaign manager, in mid-March wanted much more than this glowing endorsement. He asked Nixon for a favor: to supply Jack Tenney's HUAC file. Tenney had once had Communist sympathies, though he had since renounced them. HUAC had compiled a file on him, but never pursued an investigation because he had rejected those earlier beliefs. Nevertheless, Bill Arnold sent the file, warning Chotiner that he should not use it "in light of Tenney's complete reformation a la Whittaker Chambers. You no doubt also have considered the potential backfire danger in the use of this material." Arnold further cautioned that Nixon "distinctly does not want it to be known that we have obtained material for you and sent it to you."[65]

What Nixon authorized was, at a minimum, outrageous. He knew that HUAC files were solely for congressional use, and yet he sent Tenney's files to his opponent to use against him. Nixon was sufficiently concerned about his action that Arnold pointedly told Chotiner that he was not to disclose where the information had originated. Files were regularly leaked. The senator owed both Chotiner and Holt debts of gratitude and wished to accommodate them. However, as a lawyer, Nixon's action smacked of a violation of ethics and wrongdoing. At the very least, Nixon had compromised his congressional integrity.

Holt beat Tenney, though the file did not seem to come into play. Afterwards, Nixon called upon Republicans from that district to unite behind Holt's candidacy and elect him. The senator ironically added that he did not disapprove of Tenney, but just liked Holt more. If Tenney had proved triumphant, Nixon would have backed him fully.[66]

Besides the various primary considerations, Nixon remained intimately involved in discrediting Communists. Although no longer on HUAC, he followed its activities. Still angry at the loss of America's vital atomic secrets, he concentrated on removing spies from the government. To prevent further betrayal, he staunchly supported federal loyalty procedures. By early 1952, he learned that the FBI had already conducted 18,424 loyalty investigations; 2,072 federal employees had resigned during those reviews; and 2,028 left prior to the adjudication of their cases. The loyalty boards rated 580 people ineligible for employment and reinstated 220 after they successfully appealed to the loyalty review board. Within the State Department, 33 workers had resigned during their probes, and 17 more had left because they were found to be disloyal or poor security risks.[67]

Toward the end of January, in preparation for a television debate against Francis Biddle, former U.S. Attorney General under Franklin Roosevelt and current president of the Americans for Democratic Action, Nixon voiced his suspicions about ADA's motives. While the group professed to be "a liberal anti-communist group," according to Nixon, it had attempted to repeal the Smith Act under which eleven Communist leaders in New York were convicted; therefore, "one might well wonder just how anti-communist the organization is." Nixon also had concerns about the American Civil Liberties Union, observing that its branch in California had "quite a few left-wingers in its membership."[68]

When multimillionaire Howard Hughes, managing director of RKO Pictures Corporation, filed the first motion picture studio action in Los Angeles Superior Court against Paul Jarrico, a screenwriter who had been subpoenaed by HUAC and invoked the Fifth Amendment, Nixon praised Hughes. He had refused to compromise with the Screen Writers Guild and asked the court for declaratory judgment against Jarrico.[69]

Despite this hard-line position, Nixon firmly believed that Communists should have the opportunity to speak in public as long as they openly identified themselves. David Smith, Nixon's campaign treasurer for Northern California in 1950, served on the Berkeley school board that had allowed Paul Robeson to sing at the Berkeley High School Community Theatre. Since Robeson was accused of being a Communist, Smith had received a considerable amount of criticism. Nixon privately assured Smith that his judgment was "sound." Differing with many anti-Communists in this regard, Nixon maintained, "I would even go so far as to allow an admitted card-carrying Communist to make a speech in a public hall *provided* the meeting was advertised as a Communist meeting and the speaker was properly labeled as such." As for Robeson, Nixon thought that if no one paid him any attention, "he would draw far smaller crowds than he does." The senator advised Smith not to worry; everything would turn out all right.[70]

Once Communists revealed themselves, the senator had "no fear that democracy and the American way of life will suffer by comparison in the open market place of public expression." The nation had laws against anyone seeking to overthrow the government by violent means, and "from expressions of political opinion short of that. . . . I do not believe that we should follow the example of the totalitarian nations through the suppression of a free expression of ideals."[71]

Another side of Nixon's role in the fight against communism resurfaced in 1952 with the revival of the question of Hiss's innocence or guilt. During Nixon's first year in the Senate, the case had left the front pages and Nixon had mainly wondered about its lasting scars. For example, since he believed that the *Washington Post* rigidly adhered to Hiss's innocence in its editorials, "I rather imagine it will take some time to heal some of the sore spots which developed by reason of the somewhat prominent part I played in the investigation." After the defendant had exhausted his appeals, the senator saw no reason "for elation or gratification because not since the days of Benedict Arnold have the American people been the victim of such a brazen and inexplicable act of treachery by a man who commanded the faith and confidence of our highest officials." Nixon now urged Hiss to admit his guilt and disclose what he knew about the Red spy network in America.[72]

But in 1952 the case returned to the headlines. The *St. Louis Post-Dispatch* on April 24 editorialized that Hiss's attorneys had presented evidence to the trial judge that Chambers had framed their client by using a fake typewriter. Another affidavit alleged that Priscilla Hiss did not copy the State Department documents; someone else did. Edith Murray, an African American maid, confirmed that the Hisses and Chamberses had an intimate social relationship, but her testimony was being questioned. Finally, some information had surfaced that the Chamberses might have left the Communist Party earlier than he alleged. The paper believed all of these unresolved questions demanded a new trial. After reading the article, Nixon declared that the people at the *Post-Dispatch* had never "retreated from their position of almost hysterical defense of

Hiss even in spite of the damaging testimony against him in both the Committee hearings and the trial."[73]

In regard to Whittaker Chambers, Nixon never wavered. No matter what this former Communist had done in the past, "the American people are unquestionably indebted to him for the fearlessness with which he has acted in exposing communist infiltration into our government." The senator further asserted that Chambers deserved "the loyal support of all honest citizens"; and another time, Nixon maintained that he had the "highest opinion" of the former Soviet agent. After Mount Mary College gave Chambers a Doctor of Laws degree at its June commencement, Nixon praised Chambers for contributing to the cause of free people everywhere and hoped that "other institutions of higher learning in this country will appropriately recognize the great service Mr. Chambers has rendered."[74]

Chambers published his memoirs, *Witness,* that spring. Nixon reviewed the book in the *Saturday Review,* as did Arthur Schlesinger, Jr., who pronounced it a well-written, important study; Richard Morris, a prominent Columbia historian, on the other hand, was dubious about Chambers's judgments. Nixon had no such doubts, stating that Chambers had composed "a great book, and that the verdict of history will find it so." Chambers had presented an excellent description of HUAC, Hiss, and the hearings. The former spy demonstrated the hold of the Communist faith and the need to oppose it. To Nixon, Chambers was a "brilliant," "shy," and "deeply religious man," who had done a tremendous service exposing the Communist peril.[75]

Chambers appreciated his friend's sympathetic review. The book, after all, was a counterattack against the enemy, and the "fight would have gone better in the past if there had been less apologetics." These were mere tactics in the struggle against communism. "For your personal generosity, I am truly grateful."[76]

Father Cronin also reviewed *Witness* and hoped that Nixon would introduce him to its author. The priest compared this book to the *Confessions of Saint Augustine* and John Henry Cardinal Newman's *Apologia Pro Vita Sua.* If mankind did not choose God, Chambers noted that another ideal was available in communism. He took the reader on the tortuous path that led him to espionage and returned him to religion. Cronin reveled in it. "During the dark years 1945–1948," Cronin remembered, "only a few persons, notable among them . . . Nixon . . . believed these stories and strove to bring them to light. As for the rest, there was some scepticism, much disbelief, and even systematic efforts to conceal or discredit the facts." Chambers brought out these sordid events so that people could read the truth.[77]

Besides coming to Chambers's assistance, Nixon also defended Norman Chandler, publisher of the *Los Angeles Times,* in his battle against the federal government's attempt to take over the water rights to the Santa Margarita River basin. The Fallbrook Case involved a legal battle between the recently established U.S. Marine base at Camp Pendleton and fourteen thousand landowners in the farming region just north of San Diego. Chandler entreated the senator to move aggressively with congressional action to prevent the U.S. Attorney General from "this intolerable seizure of private rights." Some questioned the nature of the dispute, hearing rumors that powerful land development companies had a large stake in it. Both Nixon and Knowland co-sponsored a bill to block the federal action. When *U.S.* v. *Fallbrook Public Utility District et al.* was filed in January 1951 asserting the U.S. government's title to the Santa Margarita River's water, both California senators wrote the president on April 3, asking for a conference of all parties to find an equitable solution to protect the citizens of the region and to secure the water supply for Camp Pendleton.[78]

When that offer produced no results, Nixon and Knowland tried to push the Fallbrook bill through the Senate in June after the legislation had unanimously passed the House. The *Los Angeles Times* offered its wholehearted backing in a series of articles designed to present the side of private rights. In late June, according to the newspaper, the issue spotlighted the struggle of the ordinary citizen versus the vast powers of the federal government: thousands of small farmers were fighting a federal "water grab." The Senate voted to cut off funding in the U.S. Attorney General's budget to prosecute this case by the end of the month, but Congress had to pass legislation preventing any repetition. Nixon and Knowland presented a bill to assure fair distribution of water to protect military and civilian needs; their measure would also stop the protracted and expensive litigation facing hundreds of small property owners in the Santa Margarita watershed.[79]

According to the general manager of the Fallbrook Public Utility District, Gordon Tinker, who has been involved with this dispute since 1980, forty-eight years have elapsed since the filing of the litigation, without resolution. Currently, a U.S. federal district court has appointed James Jenks watermaster to oversee the water rights in the watershed, but this is not a permanent solution. Tinker believes that the parties are earnestly looking for a resolution to the water issue and optimistically hopes that this will occur shortly after the turn of the twentieth-first century.[80]

As for other legislation before the Senate, Nixon voted to reduce government expenditures and opposed legislation like the St. Lawrence Seaway bill because the current budget's expenses already exceeded income. He voted for the Defense Production Act, with mandatory controls due to the threat of inflation and the high cost of living; he favored ending rent requirements the same day as price and wage controls, as well as removing controls on fresh fruits and vegetables. While some retailers criticized him for voting against the discontinuation of price controls on September 1, he continued working to terminate the inequities in the legislation and looked forward to the time when all such controls ceased. He also amended his bill on public housing authorization, which followed the Los Angeles City Council vote to rescind a public housing project, thereby removing those federal funds from the city's coffers.[81]

Nixon supported the Universal Military Training legislation because some form of military training was a necessity. He also voted for the Japanese Peace Treaty: John Foster Dulles had helped negotiate it, and Knowland, one of the administration's most vocal opponents on Far Eastern policy, as well as General MacArthur, approved. It passed the Senate by a vote of 66 to 10.[82]

The political picture once more altered radically in late March 1952, when President Truman announced that he would not seek or accept any reelection draft. Nixon chose an April Fool's Day address before the National Metal Trades Association annual dinner in New York to make remarks on the decision. Declaring that the president had lost the confidence of the people, Nixon predicted that Truman would handpick his successor, who would then owe allegiance to the White House. "Those who believe that the country needs new ideas and new leadership in the field of foreign policy," the senator asserted, "will have no choice except to vote for the Republican candidate." Neither of the Democratic front-runners, Senator Kefauver and Illinois governor Adlai Stevenson, would be forceful. The latter had been a character witness for Hiss. Nixon did not question the governor's individual right to defend this traitor, "but the voters also have a right to question whether a man who showed such lack of judgment is competent to deal effectively and realistically with the Communists at home and abroad." Kefauver, on several occasions, also voted against HUAC appropriations. Once again, Nixon raised the issue of "judgment rather than loyalty." In addition, both men had close bonds to the administration and would be unable to unravel the scandal-plagued administration.[83]

Several months later, Nixon spoke before the national convention of the Liquefied Petroleum Gas Association at a Palmer House luncheon audience in Chicago, noting that the Democratic draft for Stevenson was gaining momentum. He would be the toughest opponent that the Republicans would face, and while his affidavit favoring Hiss would hurt Stevenson, he could "get over" that political liability. Nixon anticipated a close race, whichever Democrat won its party's nomination, because the GOP needed millions of Democratic votes to win. "Those who contend that all the Republicans have to do to win is to get all the Republicans to go to the polls and vote are just whistling in the dark."[84]

The prelude to the conventions turned ugly when, a week after Truman announced his decision not to seek reelection, he seized the steel industry. The federal government technically ran the facilities, but management and labor continued under their traditional roles, without approving a new contract. Serving on the Senate Labor and Public Welfare Committee, Nixon had earlier called for more democratic practices within unions and worried that they exerted too much influence in a Democratic administration that had seized the railroad industry over a year and a half ago and had made no progress toward a labor settlement. The committee discussed pay raises for railroad employees as a solution, but in the end did nothing.[85]

Nixon was especially irritated that organized labor had continually attacked the Taft-Hartley Act, blocking any supplemental legislation, no matter how meritorious. Labor leaders knew that the act was not as terrible as they portrayed it, but any corrective bill was unlikely, "due largely to the vociferous clamor which has been set up by labor against Taft-Hartley itself." The act's injunctive provisions did not prevent all strikes, only those when and where the president and the courts feared for the national health and safety.[86]

By late spring, the growing federal tendency to establish administrative policies that had the same force as law, especially in the railroad seizure, deeply troubled Nixon. He foreshadowed action to curb the authority of special government boards and denounced the Wage Stabilization Board proposals to end the steel dispute that included employers granting CIO demands for a union shop. That, to Nixon, circumvented the Taft-Hartley Act: "Perhaps the time has come, at last, for Congress to review these blank-check powers we have given the President and to get back legislative authority it delegated because of alleged emergency situations." The senator was "hopeful we can still avert a steel strike and at the same time do justice to the public interest involved."[87]

Truman seized the steel industry on April 8 to avoid a strike that the unions had called for the next day. As with the continuing Korean "police action," the president as commander in chief invoked his executive powers without congressional approval, precipitating a legal and political controversy over presidential prerogatives. Some, like Taft, considered impeachment, and while politicians angrily debated, the industry filed suit to overturn Truman's decision before a federal district court.[88]

Nixon gave a speech on April 21 to attack the seizure as possibly posing "just as great a potential threat to labor as it does to management." The president had stopped the strike to force a wage increase that labor applauded. The previous year, Truman had seized the railroads to prevent a strike, and those unions condemned his action, for it also halted a wage increase. Nixon argued that seizures should only be allowed by congressional legislation. What Truman had done was to enforce a Wage Stabilization Board order compelling an increase in wages, and thus, labor leaders had a new way to circumvent the Taft-Hartley Act.[89]

Before more than a thousand cheering Republicans in San Francisco, eight days later, Nixon praised Judge David A. Pine's decision invalidating Truman's seizure. No one, including the president, was above the U.S. Constitution. Nixon hoped that the Supreme Court would sustain the judge, for the president had seized a nationwide industry without the authority of law. A month later, in a six-to-three decision, the highest court of the land returned the mills to their owners.[90]

At the end of April, Nixon insisted that all candidates make their positions clear on Truman's seizure of the steel industry. To the senator, the president had taken over a nationwide industry without the force of law, and every Republican candidate before the upcoming national convention should disavow publicly, without equivocation, "any claim to the arbitrary power to seize any industry in the United States except as that power is granted to him by the people's representatives in Congress." Nixon especially called on Eisenhower to express his opinions. "If General Eisenhower does not speak out," Nixon cautioned, "his inaction may well lead to his defeat for the nomination."[91]

While focusing on the steel seizure, Nixon was also concerned over the success of the Warren slate in the primary. He remained convinced that its victory was an integral part of the statewide strategy of giving California Republicans a major voice in choosing their presidential nominee. Nixon expected to follow any nominee who would "provide the American people the one sure means at their disposal to bring a halt to the continuing trend, under the present administration, toward complete socialization of every basic American industry and profession."[92]

Throughout April, Nixon held out Warren as "the front-running dark horse." A consistent theme of the senator's was that the GOP needed Democratic and independent voters to win the election. Warren drew them to him. The *Los Angeles Times* reaffirmed that logic when it endorsed the Warren delegation. The newspaper conceded that Warren had made enemies during his tenure in office, but with Taft and Ike battling each other for the nomination, Warren was a possible compromise candidate who could do the job.[93]

Not everyone concurred. Perry was still so angry that he refused to go to an event at which both Warren and Nixon appeared because he did not wish publicly to exhibit his antipathy toward the governor. Perry felt that Knowland and Nixon reflected the spirit of the California GOP, and Warren quickly needed to release the delegation into their hands. John Pierce, Republican national committeeman from Los Angeles, "shuddered a couple of times [when the senators decided to back Warren] and steeled myself for the argument that I knew would take place." The rank and file booed him for supporting the governor; others needed to step forward to carry out the party's program. Brennan even warned one Nixon follower that the two senators headed the delegation, and "it would be a catastrophe and would put a black mark against them for the rest of their political careers not to have a victory for the Warren delegation."[94]

Tom Bewley, an alternate to the convention, attended a Warren delegation meeting on April 23 with eighty to one hundred people present, including Kyle Palmer. This gathering did not compare with those who went to Nixon's political breakfasts. "Frankly," Bewley told Nixon, "the delegates and alternates who were chosen as friends of yours stand out among the entire group." Some cheered Warren for president, and Brennan, who chaired the meeting, asserted that Warren represented the best of California's Republican Party. Bewley discounted the hoopla: "My personal opinion is that there is nobody in the group as cold-blooded as Murray Chotiner and he is the type of fellow that we need badly."[95]

The battle between the Warren and Werdel delegations grew in intensity throughout May. Nixon publicly backed Warren, but would not attack the opposition since the Bakersfield congressman and many inside his group were friends. Nixon added: "I believe Republicans should attempt to sell the merit of their own candidate rather than to tear down the reputations of the other candidates."[96]

By the end of the month, despite his sunny claim that "From all reports the Warren Delegation is going to win a hands down victory," Nixon was hedging, besieged with advice to drop Warren. Bewley had spoken with a number of Nixon's banking associates who unanimously wished him to take no further action on Warren's behalf. The senator rejected that counsel, and on the day before the California primary in early June, he issued a statement calling for Californians to vote for Warren. However, he continued, the delegation was not a rubber stamp for the governor, and if he released it, "we shall be free to look over the field and select the man best qualified to carry the Republican banner in the campaign next November."[97]

In fact, Nixon's swing-vote strategy was looking increasingly likely of success. At the convention, nominees needed 604 votes to win. Based on primaries and caucuses so far, neither Taft nor Ike was close to that magic number. California's seventy votes might be the key to the presidential sweepstakes. As for Warren, Nixon assured Perry that he had no intention of blindly following the governor.[98]

Nixon's public comments on the presidential hopefuls indeed seemed to edge away from Warren. The best Nixon could say about the governor was that he and MacArthur were "the strongest dark horses at the moment." Senator Everett Dirksen was also a possibility; however, his close ties with the ultraconservative *Chicago Tribune* would hurt his chances. Between the front-runners, Taft and Ike, Nixon felt that the Ohio senator was running ahead. To have a chance, Ike needed to leave Paris immediately and return to the United States.[99]

Nixon acknowledged his "high opinion" of Taft—an oblique compliment, for Nixon added that any Republican contender would be an improvement over Truman. In the middle of the month, Nixon told a Quaker audience that the Ohio senator was well qualified, honest, organized, and a liberal except on labor and foreign policy issues. One weakness that stood out was that Taft was cold. To another group, Nixon spotlighted the Ohioan's effectiveness and experience, but he had an unpleasant personality, spoke poorly, and sometimes could be too intellectual.[100]

Nixon gravitated closer to Eisenhower as the Republican presidential standard-bearer because he was a winner. In the middle of April, the senator thought that the two major candidates were deadlocked and predicted that "Ike will make a break between now and July." Toward the end of the month, he warned Dana Smith that Eisenhower's greatest weakness would "be a 'me too' candidate and that he is too closely surrounded and advised by out-right new dealers."[101]

Nixon knew that Eisenhower proponents in San Francisco were spreading rumors that the senator met with them and pledged his support to the general if Warren could not be nominated. "This, of course, is completely untrue," Nixon trumpeted, "and could have the effect of very seriously damaging the Eisenhower cause." However, he agreed to meet with the organization under the guise of a Young Republicans gathering to give them advice on how to proceed. If they breached this confidence, any future conversations would be "completely noncommittal."[102]

To "make some good contacts for the Convention," Nixon accepted an invitation to speak before the New York State Convention at the Waldorf-Astoria on May 8. He arrived at his suite on the fourth floor for the annual $100-a-plate fund-raiser. Senator Irving Ives of New York and Governor Dewey spoke first, introducing the senator graciously, and then he presented the principal address.[103]

In his remarks, Nixon emphasized that Republicans had to appeal to Democrats in order to win the presidency. The GOP had to present positive foreign policy initiatives, but they could not be isolationist. He praised Senator Arthur Vandenberg of Michigan and John Foster Dulles, who cooperated with the administration on some global issues, but still had been consistently critical of American policies in East Asia. Nixon declared: "The Administration's policy has failed not because it was internationalist but because our State Department policy makers failed to recognize that Communists in China and Korea were just as great a threat to American security as Communists in Greece and Germany."

Afterwards, Thomas Dewey, who had already openly declared his support for Eisenhower and formed a pro-Ike New York delegation to the convention, was so taken by the speech that he invited Nixon to his hotel suite for a nightcap, along with several other Eisenhower advocates. There the governor discussed the possibility of selecting Nixon as the vice-presidential candidate on the general's ticket. Nixon knew that Dewey was close to Ike, and the governor's approval improved his prospects. His kingmaker strategy now held out hope of a great personal reward.[104]

Toward the end of that month, as the California primary neared, Nixon gave a speech supporting the favorite-son slate. Sure enough, Warren won easily, by almost two to one. Nixon was pleased, wishing that the slate would "be able to use its weight to select the very strongest man possible for the nomination." The final tally was 1,029,495 (66.4%) for Warren to 521,110 (33.6%) for Werdel, but what impressed outsiders was that the anti-Warren forces received over a half-million votes. The opposition's rallying cry was that the governor was not really a presidential candidate; in reality, he was just searching for a job in the new GOP administration. As a consequence of the extent of Warren's opposition in California and his lackluster performances in the Wisconsin and Oregon primaries, his fortunes as a contender had seriously diminished.[105]

Nixon also worked for William Knowland's reelection. At the end of February, the junior senator, who had recently spent a week at home, said that he had been impressed with the senior senator's "great strength" throughout the state, and that even though he would not make a public pronouncement, "I am sure he will win in the primary unless a far more potent candidate develops than is now on the scene." Knowland's chief opponent, due to the practice of crossfiling, was Democratic congressman Clinton McKinnon from San Diego, twice elected to the House, albeit narrowly.[106]

Chotiner once again managed Knowland's campaign and was rewarded with the results of the June 3 primary that gave his candidate an overwhelming victory on both ballots. Knowland rolled up 1,499,290 votes to 185,827 for both of his Republican challengers, won the Democratic one assuring his reelection, and amassed a total vote of 2,450,435, more than any other candidate had ever received in a California primary. Knowland's stock had risen, and *Time* declared that the senator's "bark & grain of vice-presidential timber" looked promising.[107]

Writing to Harry Bullis, board chairman of General Mills, to thank him for his support in the primaries, Ike confided on May 12 that he would return to the United States within three weeks to run for the White

House. To Sulzberger, the general expressed his call to duty over his reluctance to enter the fray: "Anybody is a damn fool if he actually seeks to be President. You give up four of the very best years of your life. Lord knows it's a sacrifice. Some people think there's a lot of power and glory attached to the job. On the contrary, the very workings of a democratic system see to it that the job has very little power."[108]

Nixon was not privy to Ike's presidential ambivalence, and therefore took the only course available to him. He backed Warren in the face of severe criticism from some of his closest allies. Nixon did this because he knew that the governor could draw Democrats and independents. If Warren lost at the convention, as expected, the senator could then form a powerful delegate bloc to select someone else.

Nixon critics have since attacked him for subverting Warren's opportunity to win the nomination while concentrating on his own vice-presidential ambitions. He did not subvert Warren; in fact, despite intense conservative unhappiness, Nixon stuck with Warren as a matter of practical politics, just as politicians have done for ages.

As for his vice-presidential possibilities, Nixon played coy. On June 22, 1951, Dick Cantwell of the Republican Club of Azusa in the 12th congressional district asked for permission to endorse Nixon for the vice presidency in 1952. Wiring back six days later, the senator expressed his appreciation, but added: "MOVEMENT TO PROMOTE MY CANDIDACY FOR HIGHER OFFICE TOO PREMATURE AT THIS TIME."[109]

Fans across the country throughout 1951 and into 1952 urged Nixon to reach higher and try for the presidency. Just after Independence Day, 1951, Chotiner acknowledged that some individuals had been advancing Nixon's name for president, letters to which he had to reply to squelch any serious effort. Chotiner told Nixon that he was "deeply convinced that your future and the future of our country are interwoven, and I would not like to see anything happen prematurely which might jeopardize that development." Joseph Davis of Chula Vista, California, early in 1952 wrote in "Voice of the People" in the *San Diego Evening Tribune* that the GOP should consider Nixon because he was "brilliant, fearless and able. We can argue about his qualifications, but there can be no doubt in anyone's mind but that he'd clean up the mess, and quickly, were he president."[110]

These compliments were flattering, but little more. Nixon knew that he had no chance for the presidency, and he also realized that he would not be considered for the second spot on any ticket until the convention chose its presidential nominee in what was shaping up to be a deeply divisive struggle based on ideological beliefs. Any thought that Nixon dumped Warren to advance his own personal goals fails on the weight of its own logic. After the June primary, the senator was pledged to California's favorite son. He had no bargaining power for its delegation.

# Chapter 20

# THE 1952 CONVENTION

E isenhower landed in the United States on June 1, 1952, shortly before the California primary. Three days after his arrival, he returned
to his boyhood hometown of Abilene, Kansas, to give his first major televised speech at an outside auditorium. Rain started to fall at noon and
quickly turned into what the general described as a "gully washer." Ike,
who wore a rumpled raincoat, addressed only a handful of the most
hearty who sat in the pouring rain. Any speech under these adverse conditions would have been difficult at best, but this one, poorly presented,
was a dismal flop. Ike outlined his domestic agenda based on the evils of
governmental centralization, and his proposed foreign policy, resting on
America assuming its international responsibilities as a superpower. The
following morning, he appeared in front of the press corps for a question
and answer session; the general was far more comfortable in that venue,
and the media gave him high marks.[1]

While Eisenhower embarked on this unfamiliar and hostile political
terrain, Robert Agnew, the treasurer of the Young Republicans of California, asked the Republican National Committee on June 6 to make
Nixon a keynote speaker at the Chicago convention, due to his popularity within the GOP. The next day, twenty-one congressmen, including
many in the Chowder and Marching Club such as Kenneth Keating,
Gerald Ford, and Pat Hillings, seconded the idea. The *San Diego Union*
also applauded it. Since Nixon was pledged to California's favorite son,
the paper said, he was "not considered a presidential candidate" and had

not become involved in the battle that pitted Taft against Eisenhower. The senator had an unblemished national reputation, made a good presentation on television, and was an "outstanding speaker." Finally, the newspaper noted, "The selection of Sen. Nixon, who is 39, would appeal to young voters who are needed if the Republicans are to win in 1952."[2]

While such accolades were flattering, Nixon's chances of speaking at the convention were virtually nil. He understood that his call for Gabrielson's resignation in October 1951 over his dealings with the Reconstruction Finance Corporation and his disapproval of the chairman's stewardship made such a request "pretty slim." While Nixon expected Gabrielson's negative response, he never imagined that the Werdel group was so embittered over the primary fight that some of its members would send letters to the arrangements committee objecting to his selection. Gabrielson, Nixon now anticipated, would use them "as a graceful way of backing up his own objection to my selection."[3]

McIntyre Faries, California's Republican national committeeman, immediately recognized that Gabrielson would reject the request, and therefore never entered Nixon's name for formal consideration. Senator Lodge, in the meantime, shrewdly wrote Gabrielson, a staunch Taft activist, repeating the call to have Nixon give a keynote address, with a copy of the letter going to "Dick." Lodge had earlier shown his high regard for Nixon by asking him that spring to speak in Chicago "to give the Party's Illinois prospects a helpful shot in the arm." Nixon, in a "Dear Cabot" letter, replied warmly: "I rather imagine that he [Gabrielson] will file it in the usual place but I do want you to know how much I appreciate your going to bat for me."[4]

During the second week of June, Nixon expressed his bleak outlook about the convention: "I don't believe that any of us should have any illusions on the possibilities of Warren being selected for the top spot. He just doesn't have the support in the Midwest and East which a dark horse needs." Since Knowland had won his primary by a tremendous number of votes, he had replaced the governor as a possible dark horse presidential hopeful and a likely vice-presidential prospect. Taft, according to Nixon, was close to a first ballot nomination: "I am also convinced that he cannot win if nominated. I believe that even if Eisenhower is nominated he will have a tough job to win but that at least there would be a fair chance of pulling it off." Knowland disagreed, and Nixon warily anticipated: "When Warren releases the Delegation, a split might develop between Bill and myself as to whether we should go to Taft or Eisenhower."[5]

This was not the only situation that had upset the junior senator. Since his first election in 1946, the Republican finance committee had refused to assist him monetarily, and he was angry, "particularly in view of the penny-pinching attitude the Los Angeles group has had in the past." He regularly appeared, without charge, at party fund-raisers, when he could have accepted lucrative speaking engagements. He had spent his own money for expenses dealing with the convention when the party should have paid for it. As a consequence of the finance committee's inconsiderate treatment, he had decided to have "a showdown" to obtain assistance for his programs. He wanted $10,000 from the Southern California and $5,000 from the Northern California Republican organizations that would pay for special mailings like Christmas cards, traveling expenses, media needs; besides, that financial group's responsibility was to aid him in upcoming election campaigns. "I feel very strongly on this matter and, frankly, I intend to condition my future cooperation with Republican Finance on whether they support our program."[6]

Nixon further complicated the California political panorama by sending out a questionnaire to twenty-three thousand of his constituents—mainly those who supported him in the last election—about whom they would endorse as the Republican presidential nominee. The senator did not release the results, but when the count of those who responded was totaled, 3,784 favored Ike and 3,902 were for Taft. The Nixon poll did not provide a clear-cut choice, but in national polls of likely voters across the country, Ike had a solid lead.[7]

Some Warrenites damned Nixon for sending out the questionnaire because it implied that the governor was unelectable. Nixon retorted that Taft and Ike forces were flooding the California delegation with requests to switch to their candidate if the governor withdrew. Since partisans promoted their own choices, Nixon sent out his poll to reflect a much broader range of feelings. As long as Warren felt that he had an opportunity to win, Nixon would support him; but if he released the delegation, the senator wanted to make his best-informed choice based on the relative strengths and weaknesses of the other contenders.[8]

To make this point vividly, the senator wired the Associated Press on June 20: "I BELIEVE THAT SINCE DELEGATION IS PLEDGED TO WARREN IT WOULD BE IMPROPER FOR DELEGATES TO EXPRESS PREFERENCE ON SECOND

Shortly after Nixon's statement, Senator Knowland announced that the governor would wait for several ballots at least, watching for a deadlock, before releasing his delegation, for Ike and Taft could easily lose: "If Eisenhower and Taft deadlock, I believe Gov. Warren is the logical compromise candidate and will be nominated." If the governor did withdraw from consideration, Taft's backers thought that twenty Californians favored him, and the remaining fifty were Ike loyalists.[10]

Knowland's stature had risen significantly due to his primary victory, and his name was emerging with growing frequency for the second spot on the ticket. In the middle of June, Nixon, during a national radio broadcast, acknowledged the senior senator as a possible choice due to his stunning primary victory. The *Wall Street Journal* lumped Knowland as a potential running mate along with Nixon, Governors Warren, Sherman Adams, John Fine of Pennsylvania, Alfred Driscoll of New Jersey, and Senator Dirksen. Taft supporters also were increasingly discussing the possibility of Knowland serving on the Ohioan's ticket.[11]

Nixon described the rising political heat in the capital: "It's hotter than h--l back here and I'm not speaking just of the weather. The boys realize they are playing for big stakes and they're putting the pressure on as I have never seen it put on before. I still think it's fifty-fifty with a slight edge to Taft." Indeed, on June 25, the *Los Angeles Times* endorsed Taft for president, but indicated that Warren also stood an excellent chance.[12]

By the end of the month, *Time* magazine counted 464 delegates for Taft, 389 for Ike, and 76 for Warren. With 1,206 voting delegates, the winner would need 50 percent (603) plus one. The Gallup poll provided data illustrating that the general would draw more votes than the Ohio senator, and few political analysts forecast that Taft could carry California or New York, the largest electoral plums. Eisenhower, according to the magazine, was much more likely to be triumphant than Taft.[13]

In the middle of June, Nixon received a call that placed him in the center of the preconvention activities. Robert Kirkwood, chairman of the platform committee for the Republican State Central Committee, had announced that the state delegation unanimously appointed Nixon and Mrs. Mildred Younger, an avowed Warren supporter, as the California representatives to the resolutions committee to help draft the final version of the GOP platform. Nixon reluctantly agreed, and on June 26, discussed the reasons for his trepidation: "It's a mean, thankless assignment because platforms usually don't mean too much in campaigns but we'll do our best to hammer something out which will command the support of all the rival candidates."[14]

At first not realizing the initial advantage of coming early to Chicago, Nixon soon understood the opportunity that had been supplied to him. He had arrived by plane as a California representative to hold hearings on the various issues concerning the platform. He came in during the debate over the seating of the contested delegates from Georgia, Louisiana, and Texas. Republicans from those states did not normally play a major role because the South had voted solidly Democratic for decades. When the southern delegations to GOP national conventions were counted, they had the same voting rights as anyone else, but traditionally dealmakers ignored them in choosing the presidential nominee.

This convention was different; in fact, the importance attached to the composition of the delegates from those three southern states materially helped to influence the outcome. The RNC was hearing challenges in all three delegations over how many delegates belonged to either Eisenhower and Taft. Texas was by far the largest prize and generated the greatest amount of attention. During the primary process in that state, traditional Republicans held informal caucuses, sometimes in people's homes, where they picked delegates to the national convention. This atmosphere changed when large numbers of Eisenhower supporters, many of whom were registered Democrats, decided to vote in the GOP caucuses and carry them for their man. Faced with defeat, GOP partisans for Taft rejected the majority for not having the proper credentials. Democrats who temporarily crossed party lines for Ike, they charged, were not Republican voters. Therefore, the regular party members chose Taft slates, and the Eisenhower advocates selected their own delegations. Both sets arrived at the national convention, and the committee that would decide on which one to seat was stacked with Taft supporters.[15]

Throughout the acrimonious debates over these states' delegations, the Eisenhower faction accused Taftites of trying to steal the presidential nomination with fraudulent delegates. All through June, the country listened to charges and countercharges in the media. Raymond Moley, who was present in Texas and saw Democrats switching to Republicans, wrote in *Newsweek* that the Taft organization should not accept the shenanigans of its followers. Henry Zweifel, a traditional GOP leader from Fort Worth, supplied his own test for Republican allegiance and kicked the Eisenhower followers out of the delegation. This kind of dissension could seriously damage any party at a time when it faced its greatest opportunity.[16]

Senator Lodge reinforced his camp's allegations by informing Nixon on June 25 that Ike would win the nomination if the convention was open and not tainted by corruption. At the end of the month, Andrew Dunlap, a prominent GOP leader from Los Angeles, wrote Nixon that he had conducted his own political survey and unhappily found that Taft could not be elected. Ike, Dunlap determined, would receive great numbers of Democratic and independent ballots because voters did not appreciate politicians like Taft. "The Texas 'steal' has greatly harmed Taft with everybody," Dunlap concluded: "Just proves 'that all politicians are crooks.' These comments are heard everywhere the matter is discussed except with the 'Old Guard.'" If the Ohio senator were nominated, he would lose.[17]

At the height of the dispute, the governors met in Houston for their forty-fourth annual conference, in late June. Assembling as an independent body, Tom Dewey, Sherman Adams, Dan Thornton of Colorado, and Arthur Langlie of Washington presented a resolution to their assembled GOP colleagues: that none of the contested delegations could participate in the voting for the admission of any delegations to the national convention until their right to be seated was accepted or rejected. All twenty-three governors there, as well as the two who were absent, signed what was to become known as the "Houston Manifesto," which was released on July 2.[18]

The Republican National Committee convened in Chicago one day earlier, with Taft's followers in control of the national machinery. The next day, his supporters on that body dutifully voted to seat the contested Georgia slate. Nixon, through a press interview, sternly warned against any abuse of its majority. The Georgia decision, he said, opened the question of whether or not the convention was going to be conducted "with complete integrity and fair play." If the GOP was going to survive, it could not be "a closed corporation," but instead, had to be "open to all people who want a change of Administration in Washington." The Republican presidential candidate had to be decided by "the will of the people," and not by "a small clique of politicians who happen to control the party machinery." If Republican hands were not clean, then a potential overriding issue against Democratic corruption would disappear.[19]

The California senator made two other critical public statements. First, on the evening of July 2, he stated that while Warren would not accept the vice presidency, Knowland would be an "outstanding candidate" for either the Taft or the Eisenhower tickets. On the following day, Nixon said while that he was neutral over the struggle between Ike and Taft, the latter's organization had been accused of trying to steal the nomination after the Georgia decision to seat the Taft delegation. "If the Republican Party approves the Texas grab [of the delegates by Taft forces], we will be announcing to the country that we believe ruthless machine politics is wrong only when the Democrats use it." The logical conclusion was: "The Republican Party can't hope to win this November if it limits its membership to the minority which has not been large enough to win four national elections."[20]

While Nixon was busily working on the resolutions committee in Chicago and following the preconvention political maneuvering, Governor Warren, his wife, and three daughters boarded a special Western Pacific train in Sacramento on July 3. That train hooked up with a southern one in Salt Lake City where eighteen cars were joined together to proceed on their journey eastward. As they sped toward Chicago, San Francisco reporter R. W. Jimerson and *Los Angles Times* correspondent Chester Hanson listened to the governor make several candid statements. First, without alluding to his signing of the Houston Manifesto, he voiced his displeasure over the RNC's decision on the seating of the pro–Taft Georgia delegation. Second, he expressed his dislike for Taft, without specifically referring to him, by opposing any "reactionary" nominee. Third, not being a delegate, he would not attend the convention and refused to discuss when and if he would release the delegation. Furthermore, he was silent on the delegation's second choice for president, but admitted that between forty to fifty-five of the members probably favored Ike, as the governor apparently did. As for any vice-presidential aspirations, his advisers had suggested that he reject any offer.[21]

While the governor was on the train, his headquarters on the fifteenth floor of the Conrad Hilton Hotel, four floors above Ike's and six above Taft's, started its operations under Murray Chotiner's direction. Chotiner had ordered up to one thousand Warren badges, six inches in diameter—outdoing the Taft badge by two inches and Ike by one. When asked who would get them, the lawyer responded: "Anyone who'll wear 'em."[22]

Initially, Nixon intended to ride with the delegation from California to Illinois, but his duties in Chicago during the platform considerations changed his plans. Instead, he flew out from Chicago to Denver, Colorado, to meet the train, and when the Warren special pulled into the station at 7:00 P.M., Nixon boarded and joined his fellow delegates on their way to the convention.[23]

He was greeted by his confidant, Congressman Pat Hillings, and according to Hillings's recollection, Warren invited them plus several more people to dinner, where they had "a very friendly meeting" in which the governor asked what the senator had learned at the preconvention. Nixon candidly replied that the gathering had shaped up as a battle of Ike versus Taft, and Warren did not have much of a chance.[24]

In a long talk the next morning with Warren, Nixon told the governor that both of his appointed national committee persons were voting with the Eisenhower forces on all the controversial issues before the RNC. Both Nixon and Warren agreed that the Ike faction had a major issue over the seating of the southern delegates, which could preoccupy the convention for several days. Drew Pearson, too, recognized the significance of this dispute, for it smacked of corruption. To the reporter, "The swing to Ike has already started."[25]

The train roared into Chicago late on the afternoon of July 5 after losing several hours in the Rockies, but it had made up some time traveling at ninety miles an hour over the prairies and had a fast run through Nebraska, Iowa, and Illinois. A brass band played "California, Here I Come"; delegates wore orange-colored baseball caps with Warren initials on them, and were armed with their own whistles and banners.[26]

Nixon later gave Warren a "shot in the political arm" by declaring that the governor was "the strongest dark horse" and could become a front-runner if a stalemate occurred after the second or third ballot. As for the rumors about Nixon for vice president, he was not even considering them because his chances were so remote; Nixon felt that Knowland was the "logical choice" for vice president under either nominee.[27]

The California delegation had allocated a large block of rooms at the Hotel Knickerbocker, located at 163 East Walton Place, just off Michigan Boulevard, near the lake and the Drake Hotel. After the members registered, they listened to Knowland speak at the delegation caucus, where he stressed that Governor Warren had a better opportunity now to be nominated for president than he had had in the last six months. Many had heard stories that Knowland was throwing the California delegation to Taft for the vice-presidential nomination, but Knowland emphatically denied those rumors. Some asked for unity because they needed to "stick together." As for the governor, he called for a fair convention and an end to gossip: "You are bound to hear that Bill Knowland and I have made a lot of deals unbeknown to you. I will hear that you have made a lot of deals unbeknown to me. You will trust me and I'll trust you and we can't go wrong."[28]

While Warren tried to keep his delegation united, Eisenhower took a three-day train ride from Denver to the convention, arriving on July 5. He went to his private suite at the Blackstone Hotel, where he left Mamie, who was unwell, and then went over to his convention headquarters on the eleventh floor of the Conrad Hilton, where Lodge had him continually meeting delegates. As one group left, Eisenhower greeted people in another room. In order to waste as little time as possible, when the vacated room filled up again, the candidate reentered, and this procedure continued throughout the day. His staff appeared confident that it would prevail on contested disputes regarding the several delegations.[29]

Cyrus Sulzberger arrived in Chicago on Sunday morning, July 6: "It's hot as hell but there is a real atmosphere of excitement." After registering, he went to see Ike at the Blackstone. The general looked good and commented that he had had all of his clothes made "very cheap from a Jewish friend in New York." Possibly wearing one of those creations, Ike and Mamie held a reception in the grand ballroom of the Palmer House from 5:00 to 7:00 P.M., where, for the first time, after waiting in line for over an hour, Pat Nixon met the general and his wife.[30]

On the morning of July 7, Guy Gabrielson, the Republican National Convention chairman, struck his gavel on the podium, opening the convention from inside the mammoth 13,000-seat International Amphitheatre. Press, radio, and television were there: there were 2,000 reserved seats, and 3,618 for voting delegates and their alternates plus friends. The remaining 7,000 went to GOP officials from governors and senators to county chairmen. Unlike the modest, nascent television coverage four years earlier, the commercial networks covered this gathering from start to finish. They would take advertising breaks, but those would be eliminated during the most exciting happenings. For the first time, Walter Cronkite anchored a national convention as an eyewitness. Rather than the stage productions that eventually evolved, audiences who viewed the 1952 conventions saw national politics at its rawest.[31]

Ten minutes before the morning session, Gabrielson asked to see Lodge at a small office under the speaker's platform. Upon entering, Lodge met the chairman, three Taft campaign managers, and Knowland, to see if the Eisenhower camp would agree to a compromise over the seating of the southern delegations. Lodge ultimately rejected any negotiations, insisting upon a debate. Following the terms of the Houston Manifesto, Governor Langlie, from the convention floor, introduced what was called the Fair Play Amendment, covering the sixty-eight contested delegates, and stated that none of them, except for those who had a four-fifths vote from the 106-member RNC, would be allowed to vote on any disputes until the duly constituted delegates decided on whom to seat permanently. Instead of confronting that central issue, Congressman Clarence Brown of Ohio, Taft's chief floor strategist, surprised the Eisenhower forces by moving to exclude seven Louisiana seats that had not been questioned. The Brown proposal, which was, in fact, an amendment to an amendment, had priority. It was a test case to measure the strength of competing combatants on a relatively minor point, and the result of the roll call shocked the Taft forces, who lost, 658–548. Afterwards, by a voice vote, the convention unanimously approved of the Fair Play Amendment.[32]

While the Ike forces were taking command of the convention floor, the general was meeting with Warren for a fifty-minute "social visit" at the Blackstone. Afterwards, Warren announced that he had invited Ike to visit the California delegation and reaffirmed his support for the Fair Play Amendment. Before his delegates voted on the resolution, he told them to vote their conscience, but they already knew his public stance for the amendment, and the 57–8 California vote for the amendment demonstrated two points: first, that they overwhelmingly agreed with him; and second, that the vote gave an inclination how the members would split if Warren released them to vote their preference.[33]

That evening, General Douglas MacArthur, stepping before the microphone in a dark blue suit with a matching tie, keynoted the opening session of the convention, tagging the Democrats as the "war party" and calling on Republicans to restore traditional American values. He attacked Truman for not following his recommendations to expand the

Korean War and accused the president of promoting socialism at home. The general wished for a nationwide spiritual unity, for "an aroused countryside ready and eager to march." The delegates wildly roared their approval, but the cheering that he received did not translate into a massive swing to his dark horse cause. Late that evening, MacArthur left Chicago; he would not be asked to return. Chosen by Taft to speak, MacArthur's lackluster performance could only further depress an already dismal day.[34]

Tuesday morning, July 8, proved far more serious, with a critical vote on the contested delegations before the credentials committee. Herbert Brownell of the Ike camp had asked Kenneth T. Royall, secretary of the army under Truman, currently a partner in a prestigious Washington, D.C., law firm, and a Democrat who was campaigning for Eisenhower, to suggest a lawyer to handle the dispute over the southern delegations at the GOP convention. Royall responded that William Rogers, an attorney at the firm, would be excellent, and he presented the Eisenhower side as if it were a Supreme Court argument. At the end of the day, the Taft forces had lost sixty-eight votes from the total number of contested delegates. To Drew Pearson, Taft's apparently indestructible tower of strength seemed to be crumbling, and his sources found out that Taft had asked Knowland to switch California on the first ballot. If the Ohioan failed to win with that boost, according to Pearson, he would throw his support to the governor.[35]

Herbert Hoover, an avid Taft promoter, keynoted the second night of the convention and received a heart-warming reception. Warning that the New and Fair Deals had hampered American freedoms, the single living past president said that due to his advancing age, this would probably be his last address to a GOP convention. Responding to critics who disapproved of his foreign policy position, he said that did not propose that "we retreat into our shell like a turtle." Instead, Hoover declared, "I do propose the deadly reprisal strategy of a rattlesnake." Though welcomed fondly, the past president could not alter votes; his candidate was losing.[36]

Governor Warren also was not pleased with the day's events. According to a memoir by Paul H. Davis sent to the Hoover Institution Archives on March 2, 1959, Warren invited Davis, a confidant and a former administrator at Stanford University, who had later served as a vice president during Ike's presidency at Columbia University in the late 1940s, to lunch at his Santa Monica beach club a month and a half be-

fore the convention. The governor raised the issue of Eisenhower's qualifications and complained about the general's criticism of the contentious academic freedom issue at the University of California. This
was especially annoying since Warren was chairman of the board of re-
gents. He chuckled that, as an experienced governor of a large state, he
was better prepared for the White House than an untrained military
leader.

A month after this luncheon, Davis offered to assist Warren at the
convention. He accepted and had his friend go to Chicago as a lobbyist
for the governor's nomination; his real purpose, however, was, if necessary, to carry private messages to Eisenhower from Warren. On July 8,
the governor sent for Davis to relay orally a confidential message to the
general:

> The problem is this. We have a traitor in our delegation. It's Nixon. He,
> like all the rest, took the oath that he would vote for me, until such time
> as the delegation was released, but he has not paid attention to his oath
> and immediately upon being elected, started working for Eisenhower
> and has been doing so ever since. I have word that he is actively in touch
> with the Eisenhower people. I wish you would tell General Eisenhower
> that we resent his people infiltrating, through Nixon into our delega-
> tion, and ask him to have it stopped.

At the conclusion of that somber conversation, Davis went to Ike's
suite at the Blackstone Hotel for a long session with the general while
hundreds of people in the corridors were clamoring for audiences with
Ike. After Davis delivered Warren's message, Eisenhower replied: "Well,
I am not at all sure that his information is correct, for my understanding
is that we are definitely letting the California delegation alone and not
trying to interfere with it in any way whatsoever. In fact, I want the Warren candidacy to be strong, for if Taft and I get into an impossible deadlock, then I hope Warren gets the nomination." This would eliminate
MacArthur as a viable candidate, a possibility that Eisenhower vehemently opposed. If, however, anyone in the Ike camp tried to infiltrate
the governor's delegation, he wanted Davis or Warren to phone him.
The general would then halt any further intrigue.

During the conversation, Ike turned to the vice presidency: "I think
it is highly desirable that for the vice president we have a young man
such as Richard Nixon. He appears to me the aggressive, able kind of

fellow that we need in Republican leadership. We need more young men. He looks like the right type."

Davis delivered Ike's reply to Warren, and shortly thereafter, left the convention with the governor's thanks. His recollection was "TO BE OPENED ONLY AFTER THE DEATHS OF DWIGHT D. EISENHOWER AND EARL WARREN."[37]

While this mission was taking place, Eisenhower advocates were pressuring the California contingent to release its delegates early since the Ike bandwagon was gaining momentum, but Knowland argued against changing course based on innuendo. His introduction of Taft to the California delegation, however, had intensified speculation that the Ohioan was thinking about Knowland. "I want to make it quite clear. I am sticking with Governor Warren. I will stay with him for one ballot or thirty ballots, until he releases the delegation."[38]

That evening, after Harrison McCall had returning to the Knickerbocker, he saw Nixon alone in the lobby; they chatted, and Mac the senator if he would like to meet Jackie Robinson, who was talking in the corner with Paul Williams, another member of the delegation. Nixon congratulated Robinson on hitting a home run the day before, where the National League beat the American League at the All-Star Game. The senator then recalled the first time that he had seen Robinson play during a UCLA-Oregon football game. Nixon described an unusual play that was run, and Robinson told him why it was used. As McCall and Nixon walked away, Mac stated that "while Robinson had undoubtedly met a lot of notables during his career, nevertheless I was sure there was one person he would never forget."[39]

By the next morning,, while Eisenhower's strength was mounting, rumors circulated that the vice-presidential nomination was wide open. MacArthur's was the most discussed person, with Knowland and Nixon closely behind. Everett Dirksen, a conservative, and Governor Driscoll of New Jersey, a moderate, were also mentioned. But John S. Knight, editor and publisher of the *Chicago Daily News*, greeted the delegates with a front-page editorial predicting not only that Ike would be the GOP presidential nominee, but that Nixon would probably take the second spot in the ticket. Knight felt that the 548 votes that Taft had received on the Brown amendment might well represent his maximum strength. If large states like California, Michigan, and Pennsylvania swung to the general, the Ohio senator's base would crack and Ike would triumph.

Knight had two reasons for predicting Nixon's selection: he was "(1) an able, intelligent senator and a good speaker and (2) the Californian is given credit for landing Alger Hiss behind bars." Since Stevenson looked like the Democratic nominee and had acted as a character reference for Hiss, Nixon could tacitly or openly question the Illinois governor's judgment. Eisenhower, furthermore, encouraged a youth movement within his camp, while Taft spoke for older GOP stalwarts. Nixon, due to his age, could directly speak to the issues of young adults.[40]

Speaking for Eisenhower, Dewey told the press that Ike would not discuss vice-presidential prospects until after the presidential nomination. Lodge reiterated the governor's stance: the Eisenhower organization was totally focused on getting its man nominated. Nobody had even looked at vice-presidential contenders.[41]

Nonetheless, correspondents started to interview Pat Nixon. She had heard about Knight's prediction and knew that her husband "might be considered," but she insisted that neither of them took it "seriously." She described herself as "his Man Friday," as well as "chief cook, bottle washer, chauffeur and what-not" for the family. She did all the housework and loved to cook. Dick favored Mexican food and especially was "crazy about enchiladas." She had left her children at their new home in Washington, D.C., because the convention was "too hectic" for them; however, "our next project is to get a dog for the children." It was a standard, wholesome, winning formula for a candidate's wife.[42]

That same Wednesday morning, Eisenhower went to woo the California delegation. Nixon greeted him at curbside and ushered him in to meet the delegation at the top of the hotel. All seventy delegates, many alternates, and newspapermen jammed in to see the general, with an overflow crowd of two to three hundred who sat or stood in the corridor. In what was not one of his best talks, the general haltingly described himself as a "militant Republican," who would install a "clean new group" if he were nominated. He also praised Warren, Knowland, and Nixon for their contributions to the nation, and promised to support whomever the convention nominated. With the exception of the few Taft supporters, when Ike finished, most delegates rose and applauded loudly.[43]

That afternoon, Senator Joe McCarthy went before the convention, advising the delegates that he would not soften his stand on communism because "a rough fight is the only fight Communists can understand." The controversial speaker, who by this time had lost some credibility with his wild accusations against the Democrats, did not move many. Those who believed him carried fish-shaped placards, a reference to Truman's "red herring" remarks in defense of Acheson, Hiss, and Owen Lattimore. The Wisconsin senator tried to rally the troops:

> I say, one Communist in a defense plant is one Communist too many.
> One Communist on the faculty of one university is one Communist too many.
> One Communist among the American advisers at Yalta was one Communist too many.
> And even if there were only one Communist in the State Department, that would be one Communist too many.[44]

The real battle on the floor now amounted to a formal ratification of Ike by way of the delegation fights in Georgia and elsewhere. Though the credentials committee had passed on Taft's delegates, the issue was reopened on the floor that evening and assigned to Dirksen to present the credential committee's majority argument. With thousands watching on the convention floor and millions viewing and listening over radio and television, Ev reminded all present of the responsibilities that they faced and the glaring fact that the GOP had not won a presidential election for two decades. Dewey, an influential leader of the pro-Ike forces, was seated in the front row of the New York delegation, wearing a grim smile while Ev tried to persuade the delegates to accept the majority opinion opposing the seating of Ike's delegates. He was visibly frustrated by the parliamentary setbacks and the likelihood that his friend Taft would lose. Dirksen's voice rose as he looked down at Dewey. Pointing and shaking his finger at him, Dirksen reminded the New Yorker that he had tirelessly campaigned for him in 1944 and 1948. Without carefully considering his words, and not meaning to evoke controversy, Ev fervently appealed: "Reexamine your hearts before you take this action in support of the Minority Report, because we followed you before and you took us down the path of defeat." Thunderous applause and a eruption of booing ensued. At least one fistfight broke out. After the mayhem stopped and order was restored, the pro-Eisenhower delegation won by a vote of 607 to 531. It was a long, straight nail in Taft's coffin.[45]

Lodge recalled that dramatic scene: "Those who were there will not forget that moment." Some delegates went over to Dewey and "shook their fists in his face." He sat there calmly. But he would not forgive the outburst that Dirksen unleashed when his name was raised for vice-presidential consideration.[46]

The agenda the next day, Thursday, July 10, evoked far less emotion. The 5,000-word Republican platform featured attacks on the Democrats for foreign policy failures in Europe and Asia, especially Korea. The GOP supported Israel, favored international trade, called for a stronger defense, and opposed communism. The remainder of the document addressed domestic issues: reduced government expenditures, lower inflation, a more dynamic agriculture system, continuation of the Taft-Hartley Act, wise use of natural resources, state control of water usage—which particularly applied to California—Social Security protection, opposition to compulsory federal health insurance, civil rights, immediate statehood of Hawaii and later for Alaska, full citizenship for Indians, self-government for Washington, D.C., a full merit system for civil servants, and adoption of the Hoover Commission guidelines. Finally, the GOP called for an end to the graft under Truman: "The present Administration's sordid record of corruption has shocked and sickened the American people."[47]

Nixon, who helped shape the platform, remarked that it sometimes was vague on vital issues like the open shop versus the closed one for labor, farm price supports, and civil rights: "It isn't going to make very many people happy but it may not make anybody mad."[48]

Chairman Joe Martin announced that the balloting for president and vice president would wait until Friday, but presidential nominating speeches would begin that evening. Final maneuvering commenced. Taft's followers were deserting him for a rejuvenated bid for MacArthur; Stassen denied that he was joining a pro-Eisenhower movement. The Associated Press blandly and inaccurately declared that the nomination was "wide open today."[49]

Rumors about the movements of the California delegation abounded. Columnist Marquis Childs, present at the convention, wrote that Warren hoped to win, detested Taft's views, and leaned toward Ike. Knowland, the delegation's floor manager, emphatically affirmed he would not switch to Ike and that Governor Warren should be the GOP nominee because he was the most experienced chief executive in the field: "As governor of the second largest state in the union, he has had more executive experience in civil government than any other candidate whose name is before the convention." Nixon was similarly careful: "I think Warren has a better chance now than ever before," and the delegates should not stampede to another contender. That evening, Nixon went on network television and stated that the delegation would vote for Warren, and if Ike won on the first ballot, he would do so without California's help. Nevertheless, he admitted to being pro-Ike and insisted that the rumors that the general was "soft on communism" were erroneous: "The first I heard of it was in the newspapers. I think it probably is the last I'll hear of it. I think it is just one of the rumors that comes up at a convention." This was the closest he could get to voting for Ike until Warren released him.[50]

Warren spoke to the delegation that evening, praising its members for their exemplary conduct. They had been inundated with hundreds of letters and telegrams demanding that when Warren released the delegation, they should vote for Taft. Knowland and Nixon followed with pleas to hold fast, and the senior senator felt that neither Taft nor Ike would win on the first ballot. The governor thanked Knowland and others for their assistance, but forgot to mention Nixon, who was sitting at his side. When Knowland introduced Nixon as "my good friend," the governor took the microphone and added: "I'm tremendously proud of the work Dick Nixon has done on the resolutions committee." Rumors floated that the two men had cool relations, but Nixon placed his hand on Warren's shoulder, smiled at him, and told the delegates: "No pressure has been put on anyone. All of you have been able to speak up and vote your sincere convictions."[51]

By now the *New York Herald Tribune* and the *New York Times* were reporting that Nixon was the leading contender for vice president among the convention delegates because he was known for his anti-Communist stand and for bringing Hiss to trial. Los Angeles newspapers thought that he headed the preferred list if a westerner was going to be selected, and that his age would appeal to young voters. The *Los Angeles Examiner* reported that Eisenhower's lieutenants had already approached the senator and offered him the spot; he would accept if the general directly asked him to take it. As for Nixon, when interviewed, he evaded talking about his own chances, and spoke instead about the possibilities of Warren, Taft, and MacArthur.[52]

On the floor of the convention, the presidential nominating process now began. Dirksen was first, asserting to wild cheering and demonstrations that Taft was "a leader who will boldly assert the moral purposes of the Republican party even as they were here asserted by Abraham Lincoln ninety-two years ago." Knowland followed with a rousing speech for Warren, equally vociferous, with ascending balloons, but without the marching. Governor Theodore McKeldin of Maryland hailed Eisenhower as "the man to unite our party, to unite our nation, to unite our productive forces of capital and labor in the teamwork that is essential to our times," and again pandemonium erupted. Stassen was next, and MacArthur, who had left Chicago, was nominated last.[53]

On the next morning, Friday, the 11th, the balloting began in alphabetical order by states. At the end of the calling of the roll, MacArthur had 10 votes, Stassen, 20, Warren 81, Taft 500, and Ike 595, 9 short of victory. Senator Edward Thye of Minnesota, who was pledged to its favorite son Stassen, jumped up, took the microphone, and demanded the floor. His announcement that his state was switching its nineteen votes to Eisenhower made the general the Republican presidential nominee. The remaining states promptly stampeded to make the nomination by acclamation, much to the chagrin of the disillusioned and deeply dispirited Taft supporters. By 2:00 P.M., Dwight Eisenhower was the GOP nominee for president of the United States, and the convention recessed for lunch.[54]

After the victory, Ike immediately went down the corridor to Mamie's room to tell her the news. In bed, after being awake all night with a bad case of neuritis, an inflammation of the nerves, she was still elated. The general reminisced: "both of us were somewhat overwhelmed by the future life our imaginations pictured for us."[55]

Once Ike was assured that his wife's health was improving, he kept a promise made to Senator H. Alexander Smith before the balloting that if nominated, the general would immediately go to Taft and welcome his cooperation in the general election. Eisenhower announced to his staff that he intended to walk across the street and see Taft. Even though some felt that this was inappropriate and that the senator should visit the general, Ike telephoned Taft, asked to come over, and Taft agreed. The multitude outside caused delay, for even with a Chicago police escort Ike fought for ten to twenty minutes just to cross the street from the Blackstone to the Conrad Hilton. Inside Taft's hotel, Eisenhower noticed resentment, depression, and some tears from a number of women openly crying.[56]

At the meeting, the general said that both men were tired and he did not want to discuss substantive matters, but hoped that they could "work together." Taft made only one request: reporters had bombarded him for a picture of the two of them. They stepped into the hallway, flashbulbs popped, and Taft calmly told reporters that he had congratulated the general and would promote the ticket in the November elections. Ike paid tribute to Taft as a "great American," and fought his way back to the elevator.[57]

Due to the uncertainty of the general's nomination, his campaign staff was adamant that it would not give consideration to his running mate until afterwards. While Eisenhower's speechwriters worked on his acceptance address, Brownell hurriedly called as many of the general's major supporters as he could to get a cross section of opinions. When he walked over to the Conrad Hilton headquarters, most of the "high command," approximately thirty or forty men and women, had gathered. Brownell chaired the session. It included Governors Adams, Dewey, Carlson, Fine; Senators Lodge, Duff, Saltonstall, Smith, and former senator from Kansas Harry Darby; Congressman Herter; Frank duPont from Delaware, Russell Sprague from New York, Arthur Summerfield from Michigan, and retired general Lucius Clay; Roy Roberts, president of the *Kansas City Star*; Paul Hoffman, chairman of Citizens for Eisenhower; Barak Mattingly, a member of Ike's strategy board from St. Louis; and Sinclair Weeks, chairman of the Republican national finance committee.[58]

The euphoria of getting Eisenhower nominated presented an almost anticlimactic setting for the selection process for vice president. This choice was nowhere near as intense and was accomplished haphazardly. No one rigged the process, nor was there a predestined winner. Most of the people there were exhausted and wanted to finish as quickly as possible. Brownell announced that he had invited Ike, who declined since he did not wish to sponsor any candidate. The nominee looked to those assembled for a recommendation. Brownell declared that no deals had been made and the selection was wide open. He personally wanted someone from a key state who would "balance the ticket." Most men removed their jackets, lit up cigarettes and cigars, and began their deliberations.[59]

To encourage "party harmony," Summerfield invited Senator Smith to speak first, who then sponsored Taft. After stating his case, Smith left, and after deliberating the merits, Taft was eliminated. Carlson then said that Taft had asked him to raise Everett Dirksen's name, but due to his explosion against the New York governor on the convention floor, that quickly was rejected. New Jersey governor Driscoll's name was mentioned, but the conferees dismissed any easterner. That narrowed the choice to the Midwest and West.[60]

Brownell left briefly, placing Dewey in command. Roy Roberts, a "big rumpled man" and arch rival of Truman, might have introduced Nixon's name. Upon returning, Brownell recalled that no one proposed Nixon; his name "just came up in the general discussion." Dewey followed by outlining the advantage of Nixon's youth and his ability to engage audiences with his public speaking.

Nixon's years in Congress had paid rich dividends. Congressman Herter and he had been friends since the European mission in 1947. The first time that Senator Saltonstall heard Nixon speak in Massachusetts was toward the end of 1951, and he was impressed: "It was a crackerjack! You lived up completely to your advanced billing." To the public, the reason for Nixon was obvious. Lodge described Nixon as one of the party's outstanding young leaders, who was "an outspoken foe of Communism. . . . A splendid leader . . . a young man, but not too young." He was "an ideal choice."[61]

Paul Hoffman, who had taken leave from his job as president of the Ford Foundation, was enthusiastic. As the administrator for the European Recovery Administration that implemented the Marshall Plan, he was delighted that Nixon, who forcefully backed the revitalization of Western Europe, was being considered. Everything that Hoffman heard about Nixon was "good." He had done well in his senatorial race and "was well liked in Southern California." Hoffman concluded that Nixon "would be a great deal to the ticket."[62]

Hoffman approvingly noted in later correspondence that in domestic matters, Nixon was "a middle-of-the-roader and on his legislative record has often been in opposition to the right wing of the party." If he had attempted to "out-McCarthy McCarthy," Hoffman would have voted against him. Yet when Nixon had exposed Hiss, "the consensus was that in his examination and cross-examination of Hiss he was eminently fair and courteous." Hoffman stated that Nixon was "really a very competent man of excellent character," and charges comparing him with McCarthy were false, for an "examination of his [Nixon's] voting record would result in pegging him as a forward-looking middle of the roader." Hoffman interestingly stressed that Nixon was "a Quaker by birth and upbringing, and as a member of that stalwart minority I cannot picture him in the role of a witch-hunter."[63]

Nixon seemed the logical choice as balance to the ticket. He appealed to youthful Americans because he was thirty-nine, compared to Ike, who was sixty-two. Nixon fought Communists but did not resort to "smears." He was acceptable to all GOP factions. Another benefit was that if the ticket won, the GOP would not lose Nixon's seat. Since Warren was the Republican governor of California, he would appoint another GOP senator. "Nobody sold Nixon to the committee," Mattingly reasoned. "The practical political considerations did that." Unanimity followed and the meeting ended.[64]

With Dewey sitting on the edge of the desk and a half dozen more of the deliberators surrounding Brownell, he telephoned Eisenhower with the group's recommendation and said that unless he personally intervened, Nixon would be his running mate. The general responded: "That's fine with me."[65]

The selection process took less than two hours. Herbert Trask, a reporter for *St. Louis Post-Dispatch* who interviewed several of those inside that smoke-filled room, concluded that the group paid no attention to the fact that their choice might someday have to assume the presidency. Instead, the manner in which Nixon was decided upon was as unscientific as at previous national conventions. The conferees picked their man to bring balance and votes to the ticket rather than relying on "his qualifications and experience to be a 'reserve' President."[66]

Brownell did not mention any preference during the discussions, but Ike had to be pleased with Nixon's selection. On August 2, Ike enthusiastically declared: "I wanted him as a running mate because he is dynamic, direct and square." First, both men shared similar philosophical beliefs. Second, Ike wanted a man on the ticket who was "young, vigorous, ready to learn, and of good reputation." Third, the general admired the manner in which Nixon had sought out Communists in the federal government and had conducted the Hiss inquiry. Eisenhower especially respected "the reputation that Congressman Nixon had achieved for fairness in the investigating process. Not once had he overstepped the limits prescribed by the American sense of fair play or American rules applying to such investigations. He did not persecute or defame. This I greatly admired."[67]

A decade after the fact, Eisenhower revealed that he had handwritten a short "eligible list" of qualified vice-presidential candidates before the convention and kept it in his billfold. When he met with Brownell after the nomination to choose the second spot on his ticket, the general gave Brownell the list. Eisenhower remembered that Nixon was first; Congressman Charles Halleck of Indiana, Congressman Walter Judd of

Minnesota, and Governors Thornton and Langlie were also potential running mates. The list was irrelevant; it did not seem to have anything to do with the selection process.[68]

On the Thursday evening, July 10, after returning to their hotel room from a late supper, Dick began to talk to Pat about running for the vice presidency. Remembering the campaign against Helen Gahagan Douglas, she resisted another electoral race and was especially anxious about being away from her daughters for extended periods of time.[69]

Very early in the morning of Friday, July 11, Dick woke Chotiner and had him come over to the hotel room to get his opinion. As usual, Chotiner was blunt, instinctively recognizing that Pat disapproved, but arguing: "There comes a time when you have to go up or get out." If Dick ran and lost, he still retained his Senate seat. If he won and disliked the job, he could leave after the first term as one of the youngest vice presidents in American history. That accomplishment certainly would enhance any future direction that he would take. Chotiner left after about an hour. The Nixons continued their discussion, and at dawn, Pat agreed to absorb the punishment of another campaign. This, of course, was hypothetical. Neither knew about the dynamics within the Eisenhower camp; therefore, they believed that their discussion of his selection was little more than an academic exercise.[70]

That day, Nixon went over the Stockyard Inn, where Chotiner had rented a room next to the amphitheater. After no sleep the previous night, Nixon was exhausted and hot. His room had no air-conditioning; the temperature was close to 100 degrees. Nixon was sitting shirtless on his bed, eating a ham-and-cheese sandwich, when Chotiner arrived with exciting news. He had talked to Brownell, who stated that Nixon was on the final list for vice president, and the Eisenhower committee needed a telephone number if Nixon were chosen. Trying to remain calm, Nixon responded: "It's still wishful thinking, Murray."[71]

When the telephone rang, Pat Hillings, who happened to be in the room, picked up the receiver. Brownell was calling to speak to Nixon. While Hillings waited for the senator to answer, he heard Brownell say that the committee had decided on Nixon. The congressman then screamed: "Wake up Dick! It's you." Nixon took the call. Brownell stated that the committee had unanimously selected him for the second spot on the ticket and Ike wanted to meet with him immediately at the general's suite. Almost speechless, Nixon instantly uttered his acceptance and quickly got dressed. He knew that he needed a shave and a shower, but decided not to bother in the heat. Since he had no use for his Ford that afternoon, he had loaned it to San Francisco political reporter Earl Behrens. Without it, Nixon, Chotiner, and Hillings had a policeman commandeer a car to drive them over to the Blackstone.[72]

When Nixon arrived in a wrinkled light gray suit with a five-o'clock shadow, Sherman Adams welcomed him at the door of the suite and took him inside to see Eisenhower. Ike stated that his advisers had recommended Nixon for the vice presidency; he asked Nixon to accept the nomination and join in an American crusade. Nixon replied affirmatively that he was "tremendously surprised" and hoped "to conduct a fighting campaign with a fighting candidate." The general had him read a copy of his acceptance speech and discussed some thoughts with him. Suddenly, Eisenhower remembered that he had not, as yet, resigned from the army; he immediately drafted and signed a letter to that effect, walked Nixon to the door, and shook hands. That interview lasted approximately fifteen minutes; they would meet again in the evening at the convention.[73]

During the process of Dick's anointing, Pat Nixon, Helene Drown, and Phyllis Chotiner had left the convention for lunch at the Stockyard Inn's coffeeshop. Pat had not seen her husband since breakfast. Just as she was taking the first bite out of her bacon, lettuce, and tomato sandwich, while the trio was watching a movie on television, a commentator interrupted with a news flash that Eisenhower had chosen Dick as his running mate. Her reaction: "I was so surprised my sandwich fell out of my mouth."[74]

Before rushing back to the arena, Pat freshened up and ran back to the convention hall in high heels. Upon her arrival, she told reporters that this was her first convention, and though she had heard rumors that her husband was being mentioned, she was "amazed, flabbergasted, weak and speechless."[75] To others, Pat admitted that she had heard gossip that he "might be considered."[76] Her biggest worry was her children. She hoped that the nomination would not interfere with family plans to take the girls on a two-week vacation to a Virginia beach after the convention. Telling them created a problem because they would "just think it means we'll be off campaigning again." While she enjoyed the contest, "Leaving the girls is the only thing I won't like about campaigning."[77]

At 5:25 P.M., while reporters swarmed around Pat, Dick entered the convention hall. He reiterated his pledge to put on a "fighting campaign." He then said with a grin: "I don't own a Cadillac and my wife doesn't own a mink." As Nixon pushed through the crowd, Senator Homer Ferguson of Michigan congratulated him. Nixon reminded his colleague that no one had nominated him as yet, and Ferguson assured him that this was a mere formality. Nixon then searched for Bill Knowland, who agreed to present his name to the convention. Going to the dais, Knowland in a short two-minute declaration said that Nixon would give the GOP a special "appeal to the young men and women of this nation" and would be "a great asset to that great ticket we have that is headed by Gen. Eisenhower." Knowland praised his colleague for his paramount role in the Hiss case.[78]

After Knowland's initial nomination, a celebratory tone continued throughout Nixon's anointing process. Governor Driscoll followed with the principal seconding speech, praising Nixon's battle against subversion in Congress. He knew "the smell of a red herring and the color of it, too." Former Texas congressman Ben Guill, and Congressman Cecil Harden of Indiana—who called Nixon a man of "sincerity and principle," who did "fine work" on HUAC—also seconded the nomination. Governor Frank Barrett of Wyoming shouted in his seconding: "No one has done more to put the fear of God into those who would betray their country." Finally, Governor John Fine made a motion to dispense with a roll-call vote and asked for acclamation. Chairman Joe Martin put the question to a vote at 6:35 P.M., and the delegates roared their approval. Only forty minutes had elapsed for the entire proceeding.[79]

Nixon took the rostrum. With a tremendous grin on his face, standing among the California delegation, he flung his arms around those nearest to him. He then looked for Pat as she made her way from the Distinguished Visitors Gallery to join him on the convention floor. Upon reaching him, with a feeling of exaltation, she kissed him. At the insistence of photographs who were unable to capture the moment, they had the Nixons kiss again, and then they made their way through the crowd to the platform with the band playing, "California, Here I Come," climbed the steps, and stood with Martin. Dick placed one arm around Pat and the other on Martin. Pat kissed him, and they all smiled for the cameras.[80]

At 7:30 P.M., the Eisenhowers, with Mamie feeling much better, arrived at the convention hall to a tremendous sound of cheers from those assembled. The Eisenhowers and the Nixons warmly greeted each other. Dick shook hands with Mamie and then with her husband. Pat sat down with Mamie, and they talked about the ordeal. A call for prayer interrupted Mamie's description as they all bowed their heads. Martin, as conference chairman, then introduced Ike with a six-minute speech. The general rose to a rousing ovation, approached the rostrum, and began to speak. He departed from his prepared text to pay a warm tribute to Nixon. The general congratulated the convention for having "the temerity" to select Richard Nixon: "A man who has shown statesmanlike qualities in many ways, but has a special talent, an ability to ferret out any kind of subversive influence wherever it may be found and the strength and persistence to get rid of it."[81]

During the thirteen-minute address, Eisenhower claimed that the convention had summoned him "to lead a great crusade—for freedom in America and in the world." He intended to drive out the Democratic administration, "which has fastened on every one of us the wastefulness, the arrogance and corruption in high places, the heavy burdens and the anxieties which are the bitter fruit of a party too long in power." He called for the election of Republicans throughout the nation, asked for a united effort, appealed to America's youth, and promised a brighter tomorrow with God's guidance and blessings.[82]

Still wearing the same rumpled gray summer suit, Nixon had scribbled some fragmentary notes in a small notebook for his off-the-cuff remarks that served as his acceptance speech. Starting with the ad-lib: "Haven't we got a wonderful candidate for the Presidency of the United States?", he promised "to put on a fighting campaign" to win the White House and elect a Republican Congress. He complimented Joe Martin and pledged to make him Speaker of the House, and Styles Bridges Senate majority leader.[83]

Nixon next turned to someone whom he called "a very great man." Nixon felt that Robert Taft, "one of the really great Senators, one of the greatest legislative leaders in the history of America," needed to become the chairman of the majority policy committee, and Nixon would devote himself to seeing that was accomplished. Disappointed Taft adherents used this declaration of praise to give their man a tumultuous roar of approval. The GOP, Nixon continued, had to capture the presidency as well as Congress in November because the Democrats were "unable to furnish this new vital, dynamic leadership that America needed in this critical period." He would carry that message throughout America to all Republicans so that their victory would be "a victory for America and for the cause of free peoples throughout the world."[84]

With that finale, the Eisenhowers and the Nixons stood on the platform to the adulation from the audience. With the two men standing next to each and their wives on the outside, Dick took Ike's wrist in his hand and put both hands over their heads. All were smiling, and Dick probably the widest.[85]

To Richard Milhous Nixon, "July 11, 1952, was the most exciting day of my life."[86]

He was now in the arena.

Nixon's vice-presidential nomination has sparked considerable controversy over how the senator manipulated his way to the second spot on the ticket. Some, after the fact, claimed that Nixon undermined Warren's presidential chances by sending out the Nixon poll of likely candidates and telling California delegates that the governor could not win and Eisenhower would be victorious. And clearly, Nixon and Warren disliked each another. Many have drawn the inference that the senator would do anything to destroy his antagonist.

The record does not support this allegation. First, in the face of his most fervent believers who despised Warren, Nixon actively promoted the favorite-son ticket in the primary. Second, since the delegation was bound by law to the governor on the first ballot, any potential Nixon uprising would have to await the results of that ballot. Third, Nixon and others made no secret that they favored Eisenhower and that he would be the eventual winner. However, Nixon had only ten loyalists in the state delegation to stage any coup d'état against the governor's majority; until the voting demonstrated clearly that Warren had been eliminated, Nixon would be committing political suicide to challenge the governor without the votes to support a revolt. Fourth, the senator had openly, privately, and constantly pledged to support the delegation; he reported to Warren on the train about the preconvention struggles, worked with him at keeping the delegation united at the convention, and raised the governor's name as the strongest dark horse possibility. These actions demonstrated that Nixon had not reneged on his pledge to follow the governor.[87]

The man most responsible for Warren's presidential hopes evaporating was the governor himself. A half-million voters registered their disapproval in the primary; nor had he done well in the other primaries where his name was on the ballot. Warren not only had signed the Houston Manifesto, but he also came out for it at the convention as the Fair

Play Amendment. To add to Taft's woes, Warren announced that he opposed any "reactionary nominee"—presumably referring to Taft—and admitted that the California delegation favored Eisenhower for the nomination if the favorite-son effort failed.

Another unsubstantiated charge regularly circulated was that Nixon's vice-presidential ambitions depended on the senator bringing the delegation into Ike's camp. One reporter heard gossip that some delegates stated that Nixon was "running around trying to make 'deals' all over the lot," and below the surface, was causing dissension within the delegation. Though this rumor would plague Nixon for the rest of his life, there is no evidence to support it.[88]

Some critics use Bill Knowland to support their case that Nixon tried to subvert the delegation, but forget to include what the senior senator said at the convention, and fifteen years later, when Knowland acknowledged that he was delighted to place Nixon's name into nomination for the vice presidency and declared that the junior senator was "an honorable man, and he had pledged to support Warren until Warren personally released him, and Warren did not release him." Nixon had voted, Knowland recounted, for the favorite son and made no effort to break with his pledge. James Bassett, who reported for the *Los Angeles Mirror*, reiterated that Nixon never bolted.[89]

What brought Nixon the vice-presidential nomination was the culmination of many forces pulling and pushing in the same direction. He had become a national celebrity due to the Hiss affair, but he furthered his standing within the GOP by his extensive speaking schedule and oratory skills. Although he was unable to bring any California delegates to Ike, Nixon did back the Fair Play Amendment and was sympathetic to the general's cause.

Nixon had no managers who manipulated his nomination. What occurred took place without any concerted drive. Reporters before and during the convention made Nixon a leading candidate for the second spot. John Knight, in large bold letters on the morning of July 9, called for an Ike-Nixon ticket even before the general was nominated. Just a day after the convention, Sulzberger remembered that Eisenhower had told him in Paris that he wanted "to capture the imagination of American youth." Ike leaned toward Nixon because he clearly represented that constituency.[90]

When the lieutenants from Ike's headquarters gathered at the Conrad Hilton to choose his running mate, the leaders there knew that they had to select someone who would balance the ticket and bring in votes. Some of those whom Ike wished to run beside him declined. The group in the smoke-filled room rejected Taft, any of his advocates like Dirksen, and anyone from the East. Of the choices that remained, Nixon's name kept coming up. He was the logical selection: young, patriotic, articulate, and dependable. As such, for the fourth time in six years, Nixon became a contender.

# EPILOGUE: NIXON AND HIS DETRACTORS—WHOM SHOULD WE BELIEVE?

The fundamental issue that plagued Richard Nixon throughout his political career concerned his character. In the midst of the Watergate scandal, during a question and answer session on November 17, 1973, in response to a question about his income tax filings, he insisted that he was not a crook. From the polling data taken at that time, however, Americans in overwhelming numbers rejected his assertion. They had been conditioned for almost a quarter of a century to think that he was dishonest. To legions of Nixon haters, it was a well-earned reputation.[1]

The events that forced Nixon's presidential resignation, however, cannot be traced back to his congressional ascendancy. Indeed, as we have seen, every major charge brought against him during his congressional years are not sustained by facts. His political rise demonstrates that while he was not perfect, he was a dedicated, efficient public servant. The time has come to let his record, for good and ill, speak for itself.

## THE REAL NIXON

Richard Nixon entered politics not from a sense of mission to public service but because of an accident of timing. In the fall of 1945, he was contemplating what to do after his naval discharge. Herman Perry, disappointed by the quality of prospective Republican applicants to challenge Democratic incumbent Jerry Voorhis, called upon Nixon to run for the

House. He seized the opportunity, accepted this political calling, and resolved his employment dilemma for the next fourteen years.

During that first race against Voorhis, Nixon worked much harder than his opponent and upset him by a solid margin. Six years after the election, an editorial in the *Madera News-Tribune* recounted why Nixon was victorious. He spoke to the issues of the day. "He rang doorbells, he talked on street corners and in auditoriums, he kissed babies, patted old ladies on the cheek, and otherwise made himself known wherever and whenever two people would stop and listen to him. He made friends with the press and radio, he went out of his way to be congenial and likeable." He campaigned for almost ten months; Voorhis allocated just two months. Besides staying in the capital, Voorhis made other blunders. The incumbent actually called upon his challenger to debate the issues. By doing so, Voorhis raised Nixon to the incumbent's level, allowed the challenger to appear on the same platform, provided him with the means to attack the congressman's vulnerabilities, gave Nixon's followers a chance to claim victory during the debates, and accelerated Nixon's momentum.[2]

During his reelection campaign, Nixon not only won the Republican primary but also defeated political novice Stephen Zetterberg on the Democratic ballot. Now with two years of experience, Nixon had built a record, assembled a competent campaign committee, and recognized the importance of public relations. The Democratic Party hoped that Voorhis would run again for his House seat. His refusal left a void, and Zetterberg was chosen at the last moment to become a sacrificial political lamb for a party that lacked an attractive candidate. Under such adverse conditions of the Democrats' own making, they suffered a humiliating defeat.

After three years in the House, Nixon looked forward to the possibility of running for a Senate seat. Because the Democratic incumbent, Senator Sheridan Downey, was deemed unbeatable, none of the most prominent Republicans stepped up to challenge him. Nixon, on the other hand, assumed the risk and was fortunate when Downey's health forced him to retire.

With the incumbent eliminated, Nixon's victory had as much to do with Helen Gahagan Douglas's weaknesses as with his own strengths. Her bruising primary fight first against Downey and then against his surrogate Manchester Boddy caused an enormous breach within the Democratic Party. Douglas entered the fall election without the support of a substantial number of moderate and conservative Democrats, who deserted their party to join the opposition.

At this crucial moment, anticommunism, Nixon's leading issue and Douglas's most glaring vulnerability, was gaining widespread popularity. Yet her first salvo after Labor Day in the fall campaign attacked Nixon's voting record on Korea, as if trying to beat him on his own turf. After Douglas made this disastrous decision, Nixon set the tone for the campaign by contrasting his and her judgments on matters pertaining to domestic security and Russian expansionism. The "pink sheet" became the focus of charges and countercharges, but it was mild by comparison to later (or, for that matter, earlier) standards of negative campaigning. Even without the pink sheet, anticommunism was bound to be the key issue in the race, and from the start, Douglas's chances were at best remote.

Rarely do Nixon's biographers concede that his challengers lacked managerial, tactical, and ideological skills. Instead, Voorhis and Douglas are often described as virtuous. Some writers concede that Douglas had various handicaps, but Nixon's attack politics are featured far more than hers.

The myth of Nixon as a liar is underscored by selective attention to his activities in the House and Senate. As we have seen, a full and fair version of his record shows a hardworking, promising young star. He became a defender of GOP moderation in domestic issues and a champion of internationalism in foreign affairs. He fought for the Taft-Hartley Act, and after its passage, argued for amendments to correct its ambiguities. He followed most of the Republican initiatives in the 80th Congress and agreed with his colleagues as they shrank back into the minority during the next one. Whatever problems Nixon had with Harry Truman in domestic matters, they did not interfere with support for a bipartisan foreign policy. Named to the Herter mission, he saw firsthand the abysmal postwar conditions in Europe and came away from that journey a firm convert to the objectives expressed in the burgeoning Marshall Plan.

Nixon's sharpest disagreement with the White House arose from his HUAC role. Once the new congressman was convinced that federal officials were guilty of espionage and that the administration was unwilling to halt subversion, he fought doggedly to present his case, find those who had compromised American security, and publicly expose them. When Professor Robert Carr, in his authoritative treatise on HUAC, evaluated Nixon's performance, he concluded that the congressman had acted in the most responsible and moderate manner of any of those on the controversial committee.

Nixon's HUAC service and especially the Hiss hearings have attracted the most attention. What commentators often obscure is the fact that he was far from an extremist. More than fourteen years after entering Congress, Nixon recalled his disgust with some HUAC colleagues and how he "used to boil inwardly with rage when John Rankin, of Mississippi, or one of his associates would take the Floor of the House of Representatives to spout venom against fellow-Americans because they were of the Negro race, or the Jewish faith, or perhaps Italian extraction." To Nixon, such racist slurs were "dangerous," and he wondered "whether those who professed to patriotism realized how effectively they were furthering the Communist cause when they excited bitterness among Americans by aggravating natural difference between people like those of race and religion."[3]

Nixon's signature in the struggle against communism came accidentally, with the eruption of the Chambers-Hiss volcano, demonstrating that Hiss had committed perjury, and leading to major coverage on the front pages of almost every American newspaper. From the hot August days when Chambers and Hiss confronted each other at a televised HUAC hearing, both the former spy and his antagonist were intertwined with Nixon. Some have charged that Nixon had advance knowledge of Hiss's guilt, but the evidence shows the opposite.

To examine Nixon from his contemporaries' viewpoint is paramount not from the hindsight of our knowledge of Watergate. Anticommunism was as American as apple pie in the late 1940s. From his first term, Nixon preached to an enormous national congregation who passionately considered the Red peril worthy of a life and death struggle. Nixon was a true believer. Truman's characterization of HUAC's hearings as a "red herring" not only infuriated him but also led to a stalemate in which the president refused to cooperate with the GOP and likeminded Democrats who honestly felt that Soviet penetration of American institutions was destroying the fabric of American life. This only enhanced the stature of the cause. Nixon soon turned to his oratorical skills to become a prominent GOP critic of the administration's failings on Korea, communism, and corruption.

Nixon's meteoric rise to national prominence, his principled anticommunism that stood out so clearly in contrast to Joe McCarthy's and HUAC members', his systematic and well-organized campaigns, all made him an attractive choice for Dwight Eisenhower's advisers. The general's convention lieutenants stumbled through an anticlimactic and haphazard process of choosing a running mate. Yet Nixon quickly emerged as the unanimous choice for the second spot. He was a young moderate from the West who had become a national celebrity. As he stood on the rostrum, raising Eisenhower's wrist to the rafters with the broadest smile imaginable, Nixon appeared to be the epitome of the Horatio Alger myth: a child from a relatively poor, rural setting, who had emerged from obscurity to run for the second highest elected office in America.

Nixon was hardly flawless. Sometimes he acted precipitously and imprudently. During the controversy brought on by Laurence Duggan's mysterious death, he moved too impulsively and was linked to Congressman Karl Mundt, who blurted out the tasteless phrase that he would release the names of the other Reds associated with Duggan when they too jumped out of windows. Nixon also should have never given Chotiner, and Holt, HUAC's Tenney file. As a lawyer, Nixon understood the implications of releasing confidential data to those who had no right to see it, and he knew that its only possible use would be unfair and underhanded. Finally, the senator sometimes did not fully consider the ramifications of his actions. After sending out a questionnaire to his constituents soliciting their opinions about the best presidential contender in 1952, some of Warren's followers viciously attacked Nixon for his insensitivity in not supporting their favorite son. Recognizing this action as politically unwise, Nixon never released the results and publicly reaffirmed his support for the governor.

These multifaceted character traits should have been the stuff that legends spring from. Yet something went awry. Nixon's congressional career has become the basis of myth that both masks and mingles with reality. Errors of fact have accumulated, culminating in misguided interpretations and the persistence of the derogatory Nixon legend. How did this happen?

## THE NIXON MYTH

Nixon's reputation as a congenital liar has been most actively perpetuated by a core of Nixon haters. The standard line began with Ernest Brashear's "Who Is Richard Nixon?" in the *New Republic* on September 1, 1952, and continuing the following week. Brashear identified himself as the labor editor for the *Los Angeles Daily News,* omitting to mention that he had run and lost as a Democratic candidate for the California state assembly during 1950. He was firmly on the left. Though later, reputable historians have dismissed him out of hand, his charges have nonetheless persisted.

Brashear hurled preposterous charges that cemented the foundation of Richard Nixon's demonizing. Commencing with the genesis of his decision to enter politics in late 1945, the reporter noted that Herman Perry recruited Nixon. Brashear promoted Perry from a local bank branch manager to a wealthy Bank of America "financier." Instead of "the charming fairy tale" of the Candidate and Fact Finding Committee soliciting a naive naval officer and his running under the guidance of an amateurish campaign committee, Brashear described Nixon's supporters as a clandestine organization dominated by professional politicians, monopolies, and big business. Nixon, from Brashear's vantage, almost immediately attacked Voorhis as a Red who served the CIO-PAC. For the first time in a national publication, a reporter declared that Nixon had employed anonymous telephone callers to announce that Voorhis was a Communist and then hung up. Nixon won only as a result of such underhanded practices.

Brashear described Nixon's demolition of Helen Gahagan Douglas as "one of the best-financed, well-publicized and most underhanded campaigns in California's history." She lost, he claimed, because Nixon spent between $1 million and $2 million on newspapers, billboards, radio, television, and other media promotions. His money was supposed to have come primarily from "wealthy owners of California's oil, private utilities and corporation farms." With virtually unlimited funding, his campaign staff cleverly linked Douglas to Vito Marcantonio. "The Pink Sheet," Brashear proclaimed, "was a big and masterful lie, convincingly done." Worse, Joe McCarthy "spoke throughout the state for him as part of Nixon's double-level campaign." Each of the above accusations, as we have seen, has no basis in reality. Yet they live on.[4]

Other Nixon haters have followed in Brashear's footsteps. Fawn Brodie based an entire book on the assumption that Nixon was never to be trusted. Writing in the early 1980s, she found Nixon guilty of congenital lying: the lynchpin that predetermined why he was so reprehensible. Her book became a Book-of-the-Month Club selection, and some writers (fortunately not many) still refer to it as a reputable source.

Frank Mankiewicz, former presidential campaign manager for George McGovern, cavalierly raised the charge of criminal fraud in each of Nixon's congressional campaigns, thereby effectively indicting, trying, and sentencing Nixon. In fact, Mankiewicz made his allegations without identifying any significant documentation to defend such claims. His book is so blatantly slanted that it is rarely cited, but unsuspecting readers still pull it from library shelves.

None of these Nixon haters would matter, and none would be particularly remarkable among the typical morass of partisan sniping, if their assumptions and charges had not made it into the mainstream. Unfortunately for the real record, the theme of Nixon as untrustworthy, along with many specific allegations of Red-baiting, secret financing, back-channel communication with the FBI, et al., live on in otherwise scholarly writings. Even Stephen E. Ambrose's first volume on Nixon, which dismisses Brashear, scoffs at claims of secret moneys, and describes Nixon's California supporters fairly, includes a detailed section on his vice-presidential selection that depends almost exclusively on journalistic accounts, some of which perpetuate the myths. Ambrose portrays a Nixon who manipulated his way toward the nomination, reasoning that Nixon worked for Eisenhower within the California delegation by weakening Warren's hold on its members. He states that Nixon controlled almost a third of the delegation though that figure did not in fact reach 10 percent. The facts of the matter were straightforward: Warren had absolute control over how the delegation would vote; Nixon had no ability to change that. The records of the actual decision meeting of Eisenhower's advisers show nothing predestined in Nixon's choice as vice president.[5]

Still, Ambrose's *Nixon* represented a highpoint of objectivity, after which the "congenital liar" made a comeback. The most often cited biographer for Nixon's congressional period, Roger Morris, a finalist in the National Book Award for his *Richard Milhous Nixon: The Rise of an American Politician,* paints a sinister portrait. Certain Morris conclusions are contradicted by the record, and his interpretations invariably tend toward the dark side.

In one seemingly trivial example, Morris notes that during the 1948 congressional primary election campaign, Nixon sent out postcards from "Democrats for Nixon, J. R. Blue, Chairman." Morris states that "there were questions about whether Mr. Blue was a Democrat or even existed." In fact, J. R. Blue, whose correct name was J. B. Blue, Jr., and who was indeed a Democrat, wrote and received scores of letters to and from Nixon and his campaign staff.[6]

A far less trivial example concerns the money said to have been spent on Nixon's campaigns, beginning with the very first one. Brashear claimed, without any proof other than what seemed "reasonable" to him, that Nixon had spent at least $175,000 on billboards. Nixon campaign records show this to be preposterous; with the exclusion of eleven billboards bought by the local Long Beach committee, the statewide organization purchased 774 billboards for a total charge of $26,339.33, or approximately 13 percent of the budget, just about $150,000 less than Brashear's projection.[7]

For the Senate campaign, Brashear had estimated that Nixon forces spent between $1 million and $2 million. Morris inflates these numbers, concluding that Nixon spent even more lavishly throughout his campaigns. Referring to the 1950 race against Helen Gahagan Douglas, Morris pronounces that Nixon's "further rise had been richly financed, mostly in secret." He offers no proof to back these charges. An even more recent author, Greg Mitchell, alleges in *Tricky Dick and the Pink Lady* that Morris had underestimated Nixon's vast reserves of cash. Again, no substantiated proof is offered.

In an era before television (and also before stricter Federal Election Commission requirements), the budgets for Nixon's first three contests were minuscule. Candidates budgeted their funds for billboards, mailings, newspaper advertisements, and some radio spots. Outside groups possibly could have expended large sums on pro-Nixon billboards without ever leaving any official receipts in archives; but in this case, the Nixon archives demonstrate that almost all major expenditures were done by the campaign and accounted for.

For Morris's and Mitchell's numbers to be correct, third-party money would have had to blanket the state in an unprecedented explosion. Media reports from the time mention no such blitz. Though the accusation of "secret" money can never be disproved, because it is logically impossible to prove the negative, accounting sheets are persuasive. No scrap of paper in the Nixon archive refers to a dime of outside money, nor did Nixon even need it for his victories. The time has come to bury this myth.

Prejudicial reminisces, half-truths, journalist biases, and a small sampling of documents from various archives remain the shaky foundation of Richard Nixon's historiography during his congressional career. Rave reviews greeted Morris's book, but none of the major reviewers had examined the writer's sources or the Nixon manuscripts.

Some of the Nixon myths at first glance appears to have stronger foundations. To prove that Nixon had been tipped off in advance about Alger Hiss's serving in the Russian spy network, Garry Wills in his *Nixon Agonistes* interviewed Father John Cronin in the late 1960s, resurrecting the allegation that even though Nixon denied having had any knowledge of Hiss or his espionage before his HUAC appearance, he in fact knew all about both. Cronin had made such a claim in the late 1950s, but Wills's description revitalized it a decade after the HUAC hearings.

Allen Weinstein during the mid-1970s magnified Wills's theme and based on his own interview with Cronin concluded (in an *Esquire* article, followed by his book *Perjury*) that, indeed, Nixon had not divulged the information he had earlier received concerning Hiss. Only in the late 1980s did presidential historian Herbert Parmet challenge the mainstream view. In an interview with Parmet, Cronin recanted, conceding that Nixon's version was accurate.

None of the other evidence from the hearings and Nixon's papers support Cronin's now recanted accusation. Chambers's gradual, tortuous admissions hardly seemed orchestrated. Nixon's interrogations of Hiss did not give any indication that the congressman had privileged, advanced information that Hiss was a spy. Even if Cronin's accusations were true, what relevance might they have held for a Nixon who treated Hiss carefully throughout the hearings? The power of the Cronin myth stemmed not from its plausibility, but its underlying premise: Nixon was deceitful. The truth, including the curious fact that J. Edgar Hoover used an unofficial source on the HUAC staff to report on the activities of Nixon, whom the director distrusted, should be of much greater interest.

The anti-Nixon myths have taken deep hold on our culture. On November 8, 1998, CNN aired its much-discussed multipart documentary, *Cold War*, in which Nixon was summarily dismissed as a "Redbaiter." That was the extent of the charge. Nothing more was needed. Everyone knew what that meant.[8]

Similarly, Katharine Graham, the publisher of the *Washington Post*, in her *Personal History*, awarded a Pulitzer Prize, and a national bestseller, after acknowledging her fondness for the Democratic presidential nominee, Adlai Stevenson, declared that she and many of her "friends were deeply concerned about his [Nixon's] red baiting victorious early campaign against Helen Gahagan Douglas and about his pronounced right-wing proclivities and seeming sympathy for McCarthy."[9]

Nixon's politics unquestionably were to the right of center. But Nixon's "seeming sympathy for McCarthy" is less a factual depiction than a portrayal based on the hackneyed charge of Nixon out-McCarthying McCarthy. Such unexamined claims and assumptions appeal only to the most fundamental emotions of the faithful from either end of the political spectrum. What really transpired almost seems irrelevant and inconsequential to those shouting at each other, resolving little and surrendering nothing.

WHO WAS RICHARD NIXON?

Now that an enormous amount of Nixon material has been released concerning his congressional career, who was Richard Nixon? As a rising star, was he fundamentally a Red-baiter and tool of big business? He clearly was neither. Was he a saint, as some of his staunchest defenders assert? Of course not. But he was remarkable among his congressional peers, a success story in a troubled era, one who steered a sensible anti-Communist course against the excess of McCarthy and other extreme right-wingers. Those in the smoke-filled room who selected him above all others for the vice-presidential nomination validated his meteoric rise.

In Washington, D.C., as one drives down from Capitol Hill along the Pennsylvania Avenue side of the National Archives (principal repository of government documents), an inscription looms on the pedestal beneath a female statue symbolizing the future: *What Is Past Is Prologue.* This famous line from Shakespeare's *Tempest* is meaningful only if what is past is accurately portrayed. Within the massive archives' walls does indeed lie the truth. The enormous mountain of Nixon material is staggering. The truth is there, if only we will permit ourselves to see it objectively.[10]

# Notes

*Chapter 1*

1. Hoover speech, June 11, 1954, Helzer to Hoover, Apr 11, Hoover to Helzer, Apr 16, Adams to Callahan, June 9, 1969, Webster to Rees, Apr ?, and Adams to Callahan, May 3, 1971, Nixon application file, FBI; Richard Nixon, *RN: The Memoirs of Richard Nixon* (NY: Grosset & Dunlap, 1978), 21–22; for examples of mythology, see Earl Mazo, *Richard Nixon: A Political and Personal Portrait* (NY: Harper & Brothers, 1959), 26–27; Ralph de Toledano, *One Man Alone: Richard Nixon* (NY: Funk & Wagnalls, 1969), 31; Fawn Brodie, *Richard Nixon: The Shaping of His Character* (NY: Norton, 1981), 132; Stephen E. Ambrose, *Nixon: The Education of a Politician 1913–1962* (NY: Simon & Schuster, 1987), 82; Roger Morris, *Richard Milhous Nixon: The Rise of an American Politician* (NY: Holt, 1990), 180–184.
2. Bruce Mazlish, *In Search of Nixon: A Psychohistorical Inquiry* (NY: Basic Books, 1972), 37–38; David Abrahamsen, *Nixon vs. Nixon: An Emotional Tragedy* (NY: Farrar, Straus & Giroux, 1977), 121–122; even more fantastic is Brodie, *Nixon, passim.*
3. Application, Apr 23, 1937, Nixon application file, FBI.
4. *Ibid.,* Horack to Hoover, May 3, Hoover to Horack, May 11, 1937.
5. *Ibid.,* Hanson to Hoover, July 17, 1937.
6. *Ibid.,* Hanson to director, July 19, Hoover to SAC in Los Angeles, July 23, memorandum for Keenan, July 24, Hoover to SAC in Charlotte, North Carolina, July ?, Hoover to medical officer, July 24, medical examination, July 29, RN to director, July 31, report by Ross, Aug 3, personnel recommendation, Aug 13, 1937, and Glavin to director, Mar 16, 1954.
7. RN to Horack, Oct 6, 1937, Records of the Dean, H. Claude Horack, School of Law, Nixon mss, Duke Univ.
8. Adams to Callahan, Apr 15, 1969, Nixon application file, FBI.
9. Exhibition Hall, Richard Nixon Library & Birthplace, "Nixon—A Self Portrait," Nov 1?, 1968, RNLB:19:2, RNyl; RN to Hay, Jan 6, 1949, B 39, Ancestry, RN to Lindley, B 453, Lindley, Series 320, RNln; Nixon, *RN,* 5–6.
10. Exhibition Hall, Richard Nixon Library & Birthplace, "Nixon—A Self Portrait," Nov 1?, 1968, (RNLB):19:2, RNyl; Nixon, *RN,* 8–9.
11. "Nixon: From Whittier to the White House," Jan 20, 1969, RNLB:32:4,

RNyl; Nixon, *RN,* 3 and 8; Joseph Silvestri, exhibition designer of the Richard Nixon Library & Birthplace, took me on a tour of the house and upstairs to measure the dimensions of the second floor.

12. Doris Walker, *Orange County, A Centennial Celebration: Sections of Orange* (T.x.: Pioneer Publications, 1989), 80, 91, and 97; Jessamyn West, *Hide and Seek: A Continuing Journey* (NY: Harcourt Brace Jovanovich, 1973), 114, 122, and *passim.*

13. West, *Hide and Seek,* 218–222 and 255–256; Nixon, *RN,* 13–14.

14. West, *Hide and Seek,* 238–240.

15. Interview with RN, 1958, 4–5, C 47, Stewart Alsop mss, Library of Congress.

16. Nixon, *RN,* 4–8.

17. Interview with RN, 1958, 4–5, C 47, Alsop mss.

18. *Ibid.,* 4, 5, and 8–9; "Nixon—A Self Portrait," Nov 1?, 1968, RNLB:19:2, RNyl.

19. Nixon, *RN,* 3–5.

20. *Ibid.,* 9; interview with RN, 1958, 6, C 47, Alsop mss.

21. Nixon, *RN,* 9–12; interview with RN, 1958, 5 and 11, C 47, Alsop mss; Joseph Dmohowski, "From a Common Ground: The Quaker Heritage of Jessamyn West and Richard Nixon," *California History,* vol. 73, no. 3 (Fall 1994), 227.

22. Nixon, *RN,* 12–13; Ralph de Toledano, *Nixon* (NY: Holt, 1956), 22.

23. Report by Ross, Aug 3, 1937, Nixon application file, FBI; interview with RN, 1958, 4, C 47, Alsop mss; de Toledano, *Nixon,* 22.

24. RN to Gibbons, Feb 27, 1953, B 287, Gibbons, Series 320, RNln; "Cardinal and White," 1929 and 1930, LBM22.1, Richard M. Nixon, undated, PE121, "What do the people of Whittier think of Richard Nixon?", 1952?, PE105, RNyl; report by Ross, Aug 3, Form No. 1, Aug 3, 1937, Nixon application file, FBI; Nixon, *RN,* 14–15.

25. Report by Ross, Aug 3, 1937, Nixon application file, FBI; Albert Upton, Paul Smith, undated, Moore to Editor, Nov 22, 1968, PE 123, RNyl; James Keogh, *This is Nixon,* (NY: Putnam, 1956), 28; Nixon, *RN,* 14–17.

26. *Acropolis,* 1931–34, LBM22.1, Moore to Editor, Nov 22, 1968, PE123, RNyl; Nixon, *RN,* 17–19.

27. Wallace "Chief" Newman, undated, PE123, RNyl; report by Ross, Aug 3, 1937, Nixon application file, FBI; Keogh, *This Is Nixon,* 27; Nixon, *RN,* 19–20.

28. Application, Apr 23, report by Ross, Aug 3, 1937, Nixon application file, FBI.

29. Bolich to RN, Nov 18, 1946, PPS1.245, RNyl; Nixon, *RN,* 20.

30. Report by Lopez, July 29, 1937, Nixon application file, FBI; Nixon, *RN,* 20.

31. Report by Lopez, July 29, 1937, Nixon application file, FBI.

32. *Ibid.*

33. *Ibid.;* Nixon, *RN,* 20–21.

34. Nixon, *RN,* 21; de Toledano, *Nixon,* 27; Lester David, *The Lonely Lady of San Clemente: The Story of Pat Nixon* (NY: Cromwell, 1978), 48–50.

35. Report by Lopez, July 29, 1937, Nixon application file, FBI; *Whittier News,* June 7, 1952, PPS5.SA21, RNyl; Interview with RN, 1958, 8, C 47, Alsop mss; Nixon, *RN,* 21–22.

36. Hanson to director, July 17, 1937, Nixon application file, FBI; RN to Eddy, Oct 6, 1949, B 235, Eddy, AC, Series 320, RNln; Nixon, *RN,* 22; Nixon, *Six Crises* (NY: Doubleday, 1962), 12.

37. Application, Apr 23, report by Ross, Aug 3, 1937, Nixon application file, FBI.

38. Nixon, *RN,* 22; Mazo, *Nixon,* 29; Keogh, *This Is Nixon,* 29–30; de Toledano, *One Man Alone,* 31; David, *Lonely Lady,* 41–42.
39. Interview with RN, 1958, 9 and 10, C 47, Alsop mss.
40. RN to Bancroft, June 3, 1948, PPS205.576, RNyl; Nixon, *RN,* 22–23 and 25; de Toledano, *One Man Alone,* 35–36.
41. Nixon, *RN,* 23.
42. Julie Eisenhower, *Pat Nixon: The Untold Story* (NY: Simon & Schuster, 1986), 17–33.
43. *Ibid.,* 34–49.
44. *The Cardinal,* 1938, LBM22.1, review, Feb 18, 1938, LBM22.1, RNyl; Eisenhower, *Pat Nixon,* 50–70.
45. Richard Nixon, undated, PE117, RNyl; Nixon, *RN,* 25; Eisenhower, *Pat Nixon,* 71–73; David, *Lonely Lady,* 57–58; Mazo, *Nixon,* 35.
46. Government and Navy Service, undated, B 1, Biographical, Series 435, RNln; Nixon, *RN,* 25–26; Eisenhower, *Pat Nixon,* 75.
47. Government and Navy Service, undated, B 1, Biographical, Series 435, RNln; Nixon, *RN,* 26; Eisenhower, *Pat Nixon,* 75.
48. Government and Navy Service, undated, B 1, Biographical, Series 435, RNln; Nixon, *RN,* 26–27; Eisenhower, *Pat Nixon,* 76–78; E. M. Cofer, *Carrier on the Prairie: The Story of the U.S. Air Station Ottumwa, Iowa* (Iowa: Hawley Court Press, 1996), 45, 47, 48, 77, 78, 91, and 95.
49. Government and Navy Service, undated, B 1, Biographical, Series 435, RNln; Nixon, *RN,* 27–28; Eisenhower, *Pat Nixon,* 78–79.
50. RN to PN, Aug 24, 1943, Exhibition Hall, RNyl; Government and Navy Service, undated, B 1, Biographical, Series 435, RNln; Nixon, *RN,* 28.
51. RN to PN, Sept 3, 1943, No. 60, and Jan 28, 1944, No. 76, uncatalogued, RNyl; Nixon, *RN,* 28.
52. RN to Udall, Apr 14, 1947, B 770, Udall; RN to Van Liew, Feb 7, 1951, B 780, Van Liew, Series 320, RNln; Experience on Green Island, 1946, PPS208.31, *Pomona Progress-Bulletin,* May 15, 1948, PPS205.S39, RNyl; Nixon, *RN,* 28–29; Eisenhower, *Pat Nixon,* 81.
53. Eisenhower, *Pat Nixon,* 83; Nixon, *RN,* 33.
54. Government and Navy Service, undated, B 1, Biographical, Series 435, RNln.
55. Eisenhower, *Pat Nixon,* 82 and 86–87; Nixon, *RN,* 33–34.

*Chapter 2*

1. Because of the number the Candidate and Fact Finding Committee was sometimes called the Committee of 100. Perry to Harrison, Apr 20, 1945, PE140, McLaughlin to Perry, Apr 22, 1945, PE141, memo, Sept 28, 1953, PE102, memo by Perry, Sept 28, 1954, PE102, Mac to Dreschsel, Nov 12, 1956, MC206.1, and Members of the Fact Finding Committee Nixon Committee of 109, MC206.2, Jorgensen to Woods, Jan 12, 1972, PPS1.218A, RNyl; Barnes to RN, Dec 6, 1946, B 63, S, Series 320, RNln; Jorgensen, Berkeley Oral History Project (OHP), 6; Day, Berkeley OHP, 3–6 and 19; Paul Bullock, *Jerry Voorhis: The Idealist as Politician* (NY: Vantage Press, 1978), 211–212.
2. Gaunt to Obermayer, Nov 4, 1954, B172, Committee of 100, Series 320, RNln; Balch, "Nixon v. Voorhis," 14–15.

3. Perry to RN, Sept 29, 1945, PE142, memo by Cooper, 1947?, PE109, memo, 1950–1951, PE101(1), memo by Perry, 1950–1951, PE104(1), memo by Perry, PE106(1), and "Nixon—A Self Portrait," Nov 1?, 1968, RNLB:19:2, RNyl; RN to Perry, June 14, 1948, B 3, Workers, Series 434, RNln; interview with Hubert Perry, Apr 22, 1997.

4. Perry biography, undated, PE100, RNyl.

5. *Ibid.*, and Perry to Harrison, Apr 20, 1945, PE140, RNyl.

6. Memo by Perry, 1950–1951, PE 101(1), Smith to Perry, PE 144, and Perry to Smith, Oct 3, 1945, PE 145, RNyl.

7. RN to Perry, Oct 6, 1945, PE 146, RNyl.

8. Bullock, *Voorhis,* 47–88, 112–118, and 148–149; J.L. Voorhis, "Idealist," 13–14, 18, 34–35, 39, and 52–53.

9. RN to J. Voorhis, Apr 1, 1946, B 1 Correspondence, Series 433, RNln; Bullock, *Voorhis,* 21–34; Jerry Voorhis, *Confessions of a Congressman,* (NY: Doubleday, 1948), 18; J. Voorhis, Claremont OHP, III, 4–7.

10. J.L. Voorhis, "Idealist," 1–9; J. Voorhis, Claremont OHP, I, 12–48, II, 2–50; Voorhis, *Confessions,* 16.

11. Perry to Harper, Mar 4, 1952, PE1188, memo by Perry, Sept 28, 1953, PE 102, and memo by Perry, undated, PE 106(1), RNyl.

12. C. Voorhis to J. Voorhis, Oct 12 and 15, and J. Voorhis to C. Voorhis, Oct 16, 1945, B 109, F 13, Voorhis mss.

13. Dexter to Day, Oct 8, 1945, Day, Berkeley OHP, 49; Dexter to Perry, Oct 9, 1945, PE 148, and Perry to Dexter, Oct 10, 1945, PE 150, RNyl.

14. Balch, "Nixon v. Voorhis," 19–20.

15. Day, Berkeley OHP, 1–2 and 48.

16. Day to Perry, Oct 12, 1945, PE 155, RNyl; RN to Ethel Dexter, Dec 18, 1950, B 215, Dexter, Series 320, RNln; Day to Dexter, Oct 13, 1945, and Day, Berkeley OHP, 17 and 46.

17. Perry to RN, Oct 16, 1945, PE 156, and Day to Representatives, Oct 18, 1945, PPS1.2, RNyl; C. Voorhis to J. Voorhis, Oct 16 and 23, 1945, B 109, F 13, Voorhis mss; Day to Dexter, Oct 13, 1945, Berkeley OHP, 47.

18. *Arcadia Tribune & News,* Oct 18, 1945, B 30, F 6, Voorhis mss.

19. RN to Perry, Oct 19, 1945, PE 158, RNyl.

20. RN to Jim, Oct 22, 1945, PPS1.3A, RNyl.

21. McLaughlin to Perry, Oct 21, 1945, PE 159, RNyl.

22. Nelson to Day, Oct 26, PPS1.5, memo by Perry, 1950–1951, PE 106(1), and Day to Representatives, Oct 18, 1945, PPS1.2, RNyl; *Progress-Bulletin,* Oct 31, 1945, Day, Berkeley OHP, 4–6; Balch, "Nixon v. Voorhis," 16.

23. Nelson to Day, Oct 26, PPS1.5, and Day to Nelson, Oct 27, PPS1.4, RN to Spencer, Nov 7, 1945, SP 3, and Jorgensen to Woods, Jan 12, 1972, PPS1.218A, RNyl; Garland to RN, Nov 29, and RN to Garland, Dec 11, 1950, B 282, Garland[1/2], RN to Jorgensen, Mar 19, 1952, B 392, Jorgensen (2 of 2), Series 320, RNln; Jorgensen, Berkeley OHP, 8–9; *Independent Review,* July 25, B G281[1 of 3], "Washington Merry-Go-Round," Oct 30, 1952, B G281[2 of 3], Pearson mss, LBJ; McIntyre Faries, *Rememb'ring* (Glendale, Ca.: Griffin Publishing, 1993), 201 and 205.

24. Nixon, *RN,* 35; *Whittier News,* Nov 3, 1945; Smith to Perry, Oct 27, 1945, PE 163, and memo, PE 166, RNyl; Day, Berkeley OHP, 3–6.

25. RN to Day, Nov 7, 1945, Balch, "Nixon v. Voorhis,"Appendix D; Day, Berkeley OHP, 6.

26. Bewley to RN, Nov 7, 1945, PPS1.7, RNyl.

27. RN to Bewley, Nov 21?, 1945, PE 171a, RNyl.

28. Spencer to RN, Oct 20, PPS1.3, and RN to Spencer, Nov 7, 1945, SP 3, RNyl.

29. Day to RN, Nov 12, PPS1.8, and Day to Members, Nov 15, 1945, PPS1.10, RNyl.

30. RN to Perry, Nov 15 and 26, 1945, PE 168 and 173, RNyl; Jerry Voorhis, *Out of Debt, Out of Danger* (NY: Devin-Adair Co., 1943), *passim;* J. Voorhis to C. Voorhis, Jan 21, 1944, B 109, F 8, Voorhis mss.

31. J. Voorhis to C. Voorhis, Jan 21, 1944, B 109, F8, Voorhis mss; Perry to RN, Nov 24, 1945, PE 172, and RN to Hubert Perry, Jan 13, 1987, PE uncatalogued, RNyl.

32. Rules for Candidate and Fact Finding Committee, Oct 1945, MC 2, RNyl.

33. Day to Members, Nov 15, PPS1.10, Perry to Day, PE 171, Kepple to RN, Nov 29, PPS1.12, and *Express Herald,* Nov 29, 1945, PE 175, RNyl; Gerald Kepple, OHP, 992, 5–10, California State Univ., Fullerton.

34. RN to Day, Nov 29, 1945, PPS1.13, RNyl; Eisenhower, *Pat Nixon,* 86.

35. Perry to RN, Nov 30, 1945, PE 176, RNyl.

36. RN to Perry, Dec 2, PE 178, RN to Kepple, Dec 4, PPS1.20, and RN to Martin, Dec 4, 1945, PPS1.21, RNyl.

37. Voorhis, Claremont OHP, III, 1–8 and 32; Voorhis, Berkeley OHP, 18–20; Bullock, *Voorhis,* 47–88 and 112–118; J. L. Voorhis, "Idealist," 34–35; Jerry Voorhis, *The Strange Case of Richard Milhous Nixon,* (NY: Paul S. Ericksson, 1972), 6; Voorhis, *Confessions,* 187–192.

38. RN to Day, Dec 4, 1945, PPS1.17(1), RNyl.

39. Day to Chotiner, Dec 9, 1945, Day, Berkeley OHP; Day to RN, Dec 9, 1945, PPS1.25, and Notes for Bob, 1956, PPS300.462, and Adams to Smith, Oct 31, 1972, SM1.2, RNyl; Arnold, *Back When It All Began,* preface.

40. RN to Perry, Nov 26, PE 173, Kepple to RN, Nov 29, PPS1.12, and Perry to RN, Nov 30, 1945, PE 176, RNyl; Martin to RN, Dec 5, B 479, Martin, JW, and Phillips to RN, Dec 6, 1945, B 595, Phillips, J, Series 320, RNln.

41. RN to Perry, Dec 2, PE 178, and Dec 17, 1945, PE 217, RNyl.

42. RN to Perry, Dec 17, 1945, PE 217, RNyl.

43. Spencer to RN, Dec 17, 1945, PPS1.29, RNyl.

44. O'Brien to J. Voorhis, Dec 20, 1944, J. Voorhis to Sweet, Mar 2, Speech, Aug 23, 1945, B 58, F 1, Voorhis mss; Jerry Voorhis, 1945–1946, RNLB: 112:1 and Jerry Voorhis, Apr–May 1945, RNLB: 111, RNyl.

45. C. Voorhis to J. Voorhis, Feb 16 and Mar 24, B 109, F 8, and C. Voorhis to Voorhis mss, May 19, 1944, B 109, F 9, and C. Voorhis to J. Voorhis, Mar 1, 1946, Voorhis mss.

46. C. Voorhis to Voorhis, July 17, B 109, F 12, and Dec 6, 1945, B 109, F 13, Voorhis mss.

47. C. Voorhis to J. Voorhis, July 17, 1945, B 109, F 12, and *Progress-Bulletin,* Aug 17, 1945, B 58, F 2, C. Voorhis to J. Voorhis, Oct 5, J. Voorhis to C. Voorhis, Oct 8, 1945, B 109, F 13, Voorhis mss; J. Voorhis to Preston, Aug 10, 1945, PPS1.187, RNyl.

48. C. Voorhis to J. Voorhis, July 24, B 109, F 12, C. Voorhis to J. Voorhis, Oct 12 and 15, 1945, B 109, F 13, Voorhis mss.
49. C. Voorhis to J. Voorhis, Dec 1, and J. Voorhis to C. Voorhis, Dec 5, 1945, B 109, F 13, Voorhis mss.
50. Long to J. Voorhis, Dec 3, and J. Voorhis to Long, Dec 8, 1945, B 30, F 6, Voorhis mss.
51. *Progress-Bulletin,* Dec 21, 1945, B 30, F 7, Voorhis mss.
52. McLaughlin to Brownell, Dec 22, 1945, PPS1.30, Gibbons to RN, Dec 11, PPS1.26, RN to Perry, Dec 16, PE 182, and RN to Spencer, Dec 25, SP 6, RN to Day, Dec 26, 1945, PE 183, RNyl; RN to Faries, Feb 27, 1948, B 2, Republican Convention, Series 434, RNln; Jorgensen, Berkeley OHP, 10; Balch, "Nixon v. Voorhis," 65; Eleanor Harris, "The Nixons," *The American Weekly* (Aug 24, 1952), uncatalogued, RNyl; Pat Nixon and Joe Morris, "I Say He's a Wonderful Guy," *Saturday Evening Post,* Sept 6, 1952; Lynn Bowers and Dorothy Blair, "How to Pick a Congressman," *Saturday Evening Post,* Mar 19, 1949; Eisenhower, *Pat Nixon,* 86.
53. RN to Gist, Dec 4, 1945, PPS1.18, RNyl.
54. Commander Scott, *Romance of the Highways of California* (California: Commander Scott Productions, 1945), 75–76; John Crow, *California as a Place to Live* (NY: Scribners, 1953), 107–114.
55. Evans to RN, Nov 8, PPS1.272, and RN to Evans, Nov 13, 1945, PPS1.188, RNyl; Balch, "Nixon v. Voorhis," 19.
56. Memo by Spencer, Jan 15, PPS1.33, and Gibbons to Day, Jan 25, 1946, PPS1.34, RNyl; *Metropolitan Star-News,* Feb 6, 1946, B 58, F 2, Voorhis mss.
57. Bougainville speech, 1946, PPS 208.23–30 and experiences on Green Island, 1946, PPS 208.31, RNyl; Bullock, *Voorhis,* 244.
58. Speech, Feb 5, PPS 208.2, Amberson to RN, Feb 8, 1946, PPS1.38, RNyl; *Metropolitan Star-News,* Feb 8, 1946, B 58, F 2, Voorhis mss.
59. Day to Republicans, Feb 1, PE 185, Lincoln Day Dinner, Feb 12, PPS 208.3, Lincoln Day Dinner, Feb 12, 1946, PE 186, RNyl; Day, Berkeley OHP, 7.
60. Eisenhower, *Pat Nixon,* 89.
61. *Monrovia News-Post,* Mar 11, 1946, B 109, F 14, Voorhis mss; Bowen to Arnold, Apr 6, 1948, B 2, Publicity Corres., Series 434, RNln; Eisenhower, Pat Nixon, 87.
62. RN to Ensign, Mar 29, 1945, PPS1.61A, Chotiner to Lowell, Feb 15, 1946, PPS1.42, and Calendar 1946, PPS 212(1946).1, RNyl; *Monrovia News-Post,* Mar 11, and *Whittier News,* Mar 6, 1946. Day to Shellhorn, Mar 20, 1946, RN to Minkel, Mar 29, and RN to Reuland, Mar 29, 1946, B 1, F 1, Series 433, Bowen to Arnold, Apr 6, 1948, B 2, Publicity Corres., Series 434, RNln; Eisenhower, *Pat Nixon,* 86–88.
63. RN to Smith, Mar 11, PPS1.52, and Chotiner to RN, Mar 13, PPS1.55, and RN to Spencer, Mar 29, SP 7, RN to McCall, Mar 29, 1946, MC 4, RNyl; Day to RN, Feb 18, 1948, B 1, Finance Committee, Series 434, and RN to Garland, Mar 29, 1946, B 1, F1, Series 433, and Day to RN, Feb 18, 1948, B 1, Finance, Series 434, RNln; *Progress-Bulletin,* Mar 14, 1946.
64. Balch, "Nixon v. Balch," 12–13.
65. "People's Business," Jan 2, Feb 12, and Apr 2, 1946, B 23, F 5, Voorhis mss.
66. "People's Business," Mar 5 and 26, 1946, B 23, F 5, and Statement on Labor-Management Disputes, Feb 1946, B 34, F 3, Voorhis mss.

67. C. Voorhis to J. Voorhis, Feb 8, 1946, B 109, F 14, Voorhis mss.

68. C. Voorhis to J. Voorhis, Feb 8, Mar 1 and 29, and J. Voorhis to C. Voorhis, Feb 13, 1946, B 109, F 14, Voorhis mss.

69. Long to J. Voorhis, Feb 16 and Mar 28, and J. Voorhis to Long, Feb 19, 1946, B 30, F 7, Voorhis mss.

70. RN to George, Apr 2, 1946, B 364, Hutchinson, D, Series 320, RNln; RN to Ensign, Mar 29, 1946, PPS1.61A, RNyl.

71. RN to J. Voorhis, Apr 1, B 1, Correspondence, Jan 23–Oct 31, 1946, RN to Faries, Apr 2, 1946, B 1, F 1, Series 433, RNln, and *Des Moines Tribune,* Dec 10, 1946?, and RN to Boardman, Feb 25, 1947, B 89, Boardman, Series 320, RNln.

72. J. Voorhis to RN, Apr 16, 1946, B 791, Voorhis, Series 320, RNln.

73. RN to Smith, Mar 30, 1946, B 1, F 1, Series 433, RNln; *San Dimas Press,* May 30, 1946, B 58, F 2, Voorhis mss.

74. Long to J. Voorhis, Apr 1, and Pomona newspaper clipping, Apr 10, 1946, B 30, F 7, Voorhis mss; Day to Connors, Mar 17, PPS1.58, and American Legion Post remarks, 1946, PPS 208.34, RN to Love, Apr 9, PPS1.72, and RN to Blaisdell, May 4, 1946, PPS1.09, RNyl.

75. Report of meeting, May 3, 1946, B 58, F 15, Voorhis mss; San Marino Rally, May 3, 1946, PPS 208.4.4a, RNyl.

76. Chotiner to RN, Apr 11, PPS1.81, RN to Chotiner, Nov 13, 1946, PPS1.185, RNyl.

77. David Halberstam, *The Powers That Be* (NY: Knopf, 1979), 116–122; Marshall Berges, *The Life and Times of Los Angeles: A Newspaper, a Family and a City* (NY: Atheneum, 1984), 73–75.

78. RN to Palmer, Apr 28, 1946, PPS1.90, RNyl; *LA Times,* May 21, 1946.

79. Jorgensen to RN, Apr 2, RN to Brooks, Apr 3, and King to Caroline, Apr 17, B 1, F 1, and Johnson to RN, Apr 17, 1946, B 2, F 16, Series 433, RNln; Spencer to RN, Apr 3, SP 8, and Williamson to RN, May 21, 1946, PPS1.139, RNyl; Dear Fellow Realtors, May 10, 1946, B 58, F 3, Voorhis mss.

80. Day to Lowell, Apr 10, PPS1.80, RN to Day, Apr 29, PPS1.95, RN to Day, May 5, PPS1.115, and RN to Steele, May 4, 1946, PPS1.113, RNyl.

81. Day memo, early May 1946, PPS1.04, RNyl.

82. Day to Reps, May 17, PE 188, and Day to RN, May 21, 1946, PPS1.138, RNyl.

83. J. Voorhis to Wallace, Feb 14, B 58, F 1, J. Voorhis to Long, Mar 29, B 30, F 7, C. Voorhis to J. Voorhis, Apr 3, B 109, F 14; *Monrovia News-Post,* Apr 20, B 30, F 7, "People's Business," Apr 9 and July 3, B 23, F 5, C. Voorhis to J. Voorhis, June 12, and J. Voorhis to C. Voorhis, June 20, 1946, B 109, F 15, Voorhis mss; McCall to RN, May 13, 1948, B 1, Manager, Series 434, RNln.

84. Long to J. Voorhis, Apr 4 and May 14, 1946, B 30, F 7, Voorhis mss.

85. C. Voorhis to J. Voorhis, May 13, 14, and 15, J. Voorhis to C. Voorhis, May 20, 1946, B 109, F 15, Voorhis mss.

86. J. Voorhis to Long, Apr 3 and 15, B 30, F 7, and J. Voorhis to C. Voorhis, May 9, 1946, B 109, F 15, Voorhis mss; "Elections: 1946," *New Republic,* Feb 11, 1946, 203.

87. O'Brien to J. Voorhis, Dec 20, 1944, J. Voorhis to Sweet, Mar 2, 1945, "Congressman Jerry Voorhis: His Record on Veteran Legislation," 1946, B 58, F 1, Voorhis mss.

88. J. Voorhis to Bassett, Apr 4, 1946, B 58, F 4, Voorhis mss.

89. Robert Zieger, *The CIO 1935–1955* (Chapel Hill: Univ. of NC Press, 1995), 181–187 and 308.

90. C. Voorhis to J. Voorhis, Jan 17, 21, and 25, J. Voorhis to C. Voorhis, Jan 14 and 17, and Feb 3, 1944, B 109, F 8, Voorhis mss.

91. C. Voorhis to J. Voorhis, July 17, B 109, F 12, and Dec 6, 1945, B 109, F 13, Voorhis mss; Zieger, *CIO,* 374.

92. C. Voorhis to J. Voorhis, Apr 1 and 8, J. Voorhis to C. Voorhis, Apr 6, F 109, F 14, and J. Voorhis to Long, Apr 6, 1946, B 30, F 7, Voorhis mss.

93. Kuhlman to J. Voorhis, May 20, and J. Voorhis to Kuhlman, June 5, 1946, B 58, F 9, Voorhis mss.

94. O'Halloran to J. Voorhis, May 27, and J. Voorhis to O'Halloran, June 3, 1946, B 58, F 9, Voorhis mss.

95. J. Voorhis to Grey, May 22, *Labor Herald,* May 31, B 58, F 6, and Grey to J. Voorhis, May 27, 1946, B 58, F 9, Voorhis mss; Paul Bullock, "'Rabbits and Radicals': Richard Nixon's 1946 Campaign Against Jerry Voorhis," *Southern California Quarterly,* vol. 55, no. 3 (Fall 1973), 325.

96. *Action for Today,* Apr 16, Bulletin No. 9, and Political Committee Recommendations, Mar 27, 1946, B 58, F 6, Voorhis mss.

97. *Monrovia News-Post,* Apr 4, B 30, F 7, and *Whittier News,* Apr 24, 1946, B 58, F 15, Voorhis mss.

98. J. Voorhis to C. Voorhis, May 9, 1946, B 109, F 15, Voorhis mss.

99. *South Pasadena Review,* May 24, B 58, F 3, *Claremont Courier,* May 31, 1946, B 58, F 2, Voorhis mss; *Alhambra Post-Advocate,* May 31, 1946, B 1, Campaign Ad [1/3], Series 433, RNln.

100. *Monrovia Journal,* May 30, 1946, B 58, F 2, Voorhis mss; Nixon to Bray, June 1?, 1946, PPS1.149, RNyl.

101. *LA Daily News,* May–June, B 58, F 1, *Claremont Courier,* May 31, B 58, F 2, *Covina Argus Citizen,* May 31, and *San Marino Tribune,* May 30, 1946, B 58, F 16, Voorhis mss.; Candidate's Campaign Statement of Receipts and Expenditures, Richard M. Nixon, June 4, 1946, California State Archives, Sacramento, California.

102. RN speeches, Feb 12, PPS 208.2 and 208.3, Mar 1, PPS 208.3A, May 3, PPS 208.4, May 13, PPS208.5, and PPS 208.4a, May 15, PPS 208.6, Medical Care, PPS 208.13, Bureaucracy, PPS 208.14, Housing, PPS 208.15, Education, PPS 208.22, and Farmer, 1946, PPS 208.35.3, RNyl.

103. RN speeches, Feb 12, PPS 208.2 and PPS 208.3, Mar 1, PPS 208.3A, May 3, PPS 208.4, Housing, 1946, PPS 208.15, RNyl.

104. RN speeches, Feb 12, PPS 208.3, May 3, PPS 208.4, A–Bomb, PPS 208.19.5, and Minute Women, 1946, PPS 208.21.1–2, RNyl.

105. RN speech, Alan Mechikoff, 1946, PPS 208.17, RNyl.

106. RN speeches, Feb 12, PPS 208.3, and Manifest Destiny, undated, PPS 208.12, undated 1946, PPS 208.22, RNyl.

107. RN speeches, Mar 1, PPS 208.3A, May 16?, PPS 208.16, A–Bomb, Economy, PPS 208.19.1–6, PPS 208.19.5, and Education, 1946, PPS 208.22, RNyl.

108. Hamm to J. Voorhis, May 15, B 58, F1, *Monrovia News-Post,* June 5, B 58, F 6, C. Voorhis to J. Voorhis, June 12, J. Voorhis to C. Voorhis, June 20, 1946, B 109, F 15, Voorhis mss; Balch, "Nixon v. Voorhis," 37; Candidate's Campaign

Statement of Receipts and Expenditures, Richard M. Nixon, June 4, 1946, California State Archives, Sacramento, California.

109. Gaunt to Obermayer, Nov 4, 1954, King to Wiggs, Feb 1, 1957, RN to Hayward, May 15, 1961, B 172, Committee of 100, Series 320, RNln; Allen Weinstein, *Perjury* (NY: Knopf, 1978), 7; Christopher Matthews, *Kennedy & Nixon: The Rivalry That Shaped Postwar America* (NY: Simon & Schuster, 1996), 35; Voorhis, *Confessions,* 331.

110. Charles Hogan, Oral History, I, p. 395, Women in Politics, Helen Gahagan Douglas Project.

111. Edson to Richardson, July 27, 1952, B 236, Edson, Series 320, RNln; Candidate's Campaign Statement of Receipts and Expenditures, Richard M. Nixon, June 4, 1946, California State Archives, Sacramento, California.

112. RN to Hayward, May 15, 1961, B 172, Committee of 100, Series 320, RNln.


*Chapter 3*

1. RN to Republicans, June 11, PE189, Crocker to RN, June 20, PPS1.158, Day to Lowell, June 25, 1946, PPS1.160, RNyl.

2. RN to Republicans, June 11, PE 189, Calendar, July, PPS212(1946).1, and uncatalogued photographs of the Nixons on their vacation, Summer 1946, RNyl.

3. RN to workers, July 12, PE 190, RN to Dear Friend, July 12, 1946, PPS1.16.6, RNyl.

4. Primary analysis, June 4, 1946, PPS1.232a and PPS1.232(2), RNyl.

5. Briggs to RN, June 7, 1946, PPS1.153, RNyl; *South Pasadena Review,* June 7, 1946, B 58, F 10, Voorhis mss; McCall to Marshall, Apr 19, 1948, B 2, Publicity—Newspapers, Series 434, RNln.

6. J. Voorhis to C. Voorhis, June 6, C. Voorhis to Duane, June 24, B 109, F 15, J. Voorhis to Long, June 11, 1946, B 30, F 7, Voorhis mss.

7. Day to RN, July 10, PPS1.165, Newman to Friend, Oct 14, 1946, PE 203, *The News,* July 28, 1952, PPS5.SA162, memo by McCall, Jan 3, 1959, PPS1.461, and Donald Fantz Oral History and Ralph Peck Oral History, LBM, 22.1, RNyl; Pat Nixon and Morris, "I Say He's a Wonderful Guy"; Eisenhower, *Pat Nixon,* 88.

8. *Pasadena Star-News,* Oct 3, 1972, MC 311, RNyl; Jorgensen, Oral History, 15; Balch, "Nixon v. Voorhis," 38.

9. Perry to Bryant, Aug 12, PE 191, Perry to Nutcher, Aug 22, 1946, PE 193, memo by Perry, PE106(1), and memo by Perry, Sept 28, 1953, PE102, Need for a Coordinating Group, undated, PE 195, and Jorgensen to Woods, Jan 12, 1972, PPS1.218A, RNyl; Earl Adams Oral History, 2–6 and Jorgensen Oral History, 10–11; Jorgensen to RN, Jan 26, 1948, B 1, Finance Committee, Series 434, RNln; Balch, "Nixon v. Voorhis," 39; Bowers and Blair, "How to Pick a Congressman."

10. Chotiner to RN, Aug 14, 1946, B 1, F 1, Voorhis's War and Labor Records, 1937–1941, B 2, F 14, and Voorhis Voting Record, 1937–1946, B 2, Voting Record, Series 433, Bowen to RN, Mar 31, 1947, B 1, Corres 1947, Series 434, RNln; Day, Oral History, 12–15.

11. RN to Perry, Aug 16, 1946, PE 192, RNyl.

12. RN speeches, July 27, PPS208.7, and Aug 14, 1946, PPS208.8, RNyl.

13. *Ibid.*

14. *Monrovia Daily News,* Aug 28, 1946, B 58, F 10, Voorhis mss.

15. Spencer to RN, Aug 14, 1946, SP 10, RNyl; Spencer to Crocker, Aug 27, 1946, B 1, Campaign Analysis, Series 433, RNln.

16. *Monrovia News-Post,* Sept 2, 1946, B 58, F 15, Voorhis mss.

17. RN to McCall, Sept 3, 1946, MC 6, RNyl.

18. *San Marino Tribune,* Sept 12, B 58, F 6, and *The Chamber's Ghost,* Sept 25, 1946, B 58, F 5, Voorhis mss.

19. J. Voorhis to Long, May 11 and June 14, J. Voorhis to RN, May 11, and Long to J. Voorhis, June 8 and 11, 1946, B 30, F 7, Voorhis mss.

20. J. Voorhis to mother, July 30 and Sept 11, 1945, B 109, F 12, C. Voorhis to J. Voorhis, July 10, and J. Voorhis to C. Voorhis, July 23, 1946, B 109, F 15, Voorhis mss.

21. J. Voorhis to C. Voorhis, July 27, 1946, B 109, F 15, Voorhis mss; Balch, "Nixon v. Voorhis," 40; J. L. Voorhis, "Idealist," 67.

22. *Pageant* (Aug 1946); *McCall's Magazine* (Sept 1946); Perry to Elliott, Sept 4, 1946, PE 196, RNyl.

23. Paul Douglas, *In the Fullness of Time: The Memoirs of Paul H. Douglas* (NY: Harcourt Brace Jovanovich, 1971), 237.

24. *South Pasadena Review,* Aug 23, 1946, B 58, F 10, Voorhis mss; Voorhis, *Confessions,* 323.

25. Bowen to RN, May 11, 1948, B 2, Publicity—Corres, Series 434, RNln; Bullock, "Rabbits and Radicals," 321.

26. Press release, July 29, B 58, F 1, "People's Business," July 31, 1946, B 23, F 5, and J. L. Voorhis, "Idealist," 30; Balch, "Nixon v. Voorhis," 34; Voorhis, *Confessions,* 345.

27. Long to J. Voorhis, June 26, 1946, B 30, F 7, Voorhis mss; Bullock, "Rabbits and Radicals," 333.

28. Bullock to J. Voorhis, Aug 26, 1946, B 58, F 14, Voorhis mss; Bullock, "Rabbits and Radicals," 332–338.

29. *Whittier News,* Sept 11, 1946, B 58, F 6, J. Voorhis; *Alhambra Post-Advocate,* Sept 11, 1946.

30. *Alhambra Post-Advocate,* Sept 14, 1946; Balch, "Nixon v. Voorhis," 52; Bullock, *Voorhis,* 258; Bullock, "Rabbits and Radicals," 332 and 334–335.

31. Richard Dyke and Francis Gannon, *Chet Holifield: Master Legislator and Nuclear Statesman,* (Md,: Univ. Press of America, 1996), 48–70; Bullock, *Voorhis,* 258.

32. RN speech, Sept 13, 1946, PPS208.9a, RNyl; *Alhambra Valley News,* Sept 14, 1946, B 58, F 14, Voorhis mss; *Alhambra Post-Advocate,* Sept 14, 1946; *Whittier News,* Sept 14, 1946; Bullock, *Voorhis,* 260; Bullock, "Rabbits and Radicals," 336–337; Eisenhower, *Pat Nixon,* 91.

33. *Action for Today,* Apr 16, 1946, B 58, F 6, Voorhis mss; Balch, "Nixon v. Voorhis," 53; Bullock, *Voorhis,* 260–262; Bullock, "Rabbits and Radicals," 337–338.

34. Chet Holifield Oral History, V. II, p. 181, Women in Politics, Helen Gahagan Douglas Project.

35. Spencer to RN, Sept 14, 1946, SP 12, RNyl.

36. Mac to RN, Jan 18, 1950, MC 128, and curatorial department, plastic thimble, 92.39.01, RNyl; Balch, "Nixon v. Voorhis," 64.

37. J. Voorhis to NC-PAC, Sept 18, 1946, B 58, F 5, Voorhis mss; *Alhambra Post-Advocate,* Sept 19, 1946.

38. *Pomona Progress-Bulletin,* Oct 21, 1946, B 1, Campaign Ads [2/3], Series 433, RNyl; Bullock, "Rabbits and Radicals," 340.
39. Rayburn to J. Voorhis, Sept 14, and J. Voorhis to Rayburn, Oct 1, 1946, B 58, F 3, Voorhis mss.
40. *Alhambra Post-Advocate,* Sept 20, and *Whittier News,* Sept 21, 1946.
41. *Whittier News,* Sept 21, 1946.
42. J. Voorhis to C. Voorhis, July 5, B 109, F 15, anonymous to J. Voorhis, Oct 18, and Cleveland to Friend, Sept 18, 1946, B 58, F 1, Voorhis mss; RN to Goodson, Oct 26, 1946, B 1, Campaign Ads [3/3], Series 433, RNln; Whittier Narrows Dam speech, 1946, PPS208.32–33, RNyl; Zetterberg (Claremont), Oral History, 24; Balch, "Nixon v. Voorhis," 51.
43. McCall to Hope, Sept 24, 1946, MC 6A, RNyl.
44. *Alhambra Post-Advocate,* Sept 20, 1948, PPS205.S134, RNyl; Arnold, *Back When It All Began,* preface.
45. *Ibid.,* Introduction and 2.
46. McCall to J. Voorhis, Sept 25, and J. Voorhis to McCall, Sept 30, B 58, F 5, and RN to J. Voorhis, Oct 2, 1946, B 58, F 15, Voorhis mss; J. Voorhis to Schiefer, Sept 21, and McCall to J. Voorhis, Sept 25, 1946, B 1, F 1, Series 433, RNln.
47. McCall to RN Committee, Oct 7, 1946, PE 201, RNyl; *Whittier News,* Oct 11, 1946.
48. RN to Kinnett, May 20, PPS1.134, RN to Spencer, Nov 20, SP 13, and Perry to Jorgensen, Oct 5, 1946, PE202, clipping, Oct 9, 1950, PPS266.98, RNyl; *Alhambra Post-Advocate,* Oct 16, 1946; Wallace Black Oral History, 812, p. 13.
49. RN to Stassen, May 20, 1946, B 724, Stassen 1956, Series 320, RNln; RN to PN, Feb 11, 1944, uncatalogued, RNyl; Ivan Hinderaker, "Harold Stassen and Developments in the Republican Party in Minnesota, 1937–1943," Ph.D. thesis: Univ. of Minn., 1949, 40–114, 129–604, and 627–780; Alec Kirby, "Childe Harold's Pilgrimage: A Political Biography of Harold Stassen," Ph.D. thesis: George Washington Univ., 1992, 8–27.
50. Parker to Stassen, Dec 4, 1945, B 724, Stassen 1956, Series 320, RNln.
51. RN to Stassen, May 20, and Stassen to RN, May 24, 1946, B 724, Stassen 1956, and memo by McCall, Jan 3, 1959, B 724, Stassen, Series 320, Stassen to RN, July 29, 1946, B 1, F 1, Series 433, and RN to Smith, Jan 8, 1947, B 1, Corres 1947, Series 434, RNln; McCall to Hope, Sept 24, 1946, MC 6A, RNyl; see Arnold, *Back When It All Began,* 30–31, for a different perspective.
52. Leo Katcher, *Earl Warren: A Political Biography* (NY: McGraw-Hill, 1967), 7–205; Ed Cray, *Chief Justice: A Biography of Earl Warren* (NY: Simon & Schuster, 1997), 15–194 and 208.
53. Faries, *Rememb'ring,* 116, 128, 177, and 191.
54. *Ibid.,* 5–105, 123–128, 154, 190–191, and 201–202.
55. "Richard Nixon: Young Rebel?", *Fortnight,* Dec 31, 1948, PPS296(1948), RNyl; Katcher, *Earl Warren,* 103–204; Arnold, *Back When It All Began,* 25–26.
56. J. Voorhis to C. Voorhis, Feb 11, 1944, B 109, F 8, J. Voorhis to McNitt, Oct 8, B 58, F 15, and Cuneo to J. Voorhis, Oct 11, B 58, F 9, Voorhis Radio Address, Oct 11, 1946, B 58, F 2, Voorhis mss.
57. *Whittier News,* Oct 12, 1946.
58. "Chief" Wallace Newman to Friend, Oct 14, 1946, PE 203, RNyl; *Monrovia Daily News-Post,* Oct 18, 1946, B 58, F 15, Voorhis mss.

59. *Pomona Progress-Bulletin,* Oct 17, 1946, B 1 Campaign Ads[2/3], Series 433, RNln.

60. Speech, Oct 23, 1946, B 58, F 3, *Whittier News,* Oct 24, 1946; Voorhis mss; Balch, "Nixon v. Voorhis," 61–62

61. "Truth About Jerry Voorhis," Oct 28, 1946, B 58, F 1, Voorhis mss; Voorhis, *Confessions,* 338–339; Bullock, "Rabbits and Radicals," 342–346.

62. McCall to Friend, Oct 24, 1946, PE 204, RNyl; Newman to Friend, Oct 26, 1946, B 1, F 1, Series 433, RNln.

63. *Rosemead Review,* Oct 24 and *Covina Argus-Citizen,* Oct 25, B 1, Campaign Ads[1/3], *San Gabriel Sun,* Oct 24, San Dimas clipping, Oct 24, B 1, campaign ad [2/3], *Glendora Press-Gleaner,* Oct 25, B 1, F 4, Series 433, and radio broadcast, Oct 25, 1946, B 2, Publicity—Newspapers, Series 434, RNln.

64. Memo by Nixon, Sept–Nov 1946, MC 7, and memo by Charles Cooper, PE 109, RNyl; Eisenhower, *Pat Nixon,* 90.

65. Clipping, Oct 9, 1950, PPS266.98, RNyl.

66. Voorhis-Nixon Debate, Oct 28, 1946, PPS1.168, RNyl; *Alhambra Post-Advocate,* Oct 29, 1946; Balch, "Nixon v. Voorhis," 62.

67. Voorhis speech, Oct 28, 1946, B 58, F 13, Voorhis mss.

68. Balch, "Nixon v. Voorhis," 63.

69. Faries, *Rememb'ring,* 190–191, 202, and 205.

70. *Whittier News,* Oct 29, 1946.

71. Mowlock to Nixon, Oct 29, 1946, B 1, F 1, Series 433, RNln; Perry to RN, Oct 29, 1946, PPS1.169, Donald Fantz Oral History, LBM 22.1, RNyl.

72. RN to Mac, Dec 7, 1954, MC 196, and RN to Mac, Nov 5, 1971, MC 302, RNyl; Voorhis, *Confessions,* 345; Nixon, *RN,* 40.

73. Statement of Vote, Nov 5, 1946, PPS1.455, Republican National Committee, The 1946 Elections, PPS1.458, and Research Division, Jan 8, 1947, PE 219A.1–2, RNyl; Balch, "Nixon v. Voorhis," 66; Bullock, *Voorhis,* 281.

74. *Monrovia Journal,* Nov 7, 1946, B 58, F 16, Voorhis mss.

75. Kruse to RN, Nov 6, PPS1.300, Hodge to RN, Nov 6, PPS1.289, Warren to Nixon, Nov 7, PPS1.410, Houser to RN, Nov 7, PPS1.392, Roper to RN, Nov 11, PPS1.345, and Boardman to RN, Nov 20, 1946, PPS1.242, RNyl.

76. Cooper to RN, Nov 11, PPS1.260, and Bruce to RN, Nov 9, 1946, PPS1.251, RNyl.

77. Laycock to RN, Nov 9, 1946, PPS1.302, RNyl; Hoeppel to RN, Nov 9, 1946, B 1, F 2, Series 433, RNln.

78. Walker to RN, Nov 8, 1946, B 1, F 2, Series 433, Folger to RN, Dec 26, 1946, and RN to Folger, Jan 11, 1947, B 1, Corres 1947, Series 434, RNln; Perry to Smith, Nov 19, PE 214, Elliott to Perry, Dec 18, 1946, PE 218, RNyl.

79. *Newsweek,* Nov 18, 1946, 34–35 and 39; *Time,* Nov 18, 1946, 26; Putzel to RN, Nov 13, PPS1.333, Paul to RN, Nov 13, PPS1.327, Wyman to RN, Nov 14, PPS1.371, Williams to RN, Nov 16, PPS1.369, Wilma to PN, Nov 17, PPS1.379, Keiffer to RN, Nov 20, PPS1.296, and Bolich to RN, Nov 18, 1946, PPS1.245, RNyl; McCown to RN, Nov 22, 1946, B 1, F 2, Series 433, and Perry to RN, Jan 8, 1947, B 589, B Perry, Series 320, RNln.

80. Voorhis statement, Nov 7, 1946, B 58, F 2, and *San Dimas Press,* Nov 7, 1946, B 58, F 16, Voorhis mss.

81. Smith to J. Voorhis, Nov 5, Bullock to J. Voorhis, Nov 6, Henderson to J.

Voorhis, Nov 7, Walp to J. Voorhis, Nov 8, and Bacon to J. Voorhis, Nov 15, 1946, B 58, F 17, Voorhis mss.

82. McLaughlin to J. Voorhis, Nov 25, 1946, PPS1.203, RNyl; Voorhis, *Confessions,* 349; Richard Gardner, "Fighting Quaker (The Story of Richard Nixon)," Unpublished ms, 1953, Special Collections, Whittier College, California.

83. C. Voorhis to J. Voorhis, Nov 25, J. Voorhis to C. Voorhis, Dec 31, 1946, B 109, F 15, Voorhis mss.

84. Voorhis, *Confessions,* 331–342; McCall to RN, Feb 3, and RN to McCall, Feb 18,1948, B 1, Manager, Series 434, RNln.

85. Ernest Brashear, "Who Is Richard Nixon?", *New Republic,* 127 (Sept 1, 1952), 9 and 11; Candidate's Campaign Statement of Receipts and Expenditures, Richard M. Nixon, Nov 5, 1946, California State Archives, Sacramento, California.

86. Bullock, *Voorhis,* 262–276; Bullock to J. Voorhis, Nov 6, 1946, B 58, F 17, Voorhis mss.

87. *Chicago Daily News,* Oct 31, 1958, PPS299.69.S8, RNyl.

88. Douglas, *In the Fullness of Time,* 237; Bullock, "Rabbits and Radicals," 350–351.

89. Eisenhower, *Pat Nixon,* 90.

90. Morris, *Nixon,* 335.

91. "The Merry-Go-Round," Sept 24, 1952, PPS10.607.2, RNyl.

92. Day to Lewis, Sept 24, 1952, PPS10.607.1, RNyl.

93. *Daily Report* (Ontario-Upland, Ca), Sept 24, 1952, PPS10.607.2, RNyl.

*Chapter 4*

1. Calendar 1946, PPS 212(1946), Dinner, Nov 13, Dinner Honoring, Nov 21, Nixon Victory Dinner, Nov 26, 1946, uncatalogued, RNyl; Ward to RN, Nov 9, B 547, NAACP—Monrovia, Shellenberger to RN, Nov 27, B 690, Shellenberger, Gerhart to RN, Dec 2, 1946, B 286, Gerhart, Series 320, RNln; *Whittier News,* Nov 14, 1946.

2. Brown to RN, Nov 11, PPS1.249, and RN to Terrill, Nov 14, 1946, PPS1.435, RNyl; RN to Rasmussen, Nov 21, 1946, B 1, F 2, Series 433, RNln.

3. David Lawrence, *The Editorials of David Lawrence* (Washington, D.C.: U.S. News & World Report, 1970), 111–112; RN to Lawrence, Nov 14, 1946, PPS1.198, RNyl.

4. Perry to Beise, Jan 22, 1947, PE 224, Margaret Kroener Oral History, Phyllis Andrews Oral History, and Margaret Robbins Oral History, LBM 22.1, RNyl; author's interview with Hubert Perry, Apr 22, 1997.

5. Memo by Cooper, 1947?, PE 109, RNyl; RN to Marshall, Nov 13, and Marshall to RN, Nov 18, 1946, B 477, Marshall, JP, RNln; *Whittier News,* Nov 27, 1946.

6. RN to Cherniss, Dec 24, B 144, Cherniss, RN to Garland, Dec 24, 1946, B 282, Garland [½], and RN to Hahn, Jan 7, 1947, B 310, Hahn, AW, Series 320, RNln; RN to Mac, Dec 22, MC 9B and News Release, Dec 28, 1946, PPS 205.3007, RNyl; *Washington Post,* Dec 29, 1946.

7. Kruse to RN, Dec 17, 1946, B 430, Kruse, Series 320, RNln; RN to Mac, Dec 22, MC 9B, and Mac to RN, Dec 26, 1946, MC 9C, RNyl.

8. RN to Marshall, Nov 13, B 477, Marshall, JP, Series 320, and RN to Gearhart,

Nov 19, 1946, B 1, F 2, Series 433, RNln; news release, Dec 28, 1946, PPS 205.3007, RNyl.

9. RN to Marshall, Nov 13, Marshall to RN, Nov 18, 1946, B 477, Marshall, JP, Hass to RN, Jan 2, RN to Ewing, Jan 7, B 325, Hass, E, and RN to Carroll, Jan 9, B 135, Carroll, W, RN to Budlong, Feb 20, B 111, Budlong, RN to Patch, June 13, 1947, B 580, Patch, R, Series 320, RNln; RN to Mac, Dec 22, MC 9B and news release, Dec 28, 1946, PPS 205.3007, RNyl; Arnold, *Back When It All Began,* 1.

10. 1951, *The Congressional Club,* PPS266.122, RNyl; Donald Thompson to author, Mar 12, 1996, Gellman mss; Eisenhower, *Pat Nixon,* 94.

11. RN to Spencer, Mar 27, SP 15, 1947, RNyl; RN to Williams, May 9, B 821, Williams, RC, and RN to Patch, June 13, B 580, Patch, R, RN to Knudsen, July 7, 1947, B 422, Knudsen, C, Series 320, RNln.

12. RN to Mac, Dec 22, MC 9B and news release, Dec 28, 1946, PPS 205.3007, RNyl; Robert Donovan, *Conflict and Crisis: The Presidency of Harry S Truman, 1945–1948* (NY: Norton 1977), 257–261.

13. Press release, Jan 9, 1947, PPS205.3008, RNyl.

14. RN to Wadsworth, Feb 2, 1950, B 793, Wadsworth, E, RN to Burke, Mar 27, B 114, Burke, Montivel, Series 320, RNln; Eisenhower, *Pat Nixon,* 94.

15. *Philadelphia Inquirer,* Jan 19, 1947; *Times Herald* (Washington, D.C.), Jan 21, 1947, PPS205.S1.3, and RN to Mac, Jan 31, 1947, MC 11, RNyl; RN to Kepple, Jan 21, 1947, B 406, Kepple, Series 320, RNln.

16. RN to Shoemaker, Jan 10, B 1, Correspondence 1947, Series 434, and RN to Smith, Jan 10, 1947, B 708, Smith (2 of 2), Series 320, RNln.

17. News release, Jan 13, 1947, PPS205.3009, RNyl; RN to Holt, Dec 15, 1952, B 349, Holt [½], RNln.

18. News release, Jan 13, 1947, PPS205.3009, RNyl; RN to Newman, Jan 17, B 599, Newman, W, RN to Mabel Boardman, Feb 25, B 89, Boardman, and RN to Anderson, Mar 28, 1947, B 41, Anderson, Jack, Series 320, RNln.

19. RN to Kepple, Jan 21, B 406, Kepple and RN to Perry, Feb 25, 1947, B 589, Perry, AW, Series 320, RNln; news release, Jan 31, PPS205.3011, and July 21, 1947, PPS205.3021, RNyl.

20. RN to Reed, Mar 10, 1947, B 623, Reed, JE, Series 320, RNln; RN article, Feb 20, PPS208(1947).5 and Mar 1, PPS208(1947).7, Mar 29, PPS208(1947).13 and RN to Perry, Mar 4, 1947, PE 242, RNyl.

21. News release, Jan 24, PPS205.3010, and RN to Perry, Apr 9, 1947, PE 258, RNyl; Udall to RN, Mar 31, and RN to Udall, Apr 14, B 770, Udall, and RN to Beuscher, May 13, 1947, B 80, Beuscher, Series 320, RNln; Thomas Becnel, *Senator Allen Ellender of Louisiana: A Biography* (Baton Rouge: Louisiana State Univ. Press, 1995), 144.

22. RN to Dullard, Feb 17, 1947, B 228, Dullard, Series 320, RNln; press release, Jan 24, PPS205.3010, RN statement, May 3, PPS208(1947).24, and RN to Perry, May 5, 1947, PE 266, RNyl.

23. RN to Lowell, Mar 18, 1947, B 463, Lowell, E, Series 320, RNln; RN to Friend, May 10, PE 268 and PPS205.10A(1), RNyl.

24. RN to Friend, May 10, PPS205.10A(1), RN to Perry, May 10, 1947, PE 267, RNyl; RN to Boardman, Mar 11, B 89, Boardman, RN to Kennedy, Apr 3, B 405, Kennedy, Rex, and RN to Reedy, Apr 9, 1947, B 583, Pearson (Correspondence [4/4]), RNln.

25. Calendar 1947, PPS 212(1947).1 and RN to Mac, Jan 10, MC, 10D, RN to Mac, Jan 31, MC 11, RN statement, May 10, 1947, PPS208(1947).25, RNyl; RN to Kepple, Jan 21, 1947, B 406, Kepple, Series 320, RNln; *Philadelphia Inquirer,* Jan 19, 1947.

26. Frank Freidel, *Franklin D. Roosevelt: A Rendezvous with Destiny* (Boston: Little, Brown, 1990), 159; William Leuchtenburg, *Franklin D. Roosevelt and the New Deal 1932–1942* (NY: Harper & Row, 1963), 151–152.

27. De Toledano, *One Man Alone,* 58; Morris, *Nixon,* 343; R. Alton Lee, *Truman and Taft-Hartley: A Question of Mandate* (Lexington: Univ. of Kentucky Press, 1966), 49–51.

28. Kruse to RN, Dec 17, 1946, B 430, Kruse, RN to Newman, Jan 17, B 599, Newman, W, and RN to Wilcox, Jan 29, 1947, B 819, Wilcox, FR, Series 320, RNln.

29. Lee, *Truman and Taft-Hartley,* 54–56.

30. RN to Lathrop, Jan 7, B 441, Lathrop, Lo, Meyer to RN, Sept 1, 1947, B 583, Pearson (Correspondence [4/4]), Series 320, RNln; RN to Perry, Feb 3, 1947, PE 231, RNyl; Alan Schaffer, *Vito Marcantonio, Radical in Congress* (Syracuse: Syracuse Univ. Press, 1966), 171–173; Salvatore John La Gumina, *Vito Marcantonio, The People's Politician* (Iowa: Kendall/Hunt, 1969), 99–100.

31. RN speech, Feb 12, PPS208(1947).3, and Hoppel to RN, Feb 13, 1947, PPS205.10, RNyl.

32. RN statement, Feb 20, PPS208(1947).6, and RN article, Feb 20, 1947, PPS208(1947).6, RNyl; House of Representatives, 80th Cong, 1st Sess, Hearings Before the Committee on Education and Labor, *Amendments to the National Labor Relations Act,* V. 2, Feb 1947 (Washington, D.C.: GPO, 1947), 665.

33. McMenamin to RN, Feb 21, Burdette to RN, Feb 24, Saunders to RN, Feb 27, 1947, B 432, Labor Sp, Series 320, RNln.

34. House of Representatives, 80th Cong, 1st Sess, Hearings Before the Committee on Education and Labor, *Amendments to the National Labor Relations Act, Bills to Amend and Repeal the National Labor Relations Act, and for Other Purposes,* V. 3, Feb 1947 (Washington, D.C.: GPO, 1947), 203–205.

35. RN to Perry, Mar 4, 1947, PE 242, RNyl; Anna Rothe, ed., *Current Biography 1949* (NY: Wilson, 1950), 33–35.

36. RN to Chapman, Feb 25, RN to Johnson, Feb 25, B 432, Labor Sp, and Arnold to Blaisdell, Feb 26, 1947, B 86, Blaisdell, Series 320, RNln; Zieger, *CIO,* 246–250.

37. RN to Beuscher, May 13, 1947, B 80, Beuscher, Series 320, RNln; U.S. Congress, *Biographical Directory of the United States Congress, 1774–1989* (Washington, D.C.: GPO, 1989), 1306; Anna Rothe and Evelyn Lohr, eds., *Current Biography 1952* (NY: Wilson, 1953), 301–302.

38. Cronin to Woods, July 26, 1956, Cronin, JF 1956 ½, James Cronin to RN, Apr 29, 1957, Cronin, JF 1957–58 2/2, Robert Cronin to RN, Apr 10, 1958, Cronin, JF 1957–58½, and *Baltimore Sun,* Dec 12, 1959, Cronin, JF 1959½, B 191, Series 320, RNln; Biography of John Francis Cronin, Peter Irons, "America's Cold War Crusade: Domestic Politics and Foreign Policy, 1942–1948," Ph.D. thesis: Boston Univ. 1973, 177, and Sharlene Shoemaker, "Suggests Ex-Boss 'Schizophrenic,'" *National Catholic Reporter,* Sept 27, 1994, CCRO 2/25, John Francis Cronin mss, Univ. of Notre Dame Archives, South Bend, Indiana; Joshua Freeman and Steve Rosswurm, "The Education of an Anti-

Communist: Father John F. Cronin and the Baltimore Labor Movement," *Labor History,* 33 (Spring 1992), 227; *NY Times,* Jan 5, 1994.

39. "Our Sunday Visitor," Apr 12, 1959, B 191, Cronin, JF, 1959, Series 320, RNln; Cronin to Vinnedge, May 30, Cronin to Reuben, June 24, 1974, and Irons, "America's Cold War Crusade," 178, CCRO 2/25, Cronin mss; Freeman and Rosswurm, "The Education of an Anti-Communist," 217–247.

40. Memo Cronin to RN, June 23, 1958, Cronin, JF, 1957–58, and "Our Sunday Visitor," Apr 12, 1959, Cronin, JF, B 191, Series 320, RNln; Cronin to Vinnedge, May 30, Cronin to de Antonio, Sept 10, and Cronin to Smith, Sept 14, 1974, CCRO 2/25, Cronin mss.

41. RN article, Mar 1, 1947, PPS208(1947).7, RNyl; House of Representatives, *Amendments to the National Labor Relations Act on Bills to Amend and Repeal the National Labor Relations Acts, and for Other Purposes,* V. 4, March 1947, 1998–2126.

42. RN article, Mar 8, 1947, PPS208(1947).8, RNyl.

43. RN articles, Mar 22, PPS208(1947).10, and Mar 29, PPS208(1947).13, RNyl, and RN to Burke, Mar 27, B 114, Burke, Montivel, and RN to Anderson, Mar 28, 1947, B 41, Anderson, Jack, Series 320, RNln.

44. RN radio speech, Apr 3, PPS208(1947).14.1, and RN address, Apr 4, 1947, PPS208(1947).15, RNyl.

45. RN to Kennedy, Apr 3, B 405, Kennedy, Rex, Series 320, RNln, and Perry to RN, Apr 11, PE 259, RN address, Apr 12, PPS208(1947).16, RN to Spencer, Apr 14, SP 17, RN speech, Apr 16, PPS208(1947).17.2, McLauglin to RN, Apr 30, PE 263, and RN address, Apr 21, 1947, PPS208(1947).19, RNyl.

46. RN to Eddy, Apr 18, 1947, B 235, Eddy, AC, Series 320, RNln; RN to Perry, Apr 17, 1947, PE 261, RNyl; James Patterson, *Mr. Republican: A Biography of Robert A. Taft* (Boston: Houghton Mifflin, 1972), 352–353; Lee, *Truman and Taft-Hartley,* 68.

47. Apr 14 and 21, 1947, Calendar, PPS212(1947).1, RNyl; *Daily News* (McKeesport, Pa.), Apr 22, 1947; Eric Goldman, "The 1947 Kennedy-Nixon 'Tube City' Debate," *Saturday Review,* Oct 16, 1976, 12–13.

48. Goldman, "The 1947 Kennedy-Nixon Debate," 12–13; Matthews, *Kennedy & Nixon,* 51–52; Nixon, *RN,* 42–43; Nixon, *Six Crises,* 298–299.

49. RN to Mac, Apr 23, 1947, MC 19, RNyl.

50. Nixon, *RN,* 43.

51. RN to Box, May 12, B 432, Labor Sp, Boales to RN, Apr 18, B 89, Boales, Williams to RN, Apr 28, B 821, Williams, RC, Jim to Dick, June 6, B 730, Stewart, James, Knudsen to RN, June 23, 1947, B 422, Knudsen, C, Series 320, RNln.

52. Patterson, *Mr. Republican,* 354–359; Donovan, *Conflict and Crisis,* 300.

53. RN to Edie, May 22, B 432, Labor Sp, Series 320, RNln; RN to Friend, May 10, PE 268, RN speech, May 27, PPS208(1947).28, radio talk, May 30, 1947, PPS208(1947).29, RNyl.

54. RN to Mac, Apr 12, MC 18, May 5, MC 20, May 6, MC 21, May 9, MC 24, May 21, MC 27A, Perry to RN, May 21, PE 274, and June 3, PE 278, announcement, May 28, PE 277(1), and news release, May 24, 1947, PPS205.3016, RNyl.

55. Gibbons to PN, May 29, 1947, PPS266.29, RNyl.

56. Press release, May 28, 1947, PPS205.3032(1), RNyl.

57. RN to Beuscher, June 10, 1947, B 80, Beuscher, Series 320, RNln, and

RN statement, June 10, 1947, PPS208(1947).30, RNyl; Lee, *Truman and Taft-Hartley,* 78–89.

58. RN press release, June 20, PPS208(1947).33, and "Under the Capitol Dome," June 24, 1947, PPS208(1947).35, RNyl.

59. News release, June 20–22, PPS205.3021A, "Under the Capitol Dome," June 24, PPS208(1947).35, press release, June 26, PPS208(1947).36, RNyl; RN to Schiefer, June 23, 1947, B 674, Schiefer, Series 320, RNln; Donovan, *Conflict and Crisis,* 302–303; Lee, *Truman and Taft-Hartley,* 100–102.

60. Patterson, *Mr. Republican,* 363–366; Donovan, *Conflict and Crisis,* 303; Lee, *Truman and Taft-Hartley,* 104–105; Susan Hartmann, *Truman and the 80th Congress* (Columbia: Univ. of Missouri Press, 1971), 90.

61. RN statement, 1947, PPS208(1947).41, RNyl.

62. Press release, Feb 13, PPS205.3012, "Under the Capitol Dome," June 28, PPS208(1947).38, July 3, 1947, PPS208(1947).41, July 26, PPS208(1947).48, press release, Nov 28, 1947, PPS205.3029, RNyl.

63. RN to Friend, June 30, PPS205.11A, RN to Perry, June 1, PE 298, RN on CBS, July 26, PPS208(1947).49.4 and July 29, PPS208(1947).49.5, and "Under the Capitol Dome," Aug 12, 1947, PPS208(1947).50A, RNyl; Hartmann, *Truman and the 80th Congress,* 74–79.

*Chapter 5*

1. Press release, Jan 13, 1947, PPS205.3009, RNyl.

2. Robert Carr, *The House Committee on Un-American Activities 1945–1950* (Ithaca: Cornell Univ. Press, 1952), 1–18 and 364–365; Walter Goodman, *The Committee: The Extraordinary Career of the House Committee on Un-American Activities* (NY: Farrar, Straus & Giroux, 1968), 3–189; Earl Latham, *The Communist Controversy in Washington: From the New Deal to McCarthy* (Cambridge, Mass: Harvard Univ. Press, 1966), 358; RN to Kepple, Jan 21, 1947, B 406, Kepple, Series 320, RNln; Joe Martin, *My First Fifty Years in Politics* (NY: McGraw-Hill, 1960), 194; Nixon, *RN,* 44.

3. *Ridgewood Herald News,* Oct 31, 1946, TH Sv.12:4, *Herald News,* Jan 15, TH Sv.12:25, *Paterson News,* Jan 16, TH Sv.12:74, *Chicago Sunday Tribune Grafic,* Apr 27, TH Sv.12:74, and *PM,* Nov 30, 1947, TH Sv.14:55–57, RNyl.

4. *PM,* Nov 30, 1947, TH Sv.14:55, RNyl; Voorhis Oral History, Claremont, 21; Carr, *House Committee,* 211–218.

5. *Easton Express,* Mar 1, TH Sv.12:41, and *Bergen Evening Record,* Sept 8, 1947, TH Sv.14:2, RNyl.

6. John Garraty, ed., *Dictionary of American Biography* (NY: Scribners, 1980), 525–526; *Current Biography 1944,* 555–558.

7. U.S. Congress, *Congressional Record,* Feb 18, 1947, 1131.

8. U.S. Congress, House of Representatives, Committee on Un-American Activities, 80th Cong, 1st Sess, *Hearings on Gerhart Eisler Investigation of Un-American Propaganda Activities in the United States,* Public Law 601 (Washington, D.C.: GPO, 1947), 1–3; *Paterson Call,* Aug 16, 1947, TH Sv.13:77, RNyl; Carr, *House Committee,* 37–39 and 226–227; Goodman, *The Committee,* 190–194; Ellen Schrecker, *Many Are the Crimes: McCarthyism in America* (Boston: Little, Brown, 1998), 122–132.

9. RN radio speech, Feb 6, 1947, PPS208(1947).2, RNyl.

10. RN speeches, *Congressional Record,* Feb 18 and Apr 22, 1947, PPS208(1947).4.2 and PPS208(1947).22, RNyl; Nixon, *RN,* 43–46.

11. *Herald News,* Mar 25, TH Sv.12:48, *NY Times,* Mar 27, 1947, TH Sv.12:56, RNyl; RN to Burke, Mar 27, 1947, B 114, Burke, Montivel, Series 320, RNln; House of Representatives, Hearings Before the Committee on Un-American Activities, 80th Cong, 1st Sess., *Investigation of Un-American Propaganda Activities in the United States,* on H.R. 1884 and H.R. 2122 (Washington, D.C.: GPO, 1947), 13, 33, 96, 241, 250–252, and 283–285.

12. Alan Harper, *The Politics of Loyalty: The White House and the Communist Issue, 1946–1952* (Greenwich, Conn: Greenwood Press, 1969), 20–59; Donovan, *Conflict and Crisis,* 292–298; Latham, *The Communist Controversy in Washington,* 363–367.

13. "The Price of Vision," TH B 1, and *Paterson Call,* July 3, 1947, TH Sv.13:63, RNyl; as quoted in Harper, *Politics of Loyalty,* 46.

14. "Open Hearing Forum," Mar 25, PPS208(1947).11, RN to Spencer, Mar 27, SP 15, and RN to Perry, Apr 2, 1947, PE 257, RNyl.

15. *Herald News,* Apr 5, 1947, TH Sv.12:58, RNyl.

16. Cantwell to RN, Apr 3, B 131, Cantwell, and Meeker to RN, May 24, B 507, Meeker, L, RN to Cobey, June 17, 1947, B 160, Cobey, Series 320, RNln; RN address, Apr 21, 1947, PPS208(1947).19, RNyl.

17. RN statement, May 10, 1947, PPS208(1947), RNyl.

18. RN to Perry, June 10, 1947, PE 282, RNyl.

19. Anna Rothe, ed., *Current History 1948* (NY: Wilson, 1949), 463–464.

20. RN statement, June 17, 1947, PPS208(1947).32, and "Washington Report," Jan 29, 1948, PPS208(1948).5, RNyl.

21. Mundt to Zentner, Apr 23, 1947, R 122, Mundt mss. Karl E. Mundt Historical and Educational Foundation, Dakota State Univ., Madison, South Dakota.

22. RN statement, May 13, PPS208(1947).26, and newspaper clipping, Dec 3, 1947, PE 334, RNyl.

23. News release, July 25, 1947, PPS208(1947).47, RNyl; House of Representatives, Hearings Before the Committee on Un-American Activities, 80th Cong, 1st Sess, *Hearings Regarding Communism in Labor Unions in the United States* (Washington, D.C.: GPO, 1947), 2–167 and 203; Carr, *House Committee,* 48; Zieger, *CIO,* 253–259.

24. RN radio interview, June 22, PPS208(1947).34, and radio broadcast, July 1947, PPS208(1947).50.1, RNyl.

25. HUAC, *Investigation of Un-American Propaganda Activities in the United States,* 292–293 and 303; news release, Apr 26, 1947, PPS205.3015, RNyl.

26. *Washington,* (D.C.) *Times Herald,* May 16, 1947, TH Sv:13:44, RNyl.

27. *Time,* Nov 3, TH Sv:14:50, and *Newsweek,* Nov 3, 1947, TH Sv: 14:28, RNyl; House of Representatives, Hearings Before the Committee on Un-American Activities, 80th Cong, 1st Sess, *Hearings Regarding the Communist Infiltration of the Motion Picture Industry* (Washington, D.C.: GPO, 1947), 1 and 29.

28. HUAC, *Hearings Regarding the Communist Infiltration of the Motion Picture Industry,* 213–218; *Newsweek,* Nov 3, 1947, TH Sv:14:28, RNyl; George Murphy with Victor Lasky, *"Say . . . Didn't You Used to Be George Murphy?"* (USA: Bartholomew House, 1970), 279–296.

29. RN to Perry, June 17, 1947, PE287, RNyl.

30. Goodman, *The Committee,* 202–224; Carr, *House Committee,* 55–76 and 369–384.

31. *Congressional Record,* Nov 24, 1947, 10792–10793, PPS208(1947).52, RNyl.

32. Eric Johnston address, Nov 19, 1947, PPS205.14, RNyl.
33. RN to Lowell, June 16, 1947, B 463, Lowell, E, Series 320, RNln; Goodman, *The Committee,* 225; Carr, *House Committee,* 75–76.


*Chapter 6*

1. RN speech, Feb 12, 1946, PPS208.3, RNyl.
2. RN speeches, PPS208.17, PPS208.18, PPS208.19, and notes on speeches, 1946, PPS208.35, RNyl.
3. RN speech, May 3, PPS208.4, and Minute Women speech, 1946, PPS208.21, RNyl.
4. *Alhambra Post-Advocate,* Sept 14 and 21, 1946.
5. RN to Perry, Mar 4, 1947, PE242, RNyl; Chestnut to RN, Mar 5, and RN to Chestnut, Mar 19, 1947, B 247, Eur Aid, Series 320, RNln.
6. RN to Perry, Mar 4, PE242, press release, Mar 10, 1947, PPS205.3013, RNyl.
7. RN to Patch, July 11, 1947, B 580, Patch, R, Series 320, RNln.
8. RN to Raab, Mar 11, 1947, B 247, Eur Aid, Series 320, RNln.
9. Barton Bernstein and Allen Matusow, eds., *The Truman Administration: A Documentary History* (NY: Harper, 1968), 251–256; Donovan, *Conflict and Crisis,* 279–289; Melvyn Leffler, *A Preponderance of Power: National Security, the Truman Administration, and the Cold War* (Stanford: Stanford Univ. Press, 1992), 147–150.
10. RN article, Mar 14, 1947, PPS208(1947).9, RNyl.
11. Spencer to RN, Mar 21, 1947, SP14, RNyl and B 717, Spencer, HL, Series 320, RNln; "Washington Report," Mar 25, 1947, PPS208(1947).12, RNyl.
12. RN to Spencer, Mar 27, 1947, B 717, Spencer, HL, Series 320, RNln.
13. RN statement, May 16, 1947, PPS208(1947).27, RNyl.
14. John Bethell, "The Ultimate Commencement Address: The Making of George C. Marshall's Routine Speech," *Harvard Magazine,* vol. 99, no. 5 (May–June 1997), 36–39.
15. Press release, July 2, 1947, PPS205.3019, RNyl; July 2, 1947, President's Appointment File, PSF, Harry S Truman mss, Harry S Truman Library, Independence, Missouri; Nixon, *RN,* 43–44.
16. *Congressional Record,* July 3, 8280, PPS208(1947).40, press release, July 10, PPS205.3020, and "Under the Capitol Dome," July 12, 1947, PPS208(1947). 43, RNyl.
17. "Under the Capitol Dome," July 12, 1947, PPS 208 (1947), 43 RNyl.
18. *Congressional Quarterly,* Aug 5, 1947, 309–312, PPS206.19, Basic Documents, 1947, PPS206.130, *BusinessWeek,* Aug 23, 1947, 8, PPS206.97, RNyl; G. Bernard Noble, "Christian A. Herter," in Robert Ferrell, ed., *The American Secretaries of State and Their Diplomacy,* V. 18 (NY: Cooper Square, 1970), 2–13.
19. Martin to Eaton, July 29, PPS206.3.2, *Congressional Quarterly,* Aug 5, PPS206.19, Eaton to Duran, July 31, 1947, PPS206.130, RNyl; Philip Pope, "Foundations of Nixonian Foreign Policy: The Pre-Presidential Years of Richard M. Nixon, 1946–1968," Ph.D. thesis: Univ. of Southern California, 1988, V. I, 28 and 53.
20. *Congressional Quarterly,* Aug 5, 315–316, PPS206.19, RN to Kersten, Aug 1, PPS206.10, and RN to Martin, Aug 4, PPS206.13, RNyl; Nixon, *RN,* 48.
21. Herter to RN, July 31, 1947, PPS206.6, RNyl.

22. RN to Kersten, Aug 1,, PPS206.10, and RN to Martin, Aug 4, 1947, PPS206.13, RNyl.

23. Arnold to Lowell, Aug 1, B 463, Lowell, E, Series 320, Arnold to Meeker, Aug 6, 1947, B 1, F 1, Series 207, RNln; RN to Garland, Aug 12, PPS206.25, Arnold to supporters, Aug 14, PPS206.31, Spencer to RN, Aug 12, PPS206.27, Frank to RN, Aug 12?, PPS206.28, and *Barron's,* Sept 15, 1947, PPS206.76, RNyl.

24. Garland to RN, Aug 16, PPS206.50; RN to Courtois, Aug 20, PPS206.51, RN to Garland, Aug 21, PPS206.53, and RN to Spencer, Aug 22, 1947, PPS206.58, RNyl; memo RN to Woods, Mar 12, 1958, B 487, Mazo, Series 320, RNln.

25. "Under the Capitol Dome," Aug 19, 1947, PPS208(1947).51, RNyl.

26. Press releases, Aug 5, PPS205.3022, and Aug 28, PPS205.3024, and RN to Mac, Aug 24, 1947, MC42, Dick to Dearest, Sept 1, 1947, PPS262.10, RNyl; Noble, "Herter," 13.

27. Press release, Aug 5, PPS205.3022, Herter to RN, Aug 6, PPS206.47 and PPS206.21, Watts to RN, Aug 15, PPS206.47, and news clipping, Joseph and Stewart Alsop, July 1947, PPS206.8, press release, July 1952, PPS5.425.3, RNyl; Woods to Allen, Sept 19, 1962, B 27, Allen, Mary, Series 320, RNln; T. Michael Ruddy, *The Cautious Diplomat: Charles E. Bohlen and the Soviet Union, 1929–1969* (Kent: Kent State Univ. Press, 1986), 70–76; Charles Bohlen, *Witness to History 1929–1969* (NY: Norton, 1973), 258–266.

28. RMS *Queen Mary,* PPS206.108G, RNyl.

29. Dick to Dearest, Sept 1, 1947, PPS262.10, RNyl.

30. Press release, Aug 5, PPS205.3022, Watts to RN, Aug 15, PPS206.47, memo 1947, PPS206.152, and Gordon to Perry, Aug 28, 1947, PE308, RNyl; Dulles to RN, Feb 20, 1961, 228, Dulles, Allen, Series 320, RNln; Peter Groce, *Gentleman Spy: The Life of Allen Dulles* (Boston: Houghton Mifflin, 1994), 279–280; *Biographical Directory of the United States Congress 1774–1989,* 1259.

31. RN to Mac, Aug 1 [he meant Sept 1], MC43, press release, Aug 28, 1947, PPS205.3024, weather information, PPS206.108B, and Dick to Dearest, Sept 1, 1947, PPS262.10, RNyl.

32. Memo on Great Britain, Great Britain NPPP, B 763, Series 320, RNln; memo on Britain, 1947, PPS206.156 and "Ambassador of Friendship Complete 1960," film, 137:2, RNyl; Nixon, *RN,* 49; *Alhambra Post-Advocate,* Nov 11, 1947.

33. Memo on Britain, 1947, PPS206.156, RNyl; *Alhambra Post-Advocate,* Nov 11, 1947; Alan Bullock, *Ernest Bevin: Foreign Secretary 1945–1951* (London: Heinemann, 1983), 446–461.

34. Memo on Britain, 1947, PPS206.156, RNyl; *Alhambra Post-Advocate,* Nov 11, 1947; Bullock, *Bevin,* 452–456.

35. *Alhambra Post-Advocate,* Nov 11, 1947.

36. Memo on Germany, 1947, PPS206.158, and memo, Sept 1, 1947, PPS206.72, RNyl; *Alhambra Post-Advocate,* Nov 12, 1947; Nixon, *RN,* 49.

37. Memo on Germany, 1947, PPS206.158, and memo, Sept 1, 1947, PPS206.72, RNyl; *Alhambra Post-Advocate,* Nov 12, 1947; Jean Smith, *Lucius D. Clay: An American Life* (NY: Holt, 1990), 423–449; John Gimbel, *The American Occupation of Germany: Politics and the Military, 1945–1949* (Stanford: Stanford Univ. Press, 1968), 134–180.

38. Memo on Germany, 1947, PPS206.158, and memo, Sept 1, 1947, PPS206.72, RNyl; *Alhambra Post-Advocate,* Nov 12, 1947; Nixon, *RN,* 11.

39. *Alhambra Post-Advocate,* Nov 12, 1947.

40. *Ibid.*

41. *Ibid.,* and memo on Germany, 1947, PPS206.158, RNyl.

42. Tentative itinerary, Aug 18, PPS206.13, and Jones to RN, Oct 14, 1947, PPS206.80, RNyl.

43. Memo on growth of political terrorism in Italy, July 11, PPS206.212, RN to Phillips, Aug 4, PPS206.14, remarks by Cottam, Sept 9, PPS206.213, and memo on Italy, 1947, PPS206.160, RNyl; James Miller, *The United States and Italy, 1940–1950: The Politics and Diplomacy of Stabilization* (Chapel Hill: Univ. of NC Press, 1986), 213–230.

44. Dick to Dearest, Sept 13, 1947, PPS262.11, RNyl.

45. Memo on Italy, 1947, PPS206.160 and tentative itinerary, Aug 18, 1947, PPS206.13, RNyl; *Alhambra Post-Advocate,* Nov 13, 1947; *Time,* May 5, 1947, 32; Nixon, *RN,* 49.

46. Memo on Italy, 1947, PPS206.160, RNyl; *Alhambra Post-Advocate,* Nov 13, 1947.

47. Memo on Italy, 1947, PPS206.160, RNyl; *Alhambra Post-Advocate,* Nov 13, 1947.

48. Memo of Piedmont Visit, Sept 13, PPS206.75, memo on conversation with Vittorio Valletta, Sept 13, PPS206.214, and Dick to Dearest, Sept 13, 1947, PPS262.11, RNyl.

49. Dick to Dearest, Sept 13, PPS262.11, and Sept 14, 1947, PPS262.12, RNyl.

50. Memo on Trieste, 1947, PPS206.161, and statement by the chairman, Oct 6, 1947, PPS206.228, RNyl; memo by RN, Aug 26–Oct 10, 1947, B 763, Trieste, Series 320, RNln; Joyce to secretary of state, Sept 20, 1947, 860.00/9–2047, RG 59, National Archives, Washington, D.C.; *Alhambra Post-Advocate,* Nov 18, 1947; Roberto Rabel, *Between East and West: Trieste, the United States, and the Cold War, 1941–1954* (Durham: Duke Univ. Press, 1988), 102; Bogdan Novak, *Trieste 1941–1954: The Ethnic, Political, and Ideological Struggle* (Chicago: Univ. of Chicago Press, 1970), 251–281.

51. Memo on Trieste, 1947, PPS206.161, and statement by the chairman, Oct 6, 1947, PPS206.228, RNyl; memo by RN, Aug 26–Oct 10, 1947, B 763, Trieste, Series 320, RNln; *Alhambra Post-Advocate,* Nov 18, 1947.

52. Memo on Trieste, 1947, PPS206.161, RNyl; memo by RN, Aug 26–Oct, 1947, B 763, Trieste, Series 320, RNln; *Alhambra Post-Advocate,* Nov 18, 1947.

53. Statement by the chairman, Oct 6, 1947, PPS206.228, RNyl; memo by RN, Aug 26–Oct 10, 1947, B 763, Trieste, Series 320, RNln; Joyce to secretary of state, Sept 20, 1947, 860.00/9–2047, RG 59, National Archives; *Alhambra Post-Advocate,* Nov 18, 1947; Rabel, *Between East and West,* 103–104.

54. Memo by RN, Aug 26–Oct 10, 1947, B 763, Trieste, Series 320, RNln.

55. Joyce to secretary of state, Sept 20, 1947, 860S.00/9–2047; RG 59, National Archives; quoted in Rabel, *Between East and West,* 105.

56. *NY Times,* Sept 18, 1947, 15:3.

57. Memo on Italy, 1947, PPS206.160, memorandum of conversation, Sept 19, PPS206.215, memorandum of conference at CGIL Headquarters, PPS206.-

216, and Dick to Dearest, Sept 19, 1947, PPS262.12, RNyl; *Alhambra Post-Advocate,* Nov 13, 1947; Nixon, *RN,* 50.

58. Tentative itinerary, Aug 18, PPS206.13, opening statement, 1947, PPS206.219, statement concerning civil government division, PPS206.220, memo of conversation, Oct 6, PPS206.88, and report on Greece, Dec 10, 1947, PPS206.110, RNyl; Lawrence Wittner, *American Intervention in Greece, 1943–1949* (NY: Columbia Univ. Press, 1982), 167–191.

59. Comments by Colonel Lehrer, Sept 22, 1947, PPS206.221 RNyl; Wittner, *American Intervention in Greece,* 222–253.

60. RN to Mac, Aug 1 [should read Sept 1], MC43, RN to Larson, Oct 15, PPS.206.82, memo of conversation, Oct 24, PPS206.88, Keeley to RN, Dec 11, PPS206.105, memo on Greece, 1947, PPS206.159, and Dick to Dearest, Sept 22, 1947, PPS262.14, RNyl; *Alhambra Post-Advocate,* Nov 19, 1947.

61. Memo of conversation, Oct 24, 1947, PPS206.88 and memo on Greece, 1947, PPS206.159, RNyl; *Alhambra Post-Advocate,* Nov 19, 1947.

62. Report on Greece, Dec 10, 1947, PPS206.110, RNyl; *Alhambra Post-Advocate,* Nov 19, 1947.

63. Tentative itinerary, Aug 18, 1947, PPS206.13, and memo on France, 1947, PPS206.157, RNyl; *Alhambra Post-Advocate,* Nov 15, 1947.

64. Memo on France, 1947, PPS206.157, RNyl; Irwin Wall, *The United States and the Making of Postwar France, 1945–1954* (Cambridge: Cambridge Univ. Press, 1991), 11–95.

65. *Alhambra Post-Advocate,* Nov 15, 1947; memo on France, 1947, PPS206.157, RNyl.

66. Tentative itinerary, Aug 18, PPS206.13, and memo by Watts, Oct [possibly 4], 1947, PPS206.78, RNyl.

67. RN to Cottam, Nov 22, PPS206.96, and Dick to Dearest, Sept 1, PPS262.10, Sept 13, PPS262.11, Sept 14, PPS262.12, and Sept 19, 1947, PPS262.13, RNyl; RN to Winterer, Mar 3, 1949, B 825, Winterer, Series 320, RNln; Eisenhower, *Pat Nixon,* 96–97.

68. Press release, Oct 14, PPS205.3025, RN to Perry, Oct 15, PE323, press releases, Oct 20, PPS205.2026, and Oct 23, 1947, PPS205.3027, and RN to Woods, Mar 12, 1958, PPS206.164, RNyl; Garland to RN, Oct 21, 1947, B 282, Garland [½], Series 320, RNln; memo from Herbert Klein, May 14, 1997, Gellman mss.

69. Klein to RN, Jan 17, *The Bulletin,* May 1, and biography of Klein, 1967, uncatalogued, RNyl; RN to Klein, Dec 22, 1947, B 3, Trip, Series 434, RNln; Herbert Klein, *Making It Perfectly Clear: An Inside Account of Nixon's Love-Hate Relationship with the Media* (NY: Doubleday, 1980), viii and 76.

70. *Alhambra Post-Advocate,* Oct 30, 1947; for similar statements, see *Wilshire Press,* Nov 6, 1947, B 247, Eur Aid, Series 320, RNln; memo RN to Woods, Mar 12, 1958, B 487, Mazo, Series 320, RNln.

71. *Alhambra Post-Advocate,* Nov 11, 1947. I found these articles cited in Philip Pope's thesis on "Foundations of Nixonian Foreign Policy" and placed copies of the news articles in Gellman mss.

72. *Alhambra Post-Advocate,* Nov 12 and 13, 1947; Rosetta R. to RN, Oct 1, PPS206.77, Jones to RN, Oct 14, PPS206.80, Angleton to RN, Oct 17, PPS206.85, RN to Jones, Nov 21, 1947, PPS206.94, and Kein to RN, Feb 15, 1948, PPS206.118, RNyl; RN to Winterer, Mar 3, B 285, Winterer, RN to Gaudio, Mar 3, 1949, and Jan 30, 1950, B 284, Gaudio, Series 320, RNln.

73. *Alhambra Post-Advocate,* Nov 14, 1947.

74. *Ibid.* Nov 15 and 18, 1947; Nixon, *RN,* 52.

75. *Alhambra Post-Advocate,* Nov 17, 1947.

76. *Ibid.* Nov 18, 1947; RN to Schiefer, Nov 24, 1947, B 674, Schiefer, Series 320, RNln.

77. *Alhambra Post-Advocate,* Nov 19, 1947.

78. Wittner, *American Intervention in Greece,* 36–166 and 254–282.

79. Statement by Marshall, Nov 10, 1947, PPS206.91, RNyl; Hartmann, *Truman and the 80th Congress,* 112 and 116.

80. RN to Dunn, Dec 18, 1947, PPS206.111, RNyl; Leffler, *A Preponderance of Power,* 188–197; Forrest Pogue, *George Marshall: Statesman 1945–1959,* (NY: Viking, 1987), 218–256; Richard Freeland, *The Truman Doctrine and the Origins of McCarthyism: Foreign Policy, Domestic Politics, and Internal Security 1946–1948* (NY: NY Univ. Press, 1985), 187–200; Michael Hogan, *The Marshall Plan: America, Britain, and the Reconstruction of Western Europe* (Cambridge: Cambridge Univ. Press, 1987), 82–87.

81. "Washington Report," Dec 11, PPS208(1947).53, press release, Dec 13, PPS208(1947).54.3, and "Washington Report," Dec 18, 1947, PPS208(1947).54(1), RNyl.

82. David Lawrence, "Nixon's Tax Returns Are 'Clean,'" Dec 1, 1952, B442, Lawrence article, RNln.

Chapter 7

1. RN to Day, Jan 7, 1948, B 1, Finance Committee, Series 434, RNln; Susan Hartmann, *Truman and the 80th Congress,* 128–131.

2. RN to Dunn, Dec 18, 1947, PPS206.111, "Washington Report," Jan 1, PPS208 (1948).1, memo on foreign aid, 1948, PPS206.127, RNyl.

3. "Washington Report," Jan 29, 1948, PPS208(1948).5, RNyl.

4. RN radio broadcast, Feb 26, 1948, MC Record #2, RNyl.

5. "Washington Report," Feb 26, 1948, PPS208(1948).10, RNyl; Donovan, *Conflict and Crisis,* 361–362.

6. Kersten radio broadcast, Feb 19, MC Record #1, RN radio broadcast, Mar 4, 1948, MC Record #3, RNyl.

7. RN radio broadcast, Mar 4, 1948, MC Record #4, RNyl; RN to Bacon, Mar 15, 1948, B 174, Condon, Series 320, RNln.

8. RN radio broadcast, Mar 18, 1948, MC Record #5, RNyl; *Newsweek,* Mar 22, 1948.

9. House Concurrent Resolution No. 170, Mar 16, PPS293.2, "Washington Report," Mar 25, PPS208(1948).14, "Washington Report," Mar 25, PPS208(1948).14, RN radio broadcast, Apr 15, MC Record #7, RN to Friend, Apr 28, PE397, RN radio broadcast, Apr 29, MC Record #9, *Alhambra Post-Advocate,* Apr 29, PPS205.S15, "Washington Report," May 6, 1948, PPS208(1948).22.2, RNyl.

10. "Washington Report," Jan 15, PPS208(1948).3, memo on foreign aid, Feb 19, PPS206.119, RN radio broadcast, Mar 11, 1948, MC Record #4, RNyl; Pope, "Foundations of Nixonian Foreign Policy," V. I, 60–62.

11. "Washington Report," Apr 1, PPS208(1948).15, RN to Friend, Apr 28, PE397, "Washington Report," May 13, 1948, PPS208(1948).23.2, RNyl; RN

to Friend, Apr 28, 1948, B 269, Form Letters, RN to Woll, May 30, 1951, B 34, American Federation of Labor, Series 320, RNln: Hartmann, *Truman and the 80th Congress,* 159–160; Noble, "Herter," 14–15; Leffler, *A Preponderance of Power,* 200–203; Hogan, *The Marshall Plan,* 102–108.

12. RN to Patch, Apr 21, 1948, B 580, Patch, R, Series 320, RNln; Perry to RN, Apr 23, 1948, PE393, RNyl.

13. RN radio broadcast, Apr 15, MC Record #7, *Pomona Progress-Bulletin,* Apr 22, PPS205.S13, "Washington Report," Apr 22, 1948, PPS208(1948).18.2, RNyl.

14. Rosetta to RN, Mar 22, PPS206.124, *Alhambra Post-Advocate,* Apr 15, PPS205.S9, "Washington Report," Apr 15, PPS208(1948).17, and Apr 29, 1948, PPS208(1948).21.2, RNyl; Leffler, *A Preponderance of Power,* 214–218.

15. RN radio broadcast, Apr 29, MC Record #9, *Alhambra Post-Advocate,* Apr 29, PPS205.S15, *Monrovia News-Post,* May 2, PPS205.S19, "Washington Report," May 6, 1948, PPS208(1948).22.2, RNyl.

16. RN, "What I Think of the Marshall Plan," *The New Dominion,* May 1948, PPS206.128 and PPS208(1948).11.2, RNyl.

17. RN to Day, Jan 7, 1948, B 1, Finance Committee, Series 434, RNln; "Washington Report," Feb 17, PPS208(1948).8.2, RN radio broadcast, Mar 11, 1948, MC Record #4, RNyl; Hartmann, *Truman and the 80th Congress,* 179–183.

18. RN to McCall, Mar 13, 1948, B 1, Manager, Series 434, RNln; Spencer to RN, Jan 2, SP21, "Washington Report," Jan 15, PPS208(1948).3, RN to Spencer, Jan 12, SP22 and Mar 8, SP26.1, "Washington Report," Mar 11, SP26.2, Perry to RN, May 13, 1948, PE405, RNyl; Hartmann, *Truman and the 80th Congress,* 169–172.

19. RN to Spencer, Jan 17, SP23, "Washington Report," Jan 23, PPS208(1948).4 and Feb 19, PPS208(1948).9, news release, Apr 26, PPS(1948).20, *Monrovia News-Post,* Apr 29, 1948, PPS205.S12, RNyl; RN to Dorn, Apr 23, 1948, B 221, Dorn, E, Series 320, RNln.

20. Press release, Jan 8, 1948, PPS208(1948).2, RNyl.

21. "Washington Report," Jan 15, PPS208(1948).3 and Feb 5, PSS208(1948).6, RN to Friend, Apr 28, 1948, PE397, RNyl; Hartmann, *Truman and the 80th Congress,* 132–136.

22. "Washington Report," Feb 12, PPS208(1948).7, Bridges to Perry, Feb 14, 1948, PE369, RNyl.

23. "Washington Report," Apr 8, 1948, PPS208(1948).16, RNyl; Hartmann, *Truman and the 80th Congress,* 137–142.

24. RN to Beuscher, Feb 9, B 80, Beuscher, RN to Friend, Apr 28, B 269, Form Letters, Series 320, Day to RN, Feb 18, RN to Day, Feb 27, B 1, Finance Committee, RN to McCall, Apr 6, B 1, Manager, RN to De La Vergne, Apr 13, 1948, B 3, Workers, Series 434, RNln; RN to Friend, Apr 28, 1948, PE397, RNyl; Hartmann, *Truman and the 80th Congress,* 147–150.

25. Thomas Hoult, "The Whittier Narrows Dam: A Study in Community Competition and Conflict." Whittier College: M.A. thesis, 1948, 4–26; Zetterberg (Claremont) Oral History, 24.

26. *Pomona Progress-Bulletin,* Apr 6, PPS205.S5, *Monrovia News-Post,* Apr 7, PPS205.S5 and Apr 15, PPS205.S9, RN radio broadcast, Apr 22, 1948, MC Record #8, RNyl; Norris Hundley, Jr., *The Great Thirst: Californians and Water, 1770s–1990s* (Berkeley: Univ. of California Press, 1992), 300–304.

27. RN to Newman, Jan 17, 1947, B 599, Newman, W, Series 320, RNln; RN to Perry, Jan 25, PE226 and Feb 3, PE231, RN to Mac, Jan 31, 1947, MC11, RNyl; Hoult, "Whittier Narrows Dam," 27.

28. RN to Perry, Mar 4, PE242, Apr 2, PE257, May 21, PE272, and June 10, PE 282, Hedges to LA County Flood Control District, May 2, PE264, Perry to RN, May 3, PE265, press release, June 27, PPS205.3017 and June 28, 1947, PPS205.3018, press release, Feb 5, PPS208(1948).6A, RN to Perry, Feb 17, 1948, PE238, RNyl; Hoult, "Whittier Narrows Dam," 27–28.

29. RN to Perry, July 31, PE305, Arnold to RN, Oct 20, PPS205.12, Perry to RN, Nov 18, PE330 and Dec 8, PE336, RN to Dayhuff, Dec 4, 1947, PE333, RNyl.

30. RN to Perry, Dec 15, 1947, PE341, Perry to RN, Jan 17, PE351, RN to Perry, Jan 20, PE354, Jan 27, PE359 and Mar 22, PE378, Perry to RN, Mar 12, 1948, PE376, RNyl; press release, Feb 5, B 3, Press Releases [2/4], RN to Day, Feb 27 and Apr 21, B 1, Finance Committee, Knowland to RN, May 3, B 1, Election [½], RN to Goodspeed, June 15, 1948, B 3, Thank you, Series 434, RNln; Hoult, "Whittier Narrows Dam," 30 and 182–183.

31. MC Record #5, Mar 18, RN to Perry, Mar 22, PE378, *Pasadena Star News,* Apr 1, PPS205.S5, *Alhambra Post-Advocate,* Apr 7, PPS205.S5, and June 15, PPS205.S83, *El Monte Herald,* May 7, PPS205.S25, *Whittier News,* Apr 24, PPS205.S13, Wheeler to RN, Aug 6, 1948, PPS205.691, RNyl; Day to RN, Mar 20, RN to Day, Mar 23, B 1, Finance Committee, RN to Cooper, Mar 23, B 2, Republican Central Committee LA, Bewley to RN, Apr 2, RN to Bewley, May 3, Goodson to RN, May 8, RN to Goodson, May 8, B 3, Workers, RN to Cleveland, June 14, 1948, B 3, Thank you, Series 434, RNln; RN to Moore, Dec 1, Moore to RN, Dec 9, 1948, Moore to RN, Jan 20, RN to Moore, Jan 25, 1949, B 114, PSL671.1, Army Corps of Engineer, Los Angeles District, Civil Works Projects, 1935–1950, RG 77, National Archives and Records Administration, Pacific Region, Laguna Niguel, California..

32. *Paterson Call,* Jan 27, TH Sv.14:73, *Washington Post,* Feb 11, 1948, TH Sv.14:73, RNyl.

33. Bannerman to RN, Dec 12, PPS205.24, RN to Bannerman, Dec 20, 1947, PPS205.24, RN to Frankel, Jan 12, 1948, PPS205.62.6, RNyl.

34. RN to Dulles, Jan 17, 1948, PPS205.82, RNyl.

35. Ernst to RN, Jan 19, PPS205.91, Lyons statement, Jan 31, PPS205.172, Dulles to RN, Feb 3, 1948, PPS205.182, RNyl; Beatrice Berle and Travis Jacobs, eds., *Navigating the Rapids 1918–1971: From the Papers of Adolf A. Berle* (NY: Harcourt Brace Jovanovich, 1973), 580–582.

36. RN to Barstow, Jan 20, PPS205.116, RN to Nolan, Jan 20, PPS205.121, RN to Godkin, Jan 23, PPS205.137, Arnold to Jacoby, Jan 27, 1948, PPS205.156, RNyl.

37. *Congressional Record,* Feb 3, 1948, PPS208(1948).5A, RNyl.

38. House of Representatives, Hearings Before the Subcommittee on Legislation of the Committee on Un-American Activities, 80th Cong, 2nd Sess, *Hearings on Proposed Legislation to Curb or Control the Communist Party of the United States* (Washington, D.C.: GPO, 1948), 1–5.

39. *Ibid.,* 16–248; RN to Mrs. McCall, Dec 8, 1947, MC46, ACLU, Jan, PPS205.173A, RN to Hampton, Feb 12, PPS205.262, Ernst to RN, Feb 13, PSS205.266, RN to Koehl, Feb 16, PPS205.277, RN to Batcheler, Feb 16,

1948, PPS205.274, RNyl; RN to Lowell, Feb 9, 1948, B 3, Workers, Series 434, RNln.

40. Bill to Perry, Feb 18, PE371, "Washington Report," Feb 19, 1948, PPS208 (1948).9, RNyl; Arnold, *Back When It All Began,* 7.

41. "Washington Report," Feb 19, 1948, PPS208(1948).9, RNyl; RN to McCall, Feb 18, B 1, Manager, RN to Blue, Feb 19, B 3, Sponsors, Democratic, Series 434, RN to Van Sickle, Mar 3, B 781, Van Sickle, J, RN to Eddy, Mar 5, 1948, B 235, Eddy, AC, Series 320, RNln.

42. *Hearings on Proposed Legislation to Curb or Control the Communist Party of the United States,* 311–455; Carr, 81; Goodman, *The Committee,* 228, Gerald Horne, *Black Liberation/Red Scare: Ben Davis and the Communist Party* (Newark: Univ. of Deleware Press, 1994) 207–208.

43. Nichols to Tolson, Feb 18, 1948, Benjamin Davis FBI file, 100-149163-69, Washington, D.C.

44. Ibid.; Curt Gentry, *J. Edgar Hoover: The Man and the Secrets* (NY: Norton, 1991), 44.

45. Carr, *House Committee,* 81; Goodman, *The Committee,* 228.

46. *Ridgewood Sunday News,* Mar 24, TH Sv.11:16, *Herald News,* June 27, TH Sv.11:45, RNyl; Robert Stripling, *The Red Plot Against America,* (Pa.: Bell Publishing Co., 1949), 85–86.

47. Condon to Thomas, July 9, B 174, Condon, Condon to RN, July 17, 1947, B 174, Condon, Series 320, RN to Day, Mar 23, 1948, B 1, Finance Committee, Series 434, RNln; Stripling, *Red Plot,* 85–88; Goodman, *The Committee,* 232.

48. Thomas, "The Price of Vision," TH, B 1, RNyl; Stripling, *Red Plot,* 86; Goodman, *The Committee,* 232; Carr, *House Committee,* 131–140.

49. RN to Harriman, Mar 5, Ernst to RN, Mar 12, 1948, B 174, Condon, Series 320, RNln; *Congressional Record,* Mar 11, PPS208(1948).13, RN radio broadcast, Mar 18, 1948, MC Record #5, RNyl; Carr, *House Committee,* 141–143; Goodman, *The Committee,* 235.

50. RN to McChesney, Mar 15, RN to Bacon, Mar 15, RN to Beuscher, Mar 15, 1948, B 174, Condon, Series 320, RNln.

51. RN to Beuscher, Apr 19, 1948, B 80, Beuscher, Series 320, RNln; Carr, *House Committee,* 151–152.

52. *Congressional Record,* Apr 22, PPS208(1948).19, *Monrovia News-Post,* Apr 24, PPS205.S15, RN statement, fall 1948, PPS208(1948).39A, RNyl; RN to Dorn, Apr 23, 1948, B 221, Dorn, E, Series 320, RNln; Robert Ferrell, ed., *Truman in the White House: The Diary of Eben A. Ayers* (Columbia: Univ. Of Missouri Press, 1991), cited hereafter as *Ayers Diary,* 255; Goodman, *Committee,* 236.

53. RN radio broadcast, Mar 27, MC Record #6a and b, "Washington Report," May 13, 1948, PPS208(1948).23.2, RNyl.

54. *NY Herald Tribune,* Apr 7, 1948, TH Sv.14:80, RNyl; House of Representatives, House Committee on Un-American Activities, 80th Cong, 2nd Sess, *Report of the Subcommittee on Legislation of the Committee on Un-American Activities on Proposed Legislation to Control Subversive Communist Activities in the United States* (Washington, D.C.: GPO, 1948), 1–7; House of Representatives, House Committee on Un-American Activities, 80th Cong, 2 Sess, *Protecting the United States Against Un-American and Subversive Activities* (Washington, D.C.: GPO, 1948), 1–14.

55. RN to Day, Apr 21, 1948, B 1, Finance Committee, Series 434, RNln; *NY Herald Tribune,* Apr 27, TH Sv:15:1, and May 2, PPS205.S19; *Pomona Progress-Bulletin,* Apr 29, 1948, PPS205.S12, RNyl.

56. Foster and Dennis to Members, May 7, 1948, R 123, Mundt mss, Karl E. Mundt Historical and Educational Foundation, Dakota State Univ., Madison, South Dakota.

57. RN to Goodson, May 8, RN to Lowell, May 8, B 3, Workers, RN to McCall, May 10, 1948, B 1, Manager, Series 434, RNln; *Ramsey Journal,* May 6, TH Sv:15:7, RN to McCall, May 10, 1948, PE403, RNyl.

58. Kaplan to Martin, May 6, PPS205.396, Fox to RN, May 8, PPS205.410, Horowitz to RN, May 12, PPS205.368, *People's World,* May 13, 1948, PPS205.516, RNyl; House of Representatives, House Committee on Un-American Activities, 80th Cong, 2nd Sess, *Report on the Communist Party of the United States as an Advocate of Overthrow of Government by Force and Violence* (Washington, D.C.: GPO, 1948), 1–3.

59. *NY Sun-Telegram,* May 15, PPS205.S40, O'Dwyer to Forbes, May 15, 1948, PPS205.526.2, RNyl.

60. Spratling to RN, May 14, 1948, PPS205.518, RNyl.

61. RN to De La Vergne, May 10, 1948, B 3, Workers, Series 434, RNln.

62. Waldman to RN, Apr 17, PPS205.342, Clark to RN, May 11, PPS205.484.1, Dulles to RN, May 11, PPS205.487, Ernst to RN, May 11, PPS205.488, Sullivan to RN, May 11, PPS205.494, Waldman to RN, May 12, PPS205.509, Richberg to RN, May 14, PPS205.520, *New Leader,* May 15, 1948, PPS205.432A, RN to Dulles, May 17, 1948, PPS205.530, RNyl.

63. *Congressional Record,* May 14, 1948, PPS208(1948).24, RNyl.

64. RN to Dulles, May 17, 1948, PPS205.530, RNyl.

65. RN radio broadcast, May 18, PPS208(1948).26, memo, May, PSS205.455.4, memo on the Town Meeting, May 19, 1948, PPS205.537, RNyl; Black to RN, May 19, B 1, Contributors—Financial, Series 434, RN to Black, June 18, B 85, Black, W, RN to Brennan, July 15, 1948, B 101, Brennan, C, Series 320, RNln.

66. *Congressional Record,* May 19, 1948, PPS208(1948).27, RNyl.

67. *Ibid.,* May 19, PPS208(1948).27, *Washington Post,* May 20, 1948, PPS205.543A, RNyl; Gerald Meyer, *Vito Marcantonio: Radical Politician 1920–1954* (Albany: State Univ. of NY, 1989), 7 and 53–172; La Gumina, *Marcantonio,* 99, 103–105, 111, 141–142, and 191–199; Schaffer, *Marcantonio,* 171–181, 184, 191–199, and 210.

68. *LA Herald-Express,* May 18, PPS205.S43, *Washington Post,* May 19, PPS205.S46, *Riverside Daily Press,* May 22, 1948, PPS205.S57, RNyl.

69. *Washington Post,* May 20, PPS205.543A, *Pomona Progress-Bulletin,* May 20, PPS205.S46, *Washington Times Herald,* May 22, 1948, PPS205.S52, RNyl.

70. Mundt to Lusk, May 19, Mundt to Thomas, May 27, 1948, R 122, Mundt mss.

71. *NY Times,* May 21, PPS205.S55, Bulwer to RN, May 22, 1948, PPS205.541, RNyl.

72. *Pomona Progress-Bulletin,* May 20, PPS205.S46, *Washington Post,* May 20, PPS205.543A, *Washington Times Herald,* May 22, PSS205.S52, *People's World,* May 29, 1948, PPS205.559, RNyl; memo by Gleason, July 29, 1952, B 538, Mundt-Nixon Bill, Series 320, RNln; Richard Walton, *Henry Wallace, Harry Truman, and the Cold War* (NY: Viking, 1976), 220–222; Ric Kabat, "From

New Deal to Red Scare: The Political Odyssey of Senator Claude D. Pepper,"
Ph.D. thesis: Florida State Univ, 1995, 267–270.

*Chapter 8*

1. RN to Dorris, Nov 6, 1947, B 222, Dorris, Series 320, RNln.
2. Boardman, Mar 11, B 89, Boardman, Lutz to RN, Apr 9, B 466, Lutz, H, RN to Blaisdell, July 3, B 86, Blaisdell, RN to Martin, July 25, B 479, Martin, N, Series 320, and Arnold to Jorgensen, Oct 15, 1947, B 1, Finance Committee, RN to Brennan, Mar 28, 1949, B 2, Republican Central Committee, Series 434, RNln; RN to Mac, Mar 21, MC16, McLaughlin to RN, Apr 30, PE263, Perry to RN, June 20, PE260, McLaughlin to Reece, Sept 16, PE311, and Bacher to McLaughlin, Oct 4, 1947, PE315, RNyl.
3. RN to Perry, Aug 24, 1947, PE306, RNyl.
4. Arnold to Lowell, Aug 1, 1947, B 463, Lowell, E, Series 320, RNln; Arnold to supporters, Aug 14, PPS206.31, RN to Mac, Aug 24, MC42, and press release, Aug 28, 1947, PPS205.3024, RNyl; *Whittier Reporter,* Oct 2, 1947.
5. RN to Perry, Nov 25, 1947, PE372, RNyl; RN to Adams, Nov 25, B 1, Fact Finding Committee, RN to Day, Nov 25, Day to RN, Dec 5, Carden to Friend, Dec 9, B 1, Finance Committee, and Williamson to RN, Dec 8, 1947, B 2, Republican Convention, Series 434, RNln.
6. Arnold to RN, Oct 20, PPS205.12, Perry to RN, Nov 6, PE329, and Nov 18, PE330, and A. L. Perry to Bryant, Dec 10, 1947, PE339, RNyl; Jorgensen to RN, Dec 22, and Day to Friend, Dec 31, 1947, B 1, Finance Committee, Series 434, RNln.
7. RN to Perry, Dec 15, PE341 and Dec 23, PE347, and Mac to RN, Dec 19, 1947, MC48, RN to Savage, Jan 12, 1948, PPS205.63, RNyl; RN to Savage, Nov 24 and Dec 8, B 1, Manager, RN to Crocker, Dec 3, B 1, Fact Finding Committee, RN to Day, Dec 17, B 1, Finance Committee, RN to Latham, Dec 18, RN to Klein, Dec 22, RN to Perry, Dec 22, RN to Bewley, Dec 23, and RN to Day, Dec 23, 1947, B 3, Trip, Series 434, RNln.
8. RN to Day, Dec 17, 1947, Day to RN, Jan 3, and RN to Day, Jan 7, 1948, B 1, Finance Committee, Series 434, RNln.
9. Lutz to RN, Jan 24, B 1, Finance Committee, and memo by Bill, early 1948, B 2, Publicity—Corres, Series 434, RNln; J. Voorhis to C. Voorhis, Dec 19, 1946, B 109, F 15, Voorhis mss.
10. RN to Cantwell, Apr 9 and Aug 22, 1947, B 131, Cantwell, Series 320, and RN to Jorgensen, Jan 19, Arnold to Jorgensen, Jan 24, 1948, B 1, Finance Committee, Series 434, RNln; RN to Mac, Aug 22, MC41, Perry to RN, Nov 6, 1947, PE329, RNyl.
11. Wilkinson to US Junior Chamber of Commerce, Oct 1, LBM 164.2, McMullen to Wilkenson, Oct 2, LBM 164.3, Wilkinson to McMullen, LBM 164.4, Nov 3, 1947, The Birth of a Committee, 1948?, LBM 164.1, Distinguished Service Award Banquet, Jan 21, 1948, PPS205.129.2, RNyl; RN to Beuscher, Feb 9, B 80, Beuscher, Series 320, RN to Lowell, Jan 27, B 3, Workers, and RN to Wilkerson, June 14, 1948, Series 434, RNln; *LA Times,* Jan 21, 1948.
12. RN to Day, Feb 9 and 24, and Day to RN, Feb 26, B 1, Finance Committee, RN to McCall, Feb 18 and 24, and McCall to Arnold, Feb 28, 1948, B 1, Manager, Series 434, RNln.

13. RN to Jorgensen, Feb 4 and Feb 19, Jorgensen to RN, Feb 15, B 1, Finance Committee, RN to Bowen, Feb 9, 1948, B 2, Publicity—Corres, Series 434, RNln.

14. RN to Day, Feb 9, De La Vergne to RN, Feb 15, B 3, Workers, Day to RN, Feb 21 and 25, B 1, Finance Committee, Muffler to RN, Apr 2, 1948, B 3, Sponsors, Endorse, Series 434, RNln; RN to McCall, Apr 12, 1948, PE389, RNyl.

15. RN to Day, Nov 25, 1947, and Jan 7, 1948, B 1, Finance Committee, RN to McCall, Feb 5, 18, and 24, McCall to RN, Feb 18, B 1, Manager, RN to Blue, Feb 19, Blue to RN, Feb 22, Blue biography, Apr 26, 1948, B 3, Sponsors, Democratic, Series 434, RNln; Monrovia-Duarte telephone book, Aug 1948 issue, p. 48, California State Library, Sacramento California.

16. RN to McCall, Mar 8 and 13, B 1, Manager, Day to RN, Mar 20, B 1, Finance Committee, Dawson to Reeves, Mar 19, 1948, B 3, Sponsors, Endorse, Series 434, RNln; Young to RN, Mar 18, PPS205.330, and RN to Young, Mar 23, 1948, PPS205.332, RNyl.

17. Arnold to Bowen, Mar 4, B 2, Publicity—Corres, RN to Day, Mar 4, and Day to RN, Mar 12, 1948, B 1, Finance Committee, Series 434, RNln; Perry to RN, Mar 12, 1948, PE376, RNyl.

18. RN to McCall, Mar 19, and McCall to RN, Mar 22, B 1, Manager, Arnold to Bowen, Mar 19, and Bowen to Arnold, Mar 20, B 2, Publicity—Corres, RN to Day, Mar 23, 1948, B 1, Finance Committee, Series 434, RNln; RN to Mac, Mar 19, 1948, MC63, RNyl.

19. Day to RN, Feb 18 and Mar 20, B 1, Finance Committee, RN to Faries, Feb 27, 1948, B 2, Republican Convention, Series 434, RNln.

20. Scott to RN, Mar 23, B 1, Opposition, Bowen to Arnold, Mar 25, B 2, Publicity—Corres, McCall to RN, Mar 25, B 1, Manager, Day to RN, Mar 27, 1948, B 1, Finance Committee, Series 434, RNln.

21. Zetterberg for Congress, 1948, Day to RN, Mar 24, B 1, Opposition, Day to RN, Apr 13, 1948, B 1, Finance Committee, Series 434, RNln; *Pasadena Star News,* Apr 7, 1948, PPS205.S5, RNyl; *LA Times,* Nov 9, 1972, B 123, F 18, Voorhis mss; Zetterberg Oral History, California State Archives, iii and 1, 2, and 48; Zetterberg Oral History (Claremont), 1–12.

22. Blue to RN, Mar 27, B 3, Sponsors, Democratic, and Arnold to McCall, Mar 29, B 1, Manager, RN to Hinshaw, Apr 2, 1948, B 1, General, Series 434, RNln; *LA Times,* Nov 9, 1972; Zetterberg Oral History (Claremont), 9.

23. RN to Blue, Mar 30, 1948, B 3, Sponsors, Democratic, Series 434, RNln.

24. *LA Times,* Nov 9, 1972.

25. Lutz to Mac, Apr 6, 1948, MC72, RNyl.

26. Klein to RN, undated, B 1, Election [½], Klein to RN, Apr 6, B 2, Publicity—Newspapers, McCall to RN, Apr 15, RN to McCall, Apr 21, McCall to Arnold, Apr 28, 1948, B 1, Manager, Series 434, RNln; RN to McCall, Apr 12, 1948, PE389, RNyl; Klein to author, Aug 27, 1991, Gellman mss.

27. RN to McCall, Apr 1 and 21, B 1, Manager, RN to Bagnall, Apr 21, 1948, B 3, Workers, Series 434, RNln.

28. RN to McCall, Apr 6, 12, and 21, McCall to RN, Apr 9, B 1, Manager, RN to Muffler, Apr 7, 1948, B 3, Sponsors, Endorse, Series 434, RNln; RN to McCall, Apr 12, PE389, and *Labor Herald,* Apr 13, 1948, PPS205.S8, RNyl.

29. Muffler to RN, Apr 2, B 3, Sponsors, Endorse, Bagnall to RN, Apr 10, RN to Bagnall, Apr 21, 1948, B 3, Workers, Series 434, RNln.

30. Clark to RN, Apr 12, 1948, B 3, Sponsors, Endorse, Series 434, RNln.

31. *Labor Herald,* May 4, PPS205.S20, *San Francisco Chronicle,* May 5, PPS205.459.2, *Eagle,* May 6, PPS205.S25, *Daily Trojan,* May 10, PPS205.S29, *LA Daily News,* May 20, 1948, PPS205.548.2, RNyl; RN to McCall, Apr 21, B 1, Manager, RN to Jorgensen, Apr 23, B 1, Finance Committee, RN to Bewley, Apr 23, 1948, B 3, Workers, Series 434, RNln.

32. *Monrovia News-Post,* May 7, PPS205.S28, *Alhambra Post-Advocate,* May 10, PPS205.S32, *Newsweek,* May 10, PPS205.S29, *Arcadia Tribune,* May 13, PPS205.S33, *San Marino Tribune,* May 13, PPS205.623.1, *Alert,* May 14, 1948, PPS205.3228, RNyl.

33. McCall to Arnold, May 14, PPS299.16(1948).2, press release, May 28, 1948, PPS205.3032, RNyl.

34. RN to Jorgensen, May 3, RN to Kruse, May 6, RN to Day, May 8, B 1, Finance Committee, RN to Bell, May 3, Goodsen to RN, May 8, 1948, B 3, Workers, Series 434, RNln; Arnold to Klein, May 12, 1948, PPS205.499, and RN radio broadcast, May 11, 1948, MC Record #11, RNyl.

35. *Pomona Progress-Bulletin,* May 12, PPS 205.S37, *Monterey Park Progress,* May 13, PPS205.S22, *San Gabriel Sun,* May 20, PPS205.S48, *San Marino Tribune,* May 20, PPS205.623.3, May 27, 1948, PPS205.623.5, RNyl; Corey to RN, May 20, B 3, Sponsors, Endorse, Marshall to McCall, May 11, 1948, B 2, Publicity—Newspapers, Series 434, RNln.

36. Kruse to RN, May 4, Day to RN, May 5, RN to Day, May 8, B 1, Finance Committee, Bewley to RN, May 3, RN to De La Vergne, May 10, and Hillings to RN, May 10, B 3, Workers, Telegram, May 5, press release, May 11, 1948, B 1, Opposition, Series 434, RNln; *South Pasadena Review,* May 7, 1948, RNyl; *LA Times,* May 12, 1948; for Zetterberg's views, see Zetterberg to author, May 20, 1998, Gellman mss.

37. Bewley to RN, May 8, 1948, B 3, Workers, Series 434, RNln; *Arcadia Tribune,* May 12, PPS205.S36, *Rosemead Review,* May 13, 1948, PPS.205.S34; RNyl; *LA Times,* May 12, 1948.

38. Day to RN, May 13, Bowen to RN, May 13, B 1, Finance Committee, Bowen to RN, May 13, 1948, B 2, Publicity—Corres, Series 434, RNln; Bowen to RN, May 13, PE404, McDonald to RN, May 13, 1948, PPS205.491.1, RNyl.

39. Arnold to McCall, May 15, B 1, Manager, RN to Day, May 17, 1948, B 1, Finance Committee, Series 434, RNln; RN to Perry, May 17, 1948, PE406, RNyl.

40. *Covina Argus Citizen,* May 21, PPS205.S55, *Pomona Progress-Bulletin,* May 22, PPS205.S56, *Whittier News,* May 24, 1948, PPS205.S59, RNyl; *LA Times,* May 23, 1948.

41. *San Marino Tribune,* May 13, PPS205.623.1, *Pomona Progress-Bulletin,* May 24, PPS205.S59, *Whittier News,* May 24, PPS205.S59, RN to Hanson, May 25, PPS205.552, *Arcadia Tribune,* May 27, 1948, PPS205.S64, RNyl; RN to Cleveland, June 14, 1948, B 3, Thank you, Series 434, RNln; *LA Times,* May 23 and 24, 1948.

42. RN to Sherwood, May 25 and July 6, B 691, Sherwood, G, RN to Williams, June 2, 1948, B 821, Williams, RC, Series 320, RNln; RN to Hanson, May 25, 1948, PPS205.552, RNyl.

43. *Pomona Progress-Bulletin,* May 26, PPS205.S60, *Azusa Herald,* May 27, PPS205.S64, *Alhambra Post-Advocate,* May 31, PPS205.S70, *Herald,* May 31?,

PPS205.S71, *South Pasadena Review,* June 1, PPS205.S73, Official CIO, before June 1, 1948, PPS205.563, RNyl; *Monterey Park Progress,* May 27, 1948, B 2, Publicity—Newspapers, Series 434, RNln; Zetterberg Oral History (Claremont), 17–19.

44. *LA Times,* Nov 9, 1972.
45. The Nixon Poll, May 28, 1948, PPS205.3032, RNyl.
46. McCall to RN, May 12, Bowen to RN, May 24 and 25, B 2, Publicity—Radio, RN to Blue, May 25, 1948, B 3, Sponsors, Democratic, Series 434, RNln; *Whittier News,* May 31, 1948, PPS205.S71, RNyl.
47. *LA Times,* June 4, 1948, PPS205.S79, RNyl; Blue to RN, June 3, RN to Owen, June 14, B 1, F 1, Series 207, RN to Bewley, June 5, RN to Day, June 5, RN to Blaisdell, June 12, 1948, B 3, Thank you, Series 434, RNln.
48. *Monrovia News-Post,* June 21, 1948, PPS205.S84, RNyl; Jorgensen to RN, June 2, Lutz to RN, June 7, RN to Lutz, June 12, *Arcadia Tribune,* June 24, RN to Lutz, July 21, B 1, Finance Committee, RN to Perry, June 29, B 3, Workers, McCall to RN, July 30, 1948, B 1, Manager, Series 434, RNln.
49. *Monrovia News-Post,* Nov?, PPS205.S163, *Alhambra Post-Advocate,* Nov 3, 1948, RNyl; Congressional Districts, Nov 2, 1948, B 1, Misc, Series 434, RNln; *Congressional Quarterly's Guide to U.S. Elections,* 2nd ed. (Washington, D.C.: Congressional Quarterly, 1985), 967; Candidate's Campaign Statement of Receipts and Expenditures, Richard M. Nixon, Nov 2, 1948, California State Archives.
50. RN to Chotiner, June 15, 1948, B 3, Thank you, Series 434, RNln; see Sam Tannenhaus, *Whittaker Chambers: A Biography* (NY: Random House, 1997), 287, for his reason why Nixon won the 1948 election; Ambrose, *Nixon,* I, 164; Jonathan Aitken, *Nixon: A Life* (Washington, D.C.: Regnery, 1993), 148; Morris, *Nixon,* 371 and 379–381.
51. Zetterberg to author, May 20, 1998, Gellman mss.
52. *LA Times,* Nov 9, 1972; Zetterberg Oral History (California), 48; Zetterberg Oral History (Claremont), 36; Frank Mankiewicz, *Perfectly Clear: Nixon from Whittier to Watergate* (NY: Quadrangle, 1973), 45–46.

Chapter 9

1. RN to Bowen, Apr 9, 1947, B 1, Correspondence 1947, Series 434, RNln.
2. RN to Smith, Jan 8, 1947, B 1, Correspondence 1947, Series 434, RNln; Stassen to RN, Nov 11, PPS1.354, Boggio to RN, Nov 16, 1946, PPS1.243, RN to Mac, July 29, MC39, RN to Perry, Aug 24, 1947, PE306, RNyl.
3. Stassen to RN, Oct 11, 1947, B 1, Presidential, Series 434, RNln.
4. Palmer to Mac, July 23, MC36, Mac to RN, Aug 5, MC24, Carver to Perry, Aug 1947, PE309, RNyl.
5. Bowen to RN, Mar 31, B 1, Correspondence 1947, Warren to RN, Nov 26, RN to Blaisdell, Dec 9, B 1, Presidential, Series 434, RN to Lowell, June 16, 1947, B 463, Lowell, E, Series 320, RNln.
6. RN to Colliau, Jan 12, 1948, B 3, Workers, Series 434, RNln; RN to Savage, Jan 12, 1948, PPS205.63, RNyl.
7. Day to RN, Feb 18 and 26, B 1, Finance Committee, Cooper to RN, Mar 14, 1948, B 2, Republican Central Committee, LA, Series 434, RNln.
8. Day to RN, Dec 5, RN to Day, Dec 17, 1947, Day to RN, Mar 20, 1948, B 1,

Finance Committee, RN to Faries, Feb 27, 1948, B 2, Republican Convention, Series 434, RNln.

9. Day to RN, Mar 20, RN to Day, Mar 23, 1948, B 1, Finance Committee, Series 434, RNln.

10. Williamson to RN, Apr 14, B 2, Republican Convention, RN to Day, Apr 21, B 1, Finance Committee, Faries to RN, May 3, 1948, B 2, Republican Convention, Series 434, RNln.

11. RN to Lowell, Jan 27, 1948, B 3, Workers, Series 434, RNln.

12. Day to RN, Mar 27, 1948, B 1, Finance Committee, Series 434, RNln; McCarthy to Dear Folks, Mar 31, 1948, RNyl.

13. RN to Latham, Apr 21, RN to Bewley, Apr 23, B 3, Workers, RN to Day, Apr 21, B 1, Finance Committee, Series 434, RN to Friend, Apr 28, 1948, B 269, Form Letters, Series 320, RNln; Kirby, "Childe Harold's Pilgrimage," 31–38 and 100–163; Robert Smith, *Thomas D. Dewey and His Time* (NY: Simon & Schuster, 1982), 485–488.

14. RN to Noid, Apr 5, 1948, B 3, Workers, Series 434, RNln; RN to Friend, Apr 28, 1948, PE397, RNyl.

15. De La Vergne to RN, Feb 5, 1948, B 3, Workers, Series 434, RNln; Walton, *Wallace, Harry Truman, and the Cold War,* 118–204.

16. Ferrell, ed., *Ayers Diary,* 248.

17. *LA Times,* May 4, PPS205.S20, *Milwaukee Sentinel,* May 5, 1948, PPS205.S21, RNyl; RN to McCall, May 7, 1948, B 1, Manager, Series 434, RNln.

18. Mundt to Dewey, Apr 29, 1948, R 122, Mundt mss.

19. RN to Stassen, May 3, RN to Schemel, May 12, B 1, Presidential, RN to Day, May 8, 1948, B 1, Finance Committee, Series 434, RNln; RN to Stassen, May 3, 1948, PPS205.457A, RNyl.

20. *Pomona Progress-Bulletin,* May 18, 1948, PPS205.S44, RNyl; Kirby, "Childe Harold's Pilgrimage,"196–222; Smith, *Dewey,* 489–494.

21. RN to Dulles, May 17, PPS205.530, *South Pasadena Review,* May 21, 1948, PPS205.S54, RNyl.

22. *Arcadia Tribune,* May 28, 1948, PPS205.S64, RNyl; Lindley to RN, May 29, RN to Pike, May 31, 1948, B 1, Presidential, Series 434, RNln.

23. RN to Runge, June 1, PPS205.572, RN to Spencer, June 18, SP27, RN to Baker, July 2, 1948, PPS205.634, RNyl.

24. Feldman to Mundt, June 2, 1948, R 180, Mundt mss; *Commonweal,* June 25, PPS205.623.2(2), and July 9, 1948, PPS205.638.2(3), RNyl.

25. RN to Brecker, June 2, PPS205.574, "Washington Report," June 10, PPS208(1948).30.2, RN to McCall, June 11, PE413, *Congressional Record,* June 19, PPS208(1948).32, RN to Simon, June 29, 1948, PPS205.631, RNyl; RN to Blue, June 11, B 3, Thank you, Series 434, RN to Harger, B 319, Harger, RN to Perry, June 19, B 553, Navy Friends, Series 320, RN to Buck, July 1, 1948, B 1, F 1, Series 207, RNln.

26. *Monrovia News-Post,* July 13, 1948, PPS205.S90, RNyl.

27. Reece to Perry, Feb 9, PE368, McCall to Faries, Feb 18, PE372, Spencer to RN, Apr 2, 1948, SP25, RNyl.

28. *LA Times,* June 18, 19, 20, and 21, 1948; *Pomona Progress-Bulletin,* June 16, 18, and 21, 1948.

29. *Pomona Progress-Bulletin,* June 16, 17, 18, and 21, 1948.

30. *Ibid.,* June 19, 1948.

31. RN to Harger, June 18, B 319, Harger, Series 320, RN to Kennedy, June 17, 1948, B 3, Thank you, Series 434, RNln; Day to RN, Aug 21, 1948, PPS205.739.1, RNyl; *LA Times,* June 21, 22, 23, 24, 25, 26, and 27, 1948; *Pomona Progress-Bulletin,* June 21, 22, 23, and 24, 1948; Smith, *Dewey,* 494–501; Robert Divine, *Foreign Policy and U.S. Presidential Elections 1940–1948,* (NY: New Viewpoints, 1974), 213–214.

32. RN to Blaisdell, June 29, B 2, Republican Convention, RN to Conner, June 29, 1948, B 3, Thank you, Series 434, RNln; *Monrovia News-Post,* June 22, PPS205.S84 and June 24, 1948, PPS205.S85, RNyl; *Pomona Progress-Bulletin,* June 23, 1948.

33. RN to Soeberg, June 28, B 712, Soeberg, RN to Sherwood, July 6, B 691, Sherwood, G, RN to Smith, July 6, B 708, Smith (1 of 2), Series 320, RN to Blaisell, June 29, B 2, Republican Convention, RN to Conner, June 29, B 3, Thank you, Warren to RN, Aug 10, 1948, B 1, Presidential, Series 434, RNln; Katcher, *Warren,* 206–228: Tyler Abell, ed., *Drew Pearson Diaries 1949–1959* (NY: Holt, Rinehart & Winston, 1974), 23.

34. RN to Perry, June 29, B 3, Workers, RN to Pike, June 29, B 2, Republican Convention, Series 434, RN to Smith, July 6, 1948, B 708, Smith (1 of 2), Series 320, RNln; Perry to RN, Aug 6, 1948, PE422, RNyl; Arnold, *Back When It All Began,* 34.

35. RN to Johnson, July 6, PPS205.637 and *Pomona Progress-Bulletin,* July 6, 1948, PPS205.S88, RNyl; Eisenhower, *Pat Nixon,* 98.

36. RN to Jorgensen, July 21, 1948, B 1, Finance Committee, Series 434, RNln; Eisenhower, *Pat Nixon,* 98.

37. Alonzo Hamby, *Man of the People: A Life of Harry S. Truman* (NY: Oxford Univ. Press, 1995), 448–451; Hartmann, *Truman and the 80th Congress,* 192–193; Donovan, *Conflict and Crisis,* 403–408.

38. RN to Bell, June 14, PPS205.614, RN to Briggs, July 2, 1948, PPS205.635, RNyl; RN to Sherwood, June 11, B 3, Thank you, RN to Blaisdell, June 27, B 2, Republican Convention, RN to Kruse, July 14, B 1, Finance Committee, RN to Gregg, July 15, B 1, Contributors—Financial, Series 434, RN to Sherwood, July 6, 1948, B 691, Sherwood, G, Series 320, RNln.

39. RN to Avedon, Jan 19, B 2, Republican Policy, RN to Jorgensen, Mar 29, B 1, Finance Committee, RN to Latham, June 14, B 3, Thank you, RN to Blaisdell, July 9, B 2, Republican Central Committee, LA, RN to Jorgensen, July 21, B 1, Finance Committee, Series 434, RN to Patch, Apr 21, B 580, Patch, R, RN to Welch, June 18, B 3, Internal Revenue, RN to Eddy, July 21, 1948, B 235, Eddy, AC, Series 320, RNln.

40. RN to Jorgensen, July 21, 1948, B 1, Finance Committee, Series 434, RNln; Hartmann, *Truman and the 80th Congress,* 194–197; Donovan, *Conflict and Crisis,* 410–412; Hamby, *Man of the People,* 452–453.

41. Newspaper clipping, July 28, PPS205.717.2, "Washington Report," Aug 5, 1948, PPS208(1948).34, RNyl.

42. *San Dimas Press,* July 29, PPS205.S96, *Claremont Courier,* July 30, 1948, PPS266.46, RNyl; Carr, *House Committee,* 87.

43. *Pasadena Star News,* July 17, PPS205.669, RN to Blair, July 29, PPS205.679.1, *Claremont Courier,* July 30, 1948, PPS266.46, RNyl.

44. Thomas to Mundt, July 26, and Mundt to Thomas, July 27, 1948, R 122, Mundt mss.

45. *NY Journal American,* late July, RN speech, Sept–Oct, PPS208(1948).36, RN speech, Oct 20, 1948, PPS208(1948).37,TH Sv:15:36, Thomas, "Russian Spies in America" and "The Price of Vision," TH, B1, RNyl; Elizabeth Bentley, *Out of Bondage* (NY: Devin-Adair, 1951), 287–308; Goodman, *The Committee,* 244–246; Stripling, *Red Plot,* 89–94; Carr, *House Committee,* 86–88; Rick Ball and NBC News, *Meet the Press: 50 Years of History in the Making* (NY: McGraw-Hill, 1998), 15–17.

46. *NY Sun,* July 28, 1948, TH Sv:15:16, RNyl.

47. House of Representatives, Committee on Un-American Activities, 80th Cong, 2nd Sess, *Hearings Regarding Communist Espionage in the United States Government* (Washington, D.C.: GPO, 1948), 501–521; RN to Dulles, Sept 7, 1948, PPS205.805, Thomas, "Russian Spies in America," TH, B 1, RNyl; Bentley, *Out of Bondage,* 309.

48. *Hearings Regarding Communist Espionage in the United States Government,* 521–562; Gary May, *Un-American Activities: The Trials of William Remington* (NY: Oxford Univ. Press, 1994), *passim; NY Times,* Aug 2, 1948.

49. *NY Daily Mirror,* Aug 2, 1948, TH Sv:15:20, RNyl.


*Chapter 10*

1. *NY Daily Mirror,* Aug 3, 1948, TH Sv:15:22, RNyl; *NY Times,* Aug 1 and 2, 1948; Hartmann, *Truman and the 80th Congress,* 198–203.

2. *NY Times,* Aug 2 and 3, 1948; Tanenhaus, *Chambers,* 3–56; Levine, "The Inside Story of Our Soviet Underworld," Aug 1948, PPS205.781, RNyl; *NY Times,* Aug 4, 1948; Berle, ed. *Navigating the Rapids,* 249–250 and 598–599.

3. Robert Herzstein, *Henry R. Luce: A Political Portrait of the Man Who Created the American Century* (NY: Scribners, 1994), 346–358; Tanenhaus, *Chambers,* 57–199.

4. HUAC, *Hearings Regarding Communist Espionage in the United States Government,* 563; *NY Times,* Aug 3, 1948; Whittaker Chambers, *Witness* (NY: Random House, 1952), 529–532 and 536–537.

5. RN radio broadcast, undated, B 610, Press Releases(2 of 2), Series 320, RNln; *Bergen Evening Record,* Aug 8, 1948, TH Sv:15:21, Thomas, "Russian Spies in America," TH, B 1, RNyl; RN, *Six Crises,* 2; Chambers, *Witness,* 538; Tanenhaus, *Chambers,* 216–222; F. Edward Hébert, *"Last of the Titans": The Life and Times of Congressman F. Edward Hébert of Louisiana* (La.: Univ. of Southwestern La., 1976), 279; Stripling, *Red Plot,* 95–98.

6. Memorandum on the Hiss-Chambers Case, Sept 7, 1948, PPS205.3065, RNyl; HUAC, *Hearings Regarding Communist Espionage in the United States Government,* 564–579; Chambers, *Witness,* 539–540; RN, *Six Crises,* 2–3.

7. HUAC, *Hearings Regarding Communist Espionage in the United States Government,* 580–582; Stripling, *Red Plot,* 97–105; *House Committee,* 115.

8. *NY Daily Mirror,* Aug 4, TH Sv:16:7, *Washington Daily News,* Aug 4, 1948, PPS205.S96, RNyl; *NY Times,* Aug 4, 1948.

9. Mundt to JD, Aug 3, 1948, R 180, Mundt mss.

10. Donald Hiss to Mundt, Aug 3, 1948, PPS205.685.2, RNyl.

11. HUAC, *Hearings Regarding Communist Espionage in the United States Government,* 585–586; Alger Hiss, *In the Court of Public Opinion* (NY: Knopf, 1957), 3–6.

12. HUAC, *Hearings Regarding Communist Espionage in the United States Government,*

587–622; *NY Daily Mirror,* Aug 3, 1948, TH Sv:15:23, RNyl; Stripling, *Red Plot,* 104–105; Goodman, *The Committee,* 250.

13. Alger Hiss to Keating, Apr 8, 1953, Series 1, B 4, F 48, Keating mss; HUAC, *Hearings Regarding Communist Espionage in the United States Government,* 642–644; Nixon, *Six Crises,* 5–6; Hiss, *In the Court,* 7– 14.

14. RN to JF Dulles, Sept 7, 1948, PPS205.804, RNyl; HUAC, *Hearings Regarding Communist Espionage in the United States Government,* 644; Stripling, *Red Plot,* 110–113 and 115–116.

15. Chambers, *Witness,* 553; Nixon, *Six Crises,* 7; Stripling, *Red Plot,* 113–114.

16. HUAC, *Hearings Regarding Communist Espionage in the United States Government,* 646–659; Alger Hiss, *Recollections of a Life* (NY: Seaver Books, 1988), 202–203; Nixon, *Six Crises,* 9.

17. Memo on the Hiss-Chambers Case, Sept 7, PPS205.3065, RN to JF Dulles, Sept 7, PPS205.804, RN speech, Sept 17, 1948, PPS208(1948).35, RNyl; *NY Times,* Aug 6, 1948; William Buckley, Jr., ed., *Odyssey of a Friend: Whittaker Chambers' Letters to William F. Buckley, Jr. 1954–1961* (NY: Putnam, 1969), 19–20; obituary of Spargo, *Washington Post,* Sept 30, 1991.

18. *NY Herald Tribune,* Aug 22, PPS205.S107, memorandum on the Hiss-Chambers Case, Sept 7, PPS025.3065, RN speech, Sept 17, 1948, PPS208(1948).35, memorandum of the Hiss-Chambers Case by RN, Feb 1, 1949, PPS205.3079, RNyl; HUAC, *Hearings Regarding Communist Espionage in the United States Government,* 659; Buckley, *Odyssey,* 20; Stripling, *Red Plot,* 116.

19. Bernstein and Matusow, eds., *The Truman Administration,* 385–386; clipping, Aug 5, PPS205.684, *NY Sun,* Aug 5, 1948, TN Sv:15:28, RNyl; *NY Times,* Aug 6, 1948.

20. HUAC, Aug 6, PPS205.3130, clipping, Aug 7, 1948, PPS205.S96, RNyl; Hébert, *"Last of the Titans,"* 285–286 and 289; Nixon, *Six Crises,* 9 and 15; Buckley, ed., *Odyssey,* 21.

21. "Seeds of Treason," Nov 1, 1950, audio recordings, B 1, RNln; HUAC, *Hearings Regarding Communist Espionage in the United States Government,* 661–672; *NY Herald Tribune,* June 4, 1952; Nixon, *Six Crises,* 15–18.

22. Memorandum on the Hiss-Chambers Case, Sept 7, PPS205.3065, RN to Dulles, Sept 7, 1948, PPS205.804, RNyl; "Seeds of Treason," Nov 1, 1950, audio recordings, B 1, RNln; HUAC, *Hearings Regarding Communist Espionage in the United States Government,* 671–672; Hébert, *"Last of the Titans,"* 286–288.

23. *NY Daily Mirror,* Aug 4, TH Sv.16:4, *Ridgewood Sunday News,* Aug 7, TH Sv:15:18, *Washington Post,* Aug 7, 1948, TH Sv.16:9, RNyl.

24. Mundt to Lovre, Aug 7, 1948, R 180, Mundt mss.; Stanley Kutler, ed., *Abuse of Power: The New Nixon Tapes* (NY: Free Press, 1997), 7; Stripling, *Red Plot,* 140.

25. RN to Mundt, May 10, 1949, PPS205.1320, RNyl; Kutler, ed., *Abuse of Power,* 261.

26. MP 76–78, fall 1953, motion picture archives, Truman mss.; Kutler, ed., *Abuse of Power,* 138.

27. *Washington Post,* Aug 8, 1948.

28. Memo to Stripling, Aug 9, 1948, PPS205.693, RNyl.

29. *Washington Post,* Aug 10, TH Sv:16:10, *Bergen Evening Record,* Aug 11, 1948, TH Sv:15:30, RNyl; HUAC, *Hearings Regarding Communist Espionage in the United States Government,* 715–800; Hébert, *"Last of the Titans,"* 290.

30. Mundt to Jung, Aug 10, 1948, Correspondence File, Robert E. Woods ms, Hoover mss; Mundt to Zech, Aug 10, 1948, R 122, Mundt mss.

31. *Rochester Times-Union,* Jan 9, *Washington Post,* Oct 24, 1957, Rogers, 1953–1959(3 of 3), transcript of Kornitzer, Mar 27, 1959, memo from Woods, June 14, Rogers 1960(2 of 2), *Boston Globe,* Aug 14–19 and 23–25, 1960, B 653, Rogers, 1960(1 of 2), Series 320, RNln; Smith, *Dewey,* 245.

32. *Rochester Times-Union,* Jan 9, 1957, Rogers, 1953–1959(3 of 3), transcript of Kornitzer, May 27, 1959, B 653, Rogers, 1960(1 of 2), Series 320, RNln; Nixon, *Six Crises,* 20.

33. RN Oral History, 1, PPS208(1965).March 5, John Foster Dulles mss, Princeton Univ., RNyl; Nixon, *Six Crises,* 20–21.

34. HUAC, *Hearings Regarding Communist Espionage in the United States Government,* 802–816; RN to Dulles, Sept 7, 1948, PPS205.805, RNyl; Nixon, *Six Crises,* 21; *NY Times,* Aug 12, 1948.

35. *NY Herald Tribune,* June 2 and 1, 1952. Andrews wrote a series of five columns based on the notes that he took in August through December 1948.

36. *Ibid.;* Richard Kluger, *The Paper: The Life and Death of the New York Herald Tribune* (NY: Knopf, 1986), 406–408; Nixon, *Six Crises,* 20; Bert Andrews and Peter Andrews, *A Tragedy of History: A Journalist's Confidential Role in the Hiss-Chambers Case* (Washington, D.C.: Luce, 1962), 72 and 227–228.

37. RN to Kersten, Aug 30, 1948, Mazo to Kersten, June 22, Kersten to RN, June 11 [should read July 11], Kersten to Mazo, July 11, 1958, Richard Nixon file, Charles Kersten mss, Special Collections/University Archives, Marquette Univ, Milwaukee, Wisconsion; JF Dulles to RN, Nov 13, 1950, PPS4.677, memorandum regarding Alger Hiss and JF Dulles relationship through Carnegie Endowment, Aug 13, 1952, PPS205.2898.2, Richard Nixon Oral History, 2–5, PPS208(1965).March 5, 1965, RNyl; Richard Nixon, "Unforgettable John Foster Dulles," *Reader's Digest* (July 1967), 100; Richard Challener, "New Light on a Turning Point in U.S. History," *University: A Princeton Quarterly* 56 (Spring 1973), 30; Nixon, *Six Crises,* 21; Grose, *Gentleman Spy,* 297–298; Ronald Prussen, *John Foster Dulles: The Road to Power* (NY: Free Press, 1982), 372–373.

38. Memorandum regarding Alger Hiss and JF Dulles relationship through Carnegie Endowment, Aug 13, 1952, PSS205.2898.2, RNyl; Challener, "New Light on a Turning Point," 2, 3, 28, 29, 30, and 33; Kohlberg to Mundt, June 4, Kohlberg to Gentlemen, Sept 22, 1948, R 122, Mundt mss; Prussen, *Dulles,* 368–372.

39. *NY Times,* Aug 13, 1948.

40. Memorandum on the Hiss-Chambers Case, Sept 7, PPS205.3065, RN speech, Sept 17, 1948, PPS208(1948).35, RN to Andrews, May 15, 1952, PPS205. 2864.1, RNyl; Nixon, *Six Crises,* 21–23; Andrews and Andrews, *Tragedy of History,* 62–63.

41. Hiss to Thomas, Aug 13, PPS205.706, Keeler to RN, Aug 14, 1948, PPS205.710, "I Cannot Tell a Lie!", PPS205.716, RNyl.

42. Memos on Hiss, Aug 13, 1948, PPS205.708.1 and PPS205.707.3, memo to RN, undated, PPS205.780.2, Electric Service, undated, PPS205.780.3, city directories and credit bureau information, undated, PPS205.780.4, RNyl.

43. HUAC, *Hearings Regarding Communist Espionage in the United States Government,* 851–877.

44. *Ibid.,* 878–906.

45. *Ibid.,* 912–933; *NY Times,* Aug 14, 1948, TH Sv:15:32, RNyl.

46. Nixon, *Six Crises,* 23.

47. Memorandum on the Hiss-Chambers Case, Sept 8, 1948, PPS205.3065, RN to Andrews, May 15, 1952, PPS205.2864.1, RNyl; radio transcript with Andrews and RN, Jan 21, 1950, Pegler mss; *NY Herald Tribune,* June 2, 1952; Andrews and Andrews, *Tragedy of History,* 72– 77.

48. *NY Herald Tribune,* June 3, 1952.

49. *Ibid.,* June 4, 1952.

50. HUAC, *Hearings Regarding Communist Espionage in the United States Government,* 935–954; Hébert, *"Last of the Titans,"* 300–303; Hiss, *In the Court,* 15–16.

51. RN to JF Dulles, Sept 7, 1948, PPS205.804, memorandum of the Hiss-Chambers Case, Feb 1, 949, PPS.205.3079, RNyl; "Seeds of Treason," Nov 1, 1950, B 1, audio recordings, RNln; Nixon, *Six Crises,* 24–30; Stripling, *Red Plot,* 122–126; Andrews and Andrews, *Tragedy of History,* 78–88; HUAC, *Hearings Regarding Communist Espionage in the United States Government,* 955–974; Hiss, *In the Court,* 17–35.

52. *NY Times,* Aug 17, 1948; Andrews and Andrews, *Tragedy of History,* 78–80.

53. Nixon, *Six Crises,* 29–31; Stripling, *Red Plot,* 126.

54. RN to Chambers, Aug 17, 1948, PPS205.722, RNyl; Stripling, *Red Plot,* 126–127; Hiss, *In the Court,* 80–81.

55. Chambers, *Witness,* 599–601; Nixon, *Six Crises,* 31.

56. Memorandum on the Hiss-Chambers Case, Sept 7, 1948, PPS205.3065, RNyl; Chambers, *Witness,* 601–602; Nixon, *Six Crises,* 31.

57. HUAC, *Hearings Regarding Communist Espionage in the United States Government,* 552–977; *NY Times,* Aug 18, 1948; RN, *Six Crises,* 31–32; Hiss, *In the Court,* 81–84.

58. Memorandum on the Hiss-Chambers Case, Sept 7, 1948, PPS205.3065, RNyl; "Seeds of Treason," Nov 1, 1950, B 1, audio recordings, RNln; Stripling, *Red Plot,* 129.

59. RN to JF Dulles, Sept 7, 1948, PPS205.804, memorandum of the Hiss-Chambers Case, Feb 1, 1949, PPS205.3079, RNyl; HUAC, *Hearings Regarding Communist Espionage in the United States Government,* 978–997; *NY Times,* Aug 18 and 19, 1948; Nixon, *Six Crises,* 32–36; Chambers, *Witness,* 613–614; Hiss, *In the Court,* 85–95.

60. HUAC, *Hearings Regarding Communist Espionage in the United States Government,* 998–1001; RN, *Six Crises,* 36–37; Hiss, *In the Court,* 97–99.

61. Chambers, *Witness,* 615.

62. *NY Times,* Aug 18, 1948.

63. Memorandum on the Hiss-Chambers Case, Sept 7, 1948, PPS205.3065, RNyl.

64. *NY Herald Tribune,* August 18, 1948, PPS205.S100, Frank Conniff, "East Side, West Side," undated, PPS205.758.1, RNyl.

65. Memorandum on the Hiss-Chambers Case, Sept 7, 1948, PPS205.3065, RNyl; HUAC, *Hearings Regarding Communist Espionage in the United States Government,* 1011–1013; *NY Times,* Aug 23, 1948; Nixon, *Six Crises,* 37–39; Prussen, *Dulles,* 372; Stripling, *Red Plot,* 132–133; Hiss, *In the Court,* 100– 101.

66. *NY Times,* Aug 18, 1948; *Newark Evening News,* Aug 19, 1948, TH Sv:15:33, RNyl.

67. *Chicago Daily News,* Aug 19, 1948, PPS205.728.1, RNyl.

68. *NY Times,* Aug 18–20, 1948.
69. RN to McKesson, Aug 20, PPS205.737, RN to Caldwell, Aug 20, 1948, PPS205.735, RNyl.
70. *NY Herald Tribune,* Aug 22, 1948, PPS205.S107, RNyl.
71. *NY Times,* Aug 22, 1948; Nixon, *Six Crises,* 39–40.
72. HUAC, *Hearings Regarding Communist Espionage in the United States Government,* 1035–1042; *NY Times,* Aug 25, 1948; RN to Stripling, Sept 1, 1948, PPS205.786, RNyl.
73. HUAC, *Hearings Regarding Communist Espionage in the United States Government,* 1075; *NY Herald Tribune,* Aug 26, 1948, PPS205.S110 and RN to Parmet, Nov 17, 1988, uncatalogued, RNyl; *NY Times,* Aug 23–26, 1948; Nixon, *Six Crises,* 41; Hiss, *In the Court,* 107.
74. HUAC, *Hearings Regarding Communist Espionage in the United States Government,* 1076–1091; "U.S. Red Probe," Aug 25, 1948, RNLB:122:3, RNyl; Hiss, *In the Court,* 102–103.
75. HUAC, *Hearings Regarding Communist Espionage in the United States Government,* 1091–1117; *NY Journal American,* Aug 19, 1948, PPS205.S103, RNyl.
76. HUAC, *Hearings Regarding Communist Espionage in the United States Government,* 1118–1126; *NY Herald Tribune,* June 4, 1952.
77. HUAC, *Hearings Regarding Communist Espionage in the United States Government,* 1127–1138 and 1174– 1176; RN to Dulles, Sept 7, 1948, PPS205.804, RNyl.
78. HUAC, *Hearings Regarding Communist Espionage in the United States Government,* 1138–1141 and 1167–1169.
79. *Ibid.,* 1145–1147.
80. *Ibid.,* 1148–1160.
81. *Ibid.,* 1161–1167; HUAC, Aug 25, 1948, RNLB:70, memo by Mills, Sept 1, 1948, PPS205.788.2, RNyl; Hiss, *In the Court,* 104–149.
82. HUAC, *Hearings Regarding Communist Espionage in the United States Government,* 1176–1206; HUAC, Aug 25, RNLB:70, 122:2, and 170:1; *NY Herald Tribune,* Aug 26, 1948, PPS205.S110, RNyl.
83. Chambers, *Witness,* 694–695.
84. Hiss, *In the Court,* 149.
85. Press clipping, Aug 26, 1948, B 344, Hiss Case, Series 320, RNln; *Christian Science Monitor,* Aug 26, PPS205.S112, RN speech, Oct 20, 1948, PPS208(1948).37, RN to Lasky, June 23, 1949, PPS205.1342, RNyl.
86. *Washington Post,* Aug 30, 1948, PPS205.S117, RNyl; *NY Times,* Aug 30, 1948.
87. RN to Kersten, Aug 30, 1948, B 1, Presidential, Series 434, RNln; RN to MacKinnon, Aug 30, PPS205.769, Mills to RN, Aug 31, 1948, PPS205.770.1, RNyl.
88. Nixon presents his position in *Six Crises,* 4; Herbert Parmet and Jonathan Aitken hold that Nixon did not know Hiss: RN to Parmet, Dec 10, 1986, and Nov 17, 1988, uncatalogued, RNyl; Herbert Parmet, *Richard Nixon and His America* (NY: Konecky & Konecky, 1990), 168–169; Aitken, *Nixon,* 155 for Cronin's recantation: "The stacked deck remark was unfair. Nixon might have read something about Hiss in my reports, I don't know whether he did or not, but we didn't discuss the case until after Hiss had made his public denial. From then on I worked with Nixon a lot and gave him everything I had on Hiss. He needed that help. He was very unsure of himself at the beginning." For early

interviews with Cronin establishing that Nixon had lied, see Mazo, *Nixon,* 51; Bela Kornitzer, *The Real Nixon: An Intimate Biography* (NY: Rand McNally, 1960), 173; de Toledano, *One Man Alone,* 76; Garry Wills, *Nixon Agonistes: The Crisis of the Self-Made Man* (Boston: Houghton Mifflin, 1969), 27. For samples of Cronin's correspondence in the 1970s, see Cronin to Reuben, July 9, Cronin to de Antonio, Sept 10, and Cronin to Toren, Oct 10, 1974, CCRO 2/25, Cronin mss; for Weinstein's accusations, see Allen Weinstein, "Nixon vs. Hiss," *Esquire,* vol. 84, no. 5 (November 1975), 76; Weinstein, *Perjury,* reissued in 1997 by Random House, 7; Victor Navasky, "Weinstein, Hiss, and the Transformation of Historical Ambiguity into Cold War Verity," in Athan Theoharis, ed., *Beyond the Hiss Case: The FBI, Congress, and the Cold War* (Philadelphia: Temple Univ. Press, 1982), 215–241. For embellishments on these arguments in the 1980s and 1990s, see Brodie, *Nixon,* 201–202; Ambrose, *Nixon,* I, 171–172; Morris, *Nixon,* 391–393; and Tom Wicker, *One of Us: Richard Nixon and the American Dream* (NY: Random House, 1991), 53.

89. John Cronin, "The Problem of American Communism in 1945," Francis Matthews mss; for another copy, CCRO 1/05, Cronin to Vinnedge, May 30, and Cronin to Reuben, June 24, 1974, CCRO 2/25, Cronin mss; Irons, "America's Cold War," 179–182; Peter Irons, "American Business and the Origins of McCarthyism: The Cold War Crusade of the United Chamber of Commerce," in Robert Griffith and Athan Theoharis, eds., *The Specter: Original Essays on the Cold War and the Origins of McCarthyism* (NY: New Viewpoints, 1974), 80.

90. Cronin, "The Problem of American Communism in 1945," 16, 37, and 50, Matthews mss.

91. *Ibid.,* 50.

92. Matthews to Cronin, Jan 5, Cronin to Matthews, Jan 18 and Mar 18, 1946, and Cronin to Schmidt, Mar 1, 1947, Cronin Correspondence, Matthews mss, Cronin to RN, June 23, 1958, B 191, Cronin, JF 1957–58, Series 320, RNyl; Calendar, Apr 12, July 6 and 26, 1948, PPS212(1948).1, RN to Stripling, Sept 29, 1948, PPS205.898.1, RN to Parmet, Dec 10, 1986, uncatalogued, RNyl; Cronin to Vinnedge, May 30, and Cronin to Smith, Sept 14, 1974, CCRO 2/25, Cronin mss; Irons, "America's Cold War," 182–183; Irons, "American Business and the Origins of McCarthyism," 80–86.

## Chapter 11

1. RN to Dulles, Sept 7, 1948, PPS205.804, RNyl; Rick Ball and NBC News, *Meet the Press,* 14–15; *NY Times,* Aug 28, 1948; Chambers, *Witness,* 709–712.

2. *NY Times,* Sept 28, 1948; RN memo, Jan 12, 1949, PPS205.1285, RNyl; memo by Pearson, undated, B F155 [1 of 3], Pearson mss; Chambers, *Witness,* 721–722.

3. RN to Mundt, May 10, 1949, PPS205.1320, RNyl; Chambers, *Witness,* 723–726; Stripling, *Red Plot,* 139–140.

4. Chambers, *Witness,* 730–750 and Stripling, *Red Plot,* 141.

5. *Washington Post,* Dec 1 and 3, 1948; *Washington Daily News,* Dec 1, 1948.

6. RN to Andrews, May 7, 1952, B 43, Andrews, Bert, Series 320, RNln; *NY Herald Tribune,* June 5, 1952.

7. Stripling, *Red Plot,* 141–142; Chambers, *Witness,* 751; Nixon, *Six Crises,* 47; Athan Theoharis and John Cox, *The Boss: J. Edgar Hoover and the Great American Inquisition* (Philadelphia: Temple Univ. Press, 1988), 252.

8. RN to Kepple, Jan 25, 1949, PPS205.1293, and Andrews, "19 Minutes That 'Made' Dick Nixon," *Denver Post,* Sept 7, 1952, PPS296(1952).8B, RNyl; RN statement, Aug 21, 1953, Nadine to Dick, Apr 19, 1954, B 43, Andrews, B, Series 320, RNln; *NY Herald Tribune,* June 5, 1952; Nixon, *Six Crises,* 48; Andrews and Andrews, *Tragedy of History,* 175–176.

9. Nichols to Tolson, Dec 2, 1948, B 71, F 19, Alger Hiss mss, Harvard Law School Library, Harvard Univ, Cambridge, Massachusetts. One story that critics use to illustrate that Nixon had "set up" the "pumpkin papers" episode was the remarks of William "Fishbait" Miller, a congressional doorkeeper. He claimed that Nixon knew about the "pumpkin papers" before leaving on his cruise because of comments that Nixon made to Fishbait upon his departure from the House Office Building. This dubious conclusion can only be considered if Fishbait remained at his post between 1:00 A.M. and 3:00 A.M., when Nixon left the building. William "Fishbait" Miller as told to Frances Leighton, *Fishbait: The Memoirs of the Congressional Doorkeeper* (NJ: Prentice-Hall, 1977), 41–42.

10. RN to Jones, Sept 28, 1948, PE425, RN to Kepple, Jan 25, 1949, PPS205.1293, RNyl; Nixon, *Six Crises,* 46 and 48; Nixon, *RN,* 68; Stripling, *Red Plot,* 144–145.

11. RN to Kepple, Jan 25, 1949, PPS205.1293, RNyl; Stripling, *Red Plot,* 145; Chambers, *Witness,* 752–754.

12. Hood to the director, Mar 30, 1949, B 70, F 19, Hiss mss; Strip to Peg, May 8, 1950, Communist Infiltration, Hiss Case, 1950–1961, Pegler mss; HUAC, 80th Cong, 2nd Sess, *Hearings Regarding Communist Espionage in the United States Government,* Part Two, 1382; Stripling, *Red Plot,* 145–146; Chambers, *Witness,* 754; Andrews and Andrews, *Tragedy of History,* 176–178.

13. Andrews to RN, Dec 2, 1948, PPS205.1003, RNyl; *Washington Post,* Dec 3, 1948.

14. HUAC, *Hearings Regarding Communist Espionage in the United States Government,* Part Two, 1383–1384; Hood to the director, Mar 30, 1949, B 70, F 19, Hiss mss; Stripling to RN, Dec 3, 1948, PPS205.1007, RNyl; *NY Times,* Dec 17, 1948; Nixon, *RN,* 68; Nixon, *Six Crises,* 48; Stripling, *Red Plot,* 146–148; Andrews and Andrews, *Tragedy of History,* 178.

15. Mundt press release, Dec 3, 1948, PPS205.1006, RNyl; *Washington Post,* Dec 4, 1948; Andrews and Andrews, *Tragedy of History,* 178.

16. *Washington Times Herald,* Dec 3, PPS205.S178, and *NY Herald Tribune,* Dec 3, PPS205.S177, *Washington Evening Star,* Dec 3, 1948, PPS205.S177, RNyl; Andrews and Andrews, *Tragedy of History,* 178 and 183; Chambers, *Witness,* 754–755.

17. Chambers, *Witness,* 755–758; RN to Mundt, May 10, 1949, PPS205.1320, RNyl.

18. *NY Times,* Dec 4, 1948; *Washington Post,* Dec 4, 1948, PPS205.S179, RNyl.

19. Hood to the director, Mar 30, 1949, B 70, F 19, Hiss mss; *NY Times,* Dec 4 and 5, 1948; Andrews and Andrews, *Tragedy of History,* 183–184.

20. Andrews to RN, Dec 4, 1948, PPS205.1008, RNyl; *NY Herald Tribune,* June 5, 1952.

21. Arnold to RN, Dec 4, PPS205.1009.1 and PPS205.1010, and Thomas to RN, Dec 4, 1948, PPS205.1015, RNyl.

22. RN to Arnold, Dec 4, 1948, PPS205.1012, PPS205.1013, and PPS205.1014, RNyl; RN to Gerhart, Jan 31, 1949, B 286, Gerhart, Series 320, RNln; *NY Times,* Dec 6, 1948; Nixon, *Six Crises,* 49; Nixon, *RN,* 68.

23. Chambers, *Witness,* 758–759; *NY Times,* Dec 11, 1948.

24. *NY Times,* Dec 6, 1948; *Washington Post,* Dec 7, 1948; Nixon, *Six Crises,* 51–52; Stripling, *Red Plot,* 148.

25. Hood to the director, Mar 30, 1949, B 70, F 19, Hiss mss; RN to Andrews, May 15, 1952, PPS205.2864.1, Andrews, "19 Minutes," PPS296(1952).8B, RNyl; *NY Herald Tribune,* June 5, 1952; Andrews and Andrews, *Tragedy of History,* 188; Stripling, *Red Plot,* 148; Chambers, *Witness,* 761–765.

26. Hood to the director, Mar 30, 1949, B 70, F 19, Hiss mss; Andrews, "19 Minutes," PPS296(1952).8B, RNyl; Andrews and Andrews, *Tragedy of History,* 188; Chambers, *Witness,* 768; Stripling, *Red Plot,* 149; Nixon, *Six Crises,* 54–55.

27. Andrews, "19 Minutes," PPS296(1952).8B, RNyl; Nixon, *Six Crises,* 55; Stripling, *Red Plot,* 149–150.

28. Hood to the director, Mar 30, 1949, B 70, F 19, Hiss mss; Stripling, *Red Plot,* 150; Nixon, *Six Crises,* 55; Chambers, *Witness,* 770; Andrews, "19 Minutes," PPS296(1952).8B, RNyl.

29. Hood to the director, Mar 30, 1949, B 70, F 19, Hiss mss; *NY Times,* Dec 7, 1948; *Washington Post,* Dec 7, PPS205.S194; *NY Post,* Dec 7, PPS205.S197, and *NY Herald Tribune,* Dec 7, 1948, PPS205.S202, RNyl; *NY Times,* Dec 8, 1948; Nixon, *Six Crises,* 56–57; Stripling, *Red Plot,* 150; Chambers, *Witness,* 771–772.

30. HUAC executive session, Dec 6, PPS205.3203; *NY Journal American,* Dec 7, PPS205.S203 and *NY Post,* Dec 7, 1948, PPS205.S197, RNyl; Chambers, *Witness,* 772–773; Nixon, *Six Crises,* 56–57; Stripling, *Red Plot,* 151–153.

31. *NY Times,* Dec 8, 1948; Chambers, *Witness,* 775.

32. HUAC executive session, Dec 7, 1948, PPS205.3207; *Washington Star,* Dec 8, 1948, PPS205.S207, RNyl; *Washington Post,* Dec 8, 1948; HUAC, *Hearings Regarding Communist Espionage in the United States Government,* Part Two, 1379–1397; *NY Times,* Dec 8, 1948.

33. *Washington Star,* Dec 8, 1948, PPS205.S206; RN memo, Jan 13, PPS205.1287, RN memo, Jan 19, PPS205.1289, and memo on the Hiss-Chambers Case, Feb 1, 1949 PPS205.3079, RN to Parmet, Dec 10, 1986, and Nov 17, 1988, uncatalogued, RNyl; memo by RN?, Jan 12, 1952, B 191, Cronin, 1956 (2/2), Series 320, RNln; *Washington Post,* Dec 9, 1948; Ralph de Toledano, *Notes from the Underground: the Whittaker Chambers–Ralph de Toledano Letters: 1949–1960* (Washington, D.C.: Regnery, 1997), 61; Nixon, *RN,* 58.

34. Cronin to RN, Jan 21, and Cronin to McCarran, Jan 21, 1953, and Cronin to RN, undated 1956, B 191, Cronin, JF 1956 2/2, Series 320, RNln; Cronin to Vinnedge, May 30, Cronin to Reuben, July 9, and Cronin to Smith, Sept 14, 1974, CCRO 2/25, Cronin mss; RN to Parmet, Dec 10, 1986, and Nov 17, 1988, uncatalogued, RNyl; Nixon, *Six Crises,* 58.

35. Nichols to Tolson, Feb 18, 1948, 100–149, 163–69, Benjamin Davis File, FBI; RN to Bell, May 3, 1948, B 3, Workers, Series 434, RNln; *The Community Press,* Jan 2, 1953, TH Sv.17:15, RNyl; Kutler, ed., *Abuse of Power,* 9 and 216.

36. Ladd to the director, Dec 8, the director to the attorney general, Dec 8, 1948, B 71, F 19, Hiss mss.

37. *Ibid.;* Whitson to Fletcher, Dec 9, Ladd to the director, Dec 9, 1948.

38. Campbell to Mundt, Dec 8, 1948, PPS205.1114.1, RNyl.

39. *NY Times,* Dec 9, 1948; Keay to Ladd, Dec 13, 1948, B 71, F 19, Hiss mss.

40. HUAC, *Hearing Regarding Communist Espionage in the United States Government,* Part Two, 1399–1428; *People's World,* Dec 9, 1948, PPS205.S211; *Washington Post,* Dec 9, 1948, PPS205.S211, RNyl; *NY Times,* Dec 9 and 10, 1948; Isaac Don Levine, *Eyewitness to History: Memoirs and Reflections of a Foreign Correspondent for Half a Century* (NY: Hawthorn Books, 1973), 179–181 and 189–200.

41. *Washington Post,* Dec 10, 1948, PPS205.S219, RNyl; *NY Times,* Dec 10, 1948; Andrews and Andrews, *Tragedy of History,* 193–194; Nixon, *Six Crises,* 59.

42. HUAC, *Hearings Regarding Communist Espionage in the United States Government,* Part Two, 1461.

43. *Ibid.,* 1463; Mundt to Hasche, Dec 11, 1948, R 123, Mundt mss.

44. Mundt to Hasche, Dec 11 and Mundt to Tostlebe, Dec 11, 1948, R 123, Mundt mss.

45. Ladd to the director, Dec 13, 1948, Hood to the director, Mar 30, 1949, B 71, F 19, Hiss mss; *NY Times,* Dec 14, 1948.

46. News clipping, Dec 14, 1948, PPS205.1240.4, RNyl; Ladd to the director, Dec 13, 1948, Hood to the director, Mar 30, 1949, B 71, F 19, Hiss mss; memo to FBI director, Dec 13, memo to FBI director, Dec 14, attorney general to FBI director, Dec 14, 1948, Chambers et al. 1948 (Folder 1), Weinstein mss, Harry Truman Library, Independence Missouri; *Seattle Post-Intelligencer,* Apr 16, 1962, B 344, Hiss Case, Series 320, RNln; *NY Times,* Dec 14, 1948; *Washington Post,* Dec 14, 1948; Andrews and Andrews, *Tragedy of History,* 199; Nixon, *Six Crises,* 60.

47. HUAC, *Hearings Regarding Communist Espionage in the United States Government,* Part Two, 1468–1474; memo by FBI, Dec 14, 1948, Chambers et al. 1948 (Folder 1), Weinstein mss; *NY Times,* Dec 14 and 15, 1948; *Washington Post,* Dec 15, 1948; Nixon, *Six Crises,* 59–60; Andrews and Andrews, *Tragedy of History,* 198.

48. *NY Times,* Dec 16, 1948; *Washington Post,* Dec 16, 1948; Nixon, *Six Crises,* 60; Andrews and Andrews, *Tragedy of History,* 214–215.

49. *Washington Post,* Dec 16, 1948, PPS205.S233, RNyl; also see Mundt to Turner, Dec 18, 1948, R 123, Mundt; Kutler, ed., *Abuse of Power,* 105, 261, and 268.

50. *NY Times,* Dec 16 and 17, 1948; *NY Herald Tribune,* Dec 16, 1948, PPS205.S234, RNyl.

51. Herin to RN, Dec 9, 1948, PPS205.1093, RNyl; *Hearings Regarding Communist Espionage in the United States Government,* Part Two, 1430–1449; *NY Times,* Dec 10, 1948; *Washington Post,* Dec 10, 1948; Nichols to Tolson, Mar 30, Ladd to Hoover, Apr 7, Fletcher to Ladd, June 28, Nichols to Tolson, June 28, 1949, B 71, F 19, Hiss mss.

52. RN to Mundt, May 10, PPS205.1320, RN to Lasky, June 23, 1949, PPS205.1342, RNyl; Lasky to Tom, late June?, 1949, B 71, F 19, Hiss mss.

53. *NY World-Telegram,* July 9, PPS205.S3.14, *Baltimore News-Post,* July 9, 1949, PPS205.S3.13, RNyl.

54. RN to Mac, July 11, B 489, McCall, H, RN to Garland, July 15, 1949, B 282, Garland [½], Series 320, RNln; RN to Mac, July 26, 1949, MC122, RNyl.

55. *Oakland Tribune,* Jan 21, PPS205.S4.73; *Washington Times Herald,* Jan 22, PPS205.S3.17.1, *Newsweek,* Jan 30, 1950, PPS205.S4.101, RNyl; Weinstein, *Perjury,* 474–497.

56. O'Brien to RN, Jan 22, PPS205.1531; *Washington Post,* Jan 22, 1950, PPS205.S4.75 and PPS205.S4.76, RNyl.

57. Hoover to RN, Jan 22, PPS320.102.4, Mills to RN, Jan 24, PPS205.1536; *Claremount Courier,* Jan 27, 1950, PPS205.1545, RNyl.

58. Hoover to RN, Jan 17, PPS320.102.2, RN to Hoover, Jan 17, PPS320.102.1, Bill to RN, Jan 23, PPS320.102.3, RN to de Toledano, Jan 23, PPS205.1535, RN to Hoover, Jan 30, PPS320.102.5.1, Hoover to RN, Feb 4, 1950, PPS320.102.6, RNyl.

59. RN to de Toledano, Jan 23, 1950, PPS205.1535, RNyl.

60. James Chace, *Acheson: The Secretary of State Who Created the American World* (NY: Simon & Schuster, 1998), 193–196.

61. David McLellan, *Dean Acheson: The State Department Years* (NY: Dodd, Mead, 1976), 219–220; Dean Acheson, *Present at the Creation: My Years in the State Department* (NY: Signet, 1970), 469–471; Chace, *Acheson,* 226–227.

62. McLellan, *Acheson,* 220–222.

63. RN, "The Hiss Case: A Lesson for the American People" (Washington, D.C.: GPO, 1950), 2–16; *Alhambra Post-Advocate,* Apr 11, 1950, PPS205.S4.121, RNyl.

64. *NY Daily Compass,* Feb 1, 1950, PPS205.S4.104, RNyl; Wechsler to RN, Feb 14, 1950, B 804, Wechsler, Series 320, RNln.

65. Holifield and Douglas to Colleague, Dec 16, 1948, R 123, Mundt mss; *LA Herald Express,* Dec 13, 1948, PPS205.S228, RNyl.

66. *Washington Post,* Dec 16, 1948, PPS205.S234, RNyl.

67. *NY Times,* Dec 21 and 22, 1948; *Washington Post,* Dec 21, 1948; Sumner Welles, et al., *Laurence Duggan, 1905–1948: In Memoriam* (Conn.: Overbrook Press, 1949), 45.

68. Welles, *Duggan,* 1–4; Duggan biographical sketch, 1–2, background on IIE, 130, and Levine, "The Strange Case of Laurence Duggan," 141–145, Lawrence Duggan file, FBI; Irwin Gellman, *Secret Affairs: Franklin Roosevelt, Cordell Hull, and Sumner Welles* (Baltimore: Johns Hopkins Univ. Press, 1995), 110–112, 139–140, and 349; Welles, *Duggan,* 5–6.

69. *Washington Times Herald,* Dec 21, 1948, PPS205.S239, RNyl; Mundt to Pearson, Dec 24, 1948, R 123, press release, Dec 21, 1948, RG III, Un-American Activities, B 694, F 3, 1950–1954, Mundt to Muloney, Jan 13, 1949, B 687, F 4a, 1949, Mundt mss; *NY Times,* Dec 21 and 25, 1948; Welles, *Duggan,* 11 and 62; Carr, *House Committee,* 153–165.

70. Mundt to Pearson, Dec 24, 1948, R 123, Mundt mss; *NY Times,* Dec 25, 1948.

71. *NY Times,* Dec 22, 1948; *Washington Post,* Dec 22, 1948; Welles, *Duggan,* 62–63.

72. *NY Times,* Dec 22, 1948; *Washington Post,* Dec 22, 1948.

73. Duggan to Welles, Oct 6, 1948, B 131, F Di-Du 1948, Sumner Welles mss, Franklin D. Roosevelt Presidential Library, Hyde Park, NY; *Washington Times Herald,* Dec 21, 1948, PPS205.S239, RNyl; *NY Times,* Dec 22, 1948; *Washington Post,* Dec 22, 1948; Welles, *Welles,* 363; Abell, ed., *Pearson Diaries,* 11–12.

74. *NY Times,* Dec 22, 1948.

75. Welles, *Duggan,* 41–47.

76. *NY Times,* Dec 23, 1948; Nichols to Tolson, Feb 24, 1953, Duggan File, FBI; Welles, *Duggan,* 58.

77. Welles, *Duggan,* 27–28; *NY Times,* Dec 24, 1948; *Washington Post,* Dec 25, 1948; Belmont to Boardman, Apr 12, 1954, Duggan file, FBI.

78. FBI interview with Duggan, Dec 10, 1948, Duggan file, FBI; *NY Times,* Dec 27, 1948; *Washington Post,* Dec 28, 1948, PPS205.S241, RNyl.

79. Rosenblatt to Mundt, undated, Dale to Mundt, Dec 22, Stowe to Mundt, Dec 23, Reade to Mundt, Dec 23, McNerney to Mundt, Dec 23, Peterson to Mundt, Dec 30, and Rolle to Mundt, Dec 31, Gillen to Mundt, Dec 31, 1948, RG III, B 685, F 8, 1948, and "The Duggan Affair," Dec 28, Kurth to Mundt, Dec 31, Bolland to Mundt, Dec 31, 1948, RG III, B 687, F 4, 1948–49, Mundt mss; *Christian Science Monitor,* Dec 27, 1948, B 344, Hiss Case, Series 320, RNln; *Washington Post,* Dec 22, PPS205.S2/30, and Dec 28, 1948, PPS205.S241; Bourne to RN, Dec 22, PE437, Zinkoff to RN, Dec 26, PPS205.1263, Tiderly to RN, Dec 26, PPS205.1262.1, and McIntyre to RN, Dec 27, 1948, PPS205.1046, RNyl.

80. Pearson, "Memo to Mundt," RG III, B 685, F 8, 1948, Mundt to Christopherson, Dec 31, 1948, R 123, Lindley to Mundt, Jan 3, R 123, and Mundt to Hasche, Jan 13, 1949, RG III, Un-American Activities, B 687, F 7, 1949, Mundt mss; memo, undated, PPS205.1130.1, RNyl; Abell, ed., *Pearson Diaries,* 94–95.

81. US Embassy file, Feb 22, 1944, 75–76, memo, Mar 20, 1945, 116, memo from Whitson, July 12, 1945, 192, memo by Nichols, Oct 9, 1947, 117, letter to Hoover, Feb 16, 123, Rushmore testimony, July 19 to 23, 124, memo to director, Sept 2, 125, interview with Duggan, Dec 10, director, Dec 22, Wechster article, Dec 27, 1948, 131, memo from Fletcher, Jan 4, 136, interview with Field, Jan 25, 139; Levine, "The Strange Case," 141–145, letter to director, Feb 9, 146, Crane interview, Feb–Mar, 148, Chambers interview, Feb–Mar–Apr, 149, and memo from Jones, Dec 20, 1950; Duggan, Feb 14, Duggan, Sept 5, 1951, Duggan, July 14, 1952, Duggan, Jan 27, 1953, Belmont to Boardman, Apr 12, 1954, Duggan File, FBI; US Department of State Division of Foreign Activities Correlation, 1945, War Branch History, Record Group 59, National Archives and Records Administration, Washington, D.C.

82. Allen Weinstein, "Was Alger Hiss Framed?", *The New York Review of Books,* Apr 1, 1976, 16; Robert Novak in Book Reviews, *The American Spectator,* vol. 28, no. 9, Sept 1995, 64; Harvey Klehr, John Haynes, and Fridrickh Firov, *The Secret World of American Communism* (New Haven: Yale Univ. Press, 1995), 117; Sobell on "Venona and the Rosenbergs" Feb 27, 1997, http:\\h-net2.msu.edu/~diplo/Sobell.htm, Gellman mss; Allen Weinstein and Alexander Vassiliev, *The Haunted Wood: Soviet Espionage in America—The Stalin Era* (NY: Random House, 1999), 3–21 and 295–296.

83. Mundt to Christopherson, Dec 31, 1948, R 123, Mundt mss; HUAC, Dec 28, 1948, PPS205.3210, RNyl.

84. House of Representatives, HUAC, 80th Cong, 2nd Sess, *Report of the Committee on Un-American Activities to the United States House of Representatives* (Washington, D.C.: GPO, 1949), 2– 24; House of Representatives, HUAC, 80th Cong, 2nd Sess, *Soviet Espionage Within the United States Government* (Washington, D.C.: GPO, 1949), 1–11.

85. RN to Bewley, Jan 2, B 80, Bewley, RN to Perry, Jan 3, B 589, Perry, RN to Harger, B 319, and Harger, Jan 11, 1949, Series 320, RN to Hillings, Jan 3, 1949, B 3, Young, Series 434, RNln; RN to Perry, Jan 3, 1949, PE504, "The

Price of Vision," TH B 1, RNyl; Mundt to Lindley, Dec 31, Mundt to Christopherson, Dec 31, and Mundt to Vessey, Dec 31, 1948, and Lindley to Mundt,
Jan 3, 1949, R 123, and Lindley, "A Code of Conduct for Congress," RG III,
b 687, F 5; Stripling to Mundt, Jan 7, 1949, R 123, Mundt mss; HUAC, *Soviet
Espionage Within the United States Government,* 11.
86. Harold Evans, *The American Century* (NY: Knopf, 1998), 416–417; Peter Jennings and Todd Brewster, *The Century* (NY: Doubleday, 1998), 312–313.


*Chapter 12*

1. Mundt to Brownell, Aug 13, 1948, R 180, Mundt mss; *NY Times,* Aug 13,
1948.
2. RN to Mullin, Aug 9, 1948, PPS205.696, RNyl; RN to Jorgensen, Aug 9, B
1, Finance Committee, Series 434, RNln.
3. RN to Blaisell, Aug 9, 1948, B 1, F 1, RN to Johnson, Aug 16, RN to McCall,
Aug 16, Arnold to Cooper, Sept 1, 1948, Series 207, B 1, F 1, Jorgensen to
RN, Aug 16, 1948, B 1, Finance Committee, Series 434, RNln.
4. RN to Kersten, Aug 30, RN to Warren, Aug 30,1948, B 1, Presidential, Series
434, RNln.
5. RN to Dunlap, Aug 31, 1948, B 1, Presidential, Series 434, RNln; RN to Day,
Aug 31, PPS205.772, RN to Scott, Aug 31, 1948, PPS205.775, RNyl.
6. RN to Bewley, Sept 1, B 80, Bewley, RN to Andrews, Sept 7, 1948, B 344,
Hiss Case, RNln; memorandum regarding Alger Hiss and JF Dulles relationship
through Carnegie Endowment, Aug 13, 1952, PPS205.2898.2, RNyl; Ronald
Prussen, *John Foster Dulles,* 372–37; Challener, "New Light on a Turning Point
in U.S. History," 31; Divine, *Foreign Policy and U.S. Presidential Elections
1940–1948,* 240; Warren Kuehl, ed., *Biographical Dictionary of Internationalists*
(Westport, Conn.: Greenwood Press, 1983), 673–676.
7. RN to JF Dulles, Sept 7, 1948, PPS205.805, RNyl.
8. *Passaic Herald News,* Sept 7, 1948, TH Sv.15:51, RNyl; Mundt to Hahn, Sept
10, 1948, R 123, Mundt mss.
9. Arnold to McCall, Sept 1, PPS205.782, memo of speaking engagements, Sept
8 through Oct 21, PPS205.798.1(1), Calendar, Sept, PPS212(1948).1; *Alhambra
Post-Advocate,* Sept 8, PPS205.S127; RN to Johnson, Sept 28, PPS205.879, and
Arnold to Whitehurst, Sept 29, 1948, PPS205.893, RNyl.
10. *Whittier News,* Sept 9, 1948, PPS205.S128, RNyl; RN to Bewley, Sept 1, 1948,
B 80, Bewley, Series 320, RNln.
11. *NY Times,* Sept 14, 1948.
12. *NY Times,* Sept 23, TH Sv.16:25, Truman, Harry S., 1954, PPS299.81.13, RNyl.
13. Truman, Harry S., 1954, PPS299.81.13, RNyl; Hartmann, *Truman and the 80th
Congress,* 204–210.
14. *Passaic Herald News,* Sept 11, TH Sv.15:54, *Bergen Evening Record,* Sept 27, TH
Sv.16:30, *Washington Post,* Sept 29, TH Sv.16:39, and *Washington Daily News,*
Oct 6, TH Sv.16:44, RN to Stripling, Oct 16, 1948, PPS205.958, RNyl.
15. *Bergen Record,* Nov 5, TH Sv.16:69, *Passaic Herald News,* Nov 8, 1948, RNyl;
TH Sv.16:71; *Counterattack,* Nov 12, 1948, B 2, Republican National Committee [½], Series 434, RNln.
16. Perry to RN, Nov 23, 1948, PE439, RNyl.
17. Mundt to Mo, Sept 20, 1948, R 123, Mundt mss; *San Francisco Chronicle,* Sept

23, PPS205.S134, *Puente Journal,* Sept 23, PPS205.S134, and *El Monte Herald,* Sept 24, PPS205.S135, *Washington Times Herald,* Sept 28, 1948, PPS205.S138, RNyl; HUAC, 80th Cong, 2nd Sess, *Report on Soviet Espionage Activities in Connection with the Atom Bomb* (Washington, D.C.: GPO, 1948), 161–184.

18. RN to Phillips, Sept 13, PPS205.833, *Monrovia News-Post,* Sept 29, PPS205.S140, and *Alhambra Post-Advocate,* Sept 29, PPS205.S141; Wilder to RN, Oct 6, 1948, PPS205.916, RNyl.

19. RN to MacKinnon, Aug 30, PPS205.769, Arnold to Schwabe, Sept 8, PPS205.810, Arnold to Jenner, Sept 9, PPS205.817, RN to Herzog, Oct 12, PPS205.936, MacKinnon to RN, Oct 6, PPS205.915, MacKinnon to RN, Oct 16, PPS205.968, and Cox to Smith, Oct 19, 1948, PPS205.967, RNyl.

20. Reid to RN, Sept 28, PPS205.887, and RN to Reid, Sept 28, PPS205.886, *NY Herald Tribune,* Oct 24, PPS208(1948).36A, and Reid to RN, Nov 2, 1948, PPS205.990, RNyl.

21. RN to Mac, Oct 26, MC92, and Romney to RN, Oct 29, 1948, PPS205.988, RNyl.

22. *Whittier News,* Nov, PPS208(1948).37A and Nov, 1948, PPS208(1948).37B, RNyl; Arnold, *Back When It All Began,* 36.

23. C. Voorhis to J. Voorhis, Oct 8, B 109, F 19 and Nov 3, 1948, B 109, F 17, Voorhis mss.

24. Memo by Arnold, Nov 1948, PPS205.992A, RNyl.

25. Brennan to RN, Nov 16, 1948, B 2, Republican Party, Series 434, RNln.

26. RN to Brady, Nov 26, RN to Johnson, Nov 29, B 1, Election [½], and RN to McLaughlin, Nov 29, 1948, B 1, Misc., Series 434, RNln; *Washington Post,* Dec 16, 1948, PPS205.S234, RNyl.

27. RN to Bewley, Jan 2, 1949, B 80, Bewley, and "Nixon's Tax Returns Are 'Clean,'" Dec 1, 1952, B 442, Lawrence article, Series 320, and "Congress Today," Dec 29, 1948, B 1, Misc, Series 434, RNln; "Richard Nixon: Young Rebel?", *Fortnight,* Dec 31, 1948, PPS296(1948).2, RNyl.

28. "Richard Nixon: Young Rebel?", *Fortnight,* Dec 31, 1948, 8–10, PPS296 (1948).2, RNyl.

*Chapter 13*

1. RN to Hillings, Jan 3, B 3, Young Republicans, Series 434, RN to Perry, Jan 3, 1949, B 589, Perry (1 of 2), Series 320, RNln; also see RN to Perry, Jan 3, 1949, PE504, RNyl.

2. RN to Swain, Jan 3, B 741, Swain, JG, and RN to Sherwood, Feb 4, B 691, Sherwood, G, RN to Blaisdell, Feb 7, 1949, B 86, Blaisdell, Series 320, RNln.

3. RN to Perry, Jan 3, B 589, Perry (1 of 2), RN to Gordon, Jan 6, B 295, Gordon, WJ, RN to Jorgensen, Jan 6, B 392, Jorgensen (2 of 2), RN to Lowell, Jan 31, B 463, Lowell, E, RN to Latham, Feb 1, 1949, B 441, Latham, EV, Series 320, RNln; RN to friend, Jan 7, 1949, PPS205.1278.1, RNyl.

4. *LA Times,* Feb 6, PPS205.1294, *Cincinnati Times-Star,* Mar 4, 1949, PPS205.1303.2, RNyl; Walter Goodman, *The Committee,* 272–282; Carr, *House Committee,* 166–169.

5. *Omaha World-Herald,* Jan 26, and RN to Waite, Mar 28, 1949, B 2, Republican Party, Series 434, RNln.

6. RN to Mac, Jan 31, MC100, RNyl; RN to Day, Jan 31, 1949, B 206, Day, 2/2, Series 320, RNln.

7. RN to Day, Jan 31, 1949, B 206, Day 2/2, Series 320, RNln; Perry to RN, Feb 1, 1949, PPS287B.2, RNyl.

8. RN to Latham, Feb 1, B 441, Latham, EV, Bewley to RN, Feb 16, B 80, Bewley, RN to Day, Mar 2, 1949, B 206, Day 2/2, Series 320, RNln.

9. "On Trial," Feb 24, 1949, audio recordings, B 1, RNln.

10. RN to Bewley, Mar 15 and 25, 1949, B 80, Bewley, Series 320, RNln; RN to Mac, Mar 15, MC110, Mac to RN, Apr 1, 1949, MC115, RNyl.

11. RN to Lowell, Jan 31, B 463, Lowell, E, RN to Day, Jan 31 and Mar 2, B 206, Day 2/2, RN to Mac, Mar 19, 1949, MC111, RNyl; RN to Bewley, Mar 15, B 80, Bewley, Series 320, RN to Price, Mar 28, 1949, B 3, Young Republican, Series 434, RNln.

12. Bowers and Blair, "How to Pick a Congressman"; RN to Bewley, Mar 15, 1949, B 80, Bewley, Series 320, RNln.

13. RN to Sherwood, Feb 4, 1949, B 691, Sherwood, G, Series 320, RN labor speech, RN notes, 1949?, B 2, Labor, Series 435, RNln; RN to Dear, undated 1949, PPS205.1514A.5, RNyl.

14. *Washington Evening Star,* Jan 10 and 11, B 44, F 18, *San Francisco News,* Jan 9, 1956, memo by Jackson, Jan 5, 1959, B 97, F 13, memo by Jackson, Jan 1960, B 132, F 4, Series 207, RNln; The Chowder and Marching Club, 1949–1955, Series 7, B 16, F 8, Keating mss; The Chowder and Marching Club, 1949–1957, PPS295.B, uncatalogued, RNyl; Patrick Hillings, *Pat Hillings: The Irrepressible Irishman: A Republican Insider* (USA: Harold Dean, 1993), 39–42.

15. Brodie, *Nixon,* book jacket and 190; also see Vamik Volkan, Norman Itzkowitz, and Andrew Dod, *Richard Nixon: A Psychobiography* (NY: Columbia Univ. Press, 1997), 53.

16. RN to Day, Mar 2, B 206, Day 2/2, Arnold to Blaisdell, Mar 30, B 86, Blaisdell, RN to Gerhart, Apr 30, B 286, Gerhart, Series 320, Republican Assembly, May, B 1, Misc, *Young Republican,* May 1949, B 3, Young Republicans, Series 434, RNln; RN to Brennan, Mar 14, PPS 3/87A, RN to McCall, Mar 19, PE509, RN to Perry, Mar 25, PE511, RN to Mac, Mar 25, MC113, RN to Perry, Apr 11, PE513, RN to Kelly, Apr 14, PPS205.1314, Arnold to Dean, Apr 19, 1949, PPS299.16(1948).8, RNyl.

17. RN to Mac, Jan 31, MC100, Feb 20, MC106, Mar 15, MC110, Mar 23, MC112, and Mar 30, MC114, RN to Friend, June 16, 1949, PE517A, RNyl; RN to Blaisdell, Feb 7, B 86, Blaisdell, RN to Williams, July 30, 1949, B 821, Williams, RM, Series 320, RNln.

18. *San Marino Tribune,* Apr 7, 1949, PPS208(1948).15, RNyl.

19. Jones to RN, May 18, 1949, PPS266.67A, RNyl.

20. Perry to RN, Nov 30, 1948, PPS287B.1, Olivari to Lodge, May 16, 1949, PE515, RNyl; RN to Bewley, July 20, RN to Bewley, Aug 19, 1949, B 80, Bewley, Series 320, RNln.

21. Bourne to RN, Feb 14, PE662, *Waukesha Daily Freeman,* Feb 20, PPS205.S4. 113, Perry to Bourne, Mar 1, PE677, RN to Perry, Mar 6, 1950, PE684, RNyl.

22. RN to Bewley, Aug 24, 1949, B 80, Bewley, Series 320, RNln; RN to Day, Aug 27, PPS287B.27, RN to Mac, Aug 29, MC126, RN to Hillings, Aug 30, PPS3/114, RN to Perry, Aug 30, 1949, PE525, RNyl.

23. RN to Bewley, May 31, June 8, July 7, and Aug 24, B 80, Bewley, RN to Downing, July 11, B 223, Downing, R, RN to Lowell, Oct 10, 1949, B 463, Lowell, E, Series 320, RNln; *LA Examiner,* Oct 29, PPS3/658.1, Helen Daniels Oral History, LBM22.1; *Whittier Star-Reporter,* Nov 24, 1949, PPS266.S4, *LA Examiner,* Oct 29, 1950, PPS3/658.1, RNyl.

24. RN to Jorgensen, Aug 11, PPS287B.22, RN to Lucas, Sept 21, 1949, PPS205.1418, RNyl; RN to Porter, Sept 26, 1949, B 2, Republican Party, Series 434, RNln.

25. RN to Chutter, Aug 2, 1949, PPS205.1395, RNyl; Lowell, E, RN to Pfeiffer, Oct 11, 1949, PPS205.1434, RN to Bewley, July 28, B 80, Bewley, RN to Lowell, Oct 10, 1949, B 463, memo by Gleason, July 29, 1952, B 538, Mundt-Nixon Bill, Series 320, RNln; Lee, *Truman and Taft-Hartley,* 155–182 and 231–236; Sean Savage, *Truman and the Democratic Party* (Lexington: Univ. Press of Kentucky, 1997), 159–162.

26. RN to Mac, July 11, MC120, RN to Cooper, Nov 22, PPS3/213, *LA Examiner,* Dec 7, 1949, PPS3/241.2, RNyl.

27. RN to Day, Aug 2, PPS287B.20, RN to Hillings, Aug 22, PPS3/111, RN to Case, Dec 30, 1949, PPS3/263, RNyl; RN to Hillings, July 20, 1949, B 342, Hillings, Series 320, RNln.

28. RN to Glaha, Dec 20, 1949, PPS205.1507, RNyl; "Nixon's Tax Returns Are Clean," Dec 1, 1952, B 442, Lawrence article, Series 320, RNln.

29. *LA Times,* Aug 22, 1949, PPS287B.23.2, *Whittier News,* Jan 9, PPS205.S4.73, *San Diego Tribune-Sun,* Feb 8, 1950, PPS205.S4.107, RNyl.

30. *Whittier Star-Reporter,* Nov 24, 1949, PPS266.S4, *San Diego Union,* May 3, 1950, PPS266.S7, RNyl.

31. *Whittier News,* Jan 6, PPS205.S4.73; RN to Jagger, Jan 12, PPS205.1521, RN to Wood, Jan 18, PPS205.1527, RN to Conway, Jan 24, PPS205.1537, Arnold to O'Brien, May 2, PPS3/467; *People's World,* May 2, 1950, PPS266.S7, memo by Gleason, July 29, 1952, RNyl; Mundt to John, June 6, 1950, R 124, Mundt mss.

32. David Oshinsky, *A Conspiracy So Immense: The World of Joe McCarthy* (NY: Free Press, 1983), 1–84.

33. *Washington Evening Star,* Jan 23, 1950, PPS205.S4.86, *NY Journal American,* Aug 3, 1960, PPS299.52–54.S24, RNyl; Ferrell, ed., *Ayers Diary,* 342; Nixon, *RN,* 137–138; Donald Crosby, *God, Church, and Flag: Senator Joseph R. McCarthy and the Catholic Church 1950–1957* (Chapel Hill: Univ. of NC Press, 1978), 43–52 and 56–57; Oshinsky, *Conspiracy So Immense,* 84–114.

34. Clipping, Feb 27, 1950, B 583, Articles[2/13], Series 320, RNln; Cronin to de Antonio, Sept 10, 1974, CCRO 2/25, Cronin mss; Abell, ed., *Pearson Diaries,* 69, 112, 115, and 118.

35. Press release, Mar 31, PPS3/929, *NY Herald Tribune,* Mar 31, PPS205.S4.121, news release, Apr 24, PPS3/946, *San Diego Union,* May 3, 1950, PPS266.S7, RNyl; RN radio broadcast, undated, 1950, B 610, Press Releases(2 of 2), Series 320, RNln.

36. *Wyoming Eagle,* Feb 7, PPS205.S4.106, *Salt Lake Tribune,* Feb 9, PPS205.S4.108, *LA Examiner,* Feb 11, 1950, PPS205.S4.107, RNyl.

37. *San Jose Mercury-News,* Feb 12, PPS205.S4.109, *San Diego Union,* Feb 14, PPS205.S4.110, *LA Times,* Feb 16, PPS205.S4.110, *LA Evening Herald and Express,* Feb 16, 1950, PPS205.S4.111, RNyl.

38. RN to Chotiner, Feb 22, PPS3/310, Ford to RN, Feb 23, PPS3/314A, *Bakersfield Press,* Feb 26, 1950, PPS205.S4.115, RNyl; interview with Betty Ford, Feb 16, 1998, C-SPAN, Washington, D.C.

39. Press release, Feb 14, PPS3/94, RN to Johnson, Feb 22, PPS3/314.1, RN to Perry, Mar 7, PE686, "Washington Report," Mar 8, PE724, Mar 15, PE691, and Mar 29, PE697A, *LA Times,* June 1, 1950, PPS205.S4.128, RNyl; radio broadcast, May 22 and May 29, press release, May 23, June 1, 1950 B 3, Press Re & Radio, Series 435, RNln.

40. *San Francisco Chronicle,* Feb 1, PPS205.S4.104, "Washington Report," Mar 1, PE679; RN to Arnold, Mar 6, PPS3/330, press release, Mar 31, 1950, PPS3/929, RNyl.

41. News release, Apr 26, 1950, PPS3/947, RNyl and B 3, Press Release (Correspondence), Series 435, RNln.

42. *LA Examiner,* Feb 21, PPS205.S4.113, *Oakland Tribune,* Apr 13, PPS266.S5, news release, May 4, 1950, PPS3/959, RNyl.

43. Press release, Mar 26, B 3, Press Release & Radio, KFI broadcast, Mar 26, 1950, B 2, Press Release[2/2], Series 435, RNln.

44. Press release, Mar 10, 1950, B 2, Press Release, Series 435, RNln; *San Diego Tribune-Sun,* May 3, PPS205.S4.125, *LA Daily News,* June 5, 1950, PPS205.S4.129, RNyl; Leffler, *The Preponderance of Power,* 266–360.

45. Press release, Apr 15, 1950, PPS3/420, RNyl; press release, May 10, 1950, B 1, Campaign Issue [½], Series 435, RNln; Glenn Speer, "Richard Nixon's Position on Communist China, 1949–1960: The Evolution of a Pacific Strategy," Ph.D. thesis: City Univ. of NY, 1992, 1–6.

46. Day to RN, Aug 21, 1948, PPS205.739.1, RNyl.

47. Douglas to RN, June 4, 1949, PPS3/94, RNyl.

48. Hundley, *The Great Thirst,* 247–267.

49. Douglas speech, Apr 27, B 170, F 3, Douglas to Williams, May 11, 1949, B 167, F 7, Helen Gahagan Douglas mss, Carl Albert Center, Univ. Of Oklahoma, Norman, Oklahoma; *New Leader,* July 16, 1949, PPS3/112, RNyl.

50. Douglas to Keating, Apr 14, 1950, B 167, F 1, Douglas mss; Helen Gahagan Douglas, *A Full Life* (NY: Doubleday, 1982), 3–288; Ingrid Winther Scobie, *Center Stage: Helen Gahagan Douglas: A Life* (NY: Oxford Univ. Press, 1992), 3–220.

51. Perry to RN, Feb 1, PPS287B.2 and Mar 30, PPS287B.3, RN to Perry, Feb 8, 1949, PPS287B.3, RNyl; Bewley to RN, Feb 16, 1949, B 80, Bewley, Series 320, RNln.

52. Jorgensen to RN, Feb 16, PPS287B.4, news release, Nov 17, 1949, PE535, RNyl.

53. RN to Day, Mar 2, 1949, Day 2/2, Series 320, RNln.

54. California Volunteers news release, May 20, 1949, PPS205.1328A, RNyl.

55. RN to Day, May 24, PPS287B.6, RN to Jorgensen, May 25, PPS287B.7, RN to Erwin, May 31, PPS3/92A, Chapel to Saunders, June 6, 1949, PPS3/96, RNyl.

56. RN to Jorgensen, May 24, PPS287B.7 and June 10, 1949, PPS287B.10, RNyl.

57. RN to Erwin, May 31, PPS3/92A, RN to Jorgensen, May 24, PPS287B.7 and June 10, 1949, PPS287B.10, RNyl; Gerald Kepple, Oral History.

58. Jorgensen to RN, June 6, 1949, PPS287B.8, RNyl.

59. RN to Hillings, June 8, B 342, Hillings, Series 320, RN to Scott, June 8, 1949, B 3, Young Republicans, Series 434, RNln; RN to Perry, June 21, 1949, PE519, RNyl.

60. Darby to Day, June 27, PPS3/100, Hillings to RN, July 2, PPS3/102, July 20, PPS3/105, and Aug 15, PPS3/108, Day to RN, July 7, PPS287B.13, RN to Day, July 15, PPS287B.15 and Aug 27, PPS287B.27, Mac to RN, July 21, MC121, Jorgensen to RN, July 21, PPS287B.16 and Aug 5, PPS287B.21.1, Saunders to RN, July 27, PPS287B.17, Aug 24, PPS287B.23.1, Aug 26, PPS287B.26, and Aug 29, PPS287B.28, RN to Jorgensen, July 28, PPS287B.18, Day to RN, before Aug 2, PPS287B.19 and before Aug 27, PPS287B.24, RN to Saunders, Aug 26, PPS287B.25, Darby to Carter, Aug 30, 1949, PPS3/113, Hillings to RN, July 2, PPS3/102, Jorgensen to RN, July 21, PPS287B.16 and Aug 5, PPS287B.21.1, Saunders to RN, July 27, PPS287B.17, Aug 24, PPS287B.23.1, Aug 26, PPS287B.26, and Aug 29, PPS287B.28, RN to Jorgensen, July 28, PPS287B.18, Day to RN, before Aug 2, 1949, PPS287B.19, RNyl.

61. RN to Hillings, June 2, B 3, Young Republicans, Series 434, RN to Hillings, June 8, 1949, B 342, Hillings, Series 320, RNln; RN to Day, Aug 2, 1949, PPS287B.20, RNyl; Hillings, *Hillings,* 7–25.

62. Day to RN, July 7, PPS287B.13, Hillings to RN, July 20, PPS3/105, Chandler to Woodward, July 19, PPS287B.17.2, Jorgensen to RN, July 21, PPS287B.16, RN to Jorgensen, July 28, 1949, PPS287B.18, RNyl.

63. RN to Pike, July 7, PPS3/103, RN to Ainsworth, July 11, PPS287B.14, RN to Day, July 15, PPS287B.15, Mac to RN, July 21, MC121, Saunders to RN, July 27, PPS287B.17, Day to RN, before Aug 2, 1949, PPS287B.19, RNyl; RN to Hillings, July 20, 1949, B 342, Hillings, Series 320, RNln.

64. RN to Jorgensen, July 29, PE523, RN to Jorgensen, Aug 11, 1949, PPS287B.22, RNyl.

65. RN to Saunders, Aug 26, PPS287B.25, RN to Day, Aug 27, PPS287B.27, RN to Mac, Aug 29, MC126, RN to Hillings, Aug 30, PPS3/114, RN to Jorgensen, Aug 30, PPS287B.29, Saunders to RN, Sept 13, PPS287B.32, news release, Sept 19, PPS3/116, Saunders to Jackson, Sept 22, PPS287B.37.1, RN to Holt, Sept 28, PPS3/120, RN to Saunders, Oct 1, PPS287B.36, Price to RN, Oct 5, PPS3/123, Hillings to RN, Oct 9, PPS3/136, Holt to RN, Oct 31, 1949, PPS3/170, RNyl.

66. Jorgensen to RN, Sept 26, 1949, PPS287B.33, RNyl.

67. Jorgensen to RN, Oct 5, PPS287B.40, Bewley to RN, Oct 5, PPS287B.39, news clipping, Oct 6, 1949, PPS3/129.3, RNyl; Scobie, *Center Stage,* 228–229.

68. Jorgensen to RN, Oct 5, PPS287B.40, Bewley to RN, Oct 5, PPS287B.39, Poulson to Carlson, Oct 6, PPS3/127, RN to Bewley, Oct 7, PPS287B.45, Crowell to RN, after Oct 24, 1949, PPS3/159, RNyl.

69. Douglas to Bozzani, Oct 14, B 166, F 3, Douglas to Burger, Oct 21, B 165, F 1, Douglas to Thompson, Oct 25, B 168, F 6, Douglas to Ashford, Oct 28, 1949, B 166, F 3, Douglas mss; Scobie, *Center Stage,* 229–230.

70. Douglas to Myers, Nov 16, B 167, F 2, Representative Nixon's Voting Record, Nov 14, B 160, F 4, Douglas to Griffin, Nov 28, 1949, B 165, F 11, Douglas mss.

71. *Whittier News,* Oct 7, PPS266.S1, RN to Saunders, Oct 7, PPS287B.47, RN to Jorgensen, Oct 7, PPS287B.46, RN to Brennan, Oct 7, PPS3/130, RN to Bewley, Oct 10, PPS287B.50, RN to Book, Oct 12, PPS205.1435, press re-

lease, Oct 13, PPS287B.48.2, RN to Cook, Oct 12, PPS3/140, RN to Lucas, Oct 12, PPS205.1439, RN to Republicans, Oct 21, PPS3/153.1, RN to Halverson, Oct 21, PPS3/154.1, Brennan to Hutchens, Oct 28, 1949, PPS3/164, RNyl.

72. RN to Saunders, Oct 7, PPS287B.47, RN to Chotiner, Oct 7, PPS3/131 and Oct 10, PPS3/138, Chotiner to RN, Oct 18, PPS3/149 and Oct 19, 1949, PPS3/150, RN to Cohen, Nov 25, 1949, PPS3/217, RNyl.

73. *Washington Post,* Apr 29, 1956, B 148; Chotiner (1956)½, *Long Beach Independent-Press Telegram,* June 14, 1959, B 147, Chotiner (1957–1958), *Beverley Hills Citizen,* Mar 31, 1960, B 148, Chotiner, Series 320, RNln; press release, July 1952, PPS5.426, affidavit, Apr 2, 1953, PPS292.11.2, *LA Examiner,* Nov 9, PPS300. 436, *Ohio State Journal,* Nov 14, 1955, PPS300.437.2, RNyl; interview with Phyllis Chotiner, B 54, F 3, Coll. 2031, Ed Cray mss, Special Collections, UCLA.

74. Voorhis, *The Strange Case of Richard Milhous Nixon,* ix–x and 3–5; Faries, *Rememb'ring,* 165 and 205; Hillings, *Hillings,* 123–124 and 197.

75. Jorgensen to Friend, Oct 25, PPS3/160, Conners to RN, Oct 31, PPS3/168, Carlson to RN, Oct 31, PPS3/165, Chotiner to Behrens, Nov 1, 1949, PPS205.1461, RNyl.

76. Speech, Nov 3, 1949, B 1, audio recordings, RNln; announcement, Nov 3, PPS3/169, *Pomona Progress-Bulletin,* Nov 4, 1949, PPS208(1949).33A, RNyl; Nixon, *RN,* 73.

*Chapter 14*

1. Chotiner to Hillings, Nov 8, PPS3/184, news release, Nov 17, PE535, Chotiner to Arnold, Dec 8, PPS3/240, Chotiner to RN, Dec 8, 1949, PPS3/241, RNyl.

2. RN to Cairns, Nov 16, PPS3/227, RN to Younger, Nov 25, 1949, PPS3/218, RNyl.

3. MacMorran to Cotton, Nov 1, Cotton to RN, Nov 2, Cotton to Cady, Nov 4, RN to Cotton, Nov 21, Cotton to Wyckoff, Nov 25, Cotton to Etienne, Nov 25, Saunders to Cotton, Nov 28, Cotton to Mattei, Dec 15, 1949, Cotton to Hancock, Feb 16, 1950, uncatalogued, CO ms, Dinkelspiel to Saunders, Nov 2, 1949, PPS3/180, RNyl.

4. Saunders to RN, Dec 21, 1949, PPS287B.57, RNyl.

5. RN to Younger, Nov 25, PPS3/218, Younger to RN, Dec 7, PPS3/238, Hillings to RN, Dec 12, PPS3/244, Day to Perry, Dec 31, 1949, PE543, RNyl; RN to Balls, Apr 29, 1952, B 349, Holt [½], Series 320, RNln.

6. Nixon contributors, Sept to Nov, SM5, Day to McMahan, Nov 8, PPS205. 1470, Brennan to Mattei, Nov 10, PPS3/185, Brennan to Palmer, Nov 14, PPS3/189, Brennan to Smith, Nov 17, PPS3/198, RN to Morgan, Nov 15, 1949, PPS3/700, Cox to RN, Jan 12, PPS3/850, Nixon contributors, Nov 1949 through Jan 1950, SM6, RNyl. The average of the monthly Consumer Price Index for 1950 was 24.067. The average of the monthly Consumer Price Index for 1997 was 160.517. The ratio of 1997 to 1950 is 6.67. For the amount spent in 1950, its equivalent in 1997 dollars would be 6.67 higher. For example, if the campaign spent $10,000 for certain services in 1950, the dollar equivalent amount to be spent in 1997 would be $67,700. Faries, *Rememb'ring,* 206.

7. James Fay, ed., *California Almanac,* 6th ed., (Ca.: Pacific Data Resources, 1993), 1; *NY Times,* Apr 16, 1950, PPS205.S4.124, RNyl.

8. Douglas to Emmons, Jan 12, B 168, F 1, Douglas to Patterson, Jan 15, B 169, F 6, Douglas speech, Jan 24, 1950, B 161, F 2b, Douglas mss; India Edwards, V. I, 17, Women in Politics Oral History Project, Helen Gahagan Douglas Project, (Berkeley, Ca.); Scobie, *Center Stage,* 231–235.

9. *Independent Review,* Feb 3, PPS205.S3.21, *LA Times,* Mar 1, 1950, PPS205.S4.116, RNyl; Douglas address, Feb 20, 1950, B 160, F 12, Douglas mss.

10. Desmond for US Senate, Apr 10, 1950, B 160, F 14, Douglas mss.

11. Lybeck to Low, Mar 1, B 168, F 1, Douglas to Bernstein, Apr 2, B 166, F 3, Douglas to Edwards, Apr 11, B 165, F 1, Lybeck to Cibert, Apr 20, B 166, F 5, Reid to Harriman, Apr 21, Douglas addition, B 3, F 19, Lybeck to Stern, Apr 21, B 168, F 7, Black to Wigham, Apr 27, B 165, F 18, Douglas to Marion, Oct 17, B 167, F 2, Douglas to Ickes, end of Oct 1950, B 180, F 22, Douglas mss; Scobie, *Center Stage,* 235–236 and 244.

12. *San Gabriel Valley Bulletin,* Feb 23, PPS205.S4.114, *LA Mirror,* Feb 28, PPS205.S4.117, *LA Times,* Mar 1, 1950, PPS205.S4.116, RNyl.

13. Douglas to Boeck, Mar 3, B 170, F 6, Douglas address, Mar 12, B 160, F 11, Douglas speech, Mar 14, 1950, B 161, F 1a, Douglas mss; Douglas address, Mar 12, 1950, PPS3/37, RNyl.

14. *LA Mirror,* Jan 28, PPS205.S4.95, *Mercury Herald,* Jan 30, PPS205.S4.98, and Jan 31, PPS205.S4.100, *LA Times,* Jan 30, PPS205.S4.99, *Independent Review,* Feb 3, PPS205.S3.22; RN to Mac, Feb 4, 1950, MC130, RNyl.

15. Mac to RN, Jan 18, MC128, RN to Mac, Jan 31, MC129, RN to Davis, Mar 8, 1950, PPS3/349, RNyl.

16. RN to Brennan, Jan 10, PPS3/273, Perry to Brennan, Jan 13, PE634(1), Saunders to Perry, Jan 18, PE641, LAT, Feb 1, PPS205.S4.104, Terry to Comrade, Feb 3, PE654.1, RN to Chotiner, Mar 6, PPS3/337, Ad, Mar 1950, PPS3/385a, RNyl.

17. Cox to Chotiner, Mar 1, PPS3/320, Cox to Brennan, Mar 17, PPS3/361, Chotiner to Bewley, Mar 21, 1950, PPS3.363, RNyl.

18. RN to Dinkelspiel, Jan 9, PPS3/271, RN to Queale, Jan 10, PPS3/274, RN to Mattei, Jan 11, PPS3/275, RN to Hancock, Feb 22, PPS3/313, Mar 2, PPS3/324 and Mar 8, PPS3/350, Queale to RN, Mar 13, PPS3/356, Hancock to Cotton, Feb 15, 1950, Cotton to Cady, Feb 24, Dinkelspiel to Cotton, Mar 6, 1950, uncatalogued, CO ms, RNyl.

19. RN to Brennan, Mar 3, PPS3/326, Brennan to RN, Mar 15, 1950, PPS287B.59, RNyl; Jorgensen to RN, Mar 17, 1950, B 1, Correspondence [½], Series 435, RNln.

20. RN to Brennan, Mar 3, PPS3/326, RN to Saunders, Mar 6, PPS3/340, RN to Chotiner, Mar 6, PPS3/333, RN to Mattei, Mar 7, 1950, PPS3/345, RNyl.

21. Brennan to RN, Mar 15, 1950, PPS287B.59, RNyl.

22. RN to Mattei, Jan 11, PPS3/275, memo by Hunt, Feb 4, PE656 and Mar 28, PE696, Jorgensen to RN, Mar 13, PPS287B.58, RNyl.

23. RN to Hillings, Jan 9, PPS3/272, McCall to RN, Jan 18, PPS205.1526, McCall to member, Jan 20, PE932, Hillings to member, Feb 9, PE934, RN to Perry, Mar 6, 1950, PE684, RNyl.

24. French to Perry, Apr 27, PE712, Perry to Brennan, Apr 28, PE713; *Whittier News,* May 4, 1950, PE942, RNyl.

25. Cox to Carden, Mar 2, PPS3/323, RN to Shuler, Mar 8, PPS209.25, *LA Examiner*, Mar 14, PPS205.S4.118, Chotiner to Moore, Mar 16, PPS3/360, *LA Times*, Mar 21, PPS205.S4.118, Arnold to Kerry, Mar 27, Hancock to Cotton, Mar 8, 1950, uncatalogued, CO mss, exhibition hall containing photographs of Nixon's senatorial campaign, RNyl; Chotiner to RN, Mar 17, B 1, Correspondence [1/2], press release, Mar 20, B 3, Press Releases(1/4), Chotiner to Polzin, Mar 22, 1950, B1, Correspondence [2/2], Series 435, RNln.
26. RN to Richmond, Jan 13, PPS3/280, Poulson to RN, Jan 23, PPS205.1534, Chotiner to Forward, Feb 3, PPS3/291, RN to Hancock, Mar 2, PPS3/324, RN to Saunders, Mar 6, PPS3/340, RN to Johnson, Mar 7, 1950, PPS3/344, RNyl; Sargent to RN, Jan 24, 1950, B 671, Sargent, W, Series 320, RN to Hunter, Mar 17, 1950, B 1, Correspondence [½], Series 435, RNln.
27. *San Francisco News*, Mar 30, B 173, F 9, *Independent Review*, Mar 31, B 174, F 10, Clarvoe to Douglas, Apr 5, 1950, B 168, F 11, Douglas mss; Edwards, V.I, 21, V.I, 113–114, Women in Politics, Helen Gehagan Douglas Project; Scobie, *Center Stage*, 237–239: Douglas, *Full Life*, 293 and 297; Faries, *Rememb'ring*, 150.
28. Douglas to Trott, Apr 4, B 165, F 18, Douglas to Silkrout, Apr 4, B 166, F 1, McCormack to Swig, Apr 22, and McCormack to Douglas, May 9, B 160, F 1, news clipping, Apr 28, 1950, B 161, F 3, Douglas mss; Scobie, *Center Stage*, 240–243.
29. Douglas to Straus, Apr 10, B 170, F 3, Douglas to Edwards, Apr 11, B 165, F 1, Ickes to Douglas, Apr 13, B 180, F 22, Douglas to Harris, Apr 15, B 166, F 6, Lybeck to Stern, Apr 21, B 168, F 7, Douglas to Stern, Apr 25, 1950, B 165, F 9, Douglas mss.
30. Douglas to Rogers, Mar 2, B 170, F 6, Douglas speech, Apr 3, B 160, F 11, Douglas to Jones, Apr 8, 1950, B 168, F 7, Douglas mss.
31. News clipping, Mar 31, B 161, F 3, Douglas to Jones, Apr 8, B 168, F 7, Ickes to Douglas, Apr 13, B 180, F 22, Douglas to Nogueras, Apr 29, 1950, B 168, F 8, Douglas mss; *Daily News*, May 16, 1950, PPS205.S4.126, RNyl; Scobie, *Center Stage*, 247.
32. Chotiner to Arnold, Apr 3, B 2, Press Release, Series 435, RNln; Chotiner to Cook, Apr 5, PPS3/401, Chotiner to Robinson, Apr 19, PPS3/427, Chotiner to Jeffrey, Apr 28, 1950, PPS3/452, RNyl.
33. Breakfast meeting, Apr 14, PE706 and April 27, PE710, Chotiner to Polzin, Apr 28, 1950, PPS3/455, RNyl.
34. *LA Times*, Apr 2, PPS205.S4.198 and May 20, 1950, PPS266.S9, RNyl; *LA Times*, Apr 2 and 23, B 2, Newspaper, Series 435, RNln.
35. Douglas, *Full Life*, 301.
36. Itinerary for Nixon, Apr 6, 1950, PPS3/895A, RNyl.
37. Memo by RN, Apr 8, 1950, PPS3/409, RNyl.
38. Press release, Apr 24, 1950, B 3, Press Re & Radio, Series 435, RNln; *LA Times*, Apr 28, 1950, PPS266.S6, RNyl.
39. RN to Chotiner, Apr 4, PPS3/400, Cox to Arnold, Apr 24, PPS3/439, *LA Times*, Apr 28, PPS266.S6, news clipping, June 1, PPS266.S11, "Ladies in the News," Nov 1, 1950, PPS266.102, RNyl; St. Johns, undated, B 3, Press Releases (Corr), press release, Nov, 1950, B 4, Press Reports, Series 435, RNln; *Yorba Linda Star*, May 5, 1950.
40. Douglas to Hickok, May 3, B 170, F 3, Douglas to Sifton, May 5, B 167, F 4, Douglas to Wilkinson, May 5, B 170, F 3, Douglas to Sifton, May 5, B 167, F 4, Douglas to West, May 17, B 167, F 6, Douglas to Falconer, May 17, B 165, F

1, Lybeck to Dieden, May 20, B 165, F 11, Douglas, May 26, B 166, F 4, Douglas to Marion, May 29, B 167, F 2, Lybeck to Cooley, May 30, B 166, F 4, Douglas to Schlaifer, June 5, 1950, B 167, F4, Douglas mss.

41. Douglas to Ricks, May 5, B 165, F 15, Douglas to Miller, May 9, B 165, F 18, Douglas to Fortune, May 12, B 166, F 5, Douglas to Weymann, May 16, B 165, F 11, Douglas mss; Scobie, *Center Stage,* 248; Douglas, *Full Life,* 300.

42. Newspaper clipping, May, B 173, F 10, Douglas mss; *LA Times,* May 11, 1950; Douglas, *Full Life,* 298–299.

43. *LA Times,* May 23, 1950; Downey radio address, May 1950, uncatalogued, CO mss, RNyl; Nixon, *RN,* 74; Douglas, *Full Life,* 300–301.

44. Lybeck to Bowers, May 24, B 166, F 3 Douglas broadcast, June 1, 1950, B 161, F1a, Douglas mss; *San Francisco Cal Bulletin,* May 27, PPS205.S4.126, RNyl.

45. RN memo, May 1, PPS3/466 and PPS3/464, Perry to Rub, May 4, news release, May 12, 1950, PPS3/964, RNyl; press release, May 10, 29 and June 1, 1950, B 3, Press Re & Radio, Series 435, RNln.

46. *San Francisco News,* May 30, PPS205.S4.126, *San Francisco Chronicle,* June 2, PPS205.S4.128, Cotton to McSorley, June 2, 1950, uncatalogued, RNyl.

47. Breakfast committee memo, Apr 14, PPS3/415 and Apr 21, PPS3/436, Perry to Giannini, May 2, PE714, Perry to Natcher, May 2, PE715, Chotiner memo, after May 12, PE727, news release, May 29, PPS3/973, memo: all township, late May, uncatalogued, CO mss, Cox to Jorgensen, June 1, PPS/484A, Dottie to Ginnie, June 2, 1950, PPS3/484B, RNyl; press release, May 8, 1950, B 2, Press Release [2/2], Series 435, RNln.

48. *LA Daily News,* June 5, 1950, PPS205.S4.131 and PPS205.S4.132, RNyl.

49. Secretary to Bryan, June 2, 1950, Series 207, B 1, F 5, RNln; clipping, June 1, PPS266.S11, Dottie to Ginnie, June 2, 1950, PPS3/484B, RNyl; Arnold to Marshall, May 27, B 477, Marshall, JP, Arnold to Shelton, May 27, 1950, B 690, Shelton, C, Series 320, RNln.

50. RN to Saunders, Mar 6, PPS3/340, news release, Apr 6, PPS3/936, Chotiner to Jeffrey, Apr 28, PPS3/452, Brewster to Carlson, May 5, PPS5.471A.2, D'Aule to members, May 15, PE723, Hunt to Perry, May 18, PE725, Committee of 10,000 certificate, Sept 19, 1950, PPS3.75B, RNyl; Arnold to Marshall, May 27, 1950, B 477, Marshall, JP, Series 320, RNln.

51. *Statement of Vote,* June 6, 1950, B 124, California—Election Results, Series 320, RNln; California Secretary of State, *Statement of Vote,* June 6, 1950, 15–16.

52. Perry to Stearns, June 6, PE746, RNyl; Tognazzini to RN, June 8, 1950, B 2, Correspondence, Congrat[2/2], Series 435, RNln.

53. Roosevelt check, Apr 25, PPS266.91.2, Roosevelt to RN, Apr 1950, PPS266.91.1, clipping, May, PPS266.91A, Roosevelt to RN, Sept 29, 1950, PPS266.100, RNyl; Douglas, *A Full Life,* 314; Morris, *Nixon,* 560; Ambrose, *Nixon,* I, 216; Arnold, *Back When It All Began,* 12; Greg Mitchell, *Tricky Dick and the Pink Lady: Richard Nixon vs. Helen Gahagan Douglas—Sexual Politics and the Red Scare, 1950* (NY: Random House, 1998), 37 and 166; Mitchell had developed some of the themes for the 1950 election in Greg Mitchell, *The Campaign of the Century—Upton Sinclair's Race for Governor of California and the Birth of Media Politics* (NY: Random House, 1992), 572–573.

54. Arnold, *Back When It All Began,* 12.

55. Scobie, *Center Stage,* 231–244.

Chapter 15

1. Brennan to Perry, June 5, PE744, Perry to Lewis, June 15, PE749, Brennan to Dirksen, July 9, 1951, PPS288.148.2, RNyl.

2. Budget summary, Aug 12, SM4.1, Robinson to Carlson, Aug 24, SM3, memo from Chotiner, Aug 24, SM2, summary of receipts and disbursements, Aug 24, SM4.2, budget summary, Aug 24, SM4.1, and Aug 31, 1950, SM4.3, RNyl.

3. Mazo to Smathers, Apr 12, Smathers to Mazo with review of recollections attached, Apr 21, 1958, B 18, F 61, George Smathers mss, Department of Special Collections, Smathers Library, Univ. of Fla, Gainesville, Florida; RN to Parmet, Dec 10, 1986, uncatalogued, RNyl; Nixon, *RN,* 75; Brian Crispell, "George Smathers and the Politics of Cold War America, 1946–1968," Ph.D. thesis, Florida State Univ., 1996, pp. 225–227; Arnold, *Back When It All Began,* 17; Tip O'Neill, *Man of the House: The Life and Political Memoirs of Speaker Tip O'Neill* (NY: Random House, 1987), 81.

4. Jeffery to Arnold, May 3, 1950, B 1, Correspondence [½], Series 435, RNln; Campaign Manual, July 20, 1950, Special Collections, Whittier College; Chotiner to Cox, July 22, PPS300.412, Lonigan to RN, July 25, PPS3/30, RN to Besler, July 31, 1950, PPS3/500, RNyl; Arnold, *Back When It All Began,* 11–12.

5. RN to Bowen, Sept 2, PPS3/528, RN memo, Sept 2, PPS3/525 and PPS3/526, RN to Bill, Sept 2, 1950, PPS3/31, RNyl.

6. Schaffer, *Marcantonio,* 175–207; Meyer, *Marcantonio,* 44–86; La Gumina, *Marcantonio,* 101–136.

7. Campaign Manual, July 20, 1950, Whittier College.

8. *LA Examiner,* June 8, PPS266.Sos6, Perry to Brennan, June 30, 1950, PE761, RNyl; Malone to RN, June 8, Leven to RN, June 8, 1952, B 2, Correspondence, Congrat, Series 435, RNln.

9. Chotiner to Bowen, Sept 13, B 3, Press Releases (Corr), Series 435, Angell to Chotiner, Sept 15, 1950, B 44, Angell, Series 320, RNln.

10. Douglas to Lambert, June 22, B 165, F 18, Douglas to Bea, June 26, 1950, Douglas addition, F 23, Douglas; Cotton to RN, June 26, 1950, uncatalogued, CO mss, RNyl; Robert Finch OH-20, Columbia Oral History Project, copy in Dwight Eisenhower Library, Abilene, Kansas; Scobie, *Center Stage,* 256–259.

11. Scobie, *Center Stage,* 253–255 and 262.

12. Claude Pepper, *Pepper: Eyewitness to a Century* (San Diego, Harcourt Brace Jovanovich, 1987), 189–211; "The Red Record of Senator Claude Pepper," 1950, B 587, Pepper, C, Series 320, RNln.

13. Mundt to RN, May 8, 1950, PPS3/471, RNyl and R 180 Mundt mss; "The Red Record of Senator Claude Pepper," 1950, B 587, Pepper, C., Series 320, RNln; Mazo to Smathers, Apr 12, Smathers to Mazo with review of recollections attached, Apr 21, 1958, B 18, F 61, Smathers mss; Pepper, *Pepper,* 189–211; Kabat, "From New Deal to Red Scare," 14–261; Crispell, "George Smathers," 225–227.

14. RN to Coleman, Sept 2, 1950, PPS3/718, RNyl; Hancock to RN, Sept 6, 1950, B 587, Pepper, C, Series 320, RNln.

15. *Merry-Go-Round,* July 11, PPS3/3a, *CIO News,* July 17, 1950, PPS205.S4.138, RNyl; Douglas address, July 22, 1950, B 160, F 11, Douglas mss; Scobie, *Center Stage,* 262.

16. Douglas to Miller, July 26, 1950, B 170, F 6, Douglas mss.

17. RN to Minehand, July 17, PE774, RN to Cotton, July 18, 1950, uncatalogued,

NOTES

RNyl; RN to Stephens, July 14, RN to Andre, July 19, 1950, B 1, Correspondence [½], Series 435, RNln.

18. Douglas to Truman, Aug 1, 1950, OF 85–A, 1949–50[2 of 3], Truman mss.
19. Douglas speech, Aug 18, 1950, PPS3/38, RNyl; Douglas speech, Aug 18, 1950, B 170, F 3, Douglas mss; Scobie, *Center Stage,* 262–263.
20. Drown memo, Aug 18, 1950, PPS3/38a, RNyl.
21. Crosby, *God, Church, and Flag,* 71.
22. *LA Examiner,* July 27, PPS205.S4.140, *LA Times,* July 30, 1950, PPS205.S4.141, RNyl.
23. *League Reporter,* Aug 14, 1950, PPS205.S3.28, RNyl.
24. Mundt to Kelly, July 27, 1950, R 124, Mundt mss; Douglas statement, Aug 29, 1950, B 171, F 3, Douglas mss; William Tanner and Robert Griffith, "Legislative Politics and 'McCarthyism': The Internal Security Act of 1950," in Griffith and Theoharis, eds., *The Specter,* 174–186.
25. Perry to RN, Aug 4, PE793, news release, Aug 9, 1950, PE805, RNyl; press release, Aug 9, B 3, Press Releases[2/4], press release, Sept 6, 1950, B 2, Press Release, Series 435, RNln.
26. Perry to RN, Aug 4, PE 793, news release, Aug 9, 1950, PE805, RNyl; press release, Aug 9, 1950, B 3, Press Releases[2/4], Series 435, RNln.
27. RN to Dilworth, Aug 1, PPS3/501, Lonigan to RN, Aug 17, 1950, PPS3/30B, RNyl; press release, Aug 24, 1950, B 2, Press Release, Series 435, RNln; Ingrid Winther Scobie, "Jack B. Tenney: Molder of Anti-Communist Legislation in California 1940–1949," Ph.D. thesis: Univ. of Wisconsin, 1970, *passim.*
28. Press release, Aug 30, 1950, B 2, Press Release, Series 435, RNln; RN to Hanrahan, Aug 28, PPS3/517, *LA Evening Herald and Express,* Aug 30, PPS205.S4.143, RN to St. Johns, Aug 30, 1950, PPS3/520, RNyl.
29. Hancock to chairmen, Aug 3, 1950, uncatalogued, CO mss, RNyl.
30. *Newsweek,* Aug 28, 1950, PPS3/516.1, RNyl.
31. Perry to *Tribune,* Aug 28, PE825, *Bulletin,* end of Aug 1950, PPS3/524, RNyl.
32. RN radio address, Aug 30, B 3, Press Release (1/4), press release, Aug 30, 1950, B 2, Press Release[2/2], Series 435, RNln; RN radio address, Aug 30, uncatalogued, CO ms, *San Francisco Examiner,* Aug 31, 1950, PPS205.SO, 144, RNyl.
33. Perry to RN, Aug 5, PE795, and Aug 28, PE824.(1), RN to Perry, Aug 31, 1950, PE829, RNyl.
34. Douglas speech, Sept, PPS3/40, memo by Mandel, Sept, PPS3/39, condemnation of RN, Sept 13, PPS3/6 and PPS3/7, RNyl.
35. Douglas address, Sept 6, 1950, B 160, F 12, Douglas and PPS3/41, RNyl.
36. Douglas to Sheppard, Sept 16, and Sheppard to Douglas, Sept 30, 1950, B 3, Press releases[3/4], Series 435, RN to Cosner, July 21, 1951, B 177, Cosner, Series 320, RNln.
37. Douglas statement, Oct 18, 1950, B 160, F 10, Douglas mss; Scobie, *Center Stage,* 265–267.
38. RN to Smith, Mar 13, 1951, B 708, Smith, R, Series 320, RNln; Murray to Dick, May 24, 1951, PPS300.53, RNyl.

*Chapter 16*

1. Press release, Sept 6, 1950, B 2, Press Release, Series 435, RNln; *LA Times,* Sept 17, 1950, PPS205.S4.150, RNyl.

516

2. *LA Herald-Express,* Sept 19, 1950, PPS205.S4.150, RNyl.
3. Press release, Sept 18, 1950, B 3, Press Releases (Corr), Series 435, RNln; *San Francisco Chronicle,* Sept 19, PPS205.S4.150, *San Francisco Cal Bulletin,* Sept 19, 1950, PPS205.S4.150, RNyl.
4. Press releases, Sept 19 and 20, 1950, B 3, Press Releases (1/4), Series 435, RNln; *LA Herald and Express,* Sept 19, PPS205.S4.149, "Nixon Day," Sept 19, PPS3/354A.2 and 354A.3, *LA Times,* Sept 21, 1950, PPS205.S4.151, RNyl.
5. Press release, Sept 25, 1950, B 4, Press Reports, Series 435, memo by Gleason, July 29, 1952, B 538, Mundt-Nixon Bill, Series 320, RNln; *LA Times,* Sept 22, PPS205.S4.153, and Sept 26, 1950, PPS205.S4.154, RNyl; Tanner and Griffith, "Legislative Politics and 'McCarthyism,'" 186–189; Douglas to Truman, Sept 20, 1950, OF Internal Security Legislation 2750 C, Truman mss; Douglas to Ickes, Sept 22, 1950, B 180, F 22, Douglas mss.
6. Press releases, Sept 26 and 27, B 2, Press Release[2/2], Sept 28, 1950, B 3, Press Release (Corr), Series 435, RNln.
7. *Independent Review,* Sept 29, 1950, PPS3/3, RNyl.
8. Roosevelt to Truman, Sept 28, and Truman to Roosevelt, Oct 10, 1950, OF 300—California, File "R," Truman mss.
9. *San Francisco Chronicle,* Oct 17 and 18, *LA Times,* Oct 18, *NY Times,* Oct 18, 1950.
10. Hicks to RN, Nov 3, 1950, PPS3/660A, RNyl.
11. *LA Times,* Oct 25, PPS205.S4.177, Amor to Democrats, Oct 26, 1950, PPS3/549, RNyl; press release, Oct 27 and 29, 1950, B 2, Democrats, Series 435, RNln.
12. *Sunnyvale Standard,* Oct 6, PPS205.S4.162, *Labor,* Oct 7, PPS205.S3.30, *Press Democrat,* Oct 8, 1950, PPS205.S4.166, RNyl.
13. Douglas speech, Oct 2, PPS3/42, press release, Oct 3, 1950, PPS3/32, RNyl.
14. Press release, Oct 5, 1950, B 2, Press Release[2/2], Series 435, RNln; Helen Daniels, Oral History, LBM22.1, RNyl.
15. Dorothy to RN, Oct 9, B667, St. Johns, A, Carillo to RN, Dec 27, 1950, B 135, Carrillo, Series 320, RNln; Adela Rogers St. Johns, *The Honeycomb* (NY: Doubleday, 1969), *passim.*
16. Chotiner to Bowen, Sept 11, 1950, B 3, Press Releases (Corr), *Sentinel,* Oct 5, B 2, Newspaper, press release, Oct 6, 1950, B 4, Press Reports, Series 435, RNln; *Sentinel,* Oct 5, 1950, PPS205.S3.35, RNyl.
17. Press release, Oct 31, 1950, B 2, Democrats, Series 435, RNln; Gutierrez address, Nov 7, 1950, PPS3/1048, RNyl.
18. TV ad, Nov 4, 1950, RNLB14:7, RNyl; Nixon for Senator, 1950, B 1, audio recordings, RNln.
19. *LA Times,* Sept 29, PPS205.S4.155, Oct 5, PPS205.S4.161 and Oct 28, PPS205.S4.178, *Daily Register,* Oct 2, PPS205.S4.158, *San Jose News,* Oct 3, PPS205.S4.159, *Sunnyvale Standard,* Oct 6, 1950, PPS205.S4.162, RNyl.
20. Defeat RN, Oct 9–13, 1950, PPS3/7, RN to Chotiner, July 17, 1951, PPS300.120, RNyl; RN to Crawford, Aug 7, 1951, B 236, Edwards, F, Series 320, RNln; Zieger, *CIO,* 311.
21. Douglas radio address, Oct 9, PPS3/44, *LA Times,* Oct 10, 1950, PPS205.S4.166, RNyl; press release, Oct 17, 1950, B 2, Press Release[2/2], Series 435, RNln.
22. Tipton to McGrath, Oct 13, 1950, B 160, F 7, Douglas mss; press releases, Oct

16 and 17, B 4, Press Reports, press release, Oct 17, 1950, B 2, Press Release, Series 435, RNln; *LA Times,* Oct 17, PPS205.S4.172 and Oct 20, 1950, PPS205.S4.175, RNyl.

23. *Evening Dispatch,* Oct 16, 1950, B 170, F 5, Douglas mss.

24. Press release, Oct 11, 1950, B 3, Press Releases(1/4), Series 435, RNln; *San Diego Evening Tribune,* Oct 12, PPS266.Sos7, *LA Times,* Oct 17, 1950, PPS205.S4.172, RNyl.

25. Arnold, *Back When It All Began,* 12.

26. *San Bernardino Daily Sun,* Oct 18, 1950, PPS205.S3.32, RNyl.

27. *San Diego Union,* Oct 15, PPS205.S4.171, Klein to Arnold, Oct 21, PPS3/547B, *LA Times,* Oct 12, PPS205.S4.168 and Oct 31, PPS205.S4.180, *LA Examiner,* Oct 26, PPS3/658B.2, *Evening Telegram,* Oct 27, PPS3/678b, *Santa Ana Register,* Oct 31, 1950, PPS3/671E.2, RNyl; press release, Oct 20, B 2, Press Release, *Santa Ana Register,* Oct 25, 1950, B 4, Scrapbook, Series 435, RNln; Klein, *Making It Perfectly Clear,* 79–80.

28. Douglas speech, Oct 23, 1950, B 160, F 12, Douglas mss; Douglas speech, Oct 23, PPS3/45, *LA Times,* Oct 24, 1950, PPS205.S4.176, RNyl.

29. Douglas to Thomas, Oct 23, 1950, B 165, F 3, Douglas mss.

30. Pinkerton to Douglas, Oct 14, 1950, B 169, F 18, Douglas mss; radio reports, Oct 22, *Washington Post,* Oct 28, 1950, B 583, Articles [2/3], Series 320, RNln; *LA Daily News,* Nov 2, 1950, PPS205.S4.186, RNyl.

31. Press release, Oct 24, 1950, B 3, Press Re & Radio, Series 435, RNln; *LA Times,* Oct 24, 1950, PPS205.S4.176, RNyl.

32. Radio broadcast, Oct 25, 1950, PPS3/1065, RNyl.

33. News release, Oct 25, 1950, B 2, Press Release, Series 435, RNln.

34. *Newsweek,* Oct 30, 1950, PPS3/582, RNyl; Stolberg to Pegler, Mar 23, 1950, Toledano, Ralph de, File, Pegler mss; de Toledano, *Notes,* 29; Ralph de Toledano, *Seeds of Treason: The True Story of the Chambers-Hiss Tragedy* (Boston: Americanist Library, 1965), *passim;* interview with Ralph de Toledano, C-SPAN, Dec 25, 1997.

35. *San Francisco News,* Oct 12, PPS3/536E and Oct 27, PPS205.S4.177, *LA Times,* Oct 30, 1950, PPS205.S4.182, RNyl.

36. The Big Lie, general election, 1950, PPS3/5, RNyl.

37. C. Voorhis to J. Voorhis, Nov 3, 1950, B 110, F 1, Voorhis mss; Abell, ed., *Pearson Diaries,* 138.

38. Clipping, Nov 2, PPS205.S4.184, *Eastside Sun,* Nov 2, PPS205.S4.184, *LA Daily News,* Nov 2, PPS205.S4.185, *Sun-Reporter,* Nov 4, 1950, PPS205.S4.190, RNyl; Connelly to Roosevelt, Nov 3, 1950, OF 300—California, File "R," Truman mss.

39. *San Francisco Chronicle,* Nov 3, 1950, PPS205.S4.187, RNyl.

40. *LA Times,* Nov 4, 1950, PPS205.S4.188, RNyl.

41. *LA Times,* Oct 28, PPS205.S4.177, clipping, Nov 4, 1950, PPS205.S4.188, RNyl; Cray, *Chief Justice,* 209–213.

42. *Daily Californian,* Oct 31, 1950, B 170, F 5, Douglas mss; news clipping, Nov 6, PPS5.S.A-14, *LA Mirror,* Nov 6, 1950, PPS205.S4.193, RNyl.

43. Douglas radio address, Nov 6, 1950, B 160, F 11, Douglas mss.

44. Chotiner to Smith, Oct 31, PPS3/611, budget summary, Nov 2, SM4.16, Knowland to RN, Nov 1, PPS3/620.B, news release, Nov 1, 1950,

PPS3/1020, RNyl; press release, Nov 1, B 2, Democrats, press release, Nov 1, 1950, B 3, Press Re & Radio, Series 435, RNln.

45. "Seeds of Treason," Nov 1, 1950, B 1, audio recording, RNln.

46. Chotiner to Ingle, May 11, PPS300.46.2, Chotiner to Beck, May 11, 1951, PPS300.46.3, RNyl; "Nixon for Senate," B 1, audio recording, RNln.

47. Press release, Oct 28, 1950, B 3, Press Releases[3/4], Series 435, RNln; news release, Nov 3, 1950, PPS3/1023, RNyl.

48. Press release, Nov 1, B 2, Democrats, press release, Nov 4, B 2, Press Releases[2/2], radio speech, undated, press release, Nov 7, 1950, B 3, Press Re & Radio, Series 435, RNln; RN to editor, Nov 1, PPS3/618.2, RN to Boddy, Nov, PPS3/685A.2, press release, Nov 4, 1950, PPS3/1026.2, RNyl.

49. *LA Examiner,* Nov 3, PPS205.S3.34.1, *Sun-Telegram,* Nov 5, PPS3/672.2, *LA Times,* Nov 7, 1950, PPS3/436.2, RNyl.

50. Nixon for Senator, 1950, B 1, audio recordings, RNln.

51. Smith to members, Sept 8, PE836, Perry to RN, Sept 16, PE850, budget summary, Sept 9, SM4.4, Sept 14, SM4.5, Cotton to Cullinan, Sept 15, uncatalogued, CO mss, Lilley to RN, Sept 12, PPS3/766, Phleger to RN, Sept 18, PPS3/797, Arnold to Dottie, Sept 21, PPS3/833, expenditures, Sept 23, SM4.6, budget summary, Sept 30, SM4.7, recapitulation of advertising, end of Sept, 1950, SM4.11, RNyl.

52. Budget summary, Oct 5, SM4.8, summary, Oct 5, SM4.9, advertising, Oct 6, SM4.10, Perry to Brennan, Oct 9, PE859.1, Smith to members, Oct 11?, PE865.2, Smith to King, Oct 11, PE864, Betty to Dottie, Oct 12, PPS3/842, statement of cash balance, Oct 12, SM4.16, budget summary, Oct 12, SM4.15, TV payments, Oct 19, SM4.12, budget summary, Oct 19, SM4.17, statement of available cash, Oct 19, 1950, SM4.18, RNyl.

53. Press release, Nov 4, 1950, B 2, Press Release, Series 435, RNln; *Alhambra Post-Advocate,* Nov 7, PPS205.S4.202, *NY Daily News,* Nov 8, 1950, PPS4.133, RNyl.

54. Senate election day, Nov 7, RNLB84:28, RN to campaigner, Nov 7, PPS3/615, RN television spots, Nov 7, 1950, RNLB14.7 through 12, RNyl.

55. *San Jose Evening News,* Nov 8, 1950, PPS205.S4.202, RNyl; Boddy to RN, Nov 8, Downey to RN, Nov 8, 1950, B 5, Telegrams, Series 435, Arnold to Parkinson, Feb 12, 1951, B 579, Parkinson, Series 320, RNln.

56. *San Francisco Chronicle,* Nov 5, PPS205.S4.191, 1950 election, undated, PPS3/1071, RNyl; *Statement of Vote,* Nov 7, 1950, B 124, California—Election Results, Series 320, Chotiner to RN, Jan 3 and 8, 1951, B 1, Campaign File, Series 435, RNln.

57. Cotton to RN, Nov 9, 1950, PPS3/686C.1, RNyl; Browing to RN, Jan 15, 1951, B 4, Scrapbook, Series 435, RNln; *Yorba Linda Star,* Nov 10, 1950.

58. *Herald-Express,* Nov 8, PPS266.Sos12, *LA Times,* Nov 8, PPS266.Sos15, *Democrat,* Nov 8, PPS4.505, *LA Examiner,* Nov 8, PPS266.Sos17, and Nov 11, PPS3/686E, *Huntington Beach News,* Nov 9, PPS4.304A, *San Francisco Examiner,* Nov 15, 1950, PPS205.S4.204, RN to Brennan, Jan, PPS288.38, Marjorie to RN, Jan 21, PPS209A.1, RN to Lionvale, Feb 1, 1951, PPS209A.9, Lionvale to Gleason, Oct 6, 1952, PPS293.106.16, RNyl; Chotiner to Jones, Oct 9, B 391, Jones, WP, McClure to RN, Dec 27, 1950, B 492, McClure, RE, Series 320, RNln.

59. Tipton to editor, Oct 28, 1950, B 160, F 5, Douglas mss; Hayes to Jordan, Nov 17, B 4, Supporters, *Stanford Univ. News,* Jan 26, 1951, B 1, Correspondence [½], Series 435, Arnold to RN, Feb 15, 1951, B 610, Press Releases(2 of 2), Series 320, RNln; *LA Times,* Jan 27, 1951, PPS288.69.2, RNyl; Robert Gottlieb and Irene Wolt, *Thinking Big: The Story of the Los Angeles Times, Its Publishers and Their Influence on Southern California* (NY: Putnam, 1977), 277–289.

60. Douglas to Reuther, Nov 13, 1950, B 181, F 5a, Douglas mss.

61. Schlesinger to Douglas, Nov 10, B 181, F 6, Outland to Douglas, Dec 4, 1950, B 181, F 4, Douglas mss; C. Voorhis to J. Voorhis, Nov 24, 1950, B 110, F 1, Voorhis mss.

62. Rule to RN, Nov 8, Stassen to RN, Nov 8, B 5, Telegrams, Series 435, Phillips to RN, Nov 15, 1950, B 595, Phillips, J, Series 320, RNln; Lane to RN, Nov 8, PPS4.132, Hoover to RN, Nov 8, PPS320.102.7, Groves to RN, Nov 9, PPS4.314, Grimm to RN, Nov 11, PPS4.607, JF Dulles to RN, Nov 13, PPS4,677, Jordan to RN, Nov 13, PPS4.691, Faries to RN, Nov 13, PPS4.679, AW Dulles to RN, Nov 15, 1950, PPS4.792, RNyl.

63. Chambers to RN, Nov 9, B 141, Chambers, W, Cronin to RN, Nov 13, 1950, B 191, Cronin (1956, 2/2), Series 320, RNln; De Toledano, *Notes,* 29.

64. Douglas to Mostek, Dec 5, B 181, F 4, Douglas to Steinberg, Dec 13, 1950, B 181, F 6, Douglas mss.

65. Douglas to Lea, Oct 31, 1952, B 174, F 1, Douglas to Edson, Sept 19, 1956, B 164, F 37, Ransom to Feuerlicht, May 25, 1962, B 173, F 14, Douglas mss; McWhorter to Scott, Feb 20, *Washington Daily News,* Nov 25, 1958, B 22, Douglas, H, Series 320, RNln.

66. *Boston Globe,* Sept 8, 1960, B 222, Douglas, H, Series 320, RNln; Douglas statement, Oct 6, 1960, B 173, F 13, Douglas to Realini, May 26, 1962, B 173, F 14, Douglas mss.

67. Bird to Douglas, Nov 23, 1955, B 173, F 14 and Oct 31, 1960, B 174, F 2, Douglas mss; Kevin Starr, *Material Dreams: Southern California Through the 1920s* (NY: Oxford Univ. Press, 1990), 365, 368, and 370.

68. *Corpus Christi* [Texas] *Times,* Mar 28, PPS299.69.S10, Morris Rubin, "The Case Against Nixon," *The Progressive* (Oct 1960), 9, 10–11, and 17, PPS299.69.14, RNyl.

69. Frank Mankiewicz, *Perfectly Clear,* 33–57; report of meeting, Sept 5, 1951, PPS300.138.2, RNyl.

70. Helen Lustig, V. I, 191, Bryon Lindsley, V. I, 125–154, Mary Keyserling V. II, 119–132, Philip Noel-Baker, V. II, 474–497, Alice De Sola, V. III, 42, Women in Politics Oral History Project, Helen Gahagan Douglas Project.

71. Douglas, *Full Life,* 244 and 341.

72. Scobie, *Center Stage,* 281.

73. Candidate's Campaign Statement of Receipts and Expenditures, Richard M. Nixon, Nov 7, Cotton to Sec of State, Nov 2, Nicholson to Sec of State, Nov 21, Kern County Committee for Nixon, Nov 2 Statement of Receipts and Expenditures, Northern California Committee for Nixon (8/1/50–11/20/50), California State Archives; Morris, *Nixon,* 616 and chaps 16–18; Mitchell, *Tricky Dick,* 170, 232, and *passim.*

74. RN to Barrows, July 26, 1952, PPS10.159, RNyl.

75. Dinkelspiel to Gotshal, Aug 18, Chotiner to Snyder, Aug 26, B 46, Anti-Semitic, Chotiner to Dear, Aug ?, B 45, Anti-Defamation, Series 320, RNln.

76. RN to Black, Dec 8, 1952, B 85, Black, T, Series 320, RNln.
77. Chotiner speech, Sept 7–10, 1955, B 148, Chotiner (1956) 2/2, Series 320, RNln.
78. Nixon, *RN,* 72–78; Key to Burger, May 26, 1958, B 791, Voorhis, J, Series 320, RNln.

*Chapter 17*

1. RN to Poor, Dec 11, 1950, PPS209.122, RNyl; RN to Ganahl, Dec 18, 1950, B 280, Ganahl, Series 320, RNln.
2. RN to Cotton, Dec 1950, B 183, Cotton, A, RN to Dear, May 9, B 318, Hanley, JM, RN to Knudsen, June 4, 1951, B 422, Knudsen, V (2 of 2), Series 320, RNln; Dulles address, Nov 27, PPS323.5.4, RN to Dye, Dec 8, 1950, PPS393.3, RNyl.
3. Dulles speech, Dec 29, 1950, PPS323.5.2, RNyl.
4. Garland to RN, Nov 29, 1950, B 282, Garland [½], Series 320, RNln; Perry to RN, Nov 29, 1950, PE904, RNyl.
5. *LA Times,* Nov 21, PPS4.980.2, *LA Herald & Express,* Nov 22, PPS266.S31, clipping, Nov 23, 1950, PPS205.S4.205, RNyl.
6. Kruse to RN, Dec 8, B 430, Kruse, Bewley to RN, Dec 12, RN to Bewley, Dec 19, B 80, Bewley, Kepple to RN, Dec 15, 1950, Series 320, RN to Greenberg, Feb 19, 1951, B 1, Correspondence [½], Series 435, RNln.
7. RN to Bewley, May 3, June 8, and July 7, 1949, Bewley to RN, Dec 12, 1950, Feb 2 and Mar 13, 1951, RN to Bewley, Feb 6, B 80, Bewley, Series 320, Bewley to RN, Mar 13, 1951, Series 207, B 2, F 1, RNln; Nixon, *Six Crises,* 80.
8. RN to Perry, Dec 20, 1950, B 589, Perry, "Nixon's Tax Returns Are 'Clean,' " Dec 1, 1952, B 442, Lawrence article, Smith to Crites, Sept 25, 1951, B 704, Smith, D, Series 320, RNln; Robinson to Smith, Feb 2, SM24, RN to Smith, May 30, SM26, Chotiner to RN, July 5, PP3300.116, Smith to Reid, Aug 21, 1951, Appendix D, SM1.1, RNyl.
9. Clara Nixon to RN, Jan 9, 1951, PPS3/698D.3, RNyl; RN to Henderson, Jan 20, 1951, B 332, Henderson, H, Holt to RN, Jan 24, 1951, B 349, Holt, M, Series 320, RNln.
10. Herbert to Nixon, Apr 23, B 729, Sterner, F, Holt to RN, May 2, B 349, Holt, M,RN to Drown, Feb 7 and July 16, B 225, Drown, 2/2, RN to Perry, May 9, B 589, Perry, Bewley to RN, June 28, 1951, B 303, Greenbaum, Series 320, RN to Arnold, Feb 20, B 1, Correspondence [½], Series 435, RN to Kiefer, July 9, B 2, F 9, Series 207, RNln; Pat Nixon to Helene, Feb ?, B 1, F 1, DR, RN to Perry, Feb 15, PE1070, Brennan to RN, June 7, PPS288.136.1, RN to Drown, June 30, PPS209.641, *Long Beach Press-Telegram,* July 15, PPS266.S34, RN to Barnes, Aug 13, PPS287.119, Woods to Perry, Oct 29, 1951, PE1152, RNyl; *U.S. News & World Report,* Oct 8, 1952, 68; Eisenhower, *Pat Nixon,* 111.
11. Pat Nixon to Helene, Feb and Nov 3, 1951, B 1, F 1, DR, RNyl.
12. Pat Nixon to Helene, Mar 12, B 1, F 1, May 20, B 1, F 2, Nov 3, 1951, B 1, F 1, DR, RNyl.
13. Pat Nixon to Helene, Feb, B 1, F 1, Nov 3, B 1, F 1, after Nov 3, 1951, B 1, F 1, DR, RNyl.
14. Pat Nixon to Helene, Nov 3, B 1, F 1, after Nov 3, 1951, B 1, F 1, DR, RNyl.
15. Pat Nixon to Helene, Feb, B 1, F 1, Nov 3, 1951, B 1, F 1, 2, DR, RNyl.

16. Pat Nixon to Helene, Feb, B 1, F 1, Nov 3, B 1, F 1, after Nov 3, 1951, B 1, F 1, DR, RNyl.

17. Diagram for Room 341, PPS293A.1, RNyl; RN to Bewley, Feb 6, 1951, B 80, Bewley, Series 320, RNln; Cox to Brennan, Mar 28, 1951, PPS288.83, RNyl; telephone interview with James Gleason, July 29, 1998; Gayle Montgomery and James Johnson, *One Step from the White House: The Rise and Fall of Senator William F. Knowland* (Berkeley: Univ. of California Press, 1998), 161.

18. Irwin to RN, Nov 7, 1950, PPS3/684A, Cox to Brennan, Mar 28, PPS288.83, RNyl; staff to Hancock, Mar 2, B 316, Hancock, Irwin to Burke, July 9, 1951, B 114, Burke, JF, Irwin to RN, Dec 16, 1950, Jan 12 and 27, Irwin to Sanner, Feb 14, *LA Times Herald,* July 6, 1952, B 372, Irwin (3 of 4), Series 320, RNln.

19. Pat Nixon to Helene, Mar 12, B 1, F 1, DR, Press release, July 1952, PPS5.425.3, RNyl; Woods to Allen, Sept 19, 1962, B 27, Allen, Mary, Series 320, RNln; Eisenhower, *Pat Nixon,* 110–111.

20. RN to Wysong, Feb 2, B 835, Wysong, RN to Armour, B 50, Armour, Arnold to Greenberg, Feb 19, B 303, Greenberg, staff to Hancock, Mar 2, B 316, Hancock, RN to Upton, Apr 10, B 777, Upton, A, Gipson to RN, June 20, 1951, B 289, Gipson, Series 320, RNln; RN to Goodwin, Mar 15, 1951, PPS209.377, RNyl.

21. Memo by Dorothy, Mar 30, 1951, B 508, memorandum before 1955, Series 320, RNln.

22. Murray to Jack, May 4, PPS300.43, RN to Chotiner, May 9, PPS300.45, Murray to Bill, May 14, 1951, PPS300.48, RNyl.

23. Perry to Brennan, May 23, PE1091, Brennan to Perry, May 29, 1951, PE1095 and PPS288.133, RNyl.

24. RN to Friend, June 15, PSS300.74A.1, RN to Chotiner, July 16, PPS300.119, Brennan to RN, Aug 9, PPS288.168.1, Chotiner to RN, Sept 11, 1951, PPS300.138.1 and PPS300.138A, RNyl; Chotiner to Irwin, Aug 17, 1951, B 46, Anti-Nixon, Series 320, RNln.

25. Montgomery and James Johnson, *One Step,* 7–54.

26. *Ibid.,* 55–63.

27. RN to Shuler, Mar 8, 1950, PPS209.25, RN to Moore, Mar 24, 1951, PPS209.394, RNyl; RN to Moseley, Mar 7, B 534, Moseley[2/2], Series 320, RN to Jorgensen, Mar 5, 1951, B 1, Correspondence [½], Series 435, RNln; Montgomery and Johnson, *One Step,* 66–72, 75–77, and 81–93.

28. RN to Butler, Dec 15, B 170, Committee Appt, RN to Albrink, Dec 19, B 24, Albrink, RN to Anderson, Dec 19, 1950, B 41, Anderson, J, RN to Butler, Jan 11, B 118, Butler, H, RN to Butler, Jan 11, B 118, Butler, H, RN to Di Giorgio, Jan 17, 1951, B 216, Di Giorgio, RN to Vanderberg, Jan 18, Vandenberg to RN, Jan 23, B 779, Vandenberg, A, McCarthy to RN, Jan 25, B 170, Committee Appt, Irwin to RN, Jan 27, 1951, B 372, Irwin (3 of 4), Series 320, RNln; clipping, Jan 12, PPS5.SA-7, *LA Times,* Jan 27, 1951, PSS288.69.4, RNyl; McCarthy, Joseph R., Lewis Summary, 1–4, Scrapbook, *Pittsburg Post-Gazette,* Jan 26, V. 94, 62 and *New Britain Herald,* Feb 13, 1951, V. 95, 114, Margaret Chase Smith mss.

29. McCarthy to RN, Dec 6, 1950, B 490, McCarthy, J, Series 320, RNln.

30. *LA Times,* Dec 13, 1950, PPS299.55.2A, Pat Nixon to Helene, after Nov 3, 1951, B 1, F 1, DR, RNyl; RN to Creel, Dec 18, 1950, B 189, Creel, Series 320, RNln; Nixon, *RN,* 137–139; Oshinsky, *Conspiracy,* 179–181.

31. Holt to RN, Dec 13, RN to Holt, Dec 19, B 349, Holt [2/2], Perry to RN, Dec 14, 1950, B 589, Perry, Chambers to RN, Jan 20, B 141, Chambers, W, RN to McCarthy, Feb 16, 1951, B 490, McCarthy, J, Series 320, RNln.

32. RN speech, May 1, Hulcy to RN, May 16, 1951, B 2, F 7, Series 207, RNln.

33. *Lincoln Evening Journal and Nebraska State Journal,* Mar 20, PPS5.SA-9, RN to Deadrich, Oct 25, 1951, PPS209.1178, *Capital Times,* Jan 28, 1952, PPS5.S(1), RNyl; Cooper to RN, Oct 22, 1951, B 179, Cooper, Ch, Series 320, RNln; Robert Griffith, *The Politics of Fear: Joseph R. McCarthy and the Senate* (Lexington: Univ. Press of Kentucky, 1970), 131–198; Oshinsky, *Conspiracy,* 191–225.

34. *San Francisco Chronicle,* Nov 11, 1950, PPS3/687.8.3, RNyl.

35. RN to Aarons, Jan 18, B 18, Aarons, RN to Creel, Jan 18, B 189, Creel, RN to Binkley, Feb 13, B 82, Binkley, RN to Sokolsky, Mar 9, 1951, B 210, DeMille Foundation, Series 320, RNln; RN to Vanasek, Jan 22, 1951, PPS209.229, RNyl.

36. RN radio talk, Mar 4, B 610, Press Releases(2 of 2), RN to Benson, July 9, B 76, Benson, G, RN to Reid, Aug 3, B 625, Reid, CT, RN to Swim, Oct 2, B 742, Swim, D, Series 320, RN speech, June 8, 1951, B 3, F 5, Series 207, RNln; RN to Cecil, Aug 8, PPS287.113, RN to Pyle, Aug 16, 1951, PPS287.125, RNyl.

37. RN to Perry, June 2, PE1101, Aug 21, PE1131 and Sept 11, PE1134, RN to Stokesbary, Aug 8, 1951, PPS287.117, RNyl; RN to Friend, Aug 18, B 269, Form Letters, RN to Caldwell, Wm, Sept 11, 1951, B 122, Caldwell, Wm, Series 320, RNln.

38. RN to Kaye, Aug 8, PPS287.114, RN to Dinwiddle, Aug 17, PPS287.128, RN to Pendleton, Aug 18, 1951, PPS287.129, RNyl; RN to Friend, Aug 18, 1951, B 269, Form Letters, Series 320, RNln.

39. Bewley to RN, May 23, B 80, Bewley, RN to Van De Water, June 6, B 780, Van De Water, RN to Benson, July 9, B 76, Benson, G, Series 320, proceedings, June 10, B 3, F 6, RN to Goodloe, July 16, 1951, B 4, F 1, Series 207, RNln.

40. Cox to Brennan, Mar 28, PPS288.83, RN to Perry, May 30, PE1097, Brennan to RN, June 19, PPS288.141, RN to Reeder, Aug 16, 1951, PPS287.126, *LA Times,* June 4, 1952, PPS5.SA21, RNyl; RN to Hornby, Apr 14, B 354, Hornby, RN to Van De Water, June 6, B 780, Van De Water, Series 320, RN to Brown, July 11, 1951, B 4, F 1, Series 207, RNln.

41. RN remarks, July 5, 1951, B 610, Press Releases(2 of 2), Series 320, RNln; RN to Perry, June 30, 1951, PE1119, RNyl.

42. RN to Udall, Mar 26, B 770, Udall, RN to Derre, Mar 26, 1951, B 212, Derre, Series 320, RNln.

43. RN to Gates, Mar 26, 1951, B 284, Gates, F, Series 320, RNln.

44. RN radio talk, Mar 4, B 610, Press Releases(2 of 2), RN to Loudon, June 14, B 610, Press Releases (1 of 2), RN to Lasky, Aug 30, 1951, B 439, Lasky (2 of 3), Series 320, RNln; RN to Hardin, Aug 30, PPS287.141, RN to Lasky, Aug 30, 1951, PPS287.144, RNyl.

45. RN to Dinwiddle, Aug 17, 1951, PSS287.128, RNyl.

46. RN to Loudon, June 14, B 610, Press Releases(1 of 2), Series 320, RN to Austin, July 25, 1951, B 4, F 1, Series 207, RNln.

47. RN to Cotton, May 4, B 183, Cotton, A, RN to Hancock, May 9, B 316, Hancock, RN radio broadcast, May 25, 1951, B 610, Press Release (2 of 2), RN to Van De Water, June 6, B 780, Van De Water, Series 320, Kelchner certificate, Apr 25, B 2, F 11, RN to Ludwig, May 11, B 3, F 6, RN to McFall, June 6, RN

to Damon, June 15, RN to Kenestrick, July 6, 1951, B 2, F 11, Series 207, RNln; RN to Jamison, May 8, PPS209.511, Pat Nixon to Helene, May 20, 1951, B 1, F 2, DR, RN to Carr, Aug 16, 1951, PPS287.121, RNyl; RN to Ike, May 9, 1951, Pre-Presidential Principle File, 1916–52, Eisenhower mss.

48. RN to Blue, Dec 4, PE906, Perry to RN, Dec 18, 1950, PE914, RNyl; Perry to RN, Dec 6, 1950, B 589, Perry, Series 320, RNln; Charles Cooper, *Whittier: Independent College in California* (Los Angeles: Ward Ritchie Press, 1967), 278–279 and 308–309.

49. Bewley to RN, Dec 12, RN to Bewley, Dec 19, B 80, Bewley, RN to Perry, Dec 20, B 589, Perry, RN to Jones, Dec 20, 1950, B 391, Jones, Wm, Series 320, RNln; Cooper, *Whittier*, 310.

50. RN to Perry, Jan 17, PE1059, Feb 19, 1951, PE1071, RNyl; Reece to Alumnus, Mar 12, RN speech, Mar 31, RN to Brennan, Mar 28, B 2, F 1, Series 207, RN to Robinson, Mar 26, 1951, B 648, Robinson, E, Series 320, RNln; Cooper, *Whittier*, 310–312.

51. Smith to RN, Apr 2, Jones to RN, Apr 2, 1951, B 2, F 3, Series 207, RN to Perry, Apr 10, B 589, Perry (1 of 2), RN to Upton, Apr 10, 1951, B 777, Upton, A, Series 320, RNln; Perry to RN, May 31, PE1099(1), RN to Perry, June 5, 1951, PE1102, RNyl; Cooper, *Whittier*, 311–313.

52. Perry to RN, June 1951, PE1103(1), RNyl and also B 589, Perry (1 of 2), Series 320, RNln; Cooper, *Whittier*, 314–326.

53. RN to Cramer, June 6, 1951, B 187, Cramer, RN to Warren, Jan 29, 1952, B 799, Warren, RL, Series 320, RNln.

54. Information sheet, Apr 27, PE1118.2, RN to Perry, June 5, PE1108.2, Woods to Trustees, June 6, 1951, PE1104, RNyl; Perry to RN, May 29, RN to Perry, June 12, Perry to Jackson, June 20, 1951, B 589, Perry(1 of 2), Series 320, RNln; Cooper, *Whittier*, 264–265 and 366.

55. *Congressional Record,* June 26, 1951, 7347 and 7349–7350; RN to Perry, Feb 2, PE1122, Hillings to RN, June 22, PE1113, Jackson to Perry, July 2, PE1120, Perry to Jackson, July 13, 1951, PE1123, RNyl; Perry to RN, July 2, RN to Perry, July 7, 1951, B 589, Perry(1 of 2), Series 320, RNln; Hope Bacon, *Let This Life Speak: The Legacy of Henry Joel Cadbury* (Philadelphia: Univ. of Pennsylvania Press, 1987), *passim.*

56. Hoover to RN, Dec 11, 1950, PPS320.102.8.1, RNyl; *NY Times,* Dec 21, 1950; Justus Doenecke, *Not to the Swift: The Old Isolationists in the Cold War Era* (Lewisburg, Pa.: Bucknell Univ. Press, 1979), 196–203.

57. RN to Hoover, Dec 22, PPS320.102.9, Hoover to RN, Dec 29, 1950, PPS320.102.10, RNyl.

58. RN to Christierson, Jan 22, 1951, B 150, Christierson, Series 320, RNln.

59. RN broadcast, Jan 9, B 610, Press Releases(2 of 2), RN to Kennedy, Jan 11, 1951, B 404, Kennedy, HW, Series 320, RNln.

60. RN to Van Horne, Jan 12, B 780, Van Horne, RN to Rogers, Jan 20, B 652, Rogers (4 of 4), RN to Lutz, Mar 7, B 466, Lutz, H, RN to Call, Feb 28, 1951, B 126, Call, M, Series 320, RNln.

61. *Congressional Record,* Feb 15, 1951, 1301–1303; RN to Cooper, Feb 7, 1951, B 179, Cooper, J [2/2], Series 320, RNln.

62. Warlick to RN, Dec 26, 1950, speech and notes, Jan 6 and Hoftyzer to RN, Jan 10, B 1, F 8, RN to Kinney, Feb 5, 1951, B 1, F 18, Series 207, RNln.

63. RN speech, Jan 8, B 1, F 9, *Washington Post,* Jan 9, 1951, B 1, F 8, Series 207, RNln.

64. Radio broadcast, Jan 25, *Waterville Morning Sentinel,* Jan 26, B 1, F 11, RN excerpts and speech, Jan 27, RN to Reid, Feb 17, B 1, F 12, Series 207, RN speech, Jan 27, 1951, B 1, Campaign Material, Series 435, RNln.

65. Banquet, Feb 9, B 1, F 15, Series 207, speech, Feb 9, 1951, B 4, Speeches, Series 435, RNln; *Louisville News,* Feb 10, PPS5.SA-7, *Courier Journal,* Feb 10, 1951, PPS5.SA-8, RNyl.

66. RN to Moore, Mar 24, PPS209.394, RN to Demarest, Apr 2, 1951, PPS209.420, RNyl; RN to Hopper, Apr 4, 1951, B 354, Hopper, Series 320, RNln; Montgomery and Johnson, *One Step,* 96–98.

67. RN to Paik, Mar 20 and Oct 30, Hannah to Woods, Apr 2, B 576, Paik, RN to Cooper, Dec 19, 1951, B 179, Cooper, C, Series 320, RNln.

68. *Congressional Record,* April 11, 1951, 3753–3757; RN speech, May 24, B 3, F 2, Series 207, RN to Howard, June 1, 1951, B 357, Howard, P, Series 320, RNln.

69. *Congressional Record,* Apr 11, 1951, 3757–3758.

70. *Ibid.,* 3759; RN comments, Apr 11, RNLB123:5, clipping, Apr 11, PPS5.A-10, Murray to Dick, Apr 16, PPS300.33, Arnold to Chotiner, Apr 23, PPS300.38, Pat Nixon to Helene, May 20, 1951, B 1, F 2, DR, RNyl; press release, Apr 12, B 269, Form Letters, Hancock to RN, Apr 16, B 316, Hancock, RN to Dunlap, Apr 17, 1951, B 230, Dunlap, A, Series 320, RNln.

71. Chotiner to RN, Apr 12, PPS300.28, Murray to Bill, Apr 13, PPS300.29.1, *LA Examiner,* Apr 13, 1951, PPS300.32.3, RNyl; Fifield to RN, Apr 13, 1951, B 257, Fifield, Series 320, RNln.

72. Powell to RN, Apr 20, B 607, Powell, D, Cramer to RN, Apr 24, 1951, B 187, Cramer, Series 320, RNln; Pat Nixon to Helene, May 20, 1951, B 1, F 2, DR, RNyl.

73. Radio script, May 1, PE1085, clipping, undated 1952, PPS299.39.19, RNyl; radio script, May 1, Berg to RN, May 2, 1951, B 2, F 5, Series 207, RNln.

74. RN to Scott, May 5, B 680, Scott (2 of 3), RN to Allan, May 5, B 393, Judgeship, RN to Knoop, June 4, B 80, Bewley, Series 320, RN speech, May 25, 1951, B 3, F 2, Series 207, RNln.

75. RN speech, May 12, B 2, F 10, Series 207, RN to Neustadter, May 21, 1951, B 228, Duke Univ., Series 320, RNln; Montgomery and Johnson, *One Step,* 99–101.

76. RN to Friend, May 31, 1951, B 269, Form Letters, Series 320, RNln and PE1098, RNyl.

77. Sec to Haussler, May 28, RN speech, June 11, RN to Owen, June 14, B 3, F 7, *National Grocers Bulletin,* July, B 3, F 9, RN speech, June 14, B 3, F 8, Kimball to Cox, June 1, B 3, F 10, Series 207, RN speech, June 15, 1951, B 4, Speeches, Series 435, RNln; RN to Bell, May 27, 1951, PPS209.402, RNyl.

78. RN to Greenbaum, July 7, B 303, Greenbaum, RN to Hornbeck, July 10, 1951, B 354, Hornbeck, L, Series 320, RNln; RN to Richman, Aug 2, 1951, PPS287.112, RNyl.

*Chapter 18*

1. Hamby, *Man of the People,* 501; also see David McCullough, *Truman* (NY: Simon & Schuster, 1992), 863–872.

2. Andrew Dunar, *The Truman Scandals and the Politics of Morality* (Columbia: Univ. of Missouri Press, 1984), 1–39.

3. *Ibid.,* 40–77.

4. *York Dispatch,* Mar 15, PPS5S.A-8, *Lincoln Evening Journal and Nebraska State Journal,* Mar 20, 1951, PPS5S.A-9, RNyl.

5. Charles Fontenay, *Estes Kefauver: A Biography* (Knoxville: Univ. of Tennessee Press, 1980), 166–229; Hamby, *Man of the People,* 588.

6. Randall Woods, *Fulbright: A Biography* (Cambridge: Cambridge Univ. Press, 1995), 154–162.

7. Dunar, *Truman Scandals,* 91–95; Jules Abels, *The Truman Scandals* (Chicago: Regnery, 1956), 83–93.

8. RN to Abshire, May 11, B 18, Abshire, "The Scandalous Years," May 22, 1951, B 653, Rogers, 1960 (1 of 2), Series 320, RNln.

9. Hamby, *Man of the People,* 505.

10. RN to Brennan, Mar 24, PPS288.81, RN to Moore, Mar 24, 1951, PPS209.394, RNyl; *Citizen-News,* Mar 31, B 348, Holt, RN to Reynolds, Apr 9, 1951, B 638, Reynolds, Ra, Series 320, RNln.

11. RN speech, Sept 16, 1951, B 4, F 4, Series 207, RNln.

12. De Toledano to RN, Sept 20, 1951, B 213, de Toledano, Series 320, RNln.

13. *Washington Post,* Sept 1, 1961, B 96, Boyle, Series 320, RNln; Savage, *Truman,* 68–70.

14. RN to Hoblick, Sept 25, 1951, B 345, Hoblick, Series 320, RNln; US Senate, 82nd Cong, 1st Sess, Hearings Before the Investigations Subcommittee of the Committee on Expenditures in the Executive Departments, *Influence in Government Procurement* (Washington, D.C.: GPO, 1951), 891–893.

15. Ibid., 917–942 and 968–969.

16. RN statement, Oct 3, 1951, B 610, Press Releases(1 of 2), Series 320, RNln.

17. RN statement, Oct 8, 1951, B 96, Boyle, Series 320, RNln; RN to Friend, Oct 15, 1951, PE1145, RNyl; Senate, *Influence in Government Procurement,* 1047–1086; US Senate, 82nd Cong, 2d Sess, Senate Permanent Subcommittee on Investigations, *Interim Report of the Committee on Expenditures in the Executive Departments* (Washington, D.C.; GPO, 1952), 1–25.

18. De Toledano, *Notes,* 67.

19. Regan to RN, Oct 5, B 624, Regan [3/3], Chadbourne to RN, Oct 9, B 140, Chadbourne, Wm, *Long Beach Press-Telegram,* Oct 12, White to RN, Oct 15, Guthrie to RN, Oct 16, Ingalls to RN, Dec 3, 1951, B 96, Boyle, Series 320, RNln; Savage, *Truman,* 71.

20. Brennan to RN, Oct 26, PPS288.192, RN to McCall, Oct 29, PPS287.151, RN to Faries, Oct 29, 1951, PPS287.150, *Hanford Daily Sentinel,* Feb 1, 1952, PPS5.SA3, RNyl; RN to Fisher, Oct 9, B 261, Fisher, O, memo by RN, Dec 17, 1951, B 508, memorandum before 1955, Series 320, RNln.

21. RN to Link, Oct 8, B 96, Boyle, RN to Cotton, Nov 23, B 183, Cotton, RN to Lutz, Dec 17, B 466, Lutz, H, RN to Jergins, Dec 17, 1951, B 382, Jergins, A, RN to Harrison, Jan 14, B 322, Harrison, De, RN to Endicott, P, Jan 31, 1952, Series 320, RNln; Woods to Holmes, Oct 10, PPS209.1096, RN to Kelley, Oct 11, PPS209.1101, memo by Grover, Dec 10, 1951, PPS290.151.2, RNyl.

22. RN to Burkhard, Dec 10, PPS209.1386, RN to Peacock, Dec 13, 1951, PPS209.1404, RNyl; RN to Hoover, Jan 9, B 6, F 1, RN to Chotiner, Feb 22, 1952, B 6, F 17, Series 207, RNln.

23. *The Advance,* Jan 11, 1952, PPS5.SA1, RNyl.
24. Dunar, *Truman Scandals,* chap 6.
25. RN remarks, Jan 30, 1952, B 610, Press Releases (2 of 2), Series 320, RNln.
26. Memo from Leece, Feb 4, PPS290.153, clipping, Feb 5, PPS290.154, and Feb 1952, PPS5.68A.2, RNyl; Dunar, *Truman Scandals,* 96–119.
27. *LA Examiner,* Feb 3, 1952, PPS5.SA4, RNyl; Cronin to Yardley, Feb 8, 1952, B 531, Morris, N, Series 320, RNln.
28. Clipping, Feb 5, 1952, PPS290.154, RNyl.
29. Memo from Leece, Feb 4, 1952, PPS290.153, RNyl.
30. *Ibid.*
31. *Ibid.*
32. Cochrane to RN, Mar 4?, 1951, PPS290.159, RNyl.
33. Chinese Embassy press release, Apr 6, 1951, PPS290.155.2, RNyl.
34. Statement by Holmes, Jan 30, PPS290.152, statement by Smith, Mar 1952, PPS290.166, RNyl.
35. RN speech, Feb 27, 1952, B 1, audio recordings, RNln.
36. Reporters Roundup, Feb 28, 1952, PPS290.157, RNyl.
37. RN to Cochrane, Mar 3, PPS290.158, *LA Times,* Mar 5, PPS5.SA11, memo from Leece, Mar 5, 1952, PPS290.161, RNyl.
38. McLaughlin to RN, Mar 3, RN to McLaughlin, Mar 7, 1952, B 503, McLaughlin, R, Series 320, RNln.
39. *Washington Post,* Mar 12, 1952, PPS290.170, RNyl.
40. Morris remarks, Mar 12, PPS290.169, *Washington Post,* Mar 13, 1952, PPS5.SA14, RNyl.
41. RN press release, Mar 12, Mundt to Hoben, Mar 22, 1952, B 531, Morris, N, Series 320, RNln; *Washington Post,* Mar 13, 1952, PPS5.SA14, RNyl.
42. Irwin to Keep, Mar 18, B 531, Morris, N, press release, June 30, 1952, B 372, Irwin (3 of 4), Series 320, RNln.
43. Bryan to RN, Mar 12, Schwab to RM, Mar 13, 1952, B 531, Morris, N, Series 320, RNln.
44. Schwartz to RN, Mar 13, 1952, B 531, Morris, N, Series 320, RNln; *Washington Times Herald,* Mar 14, 1952, PPS290.171, RNyl.
45. RN to Peterson, Mar 24, PPS299.82A.73.1, Report, Sept 28, PPS299.82A.73.1, FAILURE, Oct, 1952, PPS299.82A.45, RNyl.
46. Schedule, Mar 26, RN speech, Mar 26, 1952, B 6, F 10, Series 207, RNln; *NY Herald Tribune,* Mar 27, 1952, PPS5.SA17, RNyl.
47. Questionnaire, 1952, PPS290.157A, RNyl; RN to Wolfort, Apr 19, 1952, B 531, Morris, N, Series 320, RNln; Hamby, *Man of the People,* 590–591.
48. Report, Sept 28, 1952, PPS299.82A.73.1, RNyl.
49. RN to Bennett, May 3, 1952, B 531, Morris, N, Series 320, RNln.
50. S.2560, Jan 10, PPS293.108.6.1, *Sacramento Union,* Feb 1, PPS293.108.14.2, *Baltimore Sun,* Feb 3, PPS5.SA-11, *San Mateo Times,* Feb 7, 1952, PPS293.108.24.4, RNyl.
51. *San Mateo Times,* Feb 7, 1952, PPS293.108.24.4, RNyl.
52. RN to Anderson, Feb 21, PPS293.108.25, Hubbard to RN, Apr 8, 1952, PPS293.108.28, RNyl.
53. *Whittier News,* Feb 27, 1952, PPS5.SA11, RNyl; press release, Mar 26, 1952, B 269, Form Letters, Series 320, RNln; Dunar, *Truman Scandals,* 121–134.
54. Senate, *Influence in Government Procurement,* Mar 20, 5087–5089, PPS5.473, RN

statement, Mar 20, PPS5.471, *Washington Times Herald,* Mar 21, PPS5.474, *Telegram-Tribune,* Mar 24, 1952, PPS5.474, RNyl; Abels, *Truman Scandals,* 175–179.

55. Dunar, *Truman Scandals,* 158–159.
56. Abels, *Truman Scandals,* 3–306; Abels to Humphreys, June 20, 1958, PPS299.81. 75, RNyl; The Truman Scandals, June 1958, B 764, Truman, H, Series 320, RNln.
57. Abels, *Truman Scandals,* 307–314.
58. Hamby, *Man of the People,* 592.
59. Ferrell, ed., *Ayers Diaries,* 175–177, 245, 320, 321, 324, and 325.
60. *Ibid.,* 243, 252, and 321.

*Chapter 19*

1. RN to Mullin, Jan 3, B 3, Workers, RN to Hillings, Jan 3, RN to Stassen, May 23, RN to MacKinnon, May 24, B 3, Young, Series 434, RN to Swain, Jan 3, B 741, Swain, JG, RN to Perry, Jan 3, 1949, B 589, Perry(1 of 2), Series 320, RNln; RN to Perry, Jan 3, PE504, Saunders to RN, Oct 10, PPS287B.53, memo by Arnold?, Nov 9, 1949, PPS205.1409A, RNyl.
2. Cotton to Arnold, May 21, B 183, Cotton, A, Stassen to RN, July 25, 1951, B 725, Stassen[4/4], Series 320, RNln; RN to Saunders, Feb 20, PPS209.306, Stassen to RN, May 28, PPS209.567, RN to Stassen, May 29, PPS209.570, Cox to Peaslee, June 14, PPS209.602, Clarksboro Conference, June 23 and 24, 1951, PPS209.632.3, RNyl; Kirby, "Stassen," 238–276.
3. Patterson to RN, Aug 26, PPS209.827, RN to Smith, Aug 30, SM27, Stanley to RN, Dec 6, PPS209.1378, RN to Shanley, Dec 11, 1951, PPS209.1395, Stassen speech, May 24, 1952, PPS5.78, RNyl; C. L. Sulzberger, *A Long Row of Candles: Memoirs and Diaries [1934–1954]* (NY: Macmillan, 1969), 740; Stassen to Ike, Apr 14, 1952, B 87, Pre-Presidential, 1916–52, Principle File, Eisenhower mss; Kirby, "Stassen," 293–342.
4. Palmer to RN, Jan 29, 1951, B 577, Palmer (2 of 2), Series 320, RNln.
5. RN to Stephens, July 14, 1950, 1950, B 1, Correspondence [½], Series 435, RN to Palmer, Feb 17, 1951, B 577, Palmer (1 of 2), Series 320, RNln.
6. *Ibid.*
7. *Ibid.*
8. *News,* Apr 27, PPS288.122.1, Brennan to Caylor, May 7, PPS288.122.1, *Independent Review,* May 18, PPS288.126.1, RN to Brennan, July 13, PPS288.151, Brennan to RN, Aug 16, 1951, PPS288.171, RNyl; Arnold, *Back When It All Began,* 29–45; Montgomery and Johnston, *One Step,* 109.
9. RN to Palmer, Feb 17, 1951, B 577, Palmer (1 of 2), Series 320, RNln.
10. Kohlberg to RN, May 1, B 423, Kohlberg, A, RN to Hancock, May 9, B 316, Hancock, RN to Perry, May 9, 1951, B 589, Perry, Series 320, RNln; for Kohlberg letter also see B 136, F: Correspondence, Nixon, 1948–1952, Alfred Kohlberg mss; RN to Ike, May 9, 1951, Pre-Presidential 1916–52, Principle File, Eisenhower mss.
11. Memo, Nov 6, 1948, PPS205.994, RNyl; clipping, Sept 27 and Dec 17, 1950, PPS5.549(31), RNyl; Alfred Chandler, Jr., and Louis Galambos, eds., *The Papers of Dwight David Eisenhower: Occupation 1945,* Vol. VI (Baltimore: Johns Hopkins Univ. Press, 1978), 163, and Louis Galambos, ed., *The Papers of Dwight David*

*Eisenhower: Columbia University,* Vol. X (Baltimore: Johns Hopkins Univ. Press, 1984), 146; Nixon, *Six Crises,* 76–77; Nixon, *RN,* 80; Arnold, *Back When It All Began,* 8.

12. Jones to Mattei, July 10, Mattei to RN, July 11, RN to Newcomer, July 31, RN to Jones, Aug 1, RN to Mattei, Aug 1, 1950, B 1, F 7, Series 207, Flye to RN, Aug 17, 1951, B 266, Flye, Series 320, RNln; Perry to Lycan, July 25, 1950, PE785.1, RNyl.

13. Louis Galambos ed., *The Papers of Dwight David Eisenhower,* V.X, 76–77 and 185–186; Challener, "New Light," 31; Hiss to Ike, Sept 27 and Dec 3, 1948, B 57, Pre-Presidential, 1916–52, Principle File, Eisenhower mss.

14. Hunt to Ike, July 17, Ike to Hunt, Aug 1 and Sept 2, 1950, B 59, Pre-Presidential, 1916–52, Principle File, Eisenhower mss.

15. *LA Mirror,* July 12, 1952, PPS5.S41, RNyl; Louis Galambos, ed., *The Papers of Dwight David Eisenhower: NATO and the Campaign of 1952,* Vol. XIII (Baltimore: Johns Hopkins Univ. Press, 1989), 1307.

16. Ike to RN, May 11, 1951, B 87, Pre-Presidential, 1916–52, Principle File, Eisenhower mss; RN to Hansen, June 4, RN to McFall, June 6, Hargrove to Woods, June 17, 1951, B 2, F 11, Series 207, RNln.

17. Appointment Book 1951, B 4, Pre-Presidential, 1916–52, Miscellaneous File, Eisenhower mss; RN to Kohlberg, May 30, B 423, Kohlberg, A, RN to Van De Water, June 6, 1951, B 780, Van De Water, Series 320, RNln; for Kohlberg letter also see B 136, F: Correspondence, Nixon, 1948–1952, Kohlberg mss.

18. Clipping, June 23, 1951, B 3, F 11 (1 of 2), Series 207, RNln.

19. Clippings, Jan 17, Apr 20, July 22, and Nov 16, 1951, PPS5.549(31), RNyl; C. Voorhis to J. Voorhis, Mar 12, 1951, B 110, F 2, Voorhis mss; Abell, ed., *Pearson Diaries,* 154; Herzstein, *Luce,* 420.

20. Chotiner to RN, May 24, 1951, PPS300.53 and PPS300.74A.2, RNyl.

21. Blackwell to Nick, June 6, PPS300.61, Bennett to RN, June 6, PPS300.62, McCarthy to RN, June 6, PPS300.91, Cooley to RN, June 21, 1951, PPS300.67, RNyl.

22. Morse to RN, June 5, PPS300.96, Wherry to RN, June 8, PPS300.108, Gabrielson to RN, June 18, PPS300.75, Faries to RN, June 29, 1951, PPS300.72, RNyl.

23. RN, "The Challenge of 1952" (Washington, D.C.: GPO, 1951), 3–14, and also B 4, F 1, Series 207, RNln; *LA Times,* June 29, 1951, B 3, F 12, Series 207, RNln.

24. Derre to RN, July 6, B 212, Derre, Shellenberger to RN, July 30, B 690, Shellenberger, Series 320, *LA Times,* July 19, Hetts to RN, Sept 5, 1951, B 3, F 12, Series 207, RNln.

25. RN to Jorgensen, Mar 5, B 1, Correspondence [½], Series 435, Perry to RN, Mar 21, RN to Brennan, Mar 28, B 2, F 1, Series 207, *Hollywood Citizen-News,* Mar 31, 1951, Series 320, RNln; RN to Brennan, Mar 24, 1951, PPS288.81, RNyl.

26. RN to Forward, July 25, B 270, Forward, Perry to RN, July 26, RN to Perry, July 31, 1951, B 589, Perry (1 of 2), Series 320, RNln; Perry to RN, July 26, 1951, PE1126.1, RNyl.

27. RN to Owens, Aug 8, 1951, PPS287.116, RNyl; Irwin to von Ludlow, Nov 5, B 421, Knowland, WF, Klein to Arnold, Dec 11, 1951, B 416, Klein (1 of 2), Series 320, RNln; Montgomery and Johnson, *One Step,* 55–77 and 99–102.

28. Brennan to Warren, Knowland, RN, and Faries, Aug 18, PPS288.175, RN to Brennan, Aug 23, 1951, PPS288.178, RNyl.

29. Bewley to RN, Nov 7, B 80, Bewley, press release, Nov 8, 1951, B 799, Warren Candidacy, Series 320, RNln; Perry to RN, Nov 9, 1951, PE1155, RNyl; Montgomery and Johnson, *One Step,* 105–106; Cray, *Chief Justice,* 222.

30. RN to Smith, Oct 29, SM31, RN to Perry, Nov 14, PE1157, Cox to French, Nov 15, PPS209.1303, Baer to RN, Dec 24, 1951, PPS209.1431, RNyl; Bewley to RN, Oct 30, B 80, Bewley, Cotton to Cox, Nov 21, B 182, Cotton, RN to Forward, Nov 23, 1951, B 270, Forward, Series 320, RNln; Cray, *Chief Justice,* 221–222; Katcher, *Warren,* 273.

31. RN to Stannard, Nov 24, PE1159, RN to Wellington, Dec 18, PPS209.1412, Baer to RN, Dec 24, 1951, PPS209.1431, RNyl; RN to Christierson, Dec 10, 1951, B 6, F 4, Series 207, RNln.

32. Perry to RN, Nov 26, PE1160, Wellington to RN, Dec 7, 1951, PPS209.1384.1, RNyl; Hand to RN, Dec 5, B 317, Hand, CR, Series 320, Perry to RN, Dec 27, 1951, B 6, F 11, Series 207, RNln.

33. RN to Brennan, Dec 14, PPS288.210, Brennan to Casey, Dec 26, 1951, PPS288.216.2, RNyl.

34. Creel to Jack, July 30, 1951, B 189, Creel, Series 320, RNln; Mundt to Taft, Dec 18, 1951, R 151, Mundt; Patterson, *Mr. Republican,* 499 and 518.

35. Mac to RN, Apr 9, B 667, St. Johns, M, RN to Dunlap, Dec 19, B 230, Dunlap, A, de Toledano to RN, Dec 26, 1951, B 213, de Toledano, Series 320, RNln; clippings, Jan 14, Apr 20, and July 15, PPS5.549(31), RN to Smith, Aug 30, 1951, SM27, RNyl; Faries, *Rememb'ring,* 151.

36. Smith to RN, July 11, B 133, Carlson, Bewley to RN, July 18, B 80, Bewley, RN to Drown, Dec 13, 1951, B 225, Drown 2/2, Series 320, RNln.

37. RN to Creel, Aug 8 and 23, B 189, Creel, RN to Jorgensen, Aug 23, 1951, B 392, Jorgensen (2 of 2), Series 320, RNln.

38. Sulzberger, *Candles,* 613–617.

39. *Ibid.,* 667, 672, 683–686, and 699–705.

40. Irwin to Chotiner, Apr 30, PPS300.40, RN to Brennan, Aug 17, 1951, PPS288.174, RNyl; RN to Jorgensen, Aug 20, B 392, Jorgensen (2 of 2), RN to Cotton, Sept 11, 1951, B 183, Cotton, A, Series 320, RNln.

41. RN to Brennan, Sept 17. PPS209.924, RN to Perry, Sept 18, PE1137, Cox to Perry, Oct 19, 1951, PE1148, RNyl; Bewley to RN, Sept 20, B 123, Cal Bank, RN to Lasky, Sept 20, B 439, Lasky (2 of 3), RN to Hancock, Oct 9, B 316, Hancock, Series 320, RN to Pattee, Sept 24, B 6, F 3, RN to Brennan, Oct 23, B 6, F 1, RN to Pattee, Oct 29, 1951, B 6, F 3, Series 207, RNln; Pat Nixon to Helene, Nov 3, 1951, B 1, F 1, DR, RNyl; Aiken, *Nixon,* 197.

42. Arnold to Perry, Jan 19, 1952, PE1175.1, RNyl; also B 269, Form Letters, Arnold to RN, Nov 26, B 548, National Concerts, Series 320, RN to Warlick, Aug 9, 1951, B 4, F 8, Series 207, RNln.

43. "Nixon's Tax Returns Are 'Clean,'" Dec 1, 1952, B 442, Lawrence article, Series 320, RNln.

44. *U.S. News & World Report,* Dec 28, 1951, 14–15, PPS5.434B, RNyl.

45. Smith, *Dewey,* 581; Abell, ed., *Pearson Diaries,* 187; Sulzberger, *Candles,* 715; Henry Cabot Lodge, *The Storm Has Many Eyes: A Personal Narrative* (NY: Norton, 1973), 76–102.

46. RN to Kepple, Mar 19, B 406, Kepple, RN to Mac, Mar 19, 1952, B 677, St. Johns, M, Series 320, RNln; Sulzberger, *Candles,* 735–736.

47. RN to Ike, Jan 17, PPS324.1, Ike to RN, Jan 28, 1952, PPS324.2, RNyl, and B 87, Pre-Presidential, 1916–52, Principle File, Eisenhower mss; To Impeach Acheson, May 1949, B 1, Misc, Series 434, RN to Jones, Aug 13, 1951, B 390, Jones, RA, RN to Mac, Mar 19, 1952, B 667, St. Johns, M, Series 320, RNln.

48. RN to Ike, Jan 17, PPS324.1, Ike to RN, Jan 28, 1952, PPS324.2, RNyl.

49. Smith to Perry, Jan 5, PE1169, Cox to Smith, Jan 31, 1952, SM34.1, RNyl; RN to Drown, Feb 2, 1952, B 225, Drown 2/2, Series 320, RNln.

50. Sulzberger, *Candles,* 731–735.

51. RN to Craig, Feb 29, 1952, B 5, F 7, Series 207, RNln.

52. Lionvale to RN, Feb 5, PPS293.106.7, Bewley to Perry, Mar 24, PE1303, Perry to RN, Mar 26, 1952, PE1205.1, RNyl; Creel to RN, Apr 4, 1952, B 189, Creel, Perry to RN, Mar 26, 1952, B 589, Perry, Series 320, RNln; Mundt to Wood, Feb 16, 1952, Correspondence File, Wood mss; Doenecke, *Not to the Swift,* 221.

53. Clippings, Feb 13, Mar 2, Apr 9, and May 21, 1952, PPS5.S49(31), RNyl.

54. RN to Carlson, Jan 9, B 6, F 1, RN to Pattee, Jan 10, 1952, F 4, RN to Harris, Jan 21, 1952, B 5, F 2, Series 207, RNln.

55. *LA Examiner,* Jan 15, PE1173, Perry to RN, Jan 16, PE1174.1, *San Francisco Cal Bulletin,* Feb 21, 1952, PPS5.S3, RNyl; RN to Perry, Jan 29, 1952, B 589, Perry, Series 320, RNln.

56. Brennan to RN, Jan 29, PPS288.219, clipping from Fresno, Feb 11 and 12, PPS5.SA5 and PPS5.S2, *Oakland Tribune,* Feb 14, 1952, PPS287A.44.2, RNyl.

57. RN to Hancock, Mar 19, B 316, Hancock, Series 320, RN to Robbins, Mar 21, 1952, B 6, F 3, Series 207, RNln; RN to Fussell, Mar 21, PPS205.2797, RN to Gamble, Mar 21, 1952, PPS209.1677, RNyl.

58. *LA Times,* Mar 25, 1952; RN to Murphy, Mar 24, 1952, PPS209.1687, RNyl; Brock to RN, Mar 21 and list of delegates, June 29, 1952, B 7, F 17, Series 207, RNln; State of California, *Statement of Vote,* June 3, 1952, 4–5; Faries interview, Aug 12, 1991, Coll 2031, B 53, F 3, Cray mss; Faries, *Rememb'ring,* 210; Earl Warren, *The Memoirs of Earl Warren* (NY: Doubleday, 1977), 251; Frank Jordan, comp., Secretary of State, *Statement of Vote,* June 3, 1952, State of California, 5.

59. Bobbitt to RN, Jan 14, PPS5.60, Gamble to RN, Mar 10, 1952, PPS209.1644, RNyl.

60. RN to Perry, Jan 9, 1952, B 6, F 11, Series 207, RNln.

61. Perry to Brennan, Mar 10, PE1192, Brennan to Perry, Mar 18, PE1198, Perry to RN, Mar 26, 1952, PE1205.1, RNyl.

62. Werdel to RN, Nov 25, 1950, Ambrose to Werdel, Jan 1, B 808, Werdel, RN to Perry, Jan 29, B 589, Perry, Hancock to RN, Jan 31, B 316, Hancock, RN to Kergan, Feb 22, B 407, Kergan, RN to Ewins, Mar 19, 1952, B 248, Ewins, Series 320, RNln; *LA Examiner,* Jan 15, PE1173, Perry to RN, Jan 16, PE1174.1, *Oakland Tribune,* Feb 17, PPS5.S3, *San Francisco Cal Bulletin,* Feb 21, PPS5.S3, *LA Mirror,* Feb 29, 1952, PPS5.SA-11, RNyl; Patterson, *Mr. Republican,* 518; Cray, *Chief Justice,* 226–227: Kurt Schuparra, *Triumph of the Right: The Rise of the California Conservative Movement, 1945–1966* (NY: M. E. Sharpe, 1998), 19–21.

63. *LA Times,* Mar 29, 1952; RN to Brennan, Mar 27, 1952, PPS288.246, RNyl; RN to Polzin, Apr 23, 1952, B 604, Polzin, Series 320, RNln.

64. RN to Holt, Apr 4, B 349, Holt [2/2], RN to Balls, Apr 29, 1952, B 349, Holt [½], Series 320, RNln.

65. Tenney to RN, Nov 10, 1950, PPS4.571, *LA Mirror,* Feb 29, PPS5S.A-11, RN to Jorgensen, Feb 29, 1952, PPS209.1624, RNyl; Tenney to RN, Feb 27, Chotiner to RN, Mar 12, Wood to RN, Mar 19, Arnold to Chotiner, Mar 25, B 349, Holt [2/2], RN to Moulton, May 20, B 595, Phillips, M, RN to Langer, June 7, 1952, B 436, Langer, Wm, Series 320, RNln.

66. RN to Andre, June 11, RN to Suchman, June 27, B 349, Holt [½], *Intermountain Jewish News,* Aug 14, 1952, B 45, Anti-Defamation, Series 320, RNln; Jordan, comp., *Statement of Vote,* June 3, 1952, 11, and *Statement of Vote,* Nov 4, 1952, 14.

67. RN to Bingham, Jan 23, PPS299.53.27, memo by Jim, Jan 30, 1952, PPS299.53.27, RNyl.

68. RN to Swim, Dec 19, 1951, B 742, Swim, D, Series 320, RNln; RN to Jim, Jan 22, PPS299.53.19, memo from RN, Jan 23, PPS299.53.22.2, RN to Perry, Mar 20, 1952, PE1201, RNyl.

69. RN remarks, Apr 3, 1952, B 360, Hughes, H, Series 320, RNln; *LA Times,* Apr 4, 1952, PPS5.SA19, RNyl.

70. Smith to RN, May 15, RN to Smith, May 19, clipping, May 22, 1952, B 704, Smith, DP, Series 320, RNln.

71. RN to Henderson, May 29, 1952, B 704, Smith, DP, Series 320, RNln.

72. RN to Hotchkis, Feb 15, B 355, Hotchkis, RN press release, Mar 12, 1951, B 610, Press Releases (2 of 2), Series 320, RNln.

73. *St. Louis Post-Dispatch,* Apr 24, 1952, PPS205.2854A, RNyl; RN to Curtis, May 5, 1952, B 344, Hiss Case, Series 320, RNln.

74. Neikirk to RN, Apr 18, PPS205.2834, RN to Fitzpatrick, May 16, 1952, PPS209.1863, RNyl; RN to Hearfield, Apr 21, B 141, Chambers, W, RN to Hopkins, May 8, B 344, Hiss Case, Series 320, RN to Rentschler, July 1, 1952, B 7, F 12, Series 207, RNln.

75. *Saturday Review,* May 24, 1952, B 344, Hiss, 1 of 3, Series 320, RNln; Tanenhaus, *Chambers,* 459–471; Chambers, *Witness, passim.*

76. Chambers to RN, May 9, 1952, B 827, "Witness," Series 320, RNln; de Toledano, *Notes,* 87.

77. Cronin to RN, May 20, review of *Witness,* May 23,1952, RNyl.

78. Chandler to RN, Mar 7, PPS293.114.4, RN to Chandler, Mar 13, PPS293.114.6, RN and Knowland to Truman, Apr 3, PPS293.114.8, RN to Habrial, Apr 19, 1952, PPS205.2837, RNyl; undated memo, Nixon-Grossman, B F 163 [2 of 3], Pearson mss; author's telephone interview with Gordon Tinker, general manager, Fallbrook Public Utility District, Jan 22, 1999; Tinker to Gellman, Jan 28, 1999, and enclosure, "A Compilation of Historical Data on Water Development in the Fallbrook Area," revised Jan 1999, 7, Gellman mss.

79. *LA Times,* June 11, PPS5.SA22, June 26, PPS293.114.10A, June 28, PPS5.SA24, Eberhard to Younger, June 27, uncatalogued, RN and Knowland to Murphy, July 1, PPS293.114.13.1, RN statement, July 1–4, 1952, PPS5.398, RNyl.

80. "Compilation of Historial Data," 6–10, Gellman mss.

81. Arnold to RN, June 11, B 7, F 17, Series 207, RN to Pierce, June 19, B 596, Pierce, J, RN to Garland, June 24, 1952, B 282, Garland [½], Series 320, RNln; *Congressional Record,* June 12, 1952, 7216, PPS293.129.2(1–6), RNyl.

82. RN to Allen, Mar 11, PPS293.14.29, RN to Custodio, May 9, 1952, PPS293.15.15, RNyl; RN to Pinney, Feb 26, B 599, Pinney, RN to Bush, Feb 29, B 117, Bush, D, RN to Friend, Mar 14, B 269, Form Letters, RN to Fifield, Mar 26, RN to Everett, Apr 1, B 349, Holt [½], RN to Schultz, June 16, B 677, Schultz, Series 320, RN to Simonson, Feb 21, 1952, B 6, F 3, Series 207, RNln; Prussen, *Dulles,* 432–499; Leffler, *Preponderance of Power,* 426–432 and 462–465.

83. Clipping from Fresno, Feb 12, PPS5.SA5, *LA Times,* Mar 10, 1952, PPS5.S4, RNyl.

84. *Chicago Sun Times,* May 13, 1952, PPS5.S10 and PPS5.SA20, RNyl.

85. Shroyer to RN, Jan 8, PPS300.176.2, Arnold to Chotiner, Jan 8, PPS300.176.1, RN to Chotiner, Feb 29, PPS300.185, RN to Colbert, June 17, PPS293.128.9, RN to Perry, June 26, 1952, PPS293.128.22.1, RNyl; Perry to RN, Mar 24, 1952, B 589, Perry, Series 320, RNln.

86. RN to Kruse, June 2, 1952, B 430, Kruse, Series 320, RNln.

87. *LA Times,* Mar 23, 1952, PPS5.SA17, RNyl; RN to Koffman, Apr 4, 1952, B 423, Koffman, Series 320, RNln.

88. Donovan, *Tumultuous Years,* 382–387; Lee, *Truman and Taft-Hartley,* 211–217.

89. RN speech, Apr 21, 1952, B 6, F 19, Series 207, RNln.

90. *San Francisco Examiner,* Apr 30, PPS5.SA21, *LA Times,* Apr 30, PPS5.SA16, press release, Apr 30, 1952, SP30.2, RNyl; press release, Apr 30, 1952, B 269, Form Letters, Series 320, RNln; Maeva Marcus, *Truman and the Steel Seizure Case: The Limits of Presidential Power* (NY: Columbia Univ. Press, 1977), 38–227; Donovan, *Tumultuous Years,* 387–390; Lee, *Truman and Taft-Hartley,* 218–220.

91. *Courier,* Apr 22, PPS5.S7, *San Francisco Examiner,* Apr 30, PPS5.SA21, press release, Apr 30, 1952, SP30.2, RNyl; RN speech, Apr 21, B 6, F 19, RN remarks, Apr 28, B 7, F 4, Series 207, press release, Apr 30, 1952, B 269, Form Letters, Series 320, RNln.

92. RN to Garland, Apr 3, B 282, Garland [½], RN to Fifield, Apr 24, 1952, B 257, Fifield, Series 320, RNln; RN to Martin, Apr 4, 1952, PPS209.1728, RNyl.

93. *San Francisco Chronicle,* Apr 5, PPS5.S6 and Apr 30, 1952, PPS5.SA21, RNyl; RN remarks, Apr 29, 1952, B 7, F 5, Series 207, RNln; *LA Times,* May 11, 1952.

94. Brennan to McFie, Apr 16, B 799, Warren-Werdel, Pierce to RN, Apr 29, 1952, B 596, Pierce, J, Series 320, RNln; Perry to Brennan, Apr 21, 1952, PE1212, RNyl.

95. Bewley to RN, Apr 23, 1952, B 80, Bewley, Series 320, RNln.

96. RN to Pierce, May 2, B 596, Pierce, J, RN to Beehner, May 5, B 799, Warren-Werdel, RN to Smith, May 7, Helms to RN, May 12, RN to Smith, May 14, 1952, B 799, Warren-Werdel, Series 320, RNln; memo by Thompson, May 3, PE1231.2, Brennan to RN, May 12, 1952, PPS288.255, RNyl.

97. Bewley to RN, May 28, B 80, Bewley, RN to Hancock, May 29, B 316, Hancock (3 of 3), RN statement, May 29, B 799, Warren-Werdel, RN to Hopper, May 29, 1952, B 354, Hopper, Series 320, RNln.

98. Perry to RN, May 28, 1952, B 589, Perry, Series 320, RNln; RN to Perry, May 29, 1952, PE1236.2, RNyl.

99. *LA Herald & Express,* Apr 16, PPS5.S7, *Whittier News,* Apr 18, 1952, PPS5.SA20, RNyl; RN to Day, Apr 22, 1952, B 206, Day, R, Series 320, RNln.

100. RN to Fritz, Apr 1, 1952, PPS205.2816, RNyl; RN speech, Apr 17, B 6, F 16, RN remarks, Apr 18, 1952, B 6, F 17, Series 207, RNln.
101. RN speech, Apr 17, 1952, B 6, F 16, Series 207, RNln; RN to Smith, Apr 25, 1952, SM42, RNyl.
102. RN to Smith, Apr 25, 1952, SM42, RNyl.
103. *Ibid.,* RN to Perry, May 5, 1952, PE1217, Gleason memos, May 6, 1952, un-catalogued, RNyl; Schedule, May 8, RN speech, May 8, 1952, B 7, F 6, Series 207, RNln; Nixon, *Six Crises,* 299; Smith, *Dewey,* 583.
104. Nixon, *Six Crises,* 300; Smith, *Dewey,* 583–584; Jean Smith, *Lucius D. Clay: An American Life* (NY: Holt, 1990), 602; Herbert Brownell, *Advising Ike: The Memoirs of Attorney General Herbert Brownell* (Lawrence: Univ. Press of Kansas, 1993), 120.
105. McLaughlin to RN, June 2, B 503, McLaughlin, R, RN to Perry, June 2, B 589, Perry, Perry to RN, June 4, RN to Perry, June 6, B 589, Perry, RN to Hancock, June 6, B 123, California Campaigns (1952), RN to McLaughlin, June 6, B 503, McLaughlin, R, Drown to RN, June 9, B 225, Drown, J 1956 2/2, Holt to RN, June 17, 1952, B 348, Holt, Series 320, RNln; Brennan to Perry, June 3, PE1237, Dudley to RN, June 6, PPS209.1910, Wallace to Perry, June 20, 1952, PE1251, RNyl; *Time,* June 16, 1952, 24; Congressional Quarterly, *Presidential Elections 1789–1996,* 171; Cray, *Chief Justice,* 226–228; Katcher, *Warren,* 275–286; Warren, *Memoirs,* 250; Jordan, comp., *Statement of Vote,* June 3, 1952, 4–5.
106. RN to Knowland, Feb 29, B 421, Knowland, JR, Series 320, RN to Pike, Apr 3, B 6, F 14, Series 207, RN address, Apr 16, 1952, B 1, audio recordings, RNln; *Long Beach Press-Telegram,* Apr 17, 1952, PPS5.SA20, RNyl; Joel Treese, ed., *Biographical Directory of the American Congress 1774–1996,* (Va.: CQ Staff Directory, 1997), 1495; John Moore, ed., *Congressional Quarterly's Guide to U.S. Elections,* 2d ed. (Washington, D.C.: Congressional Quarterly, 1985), 967 and 972; State of California, *Statement of Vote,* June 3, 1952, 4–5.
107. RN to Faries, May 5, 1952, B 6, F 14, Series 207, RNln; "Political Pot," June 12, PPS5.S11, Perry to Brennan, June 13, 1952, PE1245, RNyl; *Time,* June 16, 1952, 24; Montgomery and Johnson, *One Step,* 103–104; Jordan, comp., *Statement of Vote,* Nov 4, 1952, 11.
108. Ike to Bullis, May 12, Bullis to Ike, May 16, 1952, B 15, Bullis, Harry (1), Pre-Presidential, 1916–52, Principle File, Eisenhower mss; Sulzberger, *Candles,* 740–741, 744–745, 747–750, and 752–753.
109. Cantwell to RN, June 22, RN to Cantwell, June 28, 1951, B 131, Cantwell, Series 320, RNln.
110. Chotiner to RN, July 6, 1951, PPS300.117.1, Klein to RN, Jan 3, PPS5.57A, *San Gabriel Sun,* Apr 17, 1952, PPS5.SA20, RNyl; Eckerman to RN, Jan 17, B 5, F 2, Series 207, Drown to RN, Mar 6, 1952, B 225, Drown 2/2, Series 320, RNln.

*Chapter 20*

1. Dwight Eisenhower, *The White House Years: Mandate for Change 1953–1956* (NY: Doubleday, 1963, cited hereafter as *Mandate*), 31–36.
2. Agnew to RNC, June 6, PPS5.87, Keating et. al., June 7, PPS5.88, *LA Times,* June 8, PPS5.S10, *Sentinel-News,* June 9, 1952, PPS5.115, RNyl; Drown to

RN, June 9, B 225, Drown, J, 1956 2/2, *Union,* June 9, 1952, B 416, Klein (1 of 2), Series 320, RNln.

3. RN to Agnew, June 9, 1952, PPS5.93, RNyl; RN to Brennan, June 9, 1952, B 100, Brennan, Series 320, RNln.

4. Lodge to RN, Mar 12, PPS209.1650, Faries to Bechner, June 18, PPS5.147, Lodge to RN, June 19, PPS5.153.2, RN to Lodge, June 23, 1952, PPS5.261.1, RNyl.

5. RN to Brennan, June 9, 1952, B 100, Brennan, Series 320, RNln.

6. Jean Goodrich, "Richard Nixon Trust Fund," Appendix A, RN to Smith, June 9 and Appendix B, June 16, 1952, SM1.1, RNyl.

7. Poll for Presidential Republican Convention, June, PPS5.121A.2, Arnold to RN, June 16, PPS5.131A, Trial Heats, 1950–1952, PPS5.549 (32), Jim to RN, June 16, PPS5.143.2, Denham to RN, June 17, PPS5.163, Cotton to RN, June 17, PPS5.162, Lombardi to RN, June 17, PPS5.166, Day to RN, June 18, PPS5.167, RN to Baker, June 18, PPS5.170, Mecham to RN, June 19, PPS209.1942, Bean to RN, June 19, PPS5.161.1, RN to Cogswell, June 23, PPS209.1948, *LA Times,* June 24, PPS5.S16, Hoeft to RN, June 25, PPS5.204, clippings, June 4, 11, 13, 15, 18, 22, and 27, 1952, PPS5.549 (31), Dudley to RN, June 28, PPS5.315, Zimmerman to RN, June 30, 1952, PPS5.226, RNyl; RN to Friend, June 11, B 123, California Campaigns (1952), memo by RN, June 18, B 508, Memorandum before 1955, Call to RN, June 23, B 126, Call, A, RN to Weiss, July 1, B 807, Weiss, HP, Series 320, Peterson to RN, June 25, 1952, B 7, F 17, Series 207, RNln; Warren, *Memoirs,* 25; Katcher, *Warren,* 289.

8. RN to Call, June 18, 1952, PPS5.149A, RNyl; RN to Suchman, June 27, 1952, B 349, Holt [½], Series 320, RNln.

9. RN to Randall, June 16, 1952, B 620, Randall, E, Series 320, RNln; RN to Landsberg, June 20, PPS5.240, *LA Times,* June 24, 1952, PPS5.S16, RNyl.

10. *LA Mirror,* June 21, PPS5.251, *LA Times,* June 26, PPS5.S15, Gordon Harrison, "Warren of California," *Harper's* (June 1952), PPS5.442, RNyl.

11. Dudley to RN, June 6, PPS209.1910, "Political Pot," June 12, PPS5.S11, *Wall Street Journal,* June 13, PPS5.S12, *Fort Worth Star Telegram,* June 13, PPS5.S12, Perry to Brennan, June 13, PE1245, clipping, June 24, 1952, PPS5.S16, RNyl; Herter to RN, June 16, 1952, B 334, Herter, Series 320, RNln.

12. RN to Palmer, June 20, B 577, Palmer (2 of 2), Series 320, Hillings to RN, June 25, 1952, B 7, F 17, Series 207, RNln.

13. *Time,* June 30, 1952, PPS5.223.2, RNyl.

14. Kirkwood to Faries, June 18, PPS5.267.2, Gabrielson to RN, June 18, PPS5.148, Robie to RN, June 20, PPS5.246.1, RN to Faries, June 21, PPS5.250, RN to Perry, June 26, PE1255, Kirkwood to Knowland, June 27, PPS5.311, 1952, RNyl; RN to Perry, June 26, 1952, PE1255, RNln; Smith diary, July 1, 1952, 274–275, B 282, H. Alexander Smith mss, Princeton University, Princeton, New Jersey.

15. Smith, *Dewey,* 586; Sherman Adams, *Firsthand Report: The Story of the Eisenhower Administration* (NY: Harper, 1961), 15; Herbert Parmet, *Eisenhower and the American Crusades* (NY: Macmillan, 1972), 74–77.

16. Moley, "Fair Play Is Good Politics Too," June 9, PPS5.431, "Fulton Lewis Talks About Texas," June 26, 1952, PPS5.305.2, RNyl.

17. Lodge to RN, June 25, PPS5.294, Dunlap to RN, June 30, 1952, PPS5.227, RNyl.

18. Smith, *Dewey,* 588; Patterson, *Taft,* 545; Parmet, *Eisenhower,* 80–82.
19. *NY Times,* July 3, 1952, *Washington Post,* July 3, 1952, PPS5.S19, RNyl; Parmet, *Eisenhower,* 74–79.
20. *NY Times,* July 3, 1952, *LA Times,* July 3, *Post-Gazette,* July 4, 1952, PPS5.374.2, RNyl.
21. Helene to Bruce Drown, July 3, 1952, B 1, F 1, DR, *LA Examiner,* July 4, PPS5.S19, *LA Times,* July 5, PPS5.S20, *Long Beach Press-Telegram,* July 17, 1952, PPS266.S47, RNyl; *NY Times,* July 5, 1952; Richard Bergholz interview, Coll 2031, B 53, F 3, Cray mss; Cray, *Chief Justice,* 229–230.
22. *NY Times,* July 3, 1952; Warren, *Memoirs,* 251.
23. RN to Drown, June 10, B 225, Drown, 2/2, Series 320, RN to Faries, June 11, B 7, Arnold to RN, June 11, 1952, F 17, Series 207, RNln; Woods to RN, July 1, 1952, PPS5.359, RNyl.
24. RN to Mac, May 30, B 677, St. Johns, M, Series 320, RN to Klein, July 24, 1951, B 416, Klein (1 of 2), Series 320, RNln; interview with Pat Hillings, Coll 2031, B 53, F 3, Cray mss; Hillings, *Irishman,* 53; Warren, *Memoirs,* 251; Katcher, *Warren,* 290.
25. *Ibid.;* Abell, ed., *Pearson Diaries,* 218.
26. *NY Times,* July 6, 1952; *San Francisco Examiner,* July 6, PPS5.S20, *LA Times,* July 6, 1952, PPS5.S20, RNyl; Katcher, *Warren,* 291.
27. *NY Times,* July 6, 1952.
28. Delap to RN, Apr 22, PPS5.71, memo from Delap, before July 6, PPS5.381, *LA Examiner,* July 6, PPS5.S20, *LA Times,* July 6, 1952, PPS5.S20, RNyl; *NY Times,* July 7, 1952.
29. Baley to Outland, June 17, 1952, PPS5.144, RNyl; Eisenhower, *Mandate,* 40.
30. Lodge to RN, June 27, PPS5.307, *Chicago Herald-American,* July 12, PPS5.SA30, *NY Times,* July 12, 1952, PPS5.S27, RNyl; Perry to RN, July 7, 1952, B 589, Perry (2 of 2), Series 320, RNln; Smith diary, July 7, 1952, 284, B 282, H.A. Smith mss; Sulzberger, *Candles,* 766–768; Abell, ed., *Pearson Diaries,* 218; Eisenhower, *Pat Nixon,* 114.
31. Clipping pre-convention, July 1952, PPS5.284.2, RNyl; Walter Cronkite interview, "Booknotes," May 14, 1997, C-SPAN; Smith diary, July 7, 1952, 285, B 282, H.A. Smith mss; Republican convention, July 7, 1952, EL-MP16–83, audio-visual archives, Eisenhower mss; Walter Cronkite, *A Reporter's Life* (NY: Knopf, 1996), 179–180; Parmet, *Eisenhower,* 88.
32. *NY Times,* July 8, 1952; Patterson, *Mr. Republican,* 552–555; Edward Schapsmeier and Frederick Schapsmeier, *Dirksen of Illinois: Senatorial Statesman* (Urbana: Univ. of Illinois Press, 1985), 76–78; Lodge, *The Storm,* 118–120; Parmet, *Eisenhower,* 86–89; Adams, *Firsthand Report,* 15–16; Eisenhower, *Mandate,* 43.
33. Photo, July 7, 1952, 82–1–IV-145, Eisenhower mss; *Chicago Daily News,* July 7, 1952; *NY Times,* July 8, 1952; Cray, *Chief Justice,* 237–240.
34. *NY Times,* July 8, 1952.
35. *Rochester Times-Union,* Jan 9, 1957, B 653, Rogers 1953–1959 (3 of 3), Boston *Globe,* Aug 26, 1960, B 653, Rogers 1960 (1 of 2), Series 320, RNln; Smith diary, July 8, 1952, 286, B 282, H.A. Smith mss; *Chicago Daily News,* July 8, 1952; Abell, ed., *Pearson Diaries,* 219.
36. *NY Times,* July 9, 1952.

37. Republican National Convention, July 1952, Chicago, Ill. Notes of Paul H. Davis, B 3, American subject collection, Hoover Institution Archives, Stanford University, Stanford, California; Morris, *Nixon,* 719—20.

38. *NY Times,* July 9, 1952.

39. *Ibid.;* memo by McCall, Jan 3, 1959, B 649, Robinson (1 of 2), Series 320, RNln.

40. *NY Times,* July 9 and 10, 1952; *Chicago Daily News,* July 9, 1952; clipping, July 9, 1952, PE1262, RNyl.

41. *Chicago Daily News,* July 9 and 10, 1952.

42. *Chicago Daily News,* July 10, 1952; *Burlington,* NC *Daily Times,* July 12, 1952, PPS5S.A-17, RNyl.

43. Photograph, July 9, 1952, 82-1-IV-129, Eisenhower mss; *NY Times,* July 10, 1952.

44. *Ibid.*

45. *Ibid.;* *Chicago Daily News,* July 10, 1952; Schapsmeier and Schapsmeier, *Dirksen,* 777–80; Patterson, *Mr. Republican,* 556–557; Smith, *Dewey,* 593.

46. Lodge, *The Storm,* 122.

47. 1952 Republican Platform, July 10, 1952, PPS5.403, RNyl.

48. *LA Daily News,* July 11, PPS5.SA25, Younger to RN, after nomination, 1952, PPS5.423, RNyl.

49. *Chicago Daily News,* July 10, 1952; *Ashville Citizen,* July 11, 1952, PPS5.SA-13, RNyl; Sulzberger, *Candles,* 771.

50. *Chicago Daily News,* July 10, 1952; *Washington Post,* July 10, PPS5.S21, *Los Angeles Examiner,* July 11, PPS5.S22B, *San Francisco Chronicle,* July 11, PPS5.S23, *San Francisco Cal Bulletin,* July 11, PPS5.S21, *LA Herald & Express,* July 11, PPS5. S22A, *LA Examiner,* July 11, 1952, PPS5.S4A, RNyl.

51. *LA Examiner,* July 11, 1952, PPS5.S4A, *Sun-Telegram,* July 15, 1952, PPS5.S46, RNyl: *NY Times,* July 11, 1952; Cray, *Chief Justice,* 241–242.

52. *NY Times,* July 11, PPS5.S23, *NY Herald Tribune,* July 11, PPS5.S22, *San Francisco Chronicle,* July 11, PPS5.S23, *San Francisco Cal Bulletin,* July 11, PPS5.S21, *LA Examiner,* July 11, PPS5.S22B, *Daily Mirror,* July 11, PPS5.S23, *LA Herald Express,* July 11, 1952, PPS5.S21, RNyl.

53. "The GOP Ticket," July 11, 1952, RNLB2:1, RNyl; Republican convention, July 11, 1952, audiovisual archives, EL-MP16–83, Eisenhower mss; *NY Times,* July 11, 1952.

54. "The GOP Ticket," July 11, RNLB2:1, *LA Times,* July 12, 1952, PPS5.S49, RNyl; July 11, 1952, EL-MP16–83, audiovisual archives, Eisenhower mss; *NY Times,* July 12, 1952; Eisenhower, *Mandate,* 44–45; Patterson, *Mr. Republican,* 558; Abell, ed., *Pearson Diaries,* 220; Schapsmeier and Schapsmeier, *Dirksen,* 80.

55. Sulzberger, *Candles,* 772; Eisenhower, *Mandate,* 44.

56. Smith diary, July 12, 1952, 292–293, B 282, HA Smith mss; Eisenhower, *Mandate,* 44–45; Patterson, *Mr. Republican,* 562–563.

57. Eisenhower, *Mandate,* 45; Patterson, *Mr. Republican,* 563.

58. Smith diary, July 12, 1952, 293, B 282, HA Smith mss; *LA Herald Express,* July 11, PPS5.S5, *Daily Sun,* July 12, PPS5.SA192, *Philadelphia Inquirer,* July 12, PPS5.Sos71C, *St. Louis Post-Dispatch,* Sept 28, 1952, PPS13.Sos, RNyl; Adams, *Firsthand Report,* 36; Smith, *Clay,* 601: Alan Raucher, *Paul G. Hoffman: Architect of Foreign Aid,* (Lexington: Univ. Press of Kentucky, 1985), 94.

59. *St. Louis Post-Dispatch,* Sept 28, 1952, PPS13.Sos, RNyl.

60. Smith diary, July 12, 1952, 295, B 282, HA Smith mss; Sherman Adams, Columbia Oral History Project; Adams, *Firsthand Report,* 17 and 36; Frank Carlson, OH-488, Eisenhower mss; *News,* July 11, PPS5.S23, *NY Times,* July 12, PPS5.S28, *Philadelphia Inquirer,* July 12, 1952, PPS5.Sos71C, RNyl; Smith, *Dewey,* 595–596; Brownell, *Advising Ike,* 121; Patterson, *Mr. Republican,* 564–565; Schapsmeier and Schapsmeier, *Dirksen,* 81; Internet, http://www.kcstar.com/aboutstar/history/date.htm, "K.C. DateLine," p. 5, Gellman mss.

61. Saltonstall to RN, Nov 14, 1951, Series 207, B 4, F 17, and July 5, 1952, B 669, Saltonstall, Series 320, RNln; *LA Herald Express,* July 11, PPS5.S5, *News,* July 11, PPS5.S23, *NY Herald Tribune,* July 12, 1952, PPS5.SA60, RNyl; Leverett Saltonstall interview, OH-29, 2, 12, 40, 55, and 61, Columbia Oral History Project, Eisenhower mss.

62. *St. Louis Post-Dispatch,* Sept 28, 1952, PPS13.Sos, RNyl.

63. Hoffman to Horton, July 30, Hoffman to Davison, Aug 7, Hoffman to Oliver, Sept 13, 1952, Eminent Personage File, Nixon, Richard M., 1952–1960, Paul Hoffman mss; Raucher, *Hoffman,* 80–94.

64. *St. Louis Post-Dispatch,* Sept 28, 1952, PPS13.Sos, RNyl.

65. *Philadelphia Inquirer,* July 12, PPS5.Sos71C, *St. Louis Post-Dispatch,* Sept 28, 1952, PPS13.Sos, RNyl; Eisenhower, *Mandate,* 46; Brownell, *Advising Ike,* 121.

66. *St. Louis Post-Dispatch,* Sept 28, 1952, PPS13.Sos, RNyl.

67. Galambos, ed., *The Papers of Dwight David Eisenhower,* V.XIII, 1307; Eisenhower, *Mandate,* 46–47.

68. Sulzberger, *Candles,* 773; Eisenhower, *Mandate,* 46; Brownell, *Advising Ike,* 120–121; Scheele, *Halleck,* 1–2; Charles Halleck interview, OH-489, Eisenhower mss; Nixon, *RN,* 88.

69. Eisenhower, *Pat Nixon,* 114; Nixon, *RN,* 86.

70. Eisenhower, *Pat Nixon,* 114–115; Nixon, *RN,* 86.

71. *LA Times,* July 12, PPS5.S49, *Washington Times Herald,* July 14, PPS5.SA116, *Whittier Star Reporter,* Sept 4, 1952, PPS266.S57, RNyl; Nixon, *RN,* 86; Hillings, *Irishman,* 56.

72. *LA Times,* July 12, PPS5.S49, and July 18, PPS5.S53, *NY Herald Tribune,* July 12, PPS5.SA60, *Washington Times-Herald,* July 14, PPS5.SA116, *Whittier Star Reporter,* Sept 4, 1952, PPS266.S57, RNyl; Hillings, *Irishman,* 56; Nixon, *RN,* 86–87.

73. Clipping, after convention, 1952, PPS.SA192, *NY Times,* July 12, PPS5.S28, *Washington Times-Herald,* July 14, PPS5.SA116, RNyl; RN to Adams, Dec 31, 1958, B 147, Chotiner (1957–1958), Series 320, RNln; Adams, *Firsthand Report,* 17; Nixon, *RN,* 87–88.

74. *Burlington, NC Daily Times,* July 12, PPS5.SA-17, *Chicago Herald-American,* July 12, PPS5.SA30, *Washington Times-Herald,* July 14, PPS5.SA36, *LA Herald Express,* July 12, 1952, PPS5.S37, RNyl; Eisenhower, *Pat Nixon,* 115.

75. *NY Times,* July 12, 1952, PPS5.S27, RNyl; Eisenhower, *Pat Nixon,* 115.

76. *LA Times,* July 12, PPS5.Sos*46, Burlington, NC, *Daily Times,* July 12, PPS5.SA-17, *Des Moines Register,* July 12, PPS5.Sos67D, *Chicago Herald-Tribune,* July 12, PPS5.SA30, *Washington Times-Herald,* July 12, 1952, PPS5.SA36, RNyl.

77. *Des Moines Register,* July 12, PPS5.Sos67D, *Washington Times-Herald,* July 12, PPS5.SA36, *LA Herald Express,* July 12, 1952, PPS5.S37, RNyl.

78. Republican national convention, July 11, RNLB:122:1, Knowland Nominates RN, July 11, RNLB:112:5, "Ike Accepts," July 11, RNLB:112:3, *NY Times*, July 12, PPS5.S28, *Des Moines Register*, July 12, PPS5.Sos67D, clipping, undated, PPS266.S36, *Chicago Sun-Times*, July 12, PPS266.Sos26, *Washington Times-Herald*, July 12, PPS5.SA36, Des Moines *Register*, July 12, PPS5.Sos67D, Whittier *Star Reporter*, July 13, 1952, PPS5.SA108, RNyl; Nixon, *RN*, 89.

79. Republican national convention, July 11, RNLB:122:1, *NY Herald Tribune*, July 12, PPS5.SA62, *NY Times*, July 12, PPS5.S28, *Des Moines Register*, July 12, 1952, RNyl; Nixon, *RN*, 89.

80. "The GOP Ticket," July 11, RNLB:2:1, Republican national convention, July 11, RNLB:14:16, *Whittier News*, July 12, PPS5.Sos54A, *NY Times*, July 12, PPS5.S28, clipping, undated, 1952, PPS266.S36, RNyl; July 11, EL-MP16–83, audiovisual archives, Eisenhower mss; Eisenhower, *Pat Nixon*, 116; Nixon, *RN*, 89.

81. "Ike Accepts," July 11, RNLB:112:3, "The GOP Ticket," July 11, 1952, RNLB:2:1, *Chicago Sun-Times*, July 12, 1952, PPS266.Sos26, RNyl; Ike speech, July 11, 1952, EL-MP16–93, audiovisual archives, Eisenhower mss; Sulzberger, *Candles*, 773; Eisenhower, *Pat Nixon*, 116; Eisenhower, *Mandate*, 47.

82. Ike speech, July 11, 1952, audiovisual archives, EL-MP16–93, Eisenhower mss; "Ike Accepts," July 11, RNLB:112:3, "The GOP Ticket," July 11, 1952, RNLB:2:1, RNyl; Eisenhower, *Mandate*, 45–46; *NY Times*, July 12, 1952.

83. RN acceptance, July 11, RNLB:118:12, *Chicago Herald-American*, July 12, PPS5.S63, *LA Times*, July 12, PPS5.S49, clipping, after July nomination, 1952, PPS5.SA192, RNyl; RN speech, July 11, 1952, B 7, F 16, Series 207, RNln.

84. *NY Times*, July 12, 1952.

85. Photograph, July 11, 1952, 82-1-IV-174, Eisenhower mss; *Washington Times-Herald*, July 12, PPS5.SA27, *Des Moines Register*, July 12, 1952, PPS5.Sos.67B, RNyl.

86. Nixon, *Six Crises*, 75.

87. Telephone interview with Verne Scoggins, Coll 2031, B 53, F 3, Cray mss; Montgomery and Johnson, *One Step*, 109–112; Cray, *Chief Justice*, 233–236.

88. *News*, July 11, PPS5.S23, *San Francisco Cal Bulletin*, July 15, 1952, PPS5.S46, RNyl; Montgomery and Johnson, *One Step*, 119–120.

89. *LA Mirror*, July 12, 1952, PPS5.S41, RNyl; Knowland interview, Columbia Oral History Project, OH-333, copy in Eisenhower mss.

90. Sulzberger, *Candles*, 773.


*Epilogue*

1. Nixon, *RN*, 957–958.
2. "The Saga of Dick Nixon," July 12, 1952, *Madera News-Tribune*, PPS 10.56, RNyl.
3. Unused draft column for *LA Times* syndicates, Sept 18, 1961, PPS208 (1961-A).65, RNyl.
4. Ernest Brashear, "Who Is Richard Nixon?", *New Republic* (Sept 1, 1952), 9–12.
5. Ambrose, *Nixon*, I, 253–266.

6. Morris, *Nixon,* 379; Monrovia–Duarte 1948 telephone book, 48.
7. Recapitulation of Poster Advertising, 1950 election, SM4.11, RNyl; Brashear, "Who Is Richard Nixon?", 11–12.
8. *Cold War,* CNN, Nov 8, 1999.
9. Katharine Graham, *Personal History* (NY: Vintage Books, 1998), 202.
10. Virginia Purdy, "A Temple to Clio: The National Archives Building," *Prologue* (Summer 1984).

# Bibliography

*Manuscript Collections*

Alsop, Stewart, Manuscripts Division, Library of Congress, Washington, D.C.

American Subject Collection, Hoover Institution, Stanford University, Stanford, California.

Army Corps of Engineers, Los Angeles District, Civil Works Projects, 1935–1950, Record Group 77, National Archives and Records Administration, Pacific Region, Laguna Niguel, California.

Balch, John, "Richard M. Nixon vs. Jerry Voorhis for Congress 1946," May 12, 1971, University Library, Special Collections, California State Polytechnic University Pomona, Pomona, California.

Candidate's Campaign Statement of Receipts and Expenditures, Richard M. Nixon, 1946, 1948, and 1950, California State Archives, Sacramento, California.

Cray, Ed, Special Collections Department, University Research Library, University of California, Los Angeles, California.

Cronin, John, Archivist and Curator of Manuscripts, Hesburgh Library, University of Notre Dame, Notre Dame, Indiana.

Department of State, Record Groups 59, National Archives and Records Administration, Washington, D.C.

———. War Branch History, National Archives and Records Administration, Washington, D.C.

Douglas, Helen, The Carl Albert Center, University of Oklahoma, Norman, Oklahoma.

Eisenhower, Dwight, Dwight D. Eisenhower Presidential Library, Abilene, Kansas.

Federal Bureau of Investigation, Washington, D.C.:
    Benjamin Davis file
    Laurence Duggan file
    Richard Nixon application file.

Gardner, Richard, "Fighting Quaker (The Story of Richard Nixon)." Unpublished manuscript, 1953, and Richard Nixon's 1950 Campaign Manual, Special Collections, Wardman Library, Whittier College, Whittier, California.

Gellman, Gloria Gae, Richard Nixon Library & Birthplace, Yorba Linda, California.

Hiss, Alger, Special Collections, Harvard University Law School Library, Harvard University, Cambridge, Massachusetts.

Hoffman, Paul, Harry S. Truman Presidential Library, Independence, Missouri.

Hoover, Herbert, Herbert Hoover Presidential Library, West Branch, Iowa.

Keating, Kenneth, Special Collections, University of Rochester Library, Rochester, New York.

Kersten, Charles, Special Collections, Memorial Library, Marquette University, Milwaukee, Wisconsin.

Kohlberg, Alfred, Hoover Institution, Stanford University, Stanford, California.

Lasky, Victor, The John M. Ashbrook Center for Public Affairs, Ashland University, Ashland, Ohio.

Matthews, Francis, Harry S. Truman Presidential Library, Independence, Missouri.

Monrovia-Duarte 1948 Telephone Book, California State Library, Sacramento, California.

Mundt, Karl, Karl E. Mundt Historical and Educational Foundation, Dakota State University, Madison, South Dakota.

RNln, Richard Nixon Pre-Presidential Papers, National Archives and Record Administration, Pacific Region, Laguna Niguel, California.

RNyl, Richard Nixon Library & Birthplace, Yorba Linda, California.

Pearson, Drew, Lyndon Baines Johnson Presidential Library, Austin, Texas.

Pegler, Westbrook, Herbert Hoover Presidential Library, West Branch, Iowa.

Smathers, George, Department of Special Collections, Smathers Library, University of Florida, Gainesville, Florida.

Smith, H. Alexander, Manuscripts Collections, Mudd Library, Princeton University, Princeton, New Jersey.

Smith, Margaret, Margaret Chase Smith Library, Northwood University, Skowhegan, Maine.

Truman, Harry S., Harry S. Truman Presidential Library, Independence, Missouri.

Voorhis, Horace J., Special Collections, Honnold/Mudd Library, Claremont Colleges, Claremont, California.

Voorhis, J. L., "An Idealist in Congress," Special Collections, Honnold/Mudd Library, Claremont Colleges, Claremont, California.

Weinstein, Allen, Harry S. Truman Presidential Library, Independence, Missouri.

Welles, Sumner, Franklin D. Roosevelt Presidential Library, Hyde Park, New York.

Woods, Robert E., Herbert Hoover Presidential Library, West Branch, Iowa.

*Oral Histories*

Adams, Earl, Earl Warren Oral History Project, Richard M. Nixon in the Warren Era. Bancroft Library, University of California, Berkeley, California.

Adams, Sherman, OH-162, Colombia Oral History Project, copy in Dwight Eisenhower Presidential Library, Abilene, Kansas.

Andrews, Phyllis, Richard Nixon Library & Birthplace, Yorba Linda, California.

Bergholz, Richard, B 53, F 3, Coll 2031, Cray mss.

Black, Wallace, OH-812, California State University, Fullerton, California.

Carlson, Frank, OH-488, Dwight Eisenhower Presidential Library, Abilene, Kansas.

Chotiner, Phyllis, B 54, F 3, Coll 2031, Cray mss.

Daniels, Helen, Richard Nixon Library & Birthplace, Yorba Linda, California.

Day, Roy, Earl Warren Oral History Project, Richard M. Nixon in the Warren Era. Bancroft Library, University of California, Berkeley, California.

De Sola, Alice, Women in Politics, Oral History Project, Helen Gahagan Douglas Project, V. III. Bancroft Library, University of California, Berkeley, California.

Dinkelspiel, John, Earl Warren Oral History Project, Richard M. Nixon in the Warren Era. Bancroft Library, University of California, Berkeley, California.

Edwards, India, Women in Politics Oral History Project, Helen Gahagan Douglas Project, V. I. Bancroft Library, University of California, Berkeley, California.

Fantz, Donald, Richard Nixon Library & Birthplace, Yorba Linda, California.

Faries, McIntyre, B 53, F 3, Coll 2031, Cray mss.

Finch, Robert, Columbia Oral History Project, copy in Dwight Eisenhower Presidential Library, Abilene, Kansas.

Hillings, Patrick, B 53, F 3, Coll 2031, Cray mss.

Hogan, Charles, Women in Politics, Helen Gahagan Douglas Project, V. I. Bancroft Library, University of California, Berkeley, California.

Holifield, Chet, Women in Politics, Helen Gahagan Douglas Project, V. I. Bancroft Library, University of California, Berkeley, California.

Jorgensen, Frank, Earl Warren Oral History Project, Richard M. Nixon in the Warren Era. Bancroft Library, University of California, Berkeley, California.

Kepple, Gerald OH-992, California State University, Fullerton, Fullerton, California.

Keyserling, Mary, Women in Politics, Helen Gahagan Douglas Project, V. II. Bancroft Library, University of California, Berkeley, California.

Knowland, William, OH-333, Columbia Oral History Project, copy in Dwight Eisenhower Presidential Library, Abilene, Kansas.

Kroener, Margaret, Richard Nixon Library & Birthplace, Yorba Linda, California.

Lindsley, Bryon, Women in Politics, Helen Gahagan Douglas Project, V. I. Bancroft Library, University of California, Berkeley, California.

Lustig, Helen, Women in Politics, Helen Gahagan Douglas Project, V. I. Bancroft Library, University of California, Berkeley, California.

Nixon, Richard, Princeton University, Princeton, New Jersey, and Richard Nixon Library & Birthplace, Yorba Linda, California.

Noel-Baker, Philip, Women in Politics, Helen Gahagan Douglas Project, V. I. Bancroft Library, University of California, Berkeley, California.

Peck, Ralph, Richard Nixon Library & Birthplace, Yorba Linda, California.

Robbins, Margaret, Richard Nixon Library & Birthplace, Yorba Linda, California.

Rogers, Frank, Women in Politics Oral History Project, Helen Gahagan Douglas Project, V. I. Bancroft Library, University of California, Berkeley, California.

Saltonstall, Leverett, OH-29, Columbia Oral History Project, copy in Dwight Eisenhower Presidential Library, Abilene, Kansas.

Scroggins, Verne, B 53, F3, Coll 2031, Cray mss.

Voorhis, Harold J., Special Collections, Honnold/Mudd Library, Claremont Colleges, Claremont, California.

Voorhis, Horace J., Bancroft Library, University of California, Berkeley, California.

Voorhis, Horace J., Claremont Graduate School Oral History Program, Claremont Colleges, Claremont, California.

Zetterberg, Stephen, Claremont Graduate School Oral History Program, Claremont Colleges, Claremont, California.

Zetterberg, Stephen, State Government Oral History Program, California State Archives, Sacramento, California.

*Interviews*

Walter Cronkite, "Booknotes," May 14, 1997, C-SPAN, Washington, D.C.
Betty Ford, February 16, 1998, C-SPAN, Washington, D.C.
James Gleason, July 29, 1998, telephone interview.
Hubert Perry, April 22, 1997.
Gordon Tinker, January 22, 1999, telephone interview.

*Government Documents*

State of California, Secretary of State, *Statement of Vote,* June 6, 1950; June 3, 1952; November 4, 1952.
U.S. Congress, *Biographical Directory of the United States Congress, 1774–1989.* Washington, D.C.: Government Printing Office, 1989.
———. Richard Nixon, "The Challenge of 1952." Washington, D.C.: Government Printing Office, 1951.
———. "The Hiss Case: A Lesson for the American People." Washington, D.C.: Government Printing Office, 1950.
———. *Congressional Record,* 1947–52.
House of Representatives, 80th Congress, 1st Session, Hearings Before the Committee on Education and Labor, *Amendments to the National Labor Relations Act.* V. 2, February 1947. Washington, D.C.: Government Printing Office, 1947.
———. *Amendments to the National Labor Relations Acts, Bills to Amend and Repeal the National Labor Relations Act, and for Other Purposes.* V. 3 and 4, February 1947. Washington, D. C.: Government Printing Office, 1947.
———. Committee on Un-American Activities, 80th Congress, 1st Session, *Hearings on Gerhart Eisler Investigation of Un-American Propaganda Activities in the United States.* Public Law 601. Washington, D.C.: Government Printing Office, 1947.
———. 80th Congress, 1st Session, *Hearings Regarding Communism in Labor Unions in the United States.* Washington, D.C.: Government Printing Office, 1947.
———. 80th Congress, 2d Session, *Hearings Regarding Communist Espionage in the United States Government,* Parts I and II. Washington, D.C.: Government Printing Office, 1948.
———. 80th Congress, 1st Session, *Hearings Regarding the Communist Infiltration of the Motion Picture Industry.* Washington, D.C.: Government Printing Office, 1947.
———. 80th Congress, 1st Session, *Investigation of Un-American Propaganda Activities in the United States* on H.R. 1884 and H.R. 2122. Washington, D.C.: Government Printing Office, 1947.
———. 80th Congress, 2d Session, *Protecting the United States Against Un-American and Subversive Activities.* Washington, D.C.: Government Printing Office, 1948.
———. 80th Congress, 2d Session, *Report of the Committee on Un-American Activities to the United States House of Representatives.* Washington, D.C.: Government Printing Office, 1949.
———. 80th Congress, 2d Session, *Report of the Subcommittee on Legislation of the Committee on Un-American Activities on Proposed Legislation to Control Subversive Communist Activities in the United States.* Washington, D.C.: Government Printing Office, 1948.

————. 80th Congress, 2d Session, *Report of the Subcommittee on Legislation of the Committee on Un-American Activities on Proposed Legislation to Control Subversive Communist Activities in the United States.* Washington, D.C.: Government Printing Office, 1948.

————. 80th Congress, 2d Session, *Report on Soviet Espionage Activities in Connection with the Atom Bomb.* Washington, D.C.: Government Printing Office, 1948.

————. 80th Congress, 2d Session, *Report on the Communist Party of the United States as an Advocate of Overthrow of Government by Force and Violence.* Washington, D.C.: Government Printing Office, 1948.

————. 80th Congress, 2d Session, *Soviet Espionage Within the United States Government.* Washington, D.C.: Government Printing Office, 1949.

————. Subcommittee on Legislation of the Committee on Un-American Activities. 80th Congress, 2d Session, *Hearing on Proposed Legislation to Curb or Control the Communist Party of the United States.* Washington, D.C.: Government Printing Office, 1948.

U.S. Senate, Hearings Before the Investigation Subcommittee of the Committee on Expenditures in Executive Departments, 82d Congress, 1st Session, *Influence in Government Procedure.* Washington, D.C.: Government Printing Office, 1951.

————. 82d Congress, 2d Session, *Interim Report of the Committee on Expenditures in the Executive Departments.* Washington, D.C.: Government Printing Office, 1952.


## Books

Abell, Tyler, ed. *Drew Pearson Diaries 1949–1959.* New York: Holt, Rinehart & Winston, 1974.

Abels, Jules. *The Truman Scandals.* Chicago: Regnery, 1956.

Abrahamsen, David. *Nixon vs. Nixon: An Emotional Tragedy.* New York: Farrar, Straus & Giroux, 1977.

Acheson, Dean. *Present at the Creation: My Years in the State Department.* New York: Signet, 1970.

Adams, Sherman. *Firsthand Report: The Story of the Eisenhower Administration.* New York: Harper, 1961.

Aitken, Jonathan. *Nixon: A Life.* Washington, D.C.: Regnery, 1993.

Ambrose, Stephen. *Eisenhower: Soldier, General of the Army, President-Elect 1890–1952.* New York: Simon & Schuster, 1983.

————. *Nixon: The Education of a Politician 1913–1962.* V. I. New York: Simon & Schuster, 1987.

Andrews, Bert, and Peter Andrews. *A Tragedy of History: A Journalist's Confidential Role in the Hiss-Chambers Case.* Washington, D.C.: Luce, 1962.

Arnold, William. *Back When It All Began: The Early Nixon Years.* New York: Vantage Press, 1972.

Bacon, Margaret Hope. *Let This Life Speak: The Legacy of Henry Joel Cadbury.* Philadelphia: University of Pennsylvania Press, 1987.

Ball, Rick, and NBC News. *Meet the Press: 50 Years of History in the Making.* New York: McGraw-Hill, 1998.

Becnel, Thomas. *Senator Allen Ellender of Louisiana: A Biography.* Baton Rouge: Louisiana State University Press, 1995.

Bentley, Elizabeth. *Out of Bondage.* New York: Devin-Adair, 1951.

Berges, Marshall. *The Life and Times of Los Angeles: A Newspaper, a Family and a City.* New York: Atheneum, 1984.

Berle, Beatrice, and Travis Jacobs, eds. *Navigating the Rapids 1918–1971: From the Papers of Adolf A. Berle.* New York: Harcourt Brace Jovanovich, 1973.

Bernstein, Barton, and Allen Matusow, eds. *The Truman Administration: A Documentary History.* New York: Harper, 1968.

Bohlen, Charles. *Witness to History 1929–1969.* New York: Norton, 1969.

Brodie, Fawn. *Richard Nixon: The Shaping of His Character.* New York: Norton, 1981.

Brownell, Herbert. *Advising Ike: The Memoirs of Attorney General Herbert Brownell.* Lawrence: University Press of Kansas, 1993.

Buckley, William, ed. *Odyssey of a Friend: Whittaker Chambers' Letters to William F. Buckley, Jr. 1954–1961.* New York: Putnam, 1969.

Bullock, Alan. *Ernest Bevin: Foreign Secretary 1945–1951.* London: Heinemann, 1983.

Bullock, Paul. *Jerry Voorhis: The Idealist as Politician.* New York: Vantage Press, 1978.

Carr, Robert. *The House Committee on Un-American Activities 1945–1950.* Ithaca: Cornell University Press, 1952.

Chace, James. *Acheson: The Secretary of State Who Created the American World.* New York: Simon & Schuster, 1998.

Chambers, Whittaker. *Witness.* New York: Random House, 1952.

Cofer, E. M. *Carrier on the Prairie: The Story of the U.S. Air Station Ottumwa, Iowa.* Iowa: Hawley Court Press, 1996.

Congressional Quarterly. *Congressional Quarterly's Guide to US Elections,* 2nd ed. Washington, D.C.: Congressional Quarterly, 1985.

Cooper, Charles. *Whittier: Independent College in California.* California: Ward Ritchie Press, 1967.

Cray, Ed. *Chief Justice: A Biography of Earl Warren.* New York: Simon & Schuster, 1997.

Cronkite, Walter. *A Reporter's Life.* New York: Knopf, 1996.

Crosby, Donald. *God, Church, and Flag: Senator Joseph R. McCarthy and the Catholic Church 1950–1957.* Chapel Hill: University of North Carolina Press, 1978.

Crow, John. *California as a Place to Live.* New York: Scribners, 1953.

David, Lester. *The Lonely Lady of San Clemente: The Story of Pat Nixon.* New York: Cromwell, 1978.

de Toledano, Ralph. *Nixon.* New York: Holt, 1956.

———. *Notes from the Underground: The Whittaker Chambers–Ralph de Toledano Letters: 1949–1960.* Washington, D.C.: Regnery, 1997.

———. *One Man Alone: Richard Nixon.* New York: Funk & Wagnalls, 1969.

———. and Victor Lasky. *Seeds of Treason: The True Story of the Chambers-Hiss Tragedy.* Boston: American Library, 1965.

Dike, Richard, and Francis Gannon. *Chet Holifield: Master Legislator and Nuclear Statesman.* Md.: University Press of America, 1996.

Divine, Robert. *Foreign Policy and U.S. Presidential Elections 1940–1948.* New York: New Viewpoints, 1974.

Doenecke, Justus. *Not to the Swift: The Old Isolationists in the Cold War Era.* Lewisburg, Pa.: Bucknell University Press, 1979.

Donaldson, Gary. *Truman Defeats Dewey.* Lexington, Ky.: University Press of Kentucky, 1999.

Donovan, Robert. *Conflict and Crisis: The Presidency of Harry S Truman, 1945–1948.* New York: Norton, 1977.

———. *Tumultuous Years: The Presidency of Harry S Truman, 1949–1953.* New York: Norton, 1982.

Douglas, Helen. *A Full Life.* New York: Doubleday, 1982.

Douglas, Paul. *In the Fullness of Time: The Memoirs of Paul H. Douglas.* New York: Harcourt Brace Jovanovich, 1971.

Dunar, Andrew. *The Truman Scandals and the Politics of Morality.* Columbia: University of Missouri Press, 1984.

Eisenhower, Dwight. *The White House Years: Mandate for Change 1953–1956.* New York: Doubleday, 1963.

Eisenhower, Julie. *Pat Nixon: The Untold Story.* New York: Simon & Schuster, 1986.

Evans, Harold. *The American Century.* New York: Knopf, 1998.

Faries, McIntyre. *Rememb'ring.* California: Griffin Publishing, 1993.

Fay, James, ed. *California Almanac,* 6th ed. California: Pacific Data Resources, 1993.

Ferrell, Robert, ed. *Harry S. Truman: A Life.* Columbia: University of Missouri Press, 1994.

———. *Truman in the White House: The Diary of Eben A. Ayers.* Columbia: University of Missouri Press, 1991.

Fontenay, Charles. *Estes Kefauver: A Biography.* Knoxville: University of Tennessee Press, 1980.

Freeland, Richard. *The Truman Doctrine and the Origins of McCarthyism: Foreign Policy, Domestic Politics, and Internal Security 1946–1948.* New York: New York University Press, 1985.

Freidel, Frank. *Franklin D. Roosevelt: A Rendezvous with Destiny.* Boston: Little, Brown, 1990.

Galambos, Louis, ed. *The Papers of Dwight David Eisenhower: Occupation 1945.* Vol. VI. Baltimore: Johns Hopkins University Press, 1978.

———. *The Papers of Dwight David Eisenhower: Columbia University.* Vol. X. Baltimore: Johns Hopkins University Press, 1984.

———. *The Papers of Dwight David Eisenhower: NATO and the Campaign of 1952.* Vol. XIII. Baltimore: Johns Hopkins University Press, 1989.

Garraty, John, ed. *Dictionary of American Biography.* New York: Scribners, 1980.

Gellman, Irwin. *Secret Affairs: Franklin Roosevelt, Cordell Hull, and Sumner Welles.* Baltimore: Johns Hopkins University Press, 1995.

Gentry, Curt. *J. Edgar Hoover: The Man and the Secrets.* New York: Norton, 1991.

Gimble, John. *The American Occupation of Germany: Politics and the Military, 1945–1949.* Stanford: Stanford University Press, 1968.

Goodman, Walter. *The Committee: The Extraordinary Career of the House Committee on Un-American Activities.* New York: Farrar, Straus & Giroux, 1968.

Gottlieb, Robert, and Irene Wolt. *Thinking Big: The Story of the Los Angeles Times, Its Publishers and Their Influence on Southern California.* New York: Putnam, 1977.

Graham, Katharine. *Personal History.* New York: Vintage Books, 1998.

Griffith, Robert. *The Politics of Fear: Joseph McCarthy and the Senate.* Lexington: University of Kentucky Press, 1970.

Groce, Peter. *Gentleman Spy: The Life of Allen Dulles.* Boston: Houghton Mifflin, 1994.

Gullan, Harold. *The Upset That Wasn't: Harry S Truman and the Crucial Election of 1948.* Chicago: Ivan R. Dee, 1998.

Halberstam, David. *The Powers That Be.* New York: Knopf, 1979.

Hamby, Alonzo. *Man of the People: A Life of Harry S. Truman.* New York: Oxford University Press, 1995.

Harper, Alan. *The Politics of Loyalty: The White House and the Communist Issue, 1946–1952.* Westport, Conn.: Greenwood Press, 1969.

Hartmann, Susan. *Truman and the 80th Congress.* Columbia: University of Missouri Press, 1971.

Hébert, F. Edward. *"Last of the Titans": The Life and Times of Congressman F. Edward Hébert of Louisiana.* La.: University of Southwestern Louisiana, 1976.

Herzstein, Robert. *Henry R. Luce: A Political Portrait of the Man Who Created the American Century.* New York: Scribners, 1994.

Hillings, Patrick. *Pat Hillings: The Irrepressible Irishman: A Republican Insider.* USA: Harold Dean, 1993.

Hiss, Alger. *In the Court of Public Opinion.* New York: Knopf, 1957.

————. *Recollections of a Life.* New York: Seaver Books, 1988.

Hogan, Michael. *The Marshall Plan: America, Britain, and the Reconstruction of Western Europe.* Cambridge: Cambridge University Press, 1987.

Horne, Gerald. *Black Liberation/Red Scare: Ben Davis and the Communist Party.* Newark: University of Delaware Press, 1994.

Hundley, Norris, Jr. *The Great Thirst: Californians and Water, 1770s–1990s.* Berkeley: University of California Press, 1992.

Jennings, Peter, and Todd Brewster. *The Century.* New York: Doubleday, 1998.

Katcher, Leo. *Earl Warren: A Political Biography.* New York: McGraw-Hill, 1967.

Keogh, James. *This Is Nixon.* New York: Putnam, 1956.

Klehr, Harvey, John Hayes, and Fridrickh Firov. *The Secret World of American Communism.* New Haven: Yale University Press, 1995.

Klein, Herbert. *Making It Perfectly Clear: An Inside Account of Nixon's Love-Hate Relationship with the Media.* New York: Doubleday, 1980.

Kluger, Richard. *The Paper: The Life and Death of the New York Herald Tribune.* New York: Knopf, 1986.

Kornitzer, Bela. *The Real Nixon: An Intimate Biography.* New York: Rand McNally, 1960.

Kuehl, Warren, ed. *Biographical Dictionary of Internationalists.* Westport, Conn.: Greenwood Press, 1983.

Kutler, Stanley, ed. *Abuse of Power: The New Nixon Tapes.* New York: Free Press, 1997.

La Gumina, Salvatore. *Vito Marcantonio, The People's Politician.* Iowa: Kendall/Hunt, 1969.

Latham, Earl. *The Communist Controversy in Washington: From the New Deal to McCarthy.* Cambridge, Mass.: Harvard University Press, 1966.

Lawrence, David. *The Editorials of David Lawrence.* Washington, D.C.: U.S. News & World Report, 1970.

Lee, R. Alton. *Truman and Taft-Hartley: A Question of Mandate.* Lexington: University of Kentucky Press, 1966.

Leffler, Melvyn: *A Preponderance of Power: National Security, the Truman Administration, and the Cold War.* Stanford: Stanford University Press, 1992.

Leuchtenburg, William. *Franklin D. Roosevelt and the New Deal 1932–1940.* New York: Harper & Row, 1963.

Levine, Isaac Don. *Eyewitness to History: Memoirs and Reflections of a Foreign Correspondent for Half a Century.* New York: Hawthorn Books, 1973.

Lodge, Henry Cabot. *The Storm Has Many Eyes: A Personal Narrative.* New York: Norton, 1973.

Mankiewicz, Frank. *Perfectly Clear: Nixon from Whittier to Watergate.* New York: Quadrangle, 1973.

Marcus, Maeva. *Truman and the Steel Seizure Case: The Limits of Presidential Power.* New York: Columbia University Press, 1977.

Martin, Joe. *My First Fifty Years in Politics.* New York: McGraw-Hill, 1960.

Matthews, Christopher. *Kennedy & Nixon: The Rivalry That Shaped Postwar America.* New York: Simon & Schuster, 1996.

May, Gary. *Un-American Activities: The Trials of William Remington.* New York: Oxford University Press, 1994.

Mazlish, Bruce. *In Search of Nixon: A Psychohistorical Inquiry.* New York: Basic Books, 1972.

Mazo, Earl. *Richard Nixon: A Political and Personal Portrait.* New York: Harper & Brothers, 1959.

McCullough, David. *Truman.* New York: Simon & Schuster, 1992.

McLellan, David. *Dean Acheson: The State Department Years.* New York: Dodd, Mead, 1976.

Meyer, Gerald. *Vito Marcantonio: Radical Politician 1920–1954.* New York: State University of New York, 1989.

Miller, James. *The United States and Italy, 1940–1950: The Politics and Diplomacy of Stabilization.* Chapel Hill: University of North Carolina Press, 1986.

Miller, William "Fishbait," as told to Frances Leighton. *Fishbait: The Memoirs of the Congressional Doorkeeper.* Englewood Cliffs, NJ: Prentice-Hall, 1977.

Mitchell, Greg. *The Campaign of the Century: Upton Sinclair's Race for Governor of California and The Birth of Media Politics.* New York: Random House, 1992.

———. *Tricky Dick and the Pink Lady: Richard Nixon vs. Helen Gahagan Douglas—Sexual Politics and the Red Scare, 1950.* New York: Random House, 1998.

Montgomery, Gayle, and James Johnson. *One Step from the White House: The Rise and Fall of Senator William F. Knowland.* Berkeley: University of California Press, 1998.

Moore, John, ed. *Congressional Quarterly's Guide to U.S. Elections.* 2nd ed. Washington, D.C.: Congressional Quarterly, 1985.

Morris, Roger. *Richard Milhous Nixon: The Rise of an American Politician.* New York: Holt, 1990.

Murphy, George, with Victor Lasky. *"Say . . Didn't You Used to Be George Murphy?"* USA: Bartholomew House, 1970.

Nixon, Richard. *RN: The Memoirs of Richard Nixon.* New York: Grosset & Dunlap, 1978.

———. *Six Crises.* New York: Doubleday, 1962.

Noble, Bernard. "Christian A. Herter." In Robert Ferrell, ed., *The American Secretaries of State and Their Diplomacy,* Vol. XVIII. New York: Cooper Square, 1970.

Novak, Bogdan. *Trieste 1941–1954: The Ethnic, Political, and Ideological Struggle.* Chicago: University of Chicago Press, 1970.

O'Neill, Thomas P. "Tip." *Man of the House: The Life and Political Memoirs of Speaker Tip O'Neill.* New York: Random House, 1987.

Oshinsky, David. *A Conspiracy So Immense: The World of Joe McCarthy.* New York: Free Press, 1983.

Parmet, Herbert. *Eisenhower and the American Crusades.* New York: Macmillan, 1972.

———. *Richard Nixon and His America.* New York: Konecky & Konecky, 1990.

Patterson, James. *Mr. Republican: A Biography of Robert A. Taft*. Boston: Houghton Mifflin, 1972.

Pepper, Claude. *Pepper: Eyewitness to a Century*. San Diego, Ca.: Harcourt Brace Jovanovich, 1987.

Pogue, Forrest. *George Marshall: Statesman 1945–1949*. New York: Viking, 1987.

Powers, Richard. *Not Without Honor: The History of American Anticommunism*. New York: Free Press, 1995.

———. *Secrecy Power: The Life of J. Edgar Hoover*. New York: The Free Press, 1987.

Prussen, Ronald. *John Foster Dulles: The Road to Power*. New York: Free Press, 1982.

Rabel, Roberto. *Between East and West: Trieste, the United States, and the Cold War, 1941–1954*. Durham: Duke University Press, 1988.

Raucher, Alan. *Paul G. Hoffman: Architect of Foreign Aid*. Lexington: University Press of Kentucky, 1985.

Rothe, Anna, ed. *Current Biography 1944*. New York: Wilson, 1945.

———. *Current Biography 1948–1949*. New York: Wilson, 1949–50.

———, and Evelyn Lohr, eds. *Current Biography 1952*. New York: Wilson, 1953.

Rovere, Richard. *Senator Joe McCarthy*. New York: Harper Torchbooks, 1973.

Ruddy, T. Michael. *The Cautious Diplomat: Charles E. Bohlen and the Soviet Union, 1929–1969*. Kent, Ohio: Kent State University Press, 1986.

Savage, Sean. *Truman and the Democratic Party*. Lexington: University Press of Kentucky, 1997.

Schaffer, Alan. *Vito Marcantonio, Radical in Congress*. Ithaca: Syracuse University Press, 1966.

Schapsmeier, Edward, and Frederick Schapsmeier. *Dirksen of Illinois: Senatorial Statesman*. Urbana: University of Illinois Press, 1985.

Scheele, Henry. *Charles Halleck: A Political Biography*. New York: Exposition Press, 1966.

Schrecker, Ellen. *Many Are the Crimes: McCarthyism in America*. Boston: Little, Brown, 1998.

Schuparra, Kurt. *Triumph of the Right: The Rise of the California Conservative Movement, 1945–1966*. New York: M. E. Sharpe, 1998.

Scobie, Ingrid Winther. *Center Stage: Helen Gahagan Douglas: A Life*. New York: Oxford University Press, 1992.

Scott, Commander. *Romance of the Highways of California*. Ca.: Commander Scott Productions, 1945.

Smith, Jean. *Lucius D. Clay: An American Life*. New York: Holt, 1990.

Smith, Robert. *Thomas E. Dewey and His Times*. New York: Simon & Schuster, 1982.

Spanier, John. *The Truman-MacArthur Controversy and the Korean War*. New York: Norton, 1965.

St. Johns, Adela Rogers. *The Honeycomb*. New York: Doubleday, 1969.

Starr, Kevin. *Material Dreams: Southern California Through the 1920s*. New York: Oxford University Press, 1990.

Stripling, Robert. *The Red Plot Against America*. Pa.: Bell Publishing Co., 1949.

Sulzberger, C. L. *A Long Row of Candles: Memoirs and Diaries [1934–1954]*. New York: Macmillan, 1969.

Tanenhaus, Sam. *Whittaker Chambers: A Biography*. New York: Random House, 1997.

Theoharis, Athan, and John Cox. *The Boss: J. Edgar Hoover and the Great American Inquisition*. Philadelphia: Temple University Press, 1988.

Tresse, Joel, ed. *Biographical Directory of the American Congress 1774–1996*. Va.: CQ Staff Directory, 1977.

Volkan, Vamik, Norman Itzkowitz, and Andrew Dod. *Richard Nixon: A Psychobiography*. New York: Columbia University Press, 1997.

Voorhis, Horace J. *Confessions of a Congressman*. New York: Doubleday, 1948.

———. *Out of Debt, Out of Danger*. New York: Devin-Adair Co., 1943.

———. *The Strange Case of Richard Milhous Nixon*. New York: Paul S. Eriksson, 1972.

Walker, Doris. *Orange County, A Centennial Celebration: Sections of Orange*. Tx.: Pioneer Publications, 1989.

Wall, Irwin. *The United States and the Making of Postwar France, 1945–1954*. Cambridge: Cambridge University Press, 1991.

Walton, Richard. *Henry Wallace, Harry Truman, and the Cold War*. New York: Viking, 1976.

Warren, Earl. *The Memoirs of Earl Warren*. New York: Doubleday, 1977.

Weinstein, Allen, and Alexander Vassiliev, *The Haunted Wood: Soviet Espionage in America—The Stalin Era*. New York: Random House, 1999.

———.*Perjury: The Hiss-Chambers Case*. New York: Knopf, 1978; reissued New York: Random House, 1997.

Welles, Sumner, et al. *Laurence Duggan, 1905–1948: In Memoriam*. Conn.: Overbrook Press, 1949.

West, Jessamyn. *Hide and Seek: A Continuing Journey*. New York: Harcourt Brace Jovanovich, 1973.

Wicker, Tom. *One of Us: Richard Nixon and the American Dream*. New York: Random House, 1991.

Wills, Garry. *Nixon Agonistes: The Crisis of the Self-Made Man*. Boston: Houghton Mifflin, 1969.

Wittner, Lawrence. *American Intervention in Greece, 1943–1949*. New York: Columbia University Press, 1982.

Woods, Randall. *Fulbright: A Biography*. Cambridge: Cambridge University Press, 1995.

Zieger, Robert. *The CIO 1935–1955*. Chapel Hill: University of North Carolina Press, 1995.

*Articles*

Bethell, John. "The Ultimate Commencement Address: The Making of George C. Marshall's Routine Speech," *Harvard Magazine*, vol. 99, no. 5 (May–June 1997).

Bowers, Lynn, and Dorothy Blair. "How to Pick a Congressman," *Saturday Evening Post*, March 19, 1949.

Brashear, Ernest. "Who Is Richard Nixon?", *New Republic* 127 (September 1, 1952).

———. "II Who Is Richard Nixon?", *New Republic* 127 (September 8, 1952).

Bullock, Paul. " 'Rabbits and Radicals': Richard Nixon's 1946 Campaign Against Jerry Voorhis," *Southern California Quarterly*, vol. 55, no. 3 (Fall 1973).

Challener, Richard. "New Light on a Turning Point in U.S. History," *University: A Princeton Quarterly* 56 (Spring 1973).

Dmohowski, Joseph. "From a Common Ground: The Quaker Heritage of Jessamyn West and Richard Nixon," *California History*, vol. 73, no. 3 (Fall 1994).

"Elections: 1946." *New Republic* (February 11, 1946).

Freeman, Joshua, and Steve Rosswurm. "The Education of an Anti-Communist: Father John F. Cronin and the Baltimore Labor Movement," *Labor History* 33 (Spring 1992).

Goldman, Eric. "The 1947 Kennedy-Nixon 'Tube City' Debate," *Saturday Review*, October 16, 1976.

Irons, Peter, "American Business and the Origins of McCarthyism: The Cold War Crusade of the United States Chamber of Commerce." In Robert Griffith and Athan Theoharis, eds., *The Specter: Original Essays on the Cold War and the Origins of McCarthyism*. New York: New Viewpoints, 1974.

Navasky, Victor. "Weinstein, Hiss, and the Transformation of Historical Ambiguity into Cold War Veracity." In Athan Theoharis, ed., *Beyond the Hiss Case: The FBI, Congress, and the Cold War*. Philadelphia: Temple University Press, 1982.

Nixon, Pat, and Joe Morris. "I Say He's a Wonderful Guy," *Saturday Evening Post*, September 6, 1952.

Nixon, Richard. "Unforgettable John Foster Dulles," *Reader's Digest* (July 1967).

Offner, Arnold. "'Another Such Victory': President Truman, American Foreign Policy and the Cold War," *Diplomatic History*, vol. 23, no. 2 (Spring 1999).

Purdy, Virginia. "A Temple to Clio: The National Archives Building," *Prologue* (Summer 1984).

Tanner, William, and Robert Griffith. "Legislative Politics and 'McCarthyism': The Internal Security Act of 1950." In Griffith and Theoharis, eds., *The Specter: Original Essays on the Cold War and the Origins of McCarthyism*.

Weinstein, Allen. "Nixon Vs. Hiss," *Esquire*, vol. 84, no. 5 (November 1975).

―――. "Was Alger Hiss Framed?", *New York Review of Books*, April 1, 1976.


*Unpublished Theses*

Crispell, Brian. "George Smathers and the Politics of Cold War America, 1946–1968." Ph.D. thesis: Florida State University, 1996.

Hinderaker, Ivan. "Harold Stassen and Developments in the Republican Party in Minnesota, 1937–1943." Ph.D. thesis: University of Minnesota, 1949.

Hoult, Thomas. "The Whittier Narrows Dam: A Study in Community Competition and Conflict." M.A. thesis: Whittier College, 1948.

Irons, Peter. "America's Cold War Crusade: Domestic Politics and Foreign Policy, 1942–1948." Ph.D. thesis: Boston University, 1973.

Kabat, Ric. "From New Deal to Red Scare: The Political Odyssey of Senator Claude D. Pepper." Ph.D. thesis: Florida State University, 1995.

Kirby, Alec. "Childe Harold's Pilgrimage: A Political Biography of Harold Stassen." Ph.D. thesis: George Washington University, 1992.

Pope, Philip. "Foundations of Nixonian Foreign Policy: The Pre-Presidential Years of Richard M. Nixon, 1946–1968." V. I. Ph.D. thesis: University of Southern California, 1988.

Scobie, Ingrid Winther. "Jack B. Tenney: Molder of Anti-Communist Legislation in California 1940–1949." Ph.D. thesis: University of Wisconsin, 1970.

Speer, Glenn. "Richard Nixon's Position on Communist China, 1949–1960: The Evolution of a Pacific Strategy." Ph.D. thesis: City University of New York, 1992.

# Glossary of Characters

Bert Andrews, *New York Herald Tribune* reporter in the capital who worked with Nixon.

Donald Appell, HUAC investigator during Hiss investigation.

William "Bill" Arnold, publicist for Nixon campaign in 1946 and Nixon's first congressional assistant.

Alben Barkley, Truman's vice president, 1949–53.

Elizabeth Bentley, confessed Russian courier.

Adolf Berle, assistant secretary of state under Franklin Roosevelt.

Thomas "Tom" Bewley, senior partner when Nixon practiced law in Whittier.

Jesse B. Blue, Jr., headed Democrats for Nixon in 1948 and remained an avid supporter.

Ralph Manchester Boddy, editor and publisher of the *Los Angeles Daily News,* who opposed Douglas.

Charles Bowen, early Nixon supporter who handled public relations in initial campaigns.

William Boyle, chairman of Democratic National Committee caught up in RFC scandal.

Bernard "Bernie" Brennan, major GOP activist in Los Angeles who helped direct 1950 race.

Herbert Brownell, Dewey's 1948 campaign manager and prominent Ike supporter in 1952.

Alexander Campbell, supervised the crime division of the Justice Department during the Hiss inquiry.

Whittaker Chambers, Russian spy turned Hiss informant.

Murray Chotiner, professional Republican campaign manager who ran Nixon's 1950 senatorial race.

Thomas Clark, U.S. Attorney General under Truman during the Hiss investigation.

Lucius Clay, U.S. Army general in charge of the American zone in Germany and a friend of Dwight Eisenhower.

Dan Cleveland, minister from El Monte who was active in local California politics.

Edward Condon, scientist whom Parnell Thomas tried to link to Communist espionage.

Dorothy Cox, early supporter of and secretary to Richard Nixon.

Roy Crocker, early supporter of Nixon and a successful Southern California banker.

John Cronin, anti-Communist priest who advised Nixon.

George Crosley, alias for Whittaker Chambers.

Roy O. Day, ran the first primary campaign for Nixon and remained an active supporter.

Earl Desmond, conservative state senator who ran against Douglas in the 1950 Democratic primary.

Thomas Dewey, Republican governor from New York who ran for president in 1948.

John Dinkelspiel, attorney who managed Nixon's 1950 campaign in Northern California.

Everett "Ev" Dirksen, conservative Republican congressman, then senator, from Illinois.

Thomas Donegan, special assistant to the attorney general in charge of the Hiss grand jury.

Helen Gahagan Douglas, Democratic congresswoman defeated by Nixon in 1950 Senate race.

Melvyn Douglas, actor, Helen's husband.

Sheridan Downey, senator from California 1939–50, whom Douglas initially challenged.

Helene Drown, Pat Nixon's best friend.

Jack Drown, husband of Helene and active supporter of Nixon in his early campaigns.

Laurence Duggan, former high-ranking American diplomat charged with being a Russian spy.

John Foster Dulles, prominent New York lawyer and foreign policy spokesman for the Republicans.

Gerhart Eisler, Communist who led Russian espionage in the United States in 1947.

Thomas Erwin, early Nixon supporter and member of the California assembly.

McIntyre "Mac" Faries, California Republican committeeman from Los Angeles.

Guy Gabrielson, RNC chairman who was caught up in the RFC scandal.

John "Jack" Garland, wealthy real estate developer and early Nixon supporter.

Boyd Gibbons, Jr., early supporter of Nixon and owner of an automobile dealership.

James Gleason, an administrative assistant to Senator Nixon.

Harvey Hancock, directed Nixon's 1950 campaign efforts in Northern California.

F. Edward Hébert, Democrat congressman who served on HUAC during Chambers-Hiss affair.

Christian Herter, Republican congressman from Massachusetts who led the 1947 European mission.

Patrick Hillings, supported Nixon in 1948 reelection and ran successfully in 1950 for the House.

Alger Hiss, former State Department employee whom Chambers charged with spying for Russia.

Donald Hiss, brother of Alger.

Priscilla Hiss, wife of Alger.

Chester "Chet" Holifield, liberal Democratic congressman in Southern California.

Joseph Holt, Nixon's field manager in 1950 election, who successfully ran for the House in 1952.

Herbert Hoover, U.S. president, 1929–33, who becomes an early and staunch supporter of Nixon.

J. Edgar Hoover, director of the FBI.

John "Jack" Irwin, administrative assistant to Senator Nixon.

Donald Jackson, Southern California Republican congressman and a supporter of Nixon.

Frank Jorgensen, successful insurance executive who supported Nixon's political rise.

John Kennedy, elected to the House in 1946 and served with Nixon on labor committee.

Gerald Kepple, prominent lawyer who supported Nixon in 1946 congressional contest.

Charles Kersten, elected to House in 1946 and an ally of Nixon.

Herbert Klein, reporter for *Alhambra Post-Advocate* who became an early supporter of Nixon.

William "Bill" Knowland, appointed U.S. senator in 1945 and won election in 1946.

Arthur Kruse, successful Southern California banker who supported Nixon's early campaigns.

Victor Lasky, reporter who supported Nixon during the Hiss trial.

Isaac Don Levine, editor of anti-Communist magazine *Plain Talk* who championed Chambers.

Henry Cabot Lodge, Jr., Republican senator from Massachusetts who managed Eisenhower's campaign.

Jack Long, Democratic advocate of Jerry Voorhis who worked in Voorhis's congressional campaigns.

Eunice Lowell, early Nixon supporter and major female leader in Republican circles.

Harold Lutz, early Nixon supporter and assistant to Herman Perry at Bank of America.

Donald Lycan, president of Signal Oil who provided seed money for the 1946 Nixon campaign.

Douglas MacArthur, career army officer fired by Truman from his command in Korea.

Vito Marcantonio, Radical congressman from New York.

George Marshall, secretary of state responsible for the Marshall Plan to reconstruct European finances after World War II.

Joseph Martin, Republican from Massachusetts, House Speaker in the 80th Congress.

Bert Mattei, California oil executive who raised money for Nixon in 1950 for the senatorial race.

Harrison "Mac" McCall, influential Republican who ran Nixon's first general election campaign.

Joseph McCarthy, controversial Republican senator from Wisconsin, elected in 1946.

John McDowell, Republican congressman from Pennsylvania who served on HUAC.

J. Howard McGrath, Truman's Attorney General during Boyle and Morris incidents.

Roy McLaughlin, Republican congressional nominee in 1944 who backed Nixon in 1946.

Raymond Moley, an original brain truster who turned conservative and wrote for *Newsweek*.

Newbold Morris, New York attorney assigned to abortive attempt to clean up government.

Karl Mundt, Republican from South Dakota who served in the House and Senate with Nixon.

Wallace "Chief" Newman, coached Nixon in football at Whittier College.

Louis Nichols, third-ranking member of the FBI who served as a liaison with Congress.

Francis Anthony "Frank" Nixon, Richard Nixon's father.

Hannah Nixon, Richard Nixon's mother.

Julie Nixon, second child of Richard and Pat Nixon.

Patricia Nixon, née Thelma Catherine Ryan, marries Nixon in 1940.

Patricia "Tricia" Nixon, first child of Richard and Pat Nixon.

William O'Dwyer, mayor of New York City in late 1940s, linked to charges of graft.

Kyle Palmer, chief political editorial writer for the *Los Angeles Times* who supported Nixon.

Drew Pearson, controversial liberal columnist and radio commentator from the 1940s to the 1960s.

Claude Pepper, Democratic senator from Florida who was defeated in 1950.

Herman L. Perry, political mentor to Nixon and Whittier branch manager for Bank of America.

J. Peters, head of the U.S. Communist Party espionage network.

John Rankin, Democratic congressman from Mississippi who served on HUAC with Nixon.

William P. Rogers, government attorney for Senate committee who worked with Nixon on the Hiss case.

James Roosevelt, oldest son of FDR, who ran for governor against Earl Warren in 1950.

Louis Russell, HUAC investigator and former FBI special agent.

David Saunders, supporter of Stassen for president in 1948 and Nixon for the Senate in 1950.

George Smathers, Democratic Florida congressman who defeated Pepper in the 1950 senatorial race.

Dana Smith, finance chairman for Nixon's campaign in 1950 and a strong supporter.

Paul Smith, taught Nixon history and government at Whittier College and later became college president.

Herbert Spencer, Nixon supporter who assisted in his early congressional campaigns.

Harold Stassen, Republican governor from Minnesota in 1938, candidate for president in 1948 and 1952.

Robert "Strip" Stripling, served as chief investigator for HUAC during Hiss investigation.

Cyrus Sulzberger, publisher and reporter for the *New York Times.*

Robert Taft, Republican senator from Ohio who became a leading conservative spokesman.

Jack Tenney, GOP legislator who directed Committee on Un-American Activities in California.

J. Parnell Thomas, Republican congressman from New Jersey, HUAC chairman 1947–48.

Harry S. Truman, U.S. president, 1945–53.

Arthur Vandenberg, Republican senator from Michigan who became a leading internationalist.

Harry Vaughan, personal friend and administrative assistant to Truman who was plagued by scandal.

Charles Voorhis, father of Jerry; managed Jerry's political campaigns.

Horace Jeremiah "Jerry" Voorhis, incumbent congressman in 12th congressional district, 1936–46.

Henry Wallace, vice president, 1940–44, and secretary of commerce.

Earl Warren, Republican governor of California, 1942–53.

William Wheeler, HUAC investigator during Hiss affair.

Henry Dexter White, former Treasury official under Roosevelt, accused of spying for Russians.

Rose Mary Woods, secretary to the Herter mission and Nixon's private secretary after 1951.

E. Merl Young, caught up in RFC corruption and jailed for perjury.

Mildred Younger, leading Republican woman in Southern California during Nixon's rise.

Stephen Zetterberg, Nixon's 1948 primary congressional opponent on the Democratic ticket.

# Index

Abels, Jules, Truman's scandals, 389
Abrahamsen, David, on RN rejection
  from FBI, 6
Abt, John:
  Budenz's accusations, 218; Chambers's
    accusations 199; acquaintance with
    Hiss, 200, 220
Acheson, Dean:
  American defense perimeter, 315; crit-
    icism of, 243, 364; Cronin's accusa-
    tions, 223; friendship with D. Hiss,
    242; goes to Hiss's defense, 242,
    251; McCarthy attack, 273, 354;
    McLellan evaluation of Acheson,
    243; offers resignation, 243; Perry
    accuses of treason, 346; RN calls for
    resignation, 316; Stassen calls for
    resignation, 392
*Acropolis,* Whittier College yearbook, 15
*Action for Today,* NC-PAC bulletin en-
    dorsing Voorhis, 70
Adams, Earl, early fund raiser for RN, 63
Adams, J. B., FBI special agent, 8
Adams, Sherman:
  early Eisenhower supporter, 403; pos-
    sible vice presidential candidate,
    425, 440
African Americans:
  Bert Andrews's hostility toward
    Rankin, 211; *California Eagle,* 174;
    Clark's racist views, 173; Benjamin
    Davis's position, 156–57; HUAC's
    interest, 193; number in 12th con-
    gressional district, 42; RN praise for
    Korean squadron, 324; RN support
    for, 57; Rankin's racist views, 109;
    *Sun Reporter* endorsement of Dou-

glas, 331; Truman's desegregation
  order, 192; Washington's support for
  RN, 333
Agriculture:
  Brannan Plan, 275; citrus growers' cri-
    sis, 226
Alameda Air Station, RN posting, 23
Alaska, RN favors statehood for, 275
Alhambra, description of, 42
Allis-Chalmers Manufacturing Com-
  pany:
  CIO strike, 100; HUAC investigation,
    115
Amalgamated Clothing Workers of
  America:
  Hillman as president, 51; role in
    Voorhis campaign, 53
Ambrose, Stephen, RN biographer,
  457
American Civil Liberties Union (ACLU):
  opposition to Mundt-Nixon bill, 156;
    RN opposition to, 409
American Federation of Labor (AFL):
  endorses Zetterberg, 178; support for
    Douglas, 278; support for Voorhis,
    51, 58, 69
American Friends Service Committee
  (AFSC):
  friction at Whittier College, 261–62;
    Perry criticism of, 269–70
American Labor Party (ALP), Marcanto-
  nio's role, 97, 110, 165, 308
American Legion:
  Clark's position, 173; calls to outlaw
    Communist Party, 156
American Lithofold Corporation, RFC
  probe of, 377–78

Nixon, Richard (*cont.*)
rico firing, 409; Jenkins's role, 128,
132; joins Republican Party, 18;
joins Whittier Community Players,
19; joins Wingert & Bewley, 18;
Jorgensen support, 284; Justice Department conflict, 233, 237, 244,
262; Kaufman criticism, 241; Kearns
bill, 271; JFK linkage, 102–103,
363–64; Kersten relationship, 99,
254–55; keynote speech, 422–23;
Klein friendship, 139; Knight prediction, 434; Knowland relationship,
96, 284, 352–53, 398–99; Korean
Economic Aid bill, 309, 311, 313;
Korean war, 315–16, 321; labor
connection, 56, 96, 103, 112, 123,
414–15; Lasky ties, 240; law school,
6, 7, 15–16; law school alumni association president, 18; leaves for war,
21–22; leaving military, 24, 31; legal
career, 8, 18; Lewis's position,
100–101; lifestyle, 270–71, 348–50;
linkage to Cain, 325; linkage to Mc-
Carthy, 312, 326, 332, 338, 460; Los
Angeles luncheon 1945, 31–32; *Los
Angeles Times* support, 288; loyalty
program, 243, 256, 266, 273–74;
MacArthur support, 367–68, 370;
maiden House speech, 110; Marcantonio role, 38; Mankiewicz, 339;
marriage, 20; Marshall Plan,
144–45, 147; Mattei relationship,
294; McCall bonds, 63, 65–66; Mc-
Carran Act, 313–14, 326; McCarthy
linkage, 234, 273, 321, 325, 353–54,
355, 356, 369; McGrath criticism,
325–26; Morris episode, 381, 383,
384, 385, 386; moves to Washington, D.C. in 1942, 21; Mundt-
Nixon bill, 114–15, 154, 155, 160,
162, 163, 164, 174, 177, 187, 254,
257, 271; music background, 12;
myths concerning, 5, 59, 60,
222–24, 281–82, 318, 342, 447,
448, 453, 457, 500; NCPAC,
61–62; Naval Reserve Aviation
Base, 21; New Deal, 32, 41, 89;
new technology, 57; Newman, Wallace "Chief," 15, 78, 79; Nichols
ties, 227, 236, 240; J. Nixon's birth,
192; T. Nixon's birth, 44; OPA, 21,
77, 91; Orthogonians, 15, 268;
Palmer's support, 48–49, 283; part-

time jobs, 7, 15; Pearson opposition,
97, 273; Perry's role, 26, 27, 31, 34;
pink sheet, 308; political faults, 455;
political organization, 66; political
patronage, 192; political positions,
43–44, 396–98, 413; presidential
election 1948, 253, 256–57, 260;
press coverage, 42, 55, 92–93, 95,
327, 333–34, 336; price controls,
141; primary campaign 1946, 29,
42, 46, 49, 58–59, 62; primary campaign 1948, 176–77, 179, 452; primary campaign 1950, 294, 296, 299,
303–304; pumpkin papers, 231,
232–33, 238; radio programs, 267;
Rankin criticism, 454; Reagan
meeting, 117; RFC, 376–77; RTA,
149, 300, 359; Red Chinese, 146,
333, 344, 366–67, 368; Red-baiting, 85, 459–60; Red herring, 234,
236, 240, 256, 257; relationship
during war, 22; Remington affair,
194; rent control, 95; response to
September 1945 letter, 26; returns
from war, 23; role at 1948 Republican convention, 183, 190, 195; J.
Roosevelt connection, 320, 322; T.
Roosevelt's view, 74; Russia, 56–57,
123, 140, 146; Saunders's support,
283–84, 290; senatorial ranking,
356; Smathers's advice, 310; D.
Smith connection, 291; Social Security support, 150–51, 188, 271, 275;
South Pasadena debate, 70–71;
speaking, 43, 47–48, 64, 302, 402,
418–19; H. Spencer support, 33–34,
38, 74; Spring Valley home, 347–48;
State Department criticism, 57 , 64,
276; Stassen relationship, 74–75,
181–82, 183, 184, 186, 187,
190–91, 391–92; steel seizure opposition, 415; Sulgrave Club incident,
354–55; supports Bancroft for US
Senate, 18–19; supports Willkie for
president, 19; tapped Order of the
Coif, 7; Taft relationship, 183, 184,
392–93, 417–18, 446; Taft-Hartley
Act, 97–98, 101, 105, 106, 267,
302, 356; Tenney file, 408; Terry's
role, 293; tidelands dispute, 275,
357; training at Quonset Point, 21;
Trieste visit, 133–35; Truman relationship, 55, 106, 121, 124–25,
184–85, 196, 204, 217, 239–40,

253, 256, 260, 261–62, 264, 274, 356, 366–67, 371, 413; Truman Doctrine, 122, 123; Udall friendship, 274, 319; UMT, 121, 359; UN, 272, 300, 314, 321, 358, 359; veterans, 66, 149, 275, 358; vice-presidential selection in 1952, 418–19, 420, 429, 434, 438, 441–42, 443, 444–45, 448–49; view of Zetterberg, 172; VOA, 114, 119, 145, 276, 358–59; Voorhis connection, 31, 33, 35–36, 37, 41, 47, 34, 64–65, 70, 71–73, 77–79, 80–81, 85–86, 169; Wadleigh testimony, 240; Wagner-Ellender-Taft bill opposition, 151; Wallace opposition, 121, 185; Warner testimony, 116–117; Warren relationship, 77, 182–83, 184, 261, 288, 331–32, 346, 393, 400, 405–406, 416, 417, 419, 420, 421, 423, 429, 438; wartime experiences, 43; Welch relationship,14, 17; Werdel connection, 417; "Whippoorwill Manor," 16–17; Whittier Narrows Dam, 73, 106, 152–54, 262; W. Wilson, 74; *Witness,* 411; Young Republicans support, 283

Nixon, Patricia "Tricia:" birth of, 44; kindergarten, 271; living in Virginia, 91–92; Spring Valley home, 348

Nixon, Sarah Ann, mother of Frank, 9

Nixon, Thelma "Pat" Ryan: arrival in Washington in 1946, 90; appears in *The Dark Tower,* 19; assigned to SCAT, 22; care for daughters, 254; courtship of RN, 20; debates with Voorhis, 74; delivers Julie, 191; delivers Tricia, 44; early biography, 19–20; early comparison with RN, 19; first home with RN, 270–71; first pregnancy, 24, 41; future after war, 24; greets RN returning from war, 23; headquarters' burglary in 1946, 86; interview at 1952 Republican convention, 435; lifestyle, 270–71, 348–50; Los Angeles visit in 1945, 33; marriage, 20; meets Eisenhowers, 430; moves to Washington, D.C. in 1942, 21; RN accepting vice-president nomination, 443, 444, 445; RN speech on MacArthur's firing, 366–67; press,

272, 324; relationship during war, 22; relationship to Helene Drown, 293; role in 1950 campaign, 299, 300; role in politics, 44; Spring Valley home, 347–48; Thompson's assistance, 91; work in 1946 campaign, 62; works for OPA, 21, 22

Noel-Baker, Philip, view of RN, 339
Noumea, island in New Caledonia, 22
Novak, Robert, Duggan as a Communist, 249
Nunan, Joseph, goes to jail, 389

*Oakland Tribune,* Knowland newspaper, 76
Oaks, Lieutenant, and defense of Trieste, 134
O'Dwyer, William: Duggan's death, 247; opposition to Mundt-Nixon bill, 162; role in corruption, 374, 385
Office of Price Administration (OPA): wartime price control agency, 21; RN role, 91; Voorhis support, 77
O'Halloran, C.V. role in UAW-CIO endorsement of Voorhis, 53
Oliphant, Charles, resignation, 380
O'Neill, Thomas "Tip," on Joe Kennedy's contribution to RN, 307
Order of the Coif: RN induction, 7, 17; Rogers's induction, 205
Oregon, Dewey v. Stassen debate, 185–86
Ornithology, bird-watching interest of Hiss, 210
Orthogonians, RN college social club, 268
*Out of Debt, Out of Danger,* Voorhis book, 34, 47

Palmer, Kyle: biography, 48–49; Boddy criticism, 298, 299; Douglas criticism, 298, 312; RN support, 279, 283, 298–99; Stassen view of, 182; Taft's chances for presidency in 1952, 392; Voorhis's criticism, 49
*Panama,* RN cruise ship in 1948, 228, 231
Partisan Republicans of California, 403, 407
Patterson, James, biographer of Taft, 105–106